SERMONS ON GALATIANS

SERMONS ON GALATIANS

John Calvin

Translated by Kathy Childress

THE BANNER OF TRUTH TRUST

THE BANNER OF TRUTH TRUST
3 Murrayfield Road, Edinburgh EH12 6EL
P.O. Box 621, Carlisle, Pennsylvania 17013, USA

*

First published in French
1 February 1563.
First English translation by
Arthur Golding published in 1574.

*

First Published 1997
ISBN 0 85151 699 8

*

Typeset in 12/13pt New Baskerville
at the Banner of Truth Trust, Edinburgh
Printed and bound at the Bath Press, England

Contents

Introduction

These sermons on the Epistle to the Galatians were first preached in the French language between 14 November 1557 and 8 May 1558. They were preached in Geneva twice on Sundays, and followed a series on 1 and 2 Corinthians.[1] The sermons were taken down in shorthand, transcribed and presented to the deacons of the church by Denis Raguenier, a professional scribe hired by the French emigrants in Geneva to do this work. The deacons later had them printed and the proceeds were used for the relief of poor French-speaking refugees. They were printed in Geneva at the printing house of François Perrin on the first day of February, 1563. The first English translation was that of Arthur Golding, published eleven years later, in 1574. The present volume is an entirely new translation of the original French edition.[2]

Calvin's style in these sermons is, for the most part, plain and unembellished. Referring to his own style in an unpublished letter, he spoke of his 'ordinary mode of teaching'. Calvin certainly tries to ensure that his comments will be relevant to ordinary people by applying the doctrine he

[1] Readers should refer to the Introduction to Calvin's *Sermons on Ephesians* (Edinburgh: Banner of Truth, 1973) for further information about his sermons in general.

[2] We did not know of the intention of a US publisher to republish Golding's translation (*Sermons on Galatians,* Old Paths Publications, Audubon, N.J., 1995) until our own was nearing completion. In both old and newer dress the Galatians sermons of the 1550s are thus happily available across the world.

preached to the context of his own day and age. In fact, these sermons represent a very fine balance of weighty, doctrinal teaching and practical application. There is solid, sound instruction interspersed with illustration and application to everyday living. It will be seen that, unlike his German counterpart, Martin Luther, who tended to unfold his text dogmatically and bind himself to it, Calvin frequently wanders from the text in order to answer the arguments of adversaries, always bearing in mind the possible objections of his hearers.

Upon reading this volume, it will become apparent that certain themes are reinforced through repetition, giving them due emphasis and making them more memorable. Indeed, some of these themes are almost like a refrain to which Calvin returns, regardless of the text or passage under consideration. Hence, the most important subjects in this book – human depravity, justification by faith alone, law and grace, holiness, and the errors of the Church of Rome – seem to recur in almost every sermon. This reflects his very real understanding of the central truths of the gospel. Secondary truths are, of course, addressed, but not majored upon. As we read his thoughts upon these great subjects, we cannot help but be impressed by the accuracy and precision of his doctrinal understanding, whilst underpinning it all is a clear grasp of human nature which astounds us in its depth and profundity. Some of his remarks are so penetrating that one feels them awakening the conscience and leading the soul to greater humility and deeper repentance. Such, doubtless, was his aim.

I have endeavoured to be very faithful to the original text, and yet have desired that this translation should be as readable and unstilted as possible for the modern reader, to ensure maximum fruitfulness and profitability in today's world. There will, of course, be places that will be considered stylistically 'awkward', but where possible I have attempted to render these passages as intelligible and perspicuous as I can, without abandoning accuracy and fidelity to Calvin's original. Calvin often used long sentences, with many phrases and subphrases. Most of these have been shortened to aid readability and heighten the impact of his words.

In the case of a French idiom which is not readily understood in isolation when translated literally into English, I have sought either an equivalent English idiom, or a word or phrase which encapsulates the meaning of the French. However, if it is more readily comprehensible when read in context, I have translated it directly into English and left the reader to use his imagination. In the first French edition the Scripture references are placed in the margin, but for the sake of fluency and continuity I have placed them in brackets within the text itself.

I began this translation eight years ago, having completed a B.A. Honours degree in French in 1987 at the University of London, specialising in Renaissance French literature. In my efforts to complete this work, I am greatly indebted to my husband, Gavin Childress, who has carefully edited my work and encouraged me to persevere. I am grateful for his patience with me and also for his sacrificial practical help. I would also like to thank my three young children, Miriam, James and Josiah, for bearing with me whilst I have been preoccupied with this work. I am grateful to Dr Terence Allott, who has helped me to discover the meaning of some of the archaic idioms used in the text, and also to Dr Richard Alderson, whose painstaking editing and proof-reading has ensured even more clarity and readability in the finished version. He, along with Mr Iain Murray and other staff at the Banner of Truth Trust, has been a source of great encouragement in recent days. Mr Kevin Green has earned my heartfelt gratitude for applying his expertise in computer technology. Finally, I would like to thank the staff of the Evangelical Library in London for the loan of the text and for their practical help. The assistance of all these friends has been invaluable.

I have learnt so much about myself from this volume. Calvin exposes human nature with profound insight. Similarly, he brings this world into sharp focus and enables us to see its vanity and frivolity. However, he does not leave us to wallow in despair, but points us to the Saviour of sinners, glorifying him in majestic and inspiring terms. No sinner, having read these sermons, could mistake the remedy for sin. The Lord Jesus Christ is the focal point of this book and Calvin ensures that we have proper respect and reverence for him by describing him in all his glory, attributing all praise to him and by affirming the need to obey his infallible Word. There is judgment here, enough to make the sinner quake with fear, but then there is also mercy to warm the heart and lift the fainting spirit. My prayer is that you too will be led closer to Jesus Christ by a consideration of all that follows.

KATHY CHILDRESS
London, July 1996

I

Recognising the Supreme Authority of Jesus Christ

Paul, an apostle, (not of men, neither by man, but by Jesus Christ, and God the Father, who raised him from the dead;) And all the brethren which are with me, unto the churches of Galatia (Gal. 1:1–2).

It is with good cause that Peter takes pains to warn us to be watchful and sober because our enemy is like a 'roaring lion' whose mouth is always wide open, ready to devour whatever prey he might find (*1 Pet.* 5:8). Although our Lord Jesus Christ has confirmed to us that we have been given to him by God the Father, and that those in his care shall never perish (*John* 17:12), we cannot sleep, or neglect to call upon God when we consider our great need of his aid. Faith may assure us of God's unfailing love, but we also need to be aware of our own frailty, and pray for unwavering fidelity to him on our part. It is written that faith will overcome the world (*1 John* 5:4); nevertheless, we must still be involved in the struggle! Since we have no strength of our own, we need to draw it from another source: we must ask God for it. A sense of need, as I have said, will motivate us to do just this. In this book a mirror is presented to all believers for this very purpose, and it will be most helpful to us if we learn to use it profitably!

Paul had preached throughout Galatia, which was quite a large region, and had established many churches. If ever there was a man equipped with all the graces of the Spirit of God to win souls to the gospel, it was Paul. In this he excelled above all men, not least amongst the other apostles, and fulfilled his charge admirably. He had, however, only just turned around to leave Galatia when Satan rushed in, seeking to ruin everything and to bring desolation to the entire area. Satan was hoping to win over a great multitude so that, amongst those who had been so faithfully taught, the gospel light would be almost totally extinguished. Should not such a situation cause us to bow our heads and acknowledge that God is exhorting us to take refuge in him? Should we not ask him to strengthen us to persevere to the end? Alas, we cannot even do this without his aid!

Thus, the sins of the Galatians, described here by Paul, ought to serve as a lesson to us. For God is showing us, by means of their example, what our loyalty would amount to if it had not been given to us by him! However much the gospel has been faithfully proclaimed among us, we need God to actually work in us from day to day. Otherwise, we will be so inconstant that the least thing will cause us to go astray. Moreover, as I have already said, Satan is a terrible enemy. He is always on the prowl, ready to attack us from every direction; therefore, we cannot afford to be apathetic. He can gain entrance through the tiniest opening; we may not even be aware that the door is open! Indeed, he may surprise us before we have given him a thought. In view of this, let us give heed to the warning which God is giving us in this book and put it to good use.

At the same time, however, we need to be aware of the fact that the devil has used the name of God throughout the ages as a cloak to cover his lies and disguise them as truth. By doing this, he has created discord, so that, little by little, the impact of the gospel is weakened. Take the apostles for an example of this. They had been chosen by the Lord Jesus Christ to take and spread his gospel throughout the world. They were men who were worthy of respect; because of their authority, whatever they said ought to have been believed. Their calling was genuine; people knew that they were not impostors, but that the Son of God had chosen and appointed them with his own mouth. He had even made them new creatures! Poor, unlearned folk had been changed so dramatically. It was obvious to all that their doctrine could only have been taught them from heaven, for these people knew nothing, except what they had learnt in God's school. In a moment of time he had endowed them with his gifts and graces, and made them instruments of the Holy Spirit.

Although this is true, the devil did not cease to attack the name and position of the apostles in order to create turmoil and scandal within the church. For those who had previously been with the apostles, though they were now far away in another country, were boasting that they had conversed privately with them. They were full of pride, and sought nothing more than to boost their own reputations. Others were conceited and deemed nothing good except that which they had seen in Jerusalem and Judaea. These people thought that everyone else ought to bow to their wishes and yet, at the same time, they were aiming to 'turn everything on its head', as they say. Some were driven by a worse motive: they sought an opportunity to destroy all that Paul had established. Yet all alike were claiming that their teaching did not originate in themselves, but that they had learnt it from the apostles. Satan has always sought to obscure the glory of God in this way, by casting doubt upon the gifts that God has bestowed on his creatures.

The Roman Catholic Church today continues the same kind of idolatrous practices that were common amongst the heathen, but in the name of the apostles and of the virgin Mary. The only things that have changed are the names of the idols! But superstition is as wicked and detestable today as it was amongst the first idolaters! Paul is, therefore, exhorting us to be wise. For if the devil misuses the name of God, we are to resist him. We must remember the true condition of man in this world; we must not believe everything we are told, nor allow ourselves to be 'driven with the wind and tossed'. For if we do not determine to persevere in the doctrine that has been revealed to us (once we are sure that it is the pure truth of God), then we too will go the way of the Galatians.

Let us now summarise what we ought to remember. Firstly, if God has graciously allowed us to hear his Word it is our duty to learn from it. We must not be swayed like reeds, or tossed one way then the other, fickle as children! Instead, we ought to be wise and discerning, remaining faithful to that which we know to be of God. This is the first point. However, we do not possess this needed strength in and of ourselves. Therefore, we must, in all humility and zeal, pray to God to transform us by his Holy Spirit. We must ask for such perseverance that we will never compromise our stand. Even if everything else around us were to crumble, may this foundation remain sure: that God, who cannot lie, has spoken and revealed his will to us. May we grasp this fact, without allowing ourselves to be led astray in the slightest degree. Nevertheless, the devil has many devices, designed to make us stumble, and will even, as I have said, use God's name in order to gain access to us under false pretences. Thus, we must recognise that man is but man and that God alone is God. Our Lord alone has all power over us, as the great Master of the church. Faith does not depend on man's knowledge, nor on his reputation for great wisdom, virtue or holiness! Our Lord Jesus is pre-eminent, for he is the One who sustains and upholds us. If our faith is not grounded upon God's pure, unchanging truth, then we are surely following a lie! This is what we can gather from the example of the Galatians.

It may surprise us that Paul is so harsh with the Galatians, as we shall see shortly, given that there is no question of them openly rejecting God, forsaking the gospel, blaspheming against our Lord Jesus Christ, or flagrantly setting up an idol! They were simply practising the ceremonial law! Yes, the only fault of those whom Paul opposes in this letter was their observance of the ceremonies of the Mosaic law, and the fact that they considered their neglect a sin deserving of death. At first sight, we might say that their cause was honourable. For they were not acting like the Pope, who, in his tyrannical way, issues many decrees, and commands this or that duty in order to subject poor souls to bondage. No, the Galatians probably argued something like this: 'The law did not proceed from man; God is its author. Therefore, it is to be observed.' It would seem that Paul had no reason to be so enraged against such a view, even if we admit that it was neither correct nor good. Indeed, we might conclude that we ought not to debate about outward issues, such as whether we should observe a certain day or not, or whether we should eat pork as well as lamb. If a person chooses to observe a certain law – be it abstaining from eating pig's flesh or something similar – can it be taken as an utter denial of Christianity? Yet, this is the kind of issue around which Paul's argument revolves. Paul plainly declares that the Galatians have rebelled and forsaken the Lord Jesus Christ, and even indicates that they have apostatised. We might accuse him of excessive zeal here. However, Paul is reinforcing the point that the devil sometimes uses apparently small, subtle issues to distance us from the gospel, without our even perceiving it.

How careful we need to be, therefore! Since we do not naturally possess wisdom, we truly need to be guided by God. It is not for nothing that God should refer to himself as the Spirit of wisdom (*Isa.* 11:2), for he intends us to seek wisdom in him. May we, then, make him our refuge, so that if anyone should seek to introduce us to something which appears harmless, we may be aware of the possible consequences. For if we but move away from the simplicity of the gospel, we immediately become corrupted. We saw in the previous epistle that Paul specifically warned us about the devil's use of trickery and seduction to entice us away from the teaching of the gospel (*2 Cor.* 11:3). Oh yes, he always has a good pretext! He acts much like a rake, seducing some young girl or woman. A rake does not speak in sinful or evil terms, because he knows his victim will be horrified by them. Instead, he devises a way to make her drink his fatal poison by degrees. Well, the devil works in the same way! For if he revealed his horns (as they say) at the first, and declared himself to be the enemy of God, we would flee his presence and find him detestable. But he infiltrates secretly through tiny openings. Indeed, we are astonished when we find that he has overcome us in one area or another, for all the while we were convinced that we were holding fast to the Lord Jesus Christ, as members of his church. Such is Satan's work that we are at first unaware of it, until we finally come to realise that he has totally deceived us! Therefore, when we find that the devil tempted and corrupted the churches here mentioned over the question of the use of the ceremonial laws of Moses, let us beware, so that we may persevere, without being led astray in any direction from the simplicity of the gospel.

So, with regard to Paul's disputing about the status of the ceremonial law, we must be sure to learn from all that is recorded here, and especially to be on our guard against the subtle devices of Satan. If he tries to undermine us, we must simply remember the business we are about and hold on to what we have been taught. For we can be assured that we will never find anything in the teaching of the gospel which is not the pure Word of God. As I have already said, our faith is to be based on this one fact. The moment we stray from this, even just a little, we are engaged in something dangerous and also despicable. Only corruption results from any such dilution of the pure truth of God.

* * *

Let us now turn to deal with the order in which Paul treats the subject before us, point by point. Paul firstly confirms his own authority, which some had sought to deny, in order that we might hear and receive what he says. Those 'dogs' who opposed him suggested that the other apostles taught a different message from that of Paul. Since Paul had not lived with the Lord Jesus Christ while he walked upon this earth, it may at first seem true that the other apostles were in a degree above him, and should, therefore, be heeded more than Paul. Moreover, people wondered who had set Paul in his position. Believing he might be an impostor, they supposed that, more than anything else, he was highly presumptuous! Paul, therefore, had to deal with this and prove that he had truly been sent by God. Furthermore, as I have already indicated, the devil had incited others from Jerusalem to claim that theirs was the mother church and, therefore, the most holy church in all Christendom, pretending to be zealous for the purity of the gospel! Because of all this, Paul had constantly to demonstrate that he had not promoted himself, nor usurped his office. He had obeyed God's call and that of the Lord Jesus Christ, who had appointed him to be an apostle. This is why he makes himself equal to Peter, James and John, who were known as the pillars of the church, and were held in high esteem amongst the other apostles (*Gal.* 2:9). He shows by this that he is in no way inferior to them. Why does Paul do this? Because he desires that his teaching will be received; this is his chief concern. Then, after he has prepared the Galatians to obey the exhortations he gives them, he proceeds to treat the matter upon which they differed. He explains that the gospel will be overthrown if they do not exercise that liberty which was purchased for them by the blood of the Lord Jesus Christ, since they were not to remain in bondage to the ceremonial law. For, as we shall see, if we live in such bondage, we will not enjoy the fruit of our redemption and of the salvation which was procured for us by the Son of God.

Let us firstly deal with the statements pertaining to Paul's authority. He says that he is 'an apostle, not of men, neither by man, but by Jesus Christ, and God the Father, who raised him from the dead'. First of all, let us observe that Paul's foundation is the decree and ordinance of God, and that, therefore, his message ought to have been received. For indeed, 'no man can take this honour unto himself in the church, but he who is called of God' (*Heb.* 5:4), as we have seen before. Our faith is too weak by far if we rely upon men, however honourable or worthy they may be. Even if they possessed a more than angelic perfection, it would count for nothing. Faith is so precious, that we must be careful that it is completely grounded upon God and his truth. Since this is the case, it is not enough for a man to be refined or knowledgeable, or to have seen and heard and done many things, if he wishes to be heard; for these things are as useful as a wisp of smoke with regard to reaching the kingdom of heaven! Deep wisdom and great learning matter nothing; all this is but another of Satan's deceptions. We know what the Bible says about all human wisdom: it is utter foolishness, and God laughs at it; it is an abomination in his sight because it hinders obedience (*1 Cor.* 1:20). Therefore, everything that is of man and of the creature must be considered base and vile. Indeed, concerning teaching, the church needs a well-ordered system which is approved by God. For if men push themselves forward in this area, God will withdraw all the more and this will result in total confusion. We must, therefore, pay attention to what Paul tells us here. He has nothing to offer in and of himself in order to earn a position of authority, but he has been called by God. This is the first point.

Furthermore, we must remind ourselves that Paul was not, like so many fools, carelessly boasting. In their preaching, they loudly proclaim that God has sent them, when in fact they are impostors – yes, even agents of Satan sent to bring destruction! However, Paul not only protests that he has been called, but also wishes to demonstrate the reality of the fact, as we have said. It was quite well known that he had been miraculously converted to the gospel and that he had received his teaching immediately. God had worked in a surprising and unusual way in Paul's life. There had also been direct revelation to two or three men in the city of Antioch that Paul was to be an apostle to the Gentiles. And not only this; everywhere he went people could see evidence of the fact because God openly displayed his own power in Paul. Thus, when he declares here that he is an apostle, he presupposes that it had already been confirmed to some extent that it was God who had appointed him to that office, and that he had not taken it under false pretences. But we know how eager men are to seek self-advancement! Thus, it is our duty to differentiate between Paul and all those who falsely boasted and bragged that they were 'sent by God'.

The same applies to us today, for the Pope (in order to deceive this poor world of ours, and maintain his unlawful and hellish oppression) claims to be the 'Vicar of Jesus Christ', in direct succession to the apostles! And then there are those vermin of clergymen under him, known as bishops – those horned beasts! (They only possess such an honourable title because deception abounds in Popery.) If we take them at their word, they have all descended directly from the apostles! Yet we must examine what affinity there is between them. If God has authorised their calling, then they ought to bear clear and infallible testimony to this fact. However, the Pope and all his followers are found guilty of falsifying and corrupting the whole teaching of the gospel. What they call the service of God is no more than an abomination in his sight. Their entire system is built on lies and gross deception, for they have been bewitched by Satan himself, as most of us are already aware. But what cloak does Satan use to cover all this evil? It is the notion that there has been a continuous succession since the days of the apostles; thus these bishops represent the apostles today in the church, and whatever they say must be accepted. Well then, our task is to decide whether those who claim these things have anything in common with the apostles. If they are exercising the office of good and faithful pastors, then we will listen to them! But if they are living contrary to the pattern our Lord Jesus Christ ordained for his church, what can we say? Oh, but they claim to be in true succession to the apostles! Then let them first prove it. They pretend to have evidence of this, but it is most flimsy. We might as well add that there were just as many of these 'successors' in Galatia, as there were in Rome; indeed, not only there, but in several of the places where Paul had preached – in Ephesus, Colosse, Philippi, and elsewhere! So, who are the apostolic successors now? If a man believes he has the privilege of being one of Paul's successors, he must surely go out and preach the gospel. He must produce evidence of the fact before people will accept him.

Finally, we need to take note of the following: when men preach the gospel, for example, as pastors or overseers, their role does not in any way diminish the authority of God, nor do they trespass upon his territory, provided he alone is glorified and our faith is in his Word. Their role is to exhort us to remain obedient to God. This is another point. Above all, men should not arrogantly exalt themselves; they should be raised up and sent by God. He has this right as supreme Majesty. However, as I have already said, there must be sufficient evidence of a man's calling. We are to exercise discernment and not blindly accept it without due thought or consideration; for Satan's agents may constantly boast of their calling, whilst disguising their true characters, and thus deceitfully infiltrate the church. It is our duty to test all such, to see whether or not God has called them.

How does Paul speak of his calling here? 'Not,' he says, 'of men, neither by man'. When Paul says that he is an apostle 'not of men', he is making a general point which applies also to all ministers of the Word of God and pastors of the church. As we have just noted, when God chose to send prophets in former days, then pastors, to teach his people, he did not divest himself of his own authority. On the contrary, he did so to show us that we are not at liberty to govern our affairs according to our own will. At the same time, he desired to show them that they were nothing if they were not faithful to their charge. We must be obedient to God; those whom he has specifically raised up must simply be instruments or vessels of his Holy Spirit. We can see, then, that when Paul declares that he is not sent by men, he means that he has been ordained by God to serve him.

However, the second statement applies only to the apostles, for he says that he was not called 'by man'. Although God calls us today and accepts us, nevertheless, we also need to be called by man. If this were contrary to the will of God, Paul would never have allowed it. However, we know that wherever he went, he appointed ministers and pastors; therefore, this must be a lawful practice! Notice that Paul does not unwisely condemn those who are called by man.

No, but he is now dealing with that which is proper to the apostolic charge alone. This one factor distinguishes those who are called to oversee particular churches, and the apostles themselves. The distinction remains true today, and must continue until the end of the world. The apostles were appointed, not by human election, nor according to the common practice of the churches, but by the very mouth of the Son of God. Even when they had to find a substitute in Judas' place in order to complete the twelve, the apostles, though present, together with a great company of other disciples, did not dare make the choice themselves (*Acts* 1:24). If they were about to choose a pastor for the church at Jerusalem, or at Antioch, or elsewhere, they would use the appointed means; that is, they would pray to God and then choose a man whom they considered to be suited and qualified for the office. In this case, however, they submitted the matter to God's will by casting lots, for this was beyond the power of human reasoning. Why did they do this? As I have already said, the apostles had to be appointed from on high by special privilege, because they were to spread the gospel throughout the world. Now, as for Paul, he was chosen at a later point. Nevertheless, he was equally privileged, because the revelation which led him to take upon himself the office of an apostle had come directly from heaven! Furthermore, as we have seen before, he had been to the third heaven, and been blessed in countless ways (*2 Cor.* 12:2). Paul had been addressed by the Holy Spirit, pronouncing his message from on high, because God had chosen Paul to be the apostle to the Gentiles and had wanted to give him more specific instruction. Thus, as we have seen, Paul was not chosen by man. This is not to say that the present ministers and pastors of the church necessarily do wrong. No; it is rather that Paul needed to have this special honour in order to be accepted by Peter and John, and all who had lived alongside the Son of God during his time on this earth.

We have now made a brief examination of Paul's claims about himself. The lesson we ought to learn is that although we respect those who are called to be pastors, and who bring us God's Word, we are to listen to God above any other and remember that our Lord Jesus is the only head of the church. If we do not hold fast to this, then our faith is likely to be unstable, and our hearts captivated by whoever happens to be the most eloquent preacher. We will thus become most fickle, liable to change from day to day, or from moment to moment! Let us be on our guard, therefore, when we meet people with clerical titles, such as prelates or bishops, remembering that the highest privilege a person could possibly have is to be a servant of Jesus Christ and thus pleasing in his sight! How can we know whether such people are, indeed, pleasing to him? Well, firstly they need to have been appointed in a lawful way, accompanied by calling upon the name of God. Then, they need to have been selected because they possess the necessary gifts to exercise that office. This is how we may know beyond all doubt the pastors whom God owns and approves. It is not enough to have been 'called' to this position; a person must fulfil the charge which has been committed to him. Paul does not simply say that he has been ordained. No, he gives himself the title 'apostle' because he has been sent to carry the message of salvation and to preach the gospel to the world. Therefore, those who wish to be known as bishops and prelates simply must *teach.* If they are nothing more than idols, or dumb dogs, we are obliged to reject and despise them, inasmuch as they shamefully mock God's name and profane his greatness. Such people are to be abhorred, because they misuse the name of God. This is what we have learnt from our text.

Next, Paul plainly states that he has been sent 'by Jesus Christ and God the Father, who raised him from the dead'. By mentioning Jesus Christ, Paul takes us back to what we have touched upon before; namely, that if we desire to obey God and be subject to him, we must embrace the Lord Jesus Christ and listen to him alone. Since he is the only Lord, all of us, from the greatest to the least, are to submit to him and to his doctrine. For whoever does not honour the Son does not honour the Father, as it says in the fifth chapter of John's Gospel (*John* 5:23). This is worthy of our attention, because we would all like others to think that we honour God and bow our necks to his yoke! Yet, we know that the world strives against the gospel, and that none are prepared to submit to it. As soon as Jesus Christ demands that we come to him, we become sour-tempered; we are so wild that he can hardly tame us! This brings to light our inconstancy, and reveals that we really despise God, despite our previous declarations to the contrary! For God directs us to his Son, and bids us kiss him as an act of homage (*Psa.* 2:12). But as we know, and as experience too often proves, we all seem to desire to exempt ourselves from submitting to the Lord Jesus Christ. This being so, Paul reveals to us something of the glory of Jesus. Our response should be to tremble at his Word, and be silent before him when he speaks, ready to receive all of his teaching and every word that proceeds from his mouth, without contradiction. Unless we do this, God will certainly reject all our claims to serve and honour him. Thus, we are exhorted in this text to devote ourselves wholeheartedly to the Lord Jesus Christ, for he is our Shepherd. To show that we are truly his sheep, we must hear his voice rather than the voice of strangers. If God has revealed himself to us, and we have recognised the voice of the Lord Jesus Christ calling us, then we must follow as those that belong to his flock. These are the points we are to remember.

Because so many people ignore the Son of God and refuse to come to him, Paul adds the name of 'God the Father' here. Yes, it is true that all the fulness of the Godhead dwells in Christ (*Col.* 1:19; 2:9), and woe to him who seeks any other God! However, our Lord Jesus Christ appeared in human form and lived in this world as a despised man. He even emptied himself to the point of suffering a most shameful death, taking our curse upon himself. This is why God is gravely offended when we will not listen to his Son. Our Lord Jesus declared this when he said, 'He that despiseth you despiseth me; and he that despiseth me despiseth him who sent me' (*Luke* 10:16). Hence, the order which Paul uses here, for if we do not willingly submit to the Lord Jesus Christ by accepting his doctrine as infallible truth, we are showing contempt for God. We cannot then say that we wish to worship God, for he will reject all our worship. Why? Because, as I have said, if we separate the Father from the Son, we are guilty of high treason against God.

Paul then adds that Jesus Christ was 'raised from the dead'. He says this in order to give further attestation to his apostleship, that he might be included in the company of the other apostles, because he was added to their number when Jesus Christ was no longer on this earth. As we have already mentioned, there were some false apostles who sought to ruin everything, reproaching Paul and saying, 'How can this be? He cannot be a disciple of the Son of God in the way that Peter and John are; he was born at the wrong time.' How could he, therefore, prove that the message he preached had been revealed to him by Jesus Christ? Well, if a person has any doubts about the authority of the Lord Jesus Christ, Paul here declares that his resurrection ought to dispel them! For although our Lord Jesus humbled himself by taking upon him the veil of human nature, in a sense concealing his glory, his essential being was not weakened in any way. For we know that the angels acknowledged him as their sovereign King, even though he was cast into this world as a helpless baby in a stable (*Luke* 2:14). Even the stars in heaven bore witness to his birth (*Matt.* 2:2). Indeed, all the time he was here, the glory of the Lord Jesus Christ was always sufficiently evidenced. This being the case, however, it is still true to say that his glory was most nobly displayed through his resurrection. As it says in the first chapter of Romans, it was his resurrection that declared him to be the Son of God (*Rom.* 1:4). Again, we have seen in the second letter to the Corinthians that though he was crucified in weakness, he lives by the immeasurable power of the Spirit of God (*2 Cor.* 13:4). Paul is telling us that although our Lord Jesus Christ is no longer on this planet, his majesty is in no sense diminished or obscured. We are still obligated to him, to render him the obedience he deserves; we are still to receive his Word with all due reverence and without reservation. It is very important that we give thought to this warning. For there are many fickle people who say they wish to see Jesus Christ in a visible form! If they saw Jesus Christ living here in this world, they say, they would immediately believe that everything he said was true! 'Just one word from his mouth and we would be spellbound! We would not need any other teaching, nor any other teacher but him,' they say! Indeed! But the Son of God has come! Furthermore, he has fulfilled the commission which he received from his Father; that is to say, he preached the gospel, and then confirmed it by his death and passion. Then, having risen again, he sent us his apostles. Now, he reigns in sovereign power. Angels bow the knee before him and his glory surpasses that of heaven and earth combined. Is this not enough for us? It has pleased God to entrust his message – the priceless treasure of the gospel – to weak vessels. He has sent us mere mortals! Yet, he expects us to accept the message they proclaim. Is it not, therefore, a mockery to say that if Jesus Christ were amongst us we would be prepared to obey him? Indeed, even if his glory were displayed to the very demons in hell, and if all heaven and earth trembled at his presence, we would still foolishly maintain that he was too far away from us! For when the gospel is preached to us, our Lord Jesus is there, declaring that he has not forsaken us. Though he does not dwell with us in a physical sense, yet [spiritually] we are united to him. After all, he is our Head, and therefore rules over the body; there is an inseparable bond between us. Because of this bond, we must yield to him in obedience. The fact of his resurrection ought to inspire awe in us and produce deep reverence. For when we hear the name of the Lord Jesus Christ, it ought to remind us that he is the one the prophet spoke of, the name by which all men will swear, and to which they will bow the knee (*Isa.* 65:16).

Here, then, is a summary of what we must always keep in mind. Firstly, we must not measure the gospel by the reputation of those who preach it, for they will be feeble men. We are not to use this approach, otherwise our assurance of salvation will be dependent upon the merit of men, which will mean that we are resting upon this world. We are to understand, rather, that it is Jesus Christ addressing us, as it were. And how does he speak? With the authority which his Father gave him, for he was raised from the dead by the fulness of the power of the Holy Spirit. Our Lord Jesus Christ has such authority because he was raised and exalted to heaven, and now he has dominion over every creature. Since this is so, we must submit to him, and keep ourselves on a tight rein, as it were. We must receive his Word and acknowledge that he is in control of our lives. We must be willing to be taught in his name; for whenever his Word is preached, though it is uttered by the lips of men, it is spoken with the authority of God. Our faith must be totally grounded upon that Word, as much as it would be if the heavens had opened a hundred thousand times and revealed the glory of God. This, I say, is the way that we are to be instructed in this world, until the day God gathers us into his eternal kingdom. This is what we are to remember whenever we are presented with the glory of the Lord Jesus Christ.

Now let us fall before the majesty of our great God, acknowledging our faults, and praying that it may please him to make us increasingly conscious of them, that we might be brought to a better repentance. May we, who have been regenerated, really feel that we are being led by the Holy Spirit. If this is the testimony of our hearts, then we may boast without hypocrisy that we are in the world, but not of it. Indeed, we are pilgrims and strangers here and our eternal dwelling place is heaven – an inheritance above, which has been secured by faith, though we do not enjoy it at the present time. May it please him to grant this grace, not to us only, but to all peoples and nations on earth.

2

The Blood That Cleanses All Our Sinful Stains

> *Grace be to you and peace from God the Father, and from the Lord Jesus Christ, Who gave himself for our sins, that he might deliver us from this present evil world, according to the will of God and our Father: To whom be glory for ever and ever. Amen* (Gal. 1:3–5).

We all have a natural tendency to seek our own well-being. Yet we are most ignorant of the source from which all such benefits proceed. For the only true source of happiness is in the knowledge that God loves us and that we are his children. Without this knowledge, all the prosperity in the world is of no value to us; moreover, it is likely to do us harm. For until such time as God accepts us by his grace, we are all under his curse, and the good things that we receive from his hand will cost us very dear. They do not belong to us until we become members of God's family. Therefore, above all else we must seek to be acceptable to God, and to have that assurance that we are part of his household – the church. Indeed, in the Psalms, David, having condemned the folly of worldly desires (such as seeking an abundance of corn or wine, and generally thinking of one's own comfort), tells us that nothing should be more desirable to us than 'the light of his countenance' (*Psa.* 4:6–7). This involves rejoicing in his favour, and, as I said before, being confident of the fact that we are his children. In the same way, the psalmist

(*Psa.* 106:4) wishes above all else that God would remember him with the same favour which he bears toward the rest of his people. He may well have stood in need of many things, but he was prepared to ignore everything else because he was preoccupied and concerned with this one object: to be found among the number of God's elect. We know this because he specifically mentions 'the favour that thou bearest unto thy people'. Although God demonstrates tokens of his love toward all mankind in general, the whole of Adam's lineage has been cut off from him, until they are reunited through Jesus Christ. Thus, although the love of God is shown to all men by virtue of the fact that we were created in his own image, and although he causes the sun to shine upon all, provides food for all, and watches over all, yet this is nothing compared to that special love which he reserves for his elect, his flock. This is not due to any merit to be found in them, but rather because it has pleased him to make them his own.

Notice that Paul, in all his epistles, constantly reminds us of the grace of God, and the love he bears towards all believers. He says 'Grace be to you and peace'. This word 'peace' (as we have noted on previous occasions) includes all worldly prosperity. By it Paul is asking God to provide those things that he considers to be for our good, to shower his riches upon us, and reveal his bounty, in order that we might praise him for his goodness. However, all the wealth of this world will only tend to our ill, unless we have found favour with the Lord. Hence, the order in which Paul speaks here: he always places God's grace and free pardon before an increase in worldly prosperity. Thus, although we may ask God to bless us with those things which he considers we need, we must not forget the most important blessing – to be members of his church and assured of his love in our hearts. The light of his countenance, as the psalm says, should suffice us. Although God permits us to ask for good things from his hand, we must keep a tight rein on our desires. For God may afflict us with many sorrows, and at such times we need to value his grace above anything else; it should content us, even if everything else were taken away. As we have already said, if we live in comfort, surrounded by all kinds of pleasures and delights, we will still be miserable if we do not have the peace of conscience which comes from knowing that God loves and accepts us. Therefore, earthly goods should not be desired more than the love of God. For what if God, though he loves us, wishes to test our patience by causing us to suffer in this world, and subjecting us to many trials? Even then, we must prize his love above all else, and patiently bear it all, though it may seem as if all is against us.

How important it is for us to learn this lesson, as wherever we look we see men that have been led astray by their carnal appetites! Most have been blinded to such an extent that they only desire things which appeal to their natural instincts; they have no regard for God. One desires drink, another food, another clothing; these desires are vain and empty. We are to begin with the fact that God is the giver of every good gift, and whatever we have is a gift from his hand, including those commodities which meet our daily needs. If we do not ask God for these things, we are in a most pitiable, indeed, a most savage state. Yet, most people are in just such a condition. Some may seem to have more orderly conduct, but in reality they too have gone astray. Maybe they ask God to send them things which will be good and profitable for them, but they pay no attention to the fountain to which they must first resort in order to be reconciled to God. They do not much care whether God loves or hates them, as long as he spares their lives and refrains from venting his anger on them! It is all the same to them, provided he grants them what their flesh craves and longs for! Although such people seek God for their needs, they put the cart before the horse. God's love ought to come first in their lives, then they may freely ask God to display his goodness by blessing them with good things. People can never seem to control themselves in this area; they make the grandest requests it is possible for mortal beings to make. One craves wealth, another honour; they are never contented with that which God has already provided. But even if men have modest desires, and only want the barest essentials, they still forget about their need of God's grace. This shows that they are no better than the rest!

Notice, therefore, that Paul has a good reason for placing these two words together. First, he points out that we need to be accepted through God's grace, in order to know that God is our Father and that we are his children. Next, he mentions his desire that God may prosper us. Although this prosperity can be so attractive to us (as I have said), we must remember that it is only the grace of God which can afford us any real comfort. If we have to suffer great poverty in this world, and things do not happen to us as we would have liked, we ought, nevertheless, to be content with the knowledge of God's love for us.

Then, in our text, Paul mentions the Lord Jesus Christ, for it would have been impossible for God to have shown us mercy if it were not for his Son, in whom he is well pleased. (This is referred to in the seventeenth chapter of Matthew, as well as in the first chapter to the Ephesians, verse five.) If we were only to see God in all his glory, we would be fearful. For, as weak creatures in whom is to be found nothing but sin, we can have no access to such a God. Though at present we creep upon the face of this earth, we deserve to be swallowed up in the deepest pit of hell! It is for this reason that Jesus Christ was revealed. For it is only through him that we may taste the love of God and enjoy the blessings he bestows upon us. After all, these things belong to the only-begotten Son of God, who is the heir of all things, as the apostle says in the first chapter to the Hebrews (*Heb.* 1:2). Thus, because all the good gifts God grants us belong to our Lord Jesus Christ, we must seek him in order to enjoy them. Now we have seen the reason why Paul says, 'from God the Father and the Lord Jesus Christ'.

* * *

However, Paul adds that Jesus Christ 'gave himself for our sins', to give us greater assurance that God will indeed look favourably on us if we truly and sincerely seek him through his only Son. Surely, the only thing which prevents God from accepting us is our iniquity. Indeed, we know that his mercy extends even to the sparrows which fly through the air, and to dumb animals. For God causes the mountain grass to grow, and other vegetation, in order to feed the cattle, which is a token of his care for them. These are signs of his goodness, spoken of in the psalms (*Psa.* 104:14; 147:8). How could he not, then, love those whom he has created in his image, and who more closely resemble himself and his character, that is to say, mankind?

On the one hand, God, by virtue of the fact that he has made us, accepts us and calls us his own. However, on the other hand, since we have become corrupt and evil, he hates us and we have become his enemies. Indeed, there is, as it were, a mortal conflict between us, until we are accepted for the sake of the Lord Jesus Christ. Thus, in order that we might not doubt the love of God, Paul reminds us of the sacrifice by which the very memory of our transgressions is blotted out. For, having set aside all our shortcomings, God now regards us as his own, as those on whom he has set his seal. In other words, we are now those whom he has made his children and heirs.

Furthermore, this teaches us that the only way to have a peaceful conscience, and to be able to call upon God freely, is through having the sacrifice of the Lord Jesus Christ applied to our souls. It is this very sacrifice by which he made satisfaction for our sins, enabling God to call us his children. Firstly, we need to consider the benefits of the sufferings and death of the Lord Jesus Christ. It is here that we see reconciliation between God and ourselves, instead of the separation which formerly existed. Although at one time God hated us, he now deigns to accept us into his love. Why? Because our Lord Jesus Christ has atoned for all our sins and transgressions by the obedience he rendered throughout his sufferings and death. The sacrifice he offered has made satisfaction for our sins. His blood has brought us cleansing, and has washed away all our sinful stains. This is how we can be sure that God will accept us. How can we be so bold as to call upon God and take refuge in him? By fixing our eyes upon the sacrifice that our Lord Jesus Christ offered up to God. If we do not do this, then we will surely remain fearful when we consider the awesome majesty of God. For, being poor sinners, how can we do anything other than fear our Judge, who is armed ready to execute the judgment we deserve? However, the Lord Jesus Christ has put away our sin, and we can now boldly approach God without hindrance. We must bear in mind here that the sacrifice by which our Lord Jesus has reconciled us to his Father is all-sufficient. We are to place all our trust in it and not seek any other means of salvation.

Now, Paul was hoping to bring the Galatians back to the pure truth because they had been seduced and become corrupt. They had not altogether renounced Jesus Christ, but they still practised the ceremonial law as if it was a vital means of helping them obtain remission for their sins. In Popery today, likewise, people acknowledge that Jesus Christ is the Saviour of the world, yet each one seeks to 'pay' God, by presenting him with various gifts. The Galatians had already become entangled with this error. For this reason, Paul tells them that sins can only be blotted out by the sacrifice of the Lord Jesus Christ, for he wants them to trust in this alone. So then, in order to enjoy such a blessing, we too must reject all vain hopes, and all the lies that Satan places in our minds. He turns our eyes away from the Lord Jesus Christ and his grace, and would have us believe that we can have access to God through making our own satisfaction for sin. However, until we realise that there is no other cleansing from the stains of sin but the shed blood of the Lord Jesus Christ, applied by the Holy Spirit, and until we learn to trust in his grace and love alone, we will never be able to have free access to God. We will be left to our own devices as a just payment for our unbelief, for not having given the Lord Jesus Christ the honour that he deserves.

Paul refers to the sufferings and death of the Lord Jesus Christ here, to remind us that the price has been paid for our sins, and that God will no longer take them into account.

Let us notice in particular that Paul says Jesus Christ 'gave himself'. He expresses it thus to impress upon us the degree of his love. This shows us that he did not spare body or soul when he laid down his life to make the payment which God would otherwise have required of us. As our surety, he endured extreme anguish of soul, bearing God's wrath on our behalf. As for his body, it endured all the shame and disgrace and the most awful torture that a body can possibly bear. He humbled himself in this way for our salvation, to show that his love for us is boundless, as I have said.

* * *

At this point, Paul refers to 'the will of God'. He tells us that God was purposely displaying his mercy when he sent the Lord Jesus Christ to accomplish all that was necessary for our salvation. As it says in that other passage (*John* 3:16), God so loved the world that he did not spare his only-begotten Son but delivered him to death for our sakes. Paul does not want us to think that Jesus Christ came to appease God the Father in such a way as to persuade him to change his mind (although men are apt to entertain such base and earthly opinions). No; rather, he would have us see that God was not reconciled after the manner of men. Thus, he states that although Jesus 'gave himself for our sins', it was God who had ordained it. If a man is angry with his child, he can call upon a mediator to come and calm his anger in the office of a third party. But this is not what was happening when our Lord Jesus Christ sacrificed himself! Yes, he suffered in order to blot out all our iniquities and enable us to approach God, from whom we were cut off. But Paul does not mean that Jesus came of his own volition, and that God had no part in it. What, then, does he mean? Well, as we have just been saying, before we were reconciled to God, he both hated and loved us. Why did he love us? Because we were his creatures, and although we were wretched in his sight, lost and condemned because of sin, he took pity on humanity, not willing that any should perish. Thus, God loved us despite the fact that we had fallen in Adam and become totally depraved. Yet, at the same time, he hated us, because he is the source of all righteousness and had to hate the evil within us. This is why payment had to be made by the blood of the Lord Jesus Christ, in the sacrifice he offered. Yet, we must not attribute this great gift to anyone other than God himself. It was God who sent his only Son and delivered him up to death for us. Why? So that all enmity between us could be removed. This, then, is how we must understand the words of Paul, when he says that Jesus Christ 'gave himself for our sins'. We must bear in mind that this did not happen without the will of God, for he had determined thus in his eternal counsels.

Now, firstly, we must magnify the grace shown to us in the person of the Lord Jesus Christ. For if God had simply proclaimed our pardon by declaring that he had decided to receive us in mercy, despite our unworthiness, that would have been a great thing. Even then, we would never have been able to utter sufficient praise for such grace. But God has given us his own Son as a token of his love. Indeed, he has given us himself through his Son, and declared himself to be our Father. This so far outshines pardon alone that even if we employed all our faculties to worship and adore, we could never perfectly praise him for such mercy. This is our first observation upon Paul's reference to 'the will of God'. Let us remember that though God had just reason to hate and detest us, and though we were in fact his enemies, as the Scriptures say (*Rom.* 5:10), he did not utterly forsake us. Indeed, his pity was so great that he could not leave us in our lost condition. He did not only declare this with his mouth; he bestowed upon us a gift, as we have seen. His own Son met our need. Therefore, since God was so merciful and kind towards us even before we were reconciled to him, how will he regard us now that we have been reconciled, and have the gospel preached to us to grant us assurance? Now that we have been united by faith to the Lord Jesus Christ as members of his body? Can we doubt God's love for us, when Paul confirms the fact so forcefully in the fifth chapter to the Romans? In this chapter, Paul tells us that at the very time we were in mortal conflict with God, Christ came to cancel all our sins. We are now accepted by God. He has called and drawn us to himself in the gentlest possible way, and even now, his arms are stretched wide to embrace us whenever we come to him. We ought, therefore, to cast aside all doubt, and call upon God without fear, assured of our salvation because God has given abundant confirmation of the fact. This is what we need to learn from this passage.

Furthermore, we must also notice the love of the Lord Jesus Christ, who gave himself for our sins. Surely, he will not allow his sufferings and death to be of no benefit to us, nor will he allow his work to be rendered void and of no effect, by failing to produce fruit in our lives. Although he suffered once, he is our perpetual advocate and intercedes constantly on our behalf, in order that we might partake in the cleansing which he has obtained for us. Then, washed from all our stains, we can appear before God and call upon him with boldness. How we ought to store up the things which Paul brings to our attention here for the strengthening of our faith. Then we will be enabled to freely resort to God, not as strangers but as his own familiar children. At the same time, we need to reject Satan's deceptions and lies, for his only aim is to turn us away from the Lord Jesus Christ by obscuring the fact that we can only find grace through him. Though Satan cannot entirely destroy this grace, he will seek to confuse us by suggesting other means by which we may obtain God's favour. May we renounce all such things and fix our attention on the Lord Jesus Christ. He is all-sufficient, so let us loathe the false ways of 'purchasing' the favour of God which come into our minds. Jesus' sacrifice alone has secured our justification and righteousness, which means that God can now draw us to himself in mercy.

Again, this term, 'the will of God', includes the idea of his free bounty, and excludes all that men have come to believe about their own merits. For this is the way this phrase is employed elsewhere in the Holy Scriptures. As I have mentioned before, the word 'will' is elsewhere referred to as 'good pleasure'. Paul is, therefore, not only telling us that the source of our salvation and redemption is in the eternal counsels and decrees of God the Father (*Luke* 2:14), he is also demonstrating that all the praise for our justification must be attributed to God's grace, which takes no personal merit into account! Thus, he is seeking to combat all pride and presumption on our part. Let us consider for a moment; what did God see in us but wretchedness? This is why he had to exercise mercy towards us. We need to be aware that we can only lift up our eyes towards heaven and address our prayers and supplications to God because he freely permits us to do so. As John suggests (*John* 3:16), God did not wait to be loved by us! Indeed, this would have been impossible, because our hearts are given over to evil. Yet, despite the fact that we were his enemies, God demonstrated his love. As we have already seen, the reason the Lord Jesus came was to reconcile us to God the Father. This, in sum, is what Paul is teaching us in this text.

* * *

Now let us comment upon Paul's next statement, where he says that Jesus died to 'deliver us from this present evil world'. This reveals why Christ loved us so much that he was prepared to redeem us in the way he did. It is for this reason also that we have been called to know the Lord Jesus Christ – in order that we might no longer live in our filth and uncleanness, but be delivered from it. Whilst this is not the sole cause of our salvation, it is surely the end and goal that God intended for us. Thus, when we speak of salvation, we must bear the following factors in mind. We start with the free grace that God showed us when he determined in his eternal counsels to draw us to himself by the Lord Jesus Christ. This is the first cause of our salvation.

Then there is Jesus Christ himself, in whom we find all that is necessary to guarantee that salvation, for in him all our sins are blotted out. He made himself our surety, and made full satisfaction for our sins, so that nothing would prevent us from drawing near to God. This is the second point to remember.

Then there is the means by which we are united to the Lord Jesus Christ, that is to say by receiving the promises of the gospel with true faith. The sufferings and death that our Lord Jesus Christ endured are of no profit to unbelievers; in fact, their condemnation is made all the more severe by the fact that they reject the way that God has appointed. If they have trodden underfoot the blood of the Lord Jesus Christ, the ransom for their souls, then their ingratitude will be most sorely punished [see *Heb.* 10:29; *2 Pet.* 2:1]. We must receive the gospel promises by faith if we wish Jesus Christ to reveal himself to us; only then will he lead us to possess and enjoy the riches he has purchased on our behalf. These riches belong only to those who are members of his body, who have received him by faith and are united to him. As it says in the first chapter of John (*John* 1:12), the only people that God will accept and acknowledge as his children are those who believe in his only Son. This is the third thing to remember about our salvation.

The last point is that God will then glorify himself in us. This is what Paul also says in the third chapter to the Romans (*Rom.* 3:25). In that text, Paul firstly states that God has given us the Lord Jesus Christ as the means by which we may be acceptable to him, through the forgiveness of our sins, and he has granted us the gospel in order to enable us to receive this gift. Then he says that God has done this 'to declare his righteousness', that we might give him all the praise and glory when we realise that we owe everything to him. However, God is not only glorified if we confess with our mouths that he alone is the author of salvation, that it proceeds from free mercy alone. He is glorified when we are renewed by the Holy Spirit, who causes God's image to shine through us, and when we strive to devote ourselves to his service. The Scriptures say that God has not called us to worldliness or uncleanness, but to be sanctified by faith (*1 Thess.* 4:7). Thus, Paul has good reason to say that Jesus Christ has died 'to deliver us from this present evil world'. Jesus gave himself for us and blotted out the remembrance of our sins before God the Father because he did not wish us to live in our filthiness and sin. We are to be separate from the world, and live as the inheritance of God. Our whole lives should demonstrate such obedience that it becomes apparent to all that we are God's adopted children and that we love and honour him as our Father.

How we must hang our heads with shame, when we hear that we should be separate from this 'present evil world'! These words refer to man in his natural state, for the world itself contains nothing that is inherently wicked or corrupt. All the evil proceeds from the sin dwelling in us. Thus, when we read that the world is full of evil and wickedness (as it also says in John's inspired letter – *1 John* 5:19), it cannot be speaking of the sun, moon, earth, seas, nor, indeed, anything else that is in the world. It is saying that *we* are so vile that we have infected all that is in the world with our own pollution. While man remains in his natural condition, he is rotten to the core and, of necessity, displeasing to God. For it is certain that there can be no fellowship between righteousness and iniquity; yet in us there is only iniquity! Therefore, we must separate from our very natures, otherwise we will never be able to approach God. Woe to all who, in their blindness, think great things of their own free will, or power, or wisdom, or this or that! How self-satisfied we are, even when we realise that we are full of corruption within, and so much filth that we are to be pitied. Whereas we ought to be ashamed of our condition, we seem to reserve judgment and deceive ourselves through our vain imaginations. Surely, if we were to examine ourselves thoroughly, we would discover that all that is within us could aptly be described as 'evil'; this proves that we are totally corrupt. If we were to approach God just as we are by nature, he would have to remove us far from his presence. This is one observation from this text. All pride is beaten down; men cannot boast of anything save the free grace of God. We ought to feel so ashamed of our depravity that we condemn ourselves with our own mouth and act as our own judge, rather than wait for God to pronounce his sentence against us. This is what we can glean from our text.

To know whether or not the benefits of the sufferings and

death of the Lord Jesus Christ apply to us, we need to walk in the fear of God; for if we give a free rein to our lusts, the Lord Jesus will reject us. Whilst it is true that our salvation depends solely on the grace of God, and that we cannot add our works in order to gain assurance of the same, nevertheless, we must deny ourselves. Whatever we might think, our Lord Jesus Christ did not come to give us occasion to abuse the grace he has shown us, for this would be to mock him openly. If we wallow in the mire after he has washed us in his blood, we are wilfully profaning that most holy blood, which sanctifies the whole world. Since the world is subject to the curse, and since we find ourselves to be corrupt and thus condemned by God, nothing can cleanse us but the blood of the Lord Jesus Christ. What intolerable sacrilege it is, therefore, to return to the mire, as we so often do! Let us, then, be clear that the fruit of the sufferings and death of the Lord Jesus Christ does not give us licence to do wrong, nor to live according to our own lusts and desires. No, we must return to the concept of separation which Paul speaks of here; not that which is caused by our defilement of holy things and overturning of God's ways, but rather to the idea of separation from this 'present evil world'.

Thus, believers ought to devote themselves to a life of absolute purity, knowing that though they were bought by the sacrifice of our Lord Jesus Christ when he suffered and died, it was upon condition that they deny themselves. As, indeed, our Lord Jesus Christ said, 'Whosoever will come after me, let him deny himself . . . and follow me' (*Mark* 8:34). What, then, must we do, and what should be our life's aim? We are to strive to separate ourselves from the pollution of the world and to cleave, rather, to our God by living a holy life. Indeed, we will never perfectly attain to this until we have been taken out of the world, but, nonetheless, it is the goal towards which we press and to which we ought to be drawing closer. Thus, although believers have taken refuge in the mercy of God, and trust in this, realising that they can only be made righteous through having their sins forgiven, they are also working towards the goal that Paul refers to here: that is to say, to be separate from the world. We must remember both of these things. Some foolish people imagine that once they have been regenerated by the Lord Jesus Christ they have reached perfection, and no longer need have their sins forgiven. They say that we are keeping people at the ABC of the gospel, as it were, if we preach that we are justified by faith alone, and cannot be acceptable to God unless he mercifully pardons and covers our iniquity. This is devilish pride; yet Popery today is no better when it comes to an understanding of the grace of God! So then, if any should seek to bewitch us and blind us to our need of God's mercy and the remission of our sins, we are to detest such seducers, and all their blasphemies! We are to sigh and groan throughout our lives, realising that there is only one way to have assurance of salvation: that is, to realise we are condemned, and to be satisfied that the blood of the Lord Jesus Christ alone can wash and cleanse us. This is one point.

However, we are also to have this one goal: to be separate from this wicked world. How? We need to pray that, having touched us by his Holy Spirit, he will increase his gifts and graces in us and mortify the lusts of our flesh. When we are aware of such a battle occurring inside us, we must be active in the struggle; otherwise, we will come limping to God, stumbling many times on the way. We may even fall and lose our way completely. We ought always to bemoan the fact that we fail God at every turn. This is how we can be 'delivered from this present evil world'. It does not mean that we will be totally set free from sin. When Paul says that God has saved us in order that we might walk in perfection and uprightness before him, he is not suggesting that such purity can be found in any man while he lives in this world. No, for all our thoughts are continually at enmity with God. Even the most righteous man amongst us feels indebted to God, and knows that he is still dragging his feet behind him, as it were. Although this is the case, we might feel, on the other hand, that Jesus Christ has already saved us from bondage to Satan through faith, and that he will preserve us against all future attacks. Yet, if we were to examine and try our hearts, we would find that the moment we desire to do good and to honour God, our own nature leads us to do the opposite and makes us rather desire to be distant from God. Believers, therefore, have these two conflicting elements within. On the one hand, the Holy Spirit exhorts us through Peter to devote ourselves to living a holy life (*1 Pet.* 2:1); however, on the other hand, we are held back by many evil desires, and hindered from drawing near to God as we would like. Hence Paul, in the seventh chapter to the Romans, bemoans and confesses his wretchedness, in that he cannot perform the good that he desires to do, nor yet can he altogether flee the sin that he loathes and detests (*Rom.* 7:19). Here, then, is another observation about this deliverance that is mentioned here. The Lord Jesus Christ has not as yet renewed us by his Holy Spirit to the extent that we now have the ability to walk as we desire, or run with the swiftness of foot or courage that is required of us. No, rather, our deliverance makes us aim to devote ourselves to God in complete obedience, to turn our backs upon our evil ways, and die to them more and more until we are brought to perfection: in other words, until God's image is completely restored in us .

Thus, although the Galatians had rebelled in part, by giving ear to seducers who altered the gospel and had created their own, in which Jesus Christ was bound and gagged, as it were, nevertheless, Paul counts them among the believers for whom Christ's sacrifice was made. He addresses them as members of the church of God; he does not write 'To the apostates who have abandoned Jesus Christ.' Whereas he is about to point out their faults, he does not wish to exclude them altogether from the hope of salvation. The only reason he writes to them is to draw, win and direct them back to the right path. And, because he is hoping to restore them to the true way of salvation (for that was what they needed), he still connects them with the unspeakable gift purchased for us by the Son of God, counts them separate from the world, and members rather of the company of those whom God accepts and acknowledges as his children. This is because the gospel had been sown among them. Although they had become entangled with error, they had not completely forsaken God, nor were they strangers to the gospel. Hence Paul, for these reasons, still regards them as believers. In the same way, God considers us to be his servants, not because we are worthy of it, but because his Word has been preached to us. However, this can lead to our greater condemnation, if, God having called us through the gospel, we do not respond. Yet, if we truly desire to come to him despite our many sins and shortcomings, he will accept us for the sake of his Word. We are known as his church, not because we have any right to this title, but rather, in the same way that Jerusalem was known as the Holy City, because it had been promised that the gospel would proceed from her and because it was there that the Redeemer of the world was to be revealed (*Matt.* 4:5; 27:53). Likewise, we are called believers, children of God and members of the church, for the gospel is preached among us and we believe it, even though we do not treat it with the reverence and respect that it deserves.

Nonetheless, though Paul deals gently with the Galatians, he does not intend to encourage them to sin, nor does he wish to soothe them with empty flattery (though many people love to be flattered in this way!). For we shall soon see how sharply he scolds them, even calling them fools! How, then, can we reconcile the two approaches? Well, on the one hand, Paul is emphasising the grace that God had shown to that church; and on the other hand, he wants them to purge themselves from sin, for this was their urgent need. This teaches us that when God plants a church in a certain place, it does not follow that everything they do will be commendable or virtuous. Look at the way in which the Papists use the name 'church' to disguise their abominations, the most detestable and diabolical things the world has ever known. 'What!', [they say], 'The church cannot err – it is the bride of Christ, and the pillar of truth' (*1 Tim.* 3:15). Yes, but think of these churches of Galatia – what does the Holy Spirit say by the mouth of Paul? These are apostates who have denied the gospel; their heresies are more wicked and outrageous than any other. Let us, therefore, be careful not to be so attached to human beings that we cannot condemn their sins when the time comes to judge. Everything must be placed in subjection to the Word of God, and all that does not conform to it must be condemned, for God must not be robbed of his authority. All that is not according to his Word must be cast out, denounced and loathed. In addition, let us remember to encourage those who have begun the Christian life to draw closer to God, especially if they are weak or if they have gone astray. Let us treasure God's grace, that it may increase and abound in us more and more, until we are finally gathered together to be with the Lord Jesus Christ, the one who daily calls us to himself.

Now let us fall before the majesty of our great God, acknowledging our sins, and praying that he would make us increasingly conscious of them. May our consciences be truly pricked, that we might hate our sin and embrace his mercy, and may his grace be poured upon us in ever-increasing measure. May his hand support and sustain us in our weakness, until we are brought to holy perfection in the kingdom of heaven, which has been bought for us by our Lord Jesus Christ. Thus we all say, Almighty God and heavenly Father, etc.

3

On Perverting the Gospel of Christ

> *I marvel that ye are so soon removed from him that called you into the grace of Christ unto another gospel: Which is not another; but there be some that trouble you, and would pervert the gospel of Christ. But though we, or an angel from heaven, preach any other gospel unto you than that which we have preached unto you, let him be accursed* (Gal. 1:6–8).

Now we will look more deeply into the subject I touched upon this morning. I said that whereas Paul does not spare the Galatians, neither does he wish to shut the gate of salvation to them completely. He intends to bring them to repentance, and for this reason he speaks of the grace of God into which they had all been called. Yet, he does not flatter them; rather, he rebukes them for their sins. In particular, he rebukes them for their fickleness, for they had listened to deceivers who came in among them distorting the pure doctrine of the gospel. In order to make them better perceive their treachery, Paul says he marvels that they have forsaken their heavenly calling so quickly and easily. He wonders how it is that they have been led astray so swiftly, and how it is that they have remained in that state, given that they had felt and experienced the grace of God in our Lord Jesus Christ. Because he is seeking to restore them, he is not saying at the outset that they have completely turned away from the gospel, but rather that they have been overtaken by temptation through seducers, who sought no less than to pervert the truth of God. There is only one pure gospel, as also there is only one Jesus Christ on whom it is founded. It is not for us to create the gospel anew; indeed, if we seek to add anything to the pure seed which we have received from our Lord Jesus Christ, we are destroying what God has established. This, in sum, is what Paul is teaching us in this first verse.

It might seem that Paul is being overly harsh and severe in rebuking the Galatians' weakness, seeing they had never once thought of rejecting the gospel, nor Jesus Christ who had been preached to them. But Paul pays no attention to the way they viewed the situation; he sees it as it really is – in other words, that once people turn away from the truth of God, they are rejecting Jesus Christ and cutting themselves off from him. Some people may think this strange, for many would like to mix light with darkness. Indeed, the confusion that exists in Popery is an outstanding example of this. They make many wonderful claims to the effect that they are upholding the Christian faith into which they have been baptised. But, for all this, it is clear that they have turned everything upside-down. Superstitions reign, and they practise open idolatry of a worse kind than has ever been known, even among the pagans. Any reverence for God is destroyed, since each one sets himself up as a saviour in place of our Lord Jesus Christ. Now, the Papists would respond by saying that they are not apostates, and that they have not abandoned Jesus Christ. But our Lord Jesus Christ is no ghost; he cannot change according to the whims of men. In short, he cannot be separated from his church. Thus, whatever the Papists may claim, they rob Jesus Christ of all his authority. 'If there is only one mediator,' [they say], 'what about the male saints, our patrons, and the female saints, our advocates?' If we speak to them of the sacrifice by which our Lord Jesus Christ has obtained perfect justification for all believers, once and for all, [they will say], 'Are we not supposed to say Mass every day and offer Jesus Christ again as a sacrifice to appease the wrath of God?' If we speak to them of free forgiveness of sins, [they will say], 'What about the ways in which we have made satisfaction for our own sins, and thus earned God's pity?' If we say that we can only be made good by the regenerating work of the Holy Spirit, and that until God transforms us, we are full of sin and rebellion, [they will say], 'What? What about our free will?' In short, they will name the name of Jesus Christ often enough, and will still give him his title of Redeemer, but they will divide his office and put it on offer so that each man may claim a share in it for himself. They also imagine that the saints and angels in paradise are their patrons, and that, therefore, they have infinite means of coming before God, for so it seems to them. Now, we may well conclude that the Holy Spirit has good reason to call them apostates; for they have forsaken Jesus Christ, and cut themselves off from him. They even misuse his name. But Jesus Christ never changes; we have seen that Paul says in 2 Corinthians that we will not find in him yes and no (*2 Cor.* 1:19), because he remains constant. Thus, whatever the Papists babble about Christianity, it is nothing but mere hypocrisy and lies. They falsely and wickedly use the name of the Son of God, either as a mask or as an idol.

This, then, is why Paul accuses the Galatians of having been led astray. If we ask what they had done, the answer is that they sought to observe the ceremonies of the law as if they were necessary. Yes, it is true that these ceremonies had been ordained by God. Of course; yet, they were a temporary condition for the people of old, for at the coming of our Lord Jesus Christ all this had to cease. Because the Galatians were mixing old figures and the shadows of the law with the pure light of the gospel, Paul, unable to bear it, says that they have rebelled and turned away from God. But there was something worse: namely, that they were making the grace of the Lord Jesus Christ altogether void, by believing that man can merit and acquire his own justification before God, and make himself acceptable in God's service. When these deceivers introduced this particular error of keeping to the 'former shadows', it led the Galatians to believe that they were presenting God with meritorious service. Yet, our salvation must be free, or Jesus Christ is no longer anything. We call it free salvation simply because it is given to us by God, and we come to him to be fed, with nothing but a hungry desire for what we are lacking. We should approach God as miserable beggars, if we would be justified in the name of our Lord Jesus Christ. For if we imagine that we have one drop of merit, we will not be motivated to come to him. One of the learned ancients said, and not without reason, that we cannot receive the salvation offered to us in our Lord Jesus Christ unless we can first erase the memory of all our merits, and acknowledge that we are only full of wretchedness. Paul, therefore, was completely justified in saying that the Galatians had fallen away from Jesus Christ and from God the Father.

However, there was another problem: they had been deluded into believing what others desired them to believe. They had been subjected to a slavish bondage, which robbed them of the peace of conscience that they ought to have had in the Lord Jesus Christ. Indeed, together with the reconciliation we have through his sacrificial death and passion, we must also be set free from the rigours of the law to which we were once in bondage. To explain this (as we will soon see more clearly; for here I am dismissing these matters, but we will see their wider implications shortly), you know that it says in the law that all those who do not fulfil what God commands to the last letter will be accursed (*Deut.* 27:26). Yet it is impossible for us to reach such perfection. Therefore, it was necessary for our Lord Jesus Christ to obtain our liberty, and to free us from the yoke of the law, which we are unable to bear, as it says in the fifteenth chapter of Acts (*Acts* 15:10).

We have now seen, in effect, why Paul accuses the Galatians of rebelling, and why he calls them traitors to God and to our Lord Jesus Christ: they had robbed him of the loyalty that they had promised. By this, we too are being admonished to keep to the pure and simple doctrine of the gospel, without straying in one direction or another. For it is not enough to have the name and title of Christians, or to bear the mark of baptism: we must continue steadfast in the doctrine of the gospel. As we have said before, our Lord Jesus Christ cannot deny himself. He can only be known in the way he has been revealed to us by God the Father, our own various conceptions of him being irrelevant. The gospel shows us why he came, his office, the benefits that we receive from him and the strength that he gives us. If we do not have the pure and simple doctrine which our Lord Jesus Christ has revealed, we have nothing at all, but if we have been taught it, let us hold on to it to the very end. If we draw back, even just a little, it is nothing short of unfaithfulness. Indeed, we must remember that terrible Fall, where we, together with others, fell and became entangled with so many errors, lies and deceits of Satan, that Jesus Christ was totally unknown to us. Since God has now, in his goodness, taken us from such an abyss, let us resolve to have firm and constant faith, so that we are no longer shaken like reeds in the wind. Let us remain firmly rooted in the gospel, grounded upon the invincible power of our Lord Jesus Christ. In him all the promises of God are 'yes and amen' (*2 Cor.* 1:20); their truth and their fulfilment is in him. Therefore, let our faith rest steadfast in these facts. This is what we must retain in our minds from Paul's teaching in this passage.

* * *

To make the Galatians even more ashamed of themselves, he speaks to them of the calling of grace. We can relate the words, 'from him that called you', as much to Jesus Christ as to God the Father, there being no great significance in this. We can, however, understand what Paul is saying. He is criticising the Galatians for their base behaviour; for they had even less excuse for going astray, considering they had experienced the goodness of God. For if God calls us, even if he summons us in order to put us to shame, we are still his creatures, and, therefore, owe him our obedience. We must always submit to his authority, whatever he decides to do with us. It is our duty to say to him: 'Here I am. What do you require of me?' Whereas, if we make excuses when God calls us, we are perverting the proper order of things. But God not only calls us to himself, he gives us all the treasures of his goodness in our Lord Jesus Christ. He gives himself willingly to us, asking of us only that we should be his own. Since God treats us with such kindness, and ravishes all our faculties with admiration for him, this should render us most unwilling to draw back. Nevertheless, if we do happen to wander to and fro after we have come to him, we will have much less excuse, and will therefore suffer a more severe and a more terrifying condemnation, as I have already suggested.

We see now why Paul mentions the grace into which the Galatians had been called. In fact, we are more guilty today than our fathers were under the law, if we fail to abide in the pure doctrine of the gospel, without swerving from it. For although God led our forefathers to salvation under the law, yet that calling was not accompanied by such open and abundant displays of the riches of his mercy as we now have in our Lord Jesus Christ. Let us examine ourselves. If God has already made his grace known to us, may this inspire and encourage us to have even greater boldness and invincible strength, so that we may continue in our calling, until we reach the place to which he is calling us. When we compare ourselves with wretched, ignorant unbelievers, our ingratitude is all the more apparent, in that we have had fuller and nobler grace shown to us. We know that many poor souls stray far and wide. They are, however, subject to condemnation: 'For as many as have sinned without law shall also perish without law' (*Rom.* 2:12). Now, as for us, God has declared his will to us in such familiar terms, and has given us the opportunity to learn the doctrines of the gospel (if we would only apply ourselves to them); therefore, our condemnation will be even greater than theirs, if we do not make every effort to devote ourselves entirely to God, as I have already said. This makes our responsibility all the greater.

Paul adds another point here: that all this had happened so quickly. Indeed, it is terrible that the Galatians, who had been taught from the lips of the apostle, had defiled themselves during his lifetime. This made them even more blameworthy, because just three days [as it were] after receiving the gospel, they fell away by mixing false teachings with God's truth. Had they kept the faith until a good while after the death of Paul, it does not follow that this would have excused them in God's sight, if they had subsequently fallen away. For as the truth on which our faith is grounded is everlasting, although the heavens and the earth are passing away, even so our faith must endure to the very end (*Luke* 21:33). Our faith should not depend on the life or death of men; it should be anchored in heaven. Therefore, if we change from one day to the next, we shall have the more to answer for, and our ungratefulness will be even more pronounced. In fact, what Paul says here about the Galatians is far too much in evidence today. Those who have been taught the gospel become discontented after three years [or so] if they do not have some novelty or other, for they have 'itching ears'. Many vain people backslide because they are not content with the truth in the gospel. They always want to be moving house [as it were], because they need some new thing to feed their foolish imaginations. Others grow dissatisfied when they see that the gospel has not brought them any of this world's goods. There are even some who turn away when they find that they may well be persecuted, and have many enemies. They will have to suffer while others prosper (or so they think). Thus, you can see how many desert our Lord Jesus Christ, not just as one generation succeeds another, but even as those who appear to be his followers turn and rebel after three, or perhaps ten years.

How closely then do we need to hold on to this teaching, since it applies to us. Let us consider the grievance Jeremiah had against the Jews. He says, in effect, 'Go to distant lands, run to the isles, observe what is done by other people. Each one keeps to his own idols', adding, 'which are yet no gods' (*Jer.* 2:10–11). Satan had deceived them by calling this worship, and they were so set in their ways that they could not be moved. (I hope you are as steadfast as they were, since

God has revealed himself to you, and you have a full and certain knowledge of his will.) Surely, however, the same could be said of us nowadays: for we have seen how unbending the Turks[1] are! And although the wretched Jews are no better than unclean dogs, yet they are very persistent in maintaining the authority of their law. As for the Papists, their foolishness is so apparent as to make them hideous; even children could judge them. Yet for all that, they burn with such mad zeal to maintain their blasphemous practices. As for ourselves, as soon as the devil beckons with his finger, we are enticed away. It seems as if each of us is on the lookout to see if there is anything new; the slightest thing will immediately weaken us and lead us astray. There is enough sin here without going any further. We must, therefore, take heed to the accusation which is made here by the mouth of Paul against the inconstancy of those who turn away from God, so soon after he has called them into the grace of our Lord Jesus Christ.

* * *

At this point, Paul states that the cause behind all this is that, 'there be some that trouble you and would pervert the gospel of our Lord Jesus Christ'. Here, Paul is asserting that anything which we may add to the gospel is nothing but mere smoke. Eventually we will discover that it is the devil who has conceived such nonsense in order to deceive miserable fools who cannot adhere to God's truth at all. 'This is nothing other than some people troubling you,' he says. It is true that this expression 'nothing other'[2] seems to imply that the whole matter is of no importance. However, Paul is saying that the Galatians were wrong to be troubled by those

[1] 'Turks' here and throughout is a reference to Muslims.

[2] The Authorised Version of 1611 renders this 'not another [gospel]', thus reflecting a view different from that given in Calvin's French translation.

from Jerusalem and Judaea, who told them they must not separate the law from the gospel. 'No, no,' he says, 'there is only one Jesus Christ. There is only one doctrine that will lead us to him, and give us faith, through which we may obtain salvation. If we wish to have and maintain a pure knowledge of the gospel, we must realise that this is where we find perfection; those who go further are simply trouble-makers throwing everything into disarray.' This text is well worth noting. We learn from it that if our Lord has given us the privilege of being taught in his school, we must no longer have weak faith which can be blown here and there. We must have resolute determination, so that we can say, 'Here is the faith by which we are going to live and die.' We meet many who do not openly oppose the teaching of the gospel, and who even suffer us to preach the grace of our Lord Jesus Christ. Indeed, if we were to ask such people what they disagree with in the gospel, [their answer would be] 'Nothing!' But then, if they were to see an altar adorned with grotesque statues, sure enough, they would flock to it! They would go and hear Mass and do all the other excesses of the Papists; it is all the same to them. And if all this is set before them as error, they still cannot see that it makes any difference. Take good note – such base behaviour reveals that they do not have faith. How? Well, this is how we can know, and even feel, if we ourselves are believers: when we have discernment about the gospel, and conclude that it is the infallible truth of God, and that it cannot lead us astray if we follow it. However, the Papists have invented a faith (as they call it) which is veiled; this suits them fine (even though the poor souls know nothing), as long as they continue to say, 'I rely on our Holy Mother Church; I hold to what she believes.' These people openly display that they have no faith, and do not know how to be saved. It is written that we can only obtain justification and salvation through faith, when we embrace Jesus Christ as the one who communicates all blessings. Therefore, if the Lord Jesus Christ is unknown, there can be no faith. Popish leaders and teachers have been bewitched by a most awful deception of Satan to speak as they do, which proves to us that they have no knowledge of God; indeed, they are following the path of reprobates.

Let us observe, then, that when Paul tells us there is no other gospel, he wants us to abide in the Lord Jesus Christ and to remain faithful to him, now that we realise the gospel has come from him, rejecting anything which is contrary to its teaching. If we have such maturity, we will be equipped to do battle with Satan, and to oppose all the various opinions that are in the world today. We will never be shaken, whatever troubles come our way; nor will we ever lack the assurance of faith. However, if we waver, we will be just like little children: if they are offered an apple in one hand, sure enough, they will run to it. If they are then offered some other pleasant thing in the other hand, they will reach for that in the same way! Having deserted the first thing, they will rally around the second. If, I say, we are as fickle as this, then it is a sure sign that we are completely unfaithful. Know, therefore, that there must be harmony between our faith and the gospel. Having given ourselves totally to it, we will never turn aside, because we fix our faith on what is contained therein, as we have already said. Not that we can all be as well-versed as each other; for it is certain that most of those whom the Lord Jesus Christ has in his flock do not understand the tenth part of the Holy Scriptures! Yet, whatever else we do not know, we should have the following beliefs in common: that, (1) There is one God the Father, in whom we all believe, who has adopted us out of his pure mercy. (2) There is only one Jesus Christ, through whom all blessings are given to us. (3) We are made regenerate by the Holy Spirit.

Concerning our Lord Jesus Christ, we must also be aware that he is our Advocate, and that without him we cannot approach God. We would not dare to say 'our Father' unless we were members of the body of the Lord Jesus Christ – unless he spoke on our behalf as our intercessor and friend, guiding us, as it were, by the hand to bring us to God the Father. If we do not know these things, then we cannot obtain salvation. Paul accuses the Galatians of failing to recognise that there is only one gospel, which cannot be altered. He does not want them to grieve our Lord Jesus Christ, who alone is to be heeded. He also warns us of seducers, who seek to turn us from the pure simplicity of the gospel of God and of our Lord Jesus Christ. He teaches us to regard them as abhorrent, for (as we shall soon see more clearly) they pervert the gospel of the Lord Jesus Christ. How dreadful it is that the gospel, the foundation of our salvation, and the key that opens the gates of paradise, should be perverted! It is our only treasure. We were banished from the kingdom of heaven and could not come near to it, until God made a way, through the gospel, for us to be his people and for him to be our King, so that we can be led and governed by his authority. Inestimable treasures are contained in the gospel. God is reconciled with man; the gates of heaven are opened to us; our Lord Jesus Christ has been given to us as our inheritance; we are made partakers of all the good things that he has bestowed upon us; and we are assured of our eternal salvation. It were better that the whole world should perish and be consumed than that this gospel should be perverted. This is what Paul says about all those who come to trouble us, after we have been so faithfully taught, and of all those who bring us little novelties, mixing in their own inventions here and there – these people turn men from the kingdom of God, and from his royal throne, so that they are no longer governed by him, and thereby the sceptre of our Lord Jesus Christ is no longer extended to them for their salvation. If God's honour, and our own salvation, is as dear to us as it ought to be, and if sharing in all the blessings of heaven is precious to us, then whenever we are approached by such scoundrels seeking to detract from the majesty of God, the grace of the Lord Jesus Christ, and even our salvation, ought we not to shun them and cast them out as we would the most deadly plague in the world? This, in short, is what we must do: we must cling with strong affection to the gospel, and not allow anyone to corrupt it in any way. We must not let anybody confuse our minds by their claims to be bringing us an alternative view.

Even if the people who speak to us have great knowledge, and are skilful, sharp-witted and very eloquent, we must reject them as abominations, people who have come to draw us away from the purity of the gospel. This is what Paul is teaching us here.

Having spoken of this, Paul then adds, that if either he, or an angel, came to preach any other gospel than that which the Galatians had already heard, they were to reject them. They must be treated as accursed people, and as devils, and be excommunicated. We see here that Paul becomes heated (in a manner of speaking), as he is seeking to promote constancy in the faith so that we will not be shaken. Yet he does not do so without good reason. For we know how fragile we are, and not only fragile, but worse than this, we are vain and rebellious. When we are first taught from the Word of God, if we are not genuinely touched, we find it the strangest book in the world; for the teaching of the gospel is always foolishness to the human mind, as we have seen on previous occasions (*1 Cor.* 2:14). And the reason for this? Because we are vanity: our hearts have wandered and gone astray, our natures incline and tend to falsehood, and we almost wilfully desire to be beguiled. Because our minds are thus corrupted, we should not be surprised if we do not desire the Word of God and if it does not become a part of us. For our only activity is in rebelling against God. Although we think we are doing right, we are, in fact, blind. In short, the Scriptures do not say without cause that all men are 'vanity and leasing' (*Psa.* 4:2). We are in rebellion against God, pulling in the opposite direction when he calls us. God has granted us the privilege of being drawn to himself, and of realising that his truth is what we must hold to. He has so mastered us that we are no longer full of guile, but willing to be completely subject to him. Even so, the devil is still able to lead us astray at any moment, because we are so fragile and inconstant! We have seen this happen to those who were mirror-images of holiness (as it were). We have been shocked to see them change so quickly and wander from the right path. What causes this? As I have already said, even when we are in good form, we cannot remain in this state long before we travel in the opposite direction; that is, unless God works in us and strengthens us in our weakness.

This is why Paul upholds the teaching of the gospel in such a forceful way (occasion having been given him by the Galatians, who had gone astray because they had been taught to observe the ceremonies of the law). Seeing such an example and such a picture of man's great weakness and fickleness, Paul states that the truth of the gospel must supersede anything that we may devise. He also implies that we ought not to be deceived by the knowledge, skill or eloquence of men, for even if the angels from heaven had entered our ranks, we should rather count them as devils. But this, apart from anything else, must have seemed a very strange thing to say. What! The angels from heaven! But what else is it to which he refers? His own preaching. He does not simply speak of the gospel of Christ, but of the gospel which *he* had preached to them. And can he be superior to the angels from heaven? Well, in the first place, we see that it is nothing to praise the gospel in a general and vague sense; you must know its teaching. After all, there are many who will mock the folly of the Papists, but if you were to ask them the rudiments, which even little children know well, they do not know them. If one says one thing and another says something else, it is all one and the same thing to them. There is no difference; it is as if they are throwing salt, water, mustard and bitter juice together in a recipe! They will speak often enough in general terms about how we must preach the gospel, and yet they do not know what it is! In order to correct such a sin, Paul speaks of the gospel which he preached to them. By this (as I have said), he is showing us that we ought to know the substance of the doctrine which is brought to us in the name of God, so that our faith can be fully grounded upon it. Then we will not be tossed about with every wind, nor will we wander about aimlessly, changing our opinions a hundred times a day; we will persist in this doctrine until the end. This, in brief, is what we must remember.

Because Paul speaks in such bold language in defence of his teaching, this should make it all the more genuine to us. He does not speak with human arrogance or presumption, but in the name of God. Indeed, there is no question here of his boasting about himself; he proves this by saying, 'if I'. He puts himself first, as if he is saying: 'Even I myself, if I change my doctrine, or if you find I have swerved in any way, let me be regarded as a devil.' Here, Paul is showing that he was not seeking to gain a reputation for himself, nor was he fighting for his own cause, so that people would say how intelligent, wise and gifted he was. No; he puts himself on the level of all believers and says: 'Let us all embrace the whole of our Master's teaching, which God has entrusted to us, and to which we must submit our conduct. For although I have taught you this doctrine, yet it is not mine, but it is of God, who never changes. If I change, do not be shaken, nor surprised about this, but treat me as a devil, count me accursed. As for yourselves, remain grounded in the truth that you have always known. I would rather you saw me as accursed and abominable, and even the angels from heaven also, than that you forsake the truth about the Son of God and turn away from it.' We can see from this what Paul desired: that God's truth should be revered amongst men, as it deserves to be, and that it should be esteemed in such a way, that all our senses, thoughts, desires and affections should be subdued and held captive to it. It is not lawful for any living creature to change anything in the gospel, for God has spoken by the mouth of his only Son. May he be our master indeed, and may each of us obey him without question. This is what Paul desired. But since we cannot now finish commenting on the rest, it will be reserved for next Sunday, in God's good pleasure.

Now let us fall before the majesty of our great God, acknowledging our faults, and praying that he will make us ever more conscious of them. May this lead us to a right repentance, and make us grow and increase in faith, as true sacrifices to him. Since our Lord Jesus Christ gave himself for our redemption, let us also seek to dedicate ourselves fully to him. May we be led by him to persevere, so that in life and in death we seek no other contentment or rest than to acquiesce in his good will. May we glory in nothing other than the salvation which he has purchased for us. May this grace not only be granted to us, but to all peoples and nations on earth, etc.

4

Rooted in the Truth of God

But though we, or an angel from heaven, preach any other gospel unto you than that which we have preached unto you, let him be accursed. As we said before, so say I now again, If any man preach any other gospel unto you than that ye have received, let him be accursed. For do I now persuade men or God? or do I seek to please men? for if I yet pleased men, I should not be the servant of Christ (Gal. 1:8–10).

We saw, last time, that we need to have confidence in the fact that the gospel is true. For if we allow ourselves to waver, our 'faith' will be of no more value than a passing opinion. This is the kind of bold faith that we ought to have. Firstly, we need to be so fully persuaded that it is God who has taught us and revealed his will to us, that we realise that to go aside to the left or right is to cast ourselves wilfully into perdition. For this reason, we must not only believe the Word of God to be both good and holy, but we must also honour it by detesting all that is contrary and, indeed, anything that is not in complete accordance with its teaching. Paul speaks here of 'another gospel', implying that if anyone does not preach the same pure and simple gospel they have heard him preach, their message is sure to be false and corrupt. Let us, therefore, learn to so magnify the doctrine which comes from God, that we not only value it for what it is, but that we also reject all those things which lead us in the opposite direction as evil abominations.

However, Paul does not simply speak of men; he goes as far as to include the angels of heaven! He says that we must even count them accursed rather than alter our faith in the gospel. He is right to speak of himself first, because this shows us that he has no regard for his own person, and that he simply wants to honour God and ensure that his Word is accepted by all without reservation. Therefore, Paul is justified in making such a declaration; for if any man exempts his own doctrine because he enjoys some privilege or other, he is making himself a separate case. Whereas, anyone involved in teaching others should realise that he himself is on the same level as everyone else, and thus subject to obey the gospel of the Lord Jesus Christ. Our faith should not be put in any earthly master, for the Son of God alone deserves to be Lord of our lives. Interestingly, Paul also refers to angels. You see, the false apostles and deceivers who had come to Galatia were often quoting Peter, and James, and John, but Paul brushes them aside and says to us, 'Even though they may have everything in their favour, and everyone on their side, it amounts to nothing. Even if they were accompanied by the angels from heaven, God still rules over them by his Word, and every creature must be cast down. For if anyone rises up against God's truth, where his image shines forth and where both his majesty and his glory are seen, he must be condemned and counted accursed'.

At first, it seems that Paul is being rather extreme. To what purpose does he bring in the angels, seeing they, of all creatures, are devoted to doing the will of God? This is chiefly taught in Psalm 103 (verse 20), but throughout the Holy Scriptures we find that the angels are only concerned with obeying God. Therefore, since it is impossible for angels to falsify the pure truth, it might be said that Paul should not include them. Indeed, is he not wronging them? After all, God has given them grace to continue in obedience to him, and to behave graciously as he commands. No, Paul has good reason to speak as he does, because the devil will strive to use anything which could work in his favour in order to pervert pure doctrine. We know that, since time began, there have always been imposters, pretending to be working in the name of God, yet deluding and deceiving all they meet, despite their bold claims to be sent by God. Indeed, the prophets had such great difficulty battling against those who sought to deceive everyone in this way; they had to put them to the test, to see whether God was speaking through them or not. We know the words of Peter: he tells us that just as there were false prophets troubling the church and introducing confusion, we too must be ready for Satan's many agents among us today, who try to sow strife (*2 Pet.* 2:1). The church will always be subject to such things because God wants to discover and test whether we are truly his or not. Notice how quickly hypocrites waver when they are put to the test! They are so fickle and flighty that they soon scurry away. But the children of God, whose roots in the gospel are strong and deep, will never be moved. God gives Satan free rein, and allows him to raise up these false prophets, because, as it says in the thirteenth chapter of Deuteronomy, he wants to prove us to see whether we love him or not (*Deut.* 13:3). That is, are we giving him the honour that he deserves, and are we resting on him with true and unshakeable constancy? The devil has troubled the church, sowing error by masking his activity in the name of God, and the only way to overcome him is by keeping to the Word of God in its entirety.

When the heathen worshipped their idols, they did so 'in the name of God'; they believed their practices were part of true religion (as they called it). It seemed to them that the only way to be holy in this world was by following these foolish rituals. But the Holy Scriptures, on the contrary, state that all their 'gods' were nothing more than devils. What possible similarity can there be between the two? Such vain religions had to be wiped out, because the heathen were profaning God's name by attributing it to their idols. Today, we hear that the Pope and all his filthy clergy claim to be vicars of Jesus Christ, to represent the church, and to be in direct succession to the apostles. All such views must be cast down, or we will not know which beliefs to follow. This is why

Paul mentions the angels. It is as if he is saying, 'Whatever authority men claim to have, no-one has the right to judge God or his Word. For his Word must reign supreme, whilst even the best and greatest things in this world are to be despised. This not only applies to mortal creatures but also to angels, in so much that if an angel could set himself against God (which is impossible), he ought to be abhorred'. Let us not think that the angels are being wronged here. For in what else is all their glory and dignity but in worshipping their Creator and the Lord Jesus Christ, who is their Head as well as ours? So then, if Paul uses them in his argument in order to bring glory to Jesus Christ and in order to maintain the soundness of the gospel, the angels are willing to yield (as long as their name is being used for this purpose), for this is their chief desire. This is why Paul speaks of angels; he does not mean that they ever cease from their obedience to God.

Paul reiterates this same idea and says: 'If any man preach any other gospel unto you than that ye have received, let him be accursed'. Here we can observe, firstly, that God wants us to honour and serve him. He does not require us to serve him with strange customs and ceremonies, as men are inclined to do. Our chief service is to listen to him and to bridle ourselves, as it were, keeping all our desires captive to his Word when he speaks to us. This is also what he says through the prophet Jeremiah: 'Have I required sacrifices of your fathers? No, this is what I required of them, and now demand of you as the worship due to me: that you listen to my voice' (*Jer.* 7:22–23). God declares in this passage that though men may work hard to bring him their devotions, thinking this will please him, yet all are like filthy rags until a man has learnt to listen to his voice and to obey him. This point is well worth taking note of, so that we do not labour in vain, as the wretched Papists do. Men know only too well that they were created to serve God, but in seeking to do so they torment themselves and take such great pains, that all their service becomes fruitless and vain. This has been a common disease amongst mankind since time began, and it is all because men do not begin at the right point. They do not regulate their lives by the will of God, nor do they fully set themselves to undertake only that which God has commanded. To make our service acceptable to God today, we must listen to him, and allow ourselves to be taught and completely governed by his Word. Then we must make sure that our lives, thoughts and actions are fully conformable to it. How privileged we are, now that God has called us to a knowledge of the gospel! However, let us consider those wretched Papists (whom I have already mentioned), who get up early and apply themselves to some duty or other. There is no end to their devotions! Yet not only is their work vain, of no avail and a waste of time – they are also abhorrent in the eyes of God. This being the case, let us greatly rejoice in the fact that God has shown us his grace by revealing his will to us. But let us also realise that we are not to walk carelessly, but rather that we are to discern between good and evil. However, we cannot do this through our own wit or wisdom; it is only possible if God has led us to his school, and if he has accepted us. No work is more worthy of our attention than that of conforming ourselves to the rules he has given us in his Word. This is the first thing.

However, we can also see here the majesty of the gospel. We ought not to envelop ourselves in clouds of doubt by introducing men's opinions. The Papists do this today, but they have no buckler for their defence but the traditions of the church, their councils, and their antiquity. But even if they were to rally the whole world around them, would it equal the authority of the angels of heaven? Certainly not! We may, indeed, laugh at the Papists, in much the same way as Paul mocks the Galatians here! We may say that even if the Pope and all his stinking clergy had the angels on their side, this would be nothing compared to the Lord Jesus Christ, who has all sovereign authority and before whom every knee shall bow, not only things on earth, but also things in heaven, as it says in the Epistle to the Philippians (*Phil.* 2:10). In that passage, these words are applied to the Lord Jesus Christ, and God swears that every knee shall bow before him and every tongue shall confess that he alone should be glorified, (see *Isa.* 45:23). This is the extent to which we should esteem the gospel: we must never be moved by the authority of men. If we are told that such and such a person believes such and such a thing, let us remember that since God has given us the grace to commit ourselves fully to him, we must abide in him for ever and not change our minds. This is what we can learn from this passage.

Next, Paul demonstrates that he has good reason to speak of 'the gospel which we have preached unto you'. He implies that he did not teach after the manner of men, nor set men forth, nor give human counsel, but he set God forth, not seeking to please men, but Jesus Christ. He goes on to say that his gospel was not 'of man', but that it was revealed to him from above, as we have already seen. It would not have been sufficient for Paul to have spoken of the gospel in general, without mentioning that he had been a true and faithful minister. For the devil does not mind if we highly esteem the gospel; that is, as long as we do not understand it, and as long as we are still entangled in many errors, and have wandering minds! It is not enough for people to honour 'the gospel' – they must know what the gospel is, and what it contains. This is why Paul tells us that he had been faithful in preaching the gospel, and that therefore, if any were seeking to change it, they ought to be accursed. This is very important, because when the Papists read this passage, they do nothing but scoff at it. (God has also blinded them, so that they have even less sense than little children.) For they understand it thus: if a man should make another gospel, by writing another book, and it is not the gospel that Paul wrote, then it must be rejected, because the real gospel had already been sufficiently attested. Yet, they do not even consider everything that is contained in Paul's epistles to be the gospel! Rather, they imagine that he has written 'one account' of the gospel, but that if this gospel is rejected, and another gospel brought in its place, this new gospel should not be accredited or revered. We can see by this that those wretched beasts have no intelligence or understanding, nor, indeed, any discernment. How urgently we need to realise that Paul does not refer in vain to 'the gospel which he preached'; it is as if he were pointing out with his finger the very teaching in which our full trust is to be placed. Do we want to be part of the flock of the Lord Jesus Christ? It is not enough simply to accept what is said to us in his name. We must observe that which is written in the tenth chapter of John's Gospel: that is, by listening to his voice, we will be able to distinguish it from that of a stranger. We should all come to the solid conclusion that he alone is the one to whom we must flee. How can we live under the guiding hand of the good Shepherd? By not swerving aside to the left hand nor to the right when men beckon to us and seek to draw us to themselves. Let us not be like swaying reeds, but let us remain firm in the doctrine that we have received. Then we will be accepted among the number of his lambs, and he will be our Shepherd for ever.

However, let us not be like people who accept whatever they are told. For such people have no difficulty in accepting that Jesus Christ is the only one in whom we must trust in order to have assurance of salvation, if this is what they are told. But, on the other hand, if we set before them all sorts of errors and confuse their minds with this and that, it is all one and the same to them. If they have no discernment, then they certainly cannot have assurance of faith. We must be firmly persuaded that Jesus Christ is the only master, for not only has he been entrusted with this charge by God the Father, but he has also fulfilled this office perfectly. If we are not persuaded of this, then we will be liable to be carried away by every opinion and instinct that we have, and there will be no faith in us at all. This is why Paul declares that the gospel which he preached is the same gospel that the Lord Jesus commanded us to preach and to spread abroad, whereof he is the author, in the name of God the Father. This is why we need to adhere to its teaching. When Paul speaks of 'another gospel', he is thinking of the fact that people corrupt the true one and mingle other things in with it. It is as if he is saying: 'If any one adds to the doctrines of the gospel, including things that man has devised – not content with its simplicity – but deviating from it, let us remember that it will all be lies. Furthermore, let us shun such things as we would shun poison, for no poison can be as deadly as that of false teaching. If men naturally guard against things that can harm physically, why should not our souls be much more precious to us? How careful we ought to be that they are not poisoned by the deceitfulness of men!' To sum up, let us be clear that if anyone adds anything to the teaching of the Lord Jesus Christ, it is plainly going to be false. We are not only to uphold this teaching in principle, but to let it abide unrivalled [in our hearts]. Let all who are responsible for teaching others first become disciples of Jesus themselves, so that they do not teach their own ideas in the church, or ideas which have been forged in man's workshop. Instead, may they demonstrate that they are true disciples of the Lord Jesus Christ; indeed, let them teach us with his authority. This is the first point.

Secondly, we must know what is contained in the gospel. For if this word 'gospel' trips off our tongues, and yet people use this word to make us believe that chalk is cheese (as they say), what good is that? What have we gained if we simply speak honourably of the gospel, even if we acknowledge that it is God's pure truth, to which all creatures must submit? We must know the substance of the gospel: that the Son of God came down to this earth to lead us to God the Father, and to declare to us how God is to be worshipped. Also, we ought to know what the will of God is, so that we can frame our whole lives around it, not serving him according to our own desires and fancies, but yielding to him the obedience he requires and approves of above all else. Then, we also need to learn how miserable our condition is, especially if we are those who intend to seek salvation through our own goodness. For we are ignorant, weak, feeble, stubborn and full of wicked lusts. In short, we are bound by Satan's cords, and he leads us like wretched beasts, like asses and oxen which are to be sold. If we desire to be set free from this captivity and horrible tyranny, we must draw near to God alone, knowing that he is the fountain of all goodness. However, since we cannot approach God, let us come to the Lord Jesus Christ, since he has stooped down to us. Let us find in his fulness all that we are lacking and place all our trust in him, having no other refuge, no other righteousness, holiness or perfection, but being totally empty in and of ourselves, let us never cease trusting him to bring us to God the Father. We also need to know how he justifies us: that is to say, through the sacrifice of his sufferings and death. Thus, when we come to pray to God, let us come through him as our Advocate so that he may convey our words to his Father.

This, therefore, is what we should know about the gospel. There is only one law by which we must regulate our lives, and only one set of beliefs. We need to know the God that we serve and worship. Furthermore, we should see him in the person of our Lord Jesus Christ, who is the very image of the Father. We should rest on no other person but Jesus Christ, and centre all our thoughts on him, knowing that the Father has given him all that is necessary for our salvation. He also guides and governs us by the power of his Holy Spirit, so that, with his protection, we can be assured that the devil and all his demons can do us no harm, if we are kept by his power. This is what we should know about the gospel, or else what is said here will do us no good at all.

Now, Paul uses two arguments to show that he has good reason to prefer himself before those that went about disguising gospel doctrine by adding their own inventions. The first argument is that he has acted faithfully and with pure and honest affection towards the Galatians, and, indeed, towards everyone else. The second is that he has not set forth anything that has come from his own head, but that everything he has declared to them was received by revelation from the Lord Jesus Christ. Let us take good note of these two reasons and acknowledge that Paul, indeed, has good grounds to declare this teaching to be true, as he does also to declare that it is not lawful for any living creature to set himself against it. From this, a general lesson emerges about the way to be assured of one's faith. The angels will not come down in visible fashion to speak to us; we will have to be taught by men. And yet, as I have already said, we must come to the infallible conclusion that the doctrine on which our faith is grounded and based is from God and from the Lord Jesus Christ. How can we understand this? By the two things which I here set before you. Firstly, we need to be sure that those who teach us have a desire and a zeal to lead us to God. They need not be equipped with a great title or a reputation among men; no, nor with any other human honours, but they must simply be following the path that God has commanded them to tread in order to win the world over to obedience to God. This is the first thing. Secondly, apart from zeal, we should be sure that they are not taking it upon themselves to introduce anything which oversteps the boundaries God has set. Rather they should only deliver what God has commanded from hand to hand as it were, so that Jesus Christ is always heard, and so that when he speaks, every other mouth is silenced in order to listen to him. This is the way to gain knowledge of Christ's teaching.

Now, coming back to the first point (where Paul declares his affection for them), he says that he does not seek the favour of men, but of God. By this, he means that he does not have a worldly affection for them; he is simply seeking to conform himself to what God requires of him. After all, God had called him, and Jesus Christ was his Master. Therefore, he only sought to set Christ forth, and needed no backing from men (not like those who seek to allure simple, ignorant folk to their own way of thinking!). Such people justify their claims by saying: 'Listen to this! Such and such a man says it is so.' No, we should listen to God alone. Even if the whole world were to seek with one accord to turn us aside from him, surely God alone would be enough to outweigh a million worlds (if, indeed, there were as many!). Since this is so, let us mark well the lesson that we are taught here, and apply it more generally.

Paul says that he is not seeking to please men. The moment we speak to please men, God's truth becomes tainted.

He states: 'If I yet pleased men, I should not be the servant of Christ.' The devil has many ways and means of obscuring God's truth so that it seems to us that we are still close to God when we are really very far away from him. (That is, unless we have the wisdom and discernment that is being commended here.) May we know how to distinguish between what comes from God and what comes from men, so that we are not confused or taken by surprise when we come across so many contradictory views, such diversity of opinion and so many arguments and disputes. Let none of these things make us change our beliefs. Why? We should only be concerned about whether we are secure in the Lord. If we are, then we may fearlessly ignore everyone else. However, if we are not well rooted in the faith, then every gust of wind will knock us over, or at the very least cause us to sway from one side to the other. Let us, therefore, be sure that God has, indeed, had pity on us and revealed his will to us. Let us also consider those who teach us: how are their minds led and governed? Are they themselves seeking to obey God and to lead us in his way by their own example?

When Paul says that if he pleased men he would not be the servant of Christ, the implications are very far-reaching. For we know well enough what men are by nature: they are full of iniquity and rebellion against God. Therefore, if we are seeking to gratify them, we must abandon God and turn our backs upon him. Unless we try to compel them to come to God, they will go in the opposite direction and kick against him like wild beasts. Thus, we can only satisfy men by straying from God and by giving in to those who persist in troubling us. Indeed, even the righteous sometimes expect God to do just what they desire. For although they still long to serve him, they do not always have the self-control to renounce all their own opinions, lusts and desires. Because of this, everyone is tempted at some time to do this or that, but if we are not held on a tight rein and made to turn around immediately, we will be lost. In other words, there is no-one who does not seek his own gratification. This means that if those who have the responsibility to teach and build up the church are seeking to please men, they are really forsaking the Lord Jesus Christ. This text exhorts all ministers of the Word to shut their eyes to the sinful desires of men if they wish to carry out their duty faithfully. They must not swerve or be tempted to seek for favour or a good reputation amongst men. And if they are striving to lead such rebels to God, they should do it in such a way as to give to God the honour due to him and to the Lord Jesus Christ his proper authority. What must we do when we speak in his name? We must not only condemn human nature in general terms, we must also shake up men's consciences so that they are made to feel God's jurisdiction there. The gospel is not only like a spear that pricks, but also like a sword that pierces right through to the marrow of our bones, as the apostle says in the Epistle to the Hebrews (*Heb.* 4:12). We must not allow a thought or an intention to come into our minds which is not placed under the searching light of the gospel. All who are humbled in this way will inevitably bemoan themselves and face regrets and remorse; but we must close our eyes to all this and press onwards, taking no notice of what men covet or desire to hear.

However, this warning is not only for ministers of the Word of God but for all men in general. If we desire to be Christians, let us honour the Son of God by continuing to listen to his Word and obey it, even when we do not like what it says and when our natures find it unpalatable. Thus, when anyone comes to a sermon, above all else he should be ready to be rebuked where necessary, and he should realise that if he is not comforted by it, then it is to his profit. If he has itching ears, he should put this right, for he cannot benefit or profit from the teaching if this is the case. Let us all be willing to have our wounds scratched, as it were, and to be condemned, and to hear the opposite of what we would like to hear. This is how we should prepare ourselves if we wish to be good scholars under the Son of God and to attribute to him his rightful mastery over us. We must work all the harder at this if we see that our natures are pushing us to do the opposite, for we are often blinded by self-love. Each one covets to be honoured, and yet we cannot be, unless it be by flattery and deception. For what is there that is commendable in us? In God's sight there is only filth and corruption. For even all the best seeming-virtues in us are corrupt until God transforms us. Thus, it is certain that everything we are by nature must be cleansed, or else we will perish in our own wretchedness. There is no other way to be saved than to be cleansed from our sins. Yet this cleansing can only come about after we have been violently shaken and convicted by the teaching of the gospel, and when our own consciences rebuke us, even though we like to be praised and flattered at times. Let us, therefore, desire to be spoken to earnestly, shown our sins, and made ashamed of them by having our guilt uncovered, rather than seeking to hear what pleases us. For secretly to hold on to our sins is to perish in them. It will cost us very dear if, having been flattered by men, the heavenly Judge should thunder down upon us. This, then, is how we may profit from the words of Paul here. If preachers wish to gratify and please men, they are renouncing God by so doing; and if they renounce him, what will become of the rest of the people? Where will they be led except to the devil?

Thus, when we come to hear a sermon, let us bear in mind that the one who is speaking is not doing so by his own authority but in the name of our Lord Jesus Christ, who has been appointed our Judge by God the Father. And to what end does Jesus Christ judge us? To the end that we should all condemn ourselves, and then, having passed sentence, come to him to be forgiven. Now if a mortal man seeks to cover up my sins because of some supposed love he bears towards me, does this mean that the heavenly Judge will do the same? Is it not better that the one who teaches me should condemn me, and show me my sins, so that I am sorry for them and learn to dislike those things that lead to perdition? Ought I not to accept it, since God still holds out his arms to receive me, and Jesus Christ still goes before me to present me to God his Father as an acceptable sacrifice with a sweet-smelling savour? Therefore, we must either be mad or bewitched by Satan if we cannot bear to have our sores rubbed in this way, and our sins uncovered, and be shown what we need to do for our spiritual well-being. What happens when we try to cheer a sick man? We might offer him something to drink every minute of the day. We might offer him wine when he ought to have water. We might offer him something savoury and that may be the next best thing to poison for him! In short, simply seeking to please a man will certainly lead to his death. Now, which is better: that the one who is caring for the sick man should grant his every desire, or that he should help him to control his desires, even if the sick man becomes angry, and grinds his teeth, and creates a stir because he has not been given what he requested? Yet if sick people have inordinate desires, ours are surely worse! What will become of us, then, unless those who bring us the Word of God, who ought to be our physicians, take care to protect us from what they know to be harmful, and unless they show us what will be for our good? Surely, to encourage us in our natural lusts is the way to ruin us for ever? This is what we should learn here when Paul speaks of his own motives.

Then, he adds the second argument, which is that he did not receive his gospel from men, but by revelation from heaven. He is here confirming the same matter, as if he were saying that not even Peter or John could be worthy of so much reverence in themselves that men should be obliged to listen to them. This honour is reserved for God alone, and for our Lord Jesus Christ, and they must have no rival. This being the case, let us learn to look above if we need to find assurance of faith, and let us rise above all that is of the world, and forsake the things of man. However excellent a man may be, our faith should not be grounded on anything to do with the creature, nor anything else here below; it should have its foundation in God. The Papists will accuse us of pride and impudence for wanting to be wiser than the world. True, if we do rest upon our own understanding, and our own thoughts and opinions, we are displaying excessive pride. But if we are walking in humility, we will lay aside all our wisdom and reasoning, knowing that we must become fools in this world in order to obtain the wisdom of God. We need to be modest and sober, not seeking to know more than is lawful for us to know; yet at the same time we need to prize God's Word so highly that we have power to defy all that is of the world. Such glorying must be allowable, since this is the way to glorify God. Hence, we can despise all crosses and mitres, and the clamour of this world, and the horns of the Pope, who seeks to exalt himself against God. We can, I say, despise them and count them an abomination – things full of filth and rottenness by which Satan, our deadly foe, seeks to poison us. Let us be so rooted in the truth of God that we triumph over all that would oppose it. For we know that our faith will always be victorious over anything which sets itself to ruin and destroy it. (But Satan never forgets to torment us whenever possible!) Yet if we have ever been strengthened by our God, let us not fear that we might be overcome by any of Satan's temptations, but, instead, let us know that if God is on our side, we can treat all that comes from the creature as nothing more than a puff of smoke.

Now let us fall before the majesty of our great God, acknowledging our sins, and praying that he would make us increasingly more conscious of them, until the day when we are altogether set free from them. Yet, while we have to live here below, may he support us in our weakness, until he has remedied it, and until we are thoroughly transformed to enjoy the perfect righteousness to which we are called. And now let us all say, Almighty God, and heavenly Father, etc.

5

Every Good Thing Proceeds From God's Grace

> *But I certify you, brethren, that the gospel which was preached of me is not after man. For I neither received it of man, neither was I taught it, but by the revelation of Jesus Christ* . . . (Gal. 1:11–14).

We saw this morning that all those who have the responsibility and the duty of teaching the church of God must forget the favour and approval of the world; if they do not, they can never carry out their duty faithfully. For men will always desire to be pandered to, and cannot bear being reproved for their sins as they deserve. We said that each of us must rid himself of all carnal lusts in order to be true disciples of our Lord Jesus Christ. For as long as we follow our own desires, the door of the gospel will be closed to us and we will not be able to obtain entrance. Indeed, we know what the prophet Isaiah says about this: he says those who wish to hear only what is according to their wills are seeking to drive God away from them (*Isa.* 30:10–11). Granted, they did not perceive it to be the case, for in Judaea everyone claimed to be serving God – the God who had revealed himself to their father Abraham, and who had made known his law through Moses. Yes, sacrifices were being made at the temple and they were maintaining an outward show of worship; but the prophet comes to one conclusion about all this. Men wanted to be soothed and comforted, and because of this they could not bear to be led by God, nor would they allow him to lay his yoke upon their necks. This, then, is how we can be prepared to receive the doctrine of the gospel and to be edified by it: not by giving way to our own lusts, but by being ready to hear the Lord Jesus Christ speak the things which are necessary for our instruction. Beside this, we must also be cut to the heart, as it were, by the Word that is preached to us, or else we will never profit by it. As I said this morning, it is not in vain that the gospel is compared to a sharp sword (*Heb.* 4:12). In order to be true sacrifices, we need to deny all our fleshly desires, and all that God condemns, and patiently endure so that we may be wholly brought back to obeying his will.

Let us call to mind what we have already noted before; that is to say, that all men, both great and small, must bow, and the Son of God must have the pre-eminence and the mastery. He alone should be the Shepherd, and we the sheep. It is true that those who are charged with preaching the gospel may well be called shepherds, but this does not mean that they can act in their own name or by their own power, nor must they undermine the sovereignty of the Son of God. As for myself, as I speak to you now, I must not bring anything of my own, nor elevate myself above other people. In this, I am addressing the whole congregation, and therefore the message applies to myself first of all, and next to everyone else here without exception. Not even the most noble person in the world may exempt himself from the submission which is due to the Son of God. We have seen on previous occasions that the role of the gospel is to bring down the pride that is in the world, so that men will not presume to exalt themselves, nor to think highly of themselves. Instead, all who think they are the greatest are humbled and altogether crushed, in order that all may be brought into obedience to the gospel.

Why does Paul say, when seeking to attest his doctrine, that he did not receive it from men, nor learn it in their school, but that he received it from our Lord Jesus Christ, whom the Father directed us to hear (*Matt.* 3:17; 17:5)? It is because this title is special and cannot be conferred on either men or angels. Although it is true that those who speak as mouthpieces of the Lord Jesus Christ should be heeded, yet (as we have stated) this does not lessen the authority that he himself has over us. Whatever else we may say, let this be the sure and infallible rule which alone guarantees our salvation: our Lord Jesus Christ alone is to be Master and teacher, and we must be meek enough to accept his Word without question or objection. Paul is not content to say that the message he had received and preached was from Jesus Christ; he makes a point of rejecting and excluding men in order to show that their authority is insufficient as a foundation and support for our faith. For we will always be on shifting sands unless we come to God, and to the one he has appointed chief and sovereign Teacher over us. When Paul says this, we must not assume that the Galatians, or indeed anyone else, had failed to hear the like before. No, he says it because they had been so ungrateful towards God, having become entangled in many errors and misconceptions. He, therefore, brings them back to the source. It is as if he is saying: 'Until men decide to be governed simply by the pure Word of God, they will forever be on shifting sands. The moment the devil sends some trouble their way, they will be confused and not know which way to turn.'

Thus, in the first place, we must be sure that the doctrine on which we base our faith is from God and not from men. Although the revelation which was given to Paul will not be given to all alike, it should be enough for us that our Lord Jesus Christ has ratified the gospel with his own blood. Then, having also commanded his apostles to preach the gospel, he attested the fact that the doctrine they preached was authentic, so that there can no longer be any doubt. This, I say, should be enough to persuade us to hold firm and not to accept everything that men call truth. But let us also remember what we are taught by the apostle in the first chapter of Hebrews: that is to say, that God has spoken in these last days by his own Son (*Heb.* 1:2). We will find his doctrine to be perfect.

This, then, is what we should remember: the revelation which Paul speaks of here will not be common to all, but it serves to assure us that the doctrine which we have received from him is really from the Lord Jesus Christ. By disregarding what is from man, Paul is implying that our Lord Jesus Christ does not simply instruct us as if he were teaching the ABC to a child, who then has to move on to a more advanced teacher. In other words, our Lord does not teach us by halves, but in all perfection. Indeed, both in life and at death, we must abide in the doctrine we have received from him, and renounce whatever comes from men, for any mixture of the two is corrupt, as we said this morning. Peter also exhorts those who speak in the church to remember God's glory, and not introduce any views which they have conceived in their own minds. For where would we be if men mixed their own doctrines with those of the Lord Jesus Christ, if each one added his own bits and pieces so that we had a gospel full of what men had devised in their imaginations? It would produce nothing short of terrible confusion. This is why the Lord Jesus Christ can have no authority with us until men, and, indeed, all creatures, are cast down, and until we all listen to him, from the greatest to the least. This, in sum, is what we should retain in our minds. Indeed, we know that in the other passage, that is, the one to the Corinthians, Paul declares that he preaches perfect wisdom when he preaches our Lord Jesus Christ, and that we can find all we need for our salvation in him (*1 Cor.* 2:6). Also, in another passage to the Ephesians, he says that Christ's love should be all our study, in all its length and breadth (*Eph.* 3:18). We should not bring to bear our own insignificant ideas, seeking to add them to what Paul has already preached. Through this, we can see that all those who involve themselves with what has been forged and invented by men have a false Christ. They have an illegitimate gospel which God disowns. In fact, our Christianity will cease to exist, unless we continue in what we have been taught by the Son of God, our only Master, and in what the apostles have taught us in his name. This is what we ought to learn from this passage.

* * *

At this point, Paul speaks of his 'conversation', and it is here that we learn how he was truly changed by the Spirit of God. For the wonderful transformation that had been seen in him could only have come about by God laying his hand upon him and working in him in a secret and unusual way. And this, in short, is what he refers to when he says the Galatians have known his 'conversation', or his way of life. Here is a good lesson! However, in order to use it to our profit, let us note that Paul is continuing the theme he has touched upon above: namely, that we will never find in any creature a firm foundation on which to build our faith. God alone must be its author, and however much men are means and instruments, they nevertheless have to be authorised by God. We must be sure that God has sent them and approves them, and that they will only bring us that which they have learnt from him. However, if we consider for a moment Paul's virtues, he certainly merited the favour and audience of men. Yet at the same time, he admits and confesses that he is nothing in and of himself, and that everything he has is to be used solely in serving our Lord Jesus Christ, and in faithfully preaching all that he received from him.

What, then, will become of those who have neither a Christian way of life, nor sound doctrine, nor, indeed, anything else [to commend them]? Even if they call themselves prelates and attribute to themselves some nobility and superiority in order that we should accept what they say, are they really greater than Paul? No, all human pride should cease and be laid low, so that nothing will prevent us exalting Jesus Christ. John the Baptist, although he had the testimony of being the greatest man to have been born of woman (*Matt.* 11:11), says that he and all others must decrease and Jesus Christ must increase (*John* 3:30). Furthermore, Paul says in another place that the church must be built in such a way that Jesus Christ, our chief cornerstone, always has the pre-eminence (*Eph.* 2:20; *Col.* 1:18). What a terrible building it would be if we sought to exalt men to the extent that Jesus Christ was obscured by them! How much ruin and confusion this would bring! Indeed, if a man became as tall as one of the pillars of this chapel, but with a head only the size of a fist buried between his shoulders, what a monster he would be! It would be better if he were the same size as everyone else! Thus, in the same way, the church is the body of our Lord Jesus Christ, and he, the Head, must be lifted up above everyone else, and we must all look to him and stay close to him. How the Papists condemn themselves with their own tongues when they say that we can only have access to God through the apostles! They have so buried Jesus Christ that he is hidden from the world, and they have taken away everything that belongs to him. Instead of calling him Lawgiver, Judge and King to show that he alone rules (*Isa.* 33:22), men clothe themselves with his garments. Let us guard against such error. If we grow at all, let us still remain with our root and foundation in the simplicity of the gospel. Let us beware of swerving from this, even a hair's breadth.

As for what is said here about Paul's conversion, it tends to the same end: that we may know he is not exalting himself, but that God has taken him by the hand; and that we may know that he received the doctrine which he preached by revelation. Therefore, we can have no difficulty in accepting that his message proceeds from the mouth of God and is, therefore, solid, infallible truth. As we have already said, a man may wish to be heard because of his knowledge, his deep and profound wisdom, his fine way of speaking, or great eloquence, but all of these things are nothing more than a foul-smelling stench. God must have his authority and we must render him homage. And, since God has chosen to speak to us by the mouth of his only Son, may Jesus Christ alone have this honour as Master and Teacher of all his own, and may we truly be his flock and listen to his voice. The way to ensure that the Lord Jesus Christ is honoured among us is to be his true disciples and not hypocrites. The Papists will quite openly worship a grotesque image in the name of Jesus Christ; however, they are thereby trampling the gospel underfoot and blaspheming against it. What is more, these blind wretches believe that they are doing what is right! They are, however, spitting full in the face of our Lord Jesus Christ by renouncing his Word, which displays his glory and majesty, as it says in Second Corinthians (*2 Cor.* 3:18). It is not a question, therefore, of honouring our Lord Jesus Christ by having lots of ceremonies, but instead by simply submitting ourselves to his doctrine, for this is the way he makes himself known and meets with us face to face, as it were. This, in short, is what we ought to remember.

Yet, in this account of Paul's conversion, he seeks to draw our attention to the heavenly power which had been so clearly displayed. This was nothing merely human. Rather, it was God who had revealed his strength to show us that this transformation had been wrought by him, and that Paul was now a new creation. For surely, Paul declares, when God restores his image in a man, it is a more excellent work even than that of causing a man to be born into this transitory world. And this is how Paul became a new man. Furthermore, this explains why he says that, at one time, he persecuted the church of God, and sought to destroy it. He used to be a bandit (in a manner of speaking), until God changed him. Then, God made a ravening wolf become a sheep, and appointed him to be a shepherd of his church under the Lord Jesus Christ. This is how we know that Paul was sent to us by the hand of God. He bears a sure mark of this fact; we can see that he has not advanced himself. This was the work of the Holy Spirit. There was nothing of his own in the doctrine that he preached, because in order to devote and apply himself to the service of the Lord Jesus Christ, he had to deny himself completely. We know that Paul was respected amongst his own people and, therefore, if he had been driven by ambition, could have pushed himself forward. If it was a matter of having a reputation amongst men for living a holy life, he was irreproachable. He could have remained comfortable, and lived a peaceful life. Yet he regarded all that the world considered desirable, and all that he once prized, as dung and as rubbish, as he says to the

Philippians (*Phil.* 3:8). He had to reject all these things as harmful, seeing they had debarred him from coming to the Lord Jesus Christ. Therefore, not only did Paul forsake his reputation as a great scholar and a holy man, something like an angel; he also left behind the peace, the comfort and even the commodities of this world. In God's sight, he had abandoned the notion that he could obtain eternal life by his good works. He now rejected all this as an abomination, knowing that formerly he had been blinded by pride, which made him think he was worth something to God, and that made him hope to gain favour by this means. I say that he not only had to trample all of this underfoot, but hold it in absolute detestation, as he himself states. This confirms to us all the more what he has already declared about disregarding man, and, indeed, himself, even though he exercised the office of an apostle; for we can see that he had to renounce all that he once held dear. By confessing to have been a persecutor of the church of God, we notice that he does not spare himself, for it is God's honour that he seeks to uphold, as well as the authority and mastery of the Lord Jesus Christ whom he served.

Here, then, is how we should proceed if we desire to be used in the service of God: we must truly forget about our own persons and not craftily seek what will suit us, for our own pleasure and honour. Until we come to the point where we deny ourselves, we can never give ourselves fully to the service of God to which we are called. I speak primarily of those who have the responsibility to preach the gospel. Such must completely deny themselves, otherwise, they will not be able to carry out the charge which has been committed to them in a faithful manner. We also notice that Paul does not hide anything; he does not resort to any shade or cover, just so that he will be accepted amongst men. Indeed, he prefers to have the shame he merited and be humiliated in the sight of men rather than to protect himself with vain excuses. For he says that he persecuted the church, that he was a thief and a criminal, that he shed innocent blood. This does not mean that he did not strive to live in all holiness and perfection for he shone as a mirror image of great integrity. Indeed, he refers to himself as 'blameless' (*Phil.* 3:6), and not without good cause. Rather, he is saying that he was blind enough to consider himself justified in God's sight simply because there was no spot in him which men could reproach him for. However, he was full of hypocrisy, as are all those who have not been renewed by the Spirit of God. Even if everyone admires them, it is certain that until God leads them in his way, they are full of corruption. If we judge according to our natural senses, we can easily be deceived concerning good and evil. To clarify this, our Lord Jesus declares, 'that which is highly esteemed among men is abomination in the sight of God' (*Luke* 16:15). However this may be, it still remains that Paul devoted himself to living a holy life which was blameless and irreproachable. Could he not have said, once he was converted, that he had done well and that his devotion deserved to be commended? Yet, quite the opposite, he declares that he was a persecutor, and that all of this devotion meant nothing.

What is to be said about so-called devotion and service to God nowadays? How easily do these terms trot out of the mouths of the Papists! Everything is done with a good intention, and everyone has warmth and zeal (or so it seems to them), and so they believe that God is indebted and beholden to them for the things which they do. And yet we know that God has not commanded them to bring him any of the things which they offer; they are all guided by their own imaginations. Despite what they say, it is only their opinions and what they think is right, nothing more. One will say, 'It seems to me'; another will say, 'I learnt it thus; this is what I was taught'. Now if God indeed accepted all these things, he would surely have great burdens to bear. For whatever men have invented in their heads is nothing but stinking filth before him. Yet, men continue to boast foolishly about their intentions to serve God. For this cause, he says in one place by the prophet Isaiah, 'Who has required this at your hand?' (*Isa.* 1:12). 'Whoever has given you this work, let him pay you; as for me, I do not take this into account in my reckoning book. I will disclaim all this, because I demand obedience.' Paul understood this very well. If he had judged others here, it would have been less powerful and effective than speaking of himself. He does not spare himself at all, saying that all the holiness that men accredited to him was really hypocrisy, for he was a raging beast, full of pride and rebellion against God. Therefore, since even Paul makes this full and frank confession, should not every mouth be silenced, and should we not acknowledge that when we too thought we were serving God, we were really in a kind of maze, which would have led us into the very depths of hell? Indeed, when poor unbelievers torment themselves in the service of God, they are doubling their condemnation because the devil is dragging them even closer to their damnation. Let us realise, therefore, that we were rebels against God when we wanted to serve him according to our own imaginations, and that there was nothing in our lives but error, which led us astray. This meant that we were departing from God rather than drawing closer to him. In short, all worship that is man-made is a result of the lies and deceptions of Satan, whereby he seeks to plunge men into the deepest dungeons of death. Let us, then, go back to the paths of obedience and acknowledge that there is no other way to order our lives well than to be taught in the school of the Son of God.

Do we honestly believe that the superstitions which reign in this world today, and which are in fashion here, are any better than the traditions which existed in the days of Paul? It is true that there were many wicked heresies in the Jewish church. For sects had grown up, and the Pharisees (who were the most unbending and uncompromising) had added many frills and fancies to the service of God, such that it had become completely corrupted. But however this may be, Paul still had the law; he had the Holy Scriptures. As for the 'traditions' which he speaks of, to him they were accessories; but at the same time, he still desired to uphold the law of Moses, which was the Word of God, the immutable truth, and, indeed, will remain so until the end of the world.

However, he only had the letter of the law, as we have seen before in Corinthians (*2 Cor.* 3:6). But today, what can be said of even the most devoted Papists? Let them claim what they will, it is certain that the Holy Scriptures are buried, as it were, and no-one pays any attention to them. It is not that they believe they ought to be rejected – this blasphemy would be too much for them and they would be horrified – no, but whatever they claim, the gospel is nothing to them compared with what is commanded by their Holy Councils and Holy Mother Church. They are not even ashamed to say that the gospel and all of the Holy Scriptures are like a wax nose – that is to say, that there is nothing certain in them – and that they need to be interpreted by men. See how Jesus Christ is most shamefully mocked. Do we think such people can have us believe all that they have invented when they so manifestly contradict themselves? Notice, then, that if Paul condemns himself with his own mouth for not having followed the Lord Jesus Christ, there is no valid excuse which God will accept if we once stray from the simplicity of the gospel. This, in sum, is what we must retain from this passage.

From this, let us observe that God showed Paul singular grace, that through his example, we may know that we have been called to salvation purely by God's free bounty. Furthermore, if we are wretched backsliders, and have broken the oath of allegiance to Jesus Christ that we made at our baptism, we can still, despite all this, be received in mercy, if we confess freely and without hypocrisy that we have been full of confusion, and that we need God to remedy this in his great bounty. It is true that Paul had a reputation for being holy (as we have already mentioned), and that it could have been said that God would accept his service because he had received a good training. But all this could do nothing but hinder him. We have already touched upon this in the third chapter of Philippians, where Paul says that he could not embrace Jesus Christ and all the unsearchable riches which are in him, until he saw that everything he once held dear was abominable, including his own righteousness and holiness (*Phil.* 3:8). Thus we can see how God had transformed Paul's life. Indeed, in the first chapter of Timothy he describes himself as an example and pattern to others. Jesus Christ is declaring through Paul that he came for all wretched sinners, that we too might be sure of acceptance if we follow the true path (*1 Tim.* 1:16).

What had free will done for Paul in order to bring him into obedience to the gospel? God had to almost thunder from the heavens to break his arrogance and presumption! God did not simply lead him by the hand, he sent him thick scales on his eyes, so that he became like a poor blind man. Furthermore, thrown to the ground and dazed, Paul was shown the blindness of thinking highly of his own wisdom and intelligence. It was this darkness which served to bring him into new light; for if God had left him to himself, he would surely have always had these misconceptions. He would have continued to add worldly wisdom, conceived in his own brain, to the doctrine of the Lord Jesus Christ. But he would have been blind and he would have remained in that condition. For since he was held in such great reputation, he would have been tempted to retain this position; but God had to cast him down, and raise him up again, and carry him like a little child, or perhaps like a carcass or dead body. Consider the violent means by which Paul was corrected, and then we will understand that neither free will, nor devotion, nor holiness count for anything. Everything must be attributed to the pure mercy of God. Indeed, what a free and open confession Paul makes of this! Such being the case, let us also note that if God calls us to himself, it is not because we are particularly ready for it, or well equipped, but because it pleases him to draw us by his pure mercy, as we shall see again shortly in more detail. If we wish to share in the grace of our Lord Jesus Christ after Paul's example, we must tread the same path; we must recognise that there is nothing of value at all in us, and that all we are lacking must come from above. God must work in us in such a way that all the praise for our salvation will be directed to him alone, without reservation. This is why Paul adds, 'but when it pleased God to call me to preach the gospel, I did so immediately and did not even wait to confer with men'. It was enough for him that God was sending him, and that he was approved by the Master. He did not exempt himself, nor did he dispute about it; he was firmly resolved to walk in God's way and to persevere, just as we have seen, which is a sure sign that God was leading him by his Holy Spirit. This is what we ought to remember.

However, we must also notice that he says God 'separated me from my mother's womb, and called me by his grace', to the end that he might preach the gospel. Here, Paul is saying that although he was called in this way, it was not because he was suitable, or worthy in and of himself, but rather because he had been chosen by God even before his birth. This is why he uses this expression, 'from my mother's womb', for it was at that point that he was separated and dedicated to God, as it were. How, then, could he do anything in his own strength? For what could he have done, being still unborn? It was necessary for God to work. Paul says that God called him; and though it is true that he is speaking about his particular office, yet he is also more generally praising God for his goodness, and showing that all we have is from his hand – not only that which pertains to this transitory life, but also, above all, that which pertains to the eternal salvation of our souls. This cannot be discussed in all its fulness at the present time, so we will reserve some of it until later. But, to conclude, let us note that Paul reveals to us, as in a mirror, that when we yield ourselves in obedience to God, it is not that each of us progresses forward, but that a hand stretches down from above, and God draws us to himself when we could not have sought him. No doubt, men will always think of some way to commend themselves, but they are greatly deluded. The devil uses such cunning ways to obscure the grace of God, intending to leave us bereft of it. For God has every right to leave men just as they are if they wish to attribute to themselves what belongs to him. They ought rather to condemn themselves. Let us remember, therefore, that every good thing we see in this world proceeds only from the grace of God, and that nothing can be attributed to us.

In order really to experience this free bounty, we must lay down all ideas of worth or merit, and first look to God's free election, then to his calling. Why have our minds been enlightened through the knowledge of the gospel? Have we merited anything? Not at all; God chose us before we were born, indeed, even before the creation of the world, as it says in that other passage (*Eph.* 1:4). Here, then, is where we must begin. If we do not wish to be swollen with vain pride (which will eventually break our necks), let us resolve to walk in humility, bearing in mind what it says in that other passage: 'Who maketh thee to differ from another?' (*1 Cor.* 4:7). It is God, he is saying, who has done this purely out of his goodness. When Paul confesses there that it is God who makes us to differ, it is to cut down all the pretensions of man, because no-one can say that he is better than his friends. It is God who chooses us, and that before we are born! God's election is secret, until he effectually reveals that he is calling us to himself. And how does he do this? By his gospel. And here is double grace. It is grace when the doctrine is preached to us. For we know of the miserable condition of the world, in which many poor souls, many poor blind souls, are wandering aimlessly in the darkness, and there is no-one to relieve or help them. Yet we have food offered to us by our God, indeed, it is even placed in our mouths. Is he not showing us special grace by this? Yet beyond this, we are called by God from within, and touched by his Holy Spirit in such a way that his doctrine rings true. We will know that it is from God when it is sealed in our hearts by his Holy Spirit (as it says in Second Corinthians and also in the first chapter of Ephesians – *2 Cor.* 1:22; *Eph.* 1:13). In short, according to the prophet Isaiah, we must be taught by God (*Isa.* 54:13). We must be truly assured in our hearts by the Holy Spirit that the doctrine which we hold to did not come from men, but that it is the infallible truth of God. We ought to be so persuaded of this fact that our eyes are fully enlightened through it, as it were (that is unless we are still wicked and depraved). This doctrine is the one we must follow till the very end. It is also the one which will lead us to the heavenly kingdom when we have completed our course in this mortal life.

Now let us fall before the majesty of our great God, acknowledging our sins, and praying that he will make us increasingly more conscious of them, so that we will be humbled. Then, we will be better able to deny ourselves and all our evil affections and desires, and come and present ourselves to the Lord Jesus Christ, paying him the homage that he requires of us. May we not do this by way of ceremony but, rather, when he opens his mouth to show us the way of salvation, let us have attentive ears, submitting quietly to him. May we have open hearts, not hardened or rebellious, but able to bear his yoke, ready to take it upon us, and to devote our whole life to obedience so that we may be conformed to his holy will. When the name of God is thus glorified in us, may others be drawn to him, and may we all be brought back into his fold to worship him together with one accord. May our Lord Jesus Christ have all the honour and worship which belongs to him. And in order to do this may it please him to raise up true and faithful ministers of his Word, etc.

6

Paul's Call to Christ

> *But when it pleased God, who separated me from my mother's womb, and called me by his grace, To reveal his Son in me, that I might preach him among the heathen; immediately I conferred not with flesh and blood: Neither went I up to Jerusalem to them which were apostles before me; but I went into Arabia and returned again unto Damascus. Then after three years I went up to Jerusalem to see Peter, and abode with him fifteen days . . .* (Gal. 1:15–21).

We now understand the point that Paul is striving to make here: namely, that men ought not to be so elevated that, because of the regard and respect we have for their persons, God's glory is diminished or obscured. For we are inclined, at times, to esteem creatures too highly, even at the expense of the Word of God. For, although Paul identifies himself here with the other apostles, he is not seeking to draw attention to himself, but, rather, he desires that the gospel which has been committed to him should be received with all due reverence. In order to achieve this, he here sets before us God's grace, rather than his own abilities. For he does not boast or recite what he has done, as if it were his doing, but he speaks of the change that has come about, which is obviously from heaven and not a result of his own endeavours. Let us also notice how freely he declares that the fact he has changed in this way must be attributed to God's great goodness, for he speaks of the good pleasure of

God. By this, he is excluding all that is of man, so that none may think that he wishes to reserve any praise for himself.

He continues by saying that he did not have to study to gain a knowledge of the gospel, for it came to him by revelation. Thirdly, he says that it was God who called him. Finally, he says that he was not chosen as a result of his abilities, in the same way that someone may make use of us when they discover that we are well suited to a task. Rather, he says that God had already separated him when he was in his mother's womb. Therefore, we can see that Paul is not trying to elevate himself, for he simply wants to know the Lord Jesus Christ, and to ensure that the doctrine of the gospel is not weakened by men who seek to achieve a great reputation in the world. For, as we have seen, these trouble-makers who had come to Galatia were using their reputations to disguise their real intentions. Paul shows that his title was not given him by men. He is not boasting that he won it or deserved to have it, but, at the very least, he wants us to know that God has displayed his grace in him in order to authenticate the doctrine which he preached.

There is no doubt that we have in Paul a mirror image of the goodness of God such as it is shown to all. This is the grace that we are partakers of, so that all of us, from the greatest to the least, may learn to humble ourselves. When we come to know the gospel, although we do not have such a revelation of it as Paul had, nevertheless, our understanding is due (and always will be), not to us, (because men cannot save themselves), but purely to the goodness of God, who has ordained it thus. For although we may do good to people who deserve it, because of some good that we see in them, the way Paul speaks here excludes any merits that we may have. He simply sets before us that God, though he found no worth in us when it pleased him to accept us as his children and to draw us to a knowledge of his gospel, did so because of his own counsel and his own will. This is what Paul is teaching us. Faith is purely a gift from God, and men may not attribute praise to themselves for the fact that they have come into the light of the gospel, in which they have discovered their happiness and their salvation. Instead, they ought to glorify God, for they are indebted to him for choosing and calling them. The cause is found in him alone and in his pure mercy. It is the same with all the callings that God has given us. We choose men if we see they have the ability to do the work: one is fitted to lead a nation, and another to be a preacher of the Word of God, and someone else to do this or that. We can discern the gifts God has given to each one, and we are right to do so. But however this may be, the one who is chosen, no matter what dexterity he has to fulfil his office well, must still acknowledge that God had set him apart beforehand. He has not developed by his own industry, but God has worked in him. And if this is so, let us not think that a person with a more advanced and skilful mind has himself to thank for this. After all, why are we not all slow-witted, like many of the creatures we see around us, who have no powers of reasoning? Who made mankind so different from the beasts? Surely, it was God, who chose us before we were born and ordained what we would be like? The person with a more gifted mind than others should acknowledge that it is God who has created him in this way. Even when we reach adulthood, we still need God to help us along the way and guide us, even though he does so invisibly. We know how careful the heathen are to educate their children; but notice that, even so, some are more studious than others. Whatever they do, God is leading and governing from above; therefore everything must be attributed to him. This is why Paul, who says that God revealed his Son to him, and called him to preach Christ, says that he did so because he had already set him apart from others. Indeed, God separated Paul, knowing very well to what use he would put him.

This being the case, it ought to lead us to walk in humility. For even if there is any goodness in us, none of us may boast about this as if it were his own. Rather, God must be acknowledged as the author of all that he has bestowed upon us, and his goodness alone should be the fountain from which we drink. Indeed, if this applies even to the smallest mercies that we receive at his hand, then what about that inestimable benefit that he has granted us where we are called to a knowledge of the gospel, and where he opens the gates of heaven to us, in order to declare that we are his children, and that he is our Father, and where our Lord Jesus Christ is united to us in such a way that through him we are assured of eternal life? And if God gives us such treasure, can we say that any of it is our own doing? What we ought to learn from this passage is that God has reserved for himself the right to govern our lives and he it is who guides our footsteps. He knows for what purpose he has created us. If it pleases him to enlighten our minds through faith in the gospel so that we acknowledge him as our Father, we should magnify his mercy, devote ourselves to him and call upon him with great boldness. If we have done so, let us not think that this issued from our own free will, for it is due solely to the life he has given by his Holy Spirit. For the Lord Jesus Christ, who has all wisdom in himself, cannot be known by us unless he is revealed to us. As he says, 'No man can come to me, except the Father . . . draw him' (*John* 6:44). This same Jesus Christ at one time lived in this world. He preached the gospel and spread it with fervency, and yet he says that no man can come to him (that is to say, no man can obey him), unless the Father has worked in his heart by the power of his Holy Spirit.

Now, Jesus Christ is apart from us both physically and owing to our sinful human natures, and we, therefore, do not see him here below. Thus, since we cannot see him visibly, how can we come to him, unless we are drawn by the grace that is spoken of here? Again, if faith is a gift from God, and if we cannot draw near to our Lord Jesus Christ unless God the Father takes us by the hand and brings us to him, how, then, can those who seek to win others do so by their own hard work? Surely it is God who has to intervene with another power? This is why Paul says that he was enlightened, then appointed and established as a teacher and apostle to draw others (once God had put him on the right path to salvation). By this, may we realise that when it pleases

God to call someone to be responsible for preaching the gospel, he is granting him a singular mercy. God does this, not only so that we who have this role and position should walk in his fear, attributing nothing to ourselves, but also so that each of us may be a living testimony to the love that God bears to his church. If men could insinuate their way into the church, then we could say that we were being taught almost by chance. But when we know that, though no man is able to open his mouth and speak of Jesus Christ as he ought, yet God has chosen those who should teach us, then we feel great assurance of the fact that he is our Father and has not abandoned us at all. This means that the truth of the gospel will be engraved in our hearts, and we will know that this doctrine did not proceed from men, but was sent by God. Yet, however much he uses his creatures, they are still but instruments whom he controls by his Spirit. This is how we may profit from the doctrine taught us here.

When Paul writes that we are chosen and set apart for God from our mother's womb, we learn something more about the grace of God. This does not affect the truth that we were chosen before the creation of the world, as Paul says in other passages (see *Eph.* 1:4). What is important here is that he is rejecting all that can be attributed to man. When a child leaves his mother's womb, what does he bring with him? What dignity does he possess? Surely he is a poor, stinking, filthy carcass? If, then, God marks us out when there is nothing about us that makes us worthy to please him, or that merits any love or praise, then when God calls us to some honoured service, we know that it is because of his mercy, just as those whom God gathers into his fold are called objects of his grace. This is the main reason why Paul speaks of his birth: he desires to show that when God drew him to himself there was nothing good in him. It was simply that God had regard to his eternal election, which he was furthering when he ordained that this creature should come into the world (just as he had always planned). Know, therefore, that when God pours out his blessings on us, we must return to this principle: that it can all be traced back to the eternal counsels of God. We cannot understand how it is that he has chosen us, nor why, for this transcends all human understanding. However, we can conclude that God has not chosen us above those whom he has cut off because he found us worthy or fit for such a blessing. No, rather, it is because he had ordained it thus before he had created us or placed us in this world, and even before heaven and earth came into being. And this is why it is written that we must be given to our Lord Jesus Christ before we can come to him (*John* 6:37). And who is it that imparts this gift? It is not that each person offers himself of his own volition. However, we must recognise that faith involves obedience and sacrifice; we are to devote ourselves to God willingly, and present our bodies and souls to the Lord Jesus Christ because he has bought us. But I said that it is not our own free choice; therefore, it is God who leads us in this direction. Why does he do this? Because we are already his. And how is it that we belong to him? It is not through any inheritance or title that we can claim on our part, but because he has chosen us. Now the meaning of this passage is clear to us.

* * *

Now let us return to the main issue which Paul is treating; for what I have inferred so far is that although we have been adopted, we cannot usurp God's glory, as those do who boast of their own free will, and their own strengths and merits. Let us, therefore, be rid of all such arrogance and let us all confess that everything we have comes purely from the goodness of God. Let us also observe that Paul speaks of his transformation in order that we may be fully persuaded that the doctrine he preached during his life, which we now have in written form, is not of this world. Paul did not invent it in his own mind – God had prepared him for this task. We need to be grounded upon such a great truth; otherwise, whereas our faith ought to be victorious over Satan and all that sets itself against our salvation, it will be nothing better than a fleeting opinion and completely unstable. Let us consider for a moment the battles we have to endure. If we were depending upon men, where would we be? Would we be steadfast at all? When daily we are assailed by so many temptations that it seems that we will perish and sink into the pit (given that our nature is totally inclined towards rebellion, falsehood, vanity and deceit, and that there are so many lusts within, like storms and whirlwinds seeking to overturn our faith), it is only possible to survive if our source of steadfastness is that we are stayed upon God and that we know the teaching that we follow is his pure truth and has proceeded from his mouth. This must, therefore, be our first priority. The Papists, it is true, are content with what has been dreamt up by men. It is good enough for them to believe what the church believes (as they often say), and yet the devil has them in his net. They are just like wretched beasts plunged into complete darkness. But as for us, we need to be sure that we have been taught by God, and that we are following his Word.

Therefore, we need to hear Paul's doctrine preached, and to be told that Paul did not usurp his position but was used of God as an instrument that he had ordained for this very purpose. This is the way we should understand what is said here. For had Paul followed the Christian faith since his childhood, and learnt it at school, it would still have been a gift of God. Yet, we would not have had such a declaration and open testimony as we have here when he speaks of this transformation. He used to be a ravening wolf, but he became not only a sheep but a shepherd; he used to be a mortal enemy of the gospel, but here he is serving the Lord Jesus Christ; he used to be blasphemous, cruel, proud and rebellious, but now we can see a zeal which issues from the Spirit of God; we see complete humility and gentleness. This change is so great and so sudden, that we must conclude that God is displaying his power in order to teach us not to treat Paul as a mere mortal. Indeed, this is why God also took Moses into the mountain and kept him there for forty days, when he desired to declare his law. For if Moses had simply uttered words received by revelation, he would still have fulfilled his duty as a true servant of God; however, how much less impact it would have made! No, God took him on the mountain for forty days and when he returned, his face shone, and his eyes were dazed. He was unable to bear the brightness, any more than he could that of the sun, and had to put a veil over his eyes. All these things took place to attest that the law had not been devised by him, but that he was like an angel from heaven, indeed, even more noble than an angel, since God had especially appointed him for this task. It is thus with all the apostles; for Jesus Christ could well have chosen those who had long been trained in the law and in the Holy Scriptures, with fine appearances, and good reputations and high standing amongst men. But he chose poor, stupid, unlearned, labouring folk, and he made them speak in a new way, transcending by their eloquence and depth of wisdom those who were regarded as the most learned and intelligent men in the world. Because God changed them so dramatically, their doctrine was rendered more authoritative. The same applies to Paul. There is, therefore, plenty of confirmation of the fact that when we read what Paul has left to us in written form, it is really God who is speaking, and Paul is an instrument of the Lord Jesus Christ.

Then he adds, 'immediately I conferred not with flesh and blood', that is to say, with mortal man; but he went straight to Arabia, where he stayed for three years, and then returned to Jerusalem to see Peter, seeing none of the disciples except Peter and James. At first sight, it might seem that Paul is spurning the apostles rather too much. For however much he knew of the gospel, he could still have been strengthened by them. The agreement and harmony which exists between the children of God when they are together edifies them all the more, as we know from our experience. It seems as if Paul is disdaining even such means as would have been most blessed to him, and which could have served for the benefit of the whole church. Yet, there was a special reason why he went in the opposite direction, and that is that he did not want any to think that his learning came about through human means, for he was not yet well established. If he had gone to Jerusalem and met with the other apostles, men would have said, 'This man must have had some doubts and so he came here to argue about it, and in the end he was persuaded.' Thus, they would have thought that his message sprang from a human source and God's glory would have been the more diminished. But, Paul had been a man full of cruelty, seeking to wipe out all trace of the gospel, spilling the blood of martyrs, blaspheming against God, forcing even the poorest and weakest to renounce Jesus Christ. But, although Paul had been beside himself with rage, stopping at nothing to overthrow the gospel, yet he was changed in a moment, without anyone speaking to him. Furthermore, he was blinded and thrown to the ground, and lay there as dead, and was then raised up from the grave, as it were. Then, when his eyes had been miraculously opened, God sent him a man who was not at all well known, namely Ananias, who baptised him, strengthened him, and helped him receive the visible gifts of the Holy Spirit. Because of this, and because he then went to Arabia, to that country where none had ever heard of Jesus Christ (for although there had been some dispersion of the Jews, yet the gospel was still completely unknown) – because, I say, Paul acted in this way, who is there who can say he learnt anything from men, or gained anything by argument, or by reason, or by whatever other human means there may be? We are constrained to admit that everything we find in Paul had been placed there by God. Here, then, is the special reason for which he did not meet with the apostles. It is true that Paul speaks of them almost disdainfully here, calling them 'flesh and blood'. But he is simply drawing a distinction between the Lord Jesus Christ and mere men, and is not in any way demeaning the gifts they had received from God. We do well to note this. For when we speak of men, it is only right that we refer to them as 'flesh and blood', as we see from the first chapter of John (*John* 1:13). Men are by nature full of corruption. Since we readily esteem far too highly our wisdom, strength, righteousness and intellect, God cancels out all our pride and vain presumption by saying, 'Who are you? Just flesh and blood.'

Sometimes, by using this expression 'flesh and blood', the Holy Scriptures are referring to the evil nature that we have had since the Fall of Adam (*Matt.* 16:17; *John* 3:6). For that uprightness that we once had is no longer there; quite the opposite, we are utterly ignorant, indeed foolish. We are so full of filth that we can do nothing of any worth, unless God is ruling our lives. This is what is meant by 'flesh and blood'. It is written that if we have been enlightened by coming to know the Lord Jesus Christ, it is not through our natural birth, nor through flesh and blood. We are made children of God when we are born again by the Holy Spirit in a special way. For if God had left us in our condition, we would only have clung to the world. In the sixteenth chapter of Matthew, it is written that flesh and blood did not reveal to Peter, nor to his friends, that Jesus Christ was the Son of God: it was our heavenly Father (*Matt.* 16:17). Therefore we have seen that men are called 'flesh and blood' to distinguish them from God himself, to show that we are full of corruption. It is true that our souls are still immortal, but the Scripture speaks of us disdainfully in this way in order to empty us of pride. As for the apostles, they had already been made regenerate by the Spirit of God. Therefore, there was more to them than flesh and blood, as we have seen in the passage that we have just quoted. Yet, when it comes to making a comparison between them and God, all that belongs to their natures can only be summed up by the expression 'flesh and blood'. Why? Otherwise, the apostles could surely have undermined the gospel in some way through their own apparent worthiness and nobility, as did those troublemakers whom we have spoken of, when they sought to use such things to cloak their own evil deeds! Well, Paul is showing us that if God retrieved all that belonged to himself, nothing would remain either in Peter, or John, or James, except the fact that they were sons of Adam like everyone else, and full of corruption. Thus, we are not to abuse the graces that God has given us to conceal the majesty of God and of his gospel.

Now, we have seen why Paul speaks of the apostles here in this particular way. For we have already looked at his earlier declaration, that if an angel from heaven wished to contradict the gospel, he ought to be detested and considered accursed, as if he were a devil. Why? Ought he to speak so shamefully about those noble creatures, the angels, those who are called the heavenly principalities and powers of God (*Eph.* 1:21)? He is not wronging them in the least, because he is attributing all sovereign authority to the Lord Jesus Christ, who is their Head; for they must be in subjection to him. Thus, let us not think that we are being denigrated, even if we are trampled upon a hundred times, provided that God's name is exalted, and that our Lord Jesus is given the sovereignty and pre-eminence he deserves – heeded by great and small alike and submitted to in true obedience of faith.

From this, we can conclude that those wretched Papists are blind, since they worship both the apostles and the martyrs to such a degree that they rob God of his worship and service. It seems as if all that rightfully belongs to God and that should be reserved for him is put on offer among them. For what distinction do they make between him and his creatures? They virtually dispose of the Lord Jesus Christ, by robbing him of the office that he has been given. For instead of acknowledging him as the Advocate who grants us access to God the Father, and applying to him to have their prayers and supplications answered, they have an infinite multitude of advocates, patrons and intercessors! Jesus Christ is no longer anything to them. When we see that creatures have obtained such honour amongst men, whilst God is thrust into the background, as it were, and his Word treated like dirt, we know that it is the devil who has turned everything upside down. Therefore, whatever we do, though we may esteem men, we must ensure that God receives all the honour that is due to him. If we are comparing him with his creatures, let us remember that all men put together are but vanity, and that if there is anything good about them, it is a token of God's love, so that we look to him and he alone is exalted.

Also, let us learn that we cannot honour God as he deserves without being obedient to his Word. Those who hold many ceremonies in order to prove that they desire to serve God will be disowned by him unless they submit to the Lord and to his Word. Paul is contending for the authority of the gospel. To him it is not enough that people speak of God or of Jesus Christ; he wants everyone to accept without question the doctrine contained in the gospel. This shows us that religion today is in a state of decline and, in particular, there is in Popery nothing but devilish confusion. For they speak often enough about the Lord Jesus Christ, but in what manner? Do they know his power? Do they know why he was sent by God the Father, and what benefits he has brought us? They know nothing of this. They call him the Saviour of the world and yet each one of them searches for salvation in himself, or in some saint that he has made. This is their sad estate. So much the more, then, ought we to remember what is taught us here; that is to say, that when we speak of God, everything else must pale into insignificance – and the very sun and moon ought to be darkened (as the prophet says, *Isa.* 13:10), to the end that God may have all the pre-eminence. And since God will not accept the worship or service that we offer him unless we are submissive to his Word, let us accept all of the doctrine of the gospel; may nothing prevent us from holding it in such reverence that we submit to all that is contained therein. This, then, is what we ought to learn when the apostles are referred to as 'flesh and blood'.

* * *

Next, Paul adds that he went to Jerusalem to see Peter. This confirms that his journey to Arabia, to which he referred earlier, was not born of pride or disdain for the apostles. Rather, he wanted the grace of God to be seen, so that nothing in this world would act as a veil, concealing the fact that Jesus Christ had worked a wonderful miracle; for a man who had been so rebellious previously, had yielded to him.

Here, then, on the one hand, we see that Paul wanted to reserve for God everything that was his by right. And yet, on the other hand, he wanted to show that there was a good relationship between himself and the other apostles. And this is how we should be, for we will find that many people wrongly go to one or other of these extremes. There are some mockers who pretend to magnify the grace of God and yet are blasphemers, full of venom and pride, putting their own dreams and fantasies before anything else. What if we were to ask why they are like this? After all, God has apparently shown his grace to many of these people, and it would seem that they are well trained in the Holy Scriptures; also we know that they apply themselves faithfully to preaching the gospel to us. Why is it that we are not in harmony with them? 'Oh!', they would say, 'I have nothing to do with any living man upon earth: I am relying on God alone.' These are proud and arrogant people, pretending to have the Holy Spirit in their hearts, and even to have had certain revelations from the Holy Spirit, and yet they destroy the unity of the church, and despise God's grace. Therefore, we need to maintain the balance which we see here. For although, on the one hand, Paul declares that he went to Arabia immediately after his conversion so that we might see that Jesus Christ was his only Master and Teacher (as indeed he must always have pre-eminence over and above ourselves), yet he also clearly shows that he wanted to be united in sweet concord with the apostles. He desired that everyone should know that he sought to be in harmony with them as instruments together of the Holy Spirit. For (as we have already shown), if we are thus joined together, this is by no means a small aid towards the strengthening of our faith. God does not call just one man, for there are many who yield to him, and this shows us that they are led by the same Spirit and have a common desire, and work towards the same end. Because they seek the inheritance of a life in heaven, they show that they are children of God. Therefore, Paul was right to show us that he had truly joined with the other apostles and did not desire to be separated from them, for such help is necessary if we want to be strengthened in our faith.

Let us, therefore, remember the happy medium which is here commended so that we do not incline to either one or other of the extremes. There are some who are so fickle that they will abandon the doctrine of the gospel for the slightest little thing. As soon as they hear a man speak, they accept whatever he says to them. But why? If our foundation is no better than this, can we stand firm amidst all the attacks that the devil, our deadly enemy, makes upon us? Let us, then, remain firmly established in the faith, and let us all, from the greatest to the least, rest in the Lord Jesus Christ. For since he is our Head, he must be exalted; as it says in the prophet Isaiah, he is the ensign that all must seek (*Isa.* 11:10). Thus, we must learn not to fix our attention upon what men appear to be, for this detracts from the majesty of the Son of God. Also, when once we have resolved to be taught by the one who has been given to us as our teacher, let us not be so proud of him that we see no further than him, for this will only cause ruin in the church. Instead, let us seek to live in harmony with one another, and let each one contribute whatever gifts he has been given. May the unity of our faith be like a bond that knits us together so that we may become one temple of God. For it is written with good reason that we are living stones which comprise the temple of God. Thus, if each one sought to remain separate and friendless, what would become of us? Would there still be a building? No, quite the opposite, there would only be ruins. If we really desire that God should live amongst us and make his dwelling with us, then he must be worshipped in truth, and each of us must be at peace with his neighbours as far as possible. We must not distance ourselves from God in order to be closer to men; it were better for us all to disagree with one another, and for wars to flare up amongst us. No, but if we are united to God, then this shall result in sweet harmony. By this means, we can keep to the middle path that Paul followed, for he did not wish to join with the apostles if it meant obscuring the grace of God, and undermining the doctrine of the gospel. However, this did not stop him from searching them out in a foreign country, despite great difficulties, and enduring a most heavy trial when they accused him of having been a persecutor of God and his truth.

When Paul came thus to declare his unity with the other apostles, and to testify to this in front of the whole church, we not only learn that he desired to serve God, and unselfishly exalted the Word of God above all creatures, we also learn that he was very human and very humble. Likewise, we ought to be of the same mind as our brothers, and seek to submit to one another in such a way, as members of one body, with Jesus Christ as our Head. We ought not to separate or be parted over the slightest thing; nor ought we to think we are in a category apart from the rest, but, instead, let us seek to communicate one with another so that each of us guides his neighbour. May we all work towards the same end, and encourage one another, so that people may see the warm fellowship that is amongst us. It is true that we cannot be at peace with everybody; far from it! This is why Paul says in another passage that we should seek to live at peace with all men, as far as it is possible for us to do so (*Rom.* 12:18). By this, he is implying that we will be at war with many people. For the devil has many demons, and there are as many people who oppose the Word of God. We must set ourselves against them, if we want to contend for the pure doctrine of the gospel. However, when someone wishes to submit to the Lord Jesus Christ, we must welcome him, and go before him in the way. We ought to identify with him and not think that we are more important than others, so that we say, 'What! If I associate with him, it will seem as if I am lowering myself to his level.' Woe to us if we are thus proud. Let us, instead, simply desire that Jesus Christ should be our Head, and we, members of his body, worshipping him and calling upon him with one voice in unity of faith.

Now let us fall down before the majesty of our great God, acknowledging our sins, and praying that he would make us increasingly conscious of them, in order to hate ourselves and to ask that he will grant us the remedy through his Holy Spirit. Being thus freed from our sin and wretchedness, may we be renewed in his image, so that he is glorified in every aspect of our lives. In the meantime, may he support us in our frailty until he has brought us to that state of perfection from which we have all strayed. Thus we all say, Almighty God, and our heavenly Father, etc.

7

A Total Resolve to Serve and Glorify God

And was unknown by face unto the churches of Judaea which were in Christ: But they had heard only, That he which persecuted us in times past now preacheth the faith which once he destroyed. And they glorified God in me.

Then fourteen years after I went up again to Jerusalem with Barnabas, and took Titus with me also. And I went up by revelation, and communicated unto them that gospel which I preach among the Gentiles, but privately to them which were of reputation, lest by any means I should run, or had run, in vain (Gal. 1:22–2:2).

We have looked at the fact that Paul had preached the gospel everywhere without acknowledgment from any creature, content with the knowledge that he was serving God, and that his labour was pleasing to him. But he also sought fellowship and close links with the apostles, because this was necessary to strengthen those who were weak and easily turned aside, that is, without God's aid in their infirmity. Thus, we can see that whilst Paul was confident about his doctrine, at the same time he sought to draw the children of God together, that they might be united by the bands of faith, and glorify God with one heart, one soul and one voice. Yet we also notice here that Paul gave little thought to whether he ought to press onwards or go back; his main concern, though he was unrecognised by those who had become believers before him, was to serve God in the place in which he had received the call.

This point is most worthy of our attention, for Paul is demonstrating his total resolve to serve God. He did not expect to receive wages from men, or to be gratified, or even to be esteemed according to his merits. Let us, therefore, learn to be so content with the occupation to which we have been called, that even when men do not see us, we continue to perform our duty faithfully, happy in the knowledge that we are approved by God. Those who look for man's approval will always be tainted by ambition, and it will be impossible for them to walk in purity and integrity. What is more, Luke shows us that Paul needed unshakeable steadfastness in order to persevere, since men suspected his motives (*Acts* 9:26). For he says that the believers were suspicious of him, and that they avoided him when he went to Jerusalem. This was a most grievous trial for Paul, to see that he was not welcomed into the company of believers, for he had already suffered greatly. We know that when he first entered the gates of the city of Damascus, they closed upon him (as we have seen previously), and he had to be let down in a basket (*2 Cor.* 11:33). The minute he was converted to the faith of Jesus Christ, he suffered the distress of fierce persecution. Then, he travelled to Arabia, where he carried out his work faithfully. Did he then expect to have the friendship and fellowship of believers? Well, even this door was closed to him; they avoided him as they would a wild beast! Previously, he had been honoured and held in high esteem amongst the enemies of the gospel, yet now in the Jewish synagogue, he surrendered all this, to the point of being driven out of the synagogue; and still no-one would deign to give him a place in the church. He could have been so angry with such an attitude that it made him renounce it all, if his affection was fixed on things below. But since he had devoted himself entirely to serving God (though men gave him no thanks for his labour), he was determined to continue to the very end, and thus he did not swerve from the right path. Such an example should encourage us today, since so few, even in the church, approve of that which springs from a pure and godly zeal. Some are disparaging because they are world-wearied; others are so morose that you cannot please them whatever you do; others are full of wicked slanders and lies. If we know that men will always let us down in one respect or another, we will learn to devote ourselves to God in order that we might constantly press on along the path that he wishes us to tread, and not use our own weakness as an excuse. Indeed, Paul goes before us and bids us take his hand, as it were. He was frail, just as we are, yet God so strengthened him by his Holy Spirit that he was able to overcome all the obstacles. Thus, let us seek God, conscious that we are weak, that it would please him to equip us with such steadfastness that we never fail to fulfil our duty towards him. Let us do this, regardless of the extent to which some may speak evil of us, and others accuse us, and still others look down on us and disregard all our labour, though we have only sought to do them good. However much, therefore, it may seem that this is wasted effort and fruitless, let it suffice us that God accepts and owns our labour. This is what we ought to learn from this passage.

Above all else, we ought not to desire to be famous, or to make a great impact in this world, for, were to try as hard as we possibly could, we could be no better than Paul. Every time he preached the gospel, he was like a man caught up to heaven. (Although that experience of which he speaks in Second Corinthians only happened on one occasion, yet the fruit of it was displayed throughout the rest of his life – *2 Cor.* 12:2). However, even after having preached in this manner, he was 'unknown' to all the churches in Judaea. Thus, it may well have seemed that he had not been very successful, since all his work had been overlooked, and yet it was enough for him that God was building up those who lived in the remotest parts through him. We have seen, therefore, that he was not seeking to be famous, nor to acquire reputation and authority amongst men.

In referring to 'the churches of Judaea which were in Christ', he is adding this qualification because there were still some of God's seed amongst the Jews. For the promises had been given to them and, therefore, they had not been altogether cut off, unless of course they actually rejected Christ and thus denied themselves the new life which was offered to them. For as God had chosen the line of Abraham, so our Lord Jesus Christ came to this world to minister to those whom God had thus adopted. He came to fulfil the promises that had been given to their fathers. Our Lord Jesus Christ did not reject the Jews, to whom the promises belonged, as it says in the second chapter of Acts (*Acts* 2:39). The true church of God remained amongst them still; after all, their sacrament of circumcision had not been invented by man. Though they had debased themselves by introducing many errors and wicked inventions, to the extent of interfering with the true service of God, and though they corrupted true religion, yet this people were still known as God's household and flock. Therefore, the synagogues which had not yet declared their unbelief by completely cutting themselves off from Jesus Christ, are referred to here as 'churches' by Paul. Yet not perfect churches, for they had not yet been made regenerate in Jesus Christ. For the whole world was renewed when Jesus was sent to reconcile to God both those who were near and those who were afar off (*Eph.* 2:17). Those who were near, like the Jews who already had the law; those who were afar off, like the Gentiles who had no part in the heavenly kingdom, having been left by God as poor wild beasts because of their own superstitions and idolatrous practices. But Jesus Christ came to bring them all together, and reunite all who had previously been scattered. From this, we can see that the law ought to have guided the Jews to the gospel, as is apparent throughout the Holy Scriptures. It is very important for us to learn this, so that we do not think that whatever is contained in the law is of no relevance to us. For assuredly, although the ceremonies of the law are no longer practised, the truth and substance of them remain. So much is this the case that we cannot be genuine believers today if we are not also children of Abraham and disciples of Moses. This does not mean that we ought to remain under the former shadows, but we must hold together those things which cannot be put asunder, namely, the law and the gospel.

Furthermore, we ought to learn that we cannot be considered 'churches' in the sight of God today (indeed, none of the assemblies in this world can claim such an honourable title) unless we are 'in Jesus Christ'. For he is the Head and he unites us to God the Father. It is through him that we enter the kingdom of heaven. Indeed, any who do not know Jesus Christ, even if they have been baptised and call themselves Christians, are like rotten members, forever cut off, however much they number themselves among the children of God. This is what we should observe with regard to this passage.

Next, Paul says that it was commonly reported that he who had persecuted the faith in times past now preached it, and that God was glorified through this. Once again, this shows us that Paul does not utter his own praises, for he is condemning himself for having been the enemy and persecutor of the church. Whilst he is speaking of what was commonly reported amongst men, yet he repeats the facts just as they were in truth. Thus, he does not seek to hide what will be to his own reproach and shame. Anyone could have accused him of persecuting poor believers, of shedding innocent blood, and of compelling the weak to blaspheme, to the utmost of his power. But he willingly brings this accusation against himself; yet not in a manner which suggests he was half-boasting that he was such a great enemy of the gospel. It is most certain that Paul was touched with real grief for his evil deeds whenever he made such a confession; after all, he says in another passage that he is not worthy to be called an apostle (*1 Cor.* 15:9). He always felt an ache in his heart because of his rebellion against God in the past. Not only had he been inspired by evil desires, but he had become totally inflamed against the gospel. And yet, whatever he had done, he preferred to acknowledge his sin in all humility, rather than to neglect to mention something that might be to God's glory. Therefore, let us learn to be fully aware of the offences that we have committed. If it will be for the honour of God, may we not be afraid to be humiliated in the sight of men. Let us be content to bear some mark of infamy before men, if need be, so that God may have the glory. In this way, our sins will be covered by God, never to be accounted of and never to be remembered.

Therefore, when we read that it was commonly believed (and, indeed, it was the truth) that Paul destroyed the faith in times past, let us remember all the following points. We know that faith in the gospel will always be victorious over the efforts of Satan and, indeed, of all evildoers. Therefore, even at the time when Paul was inspired by the kind of raging fury that we have already alluded to, it was not possible for him to wipe out or overthrow the faith, for it is founded upon the invincible truth of God. It is not subject to the opinions of men. But here, Paul is thinking of the weakness of the ordinary folk, whom he had crushed as much as he possibly could. For he says in Acts that he not only persecuted Christians, but he also 'compelled them to blaspheme' (*Acts* 26:11). Today, if a great number of people were persecuted, some would not wish to spare their own blood, nor indeed their lives, but would confess the name of our Lord Jesus Christ. Others, however, would rather redeem for themselves this miserable life which is passing away, by recanting the faith. Such, with all in their power, thrust themselves from the kingdom of heaven, and throw themselves into Satan's net. They run headlong into eternal death, in order to escape the hand of tyrants and enemies. Thus, the Holy Spirit condemns Paul for this cruelty, for not only had he been full of pride and rebellion against God, but he had also compelled many to recant and abandon their faith in the gospel. This is how he had behaved, and this ought to serve as a lesson to us. For even though the Word may remain intact, and we can do it no harm, despite our great weaknesses, yet at the same time we can still do violence to the faith by our own actions. For if I compromise in order to satisfy the enemies of God, and if I conceal the truth or hide anything at all, then I have nullified my faith.

Yes, the Word of God will hold its own (as I have already said), and yet a man's fall will often cause a great scattering of the people. If we heard someone whom we would expect to be very faithful deny everything, many poor souls would be shaken, not knowing what to think. Whilst it is true that we should not trust in men, yet there are still many (as we will see later) whose faith needs strengthening through the good example of others. If a man casts a stumbling block in their way, they can be utterly turned away or else be so shocked that they do not know which way to turn. Knowing this to be the case, let us learn to commit ourselves to God; for the devil has many demons who are seeking to throw everything into confusion today, and whose sole employment is the suppression of the Christian faith. Let us ask God, furthermore, to strengthen us and give us such constancy that our enemies will be confounded, even when they assail us more vigorously than they do at present. Let us not be every man for himself, but let us take care of the great number of poor souls who are in the wolf's mouth, as it were. They will be tormented and threatened, and efforts will be made to make them recant by flattery and enticement. If our poor brothers are assaulted in this way, at the very least we should have enough love to pray that God would help them in their need, and give them victorious and unconquerable faith so that they will never surrender, whatever Satan and all his followers may devise against them.

Thus, we need to take serious notice of this passage, where Paul says that he destroyed and ruined the faith. For although God always preserves his truth, yet nevertheless, men are still being lost because their faith has been shaken and they have fallen away from the right path. Furthermore, we need to be strengthened, since so few persevere with the constancy that is required of them. It is to be hoped that we will not be too astonished by this, for this has been common since time began. But was Paul's preaching any less authoritative because of the many apostates who finally revealed their hypocrisy, men full of treachery? Even amongst his own friends who had joined with him, and who were as close to him as a hand in a glove, there were those who finally renounced it all. And yet Paul's doctrine is not to be rejected because of this! For he, indeed, persecuted Christians before his conversion, and though many renounced the salvation that they should have confessed, (since Jesus Christ was its author), yet for all this Christianity was not weakened! Similarly today, many poor folk find themselves overcome and give everything up, and yet others, from whom we do not expect much loyalty, persevere in the face of hardship. Let us profit from this by learning to lean upon our God, even if everyone else were heading for destruction. Let us remember that our foundation is sound and sure.

* * *

Then Paul adds that the believers 'glorified God in me'. This implies that others could see with their own eyes that this transformation had been wrought by God's hand alone. Everything comes back to the one fact that he was not an imposter, and could not be accused of preaching out of mere caprice, nor of being impetuous or presumptuous, or motivated by human impulses. It was God who had led and guided him. The believers 'glorified God in him' when they saw just how much God had worked in his life. It was a true miracle of God that such a man as Paul had been renewed and changed from being a ravening wolf to become a sheep, and finally a shepherd! This is the first thing. We learn, in short, that whenever God bestows his grace on a person, even if it enriches him beyond measure, he must not exalt himself but ensure that the praise is given to whom it belongs, and to whom it is due. Thus, let us hold on to this principle of humility. Let us not seek to be noticed, or to be esteemed above our neighbours, despite any gifts that God may have given us. May God always have the pre-eminence, and may we all learn to glorify God when we see his grace in another. This is so important, for since time began there has been such hatred between men; each is envious of his friend, because all desire to be the greatest. Surely every one of us wishes to be greater than his friends, that is, unless God has tamed us and taught us to give ourselves to meekness. Indeed, it is from this same ambition that all envy and strife proceeds, and with it all contempt, murmurings, criticisms, and the like. Contrary to this, if we hold tight to the principle that is set before us here, we will learn by and by to glorify God when we see any mark of his grace in another. For in envying someone whom God has honoured, and in seeking to deny the gifts and graces that we see in him, we are not only wronging mortal creatures, but God, the author of these very gifts. I may meet someone who can build up the church; God may have gifted him with such graces that we could profit from his labour. But, fearing that he may advance too far, and that I may have to fade into the background too much, I seek to conceal and weaken what God has done in him by my slander and other devious methods. It is just as if I were wilfully seeking to hide all the gifts of God and cause them to be despised. And where does this come from, if not from that cursed ambition that I have already described? Thus, if we stir ourselves up in this way, there will always be strife and grumbling; in short, it will lead to the kind of disunity which offends God. For whom are we wronging? I am wronging my neighbour by undervaluing him in this way, yet I am also blaspheming against God. We cannot ignore the graces and virtues of a man without adding blasphemy to it, because we are seriously offending God. How is this? It is because God desires to be known through all his gifts. Whenever he comes into our presence, we must, of necessity, worship him. If, therefore, we see some of the evidences of the Holy Spirit's workings in a man, and if we trample them underfoot, or spit at them, or loathe them, is this not an attempt, as far as it lies in us, to undermine the majesty of God? Whilst we may not admit this to be so, this does not alter the facts. We ought to give heed to what is said here regarding the believers glorifying God in the person of Paul, when they saw that God had worked in him. We are being warned by this to give God the glory that belongs to him when he grants us his gifts. For it is not that we offend or give injury to the creature, but that we are setting our faces against God, by cheating and despoiling him of what is rightfully his.

We need to adhere to this lesson all the more as we see greater malice around today than ever before. How many of us esteem the gifts of God because they are profitable for the edification and wellbeing of the whole church? The devil has so much control that he makes us ungrateful, thus preventing us from enjoying the fruit of God's gifts which we could otherwise have delighted in. If we had a fair and open-hearted spirit, then we would surely gain from the good example of others. If someone is gifted with graces from God, we would make use of them to profit our own souls. But because of our malicious spirit, we close the door so that we cannot enjoy the good things that are set before us. Indeed, there are some who are so spiteful, that out of their malice they would try to have us believe that the sun never shines! They are furious and vexed when they see that the name of God is glorified because of someone else's example. 'Why should he have that privilege?' they say. They act as if we no longer need to humble ourselves and glorify God as he deserves, when he bestows gifts upon men according to his will. Some are so wicked that they would rather dethrone God than patiently accept those whom God has gifted, and who are working to build up the church. Ought we not to welcome them, knowing that God desires to be glorified through them? You see, therefore, how full of malice and venom men are today. Since this is the case, let us hold all the more firmly to what is taught us here. That is to say, let God be glorified through all the benefits which come to us, knowing that they are bestowed out of his goodness alone, and that he is the author of all good qualities. There is no praiseworthy thing in any creature which cannot be attributed to him. Therefore, in everything and through everything let us learn to glorify God.

* * *

At this point, he adds that he went up again to Jerusalem, and communicated with those who had most authority, so that he might not in times past (or indeed in the future) have run in vain. Here we notice that Paul's appetite was never satisfied in his efforts to find suitable methods for the extension of the kingdom of our Lord Jesus Christ. He always sought to remove all obstacles, so that the gospel could have free course. As we saw this morning, he was not driven by vain presumption. But he thought that certain wicked people might accuse him of rallying around the apostles in order to learn something from them. He knew that people might well think like this, yet he did not abandon his duty, which was to seek to be united with the other apostles. I do not believe that he was seeking to acquaint himself with one man in particular, for he sought to be accepted by all. It is most certain that when Paul went to Jerusalem, he did not do so in order to find out which of them was the best teacher, but so that they would all mutually express their faithfulness in serving God and preaching the gospel. That is why Paul went there.

Can we not see his humility here? As long as the church received fruit and was strengthened in its faith, and as long as he could be assured that the apostles would allow him into their number, he was prepared to undergo anything. And coupled with his humility, we also see his zeal. He had 'run' in many a country; he had been to Arabia, and toured throughout that country, he had also been to Cilicia, the place of his birth, and to Syria, and then he had returned to Jerusalem, travelling first throughout the land of Judaea. By making all these journeys without any of his creature comforts, he was proving that he would rather die than live if by this the kingdom of our Lord Jesus Christ would be extended, and the church (as we have said) receive some fruit from his labour. Having seen such an example, may we learn to bid farewell to laziness, and to have more courage to ask God (if we are colder than we ought to be) not to let us stagnate in our sins. Let us ask that he would wake us up and give us grace, instead, to spend ourselves in his service when the opportunity arises and when the situation demands it. At the same time, may we continue to stand firm in the doctrine that Paul preached, since he so willingly worked for the glory of God and our well-being. For if he had been a deceiver, he could surely have proceeded in the manner of worldly men. But when he came, though nobody sought him out, and though he was rejected, nevertheless he sought friendship and unity with the believers. Indeed, no-one knew about his efforts and labours, and the fact that he gave himself unsparingly. This confirms that he was walking with God and that the Holy Spirit led him in all respects.

Now, when Paul says that he communicated with those who were of reputation and held in high esteem so that he might not have run (or continue to run) in vain, this does not mean that he would have failed had he not gained the favour of any particular living person. No, he was thinking of the many weak souls who could have remained in unbelief had not God drawn them by this means to a full and certain knowledge of the gospel. I said not so long ago that our faith can crumble when we falter, not in and of itself but by virtue of our infirmity. Thus, the labours of those who preach and publish the gospel are vain and fruitless if we do not profit from the preaching as much as we can (that is, if God does not bless such efforts or give the increase). When Paul says, 'lest by any means I should run, or had run, in vain', or to no profit (that is, of course, unless God were to bless his work by his own power), he does not mean that those who preach waste their efforts. For indeed, the preaching of the gospel will always be an acceptable sacrifice to God, even if the world only receives death and condemnation by it. As we saw in Second Corinthians, Paul said, 'We are unto God a sweet savour' (*2 Cor.* 2:15). God will always accept the sacrifice that we offer him, even though unbelievers see it as a stench, being poisoned against the gospel through their own corrupt natures. Thus, in this passage, Paul did not mean that he had run in vain, as if God had made him a laughing stock, or as if his preaching had been to no avail. Instead, he considered those he had instructed, and those he hoped to teach until the end of his life. He knew that they would not have been edified had they not observed a good relationship between him and the apostles, who were known to have been ordained by our Lord Jesus Christ.

At this point, we might be puzzled about whether such people were really believers, since they would not have come to believe the gospel without the assistance of men. The solution to this is simple: the Word of God alone ought to be sufficient for our faith. If we are asked what our faith is based upon and how it can be perfected, the answer is, by the Word of God. But is this so? Are there not sacraments which accompany the Word? Yes, as helps, because of our great weakness. And then there is an oath too, which God swears – all this is over and above his Word. Yes, there is a superabundance indeed! But God assists us in this way to help us when we stumble and are weakened to such a degree as to fail to rely upon his power as we should; his intention is to raise us up again by these means. Likewise, when we see there is harmony amongst the servants of God, it is sure to be of great benefit to us, and a good witness. Moreover, the blood of martyrs ought to be of great benefit to us, and serve to strengthen us. Indeed, these things act as a seal, making the doctrine of God even more authoritative in our eyes. These, then, are some helps which keep us even closer to the faith, in order to sustain and strengthen us in it. The same applies to miracles. Miracles in themselves do not give us faith in the Word of God, but they prepare us for it. God shows his power in order that we might be awakened all the more, and in order that we might respect his Word to a greater degree. Thus, miracles also serve as seals. When we come to believe in the gospel, however unstable our faith is, God grants us great strength through such means. Thus it is with the matter that Paul addresses now. For what would have happened if people had seen that men of such great authority differed and were in turmoil? What would the poor have thought, apart from being so distraught that they were made to say, 'Alas! What is this? We would not know which way to turn. If there is such strife amongst those who ought to show us the way, so that they all pull in different directions, how can we be sure this is true?' Thus, many simple folk would be disheartened. This is why Paul wished to see Peter, John and James. He desired everyone to witness the fact that they accepted him and that the gospel which he preached was not strange doctrine but the same gospel that Jesus Christ had taught his disciples, and which he had commissioned them to spread throughout the world.

Through this, we are led to understand that, added to Paul's zeal, humility, magnanimity and steadfastness, God foresaw that this harmony amongst the apostles which he speaks of here would be a further means of strengthening us. By reason of our weaknesses and imperfections, we need to make use of all the means God gives us. We ought to strive to live in such harmony with the children of God, that each of us helps his neighbour, rather than setting ourselves against one another. Woe to him who shows such ill-feeling that he makes poor, ignorant, weak folk draw back. At the same time, let us be aware of the evil that can result when those who are responsible for preaching the gospel are defamed by slander, or rendered suspect to the extent that people do not know whether or not to trust them. People wonder whether God has really chosen them to advance the kingdom of his Son by spreading the gospel in other lands, to edify multitudes by their ministry. Woe to him, therefore, who sets such a scandal in motion. Let us, as far as possible, make every effort to be in agreement with those who serve God. Let us help those who are gifted with the ability to build up the church, who have been ordained as office-bearers. Let us lend them our hands so that their labours may be fruitful, both for our benefit and for the benefit of our neighbours. By this means, God will be glorified and, more and more, we will be enabled to call upon him as our Father with one heart and voice.

Now let us fall before the majesty of our great God, acknowledging our sins, and asking him to make us increasingly conscious of them to bring us to a right repentance. Let us also ask him to display his infinite mercy towards us, until he has purged us of all our imperfections. Then we will be able to see him face to face, as he is. Let us aspire to that perfection to which he now calls us by his Word, and towards which we aim throughout our lives, knowing that we cannot reach it until we are rid of our flesh, and released from that prison in which we are now held bondage to sin. May he not only grant this grace to us, but also to all peoples and nations on earth, etc.

8

The Infiltration Which Corrupts the Truth of the Gospel

But neither Titus, who was with me, being a Greek, was compelled to be circumcised: And that because of false brethren unawares brought in, who came in privily to spy out our liberty which we have in Christ Jesus, that they might bring us into bondage: To whom we gave place by subjection, no, not for an hour; that the truth of the gospel might continue with you (Gal. 2:3–5).

Many times in our lives, we experience how much of an enemy the devil is to our souls. He is forever striving to prevent the gospel from having free course, and he will use every possible means to do so. This draws to our attention the fact that God has set the teaching of Scripture as the source of all our well-being, joy and happiness. For the devil would not bother to interfere with this teaching unless he knew that it contained all that men need for salvation. Though he strives to conceal God's glory, he cannot, for [man's salvation and God's glory] are inseparably bound together. For God in his grace has established the following pattern: he dwells amongst us in order to draw us to himself, and then our highest good is attained by cleaving to him and abiding in him. So Satan raises up numerous enemies to declare war openly on the gospel of the Lord Jesus Christ. Not only this; he also seeks to draw intruders into our ranks who will act as internal foes. This has been the case since time began, as we can see in the example which Paul describes here. We know that everyone made threats against Paul; and we know how many struggles and difficulties he had undergone because of resistance from the heathen and the unbelieving, who withstood the preaching of the gospel as much as they possibly could. But worse than this, he says that there were certain deceivers who had crept in behind their backs. The Greek word he uses suggests they did so by stealth, but we cannot adequately express it in one word in our language. He is saying that spies had infiltrated secretly amongst the believers with the sole intention of undermining the truth of the gospel. Let us be sure to notice that these rogues did not openly reject the teaching of the Lord Jesus Christ. On the contrary, they bore the name and title of Christians. And yet at the same time, they only wished to have some half-gospel, which would have been neither one thing nor the other (as we say) but a mixture according to their taste. Likewise today, there are many such people in the world who seek to design and construct a religion to suit themselves. They take some of God's pure truth and mix in lies and delusions. Notice that even at the time of Paul, there were such liberals. This is what Paul is warning us of here.

However, he says that he did not give place to them by subjection, even for a moment, so that the truth concerning the liberty of the gospel might continue. This is a summary of what is being said here. Now, first of all, we ought to be armed and equipped ready for our internal enemies; for they are seeking to confuse and corrupt the message of the gospel to such an extent that we will no longer know anything for a surety and all will be confusion. We ought not to be surprised when this happens, for it is nothing new. Let us realise that if God was testing the faithfulness of believers at the time of Paul, then it is clear that he will test us nowadays. Indeed, it is written that there must be sects and heresies amongst us, so that by our consistent obedience to God, those who have a living root will be seen and known. Such people will bear a mark which proclaims that they have truly profited in the school of the Lord Jesus Christ, that is, if they do not allow themselves to be seduced or corrupted. This is why our Lord permits such intruders who sow discord and strive to pervert pure doctrine. He could easily prevent this if it seemed good to him: but instead, he gives Satan a free rein because this is a better test of our faith. May we not go aside to the left hand nor to the right, no matter how many temptations come our way. Rather, may we always press on along the path that we have been shown, knowing that we cannot stray if we are completely grounded on the Word of God. If we can remain faithful, then it has been a good test of our faith. However, let us resist such rogues as may enter in, recognising that they are like deadly plagues and more harmful even than those who turn aside out of the way altogether and openly declare that they despise the gospel. Those who have come into our midst are much worse, and we must resist them manfully. If we give up the struggle, it is certain that before long there will be great confusion and people will no longer be able to distinguish between black and white. Let us commit ourselves, therefore, to this task.

* * *

Now, let us consider what type of person Paul is referring to here. He says that they 'came in privily to spy out our liberty which we have in Christ Jesus'. He is speaking of liberty with regard to ceremonial rites. For (as we have mentioned before, and as we will soon see at greater length), under the law, God had chosen many types which would keep our forefathers waiting for the coming of the Lord Jesus Christ and his manifestation to the world. Therefore, the sacrifices, together with all their additional requirements, (the sanctuary and all else that went with it), were of service only because our Lord Jesus Christ (who is the true fulfilment of all this) had not yet appeared. Our forefathers had to be governed and led by such shadows. This is why Paul likens them to little children who are under tutors and governors (*Gal.* 4:1–2). It was good and right that our fathers of old kept the ceremonies of the law, for they confirmed the promise of the Redeemer. This also explains why it was that the sanctuary had been made according to the pattern that Moses had seen on the mountain top. Surely, its pattern was a spiritual one – symbolic of the Lord Jesus Christ and his grace, which is now ministered to us through the gospel. Indeed, our Lord Jesus came to this world in order that such types and shadows should be no more. For this reason, when he died the veil of the temple was torn in two, to show that God desired us to approach him with greater boldness. In this passage, Paul says that we have liberty in our Lord Jesus Christ, and are no longer subject to the kind of servitude that existed at the time of the law. He continues by taking circumcision as an example, just as he does in the letter to the Colossians (*Col.* 2:11). Hence, we are circumcised, not by man's hands, but by the work of the Lord Jesus Christ within us through the power of his Holy Spirit. And instead of circumcision, which was established for the Jews, we have baptism which speaks of the same thing: that is to say, the fact that we need to be new creatures and to commit ourselves fully to God's service. Thus, we have seen the liberty which our Lord Jesus Christ has purchased for us; the ceremonies of the law have passed away and we are no longer subject to them nor bound by them.

At first sight, we might say that all this is of no great significance. For what does it matter if we have been both baptised and circumcised? Or if we acknowledge that our Lord Jesus Christ alone is the fulfilment and perfection of the law, and yet still retain the types? Well, first of all, to keep the ceremonies as if we are living under the law is to detract from the glory of the Lord Jesus Christ. For as it is written, 'the law was given by Moses, but grace and truth came by Jesus Christ'. This is how it is expressed in the first chapter of John (*John* 1:17). Thus, if we do not use the liberty which has been given to us, we are robbing him of the honour which is his due. We ought to realise that we enjoy a better and a more privileged condition today than our fathers of old, since our Lord Jesus Christ has been given to us and in him we have all that was prefigured in former days. Thus, in observing the ceremonies of the law, we wrong the Lord Jesus Christ. Here is the first thing.

Secondly, since our Lord is called the 'Sun of righteousness' (*Mal.* 4:2), we ought not to live as though there were not even a ray of light to be had. Rather, we should lift our eyes towards the truth which reveals Jesus Christ to us, through which we can gaze upon him face to face and thus come to God the Father, as it says in Second Corinthians (*2 Cor.* 3:18). Furthermore, if we take the ceremonies of the law and consider them without our Lord Jesus Christ, that is, if we separate them from him, they bring with them an obligation and a verdict of condemnation and death upon men. This is why, in the second chapter to the Colossians, Paul stresses that on the cross our Lord Jesus Christ tore up and blotted out the 'handwriting of ordinances' that was against us (*Col.* 2:14). For if the sacrifices were still performed today, we would see in them that we are all worthy of eternal death in the sight of God. How is this? Well, when poor animals were killed, it was not because they had deserved it, but to show men in a vivid picture that all were worthy of death. Therefore, if the sacrifices were still in force today, we would stand under the same sentence of death. But we have been set free through the Lord Jesus Christ. Herein is the triumph of his death, as Paul says (*Col.* 2:15).

Thirdly, our fathers of old recognised that although they had been given the law, it was only through the grace of God that they could obtain the liberty which comes from having all sins forgiven. Thus, if today we were to enforce the necessity of keeping ceremonies, it would become a yoke that we are unable to bear, as it says in the fifteenth chapter of Acts (*Acts* 15:10). For maintaining the ceremonies would cause us all to drown in despair. Is it possible for men to do what God has so rigorously and immutably commanded? Not at all; for everything that God requires and demands of us is beyond our capabilities. If we were to fail even in one point only, the weight of our sin would crush us. This is why this 'liberty' is so important; after all, we could not be assured of our salvation, nor call upon God freely unless we knew that we were no longer under the yoke of bondage with regard to the law.

There is one further point to which we will shortly come, and that is that those who wished to make believers observe such ceremonies had the perverse and wicked fancy that in doing so they would be justified and obtain God's favour. This was to deny the power of the death and passion of the Lord Jesus Christ. Now we can see that Paul had good reason to oppose the ceremonies of the law so forcefully; he did not wish them to be practised any more because they held believers in such bondage.

We also need to take heed of this, for today we have a similar disagreement with the Papists. Indeed, they have less plausibility than the deceivers of whom Paul speaks. For although the latter were servants of the devil, and sought only to pervert the truth of the gospel, they at least were able to say that they were not introducing their own ideas or traditions. Indeed, they claimed to accept the authority of God by saying that the law must be upheld, and that was their apparent excuse. The Papists, however, have no such foundation, for all their rituals have arisen according to the will of men. Yes, they have woven in a little Judaism here and there, but now they have such a mixture that it is not clear which sources they have relied upon the most. Whatever the answer may be, it is clear that all the ceremonies which are practised in Popery today have been added by men. When we oppose them, they say that we are creating a big stir over nothing. These lukewarm individuals step in, wishing to please both parties and form a bastard gospel. They reproach us as if we were seditious, and say that we are causing too much trouble in the world by our preciseness. And to prove it, they say, 'Is it right that you should argue so much about ceremonies, which are neither here nor there?' Yes indeed, for God intended the ceremonial law (which proceeded from him and came into being by his direct commandment) to cease at the coming of our Lord Jesus

Christ. Therefore, what does he think when men, in their foolhardiness, want to introduce additional rituals? If God desired his own ceremonies to be abolished, how can men press forward and introduce their own, as if they would have us believe that God has not acted wisely? Is this not an atrocious blasphemy? We know why God intended that the ceremonial law should no longer apply today: it is so that the grace of our Lord Jesus Christ can be more widely and more clearly known. For he is the 'Sun of righteousness' (*Mal.* 4:2). For this reason, it is necessary that all shadows flee away, since, as Paul says, he is the body and substance of them all (*Col.* 2:17). This being the reason, we can see that it was in fact vital that the types should fade away into the past. Now what excuse will the Papists proffer, seeing that it is obvious that all their rituals serve only to obscure the Lord Jesus Christ? Indeed, they are made so binding that if you refuse to keep them, you are guilty of mortal sin. Added to this, their rituals seem to imply that one baptism is not sufficient, but that a person needs holy water in which to be baptised afresh morning and evening. If you bring together this collection of worthless and ridiculous customs, it becomes apparent that there will always be something to keep poor souls in bondage. Should this be tolerated? Such a tight yoke is placed upon them that the poor folk are strangled by it, for they have been robbed of the liberty which was purchased for them by the death and passion of the Lord Jesus Christ. Therefore, we can see how urgent and how great the need is for us to fight against Papal tyranny with regard to rituals, seeing that our Lord Jesus Christ is not given the pre-eminence he deserves, whilst they continue to amuse themselves with such trivialities. Moreover, they keep poor consciences in a constant state of anxiety, believing as they do, that they can merit favour by what they call 'serving God'. It seems to them that this is the way for a man to be justified and to obtain salvation.

* * *

We have seen that Paul was fighting an important battle of his day. Today, we battle over this same issue, and we must not remain silent. To do so would be to betray both God and man. We have to struggle constantly against such hellish tyranny, and all the vanities, lies and delusions of Satan. He is seeking either to destroy the gospel altogether or, at the very least, to so distort it that we no longer know what is and what is not pure truth. We ought always to keep this in mind. Hence, when Paul says that he would not give way to such people, not even for a moment, this confirms to us all the more the very thing that I explained a short while ago. Peace and friendship amongst men is a wonderful thing. This is the truth, and we ought to pursue these things with all our strength. At the same time, however, God's truth ought to be so precious to us that even if we had to set the whole world on fire in order to promote it, we would be only too willing to do so! Yes, as far as we can, we are to seek peace. If only we ourselves and our possessions are at stake, let us endeavour to be at peace with our enemies and to tolerate them, seeking to win them by our patience. This is what pursuing peace entails. However, if God's truth is being ignored or misused, this no longer applies. The kind of peace that men seek will always be under God's curse if he is not acknowledged or praised as he deserves, or if his Word is not kept in all its purity, for that ought to be the knot of our bond. If we wish to please God, and if we want all things to work together for our good, surely it is God who must bind us together. Indeed, he has given us his Son, whom he calls 'our peace', so that we all surrender ourselves to him (*Eph.* 2:14). Therefore, if we desire to have a true and holy peace, we must return to this point: we must yield ourselves in obedience to the Son of God as our Head, we being one body, for there is only one church. But if others are enticing us away from the Lord Jesus Christ, rather than accepting peace on such terms we should prefer to suffer all the rage, fury and hatred of this world against us. Let us not fear the reproaches of men. Today, we may be falsely accused of having stirred up great controversy, but what can we do about it? For woe to us, if we do not abide in the gospel of truth. Since the Papists do not do this, but remain, instead, in that state of rebellion which they are still in to this day, we are obliged to be at war with them. After all, they would have us turn our backs on the peace that God gives us through his Son (who even bears this title, and not in vain, as we have already noted). When folk cry after us, we ought to be armed with the answer that Elijah gave to Ahab. He was asked, 'Art thou he that troubleth Israel?' (*1 Kings* 18:17). The prophet had been accused, much as we are today, because he had sought to bring the people back to the purity of the law, and because he opposed the superstition and idolatry which they had devised. The king believed that Elijah had come to stir up trouble, sedition and rebellion. (How the rulers of this world love to wallow in their own filthiness, not caring about whether God is worshipped and served! Provided they can maintain their position, nothing else is of any importance to them.) But the prophet answered him by saying, 'It is you, and your father's house.' It is those who fail to act according to God's will, and who do not serve him as he requires in his Word, that trouble the world. All the rebellion, strife and discord that results should be attributed to them. For (as I have already shown) it is imperative that God be not robbed of his rightful position when men are seeking to join together in harmony. Here, then, are some of the things that we should bear in mind when Paul says here that he would not for a moment be subject to those who had secretly entered the church, since they sought to pervert the gospel by mixing in their own corruptions. For indeed, the most important thing is that God's truth should be known.

Furthermore, let us not fear the slander that men will spread about us when they say that we are proud and arrogant because we refuse to submit to them. Even today, what do the Papists accuse us of, if not that we seem to be making ourselves wiser than the rest of the world, and thus displaying great pride by not conforming to what is common practice amongst men. Yes, it is an honourable thing to be obedient, as we were saying when we were speaking of peace, but at the same time, God must be obeyed above everyone else. What would become of us if we were to defy him openly and despise him in order to be subject to men and to bend our necks under their yokes, all the while ignoring God? This is why we cannot align ourselves with Papists or be in subjection to them, without turning our backs upon God, and trampling his Word underfoot. (By this, I mean that we would no longer accept its authority and no longer reverence it.) What demands would Papists make on us? They would want us to abandon the Word of God, and desert the Lord Jesus Christ, whilst accepting all that they have fabricated themselves. Of course, they would never use these exact terms, or say that you would be expected to rob God of his honour, and Jesus Christ of his pre-eminence over us; no, they would not declare this openly. Just like the deceivers whom Paul strove against: they professed that they wanted to be Christians and yet he had to go back to the touchstone and examine the whole matter thoroughly. The Papists want us to accept their traditions. And what are they? Well, we know that they virtually obscure the Lord Jesus Christ from view (as I have already said). All is corrupt; all their traditions are delusions of Satan that have been pushed to the foreground so that nothing is certain any more and no-one knows what to believe. Because such is the case, there is no doubt but that obeying men would mean being at war with God. Thus, we must resist them with, as it were, a fore-head of brass. The greatest virtue we could ever possess is seen in not conforming to the ideas of men, whatever shape or colour they may take. Instead, we ought to despise all such things as if they were filthy dung and give God his authority. We ought to listen to the Lord Jesus Christ as our Head and the One who governs us. All of us, from the greatest to the least, must submit to his leading. There is nothing for us to do other than simply to listen to him and absorb all that enables us to remain true to the faith of the gospel. This is what we ought to remember about Paul's words here.

Surely, if we are looking for a modest and peaceable man, Paul fits the description. Indeed, he is like a mirror image of all that is kind and gentle. Again, if we want to find a humble nature, what greater humility could we find than that of Paul, who made himself less than nothing? And yet at the same time, he contended for the purity of gospel doctrine, and did not care if this stirred up rage in every soul on earth. In fact, it did not matter to him if he was blamed for all the turmoil that existed in the Galatian church and elsewhere. I say he did not fear the fact that he could have been charged with such a thing, or even accused of being a rebellious or extremely arrogant man. We ought to be like this today. Yes, let us be peaceable as far as we possibly can; let us surrender all that we possess and no longer strive for the good things of this life, such as our own honour and good reputation. Let us bear all insults and injuries rather than stir up contention for our own sakes. But let us contend to the very end for God's truth. If people show contempt for us, either by rising up against us in hatred, or by seeking to weaken us, we ought not to stir up any strife over this. But if they are seeking to keep us from obeying our God, so that we bow to the tyrannical rule of men instead, then let us hold firm and show noble courage in resisting to the end. Let us despise all the lofty things of this world, but not desert the Lord Jesus Christ; he ought to reign over us and we, at the same time, ought to submit to him. This, in brief, is how we can put this passage into practice, and, indeed, the times in which we live ought to inspire us to do just that. Today, not only are we persecuted (for we have all seen the fires lit to murder the poor servants of God) but also it is likely that those wicked people who are hired by the Antichrist to pervert the truth of the gospel will accuse and condemn us as if we were subversive rebels. They will say that we are full of pride since we refuse their traditions. Do they accuse us in this malicious way? Well, let us bear it all patiently and be accused, just as Paul is saying, provided we know that we, for our part, are continuing in the truth of the gospel, not allowing creatures to reign over us instead of Jesus Christ. For every knee will have to bow before him and all must worship him.

* * *

Now the fact that Paul speaks of 'the truth of the gospel' is very significant and teaches us a very practical lesson. For he could just as well have said: 'To whom we gave place by subjection, no, not for an hour; that the gospel might continue with you.' But instead he speaks of 'the truth of the gospel', not because he is making a distinction between a false one and a true one, but he is speaking with respect to men and saying that the gospel must remain amongst us in all its truth. Why? Because, however much men may appear to be Christians, they will always try to mix in other things with their Christianity. Indeed, there are many restless souls in this world who cannot bear to be led by God alone. Each one wants to make their own contribution. This is how the Papacy today came to be in such a state of confusion. We may wonder how it is that they have been able to contrive so many fanciful, trifling things and grievous abominations, but it is simply because men could not be content to obey God and, therefore, desired to add their own whims and fancies here and there. This is the main reason why Paul speaks of 'the truth of the gospel', just as in Second Corinthians he speaks of the 'simplicity' that is in our Lord Jesus Christ (*2 Cor.* 11:3). And what is the 'simplicity' that is in Jesus Christ? It rules out anything that men might add. As I have said, men have a foolish desire to introduce what has been conceived in their own minds. It is a corrupt and abominable thing to add our own devices. This explains why Paul says that we must hold to the simplicity that is in our Lord Jesus Christ. When men, claiming to preach the gospel, seek nevertheless to make up their own many-coloured religion (as we say), it is no longer the true gospel. Much false teaching has been incorporated. Therefore, we should take note of the fact that when Paul uses this expression, he is warning us (or rather the Holy Spirit is warning us through him) that it is not enough to call ourselves Christians, and to appear to adhere to the Word of God and the doctrine of the Lord Jesus Christ. We must hold to it completely and not allow anything else to be added. Just as a little yeast can spoil the dough, so if we admit what men have devised in their heads, the whole will become corrupt. This is how pure the doctrine of the gospel ought to be: nothing must be added to it. Men must not have the audacity or the opportunity to include anything of their own. Rather, we should all be content with what our Lord Jesus Christ has revealed and should seek to be his true disciples. This means keeping our own mouths closed and not impudently taking it upon ourselves to oppose his doctrine. We must not even lift up our voices to say, 'This is what I think', or 'This is what I judge to be best'. We ought, rather, simply to accept what the Lord Jesus Christ teaches us, for he has all sovereignty over our souls. This is how we must understand what is meant here by 'the truth of the gospel'.

It is all the more important that we should put Paul's teaching into practice, since many today deliberately mix truth and error, so that nobody will trouble them about their religion. This way, they can choose the type of religion that suits them best, and the one which will be most easily accepted by the world. Having said this, it is true that there are many Papists who are so rigid that they would never allow a single point of doctrine to be dropped, for they know that if even just one deviation occurs, their whole tyrannical system will collapse and fall. For what other hold do they have, except one of tyranny and violence, when they say that we must accept all that they believe without question? Those, therefore, who fully support the Pope wish to keep the filthy abominations that they have always practised right to the end. However, there are many others who wish to see a reformation take place to the end that they might mix together in one the Pope, Muhammad and Jesus Christ, so that we can no longer discern between them! It makes no difference to them, provided they can bring the whole world together in harmony. They do not have a scrap of reverence for God. This explains why everything is so muddled and confused in our day, hence the abomination known as liberalism has arisen. Because they could not find it in their hearts to agree with Popery in every point, they thought it would be better if they were to reach a compromise between all the extremes.

Even today, many would like us to become involved. Yes, they admit that there are excesses and that these need to be corrected, but they are content only to prune some small leaf or branch, whilst the root remains the same as it always has been. Thus, the gospel of God could still be overshadowed by all the superstitions that hold sway in Popery. What? And here is the Holy Spirit condemning all such liberals and showing that these are Satan's tricks, delusions and deceptions sent to lead poor souls into perdition.

Furthermore, this detracts from the glory of the Lord Jesus Christ. How is this? Well, we have no gospel if we do not have truth in its purity, where it is not lawful for men to add anything, but where all keep to what has been revealed by our Master. Thus, we have seen that the situation around us demands that we put this teaching into practice. Then, when the enemies of God rebuke us because we will not agree with them, we must give as our reason the fact that the kind of agreement we seek is one where the Lord Jesus Christ unites us together as we all obey his Word and his doctrine. If they accuse us and say that we are proud in thus rejecting what men who call themselves our superiors have commanded, let us declare that we must obey God before anyone else. Also, we must not detract from the rightful power of the Lord Jesus Christ; rather, men must keep to their proper place. They may say, 'But listen! Would it not be better if we adopted a middle path, where we each declare that we do not wish to be separate from the rest, rather than to battle in this way and make Christianity even more fragmented?' But let us reply that it is not a question of who will win the argument, nor of each man lording it over his neighbour, but the issue at stake is this: keeping the whole Word of God. Otherwise, whatever we might call 'concord' will, in reality, be an abomination in the sight of God. How is this so? Well, it would be better if all else were to go into confusion and chaos, than that God's truth, which is so precious and so holy, be corrupted in any way. Indeed, it were better if heaven and earth were overthrown together than that we should allow such a thing to happen.

Let us, then, hold firm to this doctrine and use it to our profit, not only in resisting the attacks which are made upon us by the enemies of the truth, but also in yielding ourselves with all meekness and humility. This means being led and ruled by the Word of God alone and the doctrine of the Lord Jesus Christ. May we be strong enough not to be turned aside by men, or taken in by their reputation or authority, nor disturbed by their threats, nor by all the pride and arrogance that is in the world. Let us, instead, continuously devote ourselves to our Lord Jesus Christ. And if any should come to us with something new, let us look well to the end of the matter, to the end to which they are seeking to lead us. Since Satan has so many subtle tricks, and so many agents, let us, for our part, have the wisdom to keep ourselves in the knowledge of Jesus Christ, so that we are led to him. He alone should be our goal and our aim, since he has an abundance of riches in himself. Therefore, we may approach him to supply our wants. May everything that would prevent us coming to him be defeated.

Now let us fall before the majesty of our great God, acknowledging our sins, and praying that he would make us increasingly conscious of them, so that we can ask his forgiveness in true repentance. May we profit more and more from his Word, so that we are led to deny ourselves, and lean upon him and his strength. May he support us in our weakness, until he has brought us to that perfection to which he is calling us today. Thus, we all say, Almighty God, etc.

9

Unworthy Trophies of God's Mercy

> *But of these who seemed to be somewhat, (whatsoever they were, it maketh no matter to me: God accepteth no man's person:) for they who seemed to be somewhat in conference added nothing to me: But contrariwise, when they saw that the gospel of the uncircumcision was committed unto me, as the gospel of the circumcision was unto Peter; (For he that wrought effectually in Peter to the apostleship of the circumcision, the same was mighty in me toward the Gentiles:)* . . . (Gal. 2:6–10).

We saw this morning that the moment men add their own inventions to God's truth, the result is a false and corrupt gospel. This should keep us obedient so that none dare add anything to what we have received from above. After all, God's teaching is perfect and complete. We cannot add anything to his Word without it being a great blasphemy, for we would be tacitly accusing him of having done wrong by concealing knowledge, as if he were unwilling fully to declare the way of salvation. Let us, therefore, abide in the doctrine of the gospel. This ought to be sufficient for us, and if anyone should add to it, we are to detest them, even if it may seem to us that the issues are of no great significance. How often the devil makes use of this pretext, telling us that such small and insignificant matters ought not to perturb us! Yet, how vital it is that we listen to God above everyone else and in all circumstances! Paul could easily have let the matter of Titus' circumcision slip by him, and yet he would not compromise in this matter. He tells us the reason why: it was to ensure that the Gentiles need not be subject to such an obligation, for some were seeking to bind this burden upon them. And yet, we read that he had no scruples about circumcising Timothy. It may at first seem to us that the situation in both cases was the same, and that Paul was, therefore, being inconsistent and fickle. After all, here were two Gentiles, neither of whom had been nurtured or taught from the law of Moses from infancy. But the Jews would never accept any man who had not been circumcised, for, in their opinion, those who have not submitted to this sacrament are defiled. Paul only circumcised one of the two, and did not wish to do the same to the second; who would have thought that he could have followed such a course of action? But when everything is considered, we will see why it was he refused to circumcise Titus, and why he circumcised Timothy (*Acts* 16:3).

Circumcision in itself was, then, permissible. It was not like the idolatries of Rome today, where they profane baptism by their 'holy water'. Baptism ought to be a 'washing' which suffices us throughout life and beyond. God did not intend us to have any other sign of the spiritual cleansing which we have through the blood of our Lord Jesus Christ, and therefore with this we ought to be content. But what of this holy water? Surely this speaks of an infinite number of baptisms? As for the Mass, this is such a wicked and gross blasphemy that no-one can approach it without rejecting the death of our Lord Jesus Christ, thereby defiling themselves. Circumcision, however, did not fit into this category, because it was still practised in those days. It is true that it was abolished at the coming of the Lord Jesus Christ, but the Jews were permitted to keep it until they had been fully instructed about gospel liberty. Thus, Paul circumcised Timothy. And why? Because he knew that there were many weak believers who would have been deeply upset if he had not done so. They believed that they still had to keep the ceremonial law, for they were not, as yet, strong in their knowledge of the gospel. It is written that we must submit to one another and love constrains us to do so. It is not good if everyone does what seems right in their own eyes if they cause distress to their neighbour. We need to adapt ourselves to the needs of others so that we do not cause needless offence to any. Paul, therefore, was denying himself and considering the needs of those who were ignorant and weak, but who would be taught in good time. However, in the case of Titus, Paul knew that people sought to lay upon the Gentiles a yoke of bondage in order to maintain among the Jews a superstitious observance of the law. They should have realised that the law had served well in its day, but that its ceremonies were not permanent. Where they had not understood this point, the Jews became hardened, and resisted change; they made the Gentiles bear a yoke of bondage. This, therefore, is what Paul opposed.

We have now seen that it is not only lawful but necessary that we treat those things which are intrinsically neither good nor bad, differently according to the circumstances. For example, we must abstain from that which is lawful if we see that we are hindering someone from coming to the gospel, or if we recognise that someone is offended who is not yet very strong. Just as we have seen above, we must always consider what is expedient and most suited to the good of others. But if something is neither good nor bad, and we see a person attaching great importance to it in the pursuit of holiness or making it obligatory in order to bind poor souls, we must resist this with all our might. For example, whether we eat meat or fish is an indifferent matter, for God has neither forbidden nor commanded it. But if an ignorant brother should be offended if we were to eat meat, not knowing whether to follow Popish tradition or God's commandment, he may think that this is a mortal sin until he has been taught to know better. If we are seeking to win souls and draw them into obedience to the gospel, we must avoid all cause of offence. This is so even if we are dealing with a handful of Jews who have failed to understand our customs. We ought to abstain for a certain time from what they regard as forbidden whilst we are in their company. For, since they are armed with the authority of God's Word, they will think they have good reason to judge us, unless it has already been shown to them why it is that we can eat any meat without exception. On the other hand, however, when the Papists ask us to abstain from eating meat on Fridays and Saturdays, on fast days and other days when to them it is forbidden, we are traitors to the gospel if we agree to this. We would rather die a hundred times over than submit! Why is this? Because we must have respect to the liberty which was bought for us by the Lord Jesus Christ. If anyone should say, 'What? Do you mean we may antagonise everyone and be obstinate over such trivial issues as eating meat?', I answer that it is not simply a matter of eating meat or refraining, but of knowing whether it is better to obey God and do what he has allowed rather than to act according to the will of man. Can what God permits in his Word be condemned simply because men have so resolved according to their own whim and fancy? Surely we can see that this is to diminish God's authority by taking what belongs to him and what is his by right and giving it to mortal creatures? Further, such duties, imposed upon poor souls, serve to rob the Lord Jesus Christ of his honour. If he has obtained such liberty for us as to set us free from the ceremonies of the law, then this is a greater reason for us to cast aside and abolish all that has been invented by man, as I said this morning. Let us, therefore, understand that in all these secondary matters we must be motivated by the desire to edify. Thus, even if it is lawful for us to act or to abstain, love ought to constrain us in all our dealings with others. This involves willingness to be self-controlled, in order that we might refrain from exercising our freedom, for the sake of the edification of our neighbour. And yet at the same time, we must not disobey God's truth, or mix it with error to the confusion of others, unsure about how our lives here on earth are to be guided, or what law to follow, even if our motive is to maintain peace and unity. Rather, we must hold fast the liberty which Paul speaks of here to the best of our ability. This is what we need to remember.

* * *

He continues by saying that even the highly respected apostles 'added nothing to me', and he proceeds to name Peter, John and James, who were held in greater esteem than the others, indeed as pillars. He says that even they received and approved of the doctrine which he had been teaching. But he adds that he is not concerned about the reputation of Peter, James or John because God is no respecter of persons. This means that he does not take into account a person's appearance or reputation in the world. It would seem at first glance that Paul is here establishing himself and his own authority and worth. Many dogs had barked at him in the past, especially those who had tasted the gospel but were in reality apostates. In order to conceal the fact that they had rebelled by rejecting the Lord Jesus Christ, they pointed the finger at others. How did they do this? Well, we know that the apostles had disgraced themselves by quarrelling about which of them would be the greatest (*Luke* 22:24–26). This showed that they had failed to understand their Master's teaching, for he had instructed them to humble themselves in order that the greatest of them would become the least. We should understand, however, that Paul was not making himself superior to the other apostles here, as indeed he says himself. This means that there must be a special reason for Paul to boast in this way. Surely, he does so because of scoundrels who sought to break up the apostles and thereby to falsify and corrupt the gospel, all the while claiming that they were close friends and followers of the apostles. Just like today; many shamelessly pretend to be running the race, yet misuse the name of God's servants, unafraid to lie with open throat (as we say). They say, 'Yes, I learned it from such and such a man', whilst in truth they are speaking of things that were never in fact taught by the man in question. They will even be impudent enough to name the very cities where they heard these matters discussed, and yet, if a thorough investigation were made, we would find quite the opposite was true. Thus, Paul is right to show that man's authority is not sufficient to undermine the sovereign majesty of the Lord Jesus Christ, nor to detract from the reverence that his Word deserves.

Firstly, we note that Paul was not against Peter, James or John here, for he was very much in harmony with them. Secondly, we see that Paul was not concerned about himself but sought, instead, to uphold that which was of God, for example, the fact that he had been ordained and appointed to be an apostle. This teaches us mainly that he did not push himself forward through ambition, nor did he become an apostle by sheer accident, but that it was God who had chosen him to do this work. He then preached the doctrine which had been committed to his charge, that is to say, the truth about God and the Lord Jesus Christ. Whenever we think about what Paul legitimately could have claimed with regard to his position, it is enough to make any scoffer hold his tongue, yet at the same time it motivates us to continue steadfast in his doctrine all the more.

Although there are few today who are sufficiently audacious to demean him by denying the legitimacy of his apostleship, this lesson is still profitable for us. In what way? Well, previously Paul warned us that if even the angels in heaven rose up and preached a different gospel from that of our Lord Jesus Christ, we must count them accursed. This is very important for us today: it reveals to us that we can overcome Satan and all unbelief, and all the wiles, boasts and deceitful ways of men by which they seek to entice us away from the simplicity of our faith. I tell you, we may overcome them all. How? Well, the Word of God has such power in and of itself that it will deflect, like a shield, all that men cast at us today in their attempts to weaken us. How many weak souls have been led astray in this very way? Someone has said to them, 'The wisest and most knowledgeable people in this world – the prelates and those who lead the church, together with the kings and princes – these people hold to the faith which has been accepted down through the ages, and they live in accordance with its long-established traditions.' Such poor souls have their eyes blinded and become completely deluded by this and discouraged. In this way, God's truth is abandoned and no longer valued or held in reverence. Meanwhile, these liars gain the upper hand and people make idols of them, treacherously worshipping them instead of God.

Because this is the case today, we can see just how important it is that we are armed with the instruction that Paul gives us here. That is, we should know that God demands that we receive his Word without contradiction. For when the Lord Jesus Christ came down to this earth, he was appointed to be our Master, which means that we must all listen to him and abide by what he says without adding or subtracting from anything that he has chosen to reveal to us. Indeed, in him is all perfection of wisdom; when we have grasped this, we will be able to disregard all the boastful claims of men. Then, whenever anyone tells us that the greatest, wisest and most powerful people in this world live in such and such a way, we will be able to say, 'Yes, this may be so. But even when all these things are considered, what does it amount to in comparison with God? When we come before him, all creatures pale into insignificance.' God uses his Word as a measure to see whether we love him or not: if we have seen something of the majesty of the Word of God, then it follows that we must give assent to all that proceeds from God's holy mouth. This Word is found in the gospel; therefore, when once we have acknowledged the need to obey God, we do not have to compass land and sea to discover his will, for we have it infallibly recorded for us in the law, the prophets and the gospel. Since this is so, it is easy to see that the Holy Spirit had good reason to desire that his teaching remain until the end of time. Furthermore, we are being taught to lean upon God if we do not wish to be blown about by every wind of doctrine. We know that it is the devil who stirs up so many different opinions like whirlwinds and storms to pull us in this or that direction. But if we can but learn to be rooted in God, we will be able to persevere to the end. For if we were to base our faith upon John or Peter, our foundation would be insufficient, since they were frail creatures and we know that man is subject to lies and to vanity. Therefore, we need a more reliable and more solid base and foundation than any which we could find in this world. This draws us to reach as high as to God, when we realise that he has taught us in the person of the Lord Jesus Christ, and when we realise that men are but his instruments and nothing more.

This is how we must apply Paul's teaching to our profit when he says here that the apostles added nothing to him. It does not mean to say that he held them in contempt, or that he did not want to profit by them, for he desired this very much and sought it in every way possible, not disdaining to be taught even by the meanest sort, as we have seen. Rather, he sought to reinforce the reliability of the Word of God which he had preached; therefore, he judged all the wise and famous, and those who were foremost in reputation in the church, to be under its authority. He did so in order that Christ should have the pre-eminence and so that we would look to him and not depend upon men. May we all be rooted in the same faith so that we can all say that the Son was sent to us to declare the will of God the Father, and that it is not lawful for us to doubt in any way that which we have received from him. This is our duty today.

* * *

As for what Paul goes on to say (that it does not matter to him what the apostles were, since God is no respecter of persons), he is showing by this that he ought not to be considered inferior to John or to Peter simply because he did not believe in Jesus Christ at the time when the others were already preaching the gospel. For it is the way of the world to regard the first as the foremost. Seeing, therefore, that people might be prejudiced against his teaching, Paul says that we must not be concerned with the kind of person he used to be, nor with what sort of people the others were. Yet by this, he does not mean that we may neglect to have a full awareness of our own natures or that we do not need constantly to humble ourselves – nor does he mean that we should despise the graces that God had poured out upon Peter and John, for they are indeed worthy of our admiration. Indeed, we see from other passages that he calls himself 'one born out of due time', and says that he is 'not meet to be called an apostle' (*1 Cor.* 15:8–9). Paul, therefore, is not like many hypocrites and shameless folk, who have spent their lives as lewd or drunken men, living a dissolute and wild life, but who choose not to make mention of any of this. Such people say, 'Oh, please do not ask me any more about what sort of person I used to be.' We must not wait to be judged by others, for each of us must judge himself, as Paul exhorts (*1 Cor.* 11:28). Whenever we think about the fact that we used to be wretched unbelievers, almost like brute beasts, we ought to be ashamed of our baseness. Paul knew enough about the sort of person he used to be to hate himself and to be ashamed of his resistance to the gospel, and at the same time he did not cool in his admiration for the good that he saw in John and James. When Peter and John were flogged for the sake of the gospel, Paul was still a murderer, and thought his behaviour was justified. However, he was transformed and became the person we have already described, because God exalted him in a moment of time, ensuring that his past life would in no way hinder the usefulness of the gifts which he received for the common good of the church.

Here, then, is what we ought to learn from this: if we have been called by the gospel at a late stage in our lives, we ought always to bemoan the fact that we have spent our lives so badly. We ought also to weep, because we have lived like wretched brute beasts, not knowing that we should have worshipped the Father with our lives for all the good things that we received at his hand. We ought to feel remorse at this. Furthermore, whenever we see a wicked man converted, we should recognise that this change is a miracle brought about by God. For if a man is a brute beast, without hope of ever being brought to God, and then he is changed and becomes lamb-like in submitting voluntarily in obedience to the Lord Jesus Christ, this indicates that the hand of God has been at work. Therefore, it is very important that we remember what we once were, and for this each of us must judge our own selves. If a man is late in coming to God, we must not reject him just because it has pleased God to give him more strength and more blessing in one day than another has received in ten years, for this man could be used for our edification. Sometimes we hear people say, 'And what was this fellow like two or three years ago? He was a nobody.' Let us, instead, acknowledge that our Lord reveals himself in that person so that we might worship God. Moreover, because God's grace ought never to be without effect in a person's life, we must allow it to be applied to the profit and well-being of his children. Thus, we have seen that we should not be concerned with how a man used to live, or we will always disdain him. After all, God has perhaps humbled him by allowing him a free rein for a time. He could otherwise have continued to live a life of debauchery in ignorance, not knowing good from evil, and bereft of any outstanding or praiseworthy virtues. Yet God has made him as much of a witness as the man upon the scaffold, showing us that he intends to be served by such a person. We must, therefore, accept whoever God sends us, and whatever way he chooses to reveal himself to us. It is very important that we remember this, for there is nothing here which we can afford to ignore in our situation today.

As for Paul's expression, 'God accepteth no man's person', it means that God is not concerned with our outward appearance, or with anything that we tend to hold in esteem. He is free to bestow his grace on whomever he chooses, and distribute that grace in whatever way he chooses. Many deceive themselves about what this expression really means, and take it in the opposite way to that which was meant by the Holy Spirit. This explains why there are many fools who believe that God will not favour one person more than another, or he could be accused of having a degree of severity in his nature. This is how they become confused about the free electing grace of God. They think that he is stretching out his hands to all mankind, and that if he were to choose any, it must be a general choice of all, without excluding any. Thus, to them it is as if God's grace were flying through the air like a tennis ball, and that it is for us to stretch out our hands and catch it and apply it to our own use! In other words, it is as if all this depended upon our free will. Many people have absorbed such teaching, displaying their own gross ignorance about what this expression 'accepting of persons' means. However, the Scripture here declares that God will not withhold his grace, if it pleases him to choose a particular man and exalt him to an honourable position by pouring upon him the gifts and graces of his Holy Spirit. It does not matter to God whether such a person is white or black, old or young, upright or wicked, rich or poor, whether men love or hate him, or whether he is handsome or ugly. God does not take such trifles into consideration, for if he were to wait until he found something good in us, we would all still be in our original condition. This is what Paul means when he says that God is no respecter of persons.

* * *

Now let us gather together the lessons we ought to learn from this passage. Firstly (and we have already touched upon this), we must learn to accept God's gifts, and to make good use of them when they are offered to us. We must never reject them, as so many do, justifying their ingratitude with some excuse or other. Some use their seniority as an excuse and accuse others of some fault – may this never deter us from profiting under those whom God has sent. This applies even if they have only been Christians for three days, and can boast of nothing before men because they have not accomplished any feats of bravery or valour; it should not worry us provided the Lord Jesus Christ has equipped them with gifts which can be useful for our edification. Let each of us submit ourselves with meekness, knowing that when we reject a gift that God is presenting to us, we are not just rejecting a mortal man. For if we will not deign to accept that which is from God (since he is the source of such gifts), then we deserve to be altogether deprived of all that God desires to bestow, and of the good things that he has already placed in our hands, as it were. We do well to remember this. Furthermore, we must learn that when we come to God, we must not imagine that we have any worth of our own. He that is noble, great or rich in this world ought to cast off all pride and realise that this is nothing in God's sight. He that is poor and miserable must realise that he has not been rejected, even though men despise him. Let us apply what James says: let the one that is noble and great rejoice in that he is made low, knowing that everything he has is given to him freely through the pure mercy of God. Likewise, let him that is poor and of low degree rejoice in that God has adopted him and exalted him to a position of dignity far above that of the kingdoms of this world, if he has been pleased to accept him as one of his children. The truth is that God has respect unto our conscience; whereas men take pleasure in our appearance and in anything outward, God looks at the sincerity of our hearts. Yet, even such sincerity has been placed within us by God, for since the beginning of time we have not had any such integrity. If God were to consider all the sons of Adam, he would only find depravity in them, as it says in Psalm 14:3. We are by nature rotting in our sins. Therefore, there is nothing that could have moved God to accept us or exalt us more than others. Rather, we are trophies of his mercy and thus we ought to confess that he does not accept us because we are worthy. However, when he chose us to be his own, and set us in his way by the Holy Spirit, he then saw the integrity of our hearts. (Not that any of this was our own, but it is as if God sees himself in us.) All the gifts in all his children are as many testimonies to his mercy, for he has been very bountiful towards us. In Acts 10:34 and other such passages, this 'respect of persons' refers to appearance and such outward things as wealth, reputation, status, nobility and such like, which are delusions that make men consider they are of some worth and value to God. But it is written that the Lord looks at the heart, and is not interested in our outward appearances, as long as we submit ourselves in obedience to him, as we have already declared (*1 Sam.* 16:7). This is a summary of what we need to remember.

Paul then says that the apostles accepted him into their company and offered him the hand of fellowship, proving that the gospel which he preached was completely in accordance with their teaching and that they were all serving the same Lord Jesus Christ. Then Paul adds that they all united in accepting him as the apostle to the Gentiles, that is, to those who had not been nurtured under the law and who were not Jews by birth or parentage. Notice that Paul did not need to fight to convince the apostles, for they welcomed him as their fellow-worker; nor, indeed, did he hold them in contempt. We saw earlier that when Paul came to Jerusalem, he knew that God had appointed him, having had definite, unmistakable revelation; he had been lifted to the third heaven. Yet it was not pride that led him to undertake this journey to Jerusalem to meet with the apostles for fear that he had, or would in the future, run in vain. Instead, he wanted everyone to know that he attributed no special qualities to himself, but that he was seeking to spread the good news of the Son of God throughout the world, that all people might worship and trust in him. He was not preaching a different Jesus but the same one that Peter and John and the others preached. When Paul decided to withdraw and be apart from the others, we might have said that he did not wish to conform his doctrine to theirs, but when he came to unite with them, he proved that he was not driven by any presumption or pride. And this is why, once again, he states that the apostles welcomed him into their number. He is, therefore, not claiming to be superior to them, but rather he wishes us to recognise that they were all serving the Lord Jesus Christ, and that this makes him their equal. Therefore, we must not treat the gospel message that he taught with suspicion, but see it just as though it came from the lips of Peter or of John. When Paul handles this situation, he does not set forth himself but Jesus Christ. Whether it be Peter, or John or James who is speaking, let us remember that the Son of God is our Master and that we must receive whatever he says, whether it be through myself or another. Paul does not wish us to reverence him, any more than anyone else in this world, great or small. So then, let us remember when we look at this passage of Paul's, that in every situation and in every way he forgot about himself and did not seek his own advancement. Rather, he was content if Jesus Christ was honoured in the way that he deserves to be, and if his Word was treated with reverence. Anything else was of no significance to him.

As for the second point, that Paul was accepted as the apostle to the Gentiles, this bears out what Luke tells us when he says that Paul and Barnabas were appointed to be apostles because God had set them apart for the purpose of preaching the gospel amongst the Gentiles (*Acts* 13:2). This idea, then, had not come from man, because God had issued his irrevocable call. What Paul claims for himself in no way undermines the charge given to the other apostles. Indeed, they knew that he was not eager for self-advancement or acting rashly; they readily acknowledged that he was truly sent from God and that his calling was not based upon a man's decision. They did not dream of denying his calling because they could see that it was genuinely of God. This teaches us even more clearly that we too must submit obediently, so that the Word of God becomes a rein or a yoke to keep us from following our own imaginations, desires and lusts. We must allow ourselves to be led and governed by the hand of the Lord Jesus Christ. If it would not have been right for the apostles to have rejected Paul because he had been commissioned from heaven, what about us? What devilish arrogance it is when we cannot accept that the rules and patterns that God has laid down for his church are binding! Or when we change vocations as we are led by our senses; when we raise up or cast down according to the dictates of our foolish minds! To be guilty of causing such trouble in the church is much like seeking to pluck the sun out of the sky in spite of

God. What we must remember is that church order has been ordained by him, and that those who seek to change any aspect of this are full of the devil's pride. In the end, all who elevate themselves in this way are likely to stumble and fall to their own ruin.

Moreover, when we read that Paul was sent to the Gentiles, let us observe that this did not in any way change what our Lord Jesus Christ himself had already commanded when he said to his apostles, 'Go ye therefore, and teach all nations . . .' (*Matt.* 28:19). It might seem at first glance that the situation was changing or that a clash was emerging through the fact that Paul was sent in one direction and Peter in another. But everything fits together very well, for our Lord Jesus Christ did not speak to each apostle individually and say, 'You, Peter, you will go to all nations and encompass the whole circuit of the earth spreading my gospel, and you, John, will do the same' and so on to the others. But he did say, 'I have appointed all of you. Go and spread my gospel throughout the world', and in giving this general commission it does not mean that one could not go to one area, and another to another, or that they could not each work in the place to which God led them and granted them access. (They did indeed seek to do this whether it meant life or death for them.) However, Paul was given a special commission to go to the furthest regions where there were not so many Jews. It is true that wherever Paul went, he taught the gospel in the Jewish synagogues so that he became their apostle too, and yet at the same time, he had been set apart for the Gentiles. He took the gospel throughout the nations to those places where God was not known and where there existed no clear light of sound teaching, no law and no true religion. Paul's chief calling was to carry out this task.

With this in mind, let us consider the degree of primacy the Pope claims to have today, based on the fact that Peter (according to him) was the Bishop of Rome. It is clear that to say Peter was at Rome and that he became its bishop is sheer myth; it is another of their fanciful teachings. But if we take the case as it really was, then, according to what we have been saying, Peter was specially called to serve the Jews. Therefore, the Pope, who claims to be Peter's successor, ought to be the Bishop of the Jews and his primacy ought to begin and end there. As for Paul, it is most certain that he was not Bishop of Rome, for he never went there, except when he was taken there as a prisoner; we do not know whether he stayed there or not but it is probable that this is where he died. Thus, the Pope cannot boast that he is Paul's successor either. Yet, what a position of dignity and honour the city of Rome could have, claiming, as she does, that the apostles of our Lord Jesus Christ were there – that is, if it were not such a den of thieves and if it were not there that the servants of God were killed! Therefore, take special note of this passage and of the fact that it tells us that Peter was appointed apostle to the Jews, and that Paul was sent to the Gentiles; for this teaching directly challenges us and we ought to be the more encouraged to apply it to our profit. Indeed, we ought to hold just as firmly to the teachings of the other apostles too, for the Lord Jesus Christ must be heeded when he speaks, whether it be by the mouth of Peter, or John. They are all instruments of his Spirit and we ought not to favour one more than another. But above all else, when Paul's message points directly to us, it ought to be like a needle pricking us to action. The fact that God called Paul to work amongst the poor Gentiles – those who had been cut off from his church – the fact that he chose to draw them through Paul, ought to serve as a great encouragement to us. He strove to pull poor unbelievers out of the shadows of darkness in which they dwelt. Indeed, this was his main aim, to devote himself to us – we who have not descended from the Jews according to the flesh. However, at the same time, let us bear in mind that Jesus Christ desires that we listen to him, regardless of the persons of Peter, Paul, James, John or anyone else. Let us be content with the Master whom God the Father has given us, so that we might attain to all perfection of wisdom. Yet, let us also give heed to what we are taught by God's chosen means, such as the writings of Paul, John, James and the other apostles too, since they all draw us towards Jesus Christ. We must receive only what they teach us and close our eyes to anything else, knowing that our Lord Jesus is calling us to himself through them. And however much we follow the doctrine taught by Peter, John, James and Paul, it should always tend to one thing: that is, to join and unite us to our Lord Jesus Christ, in whom we will find an abundance of joy and of good things, such that we will glory only in him.

Now let us fall before the majesty of our great God, acknowledging our sins and asking that he will make us increasingly conscious of them. Then we will despise ourselves and ask his pardon in true repentance; thus we will also daily battle against our sins, until we are altogether rid of them. And since we are such wretched creatures that we can never be entirely free of sin, may God give us his aid until the day that he buries all our iniquities, and clothes us in his righteousness. May he show this grace not only to us, but to all peoples, etc.

10

Armed for the Fight Against Grave and Serious Error

> *But when Peter was come to Antioch, I withstood him to the face, because he was to be blamed. For before that certain came from James, he did eat with the Gentiles: but when they were come, he withdrew and separated himself, fearing them which were of the circumcision. And the other Jews dissembled likewise with him; insomuch that Barnabas also was carried away with their dissimulation . . .* (Gal. 2:11–14).

We have seen that Paul's teaching was based upon the fact that the ceremonies of the law had been abolished. Yet those who opposed him seemed to have good grounds for doing so, for they said that the law had been given by God and that because God was its author, it was not lawful to alter it in any way. However, they needed to consider the purpose for which the ceremonies had been given to the people of old. Whilst it is true that God is unchanging and that his Word abides forever, it does not follow that God will not prescribe for men what he knows to be right for them. The ceremonies were temporary, suited to the needs of the Jews. A further aspect to this which we have already touched upon is this: before the coming of Jesus Christ there were certain 'types and shadows' which served to strengthen and direct believers as they awaited the promised Redeemer. From this, we may conclude that God did not intend the ceremonies to last forever or to be a permanent practice, but they were only intended for those days. They were to serve the people as a pledge of what we now possess in our Lord Jesus Christ, who is the body and substance of the shadows that existed under the law. This is what we ought to believe. We cannot argue that God has changed, as those given to fantasy allege. Would we dare to say that God is changing his mind when he turns summer into winter? We are familiar with the different seasons of the year – the grass turns green, the trees blossom and perhaps yield their fruit; yet subsequently, in the winter, everything dies. Yes, God gave the law for man's sake (as we have already said), but the Jews needed visual aids in the form of ceremonies, because they did not have the revelation that we now have in the gospel. This is why they were necessary, but they are no longer required today because we have seen the fulfilment of those things which God promised. We are, therefore, so much more privileged than the Jews.

Paul defends his proclamation of our new 'liberty' in this passage. This is why he had to rebuke Peter, because the yoke that God had placed upon our fathers of old had been removed at the coming of our Lord Jesus Christ. If Christian people were supposed to maintain the same kind of service as the Jews, then Peter could certainly have defended his actions with all his might. Yet he allows himself to be rebuked and confesses his failing. Since Peter does this, he reveals that the apostles knew that the ancient types and shadows were to cease and be abolished at the coming of the Lord Jesus Christ. This is what Paul tells us about the situation: he rebuked Peter at Antioch, where he had lived amongst the Gentiles (not unbelievers but those who had been converted through coming to hear the gospel). Peter lived amongst them and counted them as members of the church. Then certain Jews came from Jerusalem, sent by James. Peter, worried that they might pass on a bad report of him, withdrew and pretended that he had no personal acquaintance with the Gentiles, even though they had a common faith in the gospel. He treated them as strangers, in case anyone thought he was defiling himself by keeping their company. What an awful pretence! In doing this, he was creating a split in the church. As it says in another passage, the Lord Jesus Christ was not sent for the Jews alone, for he is the light of God for the salvation of the whole world, and he broke down the dividing wall between us (*Eph.* 2:14). If, therefore, those who had once been excluded and were far away from the church had now been called into the flock, Peter was, in effect, denying the grace of God. We know what a precious thing church unity is! There is no excusing those who disrupt it. Peter's sin was that he was breaking the alliance between Jews and Gentiles, all of whom belonged to the body of the Lord Jesus Christ and were God's children. We have the same Lord and the same Redeemer, and we all gather in his name as his servants until we are welcomed into our heavenly inheritance; but Peter seemed to be trying to reduce the household of God to Jews alone. He also committed a second sin: he was denying the grace of the Lord Jesus Christ. For he came to this world to be the perfect fulfilment of all the former types and shadows. If we had to sacrifice today, as in the times of the law, we would not know that cleansing comes through the blood of the Lord Jesus Christ, who alone can pay for sin, because he lived a life of perfect righteousness on our behalf. We would not be aware of any of this. Peter's failure, therefore, was serious because he was bringing back the veil which hid the Lord Jesus Christ from view and prevented him from being known. Then there is a third failing: that of confirming the Jews in their error. Yes, we must bear with those who are ignorant and weak and not offend them above measure, even when they sin; their faults can be addressed gradually, rather than breaking the legs from under them (as we say). Yet, to encourage and nurture ignorance by seeming to approve of it is a terrible thing. When Peter withdrew from the company of the Gentiles in order to please those of his own nation, he was confirming the Jews in their wrong attitudes, since he was implying that the Gentiles were, indeed, defiled and unclean. Thus, he added to the evil that was already far too prevalent. This is why Paul says that Peter 'was to be blamed'.

We must diligently remember this, for in days gone by some have thought that all this happened by prior arrangement. They have said that Peter was angry that those of his own nation were so difficult to please, and that he had secretly agreed to this public rebuke by Paul. But all this is nonsense! Paul expressly says that Peter is blameworthy and that he felt he had to take direct action when he saw Peter was not walking in the straight and narrow way. This reveals that there had not been a secret agreement or pact; rather, Paul simply used the liberty which had been granted to him to rebuke Peter. Although he held Peter in great esteem as an apostle of Jesus Christ, he was unwilling to let the matter drop. This passage ought to teach and instruct us just how precious our liberty is, as we have already been saying. This is not only a matter which affects our actions, but one which also concerns our consciences and asks whether we are at peace with God. If it had only been a question of whether or not to eat pork (which is one of the things included in the ceremonial law), it would have been a trivial matter and it might have been overlooked. The same applies today to matters of a secondary nature. But we need to return to the root of the matter, as we have said. The shadows were there to act as a kind of schoolmaster, just as little children have governors, and cannot yet enjoy liberty. But at the advent of the Lord Jesus Christ, with the emphasis on faith, there was no longer any need for such methods to instruct the Jews. Paul, therefore, did not strive over external issues, for he willingly avoided all such conflicts. Rather, he wanted people to realise the true significance of the ceremonial law – that it was not to continue forever, but to be practised until the coming of the Lord Jesus Christ.

From this we draw the conclusion that for the Jews to abstain from eating pork or to observe various feast days, was not, in and of itself, vital to the service of God, but was intended to help people to exercise faith in Jesus Christ. Thus, the ceremonies themselves had no inherent virtue to impart; it was only that they pointed to a spiritual fulfilment. We can see clearly that God did not establish them in vain, but for the profit of his church. If we separate the ceremonies from Jesus Christ, they are of no more value than children's toys; but if we consider the one to whom they direct believers, then we will admit their great worth. Even today we can derive great benefit from them. Although no longer practised, we can better appreciate what is taught us in the gospel if we understand the ceremonial law. How is this? It is written that only the priest may enter the sanctuary, and not without a sacrifice (*Exod.* 30:10; *Lev.* 16:2–3). From this, we learn that neither man nor angel is worthy to approach God, and that we would all be banished if it were not for the entrance that has been opened for us in the person of the Lord Jesus Christ. This is one thing. Secondly, we ought also to remember that we could not please God, nor have confidence or liberty to call upon him, unless blood had been shed. This has been accomplished through the sufferings and death of the Lord Jesus Christ, by which he secured grace and favour for us. All our prayers must be offered in his name, or else God will not accept them. Also it is written that the book of the law itself was sprinkled by the blood, as well as the sanctuary (*Exod.* 24:8; *Heb.* 9:19). We learn from this that everything is unclean unless sanctified by the Lord Jesus Christ. Furthermore, we see that we can have no assurance of God's promises, and cannot apply them to our salvation unless they have been sealed with the signature of the Lord Jesus Christ. Thus, when we read that God is our Father, and that if our sins have been forgiven he accepts us as righteous and innocent in his sight, this and suchlike promises are of no effect, and cannot benefit us unless the blood of the Lord Jesus Christ is before our eyes. It is almost as if (in a manner of speaking) the Word of God must be written in red letters in the blood of the Lord Jesus Christ. This is something of the way in which we can profit from the ceremonial law today. However, these ceremonies have now been abolished, and even if they were still in use, we could not receive such good teaching by them as we have now, for we would be resting upon base and corruptible things. But if we understand the heavenly 'pattern', like that which was committed to Moses, as it says in the Epistle to the Hebrews, and as Stephen declares so plainly, then we will know why God ordained such ceremonies (*Exod.* 25:40; *Acts* 7:44; *Heb.* 8:5). The main thing we have to realise is that we are not speaking about things of no consequence here. We need to understand the ways in which these ceremonies assisted our fathers in days gone by, and also why God abolished them at the coming of the Lord Jesus Christ.

Following on from this, we notice that Paul did not spare Peter, despite the fact that they were friends, and despite the dignity and nobility of Peter's office, which might have led him to overlook the fault. Notwithstanding, Paul rebuked him sharply about the matter. We can well imagine that if this had been a small or a light thing, Paul would not have stirred up such a contention. Therefore, it proves that this was highly important. We have been warned that if God's truth is being undermined, or if any are turning from the simplicity of the gospel, we are to spare nothing and no-one. Even if the whole world were to crumble as a result, we must maintain God's cause with unshakeable constancy, without bending for anyone in any way. If anyone's fault ought to have been overlooked, it was Peter's, for the grace of the Lord Jesus Christ had been poured upon him abundantly to enable him to hold such an office. Paul might easily have fallen into line with Peter, and yet he found his sin intolerable. This ought to serve as an example to us, so that instead of being blinded by the authority of a man who is undermining God's truth, we must enter into combat, without fear.

This lesson should be most beneficial to us today because there are many who seek to avoid extremes. Although they see the abuses and corruptions around them, they prefer to steer a middle course, all to purchase peace and harmony, they say (whereas, in fact, they are in a state of great confusion when any conflict arises between the two parties!). In order to settle all disputes, such people desire both sides to join together in a union where each side compromises. But will God leave his cause to the whim of man? And can we gather ourselves against him and prosper? Today we are called upon to fight against the unyielding Papists, who have corrupted, perverted and falsified the truth of the gospel, and yet who continue to blind us with their honourable titles, veiling the truth with masks. Indeed, whenever we hear terms such as 'the holy Catholic Church', or 'the holy Apostolic See', or 'the Prelacy', or 'Christendom', or 'the Ecclesiastical Hierarchy', let us not be thrown off our feet by any of it. Why? Because God is on our side, and the defence of the truth of his gospel is so precious to him that he would not have us spare any creature in his cause. It is just as Paul said, when he told us to account angels accursed, and reject and detest them, if it were possible that they should endeavour to turn us away from pure doctrine. Why, then, should we seek to please mortal men if they are undermining the purity of the gospel by adding their own inventions? Not only this, but they even treat the Lord Jesus Christ as a subordinate in order to maintain their errors. Should we give place to such people? Woe to such a compromised peace, for it will always be the object of God's curse. Therefore, let us have such steady and constant minds that when once we are sure that the cause we are supporting is of God, we are not thrown off course by any worldly pretensions of grandeur or nobility. This is what we ought to learn.

Yet, notice furthermore how foolish the Papists really are, for these villains have the audacity to exempt themselves from all correction. The Pope seeks to magnify himself by claiming to be Peter's successor, yet he is not willing to be subject to any chastisement whatsoever! In fact, he claims that it is his role to correct everyone else, and that it is not lawful to apply this correction to himself. And where does he get this exemption from? If he claims to stand in place of Peter, we can see quite the opposite here in this passage. Peter was rebuked and he bore it; indeed, he even willingly condemned himself because he was convinced that he had done wrong. This leads us to conclude that, whichever way we seek to colour it, there is no position of dignity in this world where a man is not subject to the Word of God. However, the Pope would have us believe that our Lord Jesus has raised up 'idols' in his church (under the name of pastors), that are permitted to teach and rebuke, even to corrupt and falsify everything, without anyone uttering a word against it. The church of God would be no better than a pigsty if this were the case. She would be infected by wickedness beyond remedy. Therefore, let us take good note of this fact: God does not intend anyone in his church to enjoy the kind of pre-eminence which prevents his Word from having free course, for his Word must control even those who have a degree of superiority over others. We must give heed to the words of the Lord Jesus Christ, who has been given authority by God the Father. Indeed, we must all rally around him, and not seek for any excuse for exemption. This is what is being taught us through this incident involving Peter.

Notice also the way in which our sins ought to be rebuked; that is to say publicly, and not only in secret. This is worthy of our attention. Many people do scandalous things, and when they have upset everything and everyone, wish to be told that they have done wrong simply by a whisper in the ear. This is the common theology of the day. One asks: 'Does it not say that we should rebuke one another secretly? (*Matt.* 18:15) It cannot be right for a man to be publicly disgraced if he falls'. Yes, this is so, if his offence will not cause strife in the church. Our Lord Jesus Christ made that distinction when he said that if someone sins, and I know about it, I must rebuke him privately: but that if his sin is blatant and open, and would set a bad example if it were not dealt with, then we are no longer under an obligation to whisper secretly in the offender's ear. The rebuke must reflect the magnitude of the sin, so that others may learn from it. This not only applies to the congregation at large, but also to those in positions of the highest dignity, for they ought to set a good example to others. Indeed, Paul says in that other passage to Timothy, that those who have sinned, though they be pastors who are responsible for teaching and guiding the flock, should be rebuked before all (*1 Tim.* 5:20). He put this into practice himself here in the case of Peter! This was a grave and serious error which could have been a cause of great turmoil in the church, since it was undermining the gospel, and many were still very weak. Paul knew that Peter needed to be scolded, and did so. Let us remember all these points.

One final thing we learn is Peter's humility. The Lord Jesus Christ himself had told him that besides his ordinary name of Simon, he would be called Peter because of his firm faith. He was outstanding amongst the apostles, yet still hangs his head when he realises that he has sinned, and does not take refuge in the fact that he has attained such a high degree of honour. Because the Word of God is provided for our correction, Peter is concerned that we should always submit to it; if we do not, we are rebelling against the One who will finally destroy man's pride. Peter shows that the best a man can do is to submit to chastisement when he has done wrong, and therefore he yields to the rebuke of the apostle Paul.

When we draw together all these various lessons, we find we have a most instructive account. Firstly, we all know how important it is to feel at peace with the world. (This is why many of us are blind to our faults, because the world flatters us.) We are like this because we think we will have no friends unless we tolerate our neighbours. Well, there is, indeed, a kind of forbearance which is commendable, as we have said; it involves being gentle when we rebuke those who have fallen, and always seeking to draw them back in a friendly way. We must not be too harsh; after all, some faults can be overlooked, and do not always merit being fully exposed. If we are constantly ready to reprove others, we only make them feel exasperated. Too many people are continually on the prowl to see whether there is anything they can attack; their holiness amounts to nothing more than mocking one person or chiding another. In short, these are the world's greatest critics! We must keep ourselves from such attitudes, and not always be waiting to reprove others. However, the kind of flattery which surrounds us today is a sin which we ought to shun as we would a deadly plague. Let us, then, learn that in order to love our neighbour, we must speak freely to him, as Paul does here, especially when God's truth is at stake. We must not fear anyone, for the zeal of God must rise up within us and overwhelm us. Even if it means that we acquire a bad reputation and become the object of all kinds of calumny and slander, nevertheless, we must enter into combat. There is no excuse for treacherous dissimulation whereby we deny the truth of the gospel. Therefore, we must follow the example set for us here by Paul – what he did to his companion Peter ought to serve as a law and a rule for us. We must prove that we desire people to listen to God, and not to exchange his truth for a lie; also that none should obscure his truth, or add leaven to it. It must remain in its purity and simplicity.

Furthermore, those who are great in this world are taught here that when rebuked they are to be submissive, responding in all humility and meekness. For God did not lose any of his power when he elevated them; he always has sovereign authority over us, which he exercises through his Word. Therefore, even the greatest amongst us must bend his neck, realising the devilish confusion that results when a man believes himself to be above reproof. This is to rob the Word of God of its authority over us, which is why it is absolutely vital that we take this teaching to heart. Today, when we see man's foolish boldness in setting himself against God, let us strengthen ourselves against this, so that we will not be taken by surprise. We need to be sure of the cause which we uphold and for which we must fight. Let us rigorously despise that pestilential den containing the Pope and all his clergy. May such stinking vermin be nothing to us, since they exalt themselves above the Lord Jesus Christ. Indeed, though they use his name and seek to hide their mischief behind it, in his name, they actually tread his gospel underfoot, and even seek to bury it. Or they create such a confusing mixture of truth and error that no-one knows what is right. Seeing that they are thus possessed by the devil, let us not be afraid to arm ourselves for the battle and to fight to the end. Indeed, of all causes for battle, ours seems more favourable even than Paul's must have seemed in his day. Whilst it is true that the cause is one and the same and proceeds from the same source, yet Paul opposed ceremonies which God had appointed with his own mouth. Why was this? Well, because the gospel had been obscure as yet to them; the grace of the Lord Jesus Christ had been overshadowed and they began to stress the doctrine of man's merit instead. They had not understood the purpose for which God had given the law. Today, for the same reasons, we are fighting against the abominations which have arisen in Popery, yet with this added reason: that their doctrine has been invented by Satan and by men. We know for certain that when men rule according to their own desires, all is vanity and lies, because they do not yield themselves in obedience to God. This being the case, let us fight all the more courageously, because our Lord Jesus Christ has given us ample reason not to fear men's lofty titles, which are nothing less than Satanic delusions. This is a summary of what we need to learn.

* * *

Next, we must also notice what Paul goes on to say: that is, that he rebuked Peter when he saw that he and his friends 'walked not uprightly according to the truth of the gospel'. It was this that caused him to reprove them; he saw that this sin already had far-reaching consequences. If he had allowed them to continue in their pretence, it would probably have become too late to apply the remedy. There are two points here that we would do well to observe. As for this phrase 'the truth of the gospel', we have already said that this refers to the maintenance of its purity. Paul could just as well have said, 'they walked not uprightly according to the gospel', but he speaks of it as the 'truth'. (He has used this same expression before.) The reason he says this is because men preferred to have half a gospel, thinking they would be justified in God's sight simply if the word 'Christianity' was found often enough upon their lips. It is just the same in Popery today: they regard the term 'gospel' highly enough, yet theirs is an illegitimate gospel because of all the trimmings they have added to it. They have made the gospel unrecognisable by adding what suits their tastes; indeed, they have used such licence that now Jesus Christ is treated like a hired servant in their pay. For they make their pronouncements as if they came from heaven itself! In fact, they are not even ashamed to say that the gospel only contains the ABC of Christianity, or that it is but an introduction to it, and that the great mysteries and the important things have been revealed to them subsequently, through their councils and from the See of Rome. In this way, they mock the Lord Jesus Christ, as if they were crucifying him afresh. For what greater offence could we cause him than to suggest that he is but a schoolmaster teaching us our ABC, whilst over and above him, we have the Pope who can bring us into a state of perfection! In reality, it is quite the reverse. Thus the word 'gospel' is open to the wicked abuses of the Papists, and also to those liberals who want us to agree to their many superstitions. The latter group are content to have a little of the gospel, as long as they can keep their falsehood and error too. Such people have served to cloud the pure doctrine of the Lord Jesus Christ. This is why Paul speaks of 'the truth of the gospel' in particular: because he wants us to accept all of it and not just half. Paul would not have us add to, or take away from, what the Son of God has taught, but instead to be satisfied with the fact that he has spoken and declared it with his own mouth. For our part, let us open our ears and be attentive to what he has to say to us. None of us may say, 'This would be good', or, 'What we need is this . . .'. We must hold the pure doctrine of the gospel in such reverence that none amongst us would presume to change anything at all, but that we would all willingly accept it. This is the main point that is being brought to our attention. To summarise, we must learn to persevere as true disciples of the Lord Jesus Christ. If anyone should seek to turn us aside even just a little to make us stray into the doctrines and inventions of men, our duty is continually to resist them. Why? Because Paul's sole aim was that the gospel should remain in its purity. Let us today follow him in this respect, and we will not fall. This is the first lesson.

Secondly, we must take good note of the fact that when a sin is deepening and spreading because of silent acquiescence in it, we must deal with it. If we only respond when the illness is deep-rooted, we will be too late. When those who corrupt God's truth by adding their own inventions are drawing men to themselves and attracting a large following, it is time to arm ourselves for the fight. For if we tolerate it, we will surely be responsible for the ruin of the church which will result. Then, if after we have shown ourselves cold and indifferent, we decide to act, God will not bless us with his grace. Let us be warned, therefore, that when evil increases and becomes contagious, that is to say when one person corrupts another, we must vehemently oppose them and not allow the tares to grow, leaving the wheat choked in their midst. No, we must pull out the tares in good time. This not only applies to errors which corrupt pure gospel doctrine, but also to all corruption and vice.

However, when it comes to heresies and wicked perversions of the truth which distort everything, we should react as if we have been punched or stabbed in the stomach or neck. For in what does the life and well-being of the church consist, if not in the pure Word of God? If someone came and poisoned the meat which we needed for food, would we tolerate it? No, it would make us strike out! The same reasoning applies to the gospel. We must always raise our hands to defend the purity of its doctrine, and we must not allow it to be corrupted in any way whatever. Therefore, if sin reigns, we must deal with it at the appropriate time, for if we tolerate it, or make it a laughing matter, and then subsequently try to deal with it, we will be surprised to find that God has shut the door on us and that Satan has won. This is a just reward for our cowardice and coldness, if we are not prepared to heal the sicknesses which corrupt and infect the body of the church the moment we see them arise within her.

Here, then, is a summary of what we should learn from this passage. Firstly, we must not be so foolish or frivolous as to accept liberal teaching, which says that as long as the most prominent errors are corrected, we ought to be satisfied. No, we must not stop until the gospel's purity and integrity are restored, so that it is just as our Lord Jesus delivered it to us, without any human additions. Secondly, whenever we see evil gaining a foothold, we must take those who have gone astray and lead them back to God. But we must also seek to obstruct those who are leading others to perdition, and who seek to distort the truth. Indeed, we must rebuke such people; may all those who are zealous for God declare themselves their mortal enemies. Anything that might hold us back must be cast aside, even if it involves family or friends, or those joined by the closest possible ties in this world. All such things must be disregarded if souls purchased by the blood of the Lord Jesus Christ are being led astray to be ruined and lost forever, and if things that were once well established are being overturned. Otherwise, we will have a state of total confusion, to the extent that no-one will know that the gospel came from Jesus Christ. Little by little, the devil's ways will become the order of the day and he will drag us along with him if he once takes hold of our loose reins. If we see evil growing to this degree, each of us has a duty to stop its spread by showing that we prefer to go to war in the service of God than to have all the friends in the world and to please and gratify mortal creatures. Let us even make ourselves blind or remove an eye rather than offend God. May his truth and his glory be so precious to us that everything else is as nought in comparison. This is how we ought to apply this doctrine; the rest we can reserve until after lunch!

Now let us fall before the majesty of our great God, acknowledging our sins and asking him to be pleased to make us increasingly aware of them. And, as he desires us to come to him in repentance, may it please him to draw us to himself by his Holy Spirit, and to bear with our infirmities, until he has altogether purged and cleansed us of them, and brought us to that state of perfection to which he calls and exhorts us. Thus we all say, Almighty God, etc.

11

Even Total Observance of the Law Cannot Justify

> *But when I saw that they walked not uprightly according to the truth of the gospel, I said unto Peter before them all, If thou, being a Jew, livest after the manner of the Gentiles, and not as do the Jews, why compellest thou the Gentiles to live as do the Jews? We who are Jews by nature, and not sinners of the Gentiles, Knowing that a man is not justified by the works of the law, but by the faith of Jesus Christ . . .* (Gal. 2:14–16).

The proverb 'we must practise what we preach', has always been in common usage. For indeed, to place heavy burdens on the shoulders of others whilst remaining free from such burdens ourselves is neither just nor reasonable. Therefore, the Lord Jesus Christ reproached the Scribes and Pharisees, who thought nothing of binding heavy burdens on the poor, whilst granting themselves licence to do whatever they desired. It was largely a result of their hypocrisy, that they could be lenient and indulgent with themselves and yet most severe and strict with their neighbours. Therefore, if we are seeking to encourage our neighbours to do their duty, the right and proper approach is to begin with ourselves. If a man will not forgive his neighbour the slightest fault and yet desires to be forgiven himself for every last sin, (though he has committed gross sins and refuses to bear correction), he is making his hypocrisy plain for all to see. But there are times when even we ourselves demand of others a standard that we cannot keep.

This is what had happened in the case of Peter. Yet, although he had encouraged the Gentiles to observe the ceremonial law, he did not do so out of blatant hypocrisy, such as in the case of the person we have just described. It was not as if Peter had granted himself liberty to do as he pleased, hoping to maintain others in a position of slavery, all the while believing himself to be righteous in God's eyes. No, it was rather that he exhibited double standards because he was too eager to please his own people, the Jews. Previously, he had been content to live as a Gentile, that is to say, by not practising the ceremonial law. (Paul is not referring to unbelievers or to those who had rejected God, as we have said before; he is speaking of those Gentiles who had been converted to a knowledge of the gospel and who sought to serve God, albeit without the former ceremonies.) Peter had conformed himself to their way of life, although he was a Jew; therefore, it was a terrible sin to place a tighter bridle on the Gentiles than he was prepared to wear himself, just as we have been saying. He did not do so for his own sake, but because he wished to play two hands at once, as they say, just like people today who aim to enjoy the favour of all and be at variance with none. Thus, it is clear that there was good reason to rebuke Peter and put him to shame in front of the whole church. We must add that he acknowledged his sin, for we can learn from his example of humility. Let us be aware that there is no-one here for whom it is impossible to go astray or fall into serious errors, since none of us have perfect wisdom. Even if our lives are free from gross sins, our human frailty may still cause us to fall. Indeed, even when we are rebuked, we are likely to bare our teeth, for many of us are full of rebellion and pride. When challenged, we either swallow our venom, or else brazenly spit it out. Let us learn from the example Peter sets us here, that none of us are so advanced in holiness, wisdom or virtue that we cannot fall. Also, let us patiently heed the lesson this teaches us and use it to our profit, not afraid to hang our heads if we find good reason to accuse and condemn ourselves. This is the first thing we should glean from this passage.

However, Peter had been placed in a position of great honour, as we saw this morning, being one of the foremost pillars of the church of God and of the spiritual temple that was to be built. He had been blessed, and had received the Holy Spirit like his companions. Thus, though he had fallen once before, Jesus Christ had restored him and wiped out the memory of this particular sin, for he said, 'Feed my sheep. Take care of my lambs' (*John* 21:15). Yet, he still did not always keep to the straight and narrow way, because here he had clearly turned aside from it. Thus, we must be all the more careful not to deceive ourselves, considering that we have learnt so much in God's school as no longer to be in danger of falling. Let us keep ourselves from such presumption and remain watchful so that we do not fall prey to the wiles and ambushes of Satan. Furthermore, let us be wary of wanting to please men, for Peter himself fell into this same trap. His heart, however, was working towards an opposite goal: he desired to be completely taken up with glorifying the name of God. When ordered not to preach any longer in the name of Jesus Christ, he resisted courageously. Indeed, he spoke with the dignity of an angel when he replied, 'We ought to obey God rather than men,' (*Acts* 4:19; 5:29). There he was in front of the leaders of his people, assembled in all their pomp and with great solemnity, which would have terrified a poor man of no apparent worth like Peter, or, indeed, like John, his companion on that occasion. Yet though he made such a reply (that he would obey God rather than those who claimed to have authority over him), he still went astray later in the way that is described in our text. If ever men are seeking to lead us astray, let us be warned by the example which is related to us here, that we may all learn to keep watch over ourselves, and not allow our eyes to wander in search of the favour of this world. Even if we think we have a good excuse or believe that it will not harm us to seek to please others, let us remember, above all else, our calling and what God has commanded us to do. We must close our eyes to all that is around us and entertain but one aim: to be conformed to God's will in everything. Then we can avoid the enticements and allurements of Satan and the world, and cease from seeking to gratify creatures, by honestly considering what God demands of us, and begging him to guide and lead us by his Holy Spirit.

Furthermore, we need to consider the limits of our calling, attempting nothing which is beyond our sphere of duty. If we do not do these things, we will be deceived at every turn, just as Peter was in this case. If we compare ourselves with him, in theory he ought to have been better able than we to keep himself from falling. Nevertheless, he had to humble himself, and through his mistake we learn that we must also get rid of all pride. Then we will no longer be wise in our own conceits, constantly declaring our own fanciful notions. Instead, all our wisdom will consist in conforming ourselves to the pure Word of God.

* * *

Let us now consider how Paul proceeds. He enters deeper into the subject thus: 'We are Jews by nature, and not sinners (that is to say, condemned, defiled and miserable wretches) of the Gentiles.' We know that we cannot be justified by 'the works of the law', he says, 'for the only way to be acceptable to God is through the grace of the Lord Jesus Christ. Therefore, we have turned our backs upon the righteousness that comes through the law, and now recognise that we can only be saved if God accepts us in his free grace for the sake of his Son. If we Jews have renounced all ideas of our own merits, should not the Gentiles do the same? Surely, both are reconciled to God out of his free bounty without contributing anything in and of themselves. None can claim to have deserved anything or to have any inherent worth.' Here, Paul is entering into the main thrust of his argument against those who mixed the ceremonial law with the gospel, of whom we have been speaking. Peter did not fit into this category, for he certainly knew that the only way to approach God is through the mercy which he has shown us in the Lord Jesus Christ. Paul had already expressed his views to Peter, as we have seen, and as far as doctrine is concerned they were in complete agreement. Thus, Peter had not been ensnared by this particular error, which fully undermines the sufferings and death of the Lord Jesus Christ. Indeed, Peter would have detested such a doctrine. No – he was guilty, rather, of pretence, as we said this morning, which had the effect of hardening the Jews in their foolish errors regarding meritorious works. Of course, this was not his intention, but this is insufficient reason to excuse him. We can insist a hundred times over that we do not intend to support evil, yet if we maintain any pretence, we will surely be guilty in the eyes of God and condemned in the sight of all men.

As we have established, then, Peter agreed with Paul over matters of doctrine. They agreed that the only way to come before God and to obtain his grace and favour is to reject all that proceeds from the creature, acknowledging that all that we are by nature deserves his curse. They agreed that God will receive us out of his free mercy if we come in the name of the Lord Jesus Christ. Peter knew all of this and taught it without hesitation. Furthermore, he knew that it was not right to continue the use of the ceremonial law. He would not have granted himself liberty from the ceremonial law unless he had first understood that the Son of God had obtained this liberty for us through his sufferings and death. Yet, he was too eager to please those of his own nation, though he knew only too well how self-opinionated and wayward they were. He was simply seeking to gratify their sinful natures. Paul does not show respect of persons with regard to his friend Peter, but neither does he treat him as an imposter who does not even know the first thing about the gospel. Instead, he warns him along these lines: 'Beware of where this will lead, and the consequences it will bring. What is the purpose of keeping the ceremonial law? Is it possible for us to attain some level of holiness by it, or is it vital to our soul's salvation? Will it cause us to merit God's grace or will it lead to the remission of our sins, if we simply retain circumcision and the other rites of the law? If this is what people think, then they are discounting the death and sufferings of the Lord Jesus Christ, and you, Peter, are encouraging them in their self-deception. Where will all this lead you?' Notice that Paul does not bother to take account of Peter's own reasoning – he simply deals with the matter in hand in order to quash the pretence of those who were making the gospel gates too narrow. This occurred at a time when the church was rapidly growing, as we were saying this morning.

* * *

This subject cannot be fully covered in one day, nor even in four, so we must, therefore, confine ourselves to a few particular details in order to ascertain why Paul strove so earnestly to stop the continued use of the ceremonies. The matter regards the salvation of our souls. Indeed, our most vital study in God's school, second only to glorifying God, is how a person is saved. If we seek to compare the two things, the service of God should always be put before the good of our souls, (although the latter will increase in proportion to our service!). Indeed, the two things are inseparable. God reveals the infinite nature of his love for us in that, if anything should serve to glorify him, it will also prove beneficial to the state of our souls. Since God has loved us so much and has showered his grace upon us, we are under obligation to do our part by forgetting about self and devoting ourselves completely to him. In other words, the two main factors in our religion are, first, to recognise that God is to be served and glorified; and second, to understand how we can present ourselves to him and be accepted and acknowledged as his children, owning him as our Father. Then we can have full assurance of the salvation of our souls. Both of these factors are included in what Paul is dealing with here. For this passage addresses the subject of how God is to be served, and defines the sacrifice that God requires of us – humble confession. I speak of humility, but I do not mean simply the right facial expression, but, rather, being affected in such a way that we willingly accept God's condemnation and cast away all trust in our works or merits. Here is one important lesson.

Also, when God commanded the ceremonial law, he did not intend us to cling to such external things; he had another end in view. That is, he desired that the children of Israel exercise patience, acknowledging their poverty and misery, and rid themselves of all the corruptions of the flesh. Indeed, his design was to lead them to the Lord Jesus Christ, so that they would put their trust in him and lean on him completely for salvation. Thus, those who sought to keep the ceremonial law as if it were absolutely vital and as if it were sin not to do so, were establishing a pattern of worship to God which was against his will, and contrary to his intention. Those who did so were, therefore, false teachers, distorting the real significance of the law. This is one point. Secondly, they were instructing men to exalt themselves and to boast of their own works. This does not bring glory to God, for if we attribute to ourselves even a little merit, we are robbing and spoiling God of what rightfully belongs to him. It is devilish blasphemy to presume that we are virtuous when we do not even possess a single drop of righteousness. To believe that we can obtain salvation by our works is to enter the very mouth of hell, for we annul the death and passion of the Lord Jesus Christ, in whom all our righteousness is found. The devil can make us believe a lie, but it will lead us to perdition.

Notice that Paul also deals with the path to justification before God, that is to say, the way to be made acceptable to him. This is the most important lesson we can learn, for without this knowledge all so-called religion is but vanity and falsehood. Paul does not enter into this subject without good cause. Many will be thinking, 'What! The issue at stake is the ceremonial law. Why, then, does Paul throw himself right into the middle of the battle by raising issues such as righteousness, man's salvation and the forgiveness of sins? Why does he bring in the whole of the law?' Well, to speak of even one of the ceremonies of the law involves discussing the role and function of the whole. Let me give you an example. Today we teach that we should not uphold Popish superstitions or anything that has been invented by men. We do not only refer to abstaining from eating meat on Fridays, or to a certain vigil, or to this or that issue, but we treat the subject as a whole – whether it is right for mortal man to impose laws which subjugate consciences and lead them into tyrannical slavery. God alone reserves for himself the right to be called Lawgiver and none in the church may usurp this honourable position (*Isa.* 33:22). Because, therefore, our souls may only be governed by the pure Word of God, we conclude that there is neither Pope nor any other person, no matter what rank they hold, that has power to impose certain laws or to introduce anything which is against the doctrine we have received from God. Thus, we enter into this more general debate because the same principle is involved in each particular issue that arises. It would be frivolous if we were only to debate whether to eat fish or meat, for each one may eat according as his health requires, or according to what is available. This will not affect the salvation of our souls, nor our peace of conscience. But if we deal with the wider issue concerning whether a living creature should elevate himself to the point of imposing laws on others, this question can be addressed and fully resolved. People say that by muttering 'Our Fathers', or by going on pilgrimage to perform what the Papists call works of supererogation (which means doing more than God requires of us), they can be saved from their sin! They believe this will bring salvation by compensating for all the sins they have committed. However, if we were only to debate with them about pilgrimages, without coming to the fundamental source of the problem, it would be a cold and fruitless discussion. Rather, we need to say that the payment for all our sins was made when the Lord Jesus Christ suffered and died, and that God rejects all that we can perform, yet requires that we serve him in obedience. This is what it means to get to the root of the matter, and in this way we can reach an irrefutable conclusion. This is just the way Paul approached the matter. He not only gave his attention to what the Jews believed concerning eating pork, or the observance of this feast or that ceremony – he considered why they believed such things. They claimed that the observation of the law was vital to salvation, and this was a yoke upon the conscience that Paul found intolerable. Also he saw that they were negating the liberty which the Lord Jesus Christ obtained for us. This was a second point that constrained him to open up the whole debate. But the main offence which he counters here is the fact that those who advocated keeping the ceremonies believed this practice to be acceptable to God and to be of such value that, through them, they would obtain righteousness and salvation. In short, they thought of them as works of merit. Paul therefore declares that it is not possible for men to be justified in God's sight by their works.

We can now understand why he deals with the subject of justification in general terms, even though his opponents only claimed that we should keep the ceremonial law, and that we should continue as in the times before the coming of Jesus Christ, sacrificing and keeping the rest of the types and shadows. This shows us what fools the Papists are to say that Paul is only excluding the works of the law here and not moral good works. However, they are not the originators of such folly. The devil has always had his agents in every age who have deceived the people; this is why we should not be swayed by the authority of men, especially if they possess neither holiness nor the fear of God. It does not matter if they have great knowledge; there have been many hypocritical monks who have never even tasted the fear of God, like those whom we call 'the Early Church Fathers', who distorted the plain meaning of Holy Scripture. They were bewitched by Satan himself, yet the poor people were so blind that they did not recognise it. Such people are told here that we are not justified by the works of the law, that is, by circumcision, by abstaining from certain meats, or by keeping a certain feast (though Paul does not specifically mention any of these). Paul sets God's grace over against all our works; in brief, he shows us that we can bring nothing to God, but that it is a matter of being accepted by him. This is Paul's main contention.

If we have not understood Paul's thoughts in this passage, then the rest of the teaching in this epistle will be meaningless to us. Indeed, remember that Paul on many other occasions states simply and plainly that we are justified apart from works; for example, in the third chapter to the Romans. There, he makes a clear and certain statement about justification, saying we are justified through the remission of our sins and not by our 'works' (*Rom.* 3:28). He does not say there, 'by the works of the law'; he omits this expression in order to silence every mouth and to remove any possibility of evading the truth. Yet, when he does speak of 'the works of the law' he has good reason to do so: he intends to denigrate all the works that men do to win God's favour, and to justify themselves in his sight. As we will see shortly, if we possessed the perfection of angels, it would not mean that God was under obligation to us in any way, even though he freely promised in the law that if a man keeps his statutes, he shall live by them (*Lev.* 18:5).

Therefore, if we claim that we can obtain God's grace by our works, we cannot argue that we deserve wages or a reward because we have served him, for we belong to him and there is nothing about us that would attract him to us. How is it, then, that our works can be rewarded, as if they could satisfy God? It is only because God has promised to do this. He has drawn up a contract with us by saying, 'if a man do them, he shall live in them'. Therefore, if we could keep the law perfectly we would certainly be justified in God's sight and would merit salvation, not because of any worth in ourselves but because of the covenant that God made with us. All the righteousness that men may claim to have relates to this promise. This is why Paul repeats so frequently, 'works of the law, works of the law', for no other works can warrant acceptance with God, or any reward. This is one point.

We also learn that we cannot possibly possess such a

righteousness, because we sin. Therefore, though God declares that we will be saved if we keep the law, he is in effect revealing that all will be condemned. How is this? Well, there is no-one who can acquit himself – we are all transgressors. Thus the law can only bring us death because of our own weaknesses, but we will deal with this later when the matter arises. For the moment, it is enough to say that Paul sets out this doctrine in opposition to the Jews, who were boastful and full of vain pride, thinking God was under obligation to them because they kept the ceremonial law. 'No, no,' he says, 'this means nothing', and we will see why this is so shortly. Added to this, Paul took exception to such practices because these hypocrites, who thought of themselves as paragons of virtue in God's eyes and desired praise for their own salvation, busied themselves with trifles and never came to the root of the matter – their own consciences.

How like the Papists today, who preach so much about their own merits, and who say that they can obtain paradise by their own works. Though we are sinners, they say, we still have the means to acquit ourselves in God's sight by making satisfaction for our sins. What are they saying? When these so-called teachers go about setting people up as idols to be worshipped, and when they make great speeches about their own free will, virtue, merits and worth – what are they preaching? Are they encouraging us to live chaste lives, not to ill-treat our neighbours, to live without the slightest inclination towards avarice, to be content with what we have, to be patient in times of adversity, to suffer injustice and shame, to show that we are disciples of the Lord Jesus Christ by our self-denying lives? No, there is none of this: instead they preach about good works. By this they mean that we should be faithful in our attendance at Mass, and before entering the building take some holy water, make the sign of the cross several times, kneel in front of some pillar or other, worship some grotesque image, go on pilgrimage, observe a certain feast, say Mass, give money for the dead, or this, that or the other. These hypocrites who seek justification through their own merit believe all this folly and nonsense, for it seems to them that these things are not to be scoffed at, because they will bring them to a state of holiness and perfection. They believe that God ought to be content with their many bowings and signs and gestures, but it is not with such money that we can pay God, for his law is spiritual. God is not concerned with the appearance, with what sparkles most in the eyes of man. God utterly rejects us when we set such store by our own ceremonies. This point is worthy of our attention because men are always seeking a way to escape devoting themselves to obeying God. They think that when they have done these foolish acts of so-called devotion, they become innocent and that all their sins will be forgotten because by such means they have redeemed themselves. What we have to remember is that Paul was speaking against people who had never known what it is to serve God freely, because it had never even entered their minds that this is what he required of them.

This is the sad position of all hypocritical Papists, those rogues who exist in such abundance today. I am not only speaking of cardinals and of those horned beasts called bishops (for we all know that their stench has infected everyone), but I am speaking of all those who set themselves to teach others, as the upholders of the Catholic faith. These men are surely mockers of God, for it has never entered into their minds to examine themselves earnestly, neither have they had any moral scruples whatsoever. All their study has been to hold poor souls in Gehenna, as it were, and to teach morality to others in the hope that they will be admired for their wisdom; but as for themselves, they have never felt any pangs of conscience. They are able to speak so fluently about merit and yet do not apply their doctrine to their own lives. They have but a few trifling rituals, like babies' toys, with which they think they are able to appease God. This is why Paul first takes issue with the continued use of the ceremonial law, because this was the matter in hand, though this did not prevent him from taking the point further; that is to say, he showed that men are devoid of righteousness and can bring nothing to God. Indeed, we must come to God as beggars, confessing our poverty and hunger.

Notice, furthermore, that the Jews have always twisted the nature and usage of the sacraments by making them meritorious, which is opposite to the way we ought to understand them. God did not establish the sacraments so that if men strove to keep them they would obtain some virtue which would count for righteousness. Rather, he did so to teach them that they need to find righteousness in him. For example, when the Jews were circumcised, God was showing them in this visible way that all that proceeds from man is corrupt and that we therefore need to cut off sin. In this visible sign, the Jews should have understood that man's nature is cursed in God's eyes and that he would search in vain for one drop of purity in us. On the other hand, they had the promise that God would, nevertheless, save them by means of a Redeemer who would rise from among the human race. He would descend from the line of David. God taught these things through circumcision in a visual way. Thus, the Jews, on the one hand, were cast down as far as their own state was concerned and had to realise that in themselves they were evil, yet on the other, they were to find in Jesus Christ all that they lacked. It is the same with the ceremonial washings. When the Jews washed themselves in this way it was to show that in themselves there was nothing but filth. But what were they washing in? Water? No, they were washing in the blood of our Lord Jesus Christ. When brute beasts were sacrificed, they were acknowledging that they themselves deserved death. The animals were innocent; they were killed for the sake of men to bear away their sin. This acted as a mirror to reflect that men are all under God's curse. Yet, men could come in that way and humble themselves and call upon God, declaring that they had been bought back to God by a sacrifice, not by these shadows but by the true 'Sacrifice' which had not yet been revealed. Well, what did the Jews do? Having been circumcised, they believed that God was indebted to them; having performed their sacrifices, they thought of themselves as holy and boasted in this fact. The prophets however denounced such hypocrites for two reasons. Firstly, they declared to them that even when they had kept all the ceremonial law, they had done nothing and it was in vain (*Hos.* 6:6). In this verse God says, 'I desired mercy, and not sacrifice'. God declares that he has shown us how to please him – by being truly humble. Not by occupying ourselves with bringing lambs and oxen, for this means nothing (*Mic.* 6:8). Rather, we must 'do justly' and live upright lives in front of our neighbours if we want to serve God. Notice also what our Lord says in Jeremiah: 'For I spake not unto your fathers, nor commanded them . . . concerning burnt offerings or sacrifices: but this thing commanded I them, saying, Obey my voice . . . and walk ye in all the ways that I have commanded you' (*Jer.* 7:22–23). Then again in another passage it says, 'The Lord loves faithfulness'. We have seen that the prophets denounced hypocrisy, even though they retained the use of the ceremonies; these were of no value in and of themselves, without a clear conscience toward God and an upright walk before our fellow men. This is what the prophets taught. They taught, secondly, that even if they had done all they possibly could, they were still in debt to God, for they were expected to look beyond the ceremonies to him. Through them they ought to have recognised that God was calling them to himself, promising to show them mercy and to forgive and pardon all their sins by means of a promised Redeemer (*Jer.* 31:34).

We have now seen that the ceremonies mean nothing unless certain important conditions are met. For example, we must walk without ill-treating, annoying, harming or hurting our neighbours, and we are to live chaste and pure lives with clean consciences. Paul now leaves this point because it is no longer pertinent, but he has shown us that the shadows of the law were neither useful nor essential, and were indeed valueless; that is, if they were observed simply as they were given. They were intended to have one main purpose: to point to the grace which has now been showered upon us in the Lord Jesus Christ, on whom our souls must entirely rest. Today, this ought to be deeply engraved on our hearts and in our minds. We will have profited much, even if we have only discovered how to apply to ourselves the sacraments which the Lord Jesus Christ instituted. This is especially the case since we are going to receive the Lord's Supper next Sunday; for although we ought to have been exhorted today to make preparation for it, we did not touch upon the subject this morning. However, let us bear in mind that, if we are expecting to be justified because we have been baptised, we are, in fact, defiling an ordinance that God intended for our good. What do I mean? Well, baptism teaches us that we are full of filth and corruption within. Why else do we wash hands, face and body, but because we desire to wash off the dirt? We are told that baptism is our washing; therefore, it follows that when we come to be baptised, and when we bring our children, we are declaring that from the mother's womb our children are already lost and condemned. They are a cursed seed. This means that they must obtain cleansing, but not of themselves; they must receive it as it is offered to them in the Lord Jesus Christ. And if children are already infected when they have just been born into the world, what about us, who continually offend our God, and who drink iniquity as a fish does water, as it says in the book of Job (*Job* 15:16)?

Secondly, when we receive the Lord's Supper, what is it we are doing? Are we there to acquire some merit in God's eyes? No, we are there to confess that we are like dead men who have come to seek for life outside of ourselves. The flesh of our Lord Jesus Christ must be our meat, and his blood our drink, for in him we find all that we need. Thus, the sacraments should not make us swollen with vain pride, but they should make us walk in humility, so that, empty of pride, we only seek the provision that God has made out of his infinite bounty, and that he would bestow upon us the treasures of his grace according to our need. Our attendance at the sacraments is the means whereby God warns us about our sins in order to make us feel them keenly. He does not wish us simply to acknowledge that we are sinners with our lips, or in a half-hearted way, nor even by means of ceremonies. Rather, he would have us to be heartbroken within because we have offended him, feeling the terror of his wrath so that we tremble within ourselves and find no rest; that is, until the Lord Jesus Christ has been revealed to us. Let each one of us make sure that as we approach this holy table we are really rooted in the Lord Jesus Christ, and that we have renounced all Satan's vain delusions and the lies he places before our eyes to keep us from the grace of God. Let us, instead, embrace Jesus Christ in the merit of his death and passion, and realise that our righteousness and salvation have been accomplished through him. Moreover, since our Lord Jesus Christ has called us to be members of his body, let us be united together. Let us seek to glorify God with one heart and voice, and to live in true unity with our neighbours, just as a hand seeks to serve a foot, as much as an eye. Let us therefore demonstrate our brotherly love for one another by showing the world that we will not be separated (which would be to divide Jesus Christ himself). Instead, may we desire that he would unite us so that we may live in him and he in us, and that he would lead us by his Holy Spirit to honour and serve him above all else and to serve our neighbours as we find opportunity.

Now let us fall before the majesty of our great God, acknowledging our sins, and praying that he would make us increasingly conscious of them, to lead us to deeper repentance and to cause us to persevere to the end. May we grow in the faith of our Lord Jesus Christ, give ourselves wholly to him, and call upon God the Father in his name. We pray he will continue his grace to us until he has drawn us fully to himself and perfected our knowledge of the good that was purchased for us by the death and passion of Christ. May he not only show this grace to us, but to all peoples, etc.

12

Justification is by Grace Alone

We who are Jews by nature, and not sinners of the Gentiles, Knowing that a man is not justified by the works of the law, but by the faith of Jesus Christ, even we have believed in Jesus Christ, that we might be justified by the faith of Christ, and not by the works of the law: for by the works of the law shall no flesh be justified (Gal. 2:15–16).

Thus far, we have expounded why Paul, addressing the subject of the ceremonies, types and shadows which were practised before the coming of the Lord Jesus Christ, reaches the general conclusion that a man cannot be justified or acceptable in God's sight unless he observes the whole law. Now, at first, we might consider these things to be two separate issues; however, as we have been saying, Paul has to draw us back to basics in order to expose the folly of believing that we can obtain favour in God's eyes through our own merit. Now, we have already discussed the reason why Paul adds the word 'law'. For however much it may be commonly held that a good man can earn favour and acceptance with God, men are very seriously mistaken in such matters. Indeed, whatever we may have done, we cannot win God's favour, because he deserves the very best of all that is in our power. There is, therefore, no merit possible on our part (if, indeed, we may call it that), unless we fulfil the terms of the covenant he made with us, when he said that whosoever keeps the law shall obtain life and salvation (*Lev.* 18:5). When God uttered these words, he was prepared to accept our total obedience as worthy of salvation, but this does not, in fact, imply that we can, therefore, merit favour, for none of us have done our duty (as we shall see hereafter). Thus, the promise would have been forfeited, or at least without effect in that it would never apply to anyone, had not God sent the remedy – that is to say, unless, despite our unrighteousness, he forgave our sins, and accepted us as righteous. When Paul says that we cannot be justified by the works of the law, he means that if we claim to merit grace and salvation because God has promised that those who observe the law will be accounted as righteous, we are completely mistaken; for no-one keeps the law perfectly. We must realise that we all stand guilty before God and have the sentence of condemnation hanging over our heads.

In order to express this fact more clearly, Paul draws a comparison between the Jews and the Gentiles. He says that even though they were 'Jews by nature and not sinners of the Gentiles' they realised that they could only be acceptable to God by faith in the Lord Jesus Christ. For, although all men have fallen in Adam and therefore have no individual merit, it appeared that the Jews had a special privilege, in as much as God had adopted them as his own children and called them his servants. Yet, this is where the Jews went wrong. For when the Scriptures speak of 'the uncircumcision', they refer to the pollution which indwells us from Adam, and places us all under condemnation from our mother's womb. But the Jews believed that God had freed them from this curse upon mankind and therefore they boasted. Whilst it is true that great honour was conferred upon them, which they should have valued above all earthly good – for God had chosen them to be his people and his inheritance – yet they ought to have humbly acknowledged that in their own selves they were unworthy. Indeed, we also are used to adopting such a presumptuous attitude when we experience the grace of God; likewise the Jews, for the most part, wrongly believed they were superior to everyone else. They thought God had found something about them that made him prefer them to those he had rejected. This arrogance brought with it wicked ingratitude, for they did not attribute to God all the good things they had received from his hand, but were puffed up with pride, as if God thought they were better or more worthy of eternal salvation than the Gentiles.

To extinguish all such presumption, Paul begins his argument thus: 'we who are Jews by nature . . .' . It appears that he is saying, 'Yes, it is true that we have been shown greater grace than the Gentiles, whom God did not accept into his church'. But when he speaks like this he does not, in fact, intend to give the Jews occasion for pride; rather, he is spreading before them the things they have freely received from God to teach them that they have no grounds for boasting. In the Epistle to the Romans, Paul makes two statements which at first sight seem contradictory, yet which are in perfect harmony. On the one hand he asks, 'Do we not have more privileges than the Gentiles?', and he answers, 'Yes. For we were chosen to be his people; he gave us circumcision as a sign and seal that we are his children; he made a covenant with us; he promised to send us the Redeemer of the world. Thus, if we consider the mercies that God has showered upon us, we have been blessed indeed, and exalted far above all other peoples.' Here Paul magnifies the goodness of God towards them (*Rom.* 3:1–2). However, later he asks the same question (What advantage have the Jews?), but answers, 'None at all' (*Rom.* 3:9–10). 'For we are all under God's curse. If the Gentiles are to be condemned, then we are to be condemned twice as much, for they have the excuse of ignorance. Nevertheless, they cannot escape God, but will perish although they have never had any instruction or knowledge of doctrine. It follows, then, that we will be condemned by the law, because God has taught us and yet we have not stopped sinning or transgressing his righteous laws, so that now we are plunged into greater and deeper condemnation than even Gentiles and unbelievers', he says. Thus, the Jews were distinct from the Gentiles – not because they were more worthy or more righteous, but simply because God chose them out of his free bounty.

In the same way, the children born to believers are no better than the children of other Gentiles or even of Turks when it comes to their nature. For we are all part of a corrupt and accursed mass whom God has condemned, so that none of us may exalt ourselves and think ourselves of more worth than our friends. However, Paul declares that our children are sanctified, that they are not stained in the same way as those born to unbelievers or pagans (*1 Cor.* 7:14). It would seem that there are some contradictions here. Yet the whole hangs together very well, because, as for our natures, we are all tainted and corrupted, with only one exception [Christ]. Yet there is such a thing as a supernatural gift, that is, a privilege that God confers in order that the children of believers are dedicated to him, and he recognises and accepts them as his own. This is why the children of the church today are regarded as the people of God and amongst the number of the elect, just as under the law the Jews were separated from the rest of the world. This explains why Paul says, 'We are Jews and not sinners of the Gentiles'. By 'sinners', he means those who continue in their filth and have not been washed by the grace of God. Indeed, circumcision itself was a sign and a testimony to the fact that God accepted the family of Abraham and the race that descended from him as his own familiar and special people. In old times, this is what distinguished the Jews from unbelievers; for, although they were of equal status as children of Adam, yet God had chosen some and left others as strangers to his family. If we ask why this should be, the answer can only be purely because of God's grace, since the Jews themselves were not outstanding in any way.

* * *

Let us now follow the argument that Paul is constructing here. He says, 'Knowing that a man is not justified by the works of the law, but by the faith of Jesus Christ.' In saying this, Paul demonstrates that whatever grace they had received from God, they were not at liberty to trust in man or in themselves as if they deserved this from God. No, rather, they had to seek refuge in his free bounty, recognising that salvation is in Jesus Christ alone, who came to rescue from perdition those who were already lost. This is confirmed in that other passage, where it says that he 'came and preached peace to you which were afar off and to them that were nigh' (*Eph.* 2:17). Jesus Christ is that peace, for it is through him that God can love us and receive us in mercy. This is not only true for those who were previously far away like the Gentiles, but also for the children of Abraham, despite the dignity and nobility they already possessed (for this was not theirs by nature). Paul says that the Jews who had been converted to Christianity knew that they could not be justified by the works of the law, but only by faith in the Lord Jesus Christ, and he makes a comparison between the two in order to show that we cannot be justified by grace unless we actually renounce all personal merit.

This is well worthy of our attention. For indeed, even the Papists profess to be justified by faith, but this is only half of the truth and it is the rest of the picture which spoils the whole. Sure enough, they are persuaded of the fact that a man cannot be accounted righteous before God unless Jesus is the Mediator and unless that person rests upon him for salvation. The Papists know this only too well, and yet they so often say, 'We are justified by faith but not by faith alone.' This is the point with which they take issue, and this is the principal matter upon which we differ. Paul, however, shows their folly when he says, 'but by faith', for this expression implies that all that men bring to God to please him is rejected. The door is, therefore, tight shut to all merit, for Paul declares that the only way to come to God is through faith. We will soon see more clearly why Paul draws a comparison with the law as if here are two opposites. The law presupposes that if we fulfil what God requires of us we will be found good servants and he will give us the reward he has promised; faith, on the other hand, presupposes that we are poor, lost, condemned souls and that we are to find in Jesus Christ what we so desperately need.

Take this as an example: there are two men seeking food and shelter. One has money and wishes to be treated in accordance with his means. They both ask for something to eat, but the second man is poor and does not have a penny, so he begs for alms. They both have something in common, for they both seek food, but the first has money with which to satisfy his host. Thus, after eating and drinking well and being courteously entertained, the host, for his part, will be happy to receive his payment, no longer thinking that his guest is in any way indebted to him. Why? Well, he has been satisfied and has even gained from it. But the life of the poor man who asks for alms depends upon the one who can provide him with food and shelter, for he can give him nothing in return. In the same way, if we seek to be justified by the law we must deserve that justification; for then God will receive from us and we from him in a reciprocal manner. Is such a thing possible? Not at all, as we shall examine in more detail later. We must, therefore, conclude that we cannot obtain righteousness by the law, and that if we believe we can make God our debtor, we will only provoke his wrath. The only option is to come as poor beggars, that we may be justified by faith. Not as if faith were a virtue proceeding from us, but we must come humbly, confessing that we cannot obtain salvation except as a free gift. This, then, is why the law is put in opposition to faith. Paul is showing us that all who claim to be acceptable to God by their merits are turning their back upon the grace of the Lord Jesus Christ. We shall study this at greater length hereafter.

A man may raise this objection: the law was given by God, so therefore it cannot be placed in opposition to faith, which also proceeds from God. The answer to this is simple. God made both the day and the night, water and fire, cold and heat. Surely, the day is not in opposition to the night, but rather God in his goodness and wisdom has arranged that they appear in a suitable order; man has the brightness of the sun in which to do his work by day, and by night the sun hides itself away so that man may take his rest. Therefore, although day differs from night, there is no disharmony between them. The same applies to fire and water. Every created thing has its function – and fire and water complement each other very well; however, if we were to mix them together, then they would indeed clash! This is true of the law and the gospel. Those who believe that we are justified by the law as well as the gospel are confusing everything; it is as if they are crashing heaven and earth together! In short, it would be easier to mix fire and water than to say this: that we can merit a measure of the grace of God and yet also need the aid of the Lord Jesus Christ. If we consider what the law is and why it was given, we will discover that there is no discrepancy with the gospel, nor with faith, but that there is perfect harmony between them. This objection is thus dealt with. If we say that both faith and the law proceed from God, we are right; but we must give some thought (as we will do shortly) to the reason why God originally instituted them both.

* * *

Let us return to Paul's words – he says that we can only be justified by faith in the Lord Jesus Christ. When he speaks of justification, he means being accounted righteous in the sight of God. This expression needs to be understood because it is dealing with the whole subject of how we are saved. We would be miserable creatures indeed if, having lived a long life in this world, someone were to ask us the way of salvation and we did not know how to respond! Many fools have feasted on the bread of God without knowing how to be acceptable to him. This is why we ought to be all the more attentive to what Paul is telling us here. He says that we are justified. How? Are we already righteous – are we blameless? Not at all, but God accepts us. The word 'justification' points us to that favour which God bestows upon us when we become his children and he our Father. You may ask, why do the Scriptures use the word 'justify' when it seems so inappropriate? We could just as well say that God loves us, that he takes pity on us, that he desires to be our Father and

Saviour – why not use these expressions instead of speaking of justification? The Scriptures do not refer to it without good reason.

If we analyse salvation in its most basic sense, we will say that we are saved by the grace of our Lord Jesus Christ. However, this does not imply knowledge of our miserable condition by nature or of the remedy that we need to apply. For in order to put our trust in the Lord Jesus Christ, we must acknowledge that by the sin of Adam, as well as by our own iniquities, we are altogether lost. We ought to have already discovered this for ourselves. We will never understand that our sins condemn us in God's sight, unless we know that we need to be put right with him. In other words, we will not be aware of the righteousness of God if we simply say, 'We are saved by grace and by faith.' For God cannot once deny himself, since he embodies sovereign justice; he is all purity and perfection and, therefore, he detests what is evil. Yet we are totally corrupt and there is only wickedness in us; it follows, therefore, that God must hate us. However, if he hates us, woe unto us, for we are damned. This is why we need to be justified before we can be pleasing to God. This means we must be cleansed from our sins and transgressions; otherwise, we could never appreciate God's mercy (as I have said). If we acknowledge that we are sinners, we will realise that God hates sin, and yet though he hates it he has nevertheless provided a way to save us – by forgiving our sins, and by cleansing and purging us from them through the blood of the Lord Jesus Christ, who gives us spiritual cleansing. God washes us clean in order that he might receive us, so that sharing in his love, we may be assured of our salvation. This is why the Scriptures use the word 'justification'.

Papists may debate over its meaning like foolish beasts. 'What!', they say, 'Justified by faith? Faith does not make a person perfect – how, then, can it justify us?' They do not realise that the justification spoken of in the Scriptures refers to God covering our sins (as I have been saying) and, by virtue of his sufferings and death, cancelling them in and through the name of the Lord Jesus Christ. Whatever others may say, it is written that we are accounted righteous in God's sight when he remits and pardons our sins. In fact, Paul speaks of this in the fourth chapter to the Romans, where he says: 'Even as David also describeth the blessedness of the man, unto whom God imputeth righteousness without works, saying, Blessed are they whose iniquities are forgiven, and whose sins are covered' (*Rom.* 4:6–7; *Psa.* 32:1). Again, in another passage he says, 'For he hath made him to be sin for us, who knew no sin'; (this means that he received all the condemnation due to us for our sins), 'that we might be made the righteousness of God in him' (*2 Cor.* 5:21). Thus, we, being joined and united to his person and to his body, are accounted righteous, because his obedience was so perfect that it was sufficient to cleanse and remove our sins. We have now dealt with the meaning of the term 'justification'.

* * *

Turning our attention to the expression 'faith', Paul states here that they have 'believed' in Jesus Christ. If we were to ask a fool what he considers faith to be, he might well say 'belief', but he clearly would not understand what either word means. Are we happy to be as ignorant as such fools? Let us firstly point out that the Lord Jesus is the object of both our faith and our belief. Is salvation through faith? Yes, if we believe in the Lord Jesus Christ. Let us consider for a moment why the Lord Jesus Christ is set before us as the one in whom we must rest all our faith. It is simply because we find in him all we need for our justification. We have already said that we are accounted righteous in God's sight when he has forgiven our sins and no longer calls them into account. And how does this happen, if not by the blood of the Lord Jesus Christ which was shed for our cleansing? By his sufferings and death, he made satisfaction for our sins and appeased the wrath of God against us. We must seek no further means of payment, other than the sacrifice made by God's only Son, our Lord Jesus Christ. It is he who is called God's beloved Son (*Matt.* 3:17), so that we might be beloved in him; he is called the Righteous One (*Isa.* 53:11), so that we may partake of his righteousness; and he is called the Holy One (*Luke* 1:35), so that we may be sanctified in him. This is why our attention is drawn to the Lord Jesus Christ when we consider 'faith'.

However, the Papists form their own opinions on the subject, revealing by what they claim that they have never experienced what it is to believe. 'What!', they say, 'is it possible for a man to be justified by faith alone, seeing that even devils themselves believe?' This is indeed true, and James uses this argument (*Jas.* 2:20); however, we also see him scorning those who vainly and frivolously said they were Christians and had faith, and yet showed no fruit. The Papists have strayed even further, in that they say faith means believing in God, and that the subject of our faith is God, when by belief they mean a mere imagining that there is a God somewhere who has created the world and who now controls it. They remain at this point, asleep in their ignorance, and yet do not hesitate to call themselves good Christians and good Catholics, as they say, although they are altogether ignorant. Therefore, we should not be surprised if, devoid of discernment or intelligence, they fight against the doctrine contained in Holy Scripture, or when they deny, with incorrigible obstinacy, that man is saved by faith alone. They do not even know what faith is. How carefully, therefore, must we heed the words of Paul here which tell us that if we do not look to Jesus Christ, we cannot know what faith really is. Without him, we cannot know remission of sins, how to approach God, how to put our trust in him, or to call upon him. Neither will we know what it is to have peace of conscience, or the hope of eternal life. All this is beyond our reach until we are introduced to Jesus Christ and until we have looked to him and cast ourselves upon him. This kind of faith brings grace: when we recognise that we are wretched creatures, and abominable in God's sight, seeking the remedy in the Lord Jesus Christ. We must accept that he offered himself for us in order to redeem us from the curse under which we lived, and that he has washed us in his blood. By his obedience, he has cancelled all our transgressions so that we can be assured that God accepts and receives us as his children. This is how we can understand this passage.

* * *

Having stated that he, and all the Jews that had been converted to Christianity, had been saved by faith in the Lord Jesus Christ, Paul adds the following: 'for by the works of the law shall no flesh be justified'. We have heard this before in application to those of his own nation, but here he proclaims it in a more general sense to the whole world. When he says, 'no flesh', he primarily implies that there is no difference between the Jews and the Gentiles when it comes to the way of salvation. Although the Jews had been circumcised, chosen as God's inheritance and sanctified by him, nevertheless, they could have no hope of salvation except through God's pure grace alone. See how they are set at the same level as the Gentiles, having the same status. Paul seeks to expel all pride that men may have about their own virtues. Indeed, many of us know ourselves to be so depraved that we cannot possibly attribute any honour to ourselves, as if we should deserve anything at God's hand. Those who are drunk or debauched or who have given themselves over to all kinds of evil feel too ashamed to elevate themselves or to boast that they can persuade God to save them by their merits or good works. In fact, they hide themselves even from other people because they are ashamed of their baseness. But the bigoted, who make a show of their 'holiness' before men, are so hardened that they deceive themselves into thinking they deserve paradise – as if God were indebted to them! These hypocrites, though utterly depraved and full of ambition, avarice, wickedness and such like things, because of all their manipulations and pretences, believe that God sees nothing wrong with their corrupt practices and even persuade themselves that he will accept them because of their merits! Those who regularly attend Mass, running from the alehouse to the chapel, buying pardons and other such things, observing fasts and feast days – they are puffed up with vain pride and believe that God owes them something. By saying 'no flesh', Paul declares that it is pointless to separate ourselves from one another here below, as if one is just and the other unjust. We must all humble ourselves and judge ourselves, knowing that all our virtues are but filthy rags in God's sight, even the very best that we can do. For even if a man were perfectly righteous in our estimation, because he never harmed anyone, or because he could resist all kinds of evil and was chaste and sober – in short, though he were reputed to be an angel – yet within, there would be nothing but corruption. How is this possible? Well, we must never judge by the appearance, for all that glitters (as the proverb says) is not gold. We cannot judge what is sin or virtue without first looking within. For if a man does not ascribe to God what is rightfully his, he is not robbing men of their honour, but God. Thus, however much men might praise and commend him, he is full of pride and ambition, and nothing will humble him except coming to know the Lord Jesus Christ.

So then, even those who make a good outward show of religion shall be condemned before God. Hence, Paul intends to stop men from trusting in their own merits. But there is yet more. For when he says, 'no flesh', he not only refers to men whom God has given over, who have not been renewed by his Holy Spirit, but he also includes believers. For although God's Spirit dwells within us after he has led us to a knowledge of the gospel and grafted us into the body of the Lord Jesus Christ – although, I say, God's Spirit dwells within us, we are all included in this word 'flesh' because of what we are by nature. Thus, when Paul declares here that 'no flesh shall be justified', he means that unbelievers are condemned in Adam and remain condemned, and that believers, because they will always be imperfect and have many spots and blemishes, are condemned as much as the others. Indeed, this condemnation is a general one, for whoever seeks to be justified by the works of the law will always find himself guilty – yes, even the holiest person that ever existed. Let us take Abraham as an example of perfection, or David, who abounded in all virtues, or Noah, Job, and Daniel, whom Ezekiel names as three righteous men (*Ezek.* 14:14). They all fall into the same category as men who could only be justified in God's sight through grace.

Now then, I ask you all, where do we stand? Those who say that they will be justified by their merits, or 'meritorious works' as they call them, have they not been driven to excessive pride by the devil? For who can match David, or Noah, or Abraham, or Daniel? Surely, even those who have done well in God's school, and who are fired by true zeal in giving themselves totally to God, are convinced that they are still far from having reached the standard set by David, or even Noah or Daniel! Knowing this, therefore, we can see that the Holy Spirit is here casting down those who exalt themselves overmuch, to convince us that we have not the merest drop of righteousness, so that we seek all that pertains to our salvation in the grace of the Lord Jesus Christ. Now we understand what the statement implies when it says that 'no flesh shall be justified'. It is as if Paul were saying that, when it comes to our nature, we are only evil within, despite what appears to be the case outwardly. We may be greatly praised and respected by the world; we may be surrounded by vain flattery; but until God works in us to change us, we are full of filth. Indeed, all the virtues that men exalt are nothing short of vices that will lead men to destruction and plunge them into hell. For even those who have been renewed by the grace of God, and who have learnt to obey him by doing the things which God loves and cherishes, even they can bring nothing to God that can settle their accounts with him. They will always be in debt because all the good gifts they have proceed from God; also, even such men are corrupt through sin and infirmity. Thus, we must be stripped of all trust in our own righteousness. For, from the greatest to the least of us, we are all condemned. If we seek justification by the law, we are greatly deceived – we will never find it.

Now we can understand much more clearly the truth of

what I have been saying concerning the Lord Jesus Christ as a refuge for those who are convinced of their spiritual need. This means that the only real preparation for belief in Jesus Christ is to be touched with a real, vivid sense and awareness of our sins. This is why Christ said: 'Come unto me, all ye that labour and are heavy laden, and I will give you rest . . . and ye shall find rest unto your souls' (*Matt.* 11:28–29). Elsewhere, the Scripture clearly says that he was sent 'to preach good tidings unto the meek . . . to proclaim liberty to the captives, and the opening of the prison to them that are bound' (*Isa.* 61:1). Therefore, those who take pleasure in their sins will never come to the Lord Jesus Christ. They may boast that they have faith, for many mockers of God profane this word, holy as it is. Everyone wishes to be thought of as a Christian, and no matter how depraved they are, they will say that they believe as much as any other. But when a man speaks in this manner, it is evidence enough that he has not one drop of faith. When true believers say, 'I believe', they express it in great weakness, knowing that had not God taken pity on them, even the little they had would have been taken from them. Those who loudly boast that they have complete faith are nothing but dogs and swine, who have never once tasted true religion nor the fear of God. The term 'faith' will always be shamefully defiled by these dogs, who do nothing other than mock God. They cannot discern between good and evil, and are so foolish as to wallow in their own sins. Take a drunkard, for example, who is past shame; after drinking to excess, he longs to remain in his intoxicated state. Then there are the whoremongers, perjurers, blasphemers, and suchlike – all of whom claim to have faith; but for all that, it is certain that they are not ready to meet the Lord Jesus Christ. Why not? Because they do not realise that they can only be justified by grace. Let us remember, however, that to be thoroughly persuaded that we cannot be justified by the law, we must set God before us on his judgment throne and summon ourselves before him every morning and evening, knowing that we must give an account of our whole lives. Also, we must realise that we would be sent to the pit a hundred thousand times if God did not pity us and raise us up in his infinite mercy. Then we will know that we cannot be justified by the law, for we are all under condemnation every time we compare ourselves with God. We need to have such fear, that we cannot find rest until the Lord Jesus Christ has saved us. See, therefore, how good it is for us to be heavy laden, that is to say, to hate our sins and to be in such anguish over them that we feel surrounded by the pains of death, so that we seek God in order that he might ease us of our burden. We must, however, seek him in the knowledge that we cannot obtain salvation, full or in part, unless it is granted to us as a gift. Paul is not saying that we may find something of what we lack in Jesus Christ, and supply the rest ourselves. He says we cannot be counted righteous through our own merits, or works, but only through faith.

Let us, therefore, understand that there is no salvation whatsoever outside of Jesus Christ, for he is the beginning and the end of faith, and he is all in all. Let us continue in humility, knowing that we can only bring condemnation upon ourselves; therefore, we need to find all that pertains to salvation in the pure and free mercy of God. We must be able to say that we are saved through faith. God the Father has appointed his Son the Lord Jesus Christ that he might be both the author and finisher of our salvation. We are to deny ourselves and give ourselves to him wholly and completely, that all the praise might belong to him.

Now let us fall before the majesty of our great God, acknowledging our sins, and asking that he would make us increasingly aware of them, that we may hate them more and more, and grow in repentance (a grace that we need to exercise all our lives). May we learn so to magnify his grace, as it is shown to us in the Lord Jesus Christ, that we might be completely taken up with it; and may we not only do so with our lips, but place our entire trust in him. May we grow in that trust until we are gathered up into our eternal home, where we shall receive faith's reward. May he not only grant this grace to us, but to all peoples, etc.

13

Dead to the Law, Alive to God

> *But if, while we seek to be justified by Christ, we ourselves also are found sinners, is therefore Christ the minister of sin? God forbid. For if I build again the things which I destroyed, I make myself a transgressor. For I through the law am dead to the law, that I might live unto God. I am crucified with Christ: nevertheless I live; yet not I, but Christ liveth in me: and the life which I now live in the flesh I live by the faith of the Son of God, who loved me, and gave himself for me* (Gal. 2:17–20).

Earlier on, we saw Paul casting down all pride and trust in man's works and merits, by saying that the Jews, who enjoyed far greater privileges than others, could only be acceptable to God through faith in the gospel. It may well have seemed that the Jews possessed some righteousness in themselves which made them acceptable to God, since they had been given the law and the promise that whoever fulfils the commandments will 'live in them' (*Lev.* 18:5). It may well have seemed, then, that the Jews, considered in their own persons apart from the Lord Jesus Christ, could be judged righteous in God's sight – if they were not, then what purpose had the law served? Yet, when they came to the Lord Jesus Christ, they acknowledged that they were poor, miserable, condemned sinners. Therefore, it would appear that Jesus Christ had brought sin with him, for previously the Jews were seen as the children of God; indeed, they bore a physical sign of separation to God, and to them it was said, 'Thou art an holy people unto the Lord thy God' (*Deut.* 7:6). Thus, when we see them calling themselves wretched and accursed sinners, whose only refuge is in the grace of the Lord Jesus Christ, we might assume that it was Jesus Christ who brought sin into the world! Truly, men are likely to judge the situation in this way, but how foolish and how wrong they are! We must be absolutely clear that the Lord Jesus Christ was not the minister of sin; rather, he exposed it!

However much the Jews exercised themselves to keep the law, its function was to convince them to an ever-increasing extent that God could only be merciful to them by means of a Redeemer. Although they lived sober and chaste lives, even this was a result of grace: we must never attribute to man what does not rightfully belong to him. This is to strip God of his honour. If the Jews, led by the Holy Spirit, had some desire to live holy lives, we must not think that God owed them a reward in return. On the contrary, they were all the more indebted to God. Furthermore, we must remember that there has never been a man so perfect as to be above reproach (as we will see more fully later). Thus, we are forced to conclude that the Jews could not have been so righteous as to have no need of mercy. Their salvation was based upon the remission of their sins. Some Jews believed that the ceremonies could make them holy, as do many hypocrites today, who use ceremonies as a cloak of holiness. However, the Jews were, without question, more worthy of damnation than others. How is this? Well, without the law, as Paul says in the fifth chapter to the Romans, sin is not imputed (*Rom.* 5:13). When there is no summons to stand before God on his judgment throne, men fall asleep and are content to live in their sins. Whereas the poor Gentiles might have had some defence or excuse, or at the very least, were not as guilty before God, the Jews were doubly guilty by comparison: they had to offer sacrifices which visibly displayed that they were worthy of eternal death. Therefore, in the second chapter of Colossians and the fourteenth verse, Paul shows us that the ordinances of the law make us even more accountable to God. A debtor may not be condemned by the law of the land, and may not have done anything worthy of being brought before a judge. He may not have been made to give a written guarantee of repayment sealed with his own hand, but nevertheless, he is still bound, in terms of his conscience, to pay the debt. Likewise the Gentiles, although they have no 'handwriting of ordinances' against them, are still worthy of death. But what of the man who is condemned by the law of the land, whose debt has been recorded for all to see – what of him? There is no escape for him – he must pay the debt immediately. The Jews were in this same position. Their ceremonial washings when they entered the temple, or their own houses, along with other places, were a means of expressing that they were full of filth within. Again, when they killed animals, and watched while they were slain, they beheld a vivid picture of the death they deserved and of their cursed state. The brute beasts themselves and the blood which they shed could never have cleansed them; nor could the element of water have cleansed their souls. So then, their washing would have been meaningless had it not pointed to the spiritual cleansing which we receive in the Lord Jesus Christ. What a terrible abuse it is to believe that it is the water which cleanses us when we are baptised! The ordinance should rather point us to the blood of our Lord Jesus Christ.

Let us, therefore, conclude that although the Jews were trained in the law, this counted against them because, in terms of the judgment of God and eternal death, they were bound with tighter cords than the heathen. Thus, it is clear that Jesus Christ did not come to minister sin, but rather to expose it. For the Jews thought they could hide behind the cloak of ceremonies, these rendering them acceptable to God. They considered all other nations to be unclean; everyone else was polluted but they were holy. This was their boast, but when the Lord Jesus Christ came, he set them straight, by teaching them that they ought to have been an example to others of seeking salvation apart from works. He showed them their need to come to him humbly, confessing that they were under God's curse. Hence, the Lord Jesus Christ revealed the evil that had previously been concealed; in the same way that the sick do not always realise that they have an illness which will eventually prove fatal until the doctor reveals it. The doctor can do nothing to cure the illness until he explores what was previously unknown by the patient. In the same way, our Lord Jesus Christ had to declare that the Jews were in a state of poverty, that they might turn to him and confess their unworthiness. He taught that no other refuge could be found but in the mercy of God alone. This is a brief summary of the way in which we can answer the questions and difficulties which arise from Paul's words here.

* * *

Today, there are many who believe they are serving God and will be in paradise because they deserve it, and yet when we speak to such about the gospel, they become angry. You see, pride has already firmly shut the door. 'What!', they say, 'Do you mean that I have been wasting my time although I have been so devout all my life?' What about the man who attends Mass once or twice, mutters the prayers, makes a pilgrimage, and refuses to withhold his money and substance, but spends it all on pardons, indulgences and suchlike? If we were to tell him that we are all wretched, miserable creatures and that we can depend upon nothing but the grace of the Lord Jesus Christ – that everything we desire to bring to God is filthy and abominable in his sight, he would fly into a rage. He would say: 'Is it possible for God to ignore all the pains I have gone to in order to serve him? Surely it will all be taken into account and will lead to my salvation.' These people will happily accuse God, and blaspheme openly by protesting that their works must be taken into consideration! Although such hypocrites are aware of great sins in themselves, they seek to hide all this beneath their cloaks. This is how they proceed: one says, 'I wore a hair shirt!'. Another says, 'I rose at midnight in order to worship God!'. Still another says, 'I abstained from eating meat!'. And someone else says, 'I shut myself away in a convent, which was like being in a prison – in fact, I died to the world; and are you telling me that all this is to no avail and that God will not take it into account?'.

Such murmurings as these can be heard daily. But will such words help them to achieve what they seek? For if they were really to examine what they are, they would find that all that they have done is like a covering of paint. It is like a man who cannot be bothered to rebuild his house – he leaves the cracks there, but he fills them so that they no longer show and then paints over them. In reality, it has simply been whitewashed. Our Lord Jesus Christ speaks similarly against hypocrites who are like whitewashed sepulchres (*Matt.* 23:27). However, God is not concerned with the outward appearance, as it says in the first book of Samuel, for he searches the hearts and uncovers the hidden truth (*1 Sam.* 16:7). The same is recorded in the fifth chapter of Jeremiah and the third verse. Since this is so, all those who trust in their own devotions to save them may appear good to men, but it all amounts to no more than self-deception in the eyes of God. As soon as God blows upon their paint and make-up, it peels off. Prostitutes may take great pains to apply their make-up correctly, but when the sun shines upon them it develops a horrid crust which flakes off to reveal their shameful ugliness. The same will happen to all such hypocrites who seek to colour their true nature in God's sight – their wickedness will inevitably be revealed. Let us, therefore, understand that the Lord Jesus Christ (though he condemned the world by showing that we can only be saved through the free grace of God the Father, offered and imparted to us) does not minister sin. Sin is already within us; he simply exposes and declares it, that we might feel convicted and that all our pride might be cast into the dust. We need to be thus humbled before we can make a true confession that we are lost and acknowledge that the only remedy is to have the infinite treasure of God's mercy poured upon us. Then, indeed, all mouths will be silenced and men will no longer deceive themselves with the thought that they are righteous.

Paul uses a twofold answer to prove that Christ is not the minister of sin. But before this develops, he sets down a very direct response: 'God forbid'. This shows that he viewed it as a terrible blasphemy to suggest that the Lord Jesus Christ is to blame for our sins. He then adds, 'For if I build again the things which I destroyed, I make myself a transgressor.' In saying this, he draws us back to the plain teaching of the gospel. We preach concerning the reason why God sent his only Son: he came to bring us righteousness and to do away with sin, which held us in bondage until we were delivered and set free by the grace which the Son of God bought for us through his sufferings and death. Seeing this is so, we can understand plainly that the Lord Jesus Christ did not minister sin, as indeed it says in the epistle of John – he came to destroy sin – and we know this to be the case (*1 John* 3:8). For what does gospel doctrine teach us, but that we are full of iniquity and that we need to be cleansed by the One who was appointed to be a Lamb without blemish, and who has also brought us the Spirit of holiness? Those who are cut off from Jesus Christ are under his curse; they are steeped in their sins. Jesus Christ is the only One who can cleanse and purify them because he has shed his blood for the purpose of cleansing sin. Also, he has brought us the Spirit through whom we are renewed, to make us devoted to the service of God, and to restore God's image in us, enabling us to walk in truth and uprightness.

Having seen this, it is clear that the Lord Jesus Christ is not the minister of sin. Why not? Well, let us think for a moment of what we are – there is an abyss of iniquity in the entire human race. Our Lord Jesus Christ came to bring us the remedy. Sin was already in the world, but Jesus Christ revealed it. What harm is done by the physician in the letting of blood? Imagine a poor man who has a disease which no-one can perceive. His blood is completely diseased but no-one is aware of it because that blood remains within his veins. If he allows the physician to let his blood, he will discover that it is not blood at all, but is full of infection. What filth flows from a man's body when he allows it to be cleansed and purged of disease! But can he blame the doctor for it, or the treatment that he was given? No, for it is well known that such a remedy is applied only to those bodies which were already half-rotten. Our Lord Jesus Christ likewise by the light of his gospel exposes our spiritual diseases, the pollution and filth within which is detested by God, and of which we are ashamed. If, therefore, he cleanses us from all this, can we blame or reproach him in any way? What ingratitude this is! Thus, Paul's response is sufficient to beat back the blasphemies and murmurings of the enemies of the gospel – those who are puffed up with pride and refuse to be tamed. It does not matter what they claim about their own righteousness or holiness – it will still be found that they are full of uncleanness, which they cannot perceive (although it is, in one sense, continually making itself apparent!). This is the first point.

Secondly, Paul adds a greater, though perhaps simpler, statement when he says, 'For I through the law am dead to the law, that I might live unto God. I am crucified with Christ.' When he says he is dead to the law through the law, he is mocking those who claimed to be justified by its observance. We have already said that all his disputing and arguing was aimed at such folk. They were seducers, who sought to mix Jesus Christ with the law of Moses in order to obtain justification. The Lord Jesus Christ is not against the law, for his gospel is promised in the law, as it says in the first chapter to the Romans, and the second verse. Nevertheless, when it comes to justification (that is to say, how men are made acceptable to God and counted as innocent, pure and spotless), then the law must be separated from the Lord Jesus Christ. Why is this? The law on its own brings a curse, but Jesus Christ brings the remedy. These enemies of the gospel with whom Paul quarrels made others believe that, although we are justified by the Lord Jesus Christ, we must add certain ceremonies as a vital part of our salvation. They claimed they could merit God's grace and favour through such means. Paul rejects all of this and points to Jesus Christ alone. He says that we must not seek another means of salvation but, instead, rest content with grace, giving no place to the law. He is showing us here that he did not die through the gospel. It is as if he were saying, 'You would have me believe that I can win God's favour through the law. But I tell you the opposite, that it was not the gospel which condemned me; it was not the gospel which revealed to me my filthiness, and made me ashamed; it was not the gospel which took away from me all hope of salvation. It was the law that told me that I was actually dead, and that I was damnable in God's sight, lost and condemned. This awareness proceeded from nothing else but the law itself, and you would have me seek my justification in that very place. It is much like forcing me to take some poison in order to be nourished!' Not that evil can be imputed to the law, for this would be to dishonour God who gave it. Yet, however the case stands, due to the corruption within us, the law cannot but kill us. This truth we saw in Second Corinthians (*2 Cor. 3:7*), and Paul gives a fuller exposition in the seventh chapter to the Romans and the ninth verse. In this latter passage, Paul declares that when men think they are alive (that is, convince themselves that they are righteous and that they are in God's favour), it is a sign that the law is dead to them. In other words, its convicting power is not applied to them with any strength. For why was the law given? To set before us a rule for correct living, and that rule is the righteousness that God accepts. This is the first reason. Secondly, the law was given to act like a mirror in order that we might see our wickedness, our blemishes, our stains, our pollutions, our great iniquities, and to sink us into despair. Before we know the law, we cannot see any of this; for we do not know ourselves, nor the evil within us. However, when God sets before us what he requires and when we really understand it, we feel powerless and at our wits' end. If we think we are alive, and foolishly imagine that we are righteous and will win paradise by our good works, then the law is dead to us. It is as if we have trodden it underfoot and buried it. If, on the other hand, God gives the law power in our lives and we are touched by it, then the law is alive to us but we ourselves die, for it is a sword which thrusts us through to the heart. We must, indeed, have received this mortal wound if we have really understood what the law contains. This is what Paul refers to in the above passage.

As part of his argument, Paul says: 'I through the law am dead to the law . . .'. In effect, he is saying, 'Do not accuse the gospel of being the cause of our condemnation, as if it was when we came to know the grace of the Lord Jesus Christ that we first became the objects of God's curse – absolutely not! It is the law that will kill us, when it fulfils its true role and when we understand it as we should. What is more, we would have remained in the depths of despair, had not the Lord Jesus Christ stretched out his hand to raise us up. This is how I am dead through the law: I can have no life, I can have no assurance of salvation, I can have no comfort, or rest, or happiness. In short, there is nothing in the law to draw me closer to God. Quite the opposite: it rejects me, it turns me away, it banishes me from the kingdom of heaven, it cuts me off from all hope of salvation, it describes me as a poor, miserable, accursed creature. Indeed, it sends me into the depths of hell. This would have been my portion if I had remained under the law.' Paul is speaking here of himself rather than any other, so that his words might be better received because uttered by a man of such experience.

He speaks of himself in this same vein in the passage to the Romans we have already referred to (*Rom.* 7:9). There, he does not choose this or that person as an example, but says, 'For I was alive without the law once'. He was a Pharisee, and had a reputation for being a holy man, in fact, one of the most excellent men in Judaea, a mirror image of perfection, a little angel! 'I was alive then,' he says, 'but a complete hypocrite!' For what he believed was nonsense, and he had become so puffed up with pride that he despised Jesus Christ. This is the state of blindness in which Paul confesses himself to have been at the time (*Rom.* 7:8). He admits later that he did not even understand what it meant when he heard 'Thou shalt not covet'. It might be thought strange that a man who not only went to school, but was one of the best teachers, and was very zealous, could say that he was so dull that he did not know his own faults. Yet, Paul tells us this was so. He says that he was only concerned with outward righteousness, and appearing blameless before men who were ignorant of the evil within him. But when he understood what those words meant ('Thou shalt not covet'), he knew then that God judges man's thoughts and desires. The sting is in the tail (as the proverb says) – in other words it is the last commandment which reveals the depth of God's scrutiny. It is so deep and so keen that none of us can find acceptance in his sight. It is written in the law: 'Thou shalt not have strange gods; thou shalt not make an image and worship it; thou shalt not take the name of the Lord thy God in vain; Remember to sanctify the Sabbath day; Honour thy father and thy mother; thou shalt not kill; thou shalt not commit adultery; thou shalt not steal', etc. (*Exod.* 20:3–17). This is all very well, we think; it means I must abstain from all sexual immorality, violence and extortion, deceit and robbery. I must live soberly. It means I must also abstain from all blasphemy, and that I must honour God. All this we readily concede. However, there is a hidden corner which we do not notice and that is the secret sin of covetousness. True enough, the extent of our covetousness will not be apparent to others, but nevertheless, it is a more venomous serpent than the rest. By this last concluding commandment, God comes to search out all that is in man. This commandment, 'Thou shalt not covet', is given that we might examine what is hidden, and it will pierce to the dividing asunder of joints and marrow. Paul confesses that he did not know the meaning of sin until he had understood this last commandment. Here he does not attribute this knowledge to the gospel, but to the law.

Let us, therefore, learn from this passage that those who deceive themselves into thinking they have some personal merit have never understood the law or its function. I include the so-called great doctors who are held in such high esteem. Indeed, this applies to Papists, for those who are considered to be the pillars of the church, though they have studied theology, are ignorant of the least word of the law of God, regarding its application and proper use. They are nothing more than hypocrites, seeking to appease God's wrath with some toy or other as if he were a tiny baby. They do but play with him; yet, at the same time, are so self-opinionated that they cannot bear to be condemned. If a man tells them they must seek salvation in Jesus Christ, they say, 'Yes, but what about our own free will? What, then, is the use of our own merits and satisfactions for sin?' To their way of thinking, it were better to pluck the sun out of the sky, yes, and God from his throne also, than to deprive man of his dignity and of the merits which he plans to bring before God. Yet they are, without a shadow of a doubt, full of filth within. It is obvious that there is no fear of God to be found in their lives, no uprightness, no righteousness, nor any other virtue. They are full of pride, indeed, they are puffed up with it to the point of bursting; they are full of envy, vengeance and all immorality. Yet, they would have God to be indebted to them, which serves to prove that they have never known the law. So then, when our Lord teaches us how we should live in this world, let us always compare his doctrine with our lives, and then we shall understand the law and its perfection. In ourselves, there exists nothing more than horrible confusion, and hell itself is prepared for such sinners. Since this is the case, it should be easy for us to leave all notions that we held previously about individual merit, and cast them away, remaining silent before God as though dead, devoid of breath, because we have realised that we cannot approach God. He would just thunder against us if we came to him imagining that we deserve his mercy. This is how we are to understand that the law kills.

If we have experienced such a death, that is, if we have already been truly humbled and brought low, Paul's next statement applies to us: 'I am crucified with Christ: nevertheless I live'. Paul teaches that our Lord Jesus Christ not only brings remission of sins, but also sanctifies and renews us by the Holy Spirit. Then (although we were previously full of rebellion against God), we become devoted to his service and to pleasing him. In order to understand more clearly what Paul is teaching, we need to remember that there are two main benefits applied to us through the grace of the Lord Jesus Christ. One is remission of sins, which gives us assurance of salvation and peace of conscience; if this is our foundation, we may call God our Father. What is it that gives us the boldness to lift up our eyes to heaven and call him our Father? And what is it that gives us the boldness to proclaim that we are fellow-servants with the angels? It is the fact that our sins are no longer imputed to us, since we continually resort to the cleansing obtained for us by the sufferings and death of the Lord Jesus Christ. This is how we are justified: God overlooks our unworthiness and accepts us because he sees the obedience of the Lord Jesus Christ, through whom all our transgressions are blotted out. This is the first benefit that comes to us directly from the Lord Jesus Christ. But there is also a second. Although by nature we are perverse and our free will (as the Papists call it) is completely wild, men still believe in their own worth. This is despite the fact that they are full of malice, with twisted, sinful and corrupt personalities. Although, I say, we are in such a condition, the Lord Jesus Christ grants us grace so that we may seek what is good, and detest our sins. For as long as we remain in our sinful state, we seem to boast and revel in our fleshliness. But when once we have tasted the inestimable love of our God, and known the Lord Jesus Christ, we become so affected by his Holy Spirit that we condemn evil and seek to draw nearer to God in conformity to his holy will. This is, therefore, the second benefit. Even though we seem to be limping along the pathway, we are, nevertheless, growing daily in the knowledge of our imperfections and weaknesses. The Holy Spirit leads us in this way, and he makes it our main aim to reject what is sinful and fleshly and seek, rather, to glorify God and truly obey him in every aspect of our lives. This, then, is the second gift that the Lord Jesus Christ bestows upon us. The two things are inseparably joined together, just as the brightness of the sun cannot be separated from its heat. The remission of our sins and our justification are inseparable from the regenerative work of the Spirit of sanctification. These two benefits are thus linked together. When we say that the sun is hot, it will most likely be shining at the same time, yet the brilliance of the sun is not the same as its heat. Likewise, when we say that we have been justified through the remission of our sins, it does not mean that Jesus Christ will then allow us to mock or despise him. No, we must be truly cleansed, and learn to turn our backs on this world and even upon ourselves in order to cleave to him in true obedience.

Whatever we may say, the words of Paul in this text will always be found to be true. He says he has been crucified with Christ so that he might live unto God. If, therefore, any accuse the gospel of creating licence to do evil and to sin, we will always have this answer for such people: 'What! It is by the law that we die – because we read in it that we are accursed. The law plunges us into the depths of despair. In the gospel, we are to be crucified, yet, though the gospel speaks of a kind of death, even this is life-giving! It brings me life. As long as men live for themselves, they are dead to God – they are like rotten, corrupt corpses. But if they die to themselves, they live to God.' This is why Paul speaks of living sacrifices to God in the twelfth chapter to the Romans, verse one, showing us that we must be transformed. We must turn away from worldly wisdom and our human wills in order to offer God service that he will find acceptable. He says, 'Present your bodies a living sacrifice . . .'. In the law, there will always be the kind of death that leaves us in the depths of hell, but the death spoken of in the gospel imparts life. How is this so? Well, we are crucified with Jesus Christ so that we may live to God. This means that our old man (as Paul says in the sixth chapter to the Romans, and the sixth verse), or what we are by nature, is expelled little by little (and not all on the first day). Yet, though the progress may be slow, we can be sure that the Lord Jesus Christ is putting to death all that is worldly and fleshly in us, because we are no longer given over to this world. Indeed, we have discovered what a misery it is to be settled here below and we have realised that only by cleaving to God can true happiness be found. This is what it means to be crucified with the Lord Jesus Christ. But what does this crucifixion bring? Yes, it does involve dying, but this death will bring us life – unlike the death we experience under the sentence of the law. Thus, we have now seen something of the correct sense of this passage and we have understood Paul's true intentions in writing these words.

Today, when the enemies of the truth blaspheme against the gospel, we are provided with an answer in this passage that will silence them. If they persist and continue to bark like dogs, at least we know that whatever else they may do, they cannot bite! When we preach that we are justified through the free grace of God, what do the Papists say? They say, 'You only preach that so that you can loose the reins on your lusts, without any remorse of conscience or scruples, and everyone can do as he pleases!' This is a common blasphemy amongst the Papists. They realise that they cannot bind us by their traditions because we know them to be tyrants that have usurped God's rightful place. We have been set free by the Lord Jesus Christ so that, regarding the spiritual government of our souls, we are no longer bound by what men say we ought to do. 'You see,' they say, 'you only desire to live in pleasure and to live a loose life.' Truly, we can easily respond to this kind of statement. For the doctrine that we hold does not stir up men's lusts, nor does it give them licence or liberty in the wrong sense – quite the opposite. Yet, whatever else we say, we must certainly make this plain: if we remain in the mire with the Papists, we can expect nothing less than death. For were they not fast asleep with their senses completely dulled, they would most certainly be racked with anxiety and remorse, and would see that they are resting upon the wrong foundation. Yet, they are so blinded by their ignorance that they cannot understand anything of the judgment and justice of God. For our part, we know that the Lord Jesus Christ has obtained liberty for us, and we can be sure of our own salvation because God has freely forgiven us all our sins. We have already felt the power of the Holy Spirit drawing us to God, and we have been put to death so that we may now live unto him; therefore, we can go forward with a cheerful and courageous heart. Although by nature we have many weaknesses and cannot forget our many imperfections, we have no doubt that God will accept us. The Papists, on the other hand, cannot possess one single good desire to serve God; they only believe their case to be otherwise because they are bewitched by false assurance. What do I mean? They trust in their own merits as a way of earning God's favour. But what is the truth of the matter? Imagine, if they could bring a hundred times more merit to God than they now possess, and if God should lead them by his Holy Spirit to value the gospel (even though it were half the appreciation it deserves) – what then? They would still fall very far short of discharging their duty, even the hundredth part of it. Besides, we know that the things which they do are ridiculous! The law of God means almost nothing to them – indeed, they spend their time inventing their own rules! But now let us imagine that they were to endeavour to walk in the fear of God and that they were to learn to do the things that God commands them. Even then, they could not boast that they had reached the perfect righteousness that God requires of them. Even if they were to torment themselves to the greatest degree, how would they be able to serve God with courage and cheerfulness unless they knew that, despite their unworthiness, they were acceptable to God?

As for ourselves, we can serve God freely and boldly, even though our conscience accuses us and we know we are full of sin within. How is this possible? Well, we are not grounded upon our own merits, but purely upon the mercy of God. Because of this, we know that God accepts our works, although there is much that is wrong with them. We know that we have found acceptance with him, despite our many sins and blemishes. This is why he says, by the mouth of the prophet, that he will receive the service we render as a father accepts that of his child (*Mal.* 1:6). Picture a child who is seeking to obey his father: when his father asks him to do something, he will accept what the child does, even though the child may not understand what he is doing. The child may even break something in the process, and yet the father will not fret about the broken object when he sees his child's affection and willingness to obey. But if a man hires a servant, he will expect him to perform his task perfectly. Why? Because he is going to receive wages, and, therefore, he cannot afford to ruin what has been committed to his hands. If the task is not done well, the master will not be content with it. Our Lord, speaking of the days of gospel grace, says that he will accept our service, just as a father accepts the obedience of his child, even if all that is done is of no value. That is to say, he does not accept it because it is perfect, for it is not, but he bears with us out of his abundant mercy. He shows himself to be so bountiful and kind to us by accepting what we do as if it were fully pleasing to him, although there is no inherent merit or worth in our works at all. Thus, we can have the freedom and the courage to serve God; we can know that God will bless all that we do for him because whatever is wrong with our offerings is washed away in the blood of the Lord Jesus Christ.

However, although God is pitiful and has shown us abundant mercy, we must realise that we are not free to bolt, take the bit between our teeth and play the horse that has broken loose – not at all! On the contrary, he acts in this way in order that the sword of his Word should pierce our hearts, searching us until we are truly humbled and seek pardon from God. The Papists hinder people from approaching God, saying, 'Wretched creature, what do you think you are doing? How do you know whether God loves you or not?' We do not have any such qualms! Let us have nothing to do with this teaching. We are convinced that God regards us with pity and accepts our works – not because of their worth or merit but because we are joined to the Lord Jesus Christ. Now we have understood what Paul is saying here. We have also seen that this teaching was not only for those days; it is as necessary and useful today as ever before. For the enemies of God still fight against the gospel and spew out their blasphemies.

We must have the means to resist them; and not them only but also Satan, who since time began has craftily sought to make men believe that they can obtain life by themselves, through their own merits. He would have us sleep this sleep of death also. Let us be certain of this fact: it is better to die to the law than to live under it, for if God were to enter into account with us, we would all be lost and damned. If this is our state, let us rather choose to suffer to be crucified with the Lord Jesus Christ. If, however, we have already been reconciled to God the Father by the sacrifice Christ offered, let us be ruled by his Holy Spirit. May he renew us and enable us to truly live for God, and die to ourselves, leaving behind all pride in our own righteousness. May he help us to strive against the lusts of our flesh and to die to the world more and more.

Now let us fall before the majesty of our great God, acknowledging our faults, and praying that he would make us increasingly aware of them. May we be delivered from the filthiness in which we stand by nature, and be joined, instead, to the Lord Jesus Christ. May he draw us to God the Father and lead us ever closer to him until we are fully united forever. Thus, we all say, Almighty God, and our heavenly Father, etc.

14

Redemption by the Son of God

> *I am crucified with Christ: nevertheless I live; yet not I, but Christ liveth in me: and the life which I now live in the flesh I live by the faith of the Son of God, who loved me, and gave himself for me. I do not frustrate the grace of God: for if righteousness come by the law, then Christ is dead in vain* (Gal. 2:20–21).

This morning, we saw that when God united us to the body of the Lord Jesus Christ, he was calling each of us to be a living sacrifice. He did not wish us to remain in our natural state of death; rather, his design was that we should enjoy eternal life. Having established this, the apostle proceeds to magnify God's grace when he says, '. . . nevertheless I live; yet not I, but Christ liveth in me'. Again, he is implying that by nature we live in a cursed state. Therefore, all the good things that are showered upon us must be attributed to God's hand, and he must receive all the praise. Indeed, true faith always expresses itself by humility. It makes a man willing to count himself nothing, whilst attributing all praise to God. It would seem strange if a believer, who is a mere mortal, were to praise himself because Jesus Christ lives in him! Our life here below is subject to many infirmities. Are we, therefore, merely speculating when we say that Jesus Christ lives in us? Not at all! Paul points us to faith, and says that although our physical life appears to be crumbling because we are subject to all the afflictions of this world, yet faith has brought us new life. Christ gives us eternal life; believers, therefore, cannot be judged by their physical state or appearance; we need to look beyond outward things. The life which our Lord Jesus Christ bestows upon us is like hidden treasure; we can only understand it by faith, which is greater than anything that this world can bestow. It means that we hope for things as yet unseen and hidden from view. The way to glorify God is by esteeming his Word and his promises so highly that nothing we see in this world might hinder us from seeking him, reaching out to him, and desiring him with all our hearts.

So then, the first thing we have gleaned from this passage is that a man has not properly understood the gospel until he attributes all good gifts to the Lord Jesus Christ. Even if we were to reserve for ourselves the tiniest portion of praise, we would display great ingratitude towards God by demeaning his grace. We deserve to be stripped of such arrogance. Indeed, we are taught here that all who trust in their own merits are full of pride and deadly enemies to the glory of God. Of course, they would not admit this with their own mouths, but, nevertheless, the fact remains that all such hypocrites, thinking they will be justified because of their own worthiness, are seeking to array themselves with God's feathers. Besides, is not humility one of the principal virtues of a true believer? What possible value is his 'merit'? When believers humble themselves, it is not to win God's favour, as if they then deserved it; rather, it is to prove that there is nothing in them of which they may boast, since they have received all from the bountiful hand of God. Humility is the only response we should have towards a God who has been so kind to us, and who has given everything for our sake. Should we not seek to acknowledge just how much we owe?

This is the teaching of Paul in this passage, but the second point he makes needs some explanation. He says, '. . . the life which I now live in the flesh I live by the faith of the Son of God'. The expression 'in the flesh' used in the text signifies our earthly pilgrimage in this fleeting life. When Paul speaks of the flesh in the eighth chapter to the Romans, verse thirteen, he is referring to being given over to evil lusts, like those who have no fear of God, and who grant themselves complete liberty. It is those who follow their own natural instincts like brute beasts who are living 'in the flesh'. However, in this verse, Paul is simply using the expression to draw a contrast between our physical life and the spiritual life which we possess through faith. How can a person distinguish between believer and unbeliever? Both eat and drink. True enough, one group eats and drinks in moderation, yet even some unbelievers can be quite temperate, and are not necessarily given to drunkenness or excess! Yes, at first glance it would seem that all of us have a common experience of life. Although believers may spend their time on earth clipping their wings, as it were, pining and languishing away, all men alike must face death. Thus, if we judge by appearances, there is no difference between them. It might, therefore, seem to some that those who believe in Jesus Christ are wasting both time and energy. But they do not receive the reward of faith on this earth; even though God has called them to higher things, their life here appears to be the same as that of everyone else, for we must all alike face death.

How, then, do we know for sure that Jesus Christ lives within us? Well, he does, of course, but this fact is hidden from the world. Since Paul keeps bringing us back to the subject of faith, it is our present task to consider the nature of this faith. Faith is a belief in things which our minds cannot comprehend; faith is forsaking this world and seeking the kingdom of God; faith is esteem for the pure and simple Word which proceeds from the mouth of God, and disregard for what we see around us. If we do not have faith, we will not understand what Paul is teaching us in this passage; even if we have read it a hundred times over, we will be unable to explain the difference between life in the flesh and life by faith in the Lord Jesus Christ, or understand that Paul is referring to our outward condition when he speaks of 'the flesh'. Paul includes in his use of the expression 'in the flesh' all that pertains to this transitory life. But there is also an inward state which is hidden, which eagerly awaits that which we have been promised. For our outward man will certainly decline and decay little by little until it is completely destroyed. Even the children of God, whose youth God has promised to renew (*Psa.* 103:5), and for whom he has reserved a new set of feathers, as it were, are sometimes so unwell that we must pity them. Indeed, even the most robust people in this world grow old and die. Seeing this is so, what advantage do we have over unbelievers? The difference is not apparent to the eye, for it concerns the inner man which is hidden from view. What did Paul mean when he used this expression, 'the inner man'? He was referring to the work of the Holy Spirit within us, whereby we are assured of an eternal home in heaven, prepared for us. Here below, we are but strangers passing through the land, but we have an enduring inheritance which will never be taken from us. Paul says 'the inner man is renewed' (*2 Cor.* 4:16), whereas our bodies are decaying! Yet, even as believers see their bodies decline, they are reminded and encouraged to look above! Indeed, even those of us who are strong and full of vigour grow weary and waste away. This is why we need to be brought under the control of our Lord, so that we may be renewed in the midst of the process of decay. I suggest that we need to suffer affliction in order to strengthen our hope of eternal life, and in order to purify us and enable us to see clearly what would otherwise be obscure.

Take gold or silver, for example, which decreases in volume as soon as it is passed through the furnace. You have a large lump of metal, then you throw it into the fire, and when you take it out, there is but a small amount remaining! However, if it were not treated in this way, gold would be useless, and the same applies to silver. How apt this is as a picture of ourselves – we cannot be renewed and granted entrance to the kingdom of God unless we have first died. We will always have within us the principle of decay which will affect our bodies, but we must not be wholly concerned with what we see outwardly. Our earthly life is but a shadow, but smoke which floats past and then vanishes. However, we are, nonetheless, renewed inwardly. This experience is not common to all. Unbelievers may recognise their weaknesses, and be forced to feel the advance of death, especially when they reach old age. They know that they could be blown over by not so much as one breath. This makes them furious, and causes them virtually to despise both God and nature. Whatever else may be said of them, they are perishing without being inwardly renewed. For a grain of wheat will die, but having no roots will produce no fruit. Another grain may also perish, yet produce fruit in its season because it was planted in good soil and took root (*John* 12:24). In the same way, believers will grow old and their bodies will decay, yet they will be renewed and will receive new strength. How? They will perish in this world, only to be restored and renewed in their heavenly home. Unbelievers, in like manner, will leave this world; they will perish; they will fade and pass away; but there will be no profit in it for they will not be restored in the life to come.

Now let us be clear that when Paul says we live 'by the faith of Jesus Christ', he is warning us that nothing in this world should be allowed to prevent us from resting upon the promises of God. When considering all that is around us in this earthly life, all we see is little more than death itself. But God has revealed in his Word that when our body is dead, we live on, because our Lord Jesus Christ was sent to suffer death to lead us from death to life. We honour God when we hold such promises dear. Indeed, this promise alone ought to suffice if we would only rest upon it and, as his faithful witnesses, set our seal that God is true (as John says – *John* 3:33). Otherwise, if we entertain doubts and uncertainties, the Word of God will have no authority or value in our lives. For if we are simply looking at things as they stand at present or at things around us, we will be unable to confess that God is faithful or that what his mouth has uttered is infallible. Furthermore, we will be turning our backs upon the Lord Jesus Christ, who is the guarantor of all that is contained in the Word of God. If we have his Word, we need no longer ask (as Moses says): 'Who shall go up for us to heaven? Or who shall descend into the deep? Who will go across the seas? The Word is in your mouth (he says) and in your heart' (*Deut.* 30:12–14; *Rom.* 10:6–8). We must be content with this. Our Lord Jesus Christ gives us further confirmation of this Word, and we know that he descended to the depths – that is, he suffered the curse which was due to our sins – and he became our pledge and Advocate before the judgment throne of God the Father. He subsequently ascended into heaven and took possession of the inheritance which is prepared for us; for he was raised up on high with our flesh and our nature upon him. Having such great assurances, we will be most miserable if we fail to trust and believe.

We must, therefore, always remember what is written, so that we do not set our hopes on those things which can be seen but on things which are imperceptible to our human senses (*2 Cor.* 4:18). This is why we must learn to live by faith in Jesus Christ. However miserable we may be in this life, however many grievances we may have to bear, or fatigue or anxieties, troubles and difficulties – as long as we remain faithful, we can enjoy perfect happiness through our afflictions if they are blessed and sanctified by God through the Lord Jesus Christ. Indeed, we know that all these things work together for our good, as it says in the eighth chapter to the Romans and the twenty-eighth verse. God makes his strength perfect in our weakness (as it says in another passage – *2 Cor.* 12:9). We do not mind suffering if it helps to engrave the promises of God upon our hearts, keeping us joyful and cheerful in the midst of problems and afflictions! We can boldly ignore the mockeries and slanders of unbelievers when they reproach us thus: 'You are but poor ploughmen, but you think you have become little kings because you believe the gospel! Poor wretches, where is the joy and felicity which you say God has promised you? Where is the inestimable treasure which you value so highly? You have nothing more than those whom you call God's enemies, those who are supposed to be damned and accursed!' None of this must be allowed to shake us, as I have said, for we must hold fast to our faith. Though we may not have eyes to see what has been promised to us in the gospel, we can be absolutely sure of it! Our life is hidden, as Paul says in the third chapter to the Colossians, verse three, and the time has not yet come for it to be revealed. Where is our life but with the Lord Jesus Christ? Yes, the kingdom of the Lord Jesus has been revealed, but only in part. We have only had a taste of what is to come. Things are in such turmoil and confusion in this world that we are unable simply to assess the benefits of our salvation by what is seen; is this not so? We must accept that our life is hidden until our Lord Jesus Christ returns. Then we will see that we were not mistaken to have trusted in him or to have accepted the teachings of his gospel.

How, then, can we live by faith? We are not to be delicate people, seeking a peaceful life where all our needs and wants are met. This would make us forget what God has promised us; we would disregard it, and thereby make shipwreck of our faith. Rather, let us take the mirror of the Word of God and consider things which surpass all our understanding, which are far away from this world and invisible to all. Let us lift our eyes above – not that we can be guided to heaven by our own intellect or wisdom, for these are insufficient. But let us look beyond this world, and leave behind the things of the present, in order to ponder over the promises of God for the future. Let us be patient in affliction and suffering, for these things will come to put us to the test, and it is our duty to grapple with them until we receive the fruit of victory, when we are taken to our heavenly resting place. This is what we are to remember concerning Paul's statement here, which at first sight seems obscure. However, we have easily proven that it is not obscure in the least, now that we have examined, on the one hand, our condition in this life, and, on the other hand, the nature of faith.

* * *

Furthermore, Paul adds that Jesus Christ 'loved me and gave himself for me'. This is a declaration which men have scarcely ever understood. The term 'faith' is often misunderstood because men do not consider what faith involves. In fact, almost everyone refers to himself as a believer, yet you would be hard pressed to find even one out of a hundred professors of Christianity with an ounce of faith! As I have said, they are not seeking to understand the true nature of faith. What a short word, yet one which trails a long tail behind it, as we see by this additional statement of Paul's! He tells us that he lives by faith because Jesus Christ loved him and gave himself for him. Surely it is the same for us. When we see the Son of God, the Lord of glory, the Head of all the angels, he by whom all things were created and are sustained, giving himself to die, even undergoing a shameful death and taking our curse upon him (for he was hanged on a tree, a death that is not only despicable to men, but also one which was pronounced accursed by the very mouth of God, *Deut.* 21:23) – what a price he paid to save us from death and to bring us righteousness and salvation! When we think about such things, do we not discover that we can overcome all the obstacles Satan puts in our way in order to drag us in the opposite direction, and to take away the assurance of faith? Surely, victory over all our temptations would be easy if we could only consider the value and significance of the death and passion of our Lord Jesus Christ? Paul is thus equipping us to persevere with undaunted faithfulness, despite all the darts which Satan hurls at us to prevent us from pursuing our course. If believers are hungry and thirsty, it may perplex them to think that they are promised they will inherit the earth, whilst they are actually perishing from lack of food and water. But if they think about the Lord Jesus Christ, their worries will vanish, for he will sweeten by his sweet promises of salvation all the bitterness they are tasting. When believers are in danger, or persecuted, or wronged or ill-treated, and help seems far away, they may be tempted to think, 'Where is God? He promised that he would dwell amongst us (*Exod.* 25:8), and that he would keep us as the apple of his eye (*Psa.* 17:8); he said he would be our shield and our fortress, and yet we are like a defenceless prey.' (Surely we too would be likely to think in this way?) But once we ponder the death and passion of our Lord Jesus Christ, we are forced to conclude that the Son of God did not offer up his life in vain. The Lord Jesus Christ did not spare his own life, but humbled himself even to the extent of suffering a shameful death, yes, even a cursed death; he endured the pains of hell for a time in order to free and acquit us, to the end that we might find grace at the judgment seat of God. Can it have been to no avail? Is this possible? Even if heaven and earth were to be thrust from their places, the resulting disorder would not match that of the chaos created by the possibility of the Son of God suffering in vain!

It is now clear to us what Paul means when he declares that he lived by faith. The death and passion of our Lord Jesus Christ should be at the centre of our lives, for it is this which has delivered us from the pit of death. However, we must not only meditate upon the Lord Jesus Christ dying in the weakness of his flesh, but upon the fact that he rose again through divine and heavenly power, as it says in another text (*Rom.* 1:4). But when we do speak about the death of our Lord Jesus Christ, it is important that we understand its significance: that is, that it was a sacrifice to reconcile God and man. It was payment for all our iniquities. It was obedience which atones for our wickedness. It was cleansing to wash away all our pollution and filth. Once we appreciate the efficacy of the death of the Son of God, and then look beyond it to the glory which awaits us, we cease to think that man will remain in his natural state, and we believe that he can live by faith in the gospel. For we know that a man will never be disappointed if he trusts in the promises contained in the gospel. Thus, this is what we are to learn from Paul in this text, where he speaks of the Son of God giving his life.

Notice, however, that he does not say that he gave his life for the world in general; this would be too vague. We each need to apply to ourselves individually the fruit of the death and passion of the Lord Jesus Christ. When we find it written that the Son of God was crucified, we must not simply imagine that it was for the redemption of the world. It is for each one of us as individuals, and in our own particular circumstances, to be joined to the Lord Jesus Christ and to reach the following conclusion: 'He suffered for my sake.' Just as when we are baptised, no-one else is baptised for us; it is not as if we can sprinkle everybody at once! Rather, each one is baptised separately in order to have a special application of water to himself, thereby revealing ourselves to be members of the Lord Jesus Christ. The same applies to the Lord's Supper: each person takes a portion to show that the Lord Jesus Christ is communicated to each one of us individually. Paul, therefore, speaks of it in this way so that we cannot approach the subject and be left cold or untouched. There are many ignorant folk who believe they are Christians, yet who are little more than wretched beasts. However, if we know that the one act which accomplished the redemption of the world applies to each one of us, then we can all personally say, 'The Son of God loved me so much, that he gave himself to die for me.'

Notice too that the word 'loved' is not superfluous either. Paul is seeking to magnify the grace of the Lord Jesus Christ. It is as if he were saying, 'We are most miserable if we do not accept the wonderful gift which is being offered to us, since God's only design in sending his Son was to relieve us from our miseries. Our Lord Jesus Christ emptied himself to such a degree that he did not spare his own life for our salvation. And why did he do this? Because of his love for us.' Since this is so, we must be very foolish indeed not to accept such a gift. God loved the world so much that he did not spare his only Son but delivered him up to death for us: this doctrine appears frequently in Holy Scripture (*John* 3:16). As Paul says in the fifth chapter to the Romans, verse eight, even when we were his mortal enemies, the Lord Jesus Christ commended his wonderful love by giving himself as a sacrifice to appease God's wrath against us, and to blot out our sins so that they would no longer be taken into account. This is a guarantee of our salvation through which we enjoy great assurance. However, Paul is also reproving men for their evil ways, when they refuse to accept the gift which God has so bountifully bestowed upon us out of his free grace. For we must remember what John says in his Epistle, that we did not first love God (*1 John* 4:19). We cannot, therefore, hold him to ransom, like those who say, 'I have done such and such service for him'. Alas, what can we possibly do for him? He loved us even when we were his mortal enemies and, indeed, he came and sought us even while we were in the depths of the abyss.

Thereupon, Paul adds, 'I do not frustrate (or reject) the grace of God'. This is the practical outcome of all that we have been saying, for Paul is implying that those who ignore God's mercy displayed in the Lord Jesus Christ, and offered to us daily through the gospel, must surely be possessed by the devil. Each time the death and passion of the Lord Jesus Christ is preached to us, alongside the infinite goodness of God, an invitation is being issued; the Lord Jesus Christ is calling us to himself. He calls us to leave this world behind, despairing of all else, but trusting in him. Since this is the case, we must not 'frustrate' the grace of God. Paul is exhorting those who previously have lived lives of debauchery, and he directs them in the way they should go. In effect, he is saying, 'Ignorant people, who have never heard a word of the gospel, may have an excuse, but not us; we will be doubly worthy of damnation if we refuse the grace of God. It bespeaks an ingratitude which is inexcusable.' Paul is, therefore, drawing a contrast between those whom our Lord Jesus Christ calls to a hope of salvation through his gospel and those who prefer to wallow in their sins. Such people do not know whether there is a better life to come or not, and are, therefore, as senseless as brute beasts. Then there are some who torment their consciences over various principles to which they adhere, yet who never find relief or remedy. Nevertheless, those who have not heard about the Lord Jesus Christ will still perish without mercy – they cannot hide behind their ignorance. I am referring to all the pagan and idolatrous peoples who have ever lived – all will be silenced before him. What then will become of those who have stopped their ears to the message which God has sent them day by day? He demands that we come to him, indeed, he exhorts us and pleads with us to do so, as we saw in the second letter to the Corinthians (*2 Cor.* 5:20). Is it not a display of great humility for God to stoop down and plead with us through the person of his only Son? 'Be ye reconciled', he says. Yet what has he done and whom has he offended? Indeed, it is we who offend him every day, yet he draws near to us, expressing his desire to be reconciled with us! We are full of evil, like demons; we are lost and damned, yet he comes seeking us out and asks nothing more than to be reconciled! Paul asks, what will become of us if we reject the grace which God so bountifully offers? This is his concern in the text before us.

* * *

Finally, he concludes that if we seek to be justified by the law, Jesus Christ has died in vain. You see, in order to enjoy the grace which comes to us through the gospel, we must renounce all foolish thoughts of our 'merits'. It is self-deception to believe in one's own worth. The reality is that we can only come before God as poor beggars! Yet, we insist upon bringing God some good work or other. Our own assessment of ourselves is nothing but an abomination to God. Paul reveals to us, therefore, that there is no other way to have life through the Lord Jesus Christ, to reach his heavenly kingdom, and to benefit from his death and resurrection, than first to rid ourselves of all the vain notions which are held by the children of this world. For example, people say, 'I myself am a virtuous person and most hard-working too!' All this has to be rejected, for until we have blotted out all thought of our merits, we cannot receive the grace of the Lord Jesus Christ. Do we wish to come to him? Then let us come empty-handed, for whatever we bring to him will be like smoke in our hands. When men are swollen with pride, to the point of bursting, this is but smoke before God. But this smoke, whatever it may consist of, will prevent us receiving the benefits communicated by the Son of God through the gospel. This is the main thread of Paul's conclusion to this passage.

The Papists say that we are not good enough to obtain salvation without the help of the Lord Jesus Christ; yet by this they mean that men can half save themselves, and make up what is lacking through the grace of the Lord Jesus Christ. They think this is a suitable method of salvation. However, by saying such things they reveal that they are, in fact, mortal enemies to that grace, and that they uphold the cause of the false apostles and seducers that corrupted, tainted and falsified the truth in Galatia. For those people, too, would have professed that Jesus Christ was the Saviour of the world, and would not have treated Jesus Christ with contempt, for they professed to be Christians. But what did they really think of Jesus Christ? That he came to help men in their weakness because they could not fulfil the law alone; they needed Jesus Christ to help them because they did not have the degree of perfection required. This is exactly what the Papists say today! However, Paul concludes that if this were the case, then Jesus Christ would have died in vain. You might say, 'Not at all! His suffering and death did, indeed, bear fruit, because he has enabled us to receive the remission of our sins. Although we had the means by which to please God, they were insufficient, so Christ had to help us.' If any should give this answer, he ought to take note of the infallible principle which Paul lays down here: which is that, if we think there is anything good in us, we are accursed, until God accepts us through his pure grace alone.

This is where the Papists are mistaken, and not only they; for this same error is common amongst the Turks and, indeed, amongst all the pagans that have ever lived. Even Turks admit that they stand in need of the mercy of God, for this opinion has been held throughout the world since time began. However, they add their own works to the grace of God and say, 'Although we need God to take pity on us, we must also seek his favour through our own personal good deeds.' This is what pagans have always believed. And what about the Papists today? They believe the same thing!

Although they confess that they are poor sinners, who need the help of the Lord Jesus Christ, and that they can only approach God through his death, yet they believe in their own free will, and their own efforts and what they call 'meritorious works'. If Jesus Christ can help them, yet he cannot do it all! Here is, word for word, the doctrine of the Papists: 'We could not merit anything unless the Lord Jesus Christ had gone before us and shown us the way. He achieved the first grace for us, and it is now for us to follow and acquire the second.' If we were to ask what this first grace is, they would answer, 'the opportunity to merit'! This is the style of their speech. This 'opportunity to merit' is nothing more than men being sufficient in and of themselves to earn God's favour through their good works!

Paul shows that it is a terrible, devilish blasphemy to have such arrogance. This is why he concludes that Jesus Christ would have died in vain if we could have been justified by the law. Do we wish to possess the Lord Jesus Christ? Then, we must first know why we are coming to him. It should be because we stand condemned already by the law and are under God's curse. We are cut off from all hope of eternal life and full of depravity. We need to be cleansed by God through his Holy Spirit, and because we are so weak, we need to come to this fountain in order to receive strength. If we feel constrained by the necessity of coming to the Lord Jesus Christ, confessing that we are miserable, accursed creatures, then we too will come to the conclusion that Paul reaches: Christ would have died in vain if we could have achieved justification under the law, whether wholly or in part. We are forced to admit this. Even the most simple-minded amongst us can see clearly that if we do not receive the Lord Jesus Christ in this way, then his coming will not have profited us at all. We will possess nothing more than smoke, which soon vanishes away and prevents us from experiencing the mercy of God offered to us in the Lord Jesus Christ.

This being so, let us learn to reject such teachings, for they falsify the truth of God by mixing merit with the free remission of sins. Let us, rather, attribute everything to our Lord Jesus Christ. Furthermore, once we have learnt to rest upon him, let us delight in the spiritual blessings which he brings. May the afflictions and miseries of this life not hinder us from pursuing our course, but, instead, may we overcome all such temptations and difficulties. Indeed, may we experience fulness of joy in the midst of our sorrows and disappointments, knowing that all we suffer in this world is not worthy to be compared with the glory which has been reserved for us in the kingdom of heaven. This is the point to which Paul has led us. Firstly, he exhorts us to live a holy and well-ordered life, humbling ourselves in order to devote our lives entirely to the Lord Jesus Christ. Secondly, he encourages us to equip ourselves with patience to overcome the difficulties and problems which will come our way. We must walk in such a way in this world that we reach our heavenly inheritance, which will surpass all our expectations. Though unseen, nevertheless we can be assured of its existence since it has been promised to us. Having the pledge and guarantee of our inheritance in the Lord Jesus Christ, we can be absolutely certain that we will not reach it by chance, but, rather, by having a firm and steadfast faith and trust that in the Lord Jesus we already have the fulfilment of everything we could hope for.

Now let us fall before the majesty of our great God, acknowledging our sins, and asking him to make us increasingly conscious of them. May we be moved to true repentance, causing us to seek forgiveness from God; and may he receive us in mercy. Also, may we ask him to guide us by his Holy Spirit, so that we renounce the lusts of the flesh more and more, and all that pertains to our old Adam. Then, may we obtain that state of perfection which we fall so far short of now, but to which we are called. May he not only grant this grace to us, but to all peoples, etc.

15

The Sheer Folly of Disobeying God's Truth

> *O foolish Galatians, who hath bewitched you, that ye should not obey the truth, before whose eyes Jesus Christ hath been evidently set forth, crucified among you? This only would I learn of you, Received ye the Spirit by the works of the law, or by the hearing of faith?* (Gal. 3:1–2).

We know that God seeks to draw us to himself gently and lovingly. However, our stubborn and rebellious ways often provoke him to wrath; for we fail to respond to his patient dealings with us. Yet, throughout all gospel teaching, we see that God stretches out his arms toward us, as it were, to bring us to himself and welcome us in fatherly love. Indeed, as Moses expresses it, he is like a bird seeking to gather her young beneath her outstretched wings (*Exod.* 19:4; *Deut.* 32:11). This is how God in his infinite mercy calls us to himself; but we, like savage beasts, refuse to be led. Thus, because of our perversity, it is often necessary for him to use force, thus exposing our ingratitude and causing us to feel ashamed of ourselves.

Paul has taught us that our salvation is to be found in Jesus Christ alone, and that if we wish to receive the righteousness and benefits he wishes to bestow upon us, we must completely renounce self, knowing that we are sinful and corrupt within. Having taught us these lessons, he now sharply rebukes all those who seek to add their own acts of devotion to the grace offered them in the Lord Jesus Christ. These Galatians had been faithfully instructed. If Paul had taught elsewhere, or if they had never heard a single word of the gospel, he would not have been so severe; he would have pitied them as folk who are ignorant and blind. But since he had faithfully taught them, and dutifully laboured to instruct them in the gospel, only to find that they rebelled and became caught up with false doctrine, he is very harsh with them here. Indeed, he continues his argument by saying that Jesus Christ was crucified among them. Having seen, therefore, the treasures of God's infinite mercy displayed thus for their redemption, they had no possible excuse for turning back to their petty ways, thinking they could justify themselves and obtain salvation through ceremonial laws.

What we ought to learn from this passage is as follows: if we desire to delight in God's Word, we must be a submissive rather than a rebellious people. Remember what is written in Psalm 18:26: 'With the pure thou wilt show thyself pure; and with the froward thou wilt show thyself froward.' All who are stiff-necked and refuse to submit in obedience to God will discover that he is stronger than they are, and that unless they surrender to him, they will be broken and destroyed. Furthermore, notice that when God rebukes us for sin, it is not for us to become angry or fly into a rage as some do who grind their teeth together whenever they are scolded! They plead not to be treated harshly, for their nature requires them to be gently instructed; yet their very rebelliousness proves quite the opposite! People who speak in this way only seek the flattery of men; though they are full of evil ways, even to overflowing, they will not allow anyone to scratch their sore spots! No; they would rather play make-believe and hide their depravity. However, if rebuke comes their way they immediately become embittered against the gospel. Though once they displayed some degree of zeal, their rage will only reveal that their hearts are now full of poison and bitterness. It is a sure sign that they have never known what it is to be taught in God's school alone, as it says in that other passage where Paul says that the Word of God is not only profitable for doctrine (that is, to teach us to discern between good and evil), but is also profitable for reproof and correction (*2 Tim.* 3:16). Some careless souls need hard digs with the spur; others need to be humbled because of their arrogance; others would be untameable unless they were brought under control by a few heavy blows!

Therefore, we must all bear patiently our Lord's chastening hand, realising that it is for our good. If each of us were fully to examine our lives, we would find that every time we provoked our God, his harshness with us was completely justified. Even if a father were the gentlest we could hope for, yet if his children were difficult to manage, cruel or rebellious, he would be angry with them, as if his whole personality had altered. In order to discipline them, he would have to change his approach. It is likewise with us; we have a Father whose goodness surpasses anything we could hope for in man. However, instead of quietly obeying him and being ready to do what he commands when he so much as utters one word, our wickedness and excessive lust cause us to stray from him. We always have answers for him; although we do not speak with our mouths, there is not that silence in our hearts which will allow us to submit to God as we ought. Since we know from experience that it is necessary for God to be harsh and severe with us, let us allow him to do what he knows is best for our soul's well-being.

Let us bear in mind that the Galatians were just as frail as we are, and needed to have their ears tickled, as it were! Yet they had to be sharply reproved for their faithlessness. Those over whom Paul was set as an apostle, he sought to draw to obedience to the Lord Jesus Christ with great humility and modesty. Indeed, he compares himself (quite rightly) to a nurse caring for a little child, sparing nothing in order to show how much she loves him. We will see later in our studies that he says, 'Be as I am, for I am as ye are' (*Gal.* 4:12). In other words, I am only asking you to be like myself so that we may all be one with each other. Yet, necessity constrained him to cry out in this passage, 'Idiots, fools, people without discernment, like beasts, who has bewitched you? Are you not possessed by the devil?' Such words are hard indeed, and doubtless the people were incensed by this at first. Yet, the Galatians must have realised that Paul did not use such language without good cause. Thus, when we are reproved, may we too realise that it is for our sins, and pass judgment on them; for we will gain nothing by striking back in self-defence. If we argue, we may all plead our cause admirably with men, but in God's sight we will stand condemned.

* * *

Moreover, Paul adds a very important statement. Having said that they must have been bewitched in order to disobey the truth, he adds that 'Jesus Christ hath been evidently set forth, crucified among you'. In saying this, Paul is telling us how effectively and powerfully he had preached the gospel. It is as if he were comparing the doctrine he had taught them to a 'portrait'. Furthermore, he says that what he preached amongst the Galatians was virtually equivalent to seeing for themselves the Son of God crucified in their midst; as if they had witnessed his blood shed for the spiritual cleansing of their souls. Seeing they had been thus faithfully taught, there was no excuse for rebellion. Firstly, we learn here the true way of preaching the gospel: declaring the love of God in giving us his only Son and sending him to die for us. Indeed, in Christ are all the treasures of wisdom and knowledge, as it says in that other place, the second chapter of Colossians and the ninth verse. With this in mind, let us learn to recognise the benefits that the Lord Jesus Christ has won for us if we desire really to profit from the gospel; for unless we do, we will have nothing. Many boastfully assert that they are familiar with the Word of God, but here is the true test of this: do they know that they need God to save them from the pit of hell through his mercy? If so, do they know that they can be cleansed and purged from all their stains only in the blood of the Son of God? Do they know that it is only through him that righteousness can be obtained, through the obedience he rendered, and that there is no other payment for sin but the sacrifice he offered? We can only please God through the mediation of Christ; we cannot open our mouths to call upon him without such an intercessor. If we are thus persuaded of the benefits of the death of the Son of God, then we may claim to have some understanding of the gospel; if not, we merely follow our foolish imaginations. This is the first point.

Notice, also, that it is not good enough to have heard in passing that the Lord Jesus Christ has redeemed us at such cost – no, we must continue in the doctrine of the gospel until it is well imprinted on our hearts. Christ's blood was shed in order to bear fruit that would benefit us in every way. We must, therefore, shake off all lethargy. There are many people who consider themselves to be learned clerics the minute they have heard in passing just three words of the gospel! Yet, this will soon disappear from their memories, for they are content to have only sampled that which is meant to be diligently sought after if we are to be satisfied with the blessings which the Lord Jesus Christ has brought us. God punishes such ingratitude and the despising of his goodness. Therefore we must apply all that we have studied, in order to be strengthened in the doctrine I have been referring to: that is, we must know why the Son of God died, and appreciate the inestimable good we have received thereby.

Furthermore, we are warned in another place that they are the worst sinners in the eyes of God who, having been instructed concerning his will, turn the reins in the opposite direction. Such people do not sin through ignorance, but out of spite and disdain. It is most evident that they do not wish to be subject to him, for they are like wild beasts throwing off their yokes. Of course, even the most ignorant souls in the world will be punished for their sin, for hypocrisy reigns in us all. Yet, if we were to make a comparison between those who have never heard a single word of the truth, and ourselves, whose ears are constantly filled with invitations to come to God, we are by far the most guilty. Look at the Turks; they believe they worship the God who created heaven and earth, but because they reject the Lord Jesus Christ, their god is but an idol. The foolish acts of devotion performed by Papists show that they are similarly deceived. Not that this makes any of them less accountable before God! But what of us? We know the way of salvation; we have the voice of God resounding in our ears; we have been illuminated by the Sun of Righteousness, the Lord Jesus Christ (*Mal.* 4:2). If, therefore, we behave like wild animals, unable to discern between right and wrong, surely we must be bewitched! For if God has graciously drawn near to us and taught us so personally, he certainly has good reason to complain as he does here. 'O my people, what have I done unto thee? and wherein have I wearied thee?', he asks by the prophet Micah (*Mic.* 6:3). When God declares his case against us, it will be as follows: he will set before us all the opportunities he gave us to become his alone, which would have caused him great rejoicing. Then he will say that we set up a barrier between ourselves and him; that we did not bend our necks to take upon us his yoke; that we have withdrawn ourselves from his presence gradually as the days have passed by; that we preferred to be deceived by the tricks and illusions of Satan, than to be led by the truth that we knew to be trustworthy. Are we not indeed monsters, people who go against nature itself? Let us learn to see ourselves reflected here. What was originally written to the Galatians now applies to us today, for Paul did not write for their benefit alone. The Spirit of God is teaching us that if we have accepted the doctrine of the gospel, and soon afterwards become tempted and weaken because we do not have a firm and constant faith, then we are more worthy of damnation. We cannot hide behind an excuse; in fact, all the excuses in the world will not prevent us being convicted as most wicked people. One day we will all have to be silent before God while he points at us as examples of sheer ingratitude, and says that we are detestable to men and angels because we have failed to value the doctrine of salvation sufficiently, though the Scripture describes it as precious seed (*Matt.* 13:19).

This is what we will do well to learn: Paul is not only scolding the Galatians here, but through their example he is teaching us to walk in fear and with due reverence, provided the Lord has been gracious enough to draw us to himself and show us his will. Therefore, it is not without good cause that he uses such harsh words as these: 'O foolish Galatians, who hath bewitched you?' Listen to what Paul says in the fourth chapter to the Ephesians about the effect of the gospel: he says when we are well instructed in the gospel, 'that we henceforth be no more children, tossed to and fro' (*Eph.* 4:14). In other words, easily persuaded that white is black. Rather, we must be sure-footed, so that when the devil comes to trouble us with false doctrines and lies, we can continue on our path in the knowledge that God's truth is infallible. This is how the gospel is to be used – not only to teach us right from wrong but to arm and equip us against all Satan's devices. Then, when he stirs up heresies and other corruptions, we will be able to maintain the battle valiantly and our faith will be victorious. We must not allow ourselves to fall into the snare of the devil – a warning that Paul gives many times.

Therefore, we must indeed be bewitched and possessed by the devil if we do not accept the remedy which God sent us when he revealed himself to us. For we know for certain who it is that has spoken; if his authority means nothing, what hope is there for us? The Lord Jesus Christ has lightened our path with the midday sun, as it were; why do we, then, search out byways here and there when the road lies straight before our eyes? We are, as I have said, flying in the face of nature itself. Therefore, Paul had good reason to be so sharp with this people who had changed their doctrine, even though God had graciously revealed his truth to them. Surely it reminds us of the time when God had to reproach his ancient people through the prophet Jeremiah. 'Go,' he says, 'search across the seas and throughout the islands and in faraway lands; you will find that each nation worships its own idols. They never change their doctrine. Why, then, are you so easily swayed? Those nations do not even know upon what their beliefs are founded. But if someone attempted to change their opinions they would persist without turning aside, fully adhering to their original beliefs. You who know the God you serve – why are you still so changeable?' (see *Jer.* 2:10–11). What further evidence do we need against us at the last day, if we have thus lightly turned away from gospel doctrine, whilst wretched unbelievers persistently follow their superstitions? We have all seen just how unbending they are. Think of Turks, pagans, Jews and Papists – they do not know the God whom they worship! They have 'beliefs' rather than faith. Yet they will not let go of these false and imaginary notions. Indeed, they are so obsessed with them that we cannot envisage them ever changing their minds.

As for us, we know that the living God has called us. He is teaching us daily through men who utter nothing but that which proceeds from him and from his Spirit. We have the unfailing testimony of the law and of the gospel. If, I say, our faith is based upon this and then we later become inconsistent, having itching ears ready to receive any novelties whatsoever; and if instead of rejecting falsehood we are swayed, we wilfully reject the grace of God. It is as if we are shutting the door on him so that he cannot draw near to us. If we know that his gospel offers us inestimable treasure, and yet trample all this underfoot and defile it, do we think God will allow his grace to be thus vilified and disgraced? We cannot despise gospel teaching without profaning the blood of the Son of God, which he shed for our redemption; for we cannot separate the one from the other. Whenever God speaks to us and offers us remission of sins, he declares that he is willing to show us mercy; yet, this cannot be separated from the sprinkling of the blood of our Lord Jesus Christ. All such doctrine is of no possible avail unless the Lord Jesus Christ is there in the midst to apply to us his shed blood. However, if we despise gospel teaching, it is just as if we were to spit upon the holy blood of the Son of God, which is intolerable sacrilege. Let us, therefore, look well to ourselves and weigh up this passage, in order that we might remain faithful; for God has called us to enjoy manifold blessings!

Now, we have seen that the preaching of the gospel has not come about by accident, but was ordained so that God may display the infinite riches of his bounty towards us. Let us continue in this and be so firmly persuaded of it that nothing may ever move or shake us. This, in brief, is what we ought to retain from this passage.

Furthermore, we are shown that there are true 'portraits' of Christ that will lead us to God. The Papists say that we need relics in order to be properly in tune with the gospel. They say that images are the books of the simple and for those who do not have the capacity to learn higher doctrine! But was Paul simply addressing three or four people here? No; he was speaking to all Christians alike, great and small, without exception, when he said that when the gospel is preached, Jesus Christ is vividly portrayed and depicted. We can, therefore, contemplate him, not with our physical eyes, but with the spiritual eyes of faith. This being so, we can learn what is needful for our salvation. We do not need images or gaudy statues, or a piece of wood, or stone or any other trifles, for us to say, 'Here is a relic that will bring me closer to God'! All this is vanity and deception. We need, instead, to hear the Word of God preached, and to endeavour to become so familiar with it that we see God's express image – that is, in the person of the Lord Jesus Christ, his only Son. See what Paul says in the second letter to the Corinthians, chapter four and verse three: he declares that the doctrine he preached was only hidden from unbelievers: those who are perishing, possessed by the devil and blinded. It should not surprise us that they cannot see a thing, even in full daylight. Yet, to us his doctrine is so clear that we can easily perceive the will of God. It is declared to us so plainly each time the gospel is preached. We do not need long discourses or circuitous sermons, nor do we need to ask, 'Who will go beyond the clouds for us? Or who will cross the seas? Who will descend into the abyss?' (*Deut.* 30:12–14). Is the Word of God being faithfully preached? Then we have Jesus Christ in our midst, as it were, as if he were presented before us hanging on the cross, and he testifies to what he accomplished when he suffered to reconcile us to God the Father. Since God places before us such a sure and infallible pledge, let us be content. For even if we plead never so hard, there is no excuse for us. We will lose our cause unless we have this peace of conscience. We need to submit completely to the Word of God, which, as I have said, will bring us closer to God until, through the person of the Lord Jesus Christ, we are in full union with him.

Indeed, God condescends to us in our ignorance and weakness. Does he speak in such lofty and obscure language that we find we cannot understand him? On the contrary, he stoops down. Not content to have spoken to us, he has added the sacraments to his Word, which are the only pictures we may lawfully have. For example, when we see the water used in baptism, it is a picture to show us our pollution and the stains that need to be washed away. By whom? We must seek our cleansing from on high and be renewed by the Spirit of God. Here is a lovely picture! What makes it so beautiful? It has been ordained by God and is in complete harmony with his Word. The same applies to the Lord's Supper – when we see the piece of bread and the cup of wine, we see things which are familiar to us as means of nourishment and sustenance for the body. But these point us to the heavenly life of our souls, and show us that we only have life through the Lord Jesus Christ. The wine teaches us that Christ's blood is so efficacious that we need look nowhere else to find what we lack, for it serves as meat, drink and all that we need. Here, I say, are wonderful pictures that God sets before us. If we flap our wings in the air with impatience due to our carnal appetites, saying, 'I want much more than this!', we are despising the grace which is so freely offered. How much more, therefore, do we need to give heed to this passage where Paul, by the power and in the name of God, and with the power of the Holy Spirit, thunderously condemns all those who turn away and backslide after having been faithfully instructed in the gospel.

* * *

At this point, he adds that he would like to know how the Galatians believed a person receives the Holy Spirit. For if they had become partakers of the Spirit through the works of the law, Paul would have accepted that they had some justification; yet, since they received him through the gospel, he concludes that this ought to have been sufficient testimony against their practices. In order to fully understand what he is saying here, let us observe that the Spirit of God indwells all believers, after he has regenerated them and made them new creatures. After this, there are the spiritual gifts which God distributes in the measure and proportion which pleases him (they always serve the common good of the church). If we are Christians, we must, therefore, have the Spirit of God (as we will see hereafter), for he is called the guarantee and pledge of the inheritance which is promised to us and for which we wait (*2 Cor.* 1:22; *Eph.* 1:14). Therefore, the Spirit of God must dwell within us if we are his children. But there are also gifts, as in days gone by, when there was the gift of tongues, the gift of prophecy, the gift of healing and suchlike. Even today, God demonstrates that he has not abandoned his church. For although we are not surrounded by visible gifts as in former days, yet, God still displays his might in our midst. Paul here addresses them all. We take this reference to the 'Spirit' in its ordinary usage, to signify the renewal that occurs within the children of God; as in the third chapter of John's Gospel, verse six. Because we are born of flesh, we are full of corruption and tend towards that which is of the earth. True enough, men may boast of their great knowledge; it may seem to them that they possess a free will which is able to choose between good and evil, but this is nothing more than imagination. It is most certain that if we are left to our own natures, we tend towards all evil. The Scriptures say the same of us, for they say that every thought conceived in the human mind is only evil, and that all our desires are at enmity with God (*Gen.* 6:5; *Rom.* 8:7). Let us not deceive ourselves with vain flattery, then, but rather acknowledge that in Adam we are completely depraved and full of sin. Indeed, God reveals this evil to us when he quickens us by his Holy Spirit. He subsequently purifies our hearts so that we desire to obey him. Although we have not as yet attained the standard of perfection required, yet if we struggle against our nature and seek to do good, this is a sign that God dwells within us. It is also a sign that we are led by him as his flock and that we are his children. This can only be so, however, when God's Spirit is to us like a harness, helping us to walk in obedience to him; for we cannot count ourselves Christians unless we have such a testimony. That is to say, unless God has ratified that he is our Father by granting us his Spirit as a pledge, as Paul calls him in the first chapter of Ephesians and the fourteenth verse.

* * *

Next, Paul points out that the Galatians had received the Spirit of God through the preaching of the gospel. This being the case, we are forced to conclude that the works of the law could not justify them. Why not? Well, we must return to the principle that we have already discussed – namely, the gospel strips us of all the goodness we think we possess, and, instead, makes us feel so ashamed of ourselves that we run to God, confessing our need. For although in the law God exposes our cursed state, it is not as clear to us as it is in the gospel. Think how much hypocrites flatter themselves in the belief that they have done all that is required of them! But the gospel contains two important messages. Firstly, God declares that we are in a state of total poverty and need to come to him, begging for grace after humble confession; for we are sinners without a single drop of virtue worthy of praise. This being so, it is understandable that Paul should reiterate the second point, which is that those who have received the Spirit of God through the preaching of the gospel must empty themselves of all trust in their own merits, and realise that their salvation depends purely upon the free mercy of God.

Justification through the law and justification through the gospel are two entirely separate things, as different as fire and water. Am I saying that the gospel contradicts the law? Not at all! As we have already established, God is the author of them both, and there are no inconsistencies in him. The issue in question here is this: How is a person saved? God gave man the law in order to show him the right way to live, yet at the same time, he was seeking to condemn man, as if he were undergoing a criminal trial with the halter round his neck, even before the verdict has been pronounced. Truly, in the law we can see nothing more than the mouth of hell opening up in readiness for us, for God has prepared his vengeance against us and is armed as our enemy. This is the purpose of the law. The gospel, on the other hand, is given to us as a remedy, so that in our despair we might take refuge in the grace offered to us in the Lord Jesus Christ. It is here that we realise there is no other way but by the remission of our sins, whereby God cancels out all our offences and erases them from memory. He no longer takes them into account against us. Our justification consists in the fact that he will not impute our sins to us. When we understand God's plan and purpose in the law as well as the gospel, we can see that God is not the author of confusion. Yet, if we have been justified through the gospel, why should we seek to obtain salvation through the law? The law prepares us for the gospel, for where men are puffed up with pride, they cannot know the grace of God. If a container is full of air, and you were to try to put liquid into it, none of it would be able to enter because the air would prevent it. We might also think of the human body (for we are supposed to take examples from this world and use them to raise our thoughts heavenwards!). If a man is starving, he will, nevertheless, have such a swollen stomach that he can take nothing in – he will be full. But he will only be full of wind and not food. The wind prevents him from taking down anything that will sustain or nourish him. The same applies to our foolish pride. We think we have everything we need, but all we have is like air which excludes the grace of God. But the gospel humbles us and the Lord Jesus Christ exposes our wretchedness. We must come to him, realising that he has the answer. There is nothing good in us; we must find it all in him, all, I say, not just part.

This, then, is the reason why Paul argues that if we received the Spirit of God by means of the gospel, we must rest there and by no means look to the ceremonies of the law. We must be satisfied with the perfection of the gospel, since this is what God has given us. Indeed, let us freely rejoice in this gift! For although these remarks were addressed to the Galatians, they apply just as much to us today. Consider, I say, how much our Lord has been working in us. Then start by putting into practice what we learnt from second Corinthians – that we must be completely transformed and that the Spirit of God must dwell within us (*2 Cor.* 3:18). The true means of discerning if we are indeed children of God is this: by the Spirit of God. Have we been indwelt by the Spirit since we were in our mother's womb? Certainly not! Neither does he come upon us according to our merits (as we have been saying), but rather as it pleases God in his mercy to pour out his Holy Spirit, who draws us to the Father. If we have any will or desire to walk in the fear of our God, and if we seek to be able to call upon him with a clear conscience, it is a sign that the Spirit of God dwells within us. We need not look for other evidence, or dispute the fact at great length. But did we receive the Spirit through our own merit? The answer is most certainly, no. Thus, we must conclude that we received him by means of the gospel. In the gospel, God displays his power and might to bring about the salvation of man; this is referred to in the first chapter to the Romans, verse sixteen. If, therefore, the gospel was the instrument by which we received the Spirit of God, do we need to search for other means? Is this not a rejection of his almighty power? It is like wilfully straying from the way God has shown us to seek out other paths here or there according to our own desires. If the Galatians had no excuse for turning from the gospel to the law, what will become of us today if we seek to entangle ourselves in the superstitions conceived by men? Take the Papists, who seek justification, not through the ceremonies that God appointed in former days, but through the foolish and petty rules they have invented! What they call God's service is nothing more than a hotch-potch, where each person contributes something of their own devising. If we similarly attempt to mix human inventions with the purity of the gospel, we despise God and distance ourselves from him, rejecting his grace and preventing it from affecting us in any way. Are we not, therefore, even worse than 'foolish'?

Let us realise, in closing, that we cannot be Christians unless the Holy Spirit has first granted us the humility to confess that our salvation proceeds entirely from the grace of God. Let us adhere closely to the Lord Jesus Christ, not trusting him in part, but finding complete satisfaction in him, having received of his fulness. Let us acknowledge him as the perfection of wisdom, and also of righteousness and felicity. In him lies all our happiness, which we can possess now through the faithful preaching of the gospel. Let us be self-abasing, and rid ourselves of the pride which prevents us from approaching God. Furthermore, if our Lord has bountifully poured upon us all that is needful for salvation, let this content us and may everything else that men advance be like smoke before us. Let us despise and mistrust all else to prove how much the gospel means to us. We need to be bold and consistent enough not to be moved when the devil himself whispers in our ears. Yet, being weak, ignorant and dull people, when God tells us to come to him daily, we do it stumblingly and falteringly. We need more and more to discipline ourselves to ask God to strengthen us by his Holy Spirit, and to make us grow increasingly in the knowledge of his gospel. We must not be like those who consider they have reached their goal after the very first day, but rather, we must gradually deepen in our hope of eternal life. We must be men who are established, and whose faith increases from day to day, until that happy day when we experience what Paul describes in the fourth chapter to the Ephesians, and the fifteenth verse. Then we will be fully united to our Lord Jesus Christ.

Now let us fall before the majesty of our great God,

acknowledging our sins, and praying that he would increasingly make us feel the burden of them. May we hate ourselves and ask his pardon, and glorify him in our midst by so doing. May we be strengthened by his Holy Spirit so that we know beyond all doubt that he dwells within us, and that we have been adopted as the children of God. Thus, we all say, Almighty God, and our heavenly Father, etc.

16

The True Children of Abraham

Are ye so foolish? having begun in the Spirit, are ye now made perfect by the flesh? Have ye suffered so many things in vain? if it be yet in vain. He therefore that ministereth to you the Spirit, and worketh miracles among you, doeth he it by the works of the law, or by the hearing of faith? Even as Abraham believed God and it was accounted to him for righteousness (Gal. 3:3–6).

As we are aware, all gospel doctrine is designed to make us forsake the world and cleave to God. This is only possible if we learn to fix our gaze more and more on things above. If we desire to increase in the knowledge of God, we must first diligently endeavour to correct the weaknesses that are ours by nature. Only then may we be equipped to forsake all that the world offers. Whilst it is true that God, in his mercy, has stooped down to us, we are not to remain firmly rooted in this world. God has, indeed, chosen mortal beings as his messengers, and draws us to himself using things which we can easily relate to; for example, by means of sacraments – visual symbols, employing earthly elements. Thus, we can see that he has been willing to limit himself to such an extent as to render us without excuse. We cannot extricate ourselves on the grounds that he is way beyond our reach. Whatever we may say, it cannot be denied that the main purpose of the gospel is to strip us of all that pertains to the flesh, that we might draw near to God.

Yet, sadly, men misuse God's grace by making the visible symbols, appointed by God, the source of all their holiness. It is as if they expect to be saved by their own observances. This sin was not invented today, nor even yesterday; it has prevailed since the beginning of time and continues to this very hour. What is worse, men are not content to have simply perverted that which God has ordained to lead them to himself: they also devise and construct other barriers which distance themselves from him even further. We would, perhaps, have difficulty grasping what I am saying, had it not been so clearly demonstrated in everyday life. By the law, God appointed sacrifices which were types and shadows of the day. They were not, however, a sign that he delights in such base things, but rather an indication of the ignorance of the people, who were much like children. He was directing them to understand the nature of spiritual worship. Yet, it is written that these legal ceremonies were 'carnal'. How are we to understand this? Well, God was seeking to instruct the people how they were to approach him through means which were familiar and easily understood. Yet, at the same time, we are told that the pattern revealed to Moses on the mountain was a heavenly one. There are, therefore, these two aspects to the ceremonial law.

Washing when one entered the temple, offering sacrifices, having a candlestick and perfumed incense, and special garments for the priest to wear – all of these were external and symbolic, and could, therefore, be termed 'carnal' and temporal. However, their significance was spiritual. Yet, how did the Jews respond to all of this? They became preoccupied with the figures themselves, instead of considering why God had instituted them. They believed that in going to the temple and performing what was expected of them outwardly, they would be blameless in the eyes of God. But they were creating a god in their own image, as it were. Indeed, it is this approach that God mocks through the prophets when he says that he does not dwell in a house made by human hands, for even the heavens cannot contain him in his infinite majesty (*Isa.* 66:1). But today, the Papists are not content to misuse God's law; they add dogma upon dogma until they have filled an abyss with their follies. Yet, all the while, they claim to be worshipping God! Whatever they may say, it is a mere farce!

Let us come now to the words of our text. Paul makes a comparison between the Spirit and the flesh. What does he mean by 'the Spirit'? The term here encompasses the whole of gospel teaching, which is of a spiritual nature and designed to free us from the types and shadows under which the Jews were required to live. In the gospel, God reveals himself to us fully. Having disposed of all the types and shadows of the law, he reveals that he desires us to come to him directly, allowing nothing in this world to hold us back. Under the law, it was the High Priest alone who was able to approach God; the people had to keep at a distance. The Lord Jesus Christ is our High Priest, who has made a way whereby we may approach God the Father: through his blood, as the apostle writes in the Epistle to the Hebrews (*Heb.* 9:11). If we accept the gospel in the way in which God intends, he deals with us as if we are now ready to approach him, without the need for ceremonies; for these were originally appointed for those who were unenlightened and ignorant with regard to God's will. Paul reproaches the Galatians, who had 'begun in the Spirit'. By this, he means that they knew the teaching of the gospel, and understood things which had been hidden from the Jews by obscure types and shadows. He reproaches them because they now sought to be 'made perfect by the flesh', that is, by base and inferior means. It is as if he is saying, 'God has been gracious enough to show you his will at first hand, but you prefer to return to the ABC, and to the first principles. He has shown you high and lofty wisdom, through which you have received his incomparable love in the person of the Lord Jesus Christ. Why must you now return to your ABC and forget all that you have been taught subsequently? It is illogical and irrational, and is a despising of the grace you have been offered.' We know that, in our world, if a man wishes to learn something, he will start with the basics and, little by little, acquire greater skills in his trade. If you were to teach a child the sciences, without having taught him his alphabet, or how to read and write, or the rules of grammar (which he ought to be learning by degrees), what good is it? Likewise, take that same child when he grows up and reaches manhood, having learnt many things; what a mockery it would be to make him return to his ABC! The same applies to mechanics. We all know that if a man has just joined a workshop, to start with he will be unaware of things that he will know after a year or two. First, he will learn the basic principles, and then he will build upon that knowledge. But if after four years of learning his trade he returns to that which he learnt on the first day, he is a fool who has wasted his time.

Now let us apply this lesson to ourselves. Yes, it may be true that we need someone to break down the doctrine we cannot readily digest, due to our carnality. Yet God has graciously granted us the privilege of being taught spiritual things to a higher and greater degree than our holy fathers enjoyed under the law. Think of Abraham – he did not enjoy our privileges, yet he became the father of the faithful, and we need to be like him, as we shall see shortly. Next, there is David, a most noble king and prophet, who nevertheless had only known the things we now know in shadow form. The same is true of all those who lived under the former dispensation. This is why the Lord Jesus Christ says that the eyes that have seen what we see, and the ears that have heard the message of the gospel, are blessed (*Matt.* 13:16). For now he has been made manifest to the world. Therefore, since God is willing to draw near to us and deal with us in such a familiar way, should we shrink back and choose to draw near to God by means of ceremonies and figures rather than sound doctrine, we should be wilfully rebelling against him. What does this rebellion prove, but that we do not desire God to show us mercy and compassion or to be the God he declares himself to be. It is easy for us to understand, therefore, the point that Paul is making here. He is rebuking the Galatians for behaving like crabs in retreat! For, having been taught the spiritual doctrine of the gospel, they returned to the shadows of the law. It is like a man in our own day knowing that our worship is founded upon the gospel and that our practice is that which is laid down in God's pure Word, adding something of his own devising. He says, 'Would it not be better if we could all do it like this?'! This is returning to the flesh. Instead of God elevating us higher, we are pulled back to the things of earth. This is patently to enter into battle with God.

We must learn how to apply this lesson profitably. God has given us his Word, which we hear faithfully preached. Therefore, now that we know the manner in which he desires to be worshipped and served, let us not turn to the right hand or to the left. If we have truly profited from the Word that has been faithfully preached in the name of God, it should be evident to all that we value it. Indeed, the more advanced we become, the less excuse we have should we fall away. There are many that we know who have grown cold, or who have sought to sit on the fence. Whereas we expected them to have matured further and to have attained an even closer walk with God, they are taken up with vain fancies. Today, those who wish to escape persecution deliberately alter and falsify the Word of God by adding devices conceived in the mind of man. Knowing this to be the case, let us be all the more attentive to Paul's teaching here, that if God has granted us great knowledge, we ought not, like children, to return to our alphabets. What a terrible shame it is when those who have grown in their knowledge of the gospel, or who have had opportunity to do so, act like those who have never heard a single word of it. The apostle has to reproach the Jews in his Epistle to the Hebrews, saying, 'You ought to be teachers judging by the amount you have learnt, but instead, you are still novices' (*Heb.* 5:12). This is the first point we need to remember from this passage.

Paul's next question is, 'Have ye suffered so many things in vain? if it be yet in vain.' He wanted the Galatians to wake up to the fact that God had granted them the honour of being his witnesses – a privilege which they had soon forgotten. This is a point worthy of our attention, for God often grants his people such high privileges, for example, he uses them to declare his Word before men. If we fail in our duty, and do not endure to the end with the constancy with which we began, we ought to be doubly ashamed. Indeed, this ought to be considered a deplorable sin because it involves a double scandal. It is wicked ingratitude to stop serving our God when he has graciously stretched out his hand to us. We can even see such an attitude among the many people who boast and gloat that they have performed great wonders, when it is our Lord who has been using them as his instruments. 'What!', they exclaim, 'Have I not performed this or that miracle?' Oh yes, they will boast about their achievements, believing that God owes them something in return. Even if they have achieved a hundred times more than they say, they ought to be all the more indebted to God. They have certainly not achieved anything by their own industry, but by the power of God's Spirit. If, afterwards, they backslide, their sin and their offence is made worse. How is this? Well, they ought to have been progressing, but instead, they are withdrawing. They create more of a scandal than if they had never been in the public eye. It is as if God has placed them on a scaffold for all around to see, both far and near. For this reason, they cause offence to an innumerable multitude and their crime is even more heinous. Yet such sin is incredibly common today. Those who think they are defending the cause of the gospel believe themselves exempt from laws and rules. If we were to reprove them for their failings, they would say, 'What! Should you not rather be supporting me? I have done such and such for God.' Men will gladly excuse themselves in this way. And what is more, they proudly lift themselves up against God when he has graciously employed them in his service.

Now let us consider the words of Paul when he says, 'Have ye suffered so many things in vain?' He takes occasion to make a more serious accusation against the Galatians. They had already suffered many things for the sake of the gospel:

they had been persecuted, they had had many trials in connection with both their possessions and their persons. How is it, he is saying, that all they have undergone has not persuaded them that God has called them to glorify his name? Indeed, what we endure for the sake of the gospel marks us out, and shows that God is placing us in a position of privilege! The greatest honour we could ever have is to be witnesses to his truth. However corrupt we may be, God will ratify the eternal truth which proceeds from him. Yes, he will even vindicate his Word through us, poor creatures though we are, nothing more than smoke, vapour, shadows, and less than nothing. Since God permits and appoints us to be his true witnesses to advance and spread abroad his gospel, has he not the right to bemoan the fact that, in the face of suffering, we fall away from him?

Therefore, having begun well, may we all take heed to ourselves. This warning is most worthy of note. Even those who are least in the church have a great debt towards God. After all, he has chosen them from amongst men, has taught them gospel doctrine, and has passed by those who are 'great' and those who consider themselves more worthy and more noble. This he did in order to choose those who are despised by the world. If such people fall back, they will surely have great difficulty when they are required to give an account of themselves. What, then, will become of those whom God has chosen to be his standard-bearers, as it were? He has raised up such people to be mirrors and examples to others. If they fall away, what possible excuse can they find? What about those who have suffered for the name of the Lord Jesus Christ and for the teachings of his gospel? Some have been detained in prison, some tortured, some have been close to death. If such people apostatise, granting themselves greater freedoms than everyone else, they are (as much as lies in their power) effectively cancelling out the grace of God in their lives. They will resort to excuses, saying that they have suffered so much for the gospel's sake, and that we ought to bear with them. But those who are afflicted the most ought to keep themselves on a shorter rein! For the honour that God has granted them makes them even more indebted to him, and they ought to be vigilant and on their guard, not causing any to stumble. The gospel is attacked and ridiculed when people say, 'That man ought to have been one of God's martyrs, he has suffered so much to uphold the truth. Yet now he is a worldly man. What has happened to him?' It is the name of God that will be blasphemed. Let us learn, therefore, that if we have served God for a time, and he has blessed our labour, the church being blessed and built up, then we need to walk circumspectly and make sure that we do not fall back into the world. Let us not be like the cow who, having produced much milk, then breaks the churn and spills its contents! If our lives create a hundred times more damage in this world than good, what can we possibly say in our own defence? Therefore, if we want God to bless our service, we must serve him with a constant, firm and sure faith. Then we will remain true to our calling and continue to mature daily.

Then, because Paul's initial reproach was rather harsh, he moderates it by adding, 'If it be yet in vain'. This indicates that he anticipated better things of them. If the Galatians had fallen away for a time, this was not going to last. Having been warned and exhorted, they would return to the correct path. This passage teaches us that when we are rebuked by the Spirit of God we are not to become angry, nor to be in such despair and vexation that we take the bit between our teeth. Rather, we should be led to repentance. God does not want to cast us down, then to abandon us. No, rather, having exposed our sin, he will call us back to himself and bring us to the point of repentance. For he is ready to accept us and receive us in mercy whenever we are touched by a sense of true humility for our sins and hate ourselves for them, making full and free confession to him. Let us, therefore, learn that when we are next rebuked for the sins we have committed, we must not be sour-tempered, or seek out subtle means to justify ourselves; we must, rather, pass judgment on ourselves. We need to have a patient and tolerant spirit to endure all necessary chastisement. When rebukes seem a little too pointed and harsh, let us always remember the end they had in view, and what fruitful results there may be. Indeed, when God deals sharply with us, let us remember that he will soon afterwards be ready to forgive all our shortcomings. This is what we need to learn. It is as if Paul is saying that although we have for a time sought (as much as was in our power) to deny the grace of God in us, God, for his part, will not allow his grace in us to die, but will make it precious to us once again.

However, Paul scolds us here because he does not wish us to remain stubborn in our spirits. If we have been so foolish as to have strayed from the right path, we ought to realise that, unless we add the sin of rebellion to our iniquity, our Lord is calling us back to himself and granting us opportunities to return. Just after speaking in this way, Paul immediately adds that God had poured out the gifts of his Holy Spirit amongst the Galatians through his gospel. This ought to have been enough to keep them true to the doctrines which they had accepted, without being led astray and following other paths. When he makes reference to the Spirit of God here, he is not speaking of him in the same way as we saw this morning, when we spoke of his common operation in all believers alike. No, here he is using a different argument, as we shall see by what follows. For although God had revealed himself in general to these Galatians, and adopted them as his children, he had also appointed prophets among them, and men with special gifts. Some had the gift of tongues, others gifts of healing, and so on. All this confirmed the gospel to them. Therefore, if they returned to the ceremonial law, they had to deny the power of the Spirit of God. We have already examined one point worthy of remembrance, which is that God communicates his Spirit to all, and because our nature is full of evil, without him we could not be Christians. We need God to transform us and restore us to himself in order for us to become new creatures. This is the usual way in which God makes us partakers of his Holy Spirit; by touching us with reverence for God, enlightening us concerning the faith, causing us to seek salvation in Jesus Christ, encouraging us to take refuge in God by calling upon him, and setting us to obey his will. This is a summary of the way the Spirit of God commonly works in all believers, in all God's children. But he also grants us special gifts. For example, he gives us men who faithfully teach us about his Word and maintain law and order, and he grants many other gifts as evidences that he is in our midst, thus making us all the more dependent upon him.

Now let us examine the argument that Paul follows here. First, he accuses the Galatians of being ungrateful by refusing to acknowledge the source of their faith – the preaching of the gospel. The main reason why Paul needs to remind them of this is that men will always protest that they would never dream of rejecting the grace of God; yet, their actions prove the opposite! In what way? Some refuse to be taught anything by others; they drive away all ministers of the Word wherever possible. Some, through envy, seek to erase all memory of those whom God has appointed to sustain his people. In these various ways, people are declaring loud and clear that they wish God to keep as far away as possible. They will not come to him, even though he has provided the means by which they may draw near. They will not accept such things; they cast them aside. But when Paul accuses the Galatians, he does not simply say that they wanted nothing to do with the Spirit of God or that they were despising his gifts. Rather, he tells them that they had paid too little attention to the reasons why God had granted the blessings of his Spirit to the church. What, then, are we to retain from this passage? That if God provides the means to come to him, we must accept them and conform to his ways. For if we have the gospel preached among us, and then purposely forget what we have been told, we have rejected God, turned our backs upon him and sought to separate ourselves from his presence. Therefore, if we wish to continue to receive the grace of God, we must observe the things that he has ordained for us. This means there must be a willingness to be taught by those whom he has sent; we must all privately read the Holy Scriptures; we must respect those who have sufficient maturity to edify the church; and we must not shut the door upon the Holy Spirit. This is a summary of what we are to remember.

Paul is seeking to bring these believers back to the gospel. Let us, therefore, learn from this that if we fall away never so little, we are heading for perdition. The only way for man and God to be united is to have the gospel, as an unbreakable cord, uniting them together. Indeed, Paul refers here to 'the hearing of faith', thereby revealing how essential it is for God to go before us. Unless he stretches out his hand to us in the Lord Jesus Christ, and lifts us out of the pit of confusion we are in by nature, what will become of us? How generous he is with us: he gives himself freely to us in the person of his only Son! This is more than if we inherited heaven and earth and all the treasures they contain. If we seek out a rival to the Lord Jesus Christ, we discover him to be incomparable. Therefore, although God says that we are void of all good in ourselves, he adds that he has given all for us. He has not shown himself to be mean or sparing in any way in his dealings with us. We can find in him all that we lack and this should content us; if, therefore, we stray even just a little to the right hand or to the left, we deserve to be utterly deprived and dispossessed of all that we have already received.

Paul continues by addressing the case of Abraham, the father of all believers, because through his example God teaches us the means by which a man can be justified and saved. There are not several different ways of entering the kingdom of heaven. There is only one way: the one set down for us here through the example of Abraham. Paul says, 'Abraham believed God, and it was accounted to him for righteousness.' We, therefore, need to be 'of faith' if we want to be the children of Abraham. Here we need to bring to mind what we studied before concerning the use of the term 'faith'. It is not enough to believe that there is one God who rules the world. We need to know that this God regards us as his children. This enables us to call upon him with great liberty as our Father, because he accepts us in the name of the Lord Jesus Christ. By this word 'faith', Paul means being assured of the grace and fatherly love of our God through his promises, and having our eyes fixed upon Jesus Christ, through whom we have free access to the Father. Thus, in saying that we must be 'of faith' before we can be children of Abraham, he is, in effect, stating that we cannot be true Christians nor members of the church until we have faith. This involves being stripped of all thought of human 'merit'; furthermore, it demands that we be so broken and despairing about our state that we do not know what to do. Once he has shown us our lost and damned state due to our sin, then we will seek no other means of salvation than the free bounty of God offered to us. It also involves continuing to place our hope of salvation completely in Jesus Christ. Man, being utterly lost in himself, and knowing that he is full of sin and cursed, must come to God, setting aside all merit. He must be clothed with the grace of the Lord Jesus Christ. This is what it means to become a Christian. It is not enough to feel how lost we are. Think of Cain, who, feeling as if he were in hell, as it were, confessed his sin. Yet, he only did so out of a sense of despair, and as such he still incurred the guilt of murmuring and blaspheming against God. This is why he was cast away for ever. But as for us, we need so to taste the love of our God that we can rest upon it and be assured that he will accept us if we come to him through the gospel. We must approach him with confidence, not in our own thoughts or desires but in his promise: we will not be disappointed if we serve him and trust his Word.

This is what it means to be 'of faith'. We must still bear in mind the point which Paul is seeking to dispute here. He argues against those who sought justification in the sight of God through the works of the law. Perhaps if we only considered this phrase, 'of faith', and not the argument that Paul brings to light, we would find the expression unclear. But Paul is saying that those who claim to obtain favour from God by their merits are puffed up with pride, and their arrogance prevents them from entering paradise. God will not deign to look upon them because they rob him of the honour which is his and seek to clothe themselves, as it were, in borrowed plumes. By robbing God of his rightful place, they thus blaspheme against him. Since Paul is addressing such an issue, we have no difficulty whatsoever in seeing that his definition of those who are 'of faith' concerns those who put no trust in themselves, are utterly despairing and yet turn to Jesus Christ, entirely leaning upon and trusting in him. Such people are the true children of Abraham.

Now think how few Christians there are in the world! Yes, it is true that the word trips off everyone's tongue, but most are wickedly profaning the title. One day, God will assuredly disown all those who falsely claim to be his. In Popery, each person relies on their baptism, saying that God has given them this infallible guarantee of salvation. What! They only take the symbol and leave out the Lord Jesus Christ! Surely the Papists know nothing of what Paul is speaking about here. Worse still, they claim to have free will, meritorious deeds and satisfactions for sin. They have all this nonsense, abominations conceived by the devil, instead of the true worship of God, which they trample under foot and corrupt. Thus, ample evidence is provided to accuse them of being totally devoid of any Christianity. However, for our part, although we do not have the idolatries and superstitions which reign in Popery, we are still not yet so grounded in the gospel that we can freely offer ourselves to God, calling upon him with complete liberty, and finding ourselves gently led by him in return. Many are still like poor animals. They may protest that they do not hold to any of the superstitions or abuses of the Pope, yet when we speak to them of the rudimentary principles of the gospel, they know nothing of them! Some believe themselves to be most learned, yet when put to the test, they prove themselves to be full of nothing but hypocrisy. As the saying goes, they have been no more than chattering magpies in a cage! Thus, we need to take greater heed of Paul's teaching here. In other words, we cannot be the children of Abraham, or members of the church unless we have faith in the gospel. This involves each one of us renouncing all consideration of our own merit, and acknowledging that we are forever lost, finding ourselves in the pit of despair. Let us take refuge in the pure grace of God, and the mercy which he shows in the Lord Jesus Christ. Let us come and plunge ourselves in the blood which he shed for our cleansing, knowing that, through this, all our debts have been paid. The wrath and vengeance of God has been appeased so that now we cannot fail to experience his favour.

In order to have a better understanding of this subject, we need to examine the way in which Abraham believed in God. We need to have a clear definition of the term 'faith', for without it this teaching will be of no value to us. We have already pointed out that the Papists fight against us without knowing why or for what reason. Their wrongful attacks upon us are conducted in an impulsive and haphazard fashion. They have never understood what faith is, and they show it! I am speaking about their great men of learning – they say that faith means believing in God, but if they believe in God, so do the devils! When Paul speaks of faith, he does not mean having a vague sense that there is a God reigning in heaven, but of knowing God to be our Father. We can be assured of this because of the promises he has made. We can be joined and united to the Lord Jesus Christ, knowing that all he has is ours and that we have a share in it because we are members of his body. But when Papists speak of faith, they refer to it as something vague which will not be able to justify or save us. See how foolishly the Papists behave themselves, as if they have been completely bewitched by Satan! Indeed, it is a just punishment from God upon their pride, since they will not humble themselves to confess that they owe everything to God, having nothing in themselves that makes them worthy of his acceptance. They need to receive the grace offered to them by faith alone. This, therefore, is how we should understand the term 'faith'.

There is, however, a point here which will be of great help to us, and that is to know how Abraham believed in God. With this, we conclude. If Abraham had simply believed that there was a God in heaven, this could not have justified him, for the pagans believe as much. Or, if Abraham had simply believed that God was the Judge of all the earth, it would not have sufficed. But God said to Abraham, 'Abram, I am thy shield, and thy exceeding great reward', and 'I will be a God unto thee, and to thy seed after thee', and he also said that all nations would be blessed in him (*Gen.* 15:1; 17:7). God spoke thus with Abraham and testified that he counted him a member of his family, one of his own children, and that he would be his God. When Abraham accepted this promise, he was justified. How is this? Well, when God presented Abraham with his bounty and grace, Abraham believed and accepted God's Word. Thus, his salvation was completely secure.

Now we have a much clearer idea of what it means to be justified by faith. It does not mean we possess a vague notion that God exists, but rather, that we know him as our Father and our Saviour, since he reveals himself thus in his Word, and grants us a guarantee of it in the Lord Jesus Christ. Through him, we are united and joined to God. Although we are wretched creatures, full of wickedness, he will still accept us as his own and find us pleasing in his sight. This is only possible because our Lord Jesus Christ mediates between God and man. Having such a promise, we must rest upon it entirely and not doubt that God will be favourable to us to the end. When we call upon him, we must find all our refuge in him, leaving the world behind us and pressing on in the hope of eternal life. This is having faith, and this is being justified! This is how our father Abraham believed. Without this, we cannot be Christians. For until we know what the gospel is really about (as Paul says in the tenth chapter to the Romans, verse fourteen), we cannot call God our Father. We cannot, he says, call upon a God we have not heard of or believed in. And how can we possibly know him unless he is revealed to us? Thus, we need faith to go before us. And how do we get faith? By hearing, says Paul (*Rom.* 10:17). Therefore, we need to be taught the gospel, otherwise we cannot have faith. Through this, we can see that what the Papists call faith is pure folly. Why? Because they ignore the Word of God and, instead, call the most brutish things acts of supreme devotion: muttering words they do not understand, going on pilgrimage, etc. They will never find God while they entertain such foolish ceremonies and refuse to listen to a single drop of good doctrine. What great devotion and holiness they have! Yet we know that there is no Christianity at all without faith, and no faith without instruction in the gospel. Consequently, we cannot be Christians unless God has graciously revealed his goodness and mercy to us, as, indeed, he does daily when we hear the gospel. Then we can be assured that we are among the number of his own, and can call upon him with complete confidence; waiting to receive the perfection that he has revealed to us now by his own mouth, that is to say, through his Word.

Now let us fall before the majesty of our great God, acknowledging our sins, and asking him to make us increasingly aware of them. May this draw us to him with such repentance, that not only will we ask his forgiveness, but that he may reform and change us until we bear the marks of his children. When we appear before his judgment seat, may our Lord Jesus Christ restore in us the image of God the Father, in order that he may acknowledge us as members of his body. In the meanwhile, may he support us in our infirmities until he has purged us of them all. May he not only show such grace to us, but to all peoples, etc.

17

The Impossibility of Keeping the Whole Law of God

> *Know ye therefore that they which are of faith, the same are the children of Abraham. And the scripture, foreseeing that God would justify the heathen through faith, preached before the gospel unto Abraham, saying, In thee shall all nations be blessed. So then they which be of faith are blessed with faithful Abraham. For as many as are of the works of the law are under the curse: for it is written, Cursed is every one that continueth not in all things which are written in the book of the law to do them* (Gal. 3:7–10).

If, as we would have others believe, we are indeed Christians, we ought to be very familiar with what it means to be justified by faith. Yet, how few of those who claim to love the gospel understand the justification spoken of so frequently in the Scriptures! This being the case, it is very important that we ourselves should know this doctrine, for without it we can have no assurance of salvation. Indeed, neither can we freely call upon God or find refuge in him in time of need. This is why Paul places so much emphasis on this teaching. Last Sunday, we saw that Abraham was counted righteous because he believed God; we also learnt that we have no dignity of our own which can render us acceptable to God. We have to receive all from him. Abraham's 'belief' relates to what had been promised to him. God had freely offered himself to his servant Abraham, and he came to be counted righteous because he accepted the grace which was so liberally offered (although he realised that, in himself, he was full of iniquity and evil).

Thereupon, Paul concludes that 'they which are of faith' are the children of Abraham. Abraham is surely the father of all believers and children of God. It follows, therefore, that we must conform to the pattern he has set, otherwise the gate of heaven and the door of salvation will be closed to us and we will all be banished from God's kingdom. Paul shows us what we must do. Although we do not descend from Abraham according to the flesh, and are not connected to him in any way, yet, we need to become members of his family. The only way to do this is to partake of the promise which was made to him, and to believe it as he did. This is what it means to be 'of faith': to have recognised and acknowledged that we cannot win God's favour or approval through our own works or merit, but that we need to rest entirely on his goodness. Only then will the promise apply to us and we be adopted as his children. This is Paul's main point in this passage.

However, he adds that this is not only the case for Jews but that all in general are included. Without this additional statement, the doctrine that we have considered would be of no value to us whatsoever. For God chose Abraham and his descendants, which would suggest that we have been excluded from the hope of salvation. After all, election implies that God must reject all those who are not chosen, and because he chose the descendants of Abraham, it would seem that we must necessarily have been rejected. However, Paul quotes a double promise here. Firstly, that God would protect the line of Abraham and separate it from the rest of mankind. The second promise is that all nations would be blessed in Abraham, and in his seed (*Gen.* 12:3). If God had chosen to call his church from the family of Abraham alone, we would be lost today, but because of this second promise, we too can be saved. God has extended his grace and mercy, which at one time only applied to a certain lineage, and now we can share in this salvation. What Paul is saying here is that the Scriptures predicted that God would not only justify the Jews, but would show similar mercy to the heathen who had been cut off from his household. The Scriptures say, 'in thee shall all families of the earth be blessed'. This does not refer to a handful of people or to a certain race; God opens the door to all those who had previously been deprived of such blessings, without exception. Then Paul concludes that 'they which be of faith are blessed with faithful Abraham'. In other words, when God justified Abraham, it was not due to circumcision nor to any quality in him which made him special in man's sight. He was justified because he was a believer. God was satisfied with Abraham's faith alone. This is why he made him the father of the whole church. Since it was faith alone that enabled Abraham to be accepted by God, we must conclude that we need like faith in order to be acceptable to him; not the same measure of faith, necessarily, but we must follow his example. Even if we follow on from afar, God will accept us. This blessing, then, is not only for the physical family of Abraham but for those who were at one time cut off, provided there is that common bond of faith.

In order to benefit from this doctrine, we must remember what we have already said: that being 'of faith' means resting entirely upon the mercy of God. Paul makes a contrast between two opposites, which are no more compatible than fire and water: between the law and faith. We are not saying that the law is not God-given. Indeed, what will become of those who reject it and treat it with contempt? To do this is to violate God's authority. Paul, however, by using the terms 'law' and 'faith', is not primarily concerned with doctrine but, rather, with the question of where men place their trust for salvation. Justification by faith is taught in both the law and the prophets, as Paul says in the third chapter to the Romans, and the twenty-first verse. It is not a new thing at all. The problem is with those who do not know themselves and who, like blind hypocrites, think they can obtain God's favour by observing the law, which is in fact impossible. Those who hold fast to legal observance are, therefore, 'of the law', and believe they deserve to inherit eternal life. On the other hand, those who are weak in themselves – indeed, who are nothing, and acknowledge that they do not deserve a drop of mercy – these are 'of faith'. What determines this? They have laid their own works aside and sought justification in another. They have come as poor beggars before God and asked him to fill them because they are completely empty.

Thus, the first point is that, through faith, we are stripped of all confidence and pride in our merits and come to find all our help in God's mercy alone. However, we cannot come directly to God without a mediator. We need the Lord Jesus Christ to grant us access. Yet the term 'faith' includes all this. For faith is not something that men create in their own imaginations; it is to be assured of God's mercy when he draws near to us and tenderly declares his love for us. The promise must, therefore, come first, and faith must follow it. This implies that whoever has not been taught the gospel cannot have faith; for God must first reveal that he loves us before we can lean on his mercy or call upon him as our Father. As for the promise itself, God does not simply declare that he will have pity on us, but, rather, that he will accept us despite the fact that we are wretched sinners. He will forgive all our sins through the Lord Jesus Christ, for wherever there is remission of sins, it is through his sacrifice. There can be no pardon before God without the shedding of blood to pay for sin. Thus, the foundation of God's promise to be merciful to us is that the Lord Jesus Christ has shed his blood to cleanse us from our stains, and has made full satisfaction by appeasing the wrath of God the Father. Thus being 'of faith' means having one's eyes fixed upon Jesus Christ, and resting entirely upon his passion and death as the means to reconcile us to God.

Furthermore, let us note that Paul in this passage equates being justified with blessing. Now, out of thirty so-called Christians we would be hard-pressed to find even just one who knew how to define the word 'justification'. I say this to our shame, since our ears are constantly coming under the sound of the gospel, yet we do not properly understand this principal article of faith. Being justified does not mean possessing some sort of righteousness of our own; it is God seeing a person as righteous even though he is not. Here in this passage, we have an excellent exposition of this doctrine, for Paul uses the word 'blessed' where he had previously spoken of being justified. Indeed, in the fourth chapter of the Romans and the fifth verse, he says that justification by faith means that our sins are forgiven. When we are justified in God's sight, he is favourable and kind to us and welcomes us as his children. Why do we need to be justified? Simply because God cannot love sinners until he has forgiven their sins and blotted them out. We know that God, being a righteous God, cannot have anything to do with sin; he has to detest and abhor it. This being the case, we cannot please him in any way unless we have first been purged of all our wrongdoings; for whilst they still count against us, God can only hate us and regard us as accursed. On the other hand, when he has cancelled out all our offences he can welcome us in mercy. This is how we begin to experience his blessing. Are we blessed by God? That is to say, does he love us? Then, we must also be those who are justified. This means that although we are full of sin, God grants us a share in the righteousness of the Lord Jesus Christ. All of his obedience is written to our account. It is as if I owed a sum of money, and another were to pay on my behalf. Although I have paid nothing, I am still free of the debt. I did not have the means to pay, but I found someone else who was willing to help me. The same principle applies to us; we have no righteousness of our own, but Jesus Christ is our substitute and satisfies God the Father on our behalf. Our sins are completely washed away and are not remembered or taken account of by God. This is justification, and this is to be blessed indeed. Whereas we were once accursed and vile in his sight, we are now adopted as his children.

This exposes the folly of the Papists, who cannot be persuaded that we are justified by faith, because, they say, faith is not the greatest of virtues. When a man embraces the promises of God and rests upon them, it may not be instantly apparent to others just what a great step he has made. This man is a poor sinner who has recognised his need of God's merciful aid, and has sought refuge in him. But a man whose life appears good, and who is praised by all around him, will probably have a greater reputation for righteousness than he has! For example, if a man is known to be generous, gives away many of his possessions, and is liberal in every area of his life, he will be considered more righteous than a believer. The Papists even quote Paul in that other passage where he says that love is better than faith or hope (*1 Cor.* 13:13). Yes indeed, but it is not here a question of which is the greatest virtue, or the highest or noblest. When we say that we are justified by faith, it does not imply that there is any worth or merit in our faith which makes God obliged to accept us. Rather, God reveals his mercy and promises to be our Saviour, which causes us to come to him in faith, renouncing all trust in our own virtues. We come knowing that God sees us just as we are, worthy of his curse and his hatred. Therefore, since faith means nothing as a human virtue but receives all its worth from God's free bounty and grace, the question of human dignity or worth is irrelevant. Thus, we can say that faith is not only vital for salvation but that it is also the source of all our righteousness.

Having stated that the Gentiles are blessed in Abraham, Paul adds that they are blessed in 'faithful Abraham'. This is Paul informing us that the only way to be made acceptable to God is by faith: we need not add anything else. To do so is to make the grave mistake that the Papists continue to make to this day. Although they do not know the meaning of faith, nor what it means to be justified, they are forced to admit that faith enables them to obtain salvation. However, they say that faith is only a part of it, and that love and all kinds of other virtues are required. In other words, men need to deserve God's approval – without obedience and holiness of life all is in vain. Whilst it is true that faith is inseparable from the fear of God, faith is all that is needed for God to accept us as his children. Indeed, if he were to take our works into consideration, woe unto us! This is why he turns his back upon any examination of our persons, and accepts us only in and through the Lord Jesus Christ (or if he does consider us, he only finds that our wretched state moves him to be merciful to us). Perhaps, therefore, there is a double regard that God has to us in justifying us: firstly, he sees our miserable condition, that we are in the depths of confusion, and he is moved to take pity upon us. Then, in order not to remain at enmity with us because of our sinfulness, he sees us as we are in the Lord Jesus Christ, clothed in his righteousness, and he cancels out all our transgressions.

Thus, Paul declares that we can only be justified 'with faithful Abraham'. In effect, he is saying that Abraham, no matter how holy a person he was, contributed nothing to his being justified in God's sight. Faith (as we have already seen), entirely strips a man of the worth that he thought he had. Abraham had nothing but faith; it follows, then, that he cast aside all his works as being of no value. This being the case, let us learn not to mix the two, for this is corrupt in God's sight. Let us be content that if God knows us to be believers, we will be acceptable to him. Indeed, let us pose a question: did Abraham's virtues have any value at all in God's eyes in terms of gaining his favour? The answer to this is simple: by nature, Abraham was full of iniquity. He would have been lost, had not God rescued him from the deep pit into which he had fallen. This is demonstrated in the last chapter of Joshua, and the second verse: 'Consider from whence I took your father Abraham', he says to the Jews. 'Did not his fathers serve idols? I saved him from out of the pit of hell.' Thus, Abraham had nothing to boast about, for he could not have done anything had not God granted him grace. Even after God had given Abraham such excellent and noble qualities, and made him a most holy leader, his virtues could not have justified him. There would always have been something in him which called for rebuke, whatever the case. Even when a man forces himself, with all his strength, to obey God, he can only ever limp along, as it were. There will always be something wrong with our works, some small blemish to spoil them in God's sight and make them abominable. Thus, all of Abraham's virtues, if they had been closely examined, could only have brought him condemnation. The same could be said of David or anyone else. When it is a matter of God loving us and calling us his children, it cannot be for two or three deeds that we have performed: it must be for a perfect obedience which does not fall short in any way. This is how it is that Abraham, though he enjoyed some degree of perfection through part of his life, could not be justified through it, because he was still a man and, therefore, a sinner. God had to humble him by keeping him under his control, just as he does with all believers. Therefore, Abraham contributed nothing in and of himself; every good thing in him came from God out of his free mercy. Yet even this was not sufficient to save him, for by nature, as with all of Adam's race, he was condemned and lost. God could only accept him by pardoning his sins, and viewing him only as he stood in the faith.

Let us therefore learn that if God justifies us it is through faith, that is to say, purely out of his free grace. For our part, we must believe his promise in order to gain acceptance and approval, and also in order for our works to be received by him; not by virtue of the fact that they proceed from us, but because we perform them through the power of his Spirit. This is the only way that our works can be righteous in his sight, even worthy of reward, as the Scripture so frequently asserts. All must proceed from faith. Being justified by God, that is to say, being declared righteous, means that our works are also rendered acceptable. In other words, God declares them to be righteous, even though they have no inherent dignity and nothing which would make him obliged to receive them. We are justified by the free grace of God alone when we receive his promises by faith, and our works are justified in exactly the same way. Likewise, Abraham was justified in his person, and subsequently his works also became acceptable in the sight of God. Whatever we may say, if we go right back to the first principles of the matter, we must conclude that all God takes into account is a person's faith. For if God had examined Abraham's life, he would have been condemned just like any other mortal creature. But instead, he wanted to make Abraham his own, and the only thing which moved and motivated him to do so was his great mercy. Abraham, for his part, turned his back upon all the vain things in which men mistakenly put their trust. He knew that the mercy of God alone was sufficient to lead him to eternal life. In other words, just as Abraham only looked to the mercy of God, God only looked to the faith of Abraham. This is how he came to be justified. Thus, we too must cast aside everything that we imagine will merit the favour of God and we must not add to his Word. All these things are but falsehood and Satanic delusions. Let faith be our foundation. Let us humbly acknowledge that we are justified by God only when he pardons our sins, and that as a consequence of this, our works are declared righteous and good; not that he scrutinises them carefully, but rather, he accepts them out of fatherly love. This is what we need to learn from this passage. Finally, how do we know that the blessings of belonging to Abraham's family apply to us? Well, it is clear by what Paul says here, as, indeed, we have already indicated. He says that all nations will be blessed in him.

* * *

It now remains for us to see the opposite view of justification, which Paul sets out here. Men, when left to themselves, will always be of the opinion that they possess a righteousness of their own, unless they are persuaded otherwise. Although we are full of so many horrible sins, yet the worst of them, and that which is rooted most deeply in our natures, is that of pride and presumption – thinking that we have something special about us, when God declares that we are nothing. Indeed, God informs us that we are full of all evil, rottenness and corruption, and that all the virtue we think we have is but vanity and lies. Yet, none of this can humble us unless we perceive our need and become truly convinced of our state. Thus, we need to give careful consideration to the fact that Paul's words are uttered with the intention of drawing us to true faith and turning us away from the vain trust that we might have in our own 'merits'. He says, 'For as many as are of the works of the law are under the curse: for it is written, Cursed is every one that continueth not in all things which are written in the book of the law to do them.' When he says that all who are under the law are cursed, he means that no matter how much effort men make in the realm of works, thinking they will be able to obtain God's favour thereby, they are, in reality, under a curse. For as we have just been saying, the one who is 'of faith' will disregard his own deeds and lean upon the mercy of God alone. On the other hand, the one who is 'of the works of the law' will think that his service for God will move God to grant a reward for his merits. Paul is saying here that all such people are cursed. Why does he say this? Well, he quotes from Moses when he said, 'Cursed be he that confirmeth not all the words of this law' (*Deut.* 27:26). The passage had already said that whoever worships false gods is cursed (*Deut.* 27:15). Next, whoever blasphemes against God is cursed. Then, whoever breaks the Sabbath day of rest is cursed. Furthermore, whoever does not obey his father and mother is cursed. Next, whoever commits adultery with his neighbour's wife is cursed. Having recited all these curses – such solemn utterances – the people had to respond by saying 'Amen, Amen'. It is as if a contract was being made; God stipulates that he must be served in a certain way, without murmuring, and that we must scrupulously observe all that he commands; therefore, the people are to respond with 'Amen'. In other words, they are to say, 'Yes Lord, we accept that whoever does not serve you should be condemned.' After all this, God concludes by saying, 'Cursed be he that confirmeth not all the words of this law to do them.' This means that we must not fail in any point. And to this also the people had to say 'Amen'.

Since the law curses all those who fail to observe it perfectly, let us now consider if there is anyone to be found who can lay claim to such perfect obedience. Without doubt, we all fall short, from the greatest to the least of us. How is this? Well, think for a moment about the summary of the law, which commands us to love God with all our heart, soul, strength and mind, and our neighbour as ourselves. If each of us were to examine our own lives closely for such qualities, we would need no other judge to come and condemn us. For even if we love God sincerely and honestly from the heart, without hypocrisy, it is impossible for us not to be distracted by countless vanities in this life. Let us imagine a man who is as perfect as an angel himself: he still could not love God as he ought. You see, his entire soul must be taken up with loving God. Think of ourselves: we have only to open our eyes and we behold many vain and frivolous sights. We have only to open our ears and we hear so much that does not tend to the glory of God, even if it is not openly evil or sinful! We are expected to devote our whole being to God, so that we only think of glorifying him. Can such perfection be found? Worse still than having our minds distracted and drawn away from loving God, we know that our minds also tempt us daily to do evil so that as soon as we lift our hands, they set about things of no value. The same applies to our feet, our eyes and our ears. Furthermore, what an abyss of evil lies in the human heart! How many twisted desires lurk there, so deeply rooted in our souls? We are full of corruption. Indeed, this is why Jeremiah had to cry out that the heart of man is deceitful beyond measure, such that if a man were to seek to fathom the depths of his heart, it would be impossible to discover even the hundredth part of his wickedness (*Jer.* 17:9). God alone can be the judge of our hearts.

Thus, although God has regenerated us by his Holy Spirit, and although we make great efforts to honour and serve him, we still have a long way to go; we are still 'on the way', and we are but limping along, as it were. Besides our tardiness, there are many pitfalls along the way, and many dangers. We limp with one foot, we falter with the other, and sometimes we fall down altogether: such is our life. Therefore, according to the law, we are all accursed, even if we do not live in open sin. For as I have already declared, no-one can perfectly observe the whole law, which leads us to conclude that, under the law, we all stand condemned. This is why we need to seek our righteousness elsewhere, namely, through the mercy of God alone. Now we have seen why Paul asserts that those who trust in their merits are completely rebelling and fighting against God. God, for his part, virtually drags them by their hair, as it were, to show them the need in which they stand; if they will not come to him, how dreadfully obstinate they must be! Surely they must have been deceived by the devil himself? Paul, therefore, seeks to direct men to find their righteousness and salvation in the grace of our Lord Jesus Christ alone. Without such grace, they will never come to him, because it is our way to think of our own self-worth. Such ambition (or should we say such foolish pride?) blinds us. It prevents us from glorifying God for his righteousness, from being silenced before him in conviction for our sins, as we have seen from this passage.

Moving on, notice that Paul lays down a principle here which the Papists are not careful to uphold. For (amongst other things) they say, 'Cursed and damnable is he who claims that God has commanded us to do more than we are capable of doing.' They excommunicate and anathematise all those who consider that the righteousness of the law is beyond our human faculties to attain. It seems to them that God must not ask us to do what is impossible; we must have the means to satisfy his demands – otherwise the law is unjust. This is how they think and what they say. But here the Holy Spirit says the complete opposite, for God is not obliged to conform his demands to our abilities. Let us think about our duty. Who is there who will dare to contradict and dispute the fact that we must love God with all our hearts? If we are his people, does it not stand to reason that we ought to be completely devoted to him? Thus, we owe him the perfect love that he requires of us. When it comes to our abilities, we are not, in fact, capable of fulfilling our duty to God – that is to say, of loving him as we ought. But if a man squanders all his wealth and is left with nothing, does it mean that he will be free of debt? Not at all! We might say that it is not our fault, but it is! For we have all sinned in

Adam and original sin makes us all stand convicted and guilty before God. Thus, we cannot excuse ourselves by saying 'I am weak', or by the fact that we are perverse by nature and cannot even have a single good thought, as Paul himself says (*2 Cor.* 3:5). Yes, it is true that we cannot, of ourselves, have even one good thought, because our hearts are rebellious and full of evil and our hearts are at enmity with God. The Scriptures tell us this; nevertheless, we are still obliged to do our duty. Thus, we are commanded to obey the law even though it is impossible for us to do it perfectly. Otherwise, Paul would not have written in the eighth chapter to the Romans and the third verse, that God has sent the Lord Jesus Christ to complete that which was impossible under the law. By speaking to us in this way, he proves that we cannot observe all that God has commanded us. For if we could achieve this, we would be able to be justified through it. It is written that all those who fulfil the law perfectly will live (*Lev.* 18:5). If a man could be found who had kept the law, he would live; but Paul uses this argument to show that it is utterly false to believe that we can be justified by observance of the law. No-one can fulfil it perfectly as God requires.

Thus, considering the passage in hand, it is clear that Paul's underlying supposition is that no-one can satisfy the requirements of the law, regardless of the efforts they make. Even those whose lives are governed by the Spirit of God cannot perform his precepts faultlessly during their earthly lives, for they are granted the grace of God by measure. It is true that he is able to bestow upon us such perfection as to make our lives blameless and to grant us full powers of obedience to all his commandments, even greater than that of angels. Yet, though he keeps us in his ways and transforms and changes us, making us obedient to his will, we do not yet possess such a degree of perfection at the present time. Why not? Because God would have us wear the yoke of humility. He wants us to acknowledge our weaknesses and tremble before him; to see our condemned state so that we may always remain indebted to him. Thus, since God does not now grant us the qualities we need to observe the whole of his law perfectly, we can never fulfil what he requires of us. And because we cannot achieve this, this sentence thunders down upon our very heads: 'Cursed is he who does not keep the whole law.' Notice these words very carefully: they do not say 'Cursed is the one who has rejected the law and has altogether disobeyed it', but rather, cursed is he who fails to observe every jot and tittle of it, as I have already made clear. This is why James, in order to cast down all human pride, says that whoever offends in one point is guilty of all (*Jas.* 2:10). At first, we find such a statement most harsh. What? Does God ignore all the good we have done if we so much as commit one fault? To human opinion, this seems cruel, but James explains it by saying that if a man is guilty of murder, he is also guilty of debauchery, and that if a man is guilty of theft, he is guilty concerning the rest of God's commandments. If, therefore, I think I have pleased God because I have refrained from robbery, and yet I live an unclean life, am I not guilty of transgressing against the very holiness of God? Thus, we must not seek to divide everything up neatly, as if we would offer one portion of ourselves to God and leave the other; what will then become of us? We know that some people are taken up with one vice, and some with others; each person seeks to exempt himself because he at least keeps this or that commandment, although he may fail in another department of his life! God will not separate his commandments. He will not say to one, 'You must not steal', and to another, 'You must not commit adultery'. He says to all without exception, 'Keep yourselves from adultery, theft and murder.'

We must all, therefore, examine our lives, not against one of God's precepts but against the whole law. Can any of us truly say that we are blameless? Surely we are all put to shame when we judge ourselves by the standards of the law. If Abraham were amongst us now, it is certain that he too, though he is the best man God could possibly have chosen, would still stand condemned. This being the case, there is no longer any room for dispute; the Papists do but mock justification by faith and toy with the concept, as if they believed

God were no more than a child. Let us refrain from all such arrogance. God has pronounced such an awesome curse upon all who fail to keep the whole law. This ought to keep us in his fear and cause us to tremble before his majestic presence. Let us each be our own judge and willingly pass sentence on ourselves as we become convinced of our poverty. Let us fear when we realise how far short we fall, and let us embrace the righteousness offered to us by the Lord Jesus Christ, finding all our peace and contentment in him.

Now let us fall before the majesty of our great God, acknowledging our sins, and praying that he would make us increasingly conscious of them. May we not only come to him for pardon in true repentance, but may we also ask him to help us throughout our whole lives until he receives us into his kingdom. Until then, may he transform us continually through his Holy Spirit, witnessing with our spirits that we are truly his children, if we are living in his fear and seeking to devote ourselves to him alone. Thus, we all say, Almighty God and our heavenly Father, etc.

18

We All Stand Condemned by the Law

> *But that no man is justified by the law in the sight of God, it is evident: for, The just shall live by faith. And the law is not of faith: but, The man that doeth them shall live in them* (Gal 3:11–12).

We have seen that men must be worse than insane (whatever they say) if they do not come to the Lord Jesus Christ for salvation. For if they cling to the law, it will only bring damnation, as I have shown; this is borne out sufficiently by our own experience. Indeed, when Paul in his Epistle to the Romans seeks to prove that men are greatly deceived if they trust in their own merits, he points out that the law can only bring God's wrath and vengeance upon us (*Rom.* 4:15). For although we already stand condemned (even before God has opened his mouth in judgment against us), our evil is exposed by the law because it is written that if we transgress in just one area, we are God's enemies and have provoked his wrath against us. What can be gained by protesting when the sentence is given from the heavenly throne? There is no room for appeal. Thus, to have a proper understanding of the gospel, we must recognise that we need to lean entirely upon the Lord Jesus Christ and his mercy alone as our only hope of salvation. We all need to examine our own lives, for if we do so honestly and without hypocrisy, our spiritual standing will be abundantly clear. The Papists will not agree that faith alone can render us acceptable to God. This is because they have never been willing to place themselves before the judgment seat of God, but, instead, prefer to dwell in the darkness, as it were. Therefore, it should not surprise us if they grant themselves complete liberty to do as they please. However, the way of true, pure religion is for each of us to scrutinise our own lives. Surely, even if we were carefully to examine just one minute of our lives, we would find ourselves worthy of eternal death. Indeed, each one of us would discover ourselves to be sinners, not in just one area but a hundred thousand; not due to some one fault but to countless millions. Now if even we ourselves acknowledge that we are full of so many blemishes, surely God is aware of many more than we could ever perceive, because he sees more deeply than we can, as John writes in his epistle (*1 John* 3:20). Thus, the case is settled. The verdict is that no-one can be justified by the law; justification is through faith alone.

The apostle continues his discourse by adding another argument, which is this: if we seek our righteousness in the law, it will be clean contrary to the righteousness obtained by the elect children of God through faith. 'What is justification by the law?', Paul asks. He answers: 'The man that doeth them shall live in them.' In other words, whoever obeys God and keeps his commandments will have salvation as his reward. This is a wonderful promise, but what good will it do us? If we were to try to do perfectly all that God commands, we would find God revealing just what a grievous state of condemnation we are in, by bringing our failure to the forefront. What sort of salvation would it be, if each of us had to achieve it ourselves and deserve it? At first, when we hear that God is willing to reward with the gift of eternal life all who have honoured and served him by keeping his law, it seems like a wonderful prospect (that is, before we ponder its implications!). 'What!', we say, 'Here is God indebted to us, assuring us that we will inherit paradise if only we serve him and do his will.' But if we pause to place our lives alongside his commandments, we will find that although it appears that God is willing to be so kind and indulgent towards us as to reward us if we serve him and keep his law, the purpose of this is to plunge us deeper into the pit in which we already find ourselves by nature. What hope, therefore, can we have? The solution is set forth here by the apostle in the words of Habakkuk: 'The just shall live by faith' (*Hab.* 2:4). Let us, therefore, turn away from the promise which the law gives us, for it is of no value to us, and accept the free grace of our God, who is stretching out his arms to receive us, that is, if we first rid ourselves of all pride. This is, in effect, what Paul means here.

This argument discloses two opposites. Imagine this: one person claims that fire is a source of heat, and another arrives and rather obstinately argues the opposite. We might say to him, 'Can ice or frost create heat, then? Surely, they are opposite elements, and completely incompatible with one another!' Or imagine a quarrel about whether the heat of the sun is necessary to this life of ours or not. Well, what would happen if there were no sun in the world? We would all choke on filthy air, which is only purged by the shining of the sun. Therefore, as there are opposing forces in the realm of nature, so the apostle says that we cannot be justified by both the law and the grace of God! If we desire to be in his favour, it can only be through his own goodness and love for us, which he has revealed in the Lord Jesus Christ, and not through any dignity we possess in and of ourselves. But in order properly to understand this teaching, we need to pay careful attention to Paul's words here. He says that the righteousness of the law is achieved by observing whatever God has commanded us. This proves that keeping the law is quite sufficient to save us, for God has clearly declared, 'This is how you are to live. This is how you are to order your lives', and he has given us the ten commandments contained in the law. This law is an infallible rule for our lives, and we are not to seek for perfect righteousness anywhere else. This is why we are so opposed to the Papists, who think they are serving God so faithfully by devising their own commandments. God demands obedience. Let us be clear that the law contains the perfection of holiness in its teachings; it is not lawful to add anything to it. Man's struggle to introduce devotions which he has conceived in his own imagination is vanity.

However, the fact that the teachings of the law are sufficient to show us the nature of true righteousness, is not the end of the matter. We must move on to the next point, which is, 'Can we do what God has commanded?' We saw this morning that we fall very far short and, thus, the promise for all who keep the law is not applicable to us. The Papists are greatly deceived in this matter: they still hold to the lie that God has not commanded anything that we cannot accomplish ourselves. Yet, Paul says the very opposite. They claim in support of their error that God must, therefore, be cheating us, because he clearly says, 'The man that doeth them shall live in them.' But it is very easy to resolve this objection. Yes, we would, indeed, be most confused over the meaning of this verse, had not God granted us a remedy to this problem; otherwise, it would mean that no-one could live! As I have said, it would seem, superficially, that we have everything to gain, because God tells us that we can be acceptable in his sight by keeping the law, and he promises us a crown of glory; in fact, it would seem that we just cannot lose! But when all is taken into account, we come back to this same conclusion: no man can obtain eternal life in this way, no matter how much he desires it. Why? Because no man observes the law perfectly. It is not written that 'The man who keeps part of the law will live', but all of it. What, then, is justification by the law? A perfect obedience to it which does not fall short in any way. Such obedience cannot be found on earth: it therefore follows that we are all excluded from the promise which is given in the law.

This, however, does not mean that God is cheating us. He makes such a promise because men deceive themselves through pride and boast of their own merits; he therefore wishes to convict us of our guilt and of our inability to fulfil his demands. What would become of us if there were no law, nor such a promise as this? Think of the heathen – they have always sought to be pleasing to God through their own virtuous conduct. Yet, at the same time, they have an awareness of their shortcomings. This is why they retain the use of sacrifices. Of course, they do not understand the true purpose of sacrifice; when the heathen sacrifice something, they confess that they are in debt to God and need to find acceptance with him. Much like the Papists today, they amass many little rituals in their service to help them find reconciliation with God. Pagans throughout the ages have observed the kind of practices that the Papists use today. Whatever they may say, both groups think they can make themselves worthy of God's salvation. Now, here the Lord is saying that we are wrong if we think he will not reward us, for out of his free goodness he promises to count us righteous if we observe his law. The question is: do we keep it? No; we fall very far short, in fact so short of it that we are made to feel desperate. God has good reason for making such a promise, even though it cannot be realised in our lives. Its intention is to correct the pride which fills us to the point of bursting, and which requires a drastic remedy. And what is this remedy? Well, God knows that we begin to murmur if he does not treat us according to our desires, and therefore he is willing to pour out his grace and blessings upon us in this world, in this passing life. Furthermore, he says he is willing to reserve an immortal inheritance for us, upon condition that we serve him. If we submit to him and keep a good account with him, he says he will reward us both in this life and the next. In saying all these things, he intends that all flesh should remain silent before him, confessing that if God were to punish them, or send them many afflictions and trials, they would be well deserved. For those of us who have properly examined their lives will confess without hypocrisy that we are not even worthy to eat the bread that sustains our physical lives on this earth. How, then, could we possibly merit paradise and the glory that belongs to God alone? How could we reach this by our own virtues? Thus, men's boasting tongues are silenced, even through this most generous and bountiful promise of the Lord.

At this point, we ought to note that this same promise is free in and of itself, but that we fall so far short of its standards that it will do us no good whatsoever until we relinquish our claim upon it. This would seem rather unclear to us, if I did not expound it in more detail. The heathen, as I mentioned earlier, think that God will reward them if they live honest and blameless lives in the sight of men. But this is foolishness, even madness, for how could God possibly be indebted to us? (This is made clear in the seventeenth chapter of Luke – *Luke* 17:10.) Even if we could do better than the angels in heaven, would it mean that God would be bound to repay us? Not at all! For we belong to him; we are his possession. Our Lord Jesus Christ uses the picture of a servant; not speaking of a servant as we know it today, but, rather of a slave like the ones they used to have in those days. Even if a servant were killed a hundred times over for his master, as it were, living or dying, he is at his master's disposal. Our Lord Jesus Christ is saying to us, 'You are no more than poor mortal creatures yourselves, yet if any of you has a slave, he treats him like an ass or an ox. After working and labouring hard all day long, he returns home in the evening, but the master will not even let him sit down at his table! Even so, a servant has only done his duty and only that which he was hired to do.' Has God less authority than mortals? Even though you may be his, and are seeking to walk in obedience to his will, it can never be said that he is in any sense beholden to you. Thus (as I have already proved), although the Lord declared in the law, 'The man that doeth them shall live in them', it is important to consider what moved him to make such a bountiful promise of eternal life. It was not because he was indebted to us! If we kill ourselves, as it were, a hundred times in his service, this cannot make him obliged to pay us any wages whatever. But, in his mercy, he draws near and says, 'Although I owe you nothing, and although you can bring me nothing worthy of a reward (for you are bound to me in all points and in every respect), yet I desire to recompense you for your labour. Therefore, do your duty, do whatsoever I command and then you will not be disappointed but will receive your reward.' This is what we need to remember, and we will hear more of this shortly.

As for the Papists, they accept part of this, but not all. Most of them (I refer to those who are the Pope's closest allies) know nothing of these principles. Yet there are some who will grant that the divine promise of the law (to give life to all who have served God) does not teach that the works themselves have any merit in terms of eternal life, but only because of the promise. However, given that God has bound himself in this way, they nevertheless hope to deserve some reward at his hand. Why do they think in this way? Well, they say that, otherwise, his promise ('The man that doeth them shall live in them') was made in vain. However, these wretches do not understand what I have been expounding, namely, that God's promise does not mean that men can merit salvation by their own works, but was rather intended to convict their souls and to lead them to true humility. This they shun, through their own foolish pride and ambition.

Now we can see the purpose behind Paul's words – if we claim to be justified through the law or through our own works, we must not fail in the least duty or omit to do anything, however small. For it is written, 'The man that doeth them shall live in them'. Now, what man is so proud that he would dare boast he has fully discharged his duty towards God? None but a hypocrite who has been overtaken by devilish pride, or a profane person who despises God and who has never truly repented, whose conscience is either asleep or bewitched. Only such a person can deceive himself into thinking he deserves anything. Thus, since the righteousness of the law is unattainable, and is something from which we are utterly barred, we need to find another righteousness. Put another way, we need God to accept us through his free grace. Instead of God receiving anything from us, we need the obedience of the Lord Jesus Christ to be imputed to us, though we do not deserve it. Thus, we are delivered by God from our state of condemnation by nature through the abolition of all our offences and iniquities. In effect, this is what is meant in another passage, where Paul argues so admirably about this very doctrine (*Rom.* 3:19). In this place, too, the point at issue is the righteousness of the law. It is a wonder to me that the Papists have gone so far astray as to ignore such a clear warning as Paul makes in the latter text. They still protest thus: 'What!', they say, 'You are making a mockery of God! He has promised a reward for good works. Since he has promised on so many occasions to recompense us, how can he not carry it out? Otherwise, men might accuse him of lying.' But Paul answers them thus: 'My friends, if we think God will accept us because we deserve his favour, let us examine the promise he made us. If an argument breaks out between two men over buying or selling or some such thing, they will say, "Let us examine the contract and what is contained within it." As soon as the document has been read, the case will become plain. One of them will say, "This article belongs to you, upon condition that you pay for it. If you do not pay, you can lay no claim to it." In the same way, with reference to the way of salvation, we must come to the original and chief contract that God made with us. Now, that contract is the law. Therefore, if men are seeking to be paid according to their service, they will find that this will banish them from everlasting life rather than enable them to obtain it. For God has declared that they have to perform all that he has commanded them, before they can inherit the salvation he has in store.' All that remains is to find out whether or not it is possible for any man to perform these commandments perfectly.

Well, as we have already discovered, no-one fulfils these requirements satisfactorily; thus, the promise cannot apply to us in our natural state. However, this is not what the Papists believe. They hear the words, 'The man that doeth them shall live in them' and think the most important thing is to observe the law. It is enough for them that God has given his Word to reward them. Whilst it is true that God has indeed said this, he requires that we actually fulfil his demands. The Papists will then use the following passage, where Paul says, 'For not the hearers of the law are just before God, but the doers of the law shall be justified' (*Rom.*

2:13). They will use such quotations, but are clearly blind to their meaning, for Paul is saying that we can only be justified if we obey all that is commanded. The Jews used to glory in the law that had been given to them, saying, 'The law tells us that we are the people of God.' But there was a condition attached to this. And who has fulfilled that condition? Have you? Not in the least! Thus, we cannot be justified by hearing the law, as Paul says. How foolish if each of us simply came to church to hear the message that was being declared here, and then went away again, gratifying our own lusts. Paul says we must observe what God commands us, yet, since no-one can do this properly, we all stand condemned.

The Papists, however, fail to reach the same conclusion because they only cling to half the text: 'But the doers of the law shall be justified.' Yes, this is so if a person has kept the law, but first show me such a man. In the same Epistle to the Romans, Paul later declares that God's promise of eternal life to all who keep his law is of no value to us because we can never perform it adequately (*Rom.* 8:3). In fact, by nature we are completely hostile to God's righteous standards. Now that he has regenerated us by his Holy Spirit, we are entirely indebted to him; every good thing we possess we have received from his hand, and he simply rewards his own gifts in us. Can we, therefore, speak of merit? No. Indeed, we must go further and say that even though our Lord deigns to crown our works when they are good in his sight, they can only be partly good, for there will always be enough sin mixed in with them to condemn us. Thus, we are stripped of all confidence in our own righteousness, because our works have insufficient worth in the eyes of God. If we were being judged by the text, 'The man that doeth them shall live in them', our works would be shown to be totally offensive to God. He would say, as it were, 'You are all dead, damned and lost. Why? Because none of you have done the things I asked you to do, whereas it was your duty to do so.' This is why we need to consider the second aspect to the solution I mentioned, which is 'living by faith'.

* * *

Paul, in the passage I referred to earlier (*Rom.* 3:21–22), does not quote the words of Habakkuk as he does in Romans chapter one and the seventeenth verse. But he says that the law points to the righteousness which is by faith. The righteousness of the law (that is, the God-given rule in the law which justifies us) is that we must obey and observe all his commandments. But the righteousness of faith speaks another language. It says that it is not for man to seek to win God's favour through the way he lives his life, and thus earn his reward or crown; rather, it is for man to rest entirely upon God's Word, allowing it to dwell in his heart and upon his lips. For if we believe in our hearts that the Lord Jesus Christ has died, and confess with our lips that he has risen again, we shall be counted righteous in God's sight (*Rom.* 10:9). Notice that Paul explains his meaning at some length here for us to comprehend why he separates the righteousness of the law and the righteousness of faith, showing us that they are incompatible and can no more be mixed together than fire and water. Not that there is any contradiction between the law and the gospel (as I have already made clear), for we know that they both proceed from the same God. But we must remember God's purposes, as we have said all along. By giving us the righteousness of the law, he intended to humble us. Next, we will come before him realising we are condemned; this we would never have done if he had not revealed to us our own poverty. When we read that God promises justification if we serve him aright, he is saying in effect, 'Poor creatures, what worth or value do you have in and of yourselves? Weigh up my commandments and consider what they involve, and then reflect upon how each of you have lived. This will make you feel as if you could drown in self-despair.' Yet, though God speaks in this vein, he also grants a remedy – 'Come', he says, 'to the teachings of the gospel'. And what are they? Paul quotes the expression of Habakkuk, from chapter two and the fourth verse: 'The just shall live by his faith'. And in this passage he explains it more clearly, as we have seen, stating that we need to resort wholly to the Lord Jesus Christ. For the 'Word' that should be in our hearts and upon our lips, bringing us to God, and opening the kingdom of heaven to us, is not a Word that makes us cleave to this world below. Nor does it lead us to believe that God will praise us for our merits, allowing us to be puffed up with pride. Not at all; rather, it makes us cling to the Lord Jesus Christ. The righteousness of faith that God grants us involves the following: understanding that our sins are blotted out through the death and passion of our Lord Jesus Christ; understanding also that through his resurrection we have obtained righteousness, and are now heirs of his heavenly kingdom (whereas before we were condemned to the pit of hell, which is the heritage that belongs to us and of which we are worthy by nature). We must also realise that in Jesus Christ, all that we lost in Adam is restored to us. The curse which covered us is removed when God sets us free. This is the righteousness of faith, and indeed, when we examine the context of the verse Paul quotes from the prophet Habakkuk, we will see that it is to this very doctrine that the Holy Spirit is pointing.

Now, the prophet had spoken about the chastisements and judgments that God would send on the people; therefore, having examined the situation, we might well have concluded that all was lost. Then he says that the pride of the wicked will swell and increase, but that their feet are in a slippery place and they will stumble in the way. The more they seek to exalt themselves, the more grievous will be their fall. This is what the prophet pronounces upon the wicked. On the other hand, he says of the just that they shall 'live by faith'. Notice he says that the just shall live, implying that God's children will not find life here below. Even if they were to travel all over the world, and search high and low, they would soon realise that there is death and decay everywhere and in everything. However, though they do not enjoy this 'life' at the present time, they look forward to a life to come, and cherish it in their hearts and minds by faith. The prophet is seeking to draw the minds of God's elect away from both the world and themselves, so that they may cleave entirely to God, finding his grace alone sufficient for their salvation. Yet, Paul puts the case more briefly in our passage, because he was fully persuaded of the things I have expounded, and had already written of them – he always taught that faith leads us to find salvation in God alone. The law, though it may appear to be teaching something very different, actually shows us that there is no life in us at all, if we understand it aright. The law says, 'Work hard and do what you can to obtain paradise.' Why does it say this? Not to feed man's vain confidence in his own merits – certainly not! Rather, to prepare us to receive the grace of the Lord Jesus Christ in humility. For (as I have said), although we are far away from God, we all like to think we are worthy of his acceptance. But our Lord will be avenged on such presumptuousness. He says to us, 'Let me see what you have done, draw near and we will begin the reckoning. Whichever of us owes anything to the other will have to pay it. I will not disappoint you; I have the reward in my hand. It is all ready. If you have done what I have commanded you, do not worry, you will be well paid for your labour. Therefore, set to work and let me observe how you will serve me.' In saying this, our Lord, as I have said, prepares and disposes us to know what we are by nature. When we have acknowledged our poverty, then we will come to him to supply what we lack. Thus, the law leads to faith, albeit by a surprising route!

Whatever we may think, there will always be the paradox of which Paul speaks here. That is to say, that a person cannot be justified by faith unless he has first recognised and acknowledged in complete sincerity that he is lost. For salvation must be based upon the knowledge that we deserve damnation. It might seem as if Paul has taken the prophet's words too far, if Habakkuk was simply speaking of the afflictions of this transitory life. The just 'shall live' could mean 'shall survive', even though God may afflict and torment him. He will not fall if he rests upon the promises of God. Paul, however, is not dealing with the question of God comforting us and delivering us from the calamities to which we are subject in this world; he is concerned with the question of our eternal salvation, which is of far greater importance than anything else in this fleeting life. It might appear, therefore, as if he has misapplied the words of the prophet. But let us remember that the words themselves would have been uttered in vain if the thoughts of the prophet had gone no further than this world, for afflictions come upon all, upon good and bad alike. How, then, can we speak of living by faith, if we are constantly falling into the same trials that God has already delivered us from once, twice or three times before? If God has comforted me today in some affliction or other, and shown me his grace, tomorrow he may afflict me with another trial. What would my life be like if I had but this world alone to trust in? Therefore, to sum up, the prophet was saying that although believers may be miserable and may languish in this life, nevertheless, God blesses them in this world, and, furthermore, all the evil they endure here below shall turn to felicity. Why? Because they trust in their God. We ought to be aware, therefore, that there is a better inheritance than this, and we need to seek true, everlasting happiness – the kind that endures.

We must be careful to comment on the word 'just' here. For if Habakkuk had said, 'Wretched sinners shall live by faith', we would perhaps have imagined that his words were addressed to just a handful of people. Most will freely accept that poor sinners need to flee to God for refuge, but as for those of nobler virtues, surely they are exempt from what applies to the common people, God having exalted them to a higher degree? Surely it is their prerogative to be justified? Even today, though the Popish clergy (as they call them), with all their ceremonies, are filthy in God's sight, and ought to be abhorred by both God and man, yet they presume, because of their monkish habit and all the rest of their nonsense, that God is greatly in their debt! These bigots, having done all their babbling, and trotting up and down from altar to altar, and from chapel to chapel on various pilgrimages, hope that God will remember all their works. They hope that all of this will be put towards the payment of their account, with a hundred thousand other things that they plan to present to God! This is why the Lord Jesus Christ said that poor wretched sinners, even harlots, would enter the kingdom of heaven sooner than all these foul toads who are puffed up with pride in their own merits (*Matt.* 21:31)! Although their lives are full of wicked abominations, yet in their hypocrisy they suppose that God is bound to reward them.

Now, to eliminate all opportunity of entertaining such thoughts, the prophet expressly says, 'The just shall live by his faith.' At first, the meaning of this verse might be obscure to us. Does it mean that in order to have righteousness we must first live by faith? If this is the case, those who do not live by faith cannot be righteous. But what is the justification spoken of in the gospel? It is this – God freely granting us the means by which we may have access to him. We can be acceptable to him in the Lord Jesus Christ alone, for we cannot obtain righteousness through the law. Thus, although a man may live by faith, he is not righteous in and of himself. The prophet, therefore, means that the just are saved by the free grace of God alone. It is as if he were saying, 'Perhaps God will grant you grace to serve him acceptably, impressing upon your heart by his Holy Spirit true fear and a zeal to glorify him as he deserves. He may well enable you to struggle against the lusts of the flesh to a great extent, striving with the sin which is part of your nature. Yet for all this, you must still turn your back upon all that you have done if you are seeking to please God.' Indeed, we must rest upon the Lord Jesus Christ alone. If even those who are righteous can only be justified through faith, who is there who will dare to seek to be justified through merit? Only devils, wicked men and the enemies of God.

Thus, when the Papists boast today (as they do) about the purity of their works and meritorious deeds, they only prove that they do not know the meaning of true righteousness. They are flying in the face of both God and nature. They say they want to be righteous – what do they mean? They mean in themselves, through works of merit. But what does the prophet say? He does not say that the just shall live by their works, but that they will be saved by the grace of God alone. If the just renounce, as they ought, all trust in their own merit, it follows that those who think they can come before God in the strength of their own deeds and that he will be bound to reward them, are striking themselves off the register of the righteous. Thus, according to the statement uttered here by the prophet, the Papists are rejected by God if they continue in their errors. Paul quotes the words of David: 'Blessed is the man to whom the Lord will not impute sin.' He teaches us that the righteous are those who condemn themselves, feeling in the very depths of despair, until God, in his goodness, rescues them (*Rom.* 4:8; *Psa.* 32:1ff). When David said, 'Blessed is the man to whom the Lord will not impute sin', he was not, at this stage of his life, a wicked or dissolute man, nor one who despised God or who had never examined his conscience to expose his sin! On the contrary, God had chosen him; he had anointed him through Samuel; he had made him one of the foremost prophets. His kingdom prefigured that of the Lord Jesus Christ. In short, God had so transformed him that he was now like an angel living amongst men. Yet, he confessed and acknowledged his sins, sorrowing and mourning over them, and was in a state of torment like that of hell itself. He remained thus tortured until God came and displayed his mercy, knowing no joy or peace until God granted him forgiveness. We, too, can only be happy if God overlooks all our deeds and blots out all our sins. This joy is ours if God is gracious to us, no longer considering what we are by nature – poor, condemned sinners – and accepting us, not as we are in our own persons, but for the sake of his only Son. Indeed, David reiterates this teaching in another place (*Psa.* 143:2): 'Enter not into judgment with thy servant: for in thy sight shall no man living be justified.'

Let us, therefore, learn the following lesson: the more a man fears God, the more he will be ashamed of his sin. Consciousness of sin is not something that should last for a mere three or four months – we ought to detest our sins for the rest of our lives. After all, let us remember that the mouth of hell is open, ready to swallow us up unless God supplies the grace we need so desperately and plucks us out of the pit of death. This is why it is written that 'the just shall live by faith' – not as a doctrine that applies for three or four months only; nor is it written for those whose lives are less holy than others. God addresses these words even to the very noblest amongst us.

Now before we end, we need to comment upon the word 'live'. It does not refer to a fixed length of time, say a day or three months. It speaks, instead, of a life lived by God's grace every moment, in which we seek his presence and grace day by day to the end of our earthly lives. Although our lives are hidden in this world, as Paul says (*Col.* 3:3), and we see nothing but death in front of us, we need to rest entirely upon the promise of God. He has assured us of eternal life and this life is his to give – he will reserve it for us! He has pledged it to us by sending the Lord Jesus Christ, who died and rose again for our sakes. Now we no longer need ask, 'Who will go up for us to heaven?'. Or, 'Who will descend into the depths?' Or, 'Who will go over the sea for us?'. 'The Word is nigh thee, even in thy mouth and in thy heart' (*Deut.* 30:12; *Rom.* 10:6–8). We know that our Lord Jesus Christ descended into the deep; that is, he became a curse for us (as we shall see, God willing, in the next sermon – let this suffice us for now). Also he ascended into heaven and opened the door for us, since he entered on our behalf. Let us find great assurance in these truths and allow ourselves to be like poor, dead men in this world while we await the revelation of the life which has been promised us. There is no doubt but that God will reveal and manifest it to us in his time, and we will fully rejoice in that 'life' which his holy gospel has so long proclaimed.

Now let us fall before the majesty of our great God, acknowledging our sins, and praying that he would make us increasingly conscious of them. May we be so affected by them that we cast ourselves down before him, trembling and groaning under the burden of the weaknesses and sins which beset us, until he has fully purged us. Let us also pray that, during this mortal life, he would bear us up until he has utterly delivered us from slavery to sin and bondage to Satan; until, I say, he has granted us complete liberty. May he not only grant this grace to us, but to all peoples, etc.

19

When Curse Becomes Blessing

> *Christ hath redeemed us from the curse of the law, being made a curse for us: for it is written, Cursed is every one that hangeth on a tree: That the blessing of Abraham might come on the Gentiles through Jesus Christ; that we might receive the promise of the Spirit through faith . . .* (Gal. 3:13–18).

As we have seen, if our only hope of salvation rested upon the condition that we fulfil our duty, we would all be condemned; for we have all fallen short in many different ways and are, therefore, guilty in the eyes of God. Indeed, even the holiest amongst us can never claim to have reached a state of perfection, never again to fall, and free from all infirmity! We are, therefore, led to conclude that we will all be lost and condemned when God calls us to account. This is man's true condition, despite the high regard he may have for himself! Therefore, we need some means of escape from the curse we are under. Otherwise, what good will it do us to have our ears daily assailed by the Word of God? It will only push us closer towards eternal death. Thus, in order that the Word of God should profit and assist us to find salvation, we have to find a way of escape from the sentence of judgment pronounced upon the human race. Paul points out the way of escape to us here: 'Christ hath redeemed us from the curse of the law, being made a curse for us.' He shows us that it was not in vain that our Lord Jesus Christ hung on the tree, for he suffered to bear the curse of all those he would call to salvation.

As we have said, we are all under this curse, which means it was necessary for our Lord to take our burden of sin upon himself. In the law of Moses, it is written: 'Cursed is everyone that hangeth on a tree' (*Deut.* 21:23). Our Lord commanded that the bodies of the dead should be removed from sight, because it was a disgrace to see a human body thus defiled and therefore he desired it to be taken away. Yet, when God pronounced this curse upon all who hung upon a tree, he knew only too well what was going to happen to his only Son. For the Lord Jesus Christ did not suffer such a death by accident, nor according to the whim of man. Whilst it is true that he was crucified by unbelievers, it had been ordained by the will of God (*Acts* 2:23; 4:28). As it is written, God so loved the world that he did not even spare his only Son, but delivered him up to death for us. Indeed, if his death had been determined by Judas alone, who had him wickedly and forcibly led away, this could not be the foundation for our salvation at all! We must remember that God had appointed it thus, as Peter expounds in greater depth in Acts chapter two, verse twenty-three, where he states that the wicked hands that crucified our Lord Jesus did no more than God had previously determined in his will. Thus, when we read that our Lord Jesus Christ was crucified, we must remember that it was all for our salvation, because by this means God was seeking to reconcile us to himself. Therefore, when God said, 'Cursed is everyone that hangeth on a tree', he was not ignorant of what was going to occur, for all had been settled and predetermined.

These two facts must be carefully held together – that God has said that whoever hangs upon a tree is cursed, but that it was his will for his own Son to suffer thus. Why was this? He took our burden upon himself, as our substitute, and made himself, as it were, the chief of sinners on our behalf. Jesus Christ became a curse in order to deliver us from the curse of the law. It may seem harsh and strange at first sight that the Lord of Glory, he who has all sovereign authority, and before whom all the angels of heaven tremble and prostrate themselves, should be subject to a curse. But we must call to mind what Paul wrote in the first letter to the Corinthians, that is to say, that gospel teaching is foolishness to the human race, who regard themselves as wise (*1 Cor.* 1:18, 23). Indeed, in this way, God humbles us for our folly. For there is enough wise and good instruction, if we care to heed it, in the heaven and earth around us; yet we are blind and shut our eyes to God's wisdom displayed in nature. This is why he has opened up a new way to draw us to himself – through something which we deem foolish! Thus, we must not judge what we read here, concerning the curse to which the Son of God was subject, by our own human reasoning. Instead, we should delight in such a mystery and give glory to God that he loved our souls so much that he redeemed them at such inestimable cost to himself. Far from detracting from the majesty of our Lord Jesus Christ, or obscuring the glory which the Holy Scriptures attribute to him, this teaching provides occasion to glorify him even more. Indeed, may we all do so, for here is our Lord Jesus Christ refusing to consider it robbery (as Paul expresses it) to reveal himself in his infinite glory (*Phil.* 2:6). He willingly emptied himself; he not only took upon himself a human nature and became a man, but he also submitted to a most shameful death in the sight of both God and man. How precious to him we must have been for him to allow himself to experience such extreme suffering for our redemption! If we could but taste something of what this implies, we would forever magnify the unspeakable grace which surpasses all human understanding. However, although we cannot comprehend it fully, and can only fathom the hundredth part of it, it delights us to know that we can grasp something of its meaning, however small!

Yet, how this exposes the malice and perversity that is in man! For when Paul declares that our Lord Jesus Christ became a curse for us, it washes over us. There are even those who are so depraved that they will see this as an occasion to behave scandalously, abandoning the gospel altogether when they hear of the way in which Christ has redeemed us. Such people say, 'What! Can it be that the Son of God, the fountain of all that is good, and the one who sanctifies us, has been cursed?' To their way of thinking, God has acted in an unreasonable and disorderly fashion! But, (as I have been saying), God had to stoop to this 'folly' because we did not respond to his wisdom, though the way was clearly evident; thus he exposes our own ignorance! We can only wonder at the mysteries of God, for their significance may be obscure to us and seem strange; for in the face of such wonders, our intellect fails and our powers of reasoning are confounded!

The fact that the Son of God became a curse for us demands a fuller examination of our sinful state. Indeed, we begin to realise that we are detestable in the eyes of God, that is, until our sins and iniquities have been cleansed in the blood of the Lord Jesus Christ. For even if all the angels of heaven were to be made answerable for us, the price they would pay would be insufficient. The only one able to make satisfaction for our sins is the Lord Jesus Christ. But, when he came to this world, it was not by a display of divine and heavenly power that he paid our debt of eternal death. How, then, did he come? In weakness; indeed, not only so, but he was accursed. If this had not been the case, our burdens would have crushed us and all would have perished in the abyss. When we understand that the Son of God, the Lamb without blemish, the mirror and fountain of all righteousness, that this One was cursed for us, should we not be horrified at the thought of all our sins and engulfed in despair until God rescues us in his grace and infinite mercy? Therefore, let us be aware that when God says he has redeemed us from the curse of the law, it is to bring us to a state of complete humility. We can never be humble unless we are first stripped of self-confidence and become ashamed at what lies within us. Then we are frightened and lost, knowing that the wrath of God hangs over us until the remedy is applied to us through our Lord Jesus Christ. Thus, our whole life is detestable in God's sight and there is no means of reconciliation with him apart from the Lord Jesus Christ, who takes away the curse which is upon us and bears it himself. Now, each time that we read this passage, we should arise and present ourselves before the judgment seat of God, aware that there is a pit waiting to swallow us up if we remain as we are. Let us feel our lost condition and be ashamed before God. Furthermore, let us magnify the grace bought for us by the Son of God, and be careful not to detract from his worth in any way whatsoever, even though he became a curse. This ought, rather, to stir us to render all the praise that he deserves, for he has proved our salvation to be so precious to him.

Moreover, let us properly appreciate such a pledge of our salvation and display of the love God has for us, and let us not doubt that we are acceptable in God's sight when we approach him. For he has redeemed us at such a cost, as Peter shows in his first epistle – not with silver or corruptible things but with the Lord Jesus Christ who became a ransom for us (*1 Pet.* 1:18). Therefore, we must trust that whenever we come in his name to ask for mercy, it will be bestowed upon us. But if we come believing that we have a scrap of merit, what good is it? We know how much the Father loves the Son, and how precious his death was in his sight. For this reason, we can have full confidence that God will forgive us and be favourable and kind to us if we cleave to what Paul shows us here: namely, that our Lord Jesus Christ spared nothing for us, even to the point of bearing our curse.

* * *

However, let us turn our attention to what Paul continues to say: 'That the blessing of Abraham might come on the Gentiles through Jesus Christ; that we might receive the promise of the Spirit through faith.' By mentioning Abraham, he reveals that the promise belonged first to those who descended from him. For the gift of salvation was for the Jews until God opened the doors to everyone else, and spread his gospel abroad, that all might share in the redemption purchased by the Lord Jesus Christ. For although this promise originally belonged to the Jews and was peculiar to them, it was made applicable to the whole world. How is this possible? Because the promise originated in the Spirit and was not dependent upon observing the ceremonies. By referring us to the Spirit, Paul blots out all the false doctrines taught by seducers who sought to mix the law and the gospel together. He is revealing that now all these things are superfluous, that is to say, sacrifices, circumcision and suchlike. This is not to argue that we cannot profit by reading what is contained in the law: no, but the practice of it has been abolished. This is why we can say that the promise is a spiritual one for us today, because we no longer need the types and shadows of days gone by. Now we are simply called and invited to commune with our God. Now we are able to cry to him with complete confidence, because, having been adopted by him, we lean entirely upon the Lord Jesus Christ, who is the only foundation the gospel allows; we find all we need in him. This is, in effect, what Paul intends us to learn from this passage.

To reinforce the message, he adds another point which proves that the gospel is the perfect revelation of the way of salvation, and that we need no other teaching but the simple doctrine of justification through the free grace of our God. He tells us that the law was given four hundred and thirty years after the free promise of salvation. Now we know that a covenant made between men, if it is to be authentic, must stand, no matter what happens. It follows, therefore, that the law was not given to cancel what God had promised to Abraham and his descendants (and consequently to the rest of us). We may at first question this argument of Paul's, thinking that a second contract must annul the first. As soon as men have entered an agreement, they are liable to have second thoughts and change their minds, making the first contract null and void. The same applies to laws and statutes, for a first law can easily be broken and invalidated by a second. But Paul presupposes something which needs to be considered, which is that if a man has promised and solemnly obligated himself to do something, he cannot retrace his steps – the agreement must remain firm. Yet, if two parties were to agree together to change their previous resolutions by mutual consent, this is a different case. Indeed, such an example is almost irrelevant here if we bear in mind that men change their ideas so lightly at the slightest whim. Paul, however, presupposes that the 'person' in question has made a covenant which will endure, and which will not be disputed or contravened afterwards in any way whatsoever. If one of the parties were to break that original covenant, it would be counted terrible treachery which all men alike would judge intolerable, since the agreement was so solemnly and formally recorded that it must be upheld and maintained without the slightest contradiction. Now, is it possible that there could be less constancy in God than in a man, who is mere vanity by comparison? Therefore, I conclude that the gospel promise holds firm because the free promise was made before the arrival of the law.

All this could mystify us if it were not explained in greater detail. We have already dealt with the contrast Paul makes between the law and the gospel in previous studies. When God promised salvation, it was upon condition that we served him, completely fulfilling our duty to him. This, however, is not possible; thus, we are excluded from all hope of salvation by the law. It is not that God is unfaithful on his part: it is we who do not meet his requirements! It is like a man who says, 'I am willing to sell goods to you on condition that you have the money.' Thus, whoever does not have a penny cannot buy any of the goods, for this is the condition that was set down in the first place. Similarly, God promises that we will inherit salvation if we serve him, but this does not benefit us because we cannot fulfil what he demands. Indeed, we are so full of iniquity, so polluted and infected in his sight, that he quite justly regards us with detestation. Therefore, we all stand condemned under the law. However, God freely and graciously accepts us through the Lord Jesus Christ, who offers us the remission of our sins. In fact, he greatly desires us to accept the grace that we are offered and to lean completely on the Lord Jesus Christ, not upon ourselves.

Now Paul asks, 'Which is more ancient – the free promise of salvation or the law?' We are aware of the difference between them. Now, if the law were the more ancient, it must hold firm, because God never changes and is not subject to variation. However, if the free promise came first and was made before the law was decreed, then we must conclude that God has not changed his mind, nor withdrawn his original promise. He would not have desired the abolition of this covenant, for such would have been a withdrawal of his kindness and mercy. If, at one time, he bound himself out of his free bounty to give salvation to men on a basis other than merit, subsequently changing his mind as if he desired us to enrich him by our good works, it would be absurd! Paul tells us that the free promise was given before the law. It therefore follows that the law does not change anything about the promise; its nature and its force remain intact. Whilst it is true that the Lord Jesus Christ had not yet been born on earth when the promise was made to our father Abraham, he had already been chosen as our Mediator because, through him we would be reconciled to God.

* * *

Now, in case we think that the law must have been unnecessary, or that there must have been a change of mind on the part of God, Paul next addresses this matter. We must not become confused; though it is not possible to explain everything in an hour, nor indeed in a day, it is enough for the moment for us to have this one fact clearly understood: that the promise to ordain us to be his children was made by God before the law. Indeed, it was not made with reference to our merit or personal worthiness; God did this out of his own goodness and mercy and expected nothing from us because he knew we were full of nothing but wretched sin. This promise had its foundation in the Lord Jesus Christ, whose office was already that of Mediator, granting access to God the Father.

Having said this, we conclude that this promise will endure to the end of the world. The main reason this must be said is because the Jews tended to boast in their heritage. Paul seeks to tell them that their father Abraham did not have the law and yet was content, although he did, of course, offer sacrifices and the like. But, even though he was eventually circumcised, at the time he received the promise no written code as yet existed and not even any circumcision. For although Abraham was not circumcised when he received the promise, he was, nevertheless, justified apart from circumcision by faith alone. Therefore, Paul demonstrates to the Jews that it is very foolish indeed to count themselves in a category apart from the rest of humanity, and to base their hopes upon the types and shadows of the law, seeing that their father Abraham, the chief patriarch of the church, was justified in the same way as people today. In other words, he was justified by the mercy of God alone, having recognised that he was a poor sinner, lost and condemned in Adam, and that the only blessing he could hope for was to be included in the promise made in the name of the Lord Jesus Christ. This is what we are to remember.

Next, we must carefully consider the promise addressed directly to Abraham, which revealed to him that all nations on earth would be blessed through his seed (*Gen.* 12:3). Now, there are two main points made here. One is that the blessing is not only promised to the earthly descendants of Abraham (as we have seen), but to the whole world in general. Thus, we who descend from Gentile stock (that is, from those who are unclean and who were originally banished from the heavenly kingdom) can also share in this promise. Although we do not belong to that holy lineage that God chose at the beginning, yet now salvation extends even to us. How is this? Because it was promised that all the nations on earth would be blessed. This being the case, dare we speak as if God has withdrawn his liberal hand, and only seeks the descendants of Abraham, when he had already declared that he would reveal himself as the Saviour and Father of mankind when the time was right? Thus, the most important point here is this: though this promise was made to Abraham, it did not apply to his physical descendants alone, but to all men, even though this was not apparent at first because the fulness of time had not come, as we shall see in the following chapter.

The second point is that the blessing promised to Abraham was for his seed. Paul says that he does not refer to 'seeds' in the plural, but to one seed; we must, therefore, conclude that he is referring to Jesus Christ. We might perhaps have felt that Paul is making much of something which has little relevance; after all, the term 'seed' refers simply to descendants, not specifically to one man, nor to ten, nor to forty! Surely, it speaks of a whole race of people, the seed of Abraham being the race that descends from him. Indeed, this comprised such a great multitude that it was said to be like twelve peoples (*Gen.* 17:6); for when we refer to a people, we speak of about a hundred thousand men, and there were more than this in the tribe of Judah alone! Thus, it would seem that Paul had not properly considered what God intended by this word 'seed', when he says that it refers to just one man. But we must weigh up Paul's conclusions in order to realise that they are correct and firmly established; indeed, we shall see that his argument is utterly infallible.

Abraham did not have just one son; after Ishmael, he had Isaac. And what happened to his oldest son? He was cast out of his house, as we shall see when we come to consider the next chapter. Thus, here is Ishmael, who has all the privileges of being the first-born of Abraham's household, being cast out like a stranger, just as it is written, 'Cast out this bondwoman and her son: for the son of this bondwoman shall not be heir with my son, even with Isaac' (*Gen.* 21:10). After this, other children were born to him (*Gen.* 25:1ff). He gave each one their allotted portion and then sent them away. Only Isaac remained with Abraham. In time Isaac had two children, twins born of the same womb (*Gen.* 25:22–23). The first-born, Esau, who ought to have had the authority, was rejected and not counted as a descendant of Abraham; thus, he had no share in the promised blessings. That left only Jacob, for his father ignorantly and mistakenly blessed him, then declared that he could not withdraw that blessing, nor alter what he had said since he had been the instrument of the Holy Spirit (*Gen.* 27:37). If we take the term 'seed' to apply to those who descend from Abraham, then surely this will include such people as the Ishmaelites and Hagarenes (as they are called) and the like. If this were so, the Idumaeans, their servants, might also be counted as part of his household. But the inheritance was taken away from these people. Therefore, the phrase 'the seed of Abraham' must be understood in a rather different way.

Let us think through the issue for a moment. Without faith, what would unite the church? There would be no sure means of discerning the spiritual seed of Abraham. How would we distinguish them from the rest of mankind? The only way is by coming to the Head, in other words, to the Lord Jesus Christ. The unity of the body depends on its Head, on its Redeemer. This is why Paul says that the promise does not refer to seed in the plural, but to one man, to whom we must come if we are to discover his spiritual people. In other words, if we desire to locate the church of God, we must start with the Lord Jesus Christ, because his own will be gathered round him. All who belong to his body and cleave to him by faith are the children of God, and are his servants. These are truly the seed of Abraham. This is discussed more fully in the Epistle to the Romans, chapter nine, verse six, where it says, 'They are not all Israel who are of Israel.' How is this? Well, there was really only one child of promise: Isaac. Therefore, we must come to the Lord Jesus Christ, for in him all the promises of God are 'yes and amen', being absolutely firm and sure (*2 Cor.* 1:20). Without him, we would all be lost. This is why it is written in the first chapter of Colossians, verse twenty, that the office of the Lord Jesus Christ was to gather together all that had been scattered in heaven and on earth; without him, we would all be confounded.

Now we can see much more clearly the line of Paul's argument. Before the law was imparted to the world, that is, before we were informed of our duty to obey all that is written therein, God had already revealed his good pleasure. Seeing the human race lost and condemned, he desired to bring his elect to himself in order to bestow mercy on them. This was not only for one race but for 'all nations' as the Scripture asserts. And the source of that mercy is the Lord Jesus Christ. Indeed, when Abraham was alive, our Lord Jesus Christ had already been appointed Mediator, that through him the wrath of God against us might be appeased. Thus, when we come in his name asking for grace, it will be supplied to us and our expectations will not be disappointed. This had already been established and, happily, nothing has changed; we can be sure that God accepts us today if we are fully rooted and grounded in the Lord Jesus Christ. For the covenant made in his name shall not change – it is permanent and will always be in force. Thus, we may freely come before God and call upon him as our Father since he has adopted us as his children; not because there was anything worthy in us, but only because of his mercy are we united by faith to the Lord Jesus Christ.

However, in order to receive the grace of God and have assurance of salvation, we need to renounce all opinions we might have of our own worth. We must give heed to what is declared in this passage concerning faith, for it is only through faith that we are enabled to enjoy such blessing. Faith (as we have explained) means that we embrace the mercy of God. But we cannot have faith until we have been touched with a sense of our own poverty, for the Lord Jesus Christ, by becoming a curse for us, presents us with a picture of our cursed state. Faith, therefore, cannot exist without repentance, for it is not possible for us to come to God seeking salvation and asking him to pity our miserable condition, unless we have been convicted in our souls and led to deplore ourselves. Hypocrites who mock at God by wallowing, intoxicated, in their sins, must not expect Jesus Christ to receive them as his own; for such people may not even so much as approach him. Indeed, his invitation is intended for those who labour and are heavy laden (*Matt.* 11:28), who can bear no more and who stagger under the burden of their sins. This is how we must approach the Lord Jesus Christ, not with any merit of our own; for all the ceremonial law and all the sacrifices we could offer cannot contribute to our salvation. Rather, before God shows us mercy, we must come in a state of humility, fully aware of our miserable condition. We are first brought low in order that we might perceive the curse that we are under, before we can rejoice that we have been purchased at such inestimable cost. This has been our theme throughout our study.

Thus, it is by faith that we receive the promise of the Spirit and become united to the Lord Jesus Christ. We become part of the spiritual seed of Abraham. Although we do not physically descend from his family, it is enough that we are united together with him by faith. Indeed, we have been regenerated by incorruptible seed, as Peter says, in other words by the Word of God, the Scriptures (*1 Pet.* 1:23). Having been transformed, we understand that God accepts us as part of the body of his only Son. Though of Gentile descent, we can still be joined to his church, since faith is all that is required. Here, all pride in human virtues and merits must cease, and men must recognise that they shall be utterly confounded unless they seek God in the way that he has appointed. Having said this, let us learn not to be blown here and there, like unstable men, who will not be content with what God has declared but must always add something to it of their devising. We need to guard against such an unholy mixture. I intend to expand upon this after lunch in the will of God. Let Jesus Christ be our sufficiency, since our salvation depends entirely upon him; we will lack nothing if we have an interest in him. This is the point to which Paul frequently returns in this book. Furthermore, he desires that we hold fast to God's truth, knowing that it does not allow for any additions. Were we to add to it, we would corrupt, pervert and falsify the covenant upon which our salvation depends. Having embraced our Lord Jesus Christ, we are expected to remain fully in him, because this one man has sufficient grace for us all. In him, we can call upon God boldly, knowing that, although we descend from the accursed race of Adam, we, nevertheless, receive blessing in Jesus Christ. He now accepts us as his children and freely adopts us. He desires that this message should be heard throughout the world – there is now an open door and free access by which we may draw near to him.

Now let us fall before the majesty of our great God, acknowledging our sins, and asking that he would make us increasingly conscious of them, that we may detest them. May we spend our lives seeking and striving to honour and serve him in strict obedience. And since we cannot free ourselves owing to our great infirmity, may he bear us up until he has freed us from all the defilements of the flesh, and clothed us in his righteousness. Indeed, he has begun this work in us now and affords us solid ground of assurance that what he has begun, he will complete. Thus, we all say, Almighty God and our heavenly Father, etc.

20

Salvation Has Always Been in Christ Alone

Brethren, I speak after the manner of men; Though it be but a man's covenant, yet if it be confirmed, no man disannulleth, or addeth thereto. Now to Abraham and his seed were the promises made. He saith not, And to seeds, as of many; but as of one, And to thy seed, which is Christ. And this I say, that the covenant, that was confirmed before of God in Christ, the law, which was four hundred and thirty years after, cannot disannul, that it should make the promise of none effect. For if the inheritance be of the law, it is no more of promise: but God gave it to Abraham by promise (Gal. 3:15–18).

If God has no more authority over us than mortal man, we have cause to be greatly ashamed of ourselves. For what possible comparison can be made between the majesty of God and the condition of man, who is but a passing shadow? Yet, ordinarily speaking, men esteem themselves more highly than God! So heinous is this sin that even if we were to shine the light of the sun into the shadows of the abyss, it would not result in greater confusion than exists here, where men are regarded with more respect than the One to whom all honour is due. Yet, as I have said, this sin has abounded since time began, and is still too much in evidence today! For we are prepared to accept a man's word, either freely, or else as part of a contract which our legal system is duty-bound to uphold. But when God speaks with such clarity, sparing nothing in order to confirm the reliability of his Word, we remain hesitant or resist him completely. Surely, we must be out of our minds if we set bounds upon God's authority over us in this way, giving more credit to creatures than to the One who created and sustains the heaven and the earth by his Word alone?

Now we shall ask why Paul prefaces this passage with the words: 'I speak after the manner of men'. He could simply have said, 'A covenant has been made and it will not be withdrawn, because what God has promised is sure.' All this is true enough, but it would have been a cold way to refer to such a majestic God, and would seem as if Paul were equating God with earthly creatures. By saying that he is speaking after the manner of men, he is implying that his style and language are not adequate to describe such an awesome Being. For when God shines forth in all his glory, the sun and moon lose their brilliance; all is as darkness compared to him. What, then, of men, who are like flies or frogs in his sight, creeping upon the face of the earth? For, however much men may be puffed up with pride, in the eyes of God they are less than nothing. When we hear God's Word, therefore, we ought to feel constrained to keep silence; we ought to accept what we are told with all reverence. In other words, if God desires to give full and certain salvation to those who simply receive his promise, then let us not seek to dispute it! If an instrument is being played, men listen to it, provided it is in tune; ought we not, therefore, to listen to God, who has uttered sacred words to assure us of his good pleasure? Do we approach God with due solemnity in order to hear what he has declared and spoken? As I have already made clear, in order to take God at his word, we must strive against all our deep-rooted wickedness. For our natures are so prone to unbelief that, unless we struggle against the sin that ensnares us, we will never trust or cherish in our hearts a single word that God has uttered. This is why each one of us needs to be aware of what we are by nature when we come to be instructed in the Word of God. Then, knowing that we are full of rebellion and doubt, we must forsake all of this, asking God to touch our hearts in such a way that they heed what they hear. Indeed, it is the office of the Holy Spirit to take the truth and seal it within our hearts; for although it is true in and of itself, we do not believe it until it is confirmed by the Holy Spirit from on high. Indeed, if we were naturally inclined to believe in God, there would be no need for the Holy Spirit to work within us. He is the true seal by which God sets us apart, and through whom he engraves and imprints in our hearts what we otherwise would never have believed (*2 Cor.* 1:22; *Eph.* 1:13).

* * *

Notice that Paul uses two terms here: he says that no-one can 'disannul' or reverse that which has been agreed amongst men in a legitimate and valid manner, but he also says that no-one can 'add' anything. For even if we were not in the least rebellious, our hearts are so restless that we would make additions to the Word of God, being unable to keep to it in its simplicity. Here, then, are two sinful tendencies that are to be found in us all if we only examined ourselves as we are, without self-flattery. Firstly, we cannot fully resolve within ourselves honestly and unreservedly to say 'Amen!' to what God has declared, nor to accept his promises, nor be fearful of his threatenings. Men always hide behind excuses; we need not go too far to find plentiful examples of this, for as I have said, the tendency is within each one of us! Secondly, though we may render to God his due honour by believing his Word to be true and without error, yet we have a desire to add to it.

This is exemplified in Popery! Why is there such confusion, and such a multiplicity of ways of worshipping God? Why are there so many abuses and false practices? It is because men have not submitted to the commandments of God, but instead, have added to them, creating a confused mass of rituals devised in their own minds. Papists strive to serve God, but in what manner? Each of them has his own form of devotion, accompanied by an infinite amount of tomfoolery! They tell us that it has all been appointed by the church, whereas we know it has all been concocted by men! Why should this be? Has not God revealed to us what is pleasing to him? He tells us that his law is perfect, and that we need no other rule of life. He also informs us that he prefers obedience to all the sacrifices in the world (*1 Sam.* 15:22; *Hos.* 6:6; *Matt.* 9:13, 12:7). The law was designed to bridle man so that he would not presume to add ideas and opinions of his own. God has indeed spoken, yet we persuade ourselves that this or that would be good, and we add a hundred things which he has not required of us. What is worse, we ignore what he has commanded and strictly ordained, and exalt in its place such vain and frivolous nonsense, which not only is of no value in God's sight, but is an abomination. He disapproves of and, indeed, despises anything that man has introduced.

The fact that men seek to worship God according to their own tastes, reveals the lust and excessive pride which has always been part of human nature. Such worship flies in the face of Holy Scripture. For God tells us that the chief sacrifice he demands is for us to cast ourselves upon him, presenting to him our requests. After all, he has provided a way for us to come to him personally and with complete liberty – for he has given us the Lord Jesus Christ as our Advocate. But men would have us call upon dead saints in order to obtain favour with God; they are supposed to be interceding for us as our patrons and advocates! The same applies to other doctrines. God has directed us to pray for one another, but they tell us we must pray for the poor souls in purgatory! And who has commanded this? Men believe this to be a good idea, and notice that what man has commanded is swiftly obeyed! How audacious! God has ordained the sacraments in order to confirm his promises to us, as pledges of his abundant mercy, and to strengthen our weak faith. We have baptism, whereby God declares that we are washed and cleansed from all our sinful stains by the blood shed by his only Son. Now he accepts us as members of his body and we may join his church. But the Papists are not content with such simplicity: they prefer ornaments and candles, and other such nonsense: it is enough to horrify us! And where does all this spring from but devil-inspired audacity? To think that God has established and set down all that is pleasing and fitting in his sight, which we cannot gainsay, and here we are refusing to accept it! But as I have said, the lust of man is such that when it is stirred, he must relentlessly add, mix, change, obscure and confuse.

We must, therefore, endeavour all the more to retain what God is teaching us here through Paul. That is, since God has given his Word complete authority over us, it is not lawful for us to add anything to it. The wisest thing we could do would be to align ourselves with it and accept without the slightest reservation all that has proceeded from God's mouth. If this is true of the promise given to Abraham, surely we have stronger reasons to maintain sobriety now that we have fuller revelation in the gospel. Whilst the substance of what is preached today is no different from that which Abraham heard from the mouth of God, yet the method of instruction is clearer; for the Lord Jesus Christ, the Sun of Righteousness, has come. Although our religion would be easy if we listened to the whisperings of our sinful lusts and desires and added this or that, would it not result in unutterable sacrilege? Whatever else we do, let us learn to submit to what God has taught us, for unless we are sufficiently humble to do this, we will never succeed. For as soon as we depart from God's way even just a fraction, we find ourselves in Satan's net, to be tossed about from one side to the other until we are utterly confounded. Thus, when Paul says that the law could not cancel out the promise which had already been made, there is a principle here which applies to ourselves: let us not allow what men have invented in their foolish heads to blot out the pure doctrines of Scripture. For then we will never know who has more authority, God or man! Therefore, this teaching is designed to keep us on a tight rein so that we do not overstep the boundaries [God has set]. Our faith must always be fully governed and ruled by the simple

Word of God, and we must reject the additions that men have made. This is a brief summary of what we are to learn from this passage.

* * *

Paul says of this covenant that it was 'confirmed before of God in Christ' four hundred and thirty years before the law. This reiterates the point we mentioned this morning – that when God declared himself to be a Father to Abraham, or to Noah, or to anyone else, it was not without the mediation of the Lord Jesus Christ. For mortal conflict exists between man and God because we have been corrupted by original sin; therefore, if God were to leave us as we are, it is certain that we would all be damned. All our desires are twisted, perverse and full of rebellion; our senses are defiled by sin, so that, from the top of our heads to the soles of our feet we are full of corruption. Because we are contrary to God and his will, we must, therefore, be his enemies; for he cannot deny himself. If, therefore, God is our enemy, then we cannot approach him hoping to receive grace and favour unless Jesus Christ first comes to reconcile us. In the same way, not one of our forefathers could approach God without the help of this Mediator. This is why Paul says in the text that the covenant was confirmed 'in Christ'. Jesus Christ has no need of any of the promises which were formerly made to our fathers and which continue to this day, yet as our covenant Head, he has accepted them. With this in mind, we discover that when God dealt kindly with Abraham, it was not due to any special qualities of his but because he was a member of the church of whom Christ was the Head. Also, when God chose David to be king, he declared that his throne was to be everlasting, as long as the sun and moon were in the sky (*Psa.* 89:37); yet, this was not for any inherent dignity in David as a person but, rather, for the sake of the Lord Jesus Christ.

Similarly today, God reveals to us that if we truly seek him, we will find mercy, and that we must diligently search for him; yet, we cannot find him unless the Lord Jesus Christ gathers us into the number of those who form his body. This doctrine serves two main purposes: firstly, to work humility in us. For if we were all to consider what we really are – enemies of God – we would realise that the door is shut to us and that we cannot hope for the slightest mercy at God's hand. No, rather, we would feel him to be our Judge, ready to thunder his sentence upon us and cast us into the abyss. When we come to appreciate that it is only through the Lord Jesus Christ that the promises of God can apply to us, we are forced to hang our heads, acknowledging that his only-begotten Son alone is beloved of the Father and that we can only be accepted in him. This is the first point. Secondly, the promises serve to reassure us. For, otherwise, we might have been troubled by thoughts such as these: 'And who am I? Would God really deign to stoop to me? I am nothing but an earthen vessel – made of dust and ashes, and full of rottenness and decay. Furthermore, there is a bottomless pit full of sin within me, and yet I claim that God has come to seek me! What presumption to think that I am one of his children!' If we are tempted to think in this way, let us remember this passage, which tells us that the covenant was confirmed 'in Christ'. Therefore, although we may be full of sin, it should suffice us that there is more than sufficient worth, virtue and righteousness in the Son of God, and that, through him, the promises may be applied to us.

Now we ought to consider how we may draw near to God. For Paul writes that there is only one seed, and if men turn away from the Lord Jesus Christ even just a little, they are cut off, as it were, from the kingdom of heaven. Therefore, if this was written to destroy the pride and false presumption of those who were descendants of Abraham after the flesh, then what of us, who are like outcasts when compared to them, as Paul discusses in the tenth chapter to the Romans? All those who do not lean on the Lord Jesus Christ alone, utterly shun all possibility of salvation. For Paul says there are not two or three, but only one Mediator, just as God spoke of one seed. For as we have already seen, many of the descendants of Abraham did not inherit the promises. Likewise, unless we come to Jesus Christ and are gathered unto him, it is certain that God will disown us, declaring that we do not belong to him and that, therefore, he desires to have no further dealings with us. We see the world blown about here and there, with the Papists (as well as Turks and Jews) creating an infinite variety of ways to approach God; though they all leave aside the Lord Jesus Christ, let us learn to cleave entirely to him. For if we are part of his body by faith, then we are united to him and his promises belong to us. How is this? The promises were not committed to him for his own purposes, as I have said (for he has no need of them), but for our sake, and thus we can now partake of these same promises. This is a brief summary of what we can learn from this passage.

Another point we ought to take note of with regard to the subject Paul is dealing with here is that gospel doctrine was not new, nor something that was previously unheard of. For since the time of Abraham right until this moment, God has been calling us to be his adopted children, that we may call him our Father. In fact, this had been established even before Abraham was born; however, it was at that time that God began to proclaim publicly what is today encapsulated in the gospels, by making a full declaration of his will to Abraham. Our forefathers had no other way of obtaining salvation than that which is preached to us today. This is a very important point, for some muddle-headed fools believe that no-one had heard the gospel in those days. Indeed, there are even some profane mockers of God who seek to limit the authority of God and of his gospel by saying that the gospel has only existed for these sixteen hundred years and that previously it was unknown. What! Do we think God would have abandoned the world in this way? Can we not see with our eyes, or does it need pointing out with the finger, as it were, that God is unchanged since it pleased him to choose Abraham. Indeed, we were his even then, and the door of salvation was open to us, although all was not completely fulfilled until the fulness of time had come. We saw this point this morning and shall return to it in greater detail, as we have opportunity. This is why Paul speaks of the message of the gospel as a hidden secret (*Eph.* 3:9), and yet, God had determined it to be this way, for his promise ought to have sufficed, as we have seen. This is how we may be called descendants of Abraham: not physically, but by faith, which is all that is required to unite us to him.

Now, it is the Lord Jesus Christ who is the pledge of man's salvation. He has been revealed to assure us that we are his and that he desires us to be members of his body. The Scripture tells us that Abraham saw his day and rejoiced (*John* 8:56). The Jews boasted of the merits of the patriarch, but Jesus Christ addressed them thus: 'Your father Abraham was resting upon what he had heard of me. He, therefore, saw my day and rejoiced in that alone. His hope of salvation was based solely upon faith in the teaching which is preached to you today through the gospel.' This message is also declared by Malachi, when referring to John the Baptist: 'And he shall turn the heart of the fathers to the children' (*Mal.* 4:6). This not only applies to John the Baptist but to the gospel message in general. How, then, does God call us to himself? Well, though Abraham's body may have decayed in the earth because he lived so long ago, if we are joined to him by faith and share the same hope, calling upon God with the same mind that was in him (that is, one fixed upon the Lord Jesus Christ), then God calls us through this same promise. We have been united by faith to our father Abraham until the day comes when we will be together in the kingdom of heaven. Let us, therefore, look to the Lord Jesus Christ as the object of our faith and hope. This is what we need to remember concerning the promise which preceded the law.

Surely, Abraham's example should encourage us to imitate his faithfulness, once we understand that he was waiting for the Lord Jesus Christ long before he was manifested to the world. For he was also told that his descendants would be taken captive in a foreign land. Immediately after declaring that the world would be blessed through his seed, God said, in effect, 'Do not think that this will be fulfilled in three days, or even a hundred years, for you must die first and your family will be transported into a foreign country, where they will be oppressed by cruel and terrible tyrants. Yes, of course I will avenge them, but your people must first suffer.' Abraham heard about all this. Had the law been given at this stage? No, and it was going to be a further two thousand years before the coming of the Lord Jesus Christ. Without strength from on high, Abraham could not have believed what had been told him, for he did not enjoy the good things that were promised, nor did his children that were to come. Indeed, two thousand four hundred years had to pass, and yet, Abraham did not regret leaving his father's house, as the apostle writes in the eleventh chapter to the Hebrews (*Heb.* 11:8). He pursued his goal, though God brought him into many extremities to try his patience and faith. We have every encouragement today to resolve to walk in the path which God has called us to tread, fixing our eyes on things above until we receive that crown of glory; though it is hidden from view, and though we are called to believe things that surpass our understanding and are beyond our conception. This is how we are to put into practice the teaching of this passage.

* * *

Hereupon, Paul concludes that 'if the inheritance be of the law, it is no more of promise'. The fact is that everything was granted to Abraham by faith, which brings us to the conclusion that in our endeavours to obtain favour in the eyes of God, the law has no influence. The praise for our salvation must be rendered to God alone. Paul highlights two things here by this word 'inheritance'. One is that whatever God has promised us is a result of his bounty alone, for an inheritance is not given on the same basis as a salary. When a father grants an inheritance to his children, he may say, 'See how I have worked for you! See the result – now you can have all my wealth!' But all this blessing is only because of the blood-tie; in this way, he labours and goes to great pains to provide for those who are committed to his care. Since even our human inheritances are free, we must ensure that we do not view eternal life as wages that we have earned by our merits. Why not? Because that too is an inheritance. This is the first point: all conception of man's worth is excluded. For when a man makes his children his heirs, he does not expect them to have achieved some great task, or to be especially attractive, or to have this or that gift. No; it is enough that they are his children and that he desires to provide for them.

But there is also a second level of significance to this word: that is, that we are by nature altogether cast out of God's presence. This means that we cannot enjoy anything in this transitory life, except by the grace of God. It is true that the sun shines upon unbelievers as much as upon believers, and that we are all alike nourished by that which God provides and grants. Yet unbelievers possess nothing that is truly theirs; they are robbers, and must give account to the last drop of water of the way in which they used what they received from the hand of God. These things are unsanctified: they are polluted by the evil within those who use them. In the same way, Paul says that the things God has granted us are purified by faith (*1 Tim.* 4:5). Thus, we may lawfully make use of them; but if we remove faith, all is defiled. How is this? Well, if I have unclean hands, and I handle some of the most precious things in the world, they will become infected by the filth on my hands. The same applies to the abuse of what God has given. The unbelief within us corrupts everything and causes the whole of creation to cry out for vengeance upon such abuse, that is, unless we possess these things by faith. Thus, we cannot enjoy anything unless we are children of God. In the fourth chapter to the Romans, verse thirteen, Paul does not simply speak of Abraham gaining heaven and eternal salvation, but of Abraham inheriting the world; clearly, this does not apply to this man alone but to all in general. Thus, when God adopts us and declares that he will show us mercy, we must remember that it is his hand that will nourish us, for by feeding us he displays his love and care for us.

It is our duty now briefly to consider God's fatherly provision for all his creatures. Let us open our eyes and consider the shining rays of the sun. God is showing us by this that he is our Father. When we eat and feed our bodies, it is God who has stretched out his hand and fed us to show that he counts us as his own children. Indeed, in all things he reveals his fatherly love to confirm what he has proclaimed through the gospel; that is, that he has reserved a better inheritance for those who are his adopted children. Therefore, all of creation should direct us to the Creator in heaven. However, we are prone to use created things to serve our own lusts, and our minds remain fixed on the things of the world. Thus, although God has granted us many aids to draw us to have faith in him, these can become as many hindrances to keep our eyes on this world alone. For if we are living comfortable lives in this world, we become self-satisfied and ignore the whole question of how we may become children of God. Yet, the fact remains that we should be able to see that God is our Father. Through what he has made, he has proved how much he cares about us and we in turn should cast ourselves upon him and rest in him. Thus, we have now examined this word 'inheritance'; firstly, it implies that everything God offers to us is a result of his bounty alone, and, secondly, it shows that by nature we are cursed. Nothing belongs to us by right, not even a drop of water, unless we are chosen and appointed to be heirs for the sake of the Lord Jesus Christ.

Now we need to call to mind a point that we learnt earlier, which is that the promise was made 'in Christ', therefore, it does not begin and end with Abraham. Furthermore, the Lord Jesus Christ is called the 'heir of all things' (*Heb.* 1:2); yet, all that belongs to him he communicates to those who are members of his body. Paul also teaches that the words of Psalm eight and the sixth verse apply primarily to the person of the Lord Jesus Christ (*1 Cor.* 15:27). They tell us that 'all things are under him'. It could be said that these words apply to mankind, for God has made all the beasts of the field subject to man so that they must die in order to provide us with food, clothing and shoes. Look how fruitful the earth is for our sakes! We have been given control over creation, but only through the Lord Jesus Christ. For as I said before, if we are not joined to him, we are cut off from God's family and the inheritance cannot belong to us, just as it could not belong to any other stranger in the world.

* * *

Let us come now to the central teaching of our text, which is that this inheritance is not by the law but by faith. When Paul puts these two terms together so that they accompany one another, it is to draw a contrast between them, as we have seen. It is not that the law and faith are somehow contrary to one another. No, but when it is a question of justification, and of receiving the mercy of God, this cannot be achieved through the law because the law was not intended for that purpose (as we shall see in our next sermon). Indeed, its function is quite the reverse! Since our inheritance is obtained by faith, we must, therefore, conclude that our works are of no value, and that we are expected to come empty-handed, like poor beggars. We come asking God to fill us because we do not possess one drop of goodness in and of ourselves. These are the implications of Paul's words when he says that the inheritance is acquired by faith and not through the law, just as Abraham's inheritance was by faith.

Now, if we cannot even merit our physical nourishment, how can we deserve to inherit the kingdom of heaven? Surely, perishable meat is nothing compared to the glory of heaven? We have been told that we will see the glory of our God and that he will be our all in all (*1 Cor.* 15:28). Yet, at present we have no right to a piece of bread, for the inheritance is obtained by faith; in other words, all that God has promised men is due to his free bounty alone. How, then, can we speak of deserving the kingdom of heaven? What pride there must be in man that he should hope to reach paradise through his own virtue! Surely such people will be swept away by the fiery wrath of God? By saying that

Abraham received everything by faith, Paul clarifies and explains what we have been seeking to establish: that is, that nothing is contributed on the part of man – salvation is free. Previously, Paul had said that the promise was 'made' and 'confirmed'; here he speaks of it being 'given'. He does not refer to the promise as if it were a mutually agreed contract, as if God were saying, 'I will do this, but you must do that. I will sell, and you must buy.' Nothing of the sort! Rather, it is God who gives, and man who accepts. Seeing this is the case, we must come to God accepting his offer, knowing that whatever he grants us is a free gift. We must leave behind all thoughts of self-worth and realise that we are nothing.

Paul uses another expression here to explain the point he is making. He says that if the inheritance were by the law, then the promise, and consequently faith also, would be 'of none effect'. If the inheritance were not obtained by faith, we could have no assurance that the promise applied to us. I need to explain this, because we might find this passage difficult to understand due to its succinctness. You see, the inheritance of salvation and, indeed, of any of the good gifts which God bestows in this life, is based entirely on faith. In other words, we cannot contribute anything, for it is God who gives everything freely and abundantly. If our salvation were based upon works, or upon our worthiness in terms of what we have achieved before God, how could we be sure to obtain what has been promised? We would always stand in doubt, for we would always be asking, 'Well, what have I done? Have I reached the standard required?' In this way, faith is cancelled out. Faith should mean full assurance of God's good intentions towards us, which we would not have if this were the case, for we would never be sure [of our standing]. All would be based on supposition, and, even then, our thinking would be affected by the delusions of Satan. For all whose hopes are founded upon their own virtues have been bewitched by the devil. To believe that we will merit salvation is gross self-deception. Therefore, whilst our eyes are blinded by hypocrisy and whilst we believe in our own goodness, we can have no assurance at all, since we are without faith. For if faith is cancelled out, then so also are the promises; consequently, we can have no assurance.

In conclusion, we must add that the inheritance must be by faith in order to banish all our pride. When we claim to deserve something from God, or when we say that we have a free will to either accept or reject what God offers, we display our arrogance. It is our duty to ignore that which men are accustomed to attribute to themselves, and to trample it underfoot, as it were. We must approach God stripped of all our supposed virtues, and come empty and famished; then we must find in him all that we need. We ought to be confident that our God has plentiful supplies and is able to provide what we lack. For he has endued the Lord Jesus Christ with everything that we could hope for, as well as with all that was needful and beneficial for us. Thus, we can enjoy the inheritance that God promised at the beginning of time, because it is still offered to us today through the preaching of the gospel.

Now let us fall before the majesty of our great God, acknowledging our sins and asking him to make us increasingly conscious of them. May we walk in his fear, desiring nothing more than that we might devote ourselves entirely to him. And although he sees us surrounded and enveloped by infirmity and corruption, may he sanctify us more and more by his Holy Spirit, bearing us up until the end of our lives. May he not only grant this grace to us, but to all peoples and nations on earth, etc.

21

The Many Functions of God's Timeless Law

> *Wherefore then serveth the law? It was added because of transgressions, till the seed should come to whom the promise was made; and it was ordained by angels in the hand of a mediator. Now a mediator is not a mediator of one, but God is one* (Gal. 3:19–20).

We established last time that the law came after the promise of God to be gracious to the house of Abraham. God promised free grace, and the Jews were to lean upon this promise for their salvation, knowing that God would mercifully send them a Redeemer, through whom they would obtain remission of their sins. From this, Paul concludes that the law (which came after the promise) did not abolish that which had been ordained and established by God. However, it would be easy to assume that the law was added to strengthen the promise, as if it had been weak in isolation. Indeed, the apostle seems to argue along those lines in the Epistle to the Hebrews, where he says, in the words of Jeremiah, that God would provide a new law – the gospel. The apostle explains that the law given by Moses was imperfect and insufficient for salvation (*Heb.* 8:7). At first, it might seem that the same could apply here to the law and the promise, that the promise required a finishing touch, as if it were incomplete in and of itself, and needed to be perfected. Otherwise, surely, the law is superfluous? Yet, it would be against all reason to suppose that God would give us this doctrine for no purpose at all!

We must, therefore, give our attention to examining the function of the law, and to discovering to what end it was given, lest we mistakenly assume that the gospel promise was inadequate, and only partially beneficial for salvation. Paul states that God did not intend to provide us with a means of justification or salvation when he sent us his law; it was added, he says, 'because of transgressions'. It was not created simply to keep us on a tight rein (as the saying goes) because of all the evil and depravity in the world; for we have many ordinary laws and statutes which have been formulated to punish crime here on earth. If we were all like angels, blameless and freely able to exercise perfect self-control, we would not need rules or regulations. Why, then, do we have so many laws and statutes? Because of man's wickedness, for he is constantly overflowing with evil; this is why a remedy is required. If we were all healthy, we would have no need of medicine, but man's intemperance means that there will always be diseases, and, therefore, remedies must be sought out. The existence of so many civil laws bears testimony to the fact that we are totally evil and depraved and, therefore, need to be restrained and harnessed. But Paul does not understand the function of the law in this way – he goes much further. He declares that God gave his law in order to expose man's iniquity, which proves, therefore, that this is not a means of salvation! For heat and cold cannot originate from the same source! If a fountain is sweet, we cannot seek bitter water there; likewise, if a fountain is bitter or salted, we must seek elsewhere for sweet water. The same can be applied to the law.

Why, then, was the law given? In order that men could be doubly convicted of their sins before God and realise that their hypocrisy, self-flattery, desire to hide behind excuses, and other such sins are vain and to no avail. Hence, in the fourth chapter to the Romans, and the fifteenth verse, Paul argues that we cannot be justified by the law, since it brings upon us nothing but the wrath of God. (He is referring to

God's vengeance.) In a certain sense, it could be said that both life and death proceed from the law. For the law condemns us all and sentences all to death by showing that we are accursed and abominable in God's sight. What folly, therefore, to seek to be justified simply by its observance! Paul also states in the seventh chapter to the Romans, and the eighth verse, that the law actually causes sin to increase! We are already liable to condemnation, even before we have heard the law; as it is written, those who have sinned without the law will nevertheless perish (*Rom.* 2:12). In other words, the heathen, although they have no code from which they stray, still have the inner witness of their conscience, which acts as their judge. Thus, men are worthy of damnation well before they are summoned into God's presence and examined, God having taken his place on the judgment throne. Yet those who persist in sinning and offending God believe themselves to be faultless! For we are subject to such self-flattery, that although we are wallowing in sin, our consciences will never once feel ashamed without the law: they will remain dull and insensitive. Instead, we would feel at liberty to do whatever wicked things we desire. But when once we hear the law, we recognise sin, and are forced to humble ourselves before God (or else gnash our teeth like rebels!). God awakens us through the law and leads us to acknowledge our desperate condition. It is like a man whose face is covered with filth; people laugh at him but he does not understand why! If someone were to bring him a mirror, he would be ashamed and steal away to clean off the dirt, but he will only do this when he has discovered his ugliness! Or if a man has some sort of deformity which makes others afraid to look at him, he will not realise that he has such a disfigurement until a mirror is brought before his eyes! The same applies to us: although we are full of evil and iniquity to the extent that heaven and earth are ashamed of us, and God prepares an awful fate for us, we go on our way unperturbed! Why? Because we are unaware of our sin; we are so blinded by our own hypocrisy that we cannot perceive any danger. But the law reveals just who we are, and sets before us the judgment of God. The law teaches us that we will be condemned if we fail to do certain things. And what are these things? It is not simply a matter of guarding our feet, hands, eyes and ears; no, we must keep ourselves pure and free from all covetousness. Our integrity must be such that all our affections, thoughts and desires are centred upon God. We are not to be enticed or led astray by anything in this world. But where can such a person as this be found?

Now God has ascended his throne and sits as judge, and he has pronounced his sentence upon us – we are accursed because we are found to be transgressors, which, indeed, we are. That is the miserable condition of the human race. This is why Paul says in this passage that the law was added 'because of transgressions'. However, the law does have other functions. For example, one of the chief reasons why we need the law is to teach us how we are to worship God. It shows that we are to honour him by our obedience, rather than each person living as a law unto himself! The law helps us to distinguish between good and evil. What is the 'reasonable service' that God deserves? Is it not to submit ourselves to his will, as Paul says in the twelfth chapter to the Romans, verse one? Is this not a most excellent function of the law – to show us how we may please God and what rules we are to obey, rather than for us to be struggling in vain, believing we are serving God when we are not? But when Paul speaks of the law being added for transgressions' sake, he does not intend to give us an account of the uses of the law and the fruits it produces. We have said that the law instructs us, and teaches us to discern between good and evil; it urges us by means of goads, as it were, to give ourselves wholly to God. But Paul is referring to the law in the context of the passage he is expounding, proving that the law is not superfluous, yet, neither is it a means of justification. Indeed, its function is to confound us and reveal that we are sinners in a twofold sense, to convict us of our sin and leave us without excuse. In fact, we soon realise that there is a bottomless pit awaiting us. This is why the law was given: it was added to the promise, not because the latter was powerless without it, unable to bring salvation without assistance from another source; not at all, says Paul! It was added in order that we might realise that God is right to condemn us all, and to give our minds no rest from anxious and tortuous thoughts, in order that our despair might lead us to find hope in his promise.

If we object that the promise could have achieved this alone, the answer to this is very simple. Although God has revealed himself as Saviour, and shown us that we will be condemned unless he has mercy upon us, we cannot respond as we ought unless he first humbles us. Through his promise, he calls us to himself with the tender love of a father. This ought to be sufficient to make us aware of our sins and to make us hate them: yet, we are so comfortable in our sins that we will not give them any thought unless we are coerced. Therefore, after God had made this promise to man, we should have groaned under the burden of sin and sought refuge in the grace of the Lord Jesus Christ, but we did not, that is, until God dealt us a few mighty blows with his hammer through the law! Does this not reveal our wickedness, that we abuse God's kindness to us, and use it for an occasion to flatter ourselves? Of necessity, he deals harshly with us, and exposes what we are truly like, to alarm us so that we might run to him for grace. The word 'added' here indicates that Paul is accusing us of despising God's goodness, revealed in his gentle and gracious call. Indeed, we virtually constrain him to use force in order to humble us; only when our wills are thus inclined by force will we seek his grace in the Lord Jesus Christ.

* * *

At this point, Paul adds that the law applied 'till the seed should come to whom the promise was made'. The 'law' chiefly refers to the ceremonies, although we can also include all the qualities, circumstances and details of the law, as we say. If we take the law to refer only to the ten commandments, then what Paul says here is entirely inappropriate! For even today the law carries weight, in that it is our rule for living.

It reveals to us the will of God, keeping us from living as vagabonds, aimlessly wandering about from place to place, as it were, for the pathway is set out before us. Therefore, because the law teaches what is right, it is timeless and will endure to the end of the world. It is important for us to enter into the mind of Paul here and realise that he is referring to the promises, curses and ceremonies of the law. On the one hand, we are promised that if a man obeys, 'he shall live in them' (*Lev.* 18:5). We have already dealt with this. Next, there is the threat: 'Cursed be he that confirmeth not all the words of this law to do them' (*Deut.* 27:26). The law, as we have discovered, only promises salvation to those who have lived pure lives in all integrity. All of us fall short of this and, therefore, the promise does not apply. This is the first point. If we object that God is mocking at men, the answer is, not at all! Rather, we are so full of pride and arrogance that we think we can achieve salvation by ourselves. Therefore, God has to say, 'If you are as virtuous as you think you are, prove it to me. For my part, I have given you my law and I have prepared a reward for you if you obey it. You will not be disappointed if you serve me. Eternal life is promised you, but first you must do your duty – set to work!' Even if men were to attempt to do so with all their might, they would doubtless discover weakness of which they were previously unaware. Thus, the promises of the law do not apply to us, yet, nor are they thwarted, because they serve a rather different purpose.

The curses of the law are infallible. The following text condemns us all: 'Cursed be he that confirmeth not all the words of this law to do them.' We are obliged to fulfil them all, and there must not be one single point at which we fail. We are wrong if we believe we can serve God in part; he does not divide up his commandments in this way. He desires the one who is chaste to abstain also from plundering, pillaging, cheating, violence and everything else. Since this is the case, these warnings are binding upon us all, and Paul was aware of this.

Concerning the ceremonies, they serve to highlight our

lost condition. We have already referred to what Paul says in Colossians chapter two, and the fourteenth verse, where he describes them as ordinances which are designed to bind us and keep us in place. If a man borrows a sum of money, he then owes it and must pay it back with his own hand. This ought to be sufficient. However, if he secures a mortgage, he is obliged under penalty to pay it back, especially if it be a public matter. This makes his burden greater. The same applies to the ceremonies. The law was sufficient to condemn all mankind, for all have sinned; yet God, seeing the pride that was so deeply rooted in our hearts, added ceremonies to place us under an even more solemn obligation to him. But Paul says that all this was only 'till the seed should come'; in other words, the law cannot harness or restrain those who put their trust in the Lord Jesus Christ. Rather, it leads them to faith and they find in Christ all that is lacking in the law! Thus, when God is harsh in his condemnation, it is only to procure our salvation, and the fact that he thunders against us is an evident token of his exceptional grace towards us! How is this? I have already said, and experience bears this out, that we would never stop abusing his kindness to us, using it for our advantage if this were not the case. Therefore, God must arrest us and act as our judge, so that we hear the dreadful sentence and sink in despair. Then we expect no less than eternal death, and this verdict is confirmed and ratified by his law. Yet, all is designed to humble us in order that we might come to the Lord Jesus Christ with true zeal and in sincerity. Having experienced such anguish and torment in our consciences, we will learn to rest entirely upon him. This is why the law only applied 'till the seed should come'.

If we, then, ask how it was that our forefathers obtained salvation, the answer is that although the law reigned before the coming of the Lord Jesus Christ with regard to outward things, nevertheless, our fathers still had to rely upon the grace they had been promised (despite the fact that Christ had not yet come). We shall learn more of this presently. Now we have resolved the following point: that the law did not alter the promise, neither was it added to support the promise, as if it had been insufficient alone for salvation. Rather, it was added because of man's pride and arrogance, that we might humbly seek the mercy that is offered us in the Lord Jesus Christ, and that, through him, we might be enabled to receive and enjoy his forgiveness.

At this point Paul mentions that the law 'was ordained by angels in the hand of a mediator'. Here he authorises the law and indicates that we are to receive it with all due reverence. However, we are only to apply it in the way that God intended! To make this point, Paul speaks of angels, to demonstrate that God had many witnesses who gave authority to the law and showed how it was to be received and esteemed. But Paul's main object here is to speak of the Mediator – that is to say, the Lord Jesus Christ. Many have thought this was referring to Moses, since he was a mediator between God and man with regard to doctrine. However, this is hardly a suitable interpretation! After all, Paul firstly speaks of angels, and then of the Mediator as their head, the one who holds the position of supreme sovereignty. This cannot be applicable to Moses! Indeed, Paul's argument here is that there is no disparity between the law and the gospel concerning the free promise of salvation. In order to reiterate this, he refers to the Lord Jesus Christ, explaining that when the law was established, it was with his hand and under his leadership. This word 'hand' often implies power in Scripture, and here it is used to draw a contrast between the angels and Jesus Christ himself. Paul mentions the assembled angels because their presence should ensure that the law is heeded by men, and accepted without reservation. The angels were witnesses of God's majesty, yes, but the Mediator is even greater than they! The 'hand' here implies his headship, revealing that he has sovereign authority and, therefore, has the chief commission of ordaining the law. This ought not to seem strange to us; for when the angel appeared to Moses he said, 'I am the Lord' (*Exod.* 3:6). Yet he is called an angel! This means that he was a messenger of God as the word implies; yet he says in effect, 'I am the Lord, whose being proceeds from myself alone'. This cannot be said of any creature (including the angels) who, like ourselves, were made from nothing! It would have been blasphemy for an angel to usurp such a title, which belongs to God alone. We must, therefore, reach the conclusion that this angel was none other than the Lord Jesus Christ, who was already fulfilling his role as Mediator. This, indeed, is borne out by Paul in First Corinthians, chapter ten and verse nine, where he speaks of the rebellion of the Jews in provoking God to anger with their murmurings and foolish lusts. Paul says that they were tempting Christ himself, who led and guided them through the wilderness. Therefore, I have no difficulty in believing that our Lord Jesus Christ was already a mediator, because in many different ways he acted to reconcile men to God the Father. This is why the apostle writes in the Epistle to the Hebrews that Jesus Christ is the same, 'yesterday, and today, and forever', and that we must cleave to him and not be carried about with 'strange doctrines' (*Heb.* 13:8).

Hence, Paul is teaching us that Jesus Christ mediated between God and man in order that poor sinners might be granted relief from their troubled minds concerning the judgment of God. Now we can rejoice because God has provided a mediator through whom we may obtain grace to approach him. But the Lord Jesus Christ is also a mediator in another sense, and that is that God has always communicated to man through him. For there is such a gulf between God and ourselves, we are so alienated from him through sin, that we cannot have access to him. He can only stoop to us through a mediator. Indeed, is this not what the vision of Jacob teaches us in the twenty-eighth chapter of Genesis, verse twelve? It tells us there that Jacob saw a ladder, at the top of which God was enthroned in majesty, and the angels were ascending and descending on this ladder. There can be no doubt that this image was to reveal to Jacob that we are excluded from the kingdom of God until a means is found to reconcile heaven and earth. In other words, the Lord Jesus Christ, who is 'God manifest in the flesh'; he is higher than the heavens, yet he has identified with us in that he took our nature upon himself and became a man – frail, but without sin. Although he was perfect, he took upon himself our infirmities. This is how it was that the law was ordained by the hand of the Lord Jesus Christ. Thus, it follows that there can be no contradiction between the law and the gospel, for Jesus Christ never changes and cannot deny himself.

* * *

Now let us turn our attention to Paul's next statement. He says 'a mediator is not a mediator of one, but God is one'. By saying that the Mediator is not 'of one', he implies that the Lord Jesus Christ came to gather together in one all things in heaven and on the earth, as he says in the first chapter to the Colossians (*Col.* 1:20). Some have understood this text to mean that Jesus Christ had more than one nature; others, that if he is the Mediator for all mankind, it follows that there can be no disharmony between the law and the gospel. However, Paul is clearly referring to the bringing together of Jews and Gentiles here! In effect he is saying, 'Yes, Jesus Christ was Mediator when the law was set forth, that God might humble men through him to the end that they might receive his grace. But let us notice that, although he was already Mediator when he presented the law to the Jews, his office was to extend much further, since he was also to gather the Gentiles who were cut off from God. For though, for a time, God chose the descendants of Abraham above the rest of humanity, yet at the end of time he has made us partakers of the salvation from which we were once estranged. Those of us who were afar off have been welcomed in alongside those who were previously close to God.' Indeed, in that other passage, Paul calls Jesus Christ 'our peace', since he has reconciled and united to God both those who were already near (the Jews) and those who had no knowledge of God (*Eph.* 2:17). We have been accepted into the body of his church because of Christ's coming. Those who were once separated by a great distance have been united, not only with God, but with one another.

Now we understand Paul's teaching in this passage, but in order to profit from all we have considered, there is a specific lesson we ought to learn from this one fact: that God gave us his law through angels. That is, that these same angels will be witnesses against us if we ignore or pass by the law, or trample it underfoot, as it were. Thus, the angels will have the right to ask God to avenge our ungodly rebellion. When God chose angels to assist him in the setting forth of his law, he was not playing games; rather it was in order that we might reverence the law. Yes, it is true, we cannot perfectly fulfil what it demands; however, if we were to stop there, we would be totally engulfed in despair, and remain under the sentence of eternal death. If God has graciously taught us his will and enabled us to discern between good and evil, our response ought to be to bow our necks to receive the yoke that God places upon us, a response of submission to him. This is the first point. Secondly, the law is designed to prompt and prick our consciences, because we are so cold, lethargic and inactive that we would never come to God of our own accord. The law, therefore, should cause each one of us to examine ourselves; indeed, for our own instruction, we would do well to commit to memory the commandments of God and recite them morning and evening.

Let us, therefore, keep ourselves on a tighter rein, since the angels observe and watch over us. Having been employed by God to establish the law, they will not allow us to despise it, or to put it to an open shame as if it were worthless. Furthermore, the law is there to condemn us, and we will receive this condemnation in the presence of these same angels, regardless of how much men may have praised and applauded us. Even if the whole world were on our side, it would count for nothing. For why, then, would God have chosen to have his angels there to assist with the publication of his law, if not to teach us to be ashamed of our sinfulness, humble ourselves willingly and seek salvation in the Lord Jesus Christ?

As for the Lord Jesus Christ being the Mediator of the law, we can be sure that if we have sought refuge in his grace, the law no longer has the power to condemn us, nor to cause sin to have dominion over us. For we must bear in mind what Paul wrote in the First Epistle to the Corinthians, chapter fifteen, and the fifty-sixth verse: 'the strength of sin is the law'. The law sharpens sin, as it were, leaving us mortally wounded. Therefore, if we do not enjoy the consolation spoken of here, we will surely be seized with terror and have no assurance of salvation, despite the promises made by the Lord Jesus Christ. We will constantly be weighing these truths which seem so contradictory, saying, 'Surely the law came from God? Yet God condemns us through it! Although he sent the Lord Jesus Christ to be the remedy, there does not appear to be any way of escaping its sentence!' Thus, we will be tormented by such thoughts. But if we consider that the Lord Jesus Christ was the Mediator who established the law, we realise that if he is our Advocate today, he is able to forgive us. Thus, we do not have to be counted amongst the lost. Yes, God has indeed pronounced his curse upon us, and we have been oppressed by the torment and anguish that this has created. Our evil does at first seem to be incurable, but we know that our Lord Jesus Christ is able to fulfil both roles: that is, to teach us humility through such terrifying thoughts, and yet also to assure us of salvation. Thus, when we are cast down in this way, the only way to be raised up is to recognise that the One who was established as the Mediator of the law has been revealed to us today in this same office of Mediator, as some of us can testify from our own experience.

Finally, let us notice that he is not the Mediator for one nation alone, but for the whole world because we are all God's creatures. Yes, by the sin of Adam we were all cut off, but the Lord Jesus came to gather together things in heaven and things on earth, as we have already discussed (*Col.* 1:20). This being the case, we should never doubt that God accepts us today as heirs of his promise, because he sees us as the spiritual children of Abraham. And although we are living in days very different from the time of the ceremonial law, which divided some people from others, this does not prevent us from being able to approach God with boldness.

How is this? Because 'God is one'. There may be Jews and Greeks, and many other different nations, with a variety of languages, morals and ways of life, and certainly each individual is full of inconsistencies and subject to change, with no firm anchorage; but let us all learn to fix our eyes upon God, for he is one. He has given us his law and his gospel; let us not think that there is any contradiction between them, for they are in perfect harmony. Let us, rather, be led by these means to come to the Lord Jesus Christ. And how can we do this? Only when we are stripped of all pride, and feel that horror and repugnance that makes us detest ourselves upon the realisation that we are spiritually dead. Then we will come to the Lord Jesus Christ, knowing that God the Father accepts us if we come in his appointed way. Why? For he is one. When he gave us his law, he did not intend to diminish the authority of the promise which preceded it. When he revealed his grace more fully in the gospel, it was not because he considered the law worthless or invalid, for it provides us with a rule for living. Thus, to avoid being under its curse, the law teaches us that the only escape is found in that Seed which was promised at the beginning of time, and in whose hands our salvation is secure; that is, in the Lord Jesus Christ – the fountain and source of all blessing.

Now let us fall before the majesty of our great God, acknowledging our sins, and asking him to make us increasingly conscious of them, that we might detest them. May we not only confess them with our lips, but may our hearts also be in full submission to God's Holy Word. May his free grace comfort us, as it has been revealed to us in our Lord Jesus Christ. May his Holy Spirit continually transform us, in order that if we are full of rebellion, he may bring us under his control and make us meek, ready to follow his holy will and devote ourselves completely to him. We pray for all these things, saying, Almighty God, and our heavenly Father, etc.

22

Assessing the Degrees of Faith

Is the law then against the promises of God? God forbid: for if there had been a law given which could have given life, verily righteousness should have been by the law. But the scripture hath concluded all under sin, that the promise by faith of Jesus Christ might be given to them that believe. But before faith came, we were kept under the law, shut up unto the faith which should afterwards be revealed. Wherefore the law was our schoolmaster to bring us unto Christ, that we might be justified by faith. But after that faith is come, we are no longer under a schoolmaster (Gal. 3:21–25).

This morning we made a thorough examination of the fact that although the law could not justify us or make us acceptable to God, it was not established in vain. It was not that God's grace was weak or insufficient for our salvation, and that, consequently, it was necessary to introduce the law. No, the law was given for a totally different reason: to drive men to acknowledge that they are sinners, and to cause them to despair! For unless this happens, their consciences will not be prompted to take refuge in the Lord Jesus Christ. We can see evidence of this as we look around us. Now, however, Paul raises a different question: that is, whether the law is in keeping with the promises. For when the law promises salvation, it does so upon condition that we deserve it; but the gospel promises us acceptance with God, that we can be made acceptable to God through no merit of our own.

Naturally, it could be thought that there is a contradiction here! It is rather like being offered a house for a price, being informed of the cost, and subsequently to have someone say, 'No. You can have it for nothing!' There is a great deal of difference between the two! It seems as though God is being inconsistent. By the law, he is saying, 'Serve me and fulfil what I command and your wages are guaranteed.' Yet, in the gospel he is using a different language, saying, 'I ask nothing on your part, for you are so wretched that you cannot possibly please me; however, I will accept you into my kingdom without merit because of my free mercy. The inheritance will be assigned to you solely because it is my good pleasure to grant it to you.'

Paul is drawing our attention to the differences of style and approach in the law and the gospel. Nevertheless, it soon becomes apparent that there are, in fact, no real discrepancies. How is this? Well, we saw this morning that God did not intend to mock at us when he promised us a reward for our works. Rather, he desired that we should be struck silent before him and unable to murmur against him. For we know how ready we are to complain when God does not deal with us according to our whims and fancies; this is due to our own devilish pride. For this very reason, God cuts short all our protestations by saying that we will not be deprived of our reward if we have served him well enough! Yet, if we examine ourselves, we realise that we cannot possibly achieve justification in this way, for there is not one of us who can say that we have lived a blameless life; that is, if we judge without deceiving ourselves! Is this, then, the way God sees us? Yes, but he offers us hope in the gospel and assures us that, though we are all condemned and cannot hope to obtain justification by our works, he will justify us through his own free bounty because it pleases him to do so.

Hence, Paul writes here that if the law were given to bring justification, then we would be able to gain righteousness through it. But is this what God intended [when he gave us the law]? The answer is, most certainly not. Paul directs us to consider God's purposes. He also highlights the pride of hypocrites who say that they can be justified and reach paradise by their own efforts! Not only are they poor expositors of the law, but also such as adulterate and corrupt it. For it is vital that we reflect upon the intentions of the one who is speaking. Clearly, God did not wish us to trust in or rely upon our merits, for our natures ensure that we already lean too heavily in this direction! Indeed, this particular error has been common throughout the whole world in every generation. We need not go to school in order to persuade ourselves that we are good people, that we can win God's favour through our virtuous lives!

On the contrary, God granted us his law in order to pierce us through with a sword, as it were, and leave us mortally wounded to constrain us to take refuge in him. Since God intended the law to 'kill' us, it cannot have been sent for our justification! Therefore, those who seek life and salvation therein are deceiving themselves and mistakenly claim that God has promised it to them. They have omitted to ponder what God had in mind when he made such a promise. Paul's solution to this question of the difference between the law and the gospel is that there is no contradiction here, even though it appears God has altered his approach!

Paul continues by saying that 'the scripture hath concluded all under sin, in order that we might obtain the promise by faith in the Lord Jesus Christ'. When he says that the Scripture has 'concluded all under sin', one implication is that men are too foolish by far if they believe that the promise in Leviticus ('which if a man do, he shall live in them') suggests that a reward is due to them! For if we were to read the law in its entirety, and search its whole contents, or indeed, even if we were to read the whole of Holy Scripture, we would find that it condemns and accuses all men from the greatest to the least, without exception. If we are all condemned, even by the testimony of the law, what further witness against us do we need? Surely, we must be blinded by hypocrisy to think that we can gain God's favour, though we possess no righteousness of our own. For God has declared that when we come before his face he will cast us into the pit! Paul does not quote any text here to prove that the Scripture has concluded all under sin; he takes it to be an indisputable fact, which believers ought not to question. Indeed, since the creation of the world, man has been corrupted through Adam. Sin not only caused one man's condemnation, but that of the whole human race. We all fell in Adam's fall. In fact God declares that all our thoughts are in rebellion against him and are full of evil (*Gen.* 6:5). What is the human soul like? It is a storehouse of every kind of iniquity. Since God has made this plain, what do we gain by attributing various qualities to ourselves? All such guile increases our evildoing, because we are ignoring God and provoking him to anger.

What, then, was the function of sacrifices? Surely, to display before our eyes that if man depends upon his own efforts, he will be damned. And if the sacrifices were not convincing enough, then experience itself would teach this lesson. We must all look within ourselves and discover what we really are; then we must seek to live according to the perfect standards required of us in Holy Scripture. At this point we shall discover that all that is, in fact, required is that we embrace God's promises of mercy. For example, the promise we find in Isaiah where he says that, because of God's love for us, all our iniquities will be blotted out (*Isa.* 43:25). Even this highlights our sin, especially when we realise that God had to send Jesus Christ to be our righteousness. But if we need a more complete and forceful declaration of the fact, let us study the third chapter to the Romans, from verse nineteen. Here, Paul explains at length what he says in brief in our passage, and he helps us to understand more clearly that the Scripture has, indeed, concluded all under sin. Paul points out the traits which mark human nature before God reforms and changes it. It is as if God looked down to earth to see if there was anyone with integrity, but found that all were corrupted and ruined by evil, so that none sought him. It is clear that he is not referring to just two or three, but to all in general, with the exception of those in whom God has worked and who are now led by the Holy Spirit. Paul then quotes David who also painted a picture of what we are like by birth and by nature (*Psa.* 14:1). Then he quotes, alongside others, the fifth Psalm. Next, he quotes from Isaiah (*Isa.* 59:8, 16), who reveals that when God desired to redeem men, he had to achieve their redemption by his own strength. What would men have otherwise done? They would only have run headlong into transgression and, therefore, into damnation. They would have wandered from the path, loving (as they do) deceit, cheating, falsehood and lies. It would have been far easier for man to die a thousand deaths than for him to assist God in the work of salvation! Thus, Paul refers to all these passages to support his argument.

Now we may flatter ourselves as much as we like, but the fact remains that what God has pronounced about mankind is irrevocable. Therefore, whenever we read these passages, or hear Paul's exposition in the chapter to which I have just referred, our response ought to be that of hanging our heads, and feeling appropriately ashamed. For once we are stripped of all pride, we will come to God to supply that which we need. For the Scripture has concluded all under sin. In the eleventh chapter to the Romans, verse thirty-two, we read that God 'hath concluded them all in unbelief, that he might have mercy upon all'. Here, we are soaring much higher, for this is not the message of the law or of the prophets. Paul is referring to the secret will of God, which has decreed that we will all be condemned to perdition, in order that our only hope of salvation might be in his mercy alone. Thus, if we ask the question, why did God allow man to fall and become so miserably lost, the answer is that God desired us to lean on his grace alone. This might seem strange to people who wish to reach God in their own way. For such people are so arrogant that they find the judgments of God incomprehensible to their human reasoning, and thus condemn him as if he were wicked and cruel! But Paul wishes us to submit to this teaching, that is, that God has concluded all under sin. In other words, God could have created us stronger and more perfect than he chose to do. He could also have preserved us as he did the angels. Adam, and indeed we ourselves, could have been granted such perseverance that he could have entered his heavenly home without having to die first. But God did not plan it this way! He could even have ensured that only Adam fell and that he alone was corrupted. Why did evil have to spread so far and wide? Surely, God intended it this way! We must allow this doctrine to arrest and possess us, accepting exactly what Paul states here. In other words, that God has made us all subject to sin, that we might seek refuge in his mercy.

However, although God had decreed these things in his secret will, he also desired to declare them publicly and openly. For until men are aware that they are condemned, they will simply continue to wallow in false confidence and glorify themselves in their own eyes. We see this happening all the time! Thus, the Scripture leads us to this conclusion, in order that we might be ready to condemn ourselves with our own lips, and unfeignedly declare that we are, indeed, sinners. Why should this be necessary? Because we can only obtain the promise – that is, the free promise of justification – if we first believe. In the passage that I just cited from the eleventh chapter to the Romans, Paul said, 'that he might have mercy upon all'. But in our text he expounds the fact that not all people in general will be able to share in this mercy. Indeed, the greater part of mankind will perish in their sins because they refuse the remedy set forth in the gospel. Why, then, does Paul say 'all'? His main point is to emphasise that there is only one way for anyone to be saved; that is, when God takes pity upon us and grants us his free grace. Then, having forgiven our sins and having become reconciled to us, he can own us as his children and welcome us into the promised inheritance of the kingdom of heaven. Now we can understand why Paul speaks of God showing mercy to all; he does not mean that 'all' without exception are included – rather, he is excluding and casting out any possibility of man's so-called 'righteousness' having a part in our salvation.

Furthermore, Paul indicates the means of obtaining the promise: by faith. As it is written in the third chapter of John, verse sixteen, 'God so loved the world, that he gave his only begotten Son, that whosoever believeth in him should not perish, but have everlasting life.' Do we wish to enter into the delights of such a treasure? Well, faith is the key to open the door to these things. We are called by God, but it is not good enough to be called; we must respond. For example, if he says 'You are my people', [we must say], 'Yes Lord, you are our God'. And if he declares, 'You are my children', [we must say], 'Therefore we come to you as our Father' (*Isa.* 25:9; 63:16). We cannot respond in this way of our own volition, for it is a gift of the Holy Spirit. There is no question here of faith proceeding from men! Paul is simply proclaiming that we can bring nothing of our own which will move God to forgive us, and pluck us out of the pit of damnation in which we are engulfed. We must not entertain any thoughts of merit, but rather seek the grace which is so bountifully offered without being deserved. Our trust must be in this, for we cannot hope for salvation unless God chooses to take pity upon us.

We have already examined why this is needful: men will always seek to view themselves in a vain and presumptuous manner. Consider Adam, who was convicted of his sin and was fearful because of the majesty of God, searching for leaves to cover himself. We are just like this too, and, therefore, it is wrong for us to come before God like whitewashed walls, expecting him to accept us. For God looks for an upright heart, which no-one can claim to possess. If we remain just as we are, we are worth nothing, despite any appearance of goodness we may have! But has he transformed us? Has he given us the desire to walk in his fear, as all believers should? This does not mean that our love for God will be perfect or complete, for we fall short in many different ways. What we have is due to his free grace alone. Thus, we have no cause to exalt ourselves in order to experience peace, for we are not to lean upon our merits. Believers ought to endeavour to devote themselves wholeheartedly to God. Unless we have been sanctified by the Holy Spirit, we cannot be members of the body of the Lord Jesus

Christ. We will consider this point when opportunity arises. The Lord Jesus Christ cannot be divided or fragmented, for he is infinite, and has secured forgiveness for our sins through his sufferings and death; our sins have been cleansed and purged by his blood. We have been cleansed in order to be conformed to the image of God the Father; that we might become new creatures in him. But whatever we may say, this was not designed to embolden us to come before God believing we are worthy of his acceptance, as if we can force him to be favourably disposed towards us!

Now, if any claim to have this or that merit, let me say, firstly, that everything we have proceeds from God. On the contrary, we ought to be aware of at least a hundred faults in ourselves. For example, when we set about some good work or other and believe we have accomplished it, this good work, if examined more closely, would be found to be marred by sin! Thus, it would make us liable to condemnation! Therefore, we must be silent before him. If we desire God's mercy, the only requirement is faith, which he alone can give; yes, only faith! I do not mean that we may all feel free to do evil, as I have shown before. We must have the Holy Spirit, otherwise we will be open to all kinds of corrupt practices. This is not what I mean at all! Paul is only dealing with faith here, and with the basis of our trust as we call upon God our Father, and experience assurance of our eternal inheritance. If we trust in our works, as I have already said, we can have no assurance at all. Why not? God does not require one work, nor two, nor three, but perfect obedience, of the kind which is unknown to mortal man. And even if the angels were answerable to God, they could not attain to that perfect righteousness. How much less we, who are but vermin, and who drink iniquity as a fish drinks water (as Job expresses it, *Job* 15:16)? How can we trust such a foundation, believing that God will receive us because we are worthy? In short, we must reject all trust in our works, and confess that we are worthy of condemnation if we desire the promise to be fulfilled in us. This is a summary of what Paul is teaching us in this passage.

* * *

Next, he says that 'before faith came, we were kept under the law, shut up unto the faith which should afterwards be revealed'. The terms 'law' and 'faith' here would be unclear to us if they were not explained at greater length. For, on occasions, when the Scriptures speak of 'faith' they refer to the whole religion, including all the teachings of Holy Writ. At other times, the Scriptures are speaking of the confidence we can have when we come to call upon God. For we are not to approach him in a careless manner; we must come willing to accept the grace he offers us. Therefore, we need faith to embrace God's promise, for his pledge does not depend on merit, but is absolutely bounteous and free. The only way we can have an interest in it is through the Lord Jesus Christ. This is what Paul is referring to when he speaks of 'faith' in this text. The same definition applies to the use of the word 'faith' in the Epistle to the Romans, and, indeed, everywhere that Paul deals with the subject of justification before God. The term 'faith' means one and the same thing in these places, as I have said.

However, in this passage the word 'faith' also has a more special sense: it means the revelation which we have in the gospel. For it is certain that our forefathers had a spirit of faith; indeed, as we have said, Abraham was justified because he believed God. If we follow his example, we become his children and are granted access to the kingdom of heaven. Faith has always had this power, for there has never been any other way of joining or uniting God and man. However, we read that in the time of Abraham 'faith' had not yet been revealed, because the Lord Jesus Christ, who was the object and fulfilment of faith, had not yet appeared. Today, we are justified freely without merit; perfection is imputed to those who believe that Jesus Christ died for their sins, and rose again for their justification. For we believe in our hearts unto righteousness (as that other passage says), and we confess with our mouths unto salvation (*Rom.* 10:10). Now, if

Abraham had known the Lord Jesus Christ as we know him today, and as he was crucified amongst us (as Paul said earlier, *Gal.* 3:1), his faith would have been identical to ours. But 'faith' was somewhat obscured in his day. Yes, Abraham hoped in Jesus Christ and waited for salvation from him, and yes, he cast off all faith in himself, knowing that he possessed no virtue that could win God's approbation. Nevertheless, he was kept in the shadows, viewing Jesus Christ from afar; for he had not as yet appeared as the Sun of Righteousness; this is referred to in Malachi, chapter four and the second verse.

We can now appreciate what Paul means when he says that faith had not yet come; he is telling us that the time for revealing had not yet come. Today, we have this revelation in the gospel, but our forefathers were 'kept under the law'. There is, therefore, much that is different, but also much that is alike. If we were to enquire about the condition of our forefathers who lived under the law, we would find that it differed slightly from ours, yet was to an extent one and the same. How can it have been the same? Because God declared that he would be merciful to Abraham through our Lord Jesus Christ. Abraham realised the need to put his trust in God's grace alone and deny himself; because he believed he was counted righteous, as we have seen. The same is true of all the patriarchs and prophets. In this way, their situation was just like ours: they placed their trust in the Lord Jesus Christ, and did not hope in themselves but only in the mercy of God. Like us, they were promised an inheritance in heaven. But the difference is that, until the coming of the Lord Jesus Christ, they had sacrifices, washings and the like. Under the law, there was the priest who entered the sanctuary to mediate on behalf of the people. The people themselves had to stand a long way off, with a veil between to symbolise the separation. This is how the condition of our forefathers differed from ours. In the absence of the Lord Jesus Christ, there were ceremonies and types; but now we have the body and substance of them, as Paul says in the second chapter to the Colossians and the seventeenth verse. God no longer requires a calf, or lamb, or bullock to atone for sin, but we must be sprinkled with the blood of the Lord Jesus Christ by the power of the Holy Spirit. For in the Lord Jesus Christ we find all that is needful for salvation.

Thus, faith reigns now, that is to say, now that Jesus Christ has been fully revealed, whereas our forefathers had but a small taste of such things. This is why Paul speaks of them being 'kept' and 'shut up', as if the law kept them in bondage. Not that they did not see eternal life (which we anticipate), for we shall all be crowned together on the last day. But for a time, God had to instruct them as if they were little children, which is why he introduces this image of a schoolmaster. The third image he uses is that of a guardian or trustee, but since we will deal with this later, let us for the moment comment on Paul comparing the law to bondage. Surely this implies that God has granted us richer grace and has shown us greater kindness than was shown to those who died before the appearance of the Lord Jesus Christ? As for the second image, this indicates most clearly that the Jews were being compared to children; for this word schoolmaster means 'a teacher of children'. Today, we have reached manhood, as it were. Paul tells us that the function of the law was like that of a schoolteacher, suited to the 'childhood' of his former people. We can see from this that those believers who trusted in Jesus Christ before he had been manifested to the world were children of God in a very real sense! And if they were children, then they were heirs also. We are not to think of them as being like brute beasts, as some foolish people have judged. Some have thought that they were content just to have the fat of the land that had been promised them, and to indulge in gluttony and drunkenness. Such blasphemy is atrocious! Jesus Christ did not come that we might fill our bellies and satisfy our thirst – he came to give us eternal life! No, it is written that Abraham saw his day (*John* 8:56), and this is the means by which he enjoyed peace of conscience. We know also that David always looked beyond this world; and when Jacob was dying he proclaimed that he was waiting for God's salvation (*Gen.* 49:18), though he was drawing his last breath and could hope for nothing else in this life. Thus, our forefathers were not little children in the sense that they were not blessed by the Holy Spirit, and called by him to inherit immortality. The difference, therefore, consists only in the measure of faith. How is this? Well, the law they had was full of types and shadows, but now Jesus Christ has clearly revealed the way to heaven.

When I say that our forefathers were inferior with regard to the measure of faith, I do not mean that Abraham, David or any such saint had weaker faith than ours. Indeed, if we were to search throughout the world, we could not presume to find one person alive today who has a hundredth part of the faith of Abraham or of David! This highlights how excellent their faith was, for they overcame all the temptations which overtake us hundreds of thousands of times. What I mean is that the promises were obscured somewhat more than they are today. If one of us had to undergo the battles that Abraham and David faced, what would become of us? For Abraham was led during his lifetime through a foreign land, a land where he was refused water to drink, even though he himself had dug the wells (*Gen.* 21:25)! He was exposed to countless dangers. After God had exercised his faith through many trials (so many, in fact, that it seemed that God was leading him to the deepest pit of hell), his faith emerged victorious. As for David, for a long time he was a fugitive, being forced to flee and yet having nowhere to lodge, except amongst unbelievers and enemies of God, or amidst wild beasts in caves! He was so downtrodden that everyone cursed him as if he were the most wicked and detestable man in the world. Nevertheless, he persevered and continued to call upon God. He was never enticed to murmur or blaspheme against God, but rather glorified him, even in situations of extreme anguish. Their faith ought to make us feel ashamed of ourselves! If each of us were seriously to examine our consciences, we would find but a little portion of the faith such men had. But the greatness of their faith must not be judged by how faithful they were in trusting God.

What am I saying, then? I am assessing the degree of their faith in relation to the revelation available to them. For example, although Isaiah was outstanding and although we would have great difficulty finding such a good teacher in our world today, nevertheless, the least person who preaches the gospel faithfully will be preferred before Isaiah, as the lips of the Lord Jesus Christ declared (*Matt.* 11:11). How is this possible? Isaiah was like an angel, speaking with authority and majesty, so much so that he stirred the hearts of those who were asleep. It was as though God himself had opened his sacred mouth to speak, and not as the voice of a mortal man. Yet he only taught the people that which was appropriate to their age. In other words, he taught the people that the land of Canaan was a token of God's love, that they must keep the sacrifices, ceremonial washings and the like, and indeed all the types and shadows, demonstrating to the people how blessed they were to be the children of God. He compared the church to a palace built of gold, silver and precious stones (*Isa.* 54:11; 60:17). These things were in accordance with the shadowy nature of the law. Now we have the Lord Jesus Christ. Today, were even a simple-minded man to preach the gospel, though he may not be eloquent or dignified, he will be pointing to Jesus Christ. He will show that we are living in the fulness of time, and that our sins are forgiven because of the sufferings and death of the Lord Jesus Christ. The wrath of God against us has been appeased and victory is ours because of his death.

Thus, the difference really lies in the revelation and not in the amount of faith in the heart. Abraham may have had admirable faith, the like of which we will not find in this world today; but he was still kept in bondage to the ceremonies and other shadows. David was like an angel, and like a mirror image of all that is perfect, yet he had to submit to the common practices of the people. He had all the ceremonies which were then in use, and he only saw Jesus Christ from afar, for, as yet, there was that veil which prevented him from beholding the glory of the gospel which we have today. Yet it seems that we do not know a hundredth part of what was revealed to David and to Abraham, rendering them invincible against all sorts of temptations. They were enabled to fight powerfully in order that God might be glorified in them, and they were also strengthened to bear all the attacks to which they were subjected. However, at the same time, they still did not possess what we have today; that is, the Lord Jesus Christ as our surety, that we might call God our Father, being members of his body. He is our Head, and if we are united to him so that all his blessings are communicated to us, then we can experience fulness of joy today. This is how our faith is greater than that of Abraham: not in respect of our persons, nor with regard to the faithfulness we exhibit, but in relation to the revelation which we have received concerning the object of our faith. Hence, Paul says that our forefathers were kept under the law before the coming of our Lord Jesus Christ, as under a schoolmaster.

For our part, we ought to magnify the grace of God, as indeed our Lord Jesus Christ exhorts us to do: 'Blessed are your eyes, for they see: and your ears, for they hear. For verily I say unto you that many prophets and righteous men have desired to see those things which ye see, and have not seen them' (*Matt.* 13:16–17). Abraham is called the friend of God (*Jas.* 2:23). David was known to be a man after God's own heart (*Acts* 13:22), yet he could only see the promises fulfilled from a distance. Today, these same promises have been cast into our laps, as it were; our appetites have been satiated. Our forefathers sought Jesus Christ, who was at that time absent and hidden from sight. Now, however, our Lord Jesus Christ has descended to this world and has dwelt among us, leaving us in no doubt that all has been accomplished, as he said when he was dying (*John* 19:30). What a dreadful situation it would be, therefore, if we were not even more inspired than they to follow the gospel, now that God has come to us in such an intimate way! Since God has conferred such great privileges upon us, miserable creatures as we are – more than he granted all the holy kings and patriarchs under the law – we have greater cause to praise

God in the way that he deserves. However, we must be careful not to allow such great gifts and privileges to be turned to our greater condemnation through our lack of gratitude and failure to appreciate our blessings. For, although Abraham was like a little child (as I have explained), he was nevertheless prepared to leave the land of his birth and enter a foreign land, living like a poor vagabond. Once there, he faced troubles on every side, though he was in a state of weakness. If he had repented of his decision, could he not then have returned to his homeland? Yes, but the apostle shows us, in the eleventh chapter to the Hebrews, that Abraham persevered to the end because of his strong faith and hope. By this he demonstrated that his heart was firmly set on the kingdom of heaven, and had not become ensnared by the things of this world. Abraham, and indeed, all our holy forebears, walked in such a way that they set us a shining example, despite the fact that they had not even witnessed the fulfilment of the promises which have now been set forth in the gospel. During their lifetimes, they only experienced a small taste of what has been so plainly revealed to us today. Woe to us, therefore, if this does not urge and inspire us to embrace all that God offers.

Does he not display the infinite riches of his grace in order to win us to himself and cause us to separate ourselves from the world? He desires us to devote ourselves freely to him. We have now reached manhood, as it were, and ought to be moved and motivated by such a display of grace. Although we are weak and depraved we ought to come to God and take upon ourselves his yoke, submitting ourselves in willing obedience to him. We should take the bit in our mouths, as it were, and defy Satan and all his wiles, and everyone else, too, for that matter! If, however, we fail to overcome all these obstacles, the neglect of the grace of the gospel will cost us dear. Now is the day of salvation and the acceptable time: let us seize the opportunity and hasten to embrace it! Knowing that we are held back by such terrible weakness, we need to beg God to strengthen us to overcome our cowardice and coldness. This will cause us a great struggle within ourselves, yet in view of the fact that we are surrounded by Satan's fiery darts, such violent efforts are vital! If we walk in the fear of God, we will be enabled to combat all the schemes that Satan devises to hinder us, and to follow God's way instead. We will also be given strength to walk in the footsteps of our forefathers, who have gone before us and who await us. Then we will all be welcomed into our eternal home in heaven, at the most blessed return of our Lord Jesus Christ.

Now let us fall before the majesty of our great God, acknowledging our sins and praying that he would enable us to hate them. Then, may we not only tremble before him but also seek his pardon, being renewed in his sight through true repentance. May we grow increasingly stronger in the faith until we reach the point where we are rid of all iniquity and so perfectly conformed to his image that his glory shines through us. Then, we may enter the full possession of the promised inheritance. May he not only grant this grace to us, but to all peoples, etc.

23

Baptism Means Robing Ourselves in Jesus Christ

For ye are all the children of God through faith in Christ Jesus. For as many of you as have been baptised into Christ have put on Christ. There is neither Jew nor Greek, there is neither bond nor free, there is neither male nor female: for ye are all one in Christ Jesus. And if ye be Christ's, then are ye Abraham's seed, and heirs according to the promise (Gal. 3:26–29).

Last time, we saw that the gospel has elevated us to a position of great dignity. Not only are we called to share the privileges that our holy forefathers enjoyed, who were so greatly blessed by God; but an even greater dignity and honour has been conferred upon us because, unlike them, we have been delivered from bondage to the law. To reinforce this point, Paul states that we become children of God only through belief in the Lord Jesus Christ. The same doctrine is taught in the first chapter of the Gospel of John (*John* 1:12). In this text, our honourable status is shown to be of great worth, and rightly so! It tells us that we have the right and privilege to be called 'sons of God' by faith in the name of the Lord Jesus Christ, who is God's natural and only Son. This title of 'Son' belongs to him alone by right, but is placed upon us through grace because God has chosen to adopt us for the sake of his Son. So then, Jesus Christ is the Head of the church, but for his sake God owns and accepts us as his children.

This implies that 'to believe' means much more than people generally imagine, as I have already made clear. Those who are not familiar with Holy Scripture may find it strange that we can receive such blessing simply by believing, and may consider that faith is not enough of a virtue to earn us such a reward. However, as we have already explained, believing in Jesus Christ is not equivalent to believing a story that we have been told or that we have read; it means truly receiving him when he is presented to us by God the Father. We must embrace the Lord Jesus Christ as the One who has paid for our sin in order to reconcile us to God; we must trust in him entirely for salvation, assured that he has provided all that we need to gain our eternal inheritance. If we are certain of these things, then it will not surprise us that we become children of God simply by believing. Yet, we must remember what we said previously about faith having no merit in itself; it is not a question of weighing our faith in the balances to assess its value as a virtue! No, we become children of God through free adoption. If you are looking for a cause of this, I tell you that the true source of salvation is in the mercy of God alone when he chooses to take pity upon us. However, this is achieved by means of faith (as we have said before). When all our pride and vain presumption has been taken away, and we recognise that we are lost by nature, then we take refuge in the Lord Jesus Christ. This is what Paul is teaching us here.

Paul has developed this theme so that we might really understand that faith is sufficient on its own, and that we do not need anything else to help us obtain salvation. What else do we require, then, before God can accept us as his own? Do we think we can add anything to such an inestimable gift? To have liberty to call upon God as our Father, knowing that he has lovingly accepted us and will, therefore, treat us as his own children – surely this is the fullest and richest of blessings! How have we reached this point? Paul tells us that faith alone enables us to be partakers of these benefits. We must conclude, therefore, that the law cannot achieve any of this. Indeed, we must be full of the most wicked covetousness, or be completely out of our minds, to seek anything more than to be a son of God. In Holy Scripture, the angels are blessed to possess this very title (*Job* 1:6); the highest honour they could have had was to be called sons of God. And now we have been associated with them, even though we are but worms of the earth, in whom there is nothing but filth and corruption. God has opened the kingdom of heaven to us and made us companions with the angels, who perform his will and who are united to him. Now, I say, that we share their glory, can we be so presumptuous as to seek out other means of salvation? No, by faith alone we are able to obtain such blessings. We are to learn to reject all the possible means that may be suggested to us, for they will all serve to turn us away from the Lord Jesus Christ. Do not let others recommend any such 'aids', as if faith were insufficient. This is what Paul intends us to understand. But we will remain unaffected by this passage unless we bear in mind the fact that Paul is excluding all those who seek to bring their supposed merits or worthy deeds before God; for our worth is not assessed by our personal virtues. People who think in this way undermine the importance of the grace of the Lord Jesus Christ. But his grace cannot be treated thus, for salvation in its entirety must be attributed to grace alone. We are not to wander here and there, seeking sidepaths or byways; we are to come to God by the straight and narrow path of faith.

* * *

At this point Paul continues by saying, 'For as many of you as have been baptised into Christ have put on Christ.' Here Paul is answering a question which may have arisen in our minds; that is to say, how can we be children of God when this honour belongs to the Lord Jesus Christ alone? For the apostle teaches us that not even an angel in heaven can be called the Son of God in the way that Jesus Christ can (*Heb.* 1:5). It is true that the angels are called the sons of God, as we have already pointed out, but this has to be qualified.

Indeed, there is not a creature in existence who is worthy of this title. So then, since Jesus Christ is God's only Son, how is it that this appellation can be applied to us? Paul tells us that it results from the union that we enjoy with him, spoken of in the seventeenth chapter of John, verse twenty-three. If we were not joined to the Lord Jesus Christ, then we would not be able to know God. We would be cut off from any hope of eternal life through sin; indeed, we would be mortal enemies of God, that is, until he were to regenerate and transform us. Whatever we might think, by nature, that is to say, apart from the Lord Jesus Christ, we are not even worthy of the title of human beings – much less can we boast that God is our Father!

Paul addresses this matter (as I have said) and tells us that in baptism we have 'put on' the Lord Jesus Christ. The illustration of clothing is a very common one in the Scriptures. Jesus Christ is our garment, as it were, and he covers up all that would cause the Father to reject us. We are granted grace to come to God through the person of the Son of God, and we are no longer viewed as we are by nature. In brief, Paul highlights here the closeness that exists between the Lord Jesus Christ and those who believe in him, who are members of his body. Just as all the substance of a tree proceeds from its roots, and all the powers and faculties of the body proceed from the brain, the same applies to the relationship between the Son of God and ourselves. For (as I have said) we would not have had a single foretaste of eternal life had he not granted it to us. Therefore, in order to draw near to God, partake of his Holy Spirit and receive the gifts that pertain to eternal life, we must first be 'in Jesus Christ', and not think anything of ourselves or of our own virtues.

In the passage I have just cited from the seventeenth chapter of John, the Lord Jesus Christ, speaking of the true and perfect felicity enjoyed by his own, says, 'I in them, and thou in me, that they may be made perfect in one.' Thus, to escape the pit of death, we need to be united to the Lord Jesus Christ by the bond of faith. And Paul tells us that this occurs at baptism. Not that every baptised soul is truly a member of the body of Jesus Christ; for we see around us proof of the very opposite! Constantly, people profane and defile the holiness of baptism and become guilty of sacrilege, because they have professed to be in Jesus Christ, yet despise him. All is ruined by their filthy and depraved lifestyles. Baptism, therefore, does not make us all Christians, for we realise that becoming a child of God is too great a benefit to be bestowed through such a base element. What is water? To say that water regenerates us, delivers us from eternal death, and enables us to rise to God, is utterly to pervert the truth. Notice, therefore, first of all, that when Paul speaks of baptism here, he presupposes that we have received the grace that is offered. Many who are baptised make void the grace of God in their lives. Although it is offered to them, they render themselves unworthy of it through unbelief, wickedness and rebellion. Thus, the power of baptism is cancelled out by many. But where there is harmony and peace between God and ourselves, baptism has the effect which Paul speaks of in this text.

Thus, we can only become children of God, and put on Jesus Christ, if God draws us out of the corruption of our natural state and makes Jesus Christ our Head. Only when we are grafted into his family can we enjoy the blessings he brings. If this is our position, then all that baptism represents has been accomplished in us. If hypocrites boast because they have been baptised, Paul says to them that they are deceiving themselves with vain hopes, for he says elsewhere that the circumcision of the letter is nothing (*Gal.* 6:15). If we look no further than the outward, visible sacrament, it is not valid. The same applies to baptism; it is of no value to those who loudly declare themselves to be Christians and pillars of the church, if they defile the thing that God appointed for such noble purposes, as I have already indicated. Therefore, this text of Paul's cannot apply to all without exception. It is not for those who have only experienced the outward sign of baptism, but for those who truly understand its spiritual significance.

Secondly, Paul does not mean that the baptismal water has any power to change us or clothe us with the Lord Jesus Christ. If this were the case, God would be robbed of the praise that belongs to him alone. Rather, Paul is speaking of the means of our assurance that we are members of the body of the Lord Jesus Christ. I have already told you that the only way to be saved is through the free mercy of God; we are not to seek other paths, for this would be like a thirsty man turning his back upon a fountain [to seek water]! Let us be aware that it is only through God's mercy that we can be united to the Lord Jesus Christ, through the hidden power of the Holy Spirit. Yet, he still works through baptism as a kind of secondary instrument. For example, consider the fact that all light proceeds from God. Before the sun and the moon had their existence, there was light in the world. Yet, God has ordained the sun in order to illuminate our world. But the sun does not detract from the fact that the power belongs to God alone! Again, it is written that man shall not live by bread alone, but by every word that proceeds from the mouth of God (*Deut.* 8:3). Indeed, bread has no life in itself. So who gives us life? It is God, for we live in him, as it says in Acts chapter seventeen, verse twenty-eight. Yet, God is pleased to use bread so that its daily consumption should lead to our physical sustenance. In the same way, it is not difficult to perceive that baptism clothes us with the Lord Jesus Christ, even though this life proceeds purely from the grace of God and the hidden work and power of the Holy Spirit, who works outside the laws of nature. Baptism simply affirms this to us and is necessary because we are so base and earthly. This is God's way of drawing us to himself, little by little, because of our weakness, so that we gradually understand matters that are too lofty for us to comprehend immediately. Where are the wings we need to soar above the heavens? Surely it is difficult enough to creep upon this earth! This is why God has to stoop down to us, which he does by means of the sacraments. This, then, is how we put on the Lord Jesus Christ at baptism.

Paul employs rather different imagery, however, in the

sixth chapter to the Romans, verse five. Here, he tells us that if we have been 'planted together in the likeness of his death, we shall be also in the likeness of his resurrection'. This image of being planted or grafted in is just as appropriate as that of the 'putting on' of Christ. You take a cutting from a tree; then you make a cut in the trunk or branch of another tree, and bind on to it the cutting you took from the first tree. They will grow together and become one, because the roots will provide sap to make the sprig grow. In the same way, says Paul, we have been grafted into the Lord Jesus Christ; our old man has been crucified with him and raised in newness of life.

The first point to notice about this is how gracious and kind God has been, and indeed still is, to us, in that it pleased him to unite us to his own Son. This surpasses in greatness all the privileges our hearts could conceive or imagine. Thus, Paul proves that if we have God's Son, then everything that belongs to God is ours also to enjoy. Indeed, Paul says elsewhere, 'He that spared not his own Son, but delivered him up for us all, how shall he not with him also freely give us all things?' (*Rom.* 8:32). Indeed, there can have been no better way for God to have displayed the infinite treasures of his kindness than for him to have united us to his only Son, the Lord Jesus Christ. It is more than if he had given us heaven and earth, for when we compare Jesus Christ to all things below, or even to those things which surpass the earthly, Jesus Christ far exceeds them all! This is the first point to notice.

Secondly, notice that God has united us to the Lord Jesus Christ to show that our whole life should be in him. Surely this serves to humble us and expose just how dreadful a thing it is to remain under Adam's curse. If the Holy Scriptures had not declared that we need to be in Christ before God can look upon us, we would never have recognised sufficiently our poverty by nature, nor have hated our sin to an appropriate degree. But now we know that it is impossible to draw near to God, or have him look upon us with fatherly love and call us his own, unless we have been first clothed with the Lord Jesus Christ. Indeed, even if all the angels came to our aid, and the whole of mankind for that matter, and even if there were nothing wanting in ourselves, it would still be impossible! This leads us to abhor ourselves. Surely, we must be worse than abominable if the only way to appease God's wrath and make him favourably disposed towards us was by him covering our sins, cleansing our filthiness and washing away our iniquity! For this occurs when we put on Jesus Christ. A picture of this is found in the example of Jacob when God blessed him by the hand of his father (*Gen.* 27:27). Jacob was elected as Jacob, yet he was dressed like Esau. So he was Jacob with regard to God's calling him to that inheritance or birthright; yet he was Esau in that he had borrowed his brother's clothing! In the same manner, we are God's chosen ones, since he has promised to be merciful to us; but first and foremost, we must come to God clothed with our Lord Jesus Christ. For if we examine ourselves as we are by nature, God must surely find us detestable and abhorrent, which is a just assessment. This is Paul's warning here.

Let us profit from what we have learnt here about baptism, so that we may fight against all the temptations and obstacles that Satan puts before our eyes to shake our faith. If we are unregenerate and, therefore, unaware of our sins, or even comfortable with them, then woe to us! Yet, we may have been awakened, and understand that we must give an account of ourselves to God. We may reflect morning and evening upon the fact that God is the Judge of all the earth, and cannot relinquish his office. If this is the case, then when we examine ourselves and perceive our own sinfulness, we will rightly be afraid and even transfixed with fear. If we had no hope to comfort us, we would surely sink in despair. But let us return to thoughts of our baptism, and assure ourselves that God did not call us in vain to partake of the purity of his only Son and unite us to him. As we consider this, the blood he shed will cleanse all our stains, thus enabling us to approach God with our heads held high. Of course, we will not come proudly, like the hypocrites and the presumptuous. We will come trusting in his unspeakable kindness, because he has declared that we now share all the riches that are in our Lord Jesus Christ. If we find that we have committed so many sins that we sense the wrath of God is kindled against us, let us remember that Jesus Christ has offered a sacrifice which has made reconciliation between God and ourselves. Seeing, then, that God has manifested his love to us in this way, we can be sure that he will appear for us whenever we seek him in true faith. That is to say, whenever we approach him with steadfastness, believing that he will not forsake us now that he has shown us such bounty.

Thus, you see that our baptism becomes precious to us when we use it as a shield to deflect all assailing doubts. For we cannot even pray to God, or take refuge in him, unless we have been united to Christ in this way. Yes, it is true that I am full of sin, to the extent that I am abhorrent in the eyes of my God. But I do not come to him in my own strength. I reject all trust in myself and in my own nature, for I deserve nothing but shame and confusion. I come in the name of the Lord Jesus Christ; he goes before me and clothes me with his robe. He speaks on my behalf, and I approach God in his name, as if I were the Lord Jesus Christ himself; for God has been pleased to grant me grace to be united to him. We ought to forget about ourselves in this way when we come to God clothed with the person of the Lord Jesus Christ. When I say forget about ourselves, I do not mean that we need not acknowledge our failings and be truly humbled, bemoaning our state. Yet, at the same time, we ought to have the confidence and assurance that God will accept us if we come to him through his only Son.

However, there are very few who consider these facts. Though we all profess to follow the gospel, we will find that many do not understand the true significance of baptism, nor its efficacy, nor the purpose for which it was ordained. Such people will pay dearly for the abuse of a pledge made in God's sight. God will reveal to them that baptism is too precious a thing to misuse, since it is the means whereby we are united to the Lord Jesus Christ, and grafted into his death and resurrection. Many were baptised as infants, who have lived forty or fifty years in this world without understanding what their baptism signified. It would have been better if such people had been born dead, and buried in the earth a hundred times over, than to have profaned such a holy ordinance. Now let us look well to ourselves; although just a small amount of water has been applied to our heads, it has not been done in vain. God speaks from heaven through the ordinance of baptism, as it were, and Jesus Christ himself bears witness of the usefulness and power of the sacrament, for his death and resurrection are confirmed to us through this sign. Let us remember these things and consider the purpose of our baptism and its fruits. Let all this become well rooted in our hearts, so that whenever we see infants baptised, our own hearts may be profited. [We may ask], why is baptism solemnised before a company of believers? To commend the child to God. Also, the child is receiving heavenly citizenship, as it were, and, therefore, this ought not to carried out in secret. Indeed, it is such a noble act that it deserves more solemn and grave observance than any of the ceremonies of this world. When we witness a baptism, we become aware of the benefits that have already been bestowed upon us, which encourages us to rejoice in our own baptism to the end. Unbelievers, however, banish and exclude themselves from such adoption by God, through their disregard of such blessings. Therefore, in order to grow stronger, we need to remember that when a baptism is celebrated, it should affect us. Through another person's baptism, God is drawing us closer to himself and revealing that, though by nature we are lost and condemned, if we have been united to the Lord Jesus Christ, we are no longer viewed in our natural state. God does not see what we are in ourselves, nor what we have deserved. He sees us as if Jesus Christ were within us, for indeed, we cannot be separated from him. This is what we need to learn from this text.

* * *

Thereupon, Paul draws all this to a conclusion, saying, 'There is neither Jew nor Greek, there is neither bond nor free, there is neither male nor female: for ye are all one in Christ Jesus.' By this text, Paul seeks to underline that faith is sufficient and that every other route is excluded. Any other means dishonours the grace of the Lord Jesus Christ, as well as the power of his Holy Spirit. If anyone should say that circumcision was to our forefathers what baptism is to us, this matter has been addressed in Scripture. In the second chapter to the Colossians, verse eleven, Paul says that having been baptised, we have been circumcised, not by man's hand, nor with a visible circumcision. Yet it ought to suffice us that God acknowledges us to be partakers of the spiritual circumcision, for today, baptism is ordained for this very purpose. However, circumcision was appointed to make a distinction between Jews and Gentiles; as it says in that other passage (*Eph.* 2:14), there was a 'middle wall of partition', to distinguish the Jews as the people whom God had chosen. Now, however, the blessing extends to all, since there is no longer any such distinction between us. So then, baptism has succeeded circumcision, supplying what was lacking in the former sign, which was but a type and shadow of things to come. It was only necessary before Jesus Christ came. But now that he has been revealed, baptism has been instituted in its place.

However, let us be clear that there is nothing we can do to win God's favour, as we have said before. All that is needed is simple confession of our sins (though this were enough to drown us in despair!). Furthermore we need faith in order to receive the things that are necessary for our salvation, found in the Lord Jesus Christ. If we claim that we are too base and vile to comprehend such heavenly mysteries, we ought to consider our baptism, wherein God leads us by the hand, as it were. Through baptism, God displays before our eyes our cursed state by nature, and reveals that we need to be clothed with the Lord Jesus Christ, in order that all our sins may be covered by his perfect righteousness. We know what obedience he rendered to God the Father; thus, if we are rooted in him, we cannot fail to be accepted! In this way, God desires that we trust in him and in his Son, the Lord Jesus Christ, drinking of the fulness of that wonderful fountain. Yet, he expects us to attribute all the praise for our salvation to the power of his Holy Spirit. Thus, precisely because of our vileness and infirmity, he gave us the sacrament of baptism. Since we have all this, why do we need to seek any further? If we seek other means of salvation, or add our views and opinions according to our own will and taste, are we not wilfully robbing God? What purpose will these things serve? Such corruptions proceed from the devil.

Here Paul declares that we ought to be so closely united to the Lord Jesus Christ, that none of us would presume to rise up and set himself above the rest. We ought all to realise that everything we have is due to the grace of God alone. All of us, from the greatest to the least, must endeavour to accept this fact. With one accord, let us confess that in our Lord Jesus Christ we have everything we could possibly hope for, and, therefore, let us renounce all the different schemes and inventions that our brains conceive. However, Paul does not mean here that there are no differences of status with regard to the society of this world. For as we know, there are servants and masters, rulers and subjects; in the home, the husband is the head, and the wife must be in subjection. We know this economy to be inviolable, and that our Lord Jesus Christ did not come into this world to confuse everything by overturning what God the Father had established. When Paul says that there is 'neither bond nor free, there is neither male nor female', he means that when it is a matter of salvation, men must not come like peacocks displaying their fantails, standing gazing at their own feathers! No, we must exclude any thought of our own worthiness, and trample it underfoot, realising that it is a stumbling block which will hinder us from approaching Jesus Christ. When all, from the greatest to the least, acknowledge that we cannot contribute anything of ourselves, but that all must come from the grace and goodness of God, then our Lord Jesus Christ will become all in all to us. In other words, we will not desire to add anything to the grace that he has purchased for us. This grace is offered to us daily through the gospel, to the end that we should partake of it and enjoy it in salvation.

Thus, on the one hand we retain our worldly status; those of us who are great, and those who are in authority over others, know that God can use them in his service in that same estate. Rulers, for example, should realise that they have an even greater obligation to fulfil their duties, since God has honoured them by raising them above the station of other men. Also, private individuals, whose duty it is to obey these rulers, must be careful to submit if they do not wish to strive with God and be at war with him. Paul is, therefore, advocating sobriety and moderation, and recommending that we remain under this yoke, for it was not designed by man. God has appointed this order for us, and without it the human race could not continue. Indeed, we ought to honour and revere the way our society has been ordered, as it has been ordained directly by the Lord. Yet, when it comes to heavenly matters, we know that all the things of this world are passing and fading away; as Paul says, 'the fashion of this world passeth away' (*1 Cor.* 7:31). The kingdom of God, however, will endure.

Thus, if it is a question of our being children of God, and heirs, we cannot attain to this through wealth, nobility, dignity, power or merit. How, then? By the grace and goodness of God alone. Those who are great in this world must humble themselves, and those who are the least must wonder at God's inestimable kindness which has raised them above the heavens, though they were scarcely counted worthy to live on earth! May we learn from all these things! Surely, the most important point is that we should be seeking and endeavouring to reach our heavenly inheritance. All our efforts, thoughts and desires should be applied to attaining this one goal. Yet, in passing through this world, we must respect the various offices which our Lord has appointed for us to observe. Whenever we have to appoint a person to government – to bear the sword of God, and sit on the judgment seat, as it were – may we be careful to commend to

God those who are chosen, that they may be good and faithful rulers, and fulfil their duty well. For our part, may we obey and submit to them peaceably, seeing this is one of the first fruits of the kingdom of heaven, as it were. For through this, our Lord reveals his care of us, by watching over us; indeed, one day we shall understand this more fully, when he gathers us up into his kingdom. In order to bear the yoke that he has ordained with greater courage and joy, let us remember that it is a pleasing and acceptable sacrifice in his sight when we walk in the way that he has established. We ought to live without wronging others, and without practising violence or deceit. Also, we need to walk in all godliness and uprightness, as Paul tells us (*Tit.* 2:12). This means that God should be feared and reverenced above anything or anyone else, and that we should learn to devote ourselves to him. Our moderation should be such that we prove that we are not given over to the things of this world, although we live here. It should be like a strange land to us, because we are pressing towards our heavenly rest. Once there, we will understand what is being taught us through these verses: that is, that our union with the Lord Jesus Christ at baptism was not in vain.

Now let us fall down before the majesty of our great God, acknowledging our sins, and praying that we would be so conscious of them that we would fervently seek him. Then, may we commit our lives to the Lord Jesus Christ, that, united to him, we might be free of all the cares of this world, and press on towards the joy of the kingdom of heaven until we arrive there. Thus, we all say, Almighty God, and our heavenly Father, etc.

24

Blessed More Than the Patriarchs

Now I say, That the heir, as long as he is a child, differeth nothing from a servant, though he be lord of all; But is under tutors and governors until the time appointed of the father. Even so we, when we were children, were in bondage under the elements of the world: But when the fulness of the time was come, God sent forth his Son, made of a woman, made under the law (Gal. 4:1–4).

There has only ever been one way for mankind to be saved. Whatever circuitous routes we may invent in order to have our hopes realised, it is all self-deception. For, as we have shown before, God has rejected us all; we are children of wrath and under his curse. On our own, we can never recover what was lost in Adam, but we can if God in his infinite goodness comes to our aid and works within us. Any other ways are bound to be fruitless and to no avail. The fact is that God has established just one way by which we may escape the curse to which we are all subject. This means that our forefathers must also have been saved by the grace of God alone, just as we are today. We saw in the second letter to the Corinthians that God's promises have always been made 'in him', that is, in the Lord Jesus Christ, (*2 Cor.* 1:20). He is the pledge; he makes the promises meaningful, powerful and efficacious in our lives. This implies that believers today enjoy a common salvation with all believers that have ever lived, since the beginning of time. God willingly receives all, for we have all been reconciled to him through the grace of the Lord Jesus Christ. We have all been justified and enabled to inherit the kingdom of heaven in exactly the same manner.

However, there is a great difference between the church today and that which existed under the law. Our forefathers had to perform countless ceremonies. They were circumcised in infancy; then there were the sacrifices, ceremonial washings and the like. Today all of these have been abolished and are no longer practised. How, then, can we say that our faith is the same, now that the administration is so different, and now that God has altered everything? If we say that God is responsible for these differences, does that not make him changeable? If we say that he has done it for man's sake, then we must conclude that we are in a different category from that of our forefathers; they must have been much further off from God than ourselves!

We have already responded to the first of these objections. God is immutable, although he has altered matters of church order. If he sends good weather followed by rain, or heat after the cold, according to the season of the year, do we say that he has changed his mind, and, therefore, that he must be changeable in himself? No, on the contrary! Rather, we say that he has ordained that which is suitable to the needs of the human race. Indeed, by these variations he is admonishing us that we are not to seek our rest here below! We are to pass through this world as pilgrims, as if we were on a long journey to the kingdom of heaven.

As for the second objection, Paul shows that though we are different from our fathers who lived under the law, it does not mean that we do not have the same religion, or the same God. Likewise, it does not mean that the promises only apply to us today; because the power of the Lord Jesus Christ has always been the same from the time of Abel and, indeed, will be so until the end of the world. The difference lies in the external administration, Paul tells us. In order to clarify this point, Paul uses an example which ought to be familiar to us. If a father were to leave young orphans, he would appoint tutors and governors in his will to look after them until they should reach adulthood. Once the father had died, the children would be kept by these tutors and governors, and would not be able to enjoy the wealth that their father had left them, even though it rightfully belonged to them. They would not have the mastery; indeed, it would be more likely that they would be under strict discipline, rather than be allowed to dine whenever they felt like it! In this way, children, though they be heirs, do not have immediate liberty, because they are too weak, and have insufficient wisdom and discernment. Paul, using this illustration, shows that our forefathers, the Jews who lived under the law were God's children and heirs like us, but that the church in those days was still in infancy, as it were. Hence, restraint was called for, which was why they were in subjection and servitude to the law. Paul, therefore, compares God's law (to which the Jews were in subjection as a ceremonial yoke) to guardianship. However, we today have passed that time, he says, because God has now sent his only Son; in the Lord Jesus Christ we have grown up and reached adulthood, so that the law has become superfluous and unnecessary. In fact, we could even say that it is now contrary to God's will and to the new order he has established.

Now we have understood what Paul is seeking to teach us, and it is, indeed, a matter of great importance. We need to be aware that our Lord Jesus Christ did not appear unexpectedly, as if God suddenly decided to provide a remedy for fallen humanity! For Jesus Christ has always had power; even from the beginning people had to come to him for salvation! Faith has always been the means, as the apostle shows in the Epistle to the Hebrews. Indeed, the sacrifice Abel offered was not accepted because of its intrinsic worth, nor for the sake of the person who offered it, but rather because of faith (*Heb.* 11:4). Abel was building upon a foundation of faith. Hence, the apostle also refers to our Lord Jesus Christ as 'the same yesterday, and today, and forever' (*Heb.* 13:8). We ought to be settled in our minds about this point; thus, we need to study it thoroughly. In other words, we need to know that our hope of salvation today is not something new, but has been the same since time began. Gospel teaching has not existed for just sixteen [hundred?] years, but is the same doctrine that has been taught to all believers who have ever lived.

Returning to our text, when we come to the Lord Jesus Christ in faith, we become his adopted children. Paul sought to rebuke the folly and arrogance of those Jews who boasted of their earthly lineage. Paul tells us that the important thing is the incorruptible seed of the Word of God by which we are made regenerate. When God adopts and receives us as his children, he counts us as the spiritual descendants of Abraham. How else can we be the children of Abraham unless we have the same faith as he had? Paul had good reason to treat this subject. He wanted to teach us that right from the earliest time, there has only ever been one way that a man may be renewed unto salvation, and receive God's grace and love. That is, through trust in Jesus Christ and through taking refuge in him. This is why Paul mentions the child who is lord of the house, and heir to the inheritance, yet who cannot enjoy his privileges because of his age.

This should make us aware of the fact that if we seek to exclude our forefathers from the household of faith (as Paul describes it), we are doing them a great injustice. For they had most miserable lives in this world, in that God tested them with many afflictions. The lives of the fathers, and especially of those whom God marked out and made prominent, are shining examples of indomitable patience. For instance, think of what Abraham endured! What difficulties and struggles he experienced! And what about the temptations that Isaac, and subsequently Jacob, endured? Again, think of David and his strength of character! If these men had been carnally minded, they would have been worse than brute beasts. It follows, therefore, that their minds must have been on things above, as we have said before, for they bear testimony to this, not just by the things they said, but by their actions. Let us, therefore, give heed to the underlying message of these verses, which is that our fathers hoped for the same inheritance that we await today, through the Lord Jesus Christ. Because we have the same faith as did Abraham, David, and all the holy kings and prophets, we will be welcomed into the heavenly kingdom along with them, and will obtain the same crown of salvation, which is the end of our faith, as Peter says in his first letter (*1 Pet.* 1:9).

The point made here by Paul concerning the son as no different from a servant, serves to magnify the grace of God to us. It highlights the privileged position we have through the gospel. It is a great thing to be called children of Abraham; but how much greater is our standing when we consider that even Abraham was not raised to the height that we have reached under the gospel! For Abraham was under the yoke of the law, because our Lord Jesus Christ had not yet appeared. Today, we have been set free; thus, God has blessed us even more than the patriarchs and prophets! It is our duty to acknowledge this grace and esteem it highly, as it deserves. Next, we are to devote ourselves to God's service with even greater and more fervent zeal and desire.

However, let us be aware of the fact that Paul is not referring to each person individually here. For we all need to confess that our faith is so much weaker and feebler than that of any of the prophets or patriarchs, as our lives clearly exhibit! If, therefore, we have not reached their standards of holiness, why is it written that they are like little children, whilst we today have reached manhood? As I have just said, Paul is not referring to this or that individual here, but to that dispensation of the church. He is not speaking of people, but rather of the way that God has chosen to govern his own. This may be more clearly seen by looking at the evidence to the contrary! Paul had to rebuke the Corinthians because he was constrained to give them 'milk' as if they were infants, instead of 'strong meat' (*1 Cor.* 3:2). He makes them ashamed of their slow development, and of their perverted habits and desires, telling them that they have not grown in faith as they ought to have done by that time. They were yet in infancy, still learning the alphabet, as it were! Again, the prophet Isaiah condemns the Jews yet more harshly for this same fault. He tells them that they are like little children, repeating their alphabets, having always to return to the beginning. What they learn one day, they soon forget, rendering progress well nigh impossible (*Isa.* 28:10)! This problem is far too common in the world today! Furthermore, Paul, in the fourth chapter to the Ephesians, verse thirteen, exhorts all believers (even those who are strong and could be teaching others by proclaiming the way of salvation) – he exhorts such to grow until together they become 'a perfect man'.

It would seem that there is a contradiction here; for we are told in our text that those God receives into his church and who have become servants in the faith, have already reached manhood, no matter how foolish they may be! Even if they scarcely understand three words that relate to faith, it does not matter, provided they understand the main principles and have a rough (though limited) knowledge of the power of the Lord Jesus Christ. Paul implies that such people are like fully-grown men, no longer children kept under a schoolmaster, tutor or governor. However, in the other passage we quoted, Paul says that we need to grow; he is not referring simply to the weak and ignorant amongst us, but to those who bear the torch to enlighten others! How long do they need to grow? Not for one year, nor two, but throughout their whole lives! However long they may live in this world, they need to acknowledge their shortcomings daily, striving and endeavouring to walk more worthily.

Yet, all this agrees together very well! For, firstly, even the best of us would have to confess that we are like a little child, if we were to examine ourselves properly. However hard we try to reach God, we drag our feet, as it were. Many hindrances present themselves; even a wisp of straw is enough to stop us in our tracks, or a fly buzzing before our eyes! We are soon ready to turn back! Even those of us who are strong have to struggle against many sins. This means that we need to pray daily that God would increase our faith, and deal with the unbelief that still remains within us. This applies to us as individuals. However, with regard to the way God leads and governs his church today, we have already attained manhood. How is this? Well, we are no longer in strict subjection to the law, as our forefathers were. Nowadays, we have recourse to the Lord Jesus Christ when we sin. Of course, in the eyes of God we are spotted and stained with sin, but a way of cleansing has been prepared for us. If the blood of the Lord Jesus Christ is applied to us by faith and through the power of the Holy Spirit, then we are clean and pure, and God accepts us. Whereas we were condemned to eternal death through the sins we committed against him, now, in the Lord Jesus Christ, the price has been paid. He became our substitute in order that we might be acquitted. Hence, we are no longer under the yoke that our forefathers bore in relation to God and his plan for the church. Therefore, although we are conscious of our failings, this does not prevent us from having reached maturity, as it were, for God has given us greater privileges and a greater liberty than those who lived under the law. Now we have dealt with this difficulty. To sum up, let us remind ourselves what we have learnt. Firstly, we are to magnify the grace that God has shown us in elevating us to such a position of dignity. Yet, on the other hand, we must not think that we are somehow superior today, for we are still base and vile, and not ready to move on to higher or nobler things. Let us remember these points!

* * *

The superstitions which abound in Popery today did not originally contain the same degree of devil-inspired blasphemy when first conceived as they do now. For their ceremonies, which are considered necessary for God's service, are idolatrous, and are deceptions inspired by Satan himself. In short, they are all abominable in God's sight. Why is this? Because they suppose these things are necessary for salvation, and that men can redeem themselves through such means and acquire remission of their sins. Worse than this, these ceremonies obscure the Lord Jesus Christ and the grace which he has brought us. Men think they can save themselves through their own penances. Thus, they usurp the role of the Son of God by taking it upon themselves, as it were. These heresies are outrageous in the extreme. Yet, when all these absurdities were introduced, they did not have such negative implications. Indeed, they had a more favourable veneer! The thinking behind them was as follows: men are base and foolish, and cannot comprehend the mysteries of the kingdom of heaven unless they are treated much like children! Whilst it is true that we need to acknowledge our weaknesses and humble ourselves (as I have already said), this does not mean that we can choose whichever path we like; we must be content with the way God has appointed. A child does not select his own tutor – this would not be permitted – his father must choose one for him. It is true that, occasionally, the state has to intervene to appoint a tutor, but Paul has chosen the illustration which best suits his argument here. If, therefore, an earthly father has authority to appoint tutors for his child, why should not God have the same power? A child could not and would not choose his own tutor according to his personal taste! Since this is the case, what right or entitlement have we to invent this or that, saying to ourselves, 'We are but children; let us select ceremonies suited to our state of ignorance'? No, God has already ordained the means; are we wiser than he is? This is how it is that restless minds have introduced many ceremonies into the Christian church, using the excuse of the ignorance of the common people!

People believe we must add this and that, because, for example, baptism would be too simple if there were only water! Water is not enough [they say], for there are many poor idiots whose minds are so dull that they do not understand the meaning of the mystery; that is to say, that we are renewed by our Lord Jesus Christ. Therefore, we need holy oil, which acts as a visible sign of the Holy Spirit! We also need a candle, a white robe, some salt, then this, then that! Thus, baptism has become something elaborate, embellished according to man's fancy! But these things are like stains and blemishes; after all, did not the Lord Jesus Christ, who is the unfathomable wisdom of God the Father, know what was best for us? Why, then, do men creep about like little toads, seeking I know not what, as if that which Jesus Christ instituted was incomplete and needed perfecting? They do the same with other teachings. Even the Lord's Supper has been corrupted and perverted; more than that, it has been totally destroyed by that hellish abomination called the Mass. It would seem that it was too ordinary a thing to take a piece of bread, and drink three sips of wine. The promise is that we share in the body and blood of the Lord Jesus Christ when we take the Lord's Supper in true faith and obedience, for he alone is food for our souls. Yet, we choose to dress this up as if we were acting out a farce! There are so many actions to remember that it is most confusing! But what is it all about? Well, they say it is a sacrifice for the remission of sins, as much for the living as for the dead! This robs the Lord Jesus Christ of his honour as High Priest, which was given to him by God the Father with a solemn oath that he would have no successor. Yet, the Papists have had a million of them! And who are these people? Even if they were angels from heaven, we would still have to view them as devils. However, we choose all the vermin of this world, all the scum, people of no value, and call them successors of the Lord Jesus Christ! Papists cover themselves by claiming that they have introduced all these aids because of people's ignorance! And this is the way that all their other superstitious practices came about. For example, this is how they came to erect idols and grotesque statues. 'They are books for the ignorant', they said, and, indeed, this is one of their stock sayings. But all their impudent ways are rebuked here, where Paul points us to the order that God has established, which we must steadfastly observe.

Now then, do we desire to hold on to our heavenly inheritance, which has been secured for us by the Lord Jesus Christ? Then we must follow the order that God has set for his church, knowing that he will make up for all our shortcomings. However vile we are, he knows the way to draw us to himself. Yes, provided that we keep to the narrow way. Those who have gone astray, and who have added countless ceremonies to compensate for their own weaknesses, have effectively distanced themselves from the Lord Jesus Christ. We are all aware that, by nature, men are drawn to visible, tangible objects. Thus, by having many ceremonies, people cocoon themselves, burying themselves in them so deeply, only to find soon afterwards that they have departed from God and from the Lord Jesus Christ. We may ask, how is this so? Did not our forebears have ceremonies to help them in their infirmity at the time of the law? Yes indeed , but they had all been revealed by the Word of God! Right at the start, God declared that these things were ordained from heaven, as we are told in the twenty-fifth chapter of Exodus, and the fortieth verse. Moses was shown the pattern on the mountain that he might not be preoccupied with present, corruptible things. Indeed, knowing how inclined we are to do this, God severely reprimands us by his prophets: 'Away with your sacrifices', he says. 'Do you think that I am pleased with you when you slay your animals, believing you can appease my wrath in this way as if I were hungry or thirsty? Do you imagine that I need such gifts?' (See *Psa.* 50:8–13; and *Isa.* 66:3). Thus, God has always warned his people of the danger of superstition; although he himself appointed ceremonies, they were only necessary for a time. In the absence of our Lord Jesus Christ there were but types and shadows. Yet Paul tells us that these were the means by which our forefathers were led to seek for Jesus Christ. However, now that he has been made manifest, we no longer have need of them.

For example, if I wish to paint a person, but cannot see him in person, at the very least, I will need a picture of him to help me. However, if I see him in person, and can observe his face, I will not need a picture or any other kind of aid in order to help me paint and depict him vividly. In the same way, our forebears only had types and shadows because the Lord Jesus Christ had not been revealed. But now that he has shone upon us so clearly, as the sun of righteousness (*Mal.* 4:2), if we still retain the figures, are we not deliberately seeking to obscure Christ? The veil of the temple was torn in two at his death, to show us that today we can approach God personally, and present our spiritual sacrifices to him, that is, our prayers and requests, now that we have seen the body and substance of those former figures (which Paul refers to in Colossians chapter three). Now, we have shown that all those who have added new inventions have completely corrupted and distorted the gospel by placing veils and blindfolds over people's eyes, that they may not recognise or esteem Jesus Christ as he deserves and as is required if we are to be saved. Thus, all who do such foolish things are not seeking Jesus Christ, but precipitating their own damnation simply by being governed by their own desires. They are so single-minded about this that they will not be distracted, much like little children when they are building something; they forget to eat and drink, they are so engrossed! They will be oblivious to cold or heat, hunger or thirst. Why? Because they are transported by such follies! Then they will move their construction here or there, add this or that to it, but will not leave it alone once they have become attached to something in this way! The same applies to us when we seek to serve God according to our own wills.

Hence, we need to have a sober judgment about such things, content with the means which have been appointed to lead us to the Lord Jesus Christ. We have baptism and the Lord's Supper – let these suffice us. Curiosity can only lead to harm, if we do not acquiesce in God's will, renouncing all our own speculations and desires. It is blasphemy to think that something else might be helpful, or to believe we need some other form of Christianity or church government. It is as if we are saying that God does not know the best way to rule us; that he does not know what will be best for us. Take baptism for example: it would be too simple if it only involved water. We need something to give the ceremony more weight. Thus, we need a candle, some salt, holy oil and all the other ritual items that are included. Men have always sought to add to what God has commanded, which is unthinkable blasphemy, as I have said. It happens because men have forgotten the most important thing, and have become obsessed with trivia. The most important thing is the promise of God, for all the ceremonies in the world can only be frivolous nonsense, or even devilish lies, if they are not based upon the Word of God, taking their authority from him, and tending to his glory. For example? Well, if there were no promises attached to baptism and if we did not know why it had been instituted, what a waste of time it would be! We would do better not to practise it! Similarly, if we did not know the meaning of the Lord's Supper, it would be better to forget it altogether. But our trust lies in the fact that God's Word is behind these institutions, with promises that testify to the fact that we are cleansed and washed from all sins by the blood of the Lord Jesus Christ. Then we are made regenerate through the Holy Spirit. Thus, baptism is connected with certain promises, which in turn point us to the Lord Jesus Christ, who is the fulfilment of them all.

This is what we are reminded of when Paul ranks us in a degree which is far superior to that of the patriarchs and those who lived under the law. It is not that they were less perfect, less constant, or less faithful than we are today. No, Paul confirms the point that we have already made, which is that we have no new way of salvation set before us. God receives us in the name of the Lord Jesus Christ in the same way that he has always called his elect – those whom he chose in order that they may share in the adoption which we enjoy today. For if it were the case that men only had the opportunity to be justified and made acceptable to God since the appearing of Jesus Christ, what would become of those who lived before that event? If this were the case, how that would weaken our faith, and fill us with such confusion that we would not know what to do! What! Has not God been the Father of all his creatures since the beginning of time? Was there no salvation before the coming of the Lord Jesus Christ? The salvation which is manifested today through the gospel existed before his coming, though there were types and shadows, and though the temple veil was still hanging. Indeed, our forefathers have always looked to Jesus Christ, the same person to whom we are drawn today. This is how they were enabled to walk freely and without fear, just as today – nothing can shake us when we lean upon the Lord Jesus Christ. Through him, we are all called to an inheritance which he has secured on our behalf.

So much the more, therefore, must we loathe those devils who claim and would have us believe that our forefathers were much like brute beasts, knowing nothing of spiritual life. This blasphemy is enough to blot out all true religion. What about that awful man, that dog, who dared to suggest that Abraham knew nothing about heaven, that he never truly worshipped God, only according to his own imagination? He said that all that was written about Abraham being the father of believers was a mockery, and that he only had a most shadowy faith, knowing nothing of Jesus Christ and his coming. Well, the punishment he received was well deserved. These, I tell you, are the kind of blasphemies found in his books. Let us detest such plagues sent by Satan. Surely, this agent of the devil was subtly disguised for the express purpose of destroying faith on the earth! Indeed, the devil transfigures himself, and does not immediately expose his horns. Hence, this is a most dangerous situation, where Satan is actually seeking to ruin the foundations of our faith, even from below ground, as it were! Paul specifically warns us against this (*2 Cor.* 11:14), that we may be on our guard and keep watch, that we may not be taken by surprise. Let us, therefore, take good note of the fact that we can only be the heirs of God if we are members of the body of the Lord Jesus Christ. This is the way in which the Holy Spirit confirms our inheritance to us, that we may be better disposed to lean upon our God, and to persevere in hope until we have overcome all the struggles of our earthly life, and enter the spiritual rest that we await.

* * *

Now we must turn our attention to what is said about the fulness of time. We could ask the question that is always upon people's lips: 'Why is this so?' We could ask why God delayed, when we were all lost and condemned the moment Adam fell. Why did he not give us a remedy sooner? Paul, however, is not interested in satisfying man's curiosity; he has no time for this at all. Indeed, if God had wanted to satisfy us, he would have had to grant us all kinds of basically superfluous things, but he preferred not to, in order to test how obedient and faithful we really are. Paul, therefore, puts us in our place when he says that the fulness of time had not yet come. What does he mean by 'the fulness of time'? He is referring to a time which God has appointed according to his will, and not a time that man would choose, simply because men are not competent to judge the best time. We must submit to God and delight in that which he has established. This is what Paul was referring to when he described the time that God sent his only Son into the world as 'the fulness of time'.

Let us, therefore, learn that our highest wisdom consists in submitting to God with all sobriety, and considering all that he does to be just and good. As for ourselves, we could be highly intelligent, but it would not amount to much more than folly if we believe ourselves to be or to know something. We ought, rather, to humble ourselves before God, not like those who rashly say, 'I think such and such. That is my opinion.' There is nothing more contrary to God's Word, than a presumptuous attitude, which says, 'This is the best way to do things; this is what I judge and consider to be right.' Instead, we are to bring every thought into captivity, as the apostle says in the Second Epistle to the Corinthians, chapter ten and verse five. We must allow ourselves to become slaves so that we dare not lift our heads to dispute with God, or to claim to be clever or worthy people. We must be content with the liberty that Christ has granted to us, and yet not abuse his grace; for he has chosen us above even those who seemed to be angels in this world, yet who were unfamiliar with the liberty that we enjoy through the gospel.

Finally, Paul brings to our attention a most important fact:

namely, that we have not reached manhood today in terms of our personal holiness, but because of what the Lord Jesus Christ has done. As we have already said, we are different from our forefathers in that they were under a tutor, as it were, and we have been set free and enjoy greater liberty. Why? Because we are more worthy, or more honourable in some way? Not at all! But because the presence of God's Son has conferred this honour upon us. Do we wish to rejoice in our gospel liberty? Then let us come to the Lord Jesus Christ straight away; for, now that he has been glorified, he will introduce us to that heavenly glory, since he has gone before us. This is the main thing that Paul was seeking to bring to our attention. Of course, he adds that Christ was born of a woman, and submitted to the law, but it would not do to hurry through that right now. Therefore, I will reserve this for another time.

Now let us fall before the majesty of our great God, acknowledging our sins, and praying that he would make us increasingly conscious of them, that we might tremble and sigh in true repentance. May we reach the standard to which we are called, that is, to be free from the flesh and from all our depravity, and to experience the joy which we are daily invited to taste, and also to display integrity every day of our lives. May he grant this grace, not only to us but to all peoples and nations on earth, etc.

25

Crying Out to God in the Certainty of Our Adoption

> *But when the fulness of the time was come, God sent forth his Son, made of a woman, made under the law, To redeem them that were under the law, that we might receive the adoption of sons. And because ye are sons, God hath sent forth the Spirit of his Son into your hearts, crying, Abba, Father. Wherefore thou art no more a servant, but a son; and if a son, then an heir of God through Christ* (Gal. 4:4–7).

We have already discussed why Paul speaks here of the 'fulness of the time'. He was seeking to combat the curiosity of man, whose desire to know the secret things of God is insatiable. Indeed, men often audaciously reproach God when they discover that his will does not happen to suit them! In speaking of the coming of the Lord Jesus Christ, Paul would have believers to be content with God's chosen time scale, and, therefore, he tells us that the time had not been right until that moment. All such things are in God's hands, and are decided upon according to his good pleasure and his immutable will. We must all submit to his sovereignty.

Then Paul states that our Lord Jesus Christ was 'made of a woman, made under the law, to redeem them that were under the law'. The first thing he mentions is that Christ clothed himself with human flesh, for this was the only way he could render obedience to God on our behalf and set us free. Paul says that he was 'made of a woman'; he was conceived in a miraculous manner and was born into this world. Whilst he descended from the house of David, we know that his conception was brought about by the hidden power of the Holy Spirit. The Lord Jesus Christ took our nature upon himself, that he might live a life of obedience to God for our sake. Thus, his subjection to the law, of which Paul speaks, was not due to constraint, but was undertaken willingly. We know that the Lord Jesus Christ is Lord of all and has sovereign power; all angels and principalities must bow the knee before him and pay him homage. How, then, could he become subject to the law, seeing this, in effect, involved him in a sort of servitude? Well, it in no way detracts from the authority of the Son of God, for he stooped to our level freely and willingly. There is no contradiction here; as it is written in the second chapter to the Philippians, verse six, he 'thought it not robbery to be equal with God'. He emptied himself voluntarily. Thus, because he humbled himself out of his own pure and free bounty, he retained his position of honour, though he appeared before men in the form of a servant, as Paul expresses it.

Therefore, let us learn that though he was Lord of heaven and earth, the Lord Jesus Christ embraced servitude, that we might be set free. For we know that he was circumcised; and that when he reached manhood he meticulously observed all that was commanded in the Mosaic law. Not because he was bound to do so, but in order to abolish such servitude – to break the cords that held us in bondage. Thus, whenever the Scriptures refer to our liberty, as Paul does here, we are to focus upon the Lord Jesus Christ, knowing that his voluntary obedience was not in vain. Everything he did was with a view to accomplishing our salvation. Therefore, we are led to the conclusion that we are no longer to be subject to the law; if we are, then we are despising the work of the Lord Jesus Christ. For how terrible it would be if, having subjected himself to the law for our sakes, we now despise what he has done. It were better for heaven and earth (as we know them) to be overturned than that we should consider our Lord's humiliation and appearance here below to be a game or something trivial. What would come of such opinions?

The lesson, therefore, is that we now have freedom to worship God, no longer under the heavy yoke borne by our forefathers; we may approach him directly because the Lord Jesus Christ has come and has acquitted us. But we have already expounded the way in which we have been delivered from the law. As we have said, it is not that we no longer have a code of conduct to govern our lives; for God is still our Master and has all authority over us. No, we are not at liberty to behave in a worse manner than that of unbelievers and pagans! For even they have this same law written upon their hearts, as Paul tells us (*Rom.* 2:15). Even the person who has never attended school, never had any instruction, and has heard nothing and read nothing, knows the difference between good and evil. No, he may not have great knowledge, yet God, to remove the excuse of ignorance, has written this law upon his heart and he knows that robbery, plundering, violence, fraud, perjury, drunkenness and such like things are sins which deserve condemnation. Also, God desired that such people know their blasphemy against his name to be an abominable thing. Even pagans recognise this, without anyone telling them. How shameful, then, if we are living like lawless rebels under guise of following the Lord Jesus Christ, claiming that he has granted us liberty! In such circumstances, Satan has been unleashed and introduces nothing but chaos and disorder in the church. If this were to happen today, the church would be in an even greater state of confusion than she is already! No, when the Scriptures say that we are no longer subject to the law, they mean that the law no longer exercises the same rigorous influence over us, to tell us that whoever fails to fulfil its requirements is cursed. For although such a statement still stands and still has its own application, it paralyses us and tears us to pieces within. In short, we could have no peace unless such a verdict (that is to say, that all who fail to satisfy every detail of the law will be cursed) had been abolished. Instead, we have been assured that God pities us and bears with our weaknesses, as a father with his children, not seeing the evil that is within each one of us.

Indeed, he hides our sins from his eyes and buries them, that our service may be acceptable to him, though there is much he could condemn.

This, therefore, is what we mean when we say that we are no longer subject to the law. Not that we have no rule to live by, nor that we do not need to hear sermons about the commandments, for we need to know what God requires and to live accordingly. But we are not to lose confidence if we stumble or fall, or make mistakes; that is to say, if we do not fulfil all that is expected with the desired perfection. We are not to feel totally defeated, for we can be sure that God still holds our hand and will not bring us to account for each thing, or scrutinise us rigorously. Furthermore, it means that the ceremonies, which were in force before the coming of the Lord Jesus Christ, are no longer in use, though our forefathers were led by them in those infant days, as it were. For the sacrifice of animals forced each person to contemplate his own death, much as if the abyss of hell had been opened, ready to swallow them up. Today, however, we know that the Son of God offered himself as a sacrifice and shed his blood for us. In this way, he purchased our eternal salvation, so that we may now approach God with our heads lifted high. For we are confident that we will have eternal life through the death of the One who was not subject to death by nature, but who freely submitted to it as our substitute, in order to pardon and absolve us through the merits of his suffering and death. This is what it means, therefore, to no longer be under the law: to have been set free from its bondage and to be adopted as sons.

In saying this, however, Paul does not mean that the holy patriarchs, kings and prophets, and indeed all believers of Old Testament times, were not children of God, or that they did not understand adoption through faith. Only that this adoption had not been as clearly revealed as it has today; indeed, as we have seen, the law acted as a schoolmaster to instruct them as little children, as it were. Now we have reached manhood, due to the advent of the Son of God, and we have received even greater revelation. Now, therefore, we enjoy more fully the adoption that our forefathers only tasted, for the time of full revelation had not as yet come. God did, indeed, work in such people mightily through the Holy Spirit, according to his own good pleasure. But it was not a question of who the people were, but rather of the administration under which they lived. To explain, they served under types and shadows, which kept them bound. But now that our Lord Jesus Christ calls us to himself, the veil of the temple being torn apart, he has prepared a sanctuary for us, not one made with human hands, but one which is in heaven. We can enter with all boldness because he has gone before us. Thus we have been fully adopted, now that the law no longer holds the sway over us that it held in the days of types and shadows.

* * *

Now, to strengthen his argument, Paul adds, 'And because ye are sons, God hath sent forth the Spirit of his Son into your hearts, crying, Abba, Father.' When he refers here to the Holy Spirit, he calls him the Spirit of the Lord Jesus Christ. How else can we be called the sons of God, but by being members of the body of God's only Son, to whom the honour, dignity and right to sonship belong? The Lord Jesus Christ is the only-begotten Son of God, and neither men nor angels can claim such a title – it belongs to Jesus Christ alone. We belong to him, and he, in turn, is not willing to separate himself from us. He has become our Head, and we are joined to him, just as the parts of a human body. Similarly, we must have the Spirit of the Lord Jesus Christ, otherwise we cannot boldly approach our God or call upon him as our Father. It would be outrageous presumption to do so. For if some scoundrel or other wished to become the son of a rich man, he would be laughed to scorn and turned away in shame. But what of us poor earthworms, full of disease and corruption – how can we join the angels of heaven, and call God our Father? Indeed, even the angels cannot attribute to themselves such dignity by right, but only because the Lord Jesus Christ is their Head. To seek to be members of his body and to be in Christ, without coming in the name of the Lord Jesus Christ and with his Spirit within, is great arrogance indeed. It is like seeking to fly higher than the angels!

This is why we are taught about his intercession on our behalf, and that we must call upon the Father in his name; for if he does not plead for us, how can we hope to have our requests heard? Let us think for a moment about our weakness in prayer: though we may groan in all sincerity, and have genuine desires to lift our souls on high, we still fail God. Anyone who thinks he comes before God with perfect zeal is deceiving himself very gravely. Those who know what they are really like and who are very humble realise that they but limp and stagger, even with the strength that they have been granted. However, we can pray with confidence if we know that the Lord Jesus Christ is our Mediator, helping us to approach God. Indeed, this is why the High Priest in the Old Testament wore twelve stones on his breastplate and others upon his shoulders, upon which were inscribed the names of the tribes of Israel. For although the people were standing at the threshold, a veil existed between themselves and God, and the sanctuary was, therefore, hidden from sight; the people could not witness all that was done in the presence of God. It was sufficient for the High Priest to enter in the name of all the people, having blood in his hands in order to appease the wrath of God. He had these symbols upon his chest, on which the names of the twelve tribes, God's people, were engraved (*Exod.* 28:29). He also had them upon his shoulders, to show that he was representing the whole congregation. Thus, we pray by the Spirit of our Lord Jesus Christ to God the Father, with full confidence that he owns and accepts us as members of the body of his Son. For through him we are welcomed into the kingdom of heaven; the door is now open and we have personal access.

This is, perhaps, something that is more clearly expressed

by the word 'crying'. Paul could well have used the word 'saying', but he goes further, for a reason. For, as we have already mentioned, he is comparing our forefathers with ourselves, and showing that our position is far better, in that God has been even more merciful to us than he was to those who lived under the law. Therefore, he says that we cry out that God is our Father with a loud voice and absolute certainty, coming to him boldly to glorify him because we are his children. Yes, it is true that our fathers under the law used the same kind of language. As it is written, 'Doubtless thou art our father, though Abraham be ignorant of us, and Israel acknowledge us not' (*Isa.* 63:16). In other words, 'though we descend from these people according to the flesh, our natural ancestry is nothing compared to our spiritual parentage which you have made possible through the person of your Son. You are, therefore, our Father.' Thus, the whole church has always prayed to God in this vein, just as Isaiah tells us. And there are many such passages. Indeed, it was not possible for our forefathers to address a prayer or request to God without the underlying principle that God accepted them as his own children. Through the ages, this has always been the distinguishing mark of God's people, as opposed to pagans and unbelievers. Pagans have always prayed to God, but have always believed their prayers are subject to chance, and that they may or may not be heard and answered. Our requests must be made in faith.

What Paul tells us will always be true – that we cannot call upon God unless we have first understood his will and listened to his voice (*Rom.* 10:13–15). Thus, whilst it is certain that those who lived under the law were assured of their position as children of God, it had only been declared to them in a whisper, as it were. They prayed to God, but were surrounded by types and shadows which only permitted them a very basic knowledge of the will of God. We realise that they could only approach God by faith, for otherwise all would have been in vain, but there were many obstacles before them that they had to overcome. They could not call upon God with complete assurance, as we now can under the gospel. This is clearly expressed in the eighth chapter to the Romans, verse fifteen, where Paul says that we have not received 'the spirit of bondage again to fear; but . . . the spirit of adoption, whereby we cry, Abba, Father'. In that passage, Paul expresses, by way of two contrasting spirits, something that is a little less clear in our text due to its succinctness. He mentions the 'spirit of bondage', which indicates that the law was a fearful thing, for our fathers of old were bound to it and did not enjoy the liberty which we now have since the coming of our Lord Jesus Christ. They were much like little children. Although their fathers work hard on their behalf, they are ignorant of what is being laid up in store for them. Although their fathers love them dearly, they still have need of the rod, which makes the children even question this love. Yet they do not have the ability to govern their own affairs, neither do they understand how their fathers will provide for them. And it was the same for the people of God who lived under the law: they did, indeed, experience a degree of fear, being held by a tight rein, to which Paul refers here.

However, Paul explains that we are no longer living on Mount Sinai today; the place where thunder roared, lightning flashed, and the noise of the trumpet was heard. There, the place shook and made everyone terrified, so that they dared not approach God (*Exod.* 19:16). Indeed, the people declared, 'Let not God speak with us, lest we die' (*Exod.* 20:19). We no longer feel so afraid, says Paul, for God has granted us complete liberty since the appearing of our Lord Jesus Christ. He has entered the heavens, so that the heavenly throne no longer possesses such a threatening majesty which makes us withdraw in horror. For at that throne, we find grace and favour, and can speak personally with our God. This is all implied by this word 'crying'.

However, it is often the case that believers do not always feel this great liberty and freedom: for we are often anxious, or expressing remorse, or doubting if God will hear us at all. Sorrow can oppress us to such an extent that we have great difficulty formulating a prayer and expressing ourselves. This may all seem to contradict what Paul said in the passage to which we have been alluding. For we must surely exclude ourselves from amongst the people of God, if we have doubts about praying to God and uncertainty about the liberty of which we have been speaking. If this is our condition, what hope is there? Where is this confidence that Paul speaks of? Well, Paul removes this problem by revealing that the Spirit of God 'helps our infirmities' (*Rom.* 8:26). For we may have 'groanings which cannot be uttered', which God understands, even though men do not hear them. Thus, if we have learnt anything from the gospel, let us be fully persuaded of the fact that God counts us his children, and gently invites us to come to him, yes, even to come boldly. This is expressed in the third chapter to the Ephesians, verse twelve, where it says that by faith in Jesus Christ we have the confidence and the boldness to approach God. Thus, without confidence or boldness it would seem that we cannot possess faith, yet, since faith is never perfect and must undergo many trials, such that it appears to have been worn down, we can become so heavy-hearted (being hard-pressed by problems and afflictions) that God seems far away and that we can, therefore, hardly address a word to him in prayer. But let us, rather, return to what Paul shows us here, that the Spirit helps us in our infirmities.

Thus, we are to press on, and never cease praying to God. Even if we remain silent, or perhaps stumble over our words, being unable to pronounce even a syllable correctly – whatever our hindrances are, the Spirit of God will help us if we remember that God is still our Father and that we must seek refuge in him. Though we may not pray as freely as we would wish because we are laden with burdens, let us nevertheless go forward, not allowing our failings to close the door, but persistently calling upon God knowing that, in the end, he will have mercy upon us. This is what we must bear in mind when Paul speaks about this confident spirit, which enables us to cry out to God in the certainty of our adoption.

We must not presume, however, that we can possess this 'spirit' at all times, for we are still beset by many sins. For example, there is unbelief: if its root is not still within us, it has many means by which it seeks to entrap us. Thus, we have constantly to battle against it. But the most important thing for us to be persuaded about is that God is our Father; then we can pursue the goal that Paul sets before us here, albeit hampered by our limitations and weaknesses. Indeed, this is one of the great debates that we are having today with Papists. They say that we can never be sure of God's love; it is a matter that remains in the balance, whether God loves or hates us. However, this view undermines the true meaning and function of prayer, for the Scriptures say that we cannot pray without faith (*Jas.* 1:6–7). The man James refers to entertains no doubt whatsoever about his prayer being heard and answered. We are not to be like a reed swaying in the wind and tossed about on every side; we are to be convinced that God will keep his promises and that we will not be disappointed if we come to him, because he has bidden us to come. We must always remember this when we pray, or our prayers will be pointless.

Now, what Christianity can there possibly be in us if we do not possess the Spirit of God, as Paul says in the eighth chapter to the Romans? Again, in the fifth chapter of the same, and the fifth verse, we are told that our hope will not be in vain, because 'the love of God is shed abroad in our hearts by the Holy Ghost which is given unto us'. Without hope, we are surely banished from the kingdom of heaven and cannot call ourselves Christians. And what is this hope? It is the love of God shed abroad in our hearts, as Paul says; in other words, that we are fully satisfied and contented with the knowledge that God loves us. And how do we know this? By the Spirit. Notice that the words 'shed abroad' are used here. These words indicate that God does not express his goodness and paternal love towards us sparingly, leaving us as poor famished beggars. Rather, he lavishes it upon us so that we have more than sufficient proof that we are his own; for he has showered us with all the riches of his mercy in the Lord Jesus Christ. Now, this must surely proceed from the Spirit of God, as it is written in the first and second chapters of First Corinthians, for we could never comprehend the love God has for us with our natural minds; it is beyond human capacity (*1 Cor.* 2:9, 14). Thus, in order for us to know his love, God has to raise us far above this world, for we are unable to grasp such things by nature. If the Spirit grants us this ability, then it is certain that we do not possess it by nature, nor by inheritance; furthermore, we have not attained it by our own merits. God, in his great mercy alone, desired to assure us of his love, so that we can individually find refuge in him in time of need.

The Papists, however, judge it differently according to their own fancies, for they believe that we cannot be certain about God's love for us. Indeed, those wretches are so blind that they believe us to be presumptuous to seek such an assurance, as if we are seeking to work it up in ourselves. If we were simply to persuade ourselves that God is our Father, then we are but dreamers, as much as fools who run around our streets believing themselves to be kings or princes or some such! But if God has confirmed this fact to us, can we then be in any doubt? Is it presumption to honour God by counting him faithful, and relying upon his Word? Similarly with prayer, does he not give us every encouragement when he says, 'Come unto me' (*Matt.* 11:28)? If we had not received any instruction regarding prayer, then, indeed, we would be displaying great audacity if we were to present ourselves before him; but he bids us come. Furthermore, he does not expect us to 'seek' him out; he simply invites us to 'come' to him. When we acknowledge him as our Father, attribute to him the praise that he deserves, and seek our salvation in him, he stirs up within us the desire to pray. When he has been so bountiful to us, can we debate about whether we ought to follow him or not? Does not this blasphemy negate all the promises of God? All of this is what we are to remember when we see the word 'crying' in this text. Even if we can only babble, like those who have half lost the power of speech, being so weighed down by affliction that we can hardly utter one word or syllable, we must, nevertheless, come to God, knowing that he will meet our needs and deal with the weaknesses that hold us back. In short, whenever the Spirit moves us to experience those groanings within of which we have already spoken, we must seek the face of God, despite the fact that we may be totally confused, not knowing where to begin. We ought always to cry out to God, as we are exhorted to do here.

Paul specifies that we are to cry 'Abba, Father', which indicates that God does not only intend to save the Jews; they are not the only ones who can find refuge in him. This privilege is open to everyone, now that the gospel, which is like the key which has opened the gates of paradise, is proclaimed everywhere. Now all may enjoy this right, which was, at one time, a special privilege of the descendants of Abraham. This is why we are all able to cry 'Abba, Father'. The first word, 'Abba', means 'Father'; but Paul is deliberately using language which was peculiar to the Jews, and used most often amongst their ranks. For in those days the Hebrew language was no longer pure, since the captivity in Babylon; it was then a mixture of Hebrew and Chaldean. Paul is seeking to show that, under the gospel, God may be called upon with a loud voice by all, for his adopting grace has been made known to all nations; he has broken down the dividing wall between Jews and Gentiles, so that we are now equal and in the same condition. Thus, we can call upon God in any language, as with one voice, confident that God will receive us now that we have the liberty to address him; indeed, the gospel encourages this, and is, of course, our infallible guide. However, we also see here that each person must call upon God with his understanding. For if a man who only understands his own language tries to pray to God in Greek or Hebrew, he is a fool and is distorting and corrupting the true concept of prayer. It can only be hypocrisy and deception. We have already pointed out that we can only pray to God in faith, knowing that he will hear and answer. But what good is it if we do not know what we have to ask him? It is a pollution of such a holy thing as prayer. We know that God demands this sacrifice of us all – that we call upon him and take refuge in him – for this is a way of proving that he is our Father and the source of all good things. Thus, we must come to him as 'the rewarder', as the apostle says in the eleventh chapter to the Hebrews; he will not disappoint us if we diligently seek him (*Heb.* 11:6). On the contrary, we will discover that there is nothing better than to run to him. Thus, it is very important that we understand what we are asking when we pray to God. This is one point.

Furthermore, when we are told that we cry 'Abba, Father', it signifies that diversity of languages does not prevent there being unity in the Faith. Isaiah seems to be saying something very different when he says that everyone will speak the language of Canaan, that is to say, Hebrew (*Isa.* 19:18). Yet, we do not need to know this language to make us Christian believers! Rather, what he means is that God will be worshipped and adored in every language. He refers to the language of Canaan because it was holy and had been used to convey the very secret things of God. Because this language was special in the eyes of God, Isaiah uses it to indicate that God would be honoured by all nations. Each would have to renounce all their blasphemous and superstitious practices, and, indeed, every false way, and become one by faith. Having been taught the law and the gospel, they would profess faith, and there would ensue a harmonious and peaceful relationship between Jew and Gentile. But in our text, Paul was seeking to declare plainly that when we call upon God, we must use our own languages, and he will be able to hear and answer us all. For it is not necessary for him to attend school in order to learn this or that person's language!

Incidentally, we ought to be aware that language only serves as a means of inspiration in prayer. It is also true that it enables us to declare verbally before our fellow man that we have put our trust in God. Because it is intended to help us in our infirmity, due to our weakness and coldness, it has the effect of warming our hearts, enabling us to overcome the reticence and frailty which tends to dominate us. However, it is not that God needs language; it is not necessary for us to shout aloud if we desire our prayers to be heard.

Indeed, he knows the secret thoughts of our hearts. These are the points we must remember.

This makes us realise that the devil himself reigns in Popery, where there are no prayers, any more than there is genuine faith! They believe that there can be no true devotion or holiness without their jabbering on in an unknown tongue, using all the jargon without understanding what they are saying. Although the priests, monks and clerics tell us they understand Latin, we are well aware of the level of their intelligence! Indeed, they make babbling compulsory, though they do not even know what they are saying! For them, it is good enough simply to start out with good intentions (this is how they speak); so that before they say the words, '*Domine labia*', they purpose within themselves to pray to God and worship him. It does not then matter if they proceed to think about food, or even worse things, because they have convinced themselves that their prayers are acceptable to God. Thus, God is hidden from the poor, for they are told that it is not lawful to pray in the common tongue. This is an abomination to God. We can see how the devil has destroyed these poor folk, and bewitched them, so that they refuse the bread of life. Instead of receiving bread and meat, they are fed poison and are killed by it. Yet can we not see what Paul is teaching here: that when we pray we must not come without considering what we are about to ask, nor ignorant of our true relationship to God. If we call him our Father, then we need to remember that it is not through any personal worthiness we might have, nor through merit obtained by our works; but, rather, because he has united us to the Lord Jesus Christ and accepts us in him. For if we are part of Christ's body, God will accept us through the person of his Son.

Thus, Paul adds that if we are the sons of God, we are also his heirs. Paul is telling us that we are blessed with an inheritance now – not that we possess it in the sense that we now experience the glory which has been promised to us, but, rather, by way of contrast with our forefathers. They stood in the temple courtyard, and were separated from God by the veil and also by other types and shadows. We are not like them at all in this respect; for we draw near to God with freedom and liberty. Thus, this adoption is in our hearts in a way that was not true of those under the law, being heirs of God. However, we are still pilgrims in this world, and are absent from God (as it says in Second Corinthians – *2 Cor.* 5:6) until we have been dispossessed of our mortal bodies, and taken from this earthly pilgrimage and fleeting existence. It remains for us to praise God for his grace, that he has adopted us as his children, knowing that this has blessed us with all the happiness and joy possible. Let us glorify him for this, even in the midst of the tribulation and suffering that we must undergo. Let us have inner joy because God has called us, and has assured us that even the hardships we experience will be turned to our good and to our profit if we pursue the goal he has set us. That is to say, if we follow the Lord Jesus Christ, and renounce all else.

Now let us fall before the presence of our great God, acknowledging our sins, and praying that he would make us aware of them so that we humble ourselves before him. At the same time, let us not lose courage, since he accepts us, and willingly deigns to listen to our petitions when we come to him in complete trust. May he grant us grace to overcome all problems and hindrances, and all the arguments and questions that the devil sets in our hearts, that we may know the truth of that promise, that whoever calls upon the name of the Lord will be saved (*Joel* 2:32; *Acts* 2:21). Thus, we all say, Almighty God, and our heavenly Father, etc.

26

Backsliders Have No Excuse

> *Howbeit then, when ye knew not God, ye did service unto them which by nature are no gods. But now, after that ye have known God, or rather are known of God, how turn ye again to the weak and beggarly elements, whereunto ye desire again to be in bondage? Ye observe days, and months, and times, and years* (Gal. 4:8–10).

Earlier, we saw that the Galatians had gone astray, despite having been faithfully taught by Paul, who had laboured diligently among them. It was not that they had completely renounced Jesus Christ, nor indeed the gospel, but rather that they had allowed themselves to be deceived so easily, and to follow false doctrines (which happens to be a very common occurrence!). They still met in the name of the Lord Jesus Christ, and practised baptism as a sign of faith, but they had defiled their religion by adding superstition and idolatry. Thus, the Galatians still referred to themselves as part of the church of God, but had become enmeshed by many foolish teachings. For example, they believed that they could partly earn God's grace and favour through their observance of the ceremonies of the law. But this was a great affront to the Lord Jesus Christ. For it is impossible for him to be our Saviour if we have not put our entire trust in him, and cast away all pride. Therefore, the sin of the Galatians was that they were not living strictly by the gospel with stead-fastness and endurance, rejecting error; instead, they had been cunningly seduced away from the gospel. Hence, Paul treats them as worthy of double condemnation because God had led them into the right path, but they had become unfaithful by wandering away from it. This is why he makes a comparison with their former state. These people had been poor heathen folk, who knew nothing of true religion. God had visited them and graciously drawn them to himself by granting them a knowledge of the truth. As we said previously, this is why their crime (of mixing Satan's deceptions and lies with the pure truth of the gospel) was so heinous, as it was something for which they had no excuse whatsoever.

Next, Paul refers to them serving idols in the days when they did not know God. It is no surprise that you should do such a thing, says Paul, since you were blinded in your sins, and God had not revealed himself to you as yet. Therefore, you were unable to discern the living God from gods created in the minds of men. But you were taught the gospel, and were so blessed; this was not due to your own efforts, or wisdom, but simply because God had set his love upon you before you had even sought his face. Seeing you were drawn to him in this way, what excuse do you have for backsliding, and failing to persevere in the doctrine which you know to be infallibly true? Furthermore, says Paul, you made the wrong choice: God gave himself to you, but you left him for the sake of such trifles. For the ceremonies of the law, without the Lord Jesus Christ, are worthless. Thus, you were esteeming things of no value, whilst God meant nothing to you. At this point, Paul concludes, as a man moved with rage, that he fears he has wasted his effort, since for a long period of time he had striven to lead them to a thorough knowledge of the gospel. He mentions a specific example of what he calls, 'weak and beggarly elements': that of observing the feast days found in the law. For they regarded them as a vital means of obtaining grace in the eyes of God. This is what Paul is addressing in this passage.

We ought to take notice of the warning contained in this Scripture. If we fail to persevere with our faith in the gospel after God has called us to himself, though poor unbelievers may have their excuses, yet we shall not escape the most dreadful condemnation. For we have exhibited great ingratitude if we have not profited from the time we have spent in God's school. The heathen, though they live in ignorance, will nevertheless stand condemned likewise, for all men will be judged for their wickedness in devoting themselves to superstitious nonsense. But when we compare ourselves to them, it becomes clear that, whereas they may have a dozen or so excuses, we will not have a leg to stand on, as we say. If we have been awakened to the truth of the gospel, God has granted us singular blessing, and it will cost us very dear if we do not rightly esteem it. Let us be aware that these words were not simply addressed to one people; we are to apply Paul's warning to ourselves today in our own lives, in order that we will not stoop so low as to abandon the truth of the gospel, once we are familiar with it. It should be printed and engraved upon our hearts, so that we will never be moved by the devil. These are the points we are to remember when Paul reproaches the Galatians for their misdeeds, and accuses them of being without excuse. Those who had been awakened to the truth now corrupted it.

The next point being made here concerns the origin and source of idolatry. It always thrives where the living God is not known. For we all possess an inner conviction that there is a God who must be worshipped, and who is worthy of all adoration from great and small alike because he has granted us life. We cannot ignore the fact that we all have a seed of religion within; yet each one is enticed away by our own folly, so that we do not acknowledge God or come to him. If we had not been corrupted, and if our understanding had not been blinded by sin, God would have drawn us to himself. But his image has become so marred in us that we remain in the most terrible darkness; whereas we ought to seek God by looking above, we can only hang our heads low like wretched brute beasts. Thus, until God reveals himself to us, it is impossible for us to follow true religion. We will be led astray to follow foolish distortions of the truth. This shows us the vanity of mankind. Each person considers that he is equipped to govern himself. Even real idiots boast about their intelligence, and as for those who have gained reputation amongst men, they are so swollen with pride that they are not able to receive correction or rebuke. Whereas, if men had but a single drop of wisdom, they would begin by asking themselves which God they ought to worship. This is where men fail: they seek out the lies of Satan rather than the pure truth. They worship idols rather than the living God, that is, until God draws them to himself.

It is plain, therefore, that we cannot please God by living according to our own desires; this is not acceptable service in his eyes. We must, rather, allow ourselves to be governed only by his Word and by the Holy Spirit. We must not follow the opinions of this or that man. Paul is not simply addressing a special group in this passage, for we can see that it is impossible even for us ourselves to live an upright life, and to follow the right path, until God has first taken control and brought us to himself. Therefore, those who follow the steps of their fathers, or pursue ancient traditions etc., show that they despise God's way. How is this? Well, following their own will, they have returned to the mire, and neglected the fountain of living water, unable to discern the difference between black and white. Since this is the case, Paul seeks to remind us, by means of a vivid picture, that men can only be heading in the wrong direction until God leads them into the path of salvation; at which point they must deny themselves and all that proceeds from man, and tread it underfoot, seeking to cleave to the pure and simple truth of God. This, I say, is what we need to learn from Paul's words when he says that when they did not know God, they had served only idols.

However, let us not consider ourselves superior to the Galatians, for, as we have already mentioned, the Holy Spirit seeks to combat all pride, that men would no longer trust to their own intelligence or powers of reasoning, and do as they desire. Rather, we must acknowledge that we are utterly vile within until God illuminates our hearts through grace. Again, the fact that Paul tells us that these idols are not truly gods, implies that we must be truly bewitched if we cannot approach the One who made everything, the One who has displayed his glory in heaven and on earth, to this end – that we might know, serve and worship him. For we have only to look at our hands and feet, to see visibly displayed before us the wisdom, strength and untold goodness of our God. We have only to contemplate the sky and the stars, and we have a sufficient testimony to the sovereign Master who sustains them. If we consider the changing seasons, snow, rain, wind or heat, we see that God is revealing himself through these things. When the earth produces fruit , or even when it is dry and dead, we can still know God through this, or, at least, be convinced that he declares his own existence to us. If, today, we cannot perceive him, we will, nevertheless, have to confess that these things are so on the last day, when the books are opened. Thus, if we worship those who are not truly gods, we are effectively closing our eyes to all these signs which bear testimony to the true God who set them before us, that we might be drawn to him. All that men worship can be nothing more than vain fancy until God leads them onto the right path, for their own nature will entice them to devote themselves to all that is erroneous and illusory.

* * *

At this point, Paul says, 'But now, after that ye have known God, or rather are known of God . . .' (not that any of them showed that they had been instructed in the knowledge of God!). Paul shows, as we have already seen, that those who had been taught the truth were guilty of perjury in the eyes of God. For these people were without excuse; they could no longer plead ignorance. They could never say that they had not tasted true religion, which makes their disloyalty all the more blatant. They were like the subjects of a prince who knowingly revolt against him and break their oath of loyalty by collaborating with his mortal enemy. This is what we must learn: those of us who know God's truth cannot run after the superstitions and errors of the day, for thereby we make ourselves perjurers and counterfeits. Indeed, Isaiah has good cause to say that the idols will bow down when God is set up on high; for when he displays his majesty, all superstition will pass into oblivion (*Isa.* 46:1). By revealing himself to us, God is, in effect, taking his place on the throne and graciously becoming our King. If we cannot render ourselves subject to him, then are we not counterfeits? If, by way of reply, we claim that this is not our intention, we are nothing more than hypocrites. For we know that our Lord will not suffer a rival; indeed, he speaks of his 'jealousy', demonstrating that he desires to possess us in such a way that we belong to him entirely, and not in part (*Exod.* 20:5). Therefore, if we rove here and there, and seek to run with the hare and hunt with the hounds, we are false hypocrites. We ought, rather, to possess a strict integrity. Notice that Paul is not speaking about being deceived by Satan, or abandoning the gospel, but about being 'corrupted from the simplicity that is in Christ' (*2 Cor.* 11:3). The Galatians had not renounced Jesus Christ, nor had they discounted their baptism. They still professed to believe the gospel, but they had distorted it and thus corrupted their profession. It only takes a small amount of leaven to turn the whole lump sour. In the same way, if men desire to add anything that they have devised in their own heads to the truth of God, they will ruin everything. You may have the best wine in the world, but if you add vinegar or some other rubbish to it, you would be better off drinking plain water! This is what happens when men disguise true religion, by having the audacity to invent doctrines in their heads. It were better to know nothing at all, save that there is a God, than to have fallen from the pure doctrine of the gospel, thereby obscuring everything Christ came to do. This is intolerable, and the first point we have to observe.

Secondly, Paul tells us that the Galatians had been called to follow the gospel, and that they had not chosen it, or stepped forward, by their own free will. God had sought them out, though they were poor wandering folk, miles away from the truth. This does not only apply to them, for the prophet Isaiah speaks in the same vein of those who will one day share in the salvation purchased by the Lord Jesus Christ (*Isa.* 65:1). 'I am sought', he says, 'of them that asked not for me; I am found of them that sought me not: I said, behold me, unto a nation that was not called by my name.' Here, God displays his grace, that men may not presume to think that they have attained faith through their own wisdom. 'No', says God, 'you were all on your way to perdition and there was not one that I could draw to myself, but I took pity on your miserable condition. I showed you mercy by revealing myself to you, but it was all of grace. You would never have sought me, indeed, you were all straying further away from me.' For we were not only like wandering beasts, we were also wild and ferocious! We were completely given over to rebellion before God tamed us and made us the sheep of his pasture, living amongst us as our Shepherd. Thus, Paul has good reason to correct himself here, and say 'after that ye have known God, or rather are known of God'. He argues that though we have a knowledge of the gospel, we ought not to think of ourselves as better than others, recognising that God has gone before us. If he had not transformed us, we would have perished a hundred times over in our folly, rather than receive good instruction from God.

Now we see what is achieved by free will; though fools ignorantly boast about this, they are undermining God's grace. Whereas most confess that they need God to work in their hearts in order to awaken them to the gospel, they soon retract this by saying that this is only part of the picture, and that it seems to them that something else must be added. But all such boasting is excluded here, because we are told that God first knew us, and set us apart in order to reveal himself to us that we might draw near to him. Thus, the main point of this is to teach us that our privileges, in being permitted to hear the gospel faithfully expounded, are not due to our own worth. Each of us must apply this to ourselves as individuals. For if I think that there is something about myself that distinguishes me from other people, it is as if I am stealing or usurping the praise that should belong to

God by taking it to myself. Such sacrilege is insufferable. Let us, therefore, consider the words of Paul in that other passage (*1 Cor.* 4:7), where he says, 'For who maketh thee to differ from another?' He is speaking to those who thought highly of themselves, considering themselves to possess great virtue and noble qualities. Indeed, the Corinthians possessed spiritual gifts which might have been highly esteemed by men. Paul admits that they have great gifts, worthy of admiration, but he asks them whence they proceeded. Did they acquire them on their own because they were, in some respect, worthy of them? Certainly not!

Let us, therefore, learn that it is not enough to hear the preaching of the Word of God; we need the Holy Spirit to work in our hearts, and as experience shows us, the Holy Spirit is not given to all alike. For, indeed, unless God had shown us the way, we would never have come to him seeking the right path. Therefore, we need to remove all foolish imagination from our heads, and rid ourselves of all pride; we must not consider ourselves more gifted than others since we know the gospel. Rather, we must attribute all the praise to our God. For, even whilst we had turned our backs upon him, being a hundred thousand times condemned to perdition, he had mercy upon us and drew us to himself. Thus, when we speak of justification by faith and of being saved, we understand that all is of grace. Faith has been granted to us because we could not have manufactured it within ourselves. Now we confess with Hagar that we have now seen the One who first saw us (*Gen.* 16:13). This is a picture of the way it is with all the human race. That poor woman was in great sorrow, having been abandoned by all, and not knowing where she was going. But God took pity on her and visited her in the wilderness. It was there that she declared that God had regard to her before she had even thought about him. Thus, we must always live in fear and humility, knowing that the source of our salvation lies in God, who set us apart and acknowledged us at a time when we did not care about him. Added to our ignorance, there was disdain and hard-heartedness, each of us heading towards our own destruction and perdition until we were rescued through his infinite mercy. This is what we need to observe in this passage.

Yet, we also need to heed the warning contained in this portion of Scripture: now that God has called us to a true knowledge of his gospel, we must walk in a consistent manner along the pathway that he has shown us, for we know him to be the living fountain of all blessings. As it says in the second chapter of Jeremiah, if we go and hew out for ourselves broken cisterns which can hold no water, are we not turning our backs upon the good things that God has placed at our disposal (*Jer.* 2:13)? If a man sees food that has been prepared for him to eat, knowing that it will do him good, and he were to leave the table to go in search of filth and rubbish instead, does he not deserve to poison himself? The same applies to those who are not content with the pure doctrine of the law and the gospel of God. They have a fountain before them, from which they may drink until their thirst is fully quenched, as it says in the fifty-fifth chapter of Isaiah, and the seventh of John's gospel. But they prefer to thirst, or at least to feed on air.

It is no wonder, therefore, that such ingratitude should be doubly punished, as Paul suggests here: 'how turn ye again to the weak and beggarly elements, whereunto ye desire again to be in bondage?' Initially, we might think that Paul is too harsh and sharp-tongued in speaking in this way of the ceremonial law. For truly, although these ceremonies were indeed rudimentary (just as we teach infants their ABC), nevertheless, they prefigured the person of the Lord Jesus Christ. There were promises which led men to salvation.

Remission of sin is the highest blessing that we could hope to receive from God, for it is through this means that we may be reconciled to him; he accepts us as his own children, and we may call upon him with complete freedom. This is the true and perfect happiness enjoyed by those whose sins have been pardoned. Well, in former days, the sacrifices acted as a pledge of this blessing. When they washed themselves, they could be assured that God would purify them and that their faults would not be imputed to them; instead they would be received as clean and spotless. Why does Paul refer to things which are so full of instruction as 'weak and beggarly elements'? The Bible shows that the pattern of the sanctuary was revealed to Moses, and that was a heavenly pattern (*Exod.* 25:40). The law, therefore, cannot have been intended as a kind of game, where God was occupying man with meaningless trivia! But Paul is not concerned about how the ceremonies benefited and served our forefathers – he is simply showing that when the Lord Jesus Christ appeared, all this was abolished! Just as it is written in the second chapter to the Colossians, and the seventeenth verse, these things are 'a shadow of things to come; but the body is of Christ'. This being the case, if we stress the importance of sacrifices and of suchlike ceremonies, we are separating them from the Lord Jesus Christ, and, therefore, what good are they? There can be no value in them once they have been separated from Jesus Christ; they become like useless baggage, as I have said before. When the ceremonies were observed and used in the correct way, they were profitable exercises; our forefathers were not wasting their time, but were being confirmed in their hope of salvation. In them, they had a pledge of the fatherly love of God towards them, and were led to the Lord Jesus Christ, the fountain of all good. But if we seek to keep those same ceremonies without knowing why, it is a mockery. Even some heathen folk used to sacrifice, not to idols but to the God who created the heavens and the earth, as they thought. But all their efforts could only have served to condemn them, because they did not perform them in the way that God intended; in other words, they were not led to the Lord Jesus Christ through these things.

Thus, Paul has good reason to say that the ceremonies of the law are nothing more than 'elements', that is to say, corruptible things pertaining to this world, if they do not lead people to find their salvation in the Lord Jesus Christ. Furthermore, they are things of no value, unprofitable things if Jesus Christ is not in them, for he imparts life to everything. We must closely observe these things if we are not to be deceived. For even in the former days when everyone offered sacrifices, thinking they were worshipping God, their service was rejected if they did not have faith in Jesus Christ. Indeed, the apostle tells us in the eleventh chapter to the Hebrews, verse four, that even Abel's sacrifice was only accepted because of his faith. When heathen folk sacrifice, they imagine God to be carnal, and that, therefore, they can be reconciled to him through carnal means. But they are concerned with exterior details and do not recognise that they are guilty, and can only be redeemed by a price which is too high for them to pay. Even if we possessed a hundred worlds, it would not be sufficient to erase one offence that we have committed against God. Therefore, a heavenly sacrifice was required to pay for all our sins. The heathen are not aware of this; they are content to remain in the shadows, like the Turks and Jews of today, who wash themselves morning, midday, and evening, and perform many other such ceremonies. They are declaring their uncleanness through it all, and their need of cleansing, but they reject the Lord Jesus Christ, whose purity alone can wash us from our sins. Indeed, he has blotted out all our iniquities. Therefore, all those who maintain the ceremonial law in order to merit grace in the eyes of God, not only deceive and foolishly afflict themselves; they also provoke the wrath of God. But for our part, we know that the Lord Jesus Christ has shed his blood for the cleansing of our souls. If we, therefore, seek this cleansing from another source, we are guilty of committing an intolerable act of sacrilege.

Now, if Paul said this of legal ceremonies, what would he say about the follies that exist in Popery today? Here we have Papists, thinking that they merit salvation because they have been sprinkled with holy water, and have had a few words muttered over them, or because they keep a certain holy day, and afflict themselves by undertaking a pilgrimage. They carry a candle and place it beneath some grotesque image, sing Mass, and repeat the rosary endlessly. They genuinely believe, I tell you, that they can be reconciled to God through such means. Yet, in reality, it is certain that these people are throwing themselves headlong into hell and into the snares of Satan, as much as if they had plotted their own perdition in conjunction with him! In short, all Popish rituals represent a rejection of the Lord Jesus Christ, of the cleansing that he purchased through his death and resurrection, and also of the grace offered to us in the gospel. For no matter how many deceitful tricks they invent, they cannot contradict the words of the Holy Spirit, uttered through Paul in this text. We now understand what Paul is teaching us here.

As an example, Paul mentions that they observed 'days, and months, and times, and years'. He is not referring to the seasons, such as summer and winter, nor denying that time is divided into days, for men ought to count the passing of months and years. He is referring, instead, to the feast days appointed in the law, which those seducers sought to make the Galatians observe as a matter of necessity. They were introducing constraint and servitude in place of the liberty bought for us by the Lord Jesus Christ. This is why Paul is so vehement, and also because of the misuse of these ceremonies, as I have said, for they were intended to make manifest the Lord Jesus Christ, that he might be sought. But those who deceived the Galatians were making a very different set of obligations. In keeping the passover and other feast days, they were returning to the former figures which ought to have been abolished. When the passover was observed under the law, it was in order that the people should remember their deliverance from Egypt, and eagerly await the great redemption that they had been promised. This is why Paul tells us that our passover lamb has been sacrificed (*1 Cor.* 5:7), that is to say the Lord Jesus Christ. He is demonstrating that what was prefigured by the sacrifice of the paschal lamb under the law has today been fulfilled in the person of our Mediator. The same applies to the feast of tabernacles, in which God was reminding the Jews that they once lived in the wilderness, where there were no buildings or houses, and that they dwelt there for a long period of time, wandering about from place to place. This was a reminder to them that their life was but a pilgrimage through which we pass very quickly. The same could be said of the feast of first-fruits, when they would present the first-fruits to God. Then there were times when people would make solemn confession of their sins, which was a figure intended to lead the Jews to Jesus Christ, to whom he had been promised. Now that he has been revealed, what folly to keep all these things! We are ignoring their object and substance. We might as well seek nourishment from the colour of bread, or wine, or other foods. Can these things indeed nourish us? No, and in the same way, now that the Lord Jesus Christ has been made manifest, we no longer need the figures of the law; if we keep them, we will not be led to a knowledge of God through them since we are mis-using them.

We today need to pay most careful attention to the fact that if we fall away in the slightest degree from the truth of the gospel, we are departing from Jesus Christ himself. Yes, it is true that we have set days upon which we meet together, but not in the same manner as the Jews. What is the difference? We do not observe them as ceremonies. Under the law, if a person so much as lifted a hammer to a piece of wood on the day of rest, or did his household duties, it was a crime punishable by death. If a person dared boil a pot of water, God commanded that he be put to death. Now, these harsh laws did not exist because God delighted in idleness! No, rather, they had figurative significance; it was as if God was saying, 'I have given you Sabbath days to observe that you might know that I am the God who sanctifies you'. We enjoy the same sanctification today, but not through observing figures as our forefathers did, for this is to ignore the role of the Lord Jesus Christ. It would be to draw a veil across once again, which would blind our eyes to the light of the gospel. This is what we must remember regarding the question of observing certain days, which Paul refers to here.

But above all, we must understand that Paul is essentially declaring to us that, since we have received good things at the hands of the Lord Jesus Christ, we must remain faithful to him and rest upon him entirely. If we wander from one path to another, we will alienate ourselves from the Lord Jesus Christ, from whom we receive full and perfect life, joy, salvation and glory. Let us make sure that we are never guilty of such ingratitude. For God has drawn near to us, and even whilst we were like poor wandering animals, he gathered us to himself, became our Shepherd and made us the sheep of his flock. Therefore, we must listen to his voice and discern between false doctrine and true, recognising the subtle devices of man whenever we hear the gospel preached. May our Lord Jesus Christ reign over us, and hold us in his hand, possessing us wholly, that we might be entirely his and not in part or with exceptions, but in all sincerity. These, then, are the points we are to remember in order to profit from this passage, that we might not stand accused on the last day. God has called us to himself; may we never leave or abandon him, or nullify his promise, seeing that he has thoroughly prepared himself to keep the promises that he has made to us, not only for one day, but to continue as our Saviour and Father in life as well as in death.

Now let us fall before the majesty of our great God, acknowledging our faults and praying that he would make us increasingly conscious of them. Thus, may we be enabled to appreciate to an even greater extent the grace that we have received from him, especially when we realise that it has been communicated to those who were not worthy of it. In this way, we will be even more grateful that we have tasted his grace, and subsequently more determined to die daily to our evil desires, and to all our sins, which beset us so miserably until he has mercy upon us and showers us with grace. This grace is continually bestowed upon us, until we seek nothing more than to be completely his. Whilst we await the day when we will be bathed in light, and see him face to face, transfigured by his glory, may he continually lead us along the path of salvation, that we may walk with true perseverance. May he grant this grace not only to us, but to all the peoples and nations on earth, etc.

27

Profitable Exhortation

I am afraid of you, lest I have bestowed upon you labour in vain. Brethren, I beseech you, be as I am; for I am as ye are: ye have not injured me at all. Ye know how through infirmity of the flesh I preached the gospel unto you at the first. And my temptation which was in my flesh ye despised not, nor rejected; but received me as an angel of God, even as Christ Jesus (Gal. 4:11–14).

We have already stated on previous occasions that Paul can appear to be addressing a subject of no particular weight or importance, whereas, in fact, he is treating a vital topic. In this passage, he fears that his efforts may have been wasted and the fruit of his labour amongst the Galatians lost, because they insisted on observing certain feast days and other ceremonies of the law. They ought not to have been concerned with keeping festivals and abstaining from certain types of food, or any such thing. The most important thing is the reason behind abstinence from meat and observance of special days and ceremonies. These things can otherwise serve to eclipse the light of the gospel, indeed, almost completely extinguish it. These ceremonial requirements were appointed in former days in order to nourish and sustain our forefathers whilst they waited for their Redeemer, who had not yet been made manifest. Now that our Lord Jesus Christ has come into the world, and has perfected and accomplished all that is necessary for man's salvation, we are detracting from his glory if we keep the types and shadows in the foreground. It is much like drawing a curtain across which obscures him and prevents us from knowing and acknowledging him. Furthermore, these things tend to become compulsory, often involving the risk of committing mortal sin, which means that poor consciences are subjected to tyranny; at the same time, God loses the authority and mastery that he ought to have over us in governing our lives. What he commands must be consented to as good and necessary for us, and what he prohibits must be rejected, without contradiction, debate or argument. Even worse than this, observing the ceremonies as a means of obtaining merit in God's eyes is to despise the death and passion of the Lord Jesus Christ, who has acquitted us of all our debt to God the Father. He did not do this in order to give us licence to do evil, but that we might take refuge in him alone. When we sin, and are convicted by our accusing conscience of having transgressed the law of God, the only remedy is to present ourselves before the Lord Jesus Christ. Through the merit of his suffering and death and the shedding of his blood, we can be acquitted in the sight of God by being cleansed from our sin.

To sum up, Paul declares that men are greatly mistaken when they seek to be saved other than by Jesus Christ alone. It shows that they are altogether lost and in a desperate condition. God reveals only one way to be saved, and those who turn away from it are wilfully casting themselves headlong into hell. Because they have despised the inestimable treasure that God has offered them, they remain under the control of Satan himself. How gracious of God to call and invite us to accept his mercy and love, though we are his mortal enemies! He did not appoint angels as mediators, but sent his only Son to be the means of reconciling us to himself. If this is not sufficient for us, and if we are so vile as to search out other means of salvation with devilish greed, are we not rejecting the Lord Jesus Christ? Let us, therefore, learn that the message of the gospel compels us to abandon all that sets itself in opposition to simple faith in the

Lord Jesus Christ. He alone must be the source of our righteousness, for he alone is perfect. This is the first important lesson.

Now let us look well to ourselves. Sometimes, when we backslide, we imagine that we are committing a relatively minor and negligible offence. But how shocked we would be if God let go of his hold upon us and allowed us to fall away permanently! How few there are who persevere to the end! How easily do we excuse ourselves as if we have done nothing wrong; we allow ourselves great liberty, do we not? But God will punish such carelessness, and may even abandon us and deliver us to Satan. Thus, we are to walk circumspectly in the fear of God. Since he has graciously permitted us to taste the goodness of his Word, we must strive to obey it daily. We must beware of going astray, and remain vigilant, lest, when we believe ourselves to be simply drifting a little, we find that we have utterly fallen from grace. It is vital that we stay on the path that our Lord Jesus Christ has revealed. Yes, it is true that he does have pity on us when we fall, as we know from personal experience. He not only picks us up three or four times in our lifetime, but a hundred times a day, because we are so inconstant, and ceaselessly blown about one way, then another. Yet we are not to tempt him, and must not allow ourselves to become hardened in sin, for the devil will then be able to seduce us and draw us to his side. No, we must profit from the Word of life, to the extent that we produce fruit to the glory of God in our thoughts, words and deeds. Let us strive to this end.

* * *

In this text, Paul beseeches them to 'be as I am; for I am as ye are'. This exhortation would seem to be very far removed from the one that we have just heard from Paul's lips. In the previous verse Paul said, 'I am afraid of you, lest I have bestowed upon you labour in vain', which was rather like a thunderbolt. It was as if Paul were saying that these people were almost unteachable, for he had been disappointed when he saw that his doctrine had been poorly understood. But here he speaks in a kind and friendly tone. He addresses them as 'brethren', seeking to bring them back to himself. Indeed, he protests that he desires to be one with them and to be like them as much as possible, asking only that they in turn render the same honour to him. These two statements teach us how a man who is responsible for preaching the Word must conduct himself. He is not to encourage sin by flattery, for he must rebuke people sharply in order to bring to their senses those who have been duped by Satan, and to awake in them a fear of God's judgment. For if men are steeped in sin, they will continue to wallow in it unless they are virtually plucked out by force (though they will generally grow angry if someone should pull their ears too hard, or scratch them in a place where it did not itch, as the proverbs say!). Yet, because we all too often excuse our sin, preachers cannot afford to hold back, and if they do, they are effectively betraying us. Thus, Paul uses strong language and says that he fears that he has wasted all his efforts upon them, hoping to cause them to despair, with the intention of encouraging them to repent. Therefore, he adds soft words to his severity, showing that the door is still open if they wish to return to God's way.

Hence, there are two aspects to profitable exhortation. The first requirement is sharpness, to quicken those who are in sin, and to convict them of their wrongdoing, that they may hate it and tremble before God. Without this sorrow for sin, they can never devote themselves to following him. Yes, admittedly men can superficially alter their evil lifestyles, yet they will ultimately remain full of wickedness and rebellion, until they realise their sinful condition and discover the punishment which is due to them. Thus, the true path to repentance is to have our consciences pricked with regard to the evil within us, so that we count ourselves condemned. We need to feel anguished about our case, so that we experience no peace until God has shown us mercy. However, we must not remain under such a cloud, or else we will desire to flee the presence of God altogether, and seek to be as far from him as possible. Indeed, we might even wish him to be dethroned, as it were, that we might not have to face him as judge unless we can be sure that he will take pity upon us. But he has promised he will not disappoint us if we truly seek him. As it says in the Psalms, there is forgiveness with God, which attracts men to him, and leads them to fear him (*Psa.* 130:4). The fear that unbelievers have is more of a horror, which causes them to gnash their teeth in anger against him and to quake with rage. This kind of involuntary fear has nothing of reverence in it. We, on the other hand, having tasted the goodness of our God, are not terrified of the majesty of his presence, knowing that God has bidden us welcome. We know that God desires us to be reconciled with him when we come to him in sincerity. Indeed, he touches our hearts and grants us trust in him. When we have assurance of sins forgiven, I tell you, then we are not afraid to approach God.

The order that Paul uses here is the one that we must follow whenever we have to rebuke a person. For Paul first casts the Galatians down, when he sees them exalting themselves and offering resistance to God with such pride. But then he redresses the balance and extends a kind hand to them, for, now that they have acknowledged their failings, Paul does not wish them to regard themselves as excluded from any hope of God's mercy. Indeed, this will only be the case if we are careless about the way we seek to draw sinners to salvation. Many are quick to use harsh words, and may be perfectly justified in so doing; but their strictness can be excessive and it can leave men feeling that there is no hope for them. People can feel alienated by the unrelenting attacks upon them, and either throw caution to the winds, as it were, or become embittered against God and his Word. Those who are overly severe will justify themselves by saying that it is necessary. Yes, maybe, but it is important that those who reprove sins in the name of God also seek to bring salvation to the lost, with great care and attention. If this is the case, there will be no problem convincing a person who has gone astray that we seek their highest good, and that our rebukes, though they provoke anger, are intended to be for that person's profit. On the other hand, it is important that those who are thus harshly dealt with recognise that they need such strong medicine, for what will they gain by being angry with God? There are many who appear to be strong in the faith and to burn with fervent zeal for the gospel, but they cannot abide criticism. As long as everyone tolerates them, they say what we would all like to hear. They seem to walk hand in hand with the gospel. But, as soon as they are challenged, they turn into wild animals! What do they gain by hiding their hypocrisy from men, whilst they harden themselves against God? If they are fighting against him, it is most certain that they are going to prove to be the weaker party!

Therefore, we must allow ourselves to be harshly dealt with whenever it is necessary. This is especially true if we have not, as yet, perceived the evil that is within ourselves. We must tread very carefully and try not to excuse or defend our own actions. It is better that we examine ourselves fully and act as our own judges than that God should call us to account and be constrained to pronounce a sentence of condemnation. Thus, we must heed the correction that we are given and not be grieved by it, seeing it leads to humility on our part. But we can expect to be treated with kindness after that. Unfortunately, many people will not receive warning, because once they have heard a single word that displeases them, they become preoccupied with that word and seal up their ears and harden their hearts, so that they cannot appreciate that which is then added for their profit and for their highest good. We could speak and testify of the mercy of God, telling them that we only seek to warn them, but they are totally deaf to all this, simply because they have become embittered against God and have determined to reject his Word.

To sum up, then, we are to be patient and self-controlled, even when we are rudely assaulted by a torrent of rebukes for our faults. We must remain calm and listen to the end, right up to the final 'Amen'! Thus, we are to blend the following two things together: that is, a harshness, which provokes a keen and vivid awareness of sin, making us unhappy about our lost condition, so that we seek God's pardon. Secondly, there is a confidence in God's mercy, that when we have examined ourselves, we may be assured of his forgiveness. For though his Word condemns us, it is that he might come to our aid, and not be obliged to come against us, armed with a sword pointed at us. This is what we are to remember from this passage, where Paul is sharp on the one hand, yet willing to address the Galatians as brothers, beseeching them to emulate him, that there may be harmony and peace amongst them all.

Now, when Paul says, 'I beseech you, be as I am; for I am as ye are', he was not allowing them to be comfortable with their sins, nor ignoring their shortcomings. Neither was he resorting to flattery, as we have said. No, he was endeavouring to win them back to God, using every possible means. As we shall soon see, Paul himself uses the image of a woman in labour whose sole desire is to see a child born into the world. Though she experiences pain, she will not strangle the child as a means of vengeance, but will rather view his life as more precious than her own. Later in the text, Paul uses this very image. Thus, Paul is not attempting to draw a veil over something that ought to have been reproved, just to please men; he is acting in the best possible way to win them back. He is approaching them as gently as a nurse, as indeed he says elsewhere. This can be done without causing people to become hardened in their sin, and without being overly tolerant. For example, a nurse will stoop in order to walk along with the child she is holding by the hand. She is not intending him to fall, nor to walk with a limp, nor is she spoiling him so that he will be unable to walk properly by the time he reaches manhood. She stoops because, if she were to raise her arm, she would wrench the child's hand or, indeed, some other part of his body. In the same way, we must accommodate those who are weak. Not to harden them in their evil ways; no, everything must tend to their correction, but we must achieve this in a measured way, conscious of the manner in which we are conducting ourselves. Paul, therefore, has good reason to exhort those who are strong and more mature to assist those who are, as yet, weak and ignorant, as he does in some other passages (*Rom.* 14:1; *Gal.* 6:1).

A man may be full of noble and excellent qualities, but if he looks down on others who are not as perfect as he is, he has made his own virtues of less value than smoke. Why is this? Because God commands us to be modest and humble; indeed, these qualities lend sweetness to all others. The more a man becomes acquainted with his own nature, the more he recognises his sinfulness and helplessness. He realises that the main reason God has chosen him is to show others the way of salvation. He is more prepared to forgive and excuse others than himself. We ought to be able to discern whether the warnings of men proceed from a heart full of pure love, or from a tendency to be overly harsh and critical. For example, a man may hold back when he is rebuking another person; though aware of what the situation demands, he may refuse to show any anger when he condemns him for his vices. Yet he may still be full of anger within and utterly consumed by it – this is sheer hypocrisy! But if a man is careful about his words to others but severe with regard to himself, not seeking to exempt himself from criticism more than his neighbours, then, surely, he is fired by zeal from God and the Holy Spirit, and will be used to bring salvation. This is a summary of what Paul means when he refers to conforming himself to the Galatians.

* * *

Then Paul adds, 'ye have not injured me at all', revealing that he has no personal quarrel with them. When it comes to doctrine and to the instruction which we draw from it, the message can be ruined if we think that the teacher is unworthy in some way, that he is full of hatred or is a man given to making cutting remarks. It is impossible to take what he says in good part, once we have formed such an opinion of him. I could see a man who speaks like an angel, but if I believe that he hates me and would like to devour me, or disclose things about me that would make me ashamed, I certainly would not wish to listen to him in order to find profit for my soul. I am not saying that this is excusable, for it is a terrible sin. Even if a man truly detests us and, therefore, reproves us out of malice and spite, we ought to learn to heed what he says. The heathen seem to have learnt this lesson, for they say that often enemies are more to our profit than true friends. How is this possible? Well, often those who love each other will close their eyes to many things; they will ignore things and refuse to be bothered by them. Enemies, on the other hand, are on the watch and waiting to ambush us as soon as they notice a flaw; they will not stop talking about it ever afterwards, as Solomon suggests (*Prov.* 26:24). Sometimes, under guise of correction, they will criticise people simply because they desire to pick a quarrel. But when our enemies ambush us in this manner, God is surely using them to humble us. Even the devil can sometimes act as a doctor for us! Think of Paul, who said he was buffeted by a messenger of Satan, which helped him to overcome all pride (*2 Cor.* 12:7). Thus, when our enemies seek to dissect and criticise us, God can use this to wake us up where we have been asleep in self-deception and flattery. Indeed, if we were wise and mature, it is certain that our enemies would be more to our advantage than our friends on many occasions, as we have already suggested and as the heathen so clearly recognise. Is it not to our shame that these people, who are wretched and blind and who live in darkness, see more clearly than we who have the light of salvation? We do not seem to have learnt the lessons which these poor folk have learnt, for it is quite natural to us not to accept instruction from a person who appears to loathe us. We become embittered against them and preoccupied about their negative feelings. For this very reason, Paul protests that he has no private quarrel with the Galatians when he rebukes them.

Paul reminds them that they had been good friends at one

time. When he first came among them, it was not with great pomp, nor was he disguised in any way. According to the judgment of the world, he could easily have been held in contempt. He came amongst them to preach the pure message of the gospel, not as part of a grand parade, for, indeed, he was little noticed by the men of the world, but the Galatians received him as though he were an angel of God, or Jesus Christ himself. Why had they now changed? He had continued to fulfil his office, but why had they become alienated from him? Can it be for any other reason than that God's truth had become odious and unbearable in their eyes? Because they hated God's truth, they therefore despised Paul, who was the minister of it. How shameful! The first point we can make about this is that those who have the responsibility to teach and to bear the message of the gospel, must strive to avoid personal disputes and arguments. Indeed, all quarrelling must be banned if we do not wish the door to be closed to us. We do not have complete liberty whenever we rebuke a person, for we are to remember this statement of Paul's where he says that he does not speak out of a desire for vengeance. Even if a person has wronged us, we are not to feel any enmity towards him but to desire his salvation. This will make our words of warning more effective and hard-hitting. This is the first lesson.

Now we must apply this lesson to ourselves, and learn that, when we are reproved for our faults, we are not to erect barriers by falsely imagining that the person hates us and is, therefore, out to criticise us as part of Satan's attack upon us. Though we are naturally inclined to analyse whether or not we are being vilified and criticised out of hatred, our first thought must not be that the person is against us for any personal reason. The devil stirs up such thoughts within us. If we have fallen and someone rebukes us, the message has surely been sent to us by God, regardless of who conveys it to us. For God does not desire that we should perish, but seeks to bring us back to the right path, even if the messenger himself is motivated by less than righteous intentions! Even if he only seeks to criticise in order to avenge himself on us, God is, nevertheless, assisting us in order that we should not perish. Satan, on the other hand, will not allow us to accept this medicine, for he puts in our heads the idea that the other person is motivated by something other than holy zeal when he reproaches us for our faults. He convinces us that the person is on the attack, ready to kick us in the teeth – driven by some hidden ill-feeling towards us. Satan introduces all these imaginary ideas into our minds whenever we are checked over something, to make us angry, so that we reject what we have been told, and consequently rebel against God himself.

Let us, therefore, remember this lesson so that when we are next challenged because of our sin, we realise that the messenger has been sent to judge us on behalf of God, that we may not have to face him as our judge in this matter. When a mortal being reproves me for my sin, it is because God has ordained this and has sent the person to me in his stead. Why? That I may not have to stand before the majesty of God to give account of myself for this sin, for if I do, I will be condemned a hundred thousand times more severely. Thus, when God sends us human judges, it is because he has taken pity on us. He hopes that we will be ashamed of ourselves and return to the right path. If God is gracious enough to take pity on us in this way, we ought to take advantage of his grace, rather than become embittered against him and full of imaginary thoughts that we are hated, persecuted, envied or victims of any other kind of evil treatment that we can conceive. Let us banish all such thoughts and accept warnings and reproaches, if they are indeed true. In short, the best thing we can do when we are accused is to consider whether or not our own consciences have been telling us the same message. This is the first point, that we are not to be concerned about who has approached us, or whether he is driven by enmity or a critical spirit, but we are to heed the voice of our own conscience. Then, we must conclude that we have been rightfully challenged. How strange that those who become enraged when they are criticised, and who rant and bare their teeth, would find plenty of reasons to condemn themselves if only they searched their own hearts. But they prefer to act like madmen when face to face with God, and they despise his warnings, rather than to judge themselves and be humble before him. This, therefore, is what we must do. When rebuked, we must listen to our accusers.

Above all, we must know what we are really like. How can we do this? By examining what is written and engraved upon our consciences. If we are not aware of anything at all, let us be on our guard, for none of us are competent when it comes to judging ourselves. God has given us some ability to judge our own actions, but it is safer to accept condemnation, even if it is a fault that we were unaware of, than to resist it without thorough consideration of the extent of our guilt. Many simply shut their eyes, or blindfold themselves, so that they do not have to admit their baseness. When they are exhorted to repent, they bolt at the first opportunity. If they are thus depraved, there is no hope for them; they will not be convinced of their sin, even if they are told a hundred times over. They wipe their mouths as a gesture of self-justification and, though they are acting like little children, they do not much care because they revel in the fact that they are hardened in sin and corruption. Let us beware of ever becoming so stubborn; for it is our responsibility to judge our own shortcomings in truth and without hypocrisy. We need a spirit of humility in order to be submissive and to overcome all our pride. Then nothing will prevent us from freely confessing our failings to God. This is what we are to remember from this passage.

We might find it strange that Paul should say that the Galatians received him as 'an angel of God, even as Christ Jesus'. For however holy he was, he surely could not compare himself with angels? After all, in the seventh chapter to the Romans, Paul confesses his wretchedness, and describes himself as a poor, carnal soul who is a slave to this world and in bondage to sin. Though he was charged with fervent zeal in his desire to serve God, he recognised that he could but falter along, being hindered by many infirmities. Yet here he says that he was received as an angel; indeed, not content with this, he adds, as Christ Jesus himself, who, as we well know, is the very Son of God, the sovereign King who has authority over every creature. But Paul is not referring to his lifestyle, nor to his personal virtues, but is, rather, thinking of his doctrine. He begins by saying that they received him as an angel of God. And why not? For this very title is attributed to those who were responsible for teaching the doctrines of the law (*Mal.* 2:7). Is there not, therefore, greater reason to use it to refer to those who preach the gospel, where God displays much more of his strength and power than he ever did under the law? Because God has appointed human beings to preach in his name and with his authority, we must receive all such as angels, or messengers (for the word 'angel' means no more than this). For what good is it to hear doctrine which has not proceeded from God. It were better that the preacher were mute and unable to speak and that the congregation heard nothing at all, than for them to listen to a man speak who has not been sent by God. The best homage that we can render to God is to remain silent before him and listen to his Word, captivated and transfixed, attributing all authority to him, and submitting under his royal sceptre. If a creature usurps this authority, what will become of him? Thus, Paul has good reason to compare himself with an angel when it comes to doctrine. For he knew full well that he had not invented it all in his head, but that he had received it from God.

Hence, Paul continues by saying that he was received 'as Christ Jesus'. For our Lord Jesus Christ wishes us to receive those who have been appointed as his ministers, as if he were among us in a visible form himself. 'He that heareth you heareth me' (*Luke* 10:16). By establishing apostles and ministers of the Word, our Lord did not intend us to make idols of them; they are not to be worshipped in his stead. No, even the angels of heaven have no right to such worship, much less ourselves, who are base and vile by comparison. No, the Lord Jesus Christ is not saying anything about the nature of man by this, but rather about the need to magnify his Word, that all may submit to its precepts. Though we are mere fragile earthen vessels (indeed, we are broken vessels), and have no intrinsic value, yet we contain the treasures of the gospel and must therefore, not be despised. Whenever the gospel is preached in purity amongst us, it is, as if the Lord Jesus Christ were dwelling in our midst, and had appeared before us in person. Our duty, therefore, is to bear witness to the fear, love and obedience that we owe him by accepting his Word, though a mere mortal brings it to us. If we despise the Word preached on account of the fact that the preacher is neither a king nor a prince over us, we are really rebelling against the Lord Jesus Christ himself. He said, whoever despises us despises him, and whoever rejects us rejects him.

We must take good note of these things, for many today reject the Word of God as if it were nothing, simply because they despise the messenger. Those who cannot bear to be rebuked are ready with this response: 'Who made thee a prince and a judge over us?' They act as if God were no greater than themselves, and cannot possibly speak by the mouth of his servants. A prince would employ an official, or select a man who, though he were nobody, would be received unconditionally because of whom he represents. Therefore, when God, who has sovereign authority over us and who rules over all the principalities and powers of this world, sends his appointed servants, he expects us to heed what they say. If, however, we despise them and reject their message because we have such poor regard for their persons, where will this lead us? We might say, 'And who is this? Is he God?' But when a man faithfully preaches the Word of God (which declares that whoever rejects his message is rejecting God) and we discount his message, we are the ones who are playing at God, because we are effectively saying that God cannot speak through his appointed instruments. As I have said, woe to us if we act in this way.

Now, it were better that we were damned a hundred times over than that we should ever go up into the pulpit, unless we faithfully expound the will of God. We are only to proclaim that which he has revealed, drawing water from the pure fountain of his Word. Does this not need to be said? Do we imagine that we can rob God of his truth? No, he is inseparably bound to it. Thus, whenever we hear such detestable blasphemies as, 'The speaker wants us to think that he is God', we must regard them as wicked lies. If a man asks to be heeded without contradiction and is confident that he is speaking on behalf of God, we must listen because he is drawing attention to the authority of his Master. We are to have no dealings with any of these profane people, therefore, but must show such reverence for God that we obey what we hear in true and humble faith, though those who speak in his name may be contemptible in themselves.

Naturally, we need to distinguish, however, between those who falsely speak in the name of God and use it to hide their wickedness, and those who faithfully preach the Word that he has committed to their charge. Look at the Pope, who, scoundrel that he is, is not ashamed to say, 'Whoever listens to me, listens to God, and whoever rejects me rejects God.' He uses this very passage to justify his own position! But those who wish to be received as angels must fulfil the office of the angels and be true messengers of God, speaking on behalf of the Lord Jesus Christ who commissioned them and obtaining their message from him. They must be his true servants, and not seek any mastery for themselves. The Lord Jesus Christ must still be the Shepherd of the church, and the flock must hear his voice and follow him wherever he may lead them. But those who are false teachers, perverting the truth, usurping authority and diminishing the role of the Word of God, must be recognised for what they are. I showed this right at the outset, where I said that although the Lord Jesus Christ desires us to heed those whom he has sent in his name as if he himself were amongst us, he did not intend us to make idols of such men, so that those who speak on his behalf exercise some sort of tyrannical rule over us. Instead, his desire is that we should reverence his Word and accept it without reservation. Thus, when Paul says that he was received as an angel, even as Jesus Christ, he had not come with his own authority, but endeavoured to declare the grace of God alone, that we might follow Jesus Christ and submit to him. He sought to attribute to Christ the authority which belongs to him, that the gospel might be received unreservedly and produce the fruit that it is intended to bear; that is, that it might be the power of God to salvation to all who believe, as it says at the beginning of the Epistle to the Romans (*Rom.* 1:16).

Now let us fall before the majesty of our great God, acknowledging our sins, and asking that he would make us increasingly conscious of them, that we may be led to repentance. May he support us in our infirmity until the day that he delivers us from it completely, renewing his own image in us, that we may be wholly pure, reflecting his glory. May we daily battle against sin, that it may decrease in us, and that we may be filled, instead, with all the fruits of the Holy Spirit. Then, we may draw others to salvation. May each of us seek with one accord to serve God to his glory and to devote ourselves wholly to him. Thus, we all say, Almighty God and our heavenly Father, etc.

28

A Plain Rebuke For the Backslider

Where is then the blessedness ye spake of? for I bear you record, that, if it had been possible, ye would have plucked out your own eyes, and have given them to me. Am I therefore become your enemy, because I tell you the truth? They zealously affect you, but not well; yea, they would exclude you, that ye might affect them. But it is good to be zealously affected always in a good thing, and not only when I am present with you. My little children, of whom I travail in birth again until Christ be formed in you, I desire to be present with you now, and to change my voice; for I stand in doubt of you (Gal. 4:15–20).

It is not necessary for us to attend school in order to discover what will be good and profitable for us – this is taught by our natural instincts! We are a little too preoccupied with such things! Sadly, we do not know how to discern what is truly beneficial from what is damaging, because we are blinded by our foolish lusts, and we wilfully spoil ourselves. Although we know in our hearts what is really important, we are carried away by our own wicked desires, or else choked by the vanities of this world, so that we no longer have good judgment in such matters. Therefore, it is vital that we cry to God to grant us the wisdom to know what is right and act upon it. We need to have so much love for God that we will never fall away from him. Even those of us who are considered to be wise by this world's standards can be no better than little children, in that we keep changing our minds about everything. We leave the things that we once loved so well to run after some gaudy object that has been dangled before our eyes, and there can be no stopping us! We have all seen a child running after three or four friends, who then stumbles across something that he has been longing for. He will stop in his tracks, be it for an apple or a cherry, or whatever else, and abandon his friends in order to possess it. We are much the same: we imagine ourselves to be sensible beings who have no need of instruction regarding the difference between right and wrong. We would feel hurt if anyone were to take it upon themselves to teach us these things. Yet, experience demonstrates that we are devoid of reason and good sense in these matters.

Why is it that people struggle and torment themselves all through their lives to obtain the best for themselves, and yet it seems to elude them? As I have said, we are all obeying the same instinct within us, to seek our own highest good; young or old, we are all driven by this same principle. But let us think for a moment about what it is that we strive to obtain. Most are virtually boiling over with enthusiastic desires; indeed, are torturing themselves night and day to achieve the things that they believe will be profitable for them. And yet, are they worth the agony? Out of a million people, you would be hard pressed to find a hundred who had their ambitions under control and were organised in their strategy. It were better to remain asleep all your life than to exert so much effort for an unknown cause. Therefore, since we are now convinced that the majority cannot do what is expected of us, cannot discern between good and evil, let us realise that we need to resort to God and pray that he would lead us by his Holy Spirit. This is the very best that we can hope for in this life, and this aim should, therefore, transport us and captivate our minds. Yet, we are so easily distracted and drift here and there; we are full of fickleness and frivolity. The things that we desire on one day we despise the next!

Indeed, Paul reproaches the Galatians in this passage for

forgetting the chief source of their happiness. The words of the Lord Jesus Christ describe man's nature: that where our treasure is, our hearts will be also (*Matt.* 6:21). Our treasure is that which we desire above all else, and is that in which all our happiness lies. Yet, there are many desirable things that we can easily forgo. If a man sees something that is both beautiful and precious, he may, nevertheless, remain satisfied with his lot if he already has sufficient to content him. But, if he considers his life to be miserable and has nothing about which he may rejoice, he will surely become anxious to obtain the object of his desires. Everyday life bears this out so often! Since it is the case that our hearts will be attached to whatever we consider to be of most benefit to ourselves, we must be careful. Some devote themselves to pursuing the passing things of this world, or are so filled with ambition and self-conceit that they only seek their own glory, desiring a high status and grand reputation to boost their self-esteem. They put all their efforts into procuring such honour. Some are so possessed with greed that they never cease acquiring goods, and are never satisfied. They stop at nothing: they endure hunger and thirst, cold and heat, and dare not eat or drink, that they may amass more and more property. This is their condition. Those who seek nothing more than glory and fame in the eyes of this world suffer so many hardships, that even if they fell into the hands of a torturer himself, they would not suffer half the agony that they give themselves in pursuing these evil things. Yet, so strong is their determination that they cannot be diverted from their aim in any sense whatever. But God has graciously revealed where true happiness lies: in the kingdom of heaven. Though we know that our lives are so brief, and that we must soon die, yet, we become obsessed with vain and empty things and leave aside the priceless joy to which God has called us; we forsake the kingdom of heaven for the sake of the corruptible things of this world, which are worthless.

* * *

Consider, therefore, that the reproach which Paul addressed to the Galatians applies to us today, when he asks them, 'Where is then the blessedness ye spake of?' He presupposes that the Galatians were aware that the richest blessing God could have given them was the enlightening of their minds through knowledge of the gospel; to be aware that the world is full of vain hopes that turn us away from our heavenly inheritance. Indeed, the Lord Jesus Christ compares the gospel to a precious stone, containing, as it does, riches and treasure (*Matt.* 13:46). Even if we must leave all that we value in this world and all that we consider to be desirable, we could not possibly lose. There will be no room for regret! But we are doubly guilty if we recognise that God has weaned us away from earthly things, that we may share in the glory of heaven, and yet slide back. It takes no more than a fly to flit past our eyes, as they say, and we forget all about the greatest treasure of all. Therefore, since it has pleased God to open our eyes and draw us out of the mire into which we had fallen, along with unbelievers and ignorant folk (not only did we follow the superstitions and idolatrous practices of others, but we were also given over to our own carnal appetites and evil desires) – therefore, I say, since God has shown us where true blessedness lies and has granted us a foretaste of it, we must set our hearts on his kingdom and beware of changing course or being led astray.

If we are inclined to be fickle, let us remember that the Spirit of God condemns our faithlessness here by the mouth of Paul, asking, 'Where is then the blessedness ye spake of?' For if we were still living in ignorance, unaware of the source of true blessedness and joy, it would not be surprising if we were following the broad path like everyone else. But God has declared to us that we are to find happiness in the Lord Jesus Christ alone; he is the source of all perfection and peace. If, knowing this, we flit here and there, or become shaken, we certainly cannot use ignorance as an excuse. Therefore, the teaching of this passage is that once we know the gospel we are expected to forsake all that we prized hitherto, and all that men covet so greedily and so incessantly. That is to say, the enticements of Satan and of this world, and the passing, fading things which have no substance. We must continue to seek the Lord Jesus Christ until we enter into a full enjoyment of all the benefits he has brought us.

Paul accuses the Galatians, and says that they had only become his enemy because he had told them the truth. What a terrible thing it is to turn against one who is our friend, when he has only demonstrated his faithfulness to us. What we ought to expect from a friend, above all other things, is that he will be honest with us, and not two-faced, not practising deception or lying. All of us desire this in a friend; it is a natural instinct within us, and not something which has to be learnt at school! How, then, can we be angry and exasperated with those who are truthful, and who are thus most profitable to us? We must be bewitched by Satan if we rise up against such people and make ourselves their enemies. Paul, therefore, explains why it is that he fears for them, and had become alienated from them. He points out that they have only become his enemies because, in his integrity, he has been severe with them.

Now, although this attitude is abhorrent and we all condemn it, it is, nevertheless, as prevalent today as it ever has been. For friendships are often sustained by lies, flattery, falsehood, pretence and the like. Indeed, if a man is open and forthright in his approach, he will draw out people's hatred and ill-will on all sides. This is a cause of many of the contentions and quarrels in the world today; people have shut their ears to truth and reason. We would rather bury all that makes us uncomfortable. This was not only written for the benefit of the Galatians, therefore, for we must apply it today and use it to teach all who cannot bear to hear the truth about themselves from others. If each of us were to examine himself carefully, we would find that we are all stained with sin until God cleanses us. If we grieve those who seek to tell us the truth, we are despising the Lord; we are not simply opposing a mortal creature, but making war with God. Of course, we will claim the opposite, but it is a lie if we cannot allow God to uncover that which we would prefer to conceal. For he will reveal our faults and rebuke us for them; he will not allow us to do anything that he has forbidden, but expects us to keep ourselves on a tight rein. Therefore, if a person scolds us vehemently, and gives us good counsel, seeking to deliver us from some evil or other, and we cannot bear it, we are assuredly battling against God. These are the main points that we are to remember from this passage.

* * *

At this point, Paul once again strives to win the Galatians back with great tenderness. 'My little children', he says, 'of whom I travail in birth again until Christ be formed in you'. Although there is honey in these words, Paul also includes a remark which will convict them; for, by calling them little children, he is reminding them that they should already have been born and raised up into Christ, and have reached maturity in the faith. He adds that he is unsure about how to deal with them. They are constraining him to act contrary to his desire; hence, he cannot tell what approach is most suited to their case. He says that he has had to approach them like a different person altogether, because they had made strange and become wild. He felt they were almost beyond hope and, therefore, he was uncertain about how to handle them. This is why his manner of speaking here combines friendliness with harshness. Paul is not content with being a father figure for them, who has tender feelings towards his own children; he also compares himself to a mother who is travailing in anguish in order to give birth. Though she experiences great pain, she cares more about the child who is going to be born than she does about her own body or, indeed, her life. By using such an image, we must admit that Paul could not possibly have displayed more affection for the Galatians. He does so in order to break down any hardness in the hearts of those he is addressing, to soften them. Yet, notice that he does not flatter them, for he rebukes them for their wicked ways, in that they have not acknowledged the mother who gave birth to them, and nourished them with her own body and blood. They had become like wild animals who could not be tamed, despite the fact that they themselves had been treated so kindly. Their ingratitude, therefore, was gross. Thus, we can see that Paul is following the methods that we mentioned earlier today: that is, he is seeking, as far as possible, to win back those who had strayed through showing them love. He demonstrates a fervent desire for their salvation which is greater than we could have imagined. Nevertheless, there is vinegar mixed in with the oil, which is designed to convict them. They needed this, or else they would have remained asleep in their sins. There is no hint here of flattering those who had offended God, and who had been bewitched by Satan and poisoned, so that they were unable to perceive their corrupt ways. Paul was seeking to scrape away all of this, but he chose a route that made them realise that he desired their well-being and to see them brought back to God.

This is what we can observe from this passage, but furthermore we must comment upon the fact that Paul called them 'little children' in order to send them an oblique rebuke that they had not progressed very far along the way. Why is the gospel preached to us every day? It is written that the gospel is the incorruptible seed by which we are regenerated and made children of God (*1 Pet.* 1:23). Well, when we have been weaned from the things of this world, in time we gain strength and no longer rely upon milk for our nourishment, for we are able to digest solid food. We continue growing in strength until we reach manhood. What a dreadful shame it is, therefore, if, after having become new creatures through the message of the gospel, we remain at the breast and do not progress! We have to be carried everywhere, and are unable to eat even a morsel of bread; we are only contented when we are being suckled. Has this something to do with the nature of the gospel message? Not at all! We must, therefore, acknowledge that the fault is with us! Thus, when Paul calls the Galatians 'little children', although he is expressing on the one hand his fervent love for them, he is also criticising them. Just as the apostle writes in the Epistle to the Hebrews, they ought to have been teachers, judging by the amount of time they had been at school! They did not first hear the gospel yesterday, yet they were still at the alphabet stage (*Heb.* 5:12). 'How shameful!' says Paul. 'God has given you sufficient instruction, and has been a good teacher to you, but you have been such poor scholars.' Now apply this to ourselves. Paul had seen the Galatians born into Jesus Christ a long time before, and they, therefore, ought to have been strong in their faith. Notice, however, how weak they are, and so foolish that they do not know what to believe or follow. This is the first point.

After this, he says that he is 'travailing in birth again' until Christ is formed in them. This implies that they had been 'born' previously, but were much like little runts! Not that Paul had failed to teach them sound doctrine, but rather that they had been incapable of receiving it because they were too greatly given over to their carnal appetites. And we know that the natural man cannot understand the secret things of God (*1 Cor.* 2:14). This is why we need to be stripped of all that pertains to our natural state and be renewed by God. That which we call regeneration, or the second birth, means that our old nature must die and be completely renewed. Thus, since the Galatians had not lived according to the teachings of the gospel, Paul says that they must undergo further transformation, 'until Christ be formed in you'. This is added to sweeten the earlier part of the statement, which would have been most bitter if taken in isolation. For it was a very shameful state of affairs, that those who had received the privileges of salvation in baptism and the Lord's Supper, both men and women of all ages (some twenty, thirty, fifty or sixty years old) – that those, I say, who had claimed before God to be fully renewed in Jesus Christ should need to lay the foundations of their faith all over again. This is why Paul adds that it is only until Christ is formed in them. In effect, he is expressing his surprise at the fact that they are like little children, and that he is constrained to take them back into his womb, as it were, until the time comes when they are more mature than they were previously. He knows that the efforts he has made on their behalf have not been totally useless or in vain, but that the Galatians have, nevertheless, sinned and are not shining as he would have hoped.

Thus, Paul modifies his reproof, in which he refers to the Galatians as runts; otherwise, his remark would have been too harsh and would have caused them to despair. He said that though they had been conceived, brought forth, nursed and nourished in Jesus Christ, they now had no spiritual life; it had vanished away. But if he had stopped there, these poor people would have remained in a desperate condition. So, in order to give them courage to redress the balance, he tells them that although they have fared so badly thus far, they can return to the right road. Even those who appear to be dead can again produce new fruit, so that their earlier claim to walk according to the gospel will not have been meaningless. If a tree is half-dead and completely dry, and we put new earth around the roots and help it along, it will again produce fruit. In the same way, a man who has wandered away from the paths of the gospel can be renewed if he is warned. Not only so, but he may grow and mature beyond his former condition, for we often observe such things when God pours out his grace upon those who have strayed and brings them back to the right path. Of course, this is not always the case; therefore, we need to be on our guard, and not abuse the grace of God, as so many do who turn away from God and become accomplices of Satan. We witness many men allowing themselves to become corrupt and profane, and attempting to blot out God's truth as far as they possibly can. Many carelessly fall away, apparently lost forever; in fact, we may even question the value of having taught them anything at all. They are lost children, and appear to be void of wisdom. But if God should call them back, (as we know from countless examples), we find that what was buried hitherto shoots up again. It has been growing in well cultivated and fertilised soil, though for a time dust and rubbish have been piled on the top; nevertheless, that which has been planted, though hidden, will spring up eventually. This is the message that Paul is expounding.

Another point that we need to notice here, where Paul speaks of Christ needing to be formed within them, is that his rebuke is intended to produce obedience in them once again. At first, it is true, we may think that this statement is slightly inaccurate. After all, we are 'formed' in Jesus Christ, and not he in us, for he is our righteousness and perfection. To say that he develops within us as an infant does, and grows and matures, is inappropriate when we consider who he is. Yet, Paul uses this terminology to show us the union that we have with Jesus Christ our Head. Thus, although Jesus Christ does not increase or decrease in any sense, yet he is willing to accept in his person all that pertains to our weaknesses and sins. As I have already told you, we are born in him when we are called to a hope of salvation through the gospel. In Adam, we are all dead and condemned. There is only one way to have life, and that is by being united to the Lord Jesus Christ, who is the fountain of life, and who possesses all the fulness we require in himself. Have we been born into Jesus Christ in the way that I have described? If so, he feeds us through the teachings of the gospel until we are able to receive stronger meat, and until our faith has grown, so that we no longer resemble children. We have reached manhood, as it were, because we have prospered more and more in our knowledge of God, as Paul says in the fourth chapter to the Ephesians.

Furthermore, our Lord Jesus Christ carries our sins, and says that he will be like a little child formed within us, to show that he does not wish to be separated from us, but that we may enjoy mutual communion together. How is this possible? Is Jesus Christ weakened by this? Not at all, in himself; but because we are members of his body he says that he becomes like a child within us according to the measure of knowledge we have. The more we grow and mature, the more his influence increases and extends within us. This witnesses to the outstanding, indeed infinite, goodness of the Son of God. For he is not only willing to abase himself in order to help our infirmity in his compassion and mercy, but also he is content to express himself as if he were incomplete, like a little child, and would grow within us according to the growth of our faith. Hence, in another passage (*Eph.* 1:23), Paul refers to the church as the fulness of God and of his Son, our Saviour the Lord Jesus Christ. To imagine that God were somehow not quite complete in himself and needed us would be great blasphemy; for what can we add to him? If he were to gather us all to himself now, what would he find in us but wretchedness? For we are all plunged and drowned in sin. Nevertheless, through the mouth of Paul, he pronounces that we are his fulfilment, and that he is, therefore, incomplete. Not that he cannot exist without us, for he existed perfectly well without us in eternity past before he created the world. Though there was neither heaven nor earth, was he not content within himself? Was he not rich enough through his own glory? Yes, without doubt he was. But he does not wish to be complete and will not content himself until we are united to him. This is what is meant in this passage.

When Paul speaks of Christ being 'formed' in them, he is warning us that it is not enough to have sketchy knowledge; we need a real-life experience of him. We need to have a vision of his power, his grace and of all his benefits impressed upon our hearts to the extent that it can never be erased. Earlier in the epistle, Paul said that whenever the gospel is preached in true power, as it should be, it is as if Jesus Christ has been crucified in our midst (*Gal.* 3:1). Not only is he depicted vividly, but he is presented before us upon the cross, with his blood flowing from him, offering the ultimate sacrifice to God the Father in order to blot out all our sins and transgressions. Since God has been thus gracious to us, our response should be never to allow the message to pass us by. There are many who seem to blossom after hearing only three words of the gospel, as it were. They believe that it is sufficient, yet in reality their understanding of it is very shallow. We ought not to be surprised if they fall into temptation, however small, and become forever lost. All they thought they believed in is of no avail in such circumstances, for God is punishing them for their lack of true commitment. Therefore, now that God has graciously permitted us to know his Son, we should have this vivid picture impressed upon our hearts whenever we come to hear a sermon. We need to remind our hearts and refresh our memories, so that the devil, who seeks to cloud our minds and finally to overcome our faith, will not have the victory. Believers have a clear picture of Christ engraved deeply upon our hearts; and can say that Jesus Christ is truly formed in us.

This makes us realise that the Papists have fully renounced our Lord Jesus Christ. For they plunge everybody into darkness, and accept the fact that people only have a sketchy knowledge of him. They do not encourage too much enquiry for they believe that it is dangerous to devote oneself to studying the Scriptures. What blasphemy! How Paul reproaches the Galatians for the fact that, at one time, Christ was formed in them, but now they have strayed. How shameful for them that they did not receive the doctrine that was preached to them in a meaningful way. If, however, we have done our duty and behaved as good students under God, as he for his part has been a good and faithful teacher, then we will not have the kind of faith which is mixed-up and confused with falsity. Instead, we will have a clear sight of the Son of God, for the Second Epistle to the Corinthians tells us that the Bible is like a mirror which reflects the face of Jesus Christ (*2 Cor.* 3:18). We do not see him with our eyes, of course, for this is reserved for the last day, when we will be like God. On that day, his glory will be fully revealed. But today, we see, as far as we are able in our sinful and weak condition, the face of the Lord Jesus Christ in the gospel, in order to transform us and make us more like him.

At this point, Paul adds that he desires to be with the Galatians, 'and to change my voice; for I stand in doubt of you'. This reveals just how serious and unbearable their sin was in his eyes, for he does not even know where to begin with them. He gave birth to them in Jesus Christ, and fed them with gospel doctrine, yet now he hardly knows how to deal with them any more. A mother fully understands the temperament and nature of her child. Thus, for a mother and father to lose their control and be unsure of how to handle their child, he must be totally evil and perverse. The child must be like a serpent, full of poison, or like a lion, full of pride and waywardness, no longer manageable or teachable; he must be possessed by the devil himself. Paul accuses the Galatians of the very same thing, but before we condemn them, let us examine ourselves to be sure that we do not commit the same sin ourselves. That is to say, when God utters his voice to teach us, does he find us so fierce that he has to change his approach each time? Yes, it is true that he can turn our hearts in whichever way pleases him, but we are not now dealing with his hidden power by which he works in his elect; we are referring simply to our own nature, which is brutish when we consider it as it is. And we are examining our nature in relation to the preaching of the gospel. Are not those who faithfully devote themselves to preaching the gospel of our Lord Jesus Christ grieved continually when they find men displaying their savage opposition to it? For once we have tasted the goodness of God we need to undergo a taming process. We must learn to be attentive to the gospel. There would be no need of long exhortations if we could be easily encouraged to follow, if the beckoning of a little finger were enough to persuade us – like a child who only seeks to please his father, and has his foot poised ready to run wherever his father sends him, and his two arms stretched out ready to obey whatever he is commanded to do. But when God addresses us, we are so dull that we do not even understand what he has said, or else have stopped our ears, so that however loud he calls, it is to no avail and we remain where we are.

Thus, Paul is not only speaking to the Galatian people in this passage, but it is as if he were accusing us all of ingratitude, all of us through all the ages. God is grieved with our stubbornness and perversity, and with all the hypocrisy and hidden sin in us. Even when he speaks with gentleness, we become all the more sour-tempered, and if he is harsh, we bolt in the opposite direction to the spur. In fact, what good is his gentleness or his severity? It profits us little, and this exposes the depth of evil within us, for he cannot get through to us, no matter which approach he adopts. Let us diligently examine ourselves. For God desires to use his Word to bring us new birth, that we might be his children. Then we will one day obtain the inheritance for which he has adopted us through our Lord Jesus Christ. He purchased our salvation through the passion and death of the One who is the true and only Heir. This being the case, we need to understand the importance of each sermon or of each reading we hear from the Holy Scriptures; if we do not experience the power and efficacy of the Word of God when it is preached, or when we read it, we ought to realise that it is due to our evil hearts and dull minds. We are too obsessed with the world around us and this is holding back our progress. We need to pray that God would not allow his Word to be fruitless in our lives.

Now, once we have been regenerated by the Word of God and have become his children, we need to feed daily upon this pasture, knowing that we will need it for the rest of our lives. For we have not, as yet, reached the perfection which we are striving for, but the Word of God can encourage us along the way and give us an ardent desire to press onwards until we are fully united to the Lord Jesus Christ. We are not to prevent his work in us by closing the door to him, because he seeks to lead and guide us safely on our way. As we have seen, Paul reproached the Corinthians for the fact that they would not let him approach them, and he said that it was not his fault (*2 Cor.* 6:11–12). 'You are closed, you are barred up, so that instead of obeying God, you would rather run away from him', he says to them. 'Since you have withdrawn yourselves and gone into hiding, I must change my approach towards you.' Therefore, having seen the complaint that Paul makes, first to the Corinthians, then to the Galatians, let us not be closed, as we are by nature, but let us ask God to give his Word access to our souls. May we realise that all our lusts, our empty vanities and twisted desires are like bolts across the door, or like objects placed against it so that the Word of God is kept out. Then may we fight against this and open the way, not so that the Word gains access through a keyhole, as it were, but so that it finds the door wide open. Whenever God speaks, may we take heed and train our hearts and desires to receive the doctrine in truth and in its fulness. For it is by this that we are purified, until we reach the fountainhead of all purity.

Now let us fall down before the majesty of our great God, acknowledging our faults, and praying that we would feel the burden of them. Then may we condemn ourselves, not only with our lips, but with uprightness of heart may we engage in a fierce battle with our sins, denying ourselves increasingly, and striving to rid ourselves of all that is corrupt and depraved within us. May we continue to do this until we have been drawn fully to his side, and until we are transformed into his likeness, and enjoy immortal glory, to which we are called now, but which we can only possess through hope until the last day. May he not only reveal this grace to us, but to all peoples and nations on earth, etc.

29

Freedom From the Bondage of the Law

Tell me, ye that desire to be under the law, do ye not hear the law? For it is written, that Abraham had two sons, the one by a bondmaid, the other by a freewoman. But he who was of the bondwoman was born after the flesh; but he of the freewoman was by promise. Which things are an allegory: for these are the two covenants; the one from the mount Sinai, which gendereth to bondage, which is Agar. For this Agar is mount Sinai in Arabia, and answereth to Jerusalem which now is, and is in bondage with her children. But Jerusalem which is above is free, which is the mother of us all (Gal. 4:21–26).

Freedom is such a desirable thing to every one of us, that without it our lives would be little more than a living death, or at the very least, perpetual misery. Indeed, so far as we are able, we flee subjection and constraint, and covet liberty, which, according to the old proverb, is a priceless treasure. If this is true of our earthly lives, then it applies even more to the eternal salvation of our souls. Yet how many there are who are still in bondage, as if they have a noose tied around their necks! Although they claim to love freedom, they live as though they were bound in slavery. This freedom is particularly evident when people are able to rejoice in the liberty purchased for them by the Lord Jesus Christ, which brings rest to their souls. In the gospel, God declares that he delights to adopt us as his children, and in doing so, he frees us from Satan's snare and from the tyranny of sin. But there are very few who will accept this gift when it is presented to them, because of their cursed captivity to sin; they seem to prefer to be subject to their own carnal appetites, rather than to yield in obedience to God and walk in complete liberty. Paul, therefore, has good reason to scold the Galatians for living under the law, because they are rejecting the freedom and liberty that they should have enjoyed as children of God.

Now Paul gives us a symbol, a vivid picture illustrating that the very law itself reveals the poverty and misery of the human heart; yet the Galatians prefer to remain under it! For the house of Abraham is a clear symbol of the church of God. It tells us much about the state of the church. It is written that Abraham had two sons: Ishmael and Isaac (*Gen.* 16:1ff). Ishmael was born to Hagar, Abraham's servant, who was given to him to be his wife. But there was a serious fault here, for it was not right for him to break faith with his lawful wife, Sarah. Now, what was the reason for this union between Abraham and Hagar? It was brought about because Sarah acted hastily and rashly, believing that God was too slow about fulfilling his promise to her to provide her with offspring. She thought that she was unable to conceive. But her understanding of God's Word was poor, and she did not have the patience and contentment that faith demands. In short, this was a relationship to be condemned, an immoral union, though Abraham did not originally intend this at all. He had not been driven by wicked lust, he had simply desired to have seed through which would spring the salvation of the world. But how foolish such acts are, when we attempt this or that without being told to do so by the Word of God. When we are driven by our own rash desires, many sins occur. Thus, Ishmael was born to Hagar, the 'bondmaid', from an illicit relationship with which God was not pleased. Isaac was born to Sarah a long time after Ishmael, for Ishmael may have been sixteen years old when Isaac was born. Paul (following Moses' account) tells us that Isaac was born according to promise and Ishmael according to the flesh. Now this does not mean that Abraham was not Isaac's father, but rather that he was born through divine power; for Abraham was declining; indeed, he was half-dead and had no strength left in him! He was a hundred years old, and his wife was almost the same; she had been infertile throughout her life of roughly ninety years. The idea that she could conceive and give birth was seen as laughable when the angels brought her this message (*Gen.* 18:12). Therefore, Isaac was born according to promise, for God worked a miracle in order that he might send the Lord Jesus into this world; not following the laws of nature, but through the goodness of God alone and according to his perfect will.

Thus, in the house of Abraham, we have a figure of the church: two women, both of whom gave birth to a son. As for Hagar, Paul tells us that she represents Mount Sinai, where the law was given, and we are told that this was in Arabia, to show that it was not in the holy land chosen by God as an inheritance for his people. Sarah represents Jerusalem. Not, he says, the present city, for it has changed beyond recognition. Its inhabitants have separated themselves from the law and from pure doctrine. Now, when I say the law, I do not mean it in the way Paul refers to it in this letter – the law that engenders bondage – I mean the covenant that God made with his people through the Lord Jesus Christ. Since Jerusalem at the time of Paul had rejected Jesus Christ and, therefore, broken their covenant with God, Paul says that he must refer to it as Hagar and Sinai. For the Jews, he is saying, boast about their temple and sacrifices and the like, and that they are the chosen and elect people of God, yet they are banished and excluded from the holy land, as it were, and have a meaningless connection with the law. For if we were to see Jerusalem at the time of Paul, we would realise that it was comparable to Sinai. But there is another Jerusalem: 'Jerusalem which is above'. This corresponds to the church through which we receive regeneration in God's sight. The church, through the incorruptible seed of the gospel, engenders offspring who are freeborn. For she is 'the mother of us all'. Then Paul quotes the words of Isaiah,

'Rejoice, thou barren that bearest not' (*Isa.* 54:1). Now, Isaiah is not referring to a particular woman here, but the church of God, using this image as a simile. For a time the church had been very dissolute and, therefore, Isaiah tells us it was as if she had been cast away. A kind of divorce had occurred between God and his people. But the prophet assures the church that he will multiply her one day, and that she would have more children than if she had always prospered and flourished. This happened when the gospel was proclaimed to the world. For the church not only comprises the children of Abraham, or one particular race; but through the holy seed of the gospel, she has brought forth an infinite number of children for God, of every nation and land, even those far-distant from our own. For God has displayed his might throughout the globe. This is the meaning of the passage that we have quoted.

Paul tells us that these things are 'an allegory'. The first point we need to make here is that Paul did not wish to deny the literal meaning of Holy Scripture. There are some people who find a curious pleasure in seeking out strange interpretations of the Scriptures. By overlooking the literal interpretation, they undermine the whole. Hence, there are countless perversions and corruptions of the truth. False allegories abound today; they are adopted by multitudes, and yet are nothing more than Satanic inventions. Because such theories are accepted and applauded, the people remain bewitched by Satan. What fine expositors they make! Yet, how are they so successful? Well, if a doctrine is neither from heaven nor from earth, it is easy for poor ignorant souls to remain in suspension between the two! Paul does not intend us to interpret Moses' story of Isaac and Ishmael as a fanciful speculation – no, he is demonstrating that this historical account reveals the state of the church, though, in those days, the only church that God presided over was that of the house of Abraham. (Of course, there was Salem, whose king was Melchisedec, but this was not clearly understood at that point. Therefore, God chose to adopt a people through Abraham, and to reveal that he wished to be called upon by a people whom he had separated from the rest of mankind.) However, we must not read Moses' account coldly, without looking any further, that is, without considering what happened to this family and applying it to the church.

* * *

Now, let us come to the central theme – the law. When Paul compares Hagar, Abraham's servant, to Mount Sinai and the law which was given on that mountain, he is not referring to the substance of the law. For the law contains many promises of salvation which were fulfilled in the Lord Jesus Christ; Paul himself declares this in several other passages, as we have already seen. If we take and apply the law in its proper and legitimate usage, we will see it as an incorruptible, life-giving seed, through which God becomes our Father and sets us free. The law only engenders servitude with relation to external issues, as we have discussed before. Our forefathers of old, though they were children of God and heirs of the kingdom of heaven just like ourselves, were under tutors and governors. They were like little children, incomplete until the coming of the Lord Jesus Christ. Their ceremonies were like bridles or cords preventing those who observed them from enjoying the liberty that we have today through the Lord Jesus Christ. Yet, when Paul speaks of the law creating servitude, he is speaking here of the way in which the Galatians misapplied the law, for he continues by saying that those who are under such servitude will eventually be banished and excluded from the family and inheritance of God. Thus, although our forefathers lived in servitude with regard to external things, yet they were free; for the Spirit gave them a faith that overcame their bondage, as it says in the eighth chapter to the Romans. Without faith, they would have been cut off from any hope of salvation. To sum up, Paul refers to the law here in this negative way because of the particular interpretation these hypocrites had made of it, corrupting it by reducing it to the observance of petty rules, and by making their observation meritorious. In doing so, they were binding people's consciences so tightly that they were almost suffocated!

Now, Paul has adequately dealt with this subject on a previous occasion, but it would be helpful for us to remind ourselves of what he said. He drew a contrast between the law and the gospel; for those who seek justification through the law imagine that God is indebted to them if they fulfil their duty towards him. They have heard the promise that if a man keeps the law, he shall live (*Lev.* 18:5). They are rigorous in their law observance and even believe they have accomplished all that God requires and demands. Having such a promise before them, they await their reward, no longer believing that salvation is a free gift, but rather that they have deserved all that God has promised. Thus, eternal life becomes the expected recompense for all their meritorious deeds. So much for the law. As for the gospel, God becomes our Father when we are released from the curse of sin and Satan and, indeed, from the condemnation due to us through the law. For it is written that those who have not kept the law perfectly are accursed, as we have said before (*Deut.* 27:26). Thus, all are guilty; the whole world is plunged into despair without remedy, unless God withdraws the condemnation of poor sinners, and quashes the sentence he has pronounced upon them. We have now understood what Paul means when he refers here to the law. He is not saying that Moses' teachings are insufficient for a person to become a child of God, or that there are no promises of eternal salvation for mankind in the law, but simply that before Christ came into this world there was not the full enjoyment of liberty that we have today. More than this, he is informing us of the abuses of the law by hypocrites who had misinterpreted its purpose. They imagined that they could please God and obtain his favour by its observance. But Paul tells us that we remain in slavery until we are delivered by another kind of seed, that is to say, the gospel.

Now, when Paul says that Hagar or Sinai corresponds to 'Jerusalem which now is', he means that city which had once been God's sanctuary, and which, therefore, ought to have been the fountainhead of heavenly and pure doctrine. For both Isaiah and Micah tell us that 'out of Zion shall go forth the law, and the Word of the Lord from Jerusalem' (*Isa.* 2:3; *Mic.* 4:2). But the Jews became defiled and added their own inventions and interpretations to the purity of true doctrine. They even rejected Jesus Christ, the fountain of life. Thus, Paul tells us that this Jerusalem is like Hagar the bondmaid and Mount Sinai, which can only bring about condemnation. This is worthy of note, because it shows us that God has never favoured a place so much that he could not punish the ingratitude of its inhabitants for their misuse of his benefits; mercies which he placed at their disposal. This is Jerusalem, known as the holy city of God, his royal palace, his habitation, the place of his residence – all of these descriptions are to be found in Holy Scripture, (*Psa.* 48:1–3, 132:13; *Matt.* 4:5, 27:53). Yet, Paul tells us that it has become like Sinai, an infertile mountain in a distant and desolate area outside the borders of the holy land, which God chose as the inheritance and resting place of his elect people.

Recognising that such a change had taken place in Jerusalem, the city once chosen by God and blessed with such excellent titles, what will happen to the people who reject the gospel today? Even if they have known great honour, God can easily bring them down to ignominy. Look what is said about the towns where Jesus preached the gospel, like Capernaum and the rest; they could boast of having been first to hear the message of salvation, or that Jesus Christ preached more there than in Jerusalem itself. But we are told that such towns would be 'brought down to hell' (*Matt.* 11:23). It was for their rebellion and stubborn persistence in evil; their refusal to accept the grace that was offered to them in the preaching of the gospel. We know what Jeremiah said about Shiloh (*Jer.* 7:12). You see, the Jews boasted that they had the city of Jerusalem with its temple and altar. But Jeremiah tells them to visit Shiloh – that place where the ark rested for so many years. People would come there from all parts to worship God and bring their sacrifices, but now what would they see there? A terrifying reminder of the vengeance of God because they had misused the good things that God had originally blessed them with.

Now, let us apply this for our own instruction, so that we learn to walk in fear and wisdom, for God has been gracious to us by dwelling amongst us and establishing his royal throne to reign over us. For our part, we ought to obey him, and shelter ourselves beneath his wings in sobriety and humility. If we were to think that he is under obligation to us, then we will be audacious, opinionated and proud towards him. We would abuse the gifts that he intended to be for our well-being, and such wickedness could not go unpunished. Thus, the example of Jerusalem warns us to yield peacefully in obedience to our God, and allow him to rule over us. We must be submissive in every way, and not puffed up with pride or presumption, now that he has poured out his spiritual blessings upon us. Indeed, this ought to make us confess our dependence upon him and to humble ourselves.

Incidentally, we can see how foolish the Papists are to want to associate God with Rome; for they say it is the 'apostolic seat'. But their claims about Peter are nothing more than lies and fables. Whilst it is certain that Paul was held prisoner in Rome, and it may even be deduced that he died there, this is all that sets Rome apart. The gospel was attacked there, and that den of the devil was saturated with the blood of the martyrs, as if to provoke the wrath of God. It was here that men conspired to fight against the truth, and blot out, as far as they possibly could, the name and memory of the Lord Jesus Christ. This is all the dignity that Rome can claim! These people imagine that Rome has all the honourable titles that Jerusalem once had, though there is not a single syllable in the Scriptures to justify this. Nowhere do they tell us that God reigns there, or has chosen to dwell within its walls; nowhere is it referred to as 'mother', or as having a special honour – nothing like this at all! Paul does say that the faith of the Romans was known everywhere and that they had a good reputation (*Rom.* 1:8), but he is speaking of a mere handful of people. For those who ruled in Rome were certainly not Christians, yet there was a small group gathered together in hideouts, and these are the people that Paul praises and esteems. Therefore, we must never imagine that the whole of Rome belonged to the church of God! We saw what happened to Jerusalem – that she was compared to Hagar and Sinai, that is to say, that she had become a profane and polluted place. Her holiness had long been forgotten, because she had not continued in the pure doctrines of the gospel.

We can only conclude, therefore, that even those who are nearest to God, and who have enjoyed close communion with him, will be cast off like strangers if they do not persevere in holiness; for holiness is like a tie that keeps us closely bound to our God. We can see that the teaching of the Lord Jesus Christ is rejected, trodden under foot, held in contempt and disdain in Rome today. Furthermore, gospel teachers are persecuted by fire and their blood is shed in that place. There is no true religion there at all now, for it is full of wickedness and corruption. If a man were to enter Rome and return with the fear of God, some good seed having been sown in his heart, it would be a miracle. It is clear that Rome is the very cavern of hell. May it please God that people would suffer broken necks rather than venture upon that city! For at this time, even the nation of France has been infected by her impiety. The majority of those in France have become nothing more than dogs and pigs, with no more true religion than brute beasts. All the more reason, therefore, for us to heed this warning and to walk in wisdom and the fear of God, being careful that we are not deprived of the privileges that we have received because of our ingratitude. May God never wreak his terrible vengeance upon us, and make us trophies of dishonour and shame. Such is Paul's description of Jerusalem, which had formerly known such great honour.

Notice, furthermore, that under the figure of Abraham, God proclaims that he is the Father of all his own people. We have, therefore, been born of God in that we belong to his church. Yet it is not enough simply to claim that God is our

Father, unless we have been truly regenerated through the incorruptible seed, which is alone the guarantee of life and eternal salvation. We may ask the question, how is it possible to be members of God's family and yet be like illegitimate offspring? The answer is that, by our iniquity and wickedness, we have corrupted the Word of God, which is his seed. This is the way Peter describes it (*1 Pet.* 1:23). Yes, it is true that the Word, since it proceeds from God, is spotless in itself. It sparkles with purity, and contains all the treasures of the righteousness, goodness and mercy of God. This is the nature of the Word of God, but we have devalued it and altered it according to our own whims and fancies, and added our own impurity. So then, although we may regard ourselves as children of God, yet we are bastard children, as we shall see in greater detail this afternoon, by God's good pleasure. For Paul proceeds to show that Ishmael, though the eldest son, was finally expelled from his own family. This occurred because he was illegitimate, being born to Hagar. Therefore, we are to learn that we must be born into God's family through faith in the Word of God in its purity; God then enlightens our minds through the Holy Spirit, who reveals to us the will of God. For if we alter the Word of God beyond recognition, according to our own perceptions, though it may still be called the seed of God, it will not be so in truth, for it has been corrupted.

Thus, there are so many people around today who call themselves Christians but live under false pretences. For example, the Papists say that they believe in God and seek to adhere to the Holy Scriptures, but it is evident that they have twisted them. Instead of accepting the Holy Scriptures with all due reverence, they wrest them according to their own convenience, and even mock them and joke about them! As we have said on a previous occasion, they blasphemously treat the Scriptures like a wax nose that they can mould to whatever shape they wish! They have turned everything into confusion by their contrivances! Indeed, whatever the Papists call serving God has been hatched in their own minds. There is no question of ordering one's life according to what God has commanded and decreed. No, he is dethroned, and they usurp his lawful sovereignty and attribute such authority to themselves that they subjugate consciences and create whatever laws seem good to them. This sin is too great and too evil for words. How, then, do the Papists formulate their articles of faith? It must be according to what they have determined themselves, for there is certainly nothing in them that has been drawn from the Scriptures! Never mind what is written in the Holy Scriptures; they have conclusions of their own, which they regard as the very oracles of heaven, for they are swiftly received as commonly accepted facts. When they seek our approval of such nonsense, they say that, first and foremost, these are received doctrines: we must bow to their antiquity as if it makes them prescriptive for us, and thereupon they may just cite a few passages of Scripture which they have pulled out of context for good measure. But this is a mockery, for they have wilfully defiled the Word of God. Surely even little children, aware of such great and glaring ignorance, would spit in their faces!

Thus, the Papists are a good example of what Paul is illustrating here. In other words, there are many who boast that they are children of God, and servants of the church, who are really illegitimate. They are born of corrupt seed, for instead of adhering to pure doctrine which could bring the regeneration that leads to eternal life, they have added their own doctrines and thus violated the integrity of God's Word. We are not stretching the point too far when we say that Paul's argument is borne out by the Papists today. For what is our greatest quarrel with them at this point in time? It concerns free will, meritorious acts of service, satisfaction for sin, and the rest. The Papists say that we can obtain favour in the eyes of God by our own efforts, and that we do not need the aid and assistance of the Holy Spirit. Yes, they admit that there is some collaboration, and that God works within us up to a point; but they say that we are his helpers, and we would be most weak and useless if our virtue did not help us to gain God's favour. They also say that the grace of

God is of no effect unless we add to it something of our own doing. Thus, they are building a doctrine based upon merit; the only way you can reach the kingdom of heaven is by pleasing God. You need personal merit in order to pay for the sins you have committed. This is what the Papists spout forth! Furthermore, they conclude that it is a blasphemy to say that it is impossible to keep the law of God perfectly. They claim that anybody, if he applies himself, can fully observe its requirements. Yes, it is easy to brag in this way whilst still living in darkness, for those who say these things are themselves wicked fornicators, drunkards, blasphemers, people given to all kinds of gross and sinful behaviour. We know just how holy these monks, hypocrites, crooks and vermin are!

As for ourselves, we would say that we are born slaves of sin and under the tyrannical rule of Satan. We are held so tightly in his grip that we cannot even have one righteous thought about doing good. Our nature tends wholly towards evil, just like a donkey carrying its yoke and burden, yet our sin proceeds entirely from our own wills. We are born in sin and, therefore, can do nothing else; we continually offend God until he sets us free by his Holy Spirit and grants us his liberty. Furthermore, we believe that it is impossible to keep the law of God, but that the law simply reveals our duty; it is for each one to read his condemnation therein. We must come before God in silence, as evildoers, in order to obtain grace for the offences that we have committed. We come clothed in shame, confessing that we are lost, that God might save us through the grace of our Lord Jesus Christ. In short, we say that it is completely beyond our powers to acquit ourselves in the eyes of God. But he comes to our aid; he does not scrutinise us or enter into account with us. When we have offended him, there is no satisfaction for sin other than the sacrifice of our Lord Jesus Christ. The only way we can be cleansed is to wash ourselves in his blood.

We see, therefore, the practical application of Paul's teaching when we consider the points of conflict between the Papists and ourselves. Though they associate with the name of God, and falsely claim to honour it, and though they say they are his children because they accept the Holy Scriptures, yet they demonstrate that their mother is Hagar and Sinai, and that they are still in bondage. They still have the yoke around their necks, and refuse to come to God to accept the liberty that he offers. They would rather usurp that which God has reserved for himself alone by justifying themselves through their own merits and by seeking to fulfil the law. They are children of the bondwoman, therefore, and must remain slaves; their end is to be cast out forever. As for us, we will see the implications of this teaching later on, but, briefly, it concerns the fact that our only means of deliverance is through the gospel. Our Lord Jesus Christ himself declares in the eighth chapter of John's Gospel that it is his role to set us free, and that this privilege was given to him by God the Father, to deliver us from all condemnation. We must, therefore, come to the Lord Jesus Christ and find all that we need in him, for it is through him that we are freed from the yoke of the law. This yoke is too heavy for us to bear: not only does it weigh us down, it actually plunges us into the pit of hell. Thus, we obtain this deliverance only through the seed which brings regeneration and complete liberty. We become children of God, and not only are we known as such in the eyes of the world, but before angels. We will finally reach the inheritance that has been obtained for us at so great a cost, and which we could never have possessed by our own merits. It can only be obtained through the One to whom it all belongs, having conferred the inheritance on us through the gospel which we hear each day.

Now, let us fall down before the majesty of our great God, acknowledging our sins, and praying that he would help us to feel them more than ever before. Then we may grow and mature more and more through genuine repentance, so that, in coming to him, we may do so in all humility and without hypocrisy. We must be ashamed of our sin to the point that we seek no other remedy than the Lord Jesus Christ. Since our great God has received us and sealed us with the grace of his adoption in our hearts by his Holy Spirit, may we maintain the purity of the gospel, adding nothing of our own invention. May nothing be corrupted by our own notions, but may the Holy Spirit keep us obedient in the faith. In this way, as he has begun to show us his favour, we for our part will aim unswervingly for perfection. Thus, we all say, Almighty God and heavenly Father, etc.

30

On Discerning Who Belongs to the True Church

But Jerusalem which is above is free, which is the mother of us all. For it is written, Rejoice, thou barren that bearest not; break forth and cry, thou that travailest not: for the desolate hath many more children than she which hath an husband. Now we, brethren, as Isaac was, are the children of promise. But as then he that was born after the flesh persecuted him that was born after the Spirit, even so it is now. Nevertheless what saith the scripture? Cast out the bondwoman and her son: for the son of the bondwoman shall not be heir with the son of the freewoman. So then, brethren, we are not children of the bondwoman, but of the free (Gal. 4:26–31).

We saw this morning that many people who claim to be believers and to be associated with the name of God are, nevertheless, illegitimate children. For this reason God, disowns them, though they may be considered 'Christians' in the eyes of the world. They have corrupted that good seed, which is pure doctrine, which they need in order to be regenerated and adopted into God's family. What good is it to be regarded as part of the church if we are not truly born of the good seed which is both pure and perfect? For this to occur, we must be governed by the Word of God, without twisting it or adding to it. This is why Paul speaks here of the heavenly Jerusalem as our mother. Yes, it is true that those who contort the natural meaning of Scripture are not true children of God, and are liars and hypocrites when they address God as their Father. Yet, because they appear to be believers, Paul tells us that we may discern them by their mother, and thus know whether they are truly the legitimate children of God and acceptable to him. For the word 'church' is often used lightly. The Papists in our generation use the term as a shield to cover all their errors! Since the Word of God is against them, they make use of this; at least they have the church on their side!

Well, Paul is warning us to be careful when it comes to discerning who really belongs to the true church. For the Jews had abundant evidence to show that Jerusalem was the very place where God dwelt, since, as we saw this morning, he had chosen her and testified that she would be his everlasting resting place (*Psa.* 132:14). Yet, is it not true that this same Jerusalem was like a den of thieves, and even our Lord Jesus Christ was crucified there? In this way, through their treachery, the Jews cut themselves off from the household of God forever. Indeed, they sought, as far as they possibly could, to destroy his truth. Thus, the city of Jerusalem, though she had once been honourable, came to be regarded as dishonourable and shameful in the eyes of both believers and the angels themselves. In the same way, we must be careful today when we speak of 'the church', to ensure that we ourselves are not of that illegitimate seed; for if we have hypocritically uttered God's name before men, he will surely reject us and banish us from his family.

God bestows great honour upon the church here, when he calls her the mother of all believers. It reminds us of the words of Paul in another place, where he says that the church is the pillar which upholds God's truth in this world (*1 Tim.* 3:15). It does not mean that the truth needs to be maintained by sinners like ourselves, inclined as we are to fickleness and inconstancy, and prone to falsehood. How could the truth of God rest upon the shoulders of men, unstable as we are? Yet, through his unfailing kindness, he desired that his Word should be proclaimed here below, and committed that responsibility to those whom he has called. It is for this reason that the church is referred to here as 'the mother of us all'. As the Lord Jesus Christ declares, God alone is our Father (*Matt.* 23:9). God is our spiritual Father, and must have no rival. It is he that brings us the hope of eternal life by means of his true church, in which he has placed his incorruptible seed. As the prophet Isaiah says, 'my words which I have put in thy mouth, shall not depart out of thy mouth, nor out of the mouth of thy seed, nor out of the mouth of thy seed's seed, saith the Lord, from henceforth and for ever' (*Isa.* 59:21). Thus, God governs his people through his Word. It is this message which he has bestowed as a deposit and priceless treasure for the salvation of his church, to bring us regeneration and nourish our spiritual lives..

Therefore, we need wisdom to discern the true church of God, as I have already said. As the mother of God's children, we ought not to misuse or sully her name. Unfortunately, this is precisely what has happened and continues to occur to this day. It is a common error in our day to use the term 'church' to obscure and hide God's truth from the people. What else do the Papists do when they call themselves 'the church' so proudly and publicly? They have managed to seal up the mouth of God, as it were, and trample his Word underfoot. Indeed, they no longer even refer to it, all the while accepting unreservedly that which has been fabricated in their own minds, both declaring it and submitting to it. See how men, who are no more than earthworms and dung, consider themselves equal to God, and all is done under the auspices of the so-called 'church'. But Paul warns us here to seek for that church which upholds pure doctrine, for it is by this means alone that we are adopted as God's children. As we have seen before, the most important thing is to be grafted into the body of our Lord Jesus Christ. Firstly, we need to recognise that we are accursed by nature and that all our works are filthy rags; we are under the tyrannical rule of the devil, and the only escape is for God, in mercy and compassion, to rescue us. We can only enter the household of God through this one door, that is, through the grace of the Lord Jesus Christ. This is how the church bears us as her children, through the incorruptible seed we have been speaking about.

However, in order really to profit from this passage, there are two further points to bear in mind. Firstly, we are not to be like those who claim to be believers without ever reading or listening to the preached Word. They imagine that the Holy Spirit will reveal all to them in a vision or some such thing! In fact, the truth is, they despise doctrine and regard it as they would an alphabet for the instruction of little children. Be careful not to allow yourselves to be led astray by Satan and his wiles in this way. If we desire to be children of God, and to bear the true marks of a believer; if we desire to be acknowledged as such even by angels, we need to be teachable and, with all reverence and humility, thus to maintain order in the church. Even the greatest amongst us, and those who have been raised to honourable status, must recognise that the highest dignity men could have, be they kings or princes, is to be children of God. If a man wishes to exempt himself from this condition, he is rejecting God completely and cutting himself off from all hope of salvation. This, then, is the first point, that while we are in this world, we must make it our business to profit from the Word of God. Herein lies the key to spiritual life; for if God has granted us regeneration, we are to nourish ourselves with the teaching of Scripture for the rest of our lives. Indeed, it is the only food for our souls. Let us never proudly or presumptuously despise doctrine, as if we no longer needed to be students of the Word, for we are to accept what we are taught daily, and by this means become true children of the true church. This is the first point.

Secondly, we need to be discerning, and not like animals who are led by the reins across the fields. We need to be aware of what constitutes the true church; for God has left certain signs within it which will not fail as a means of discerning his true people. Wherever his Word is preached faithfully without any human additions, his own people will be found. This will occur where the gospel is unadulterated, and where people are led directly to God to seek in him all that they lack. They will follow the Lord Jesus Christ as the Way set before them. Ridding themselves of all pride and arrogance, they will eagerly clothe themselves with the spiritual qualities belonging to the Lord Jesus Christ. All their glory and all their teaching will proceed from the house and sanctuary of God, the true church which is our mother. They can then be sure that God accepts and receives them as his children. This, I say, is a certain and infallible means of discernment unless, of course, our minds are dull and clouded. There are many people who close their eyes and shut their ears, believing that they are justified simply because they say they belong to the church. In reality, they are hiding the fact that they follow Satan, together with all his deceptions, lies and abuses. May we not be like animals, led by our appetites, but may we be brought to the place where we are born again through the seed of his Word, and fed in the only true pasture for souls.

Paul quotes the testimony of Isaiah here (*Isa.* 54:1). In this Scripture, God is not referring randomly to any group who claim the title 'church', but only his sheep, his remnant, left to him after the terrible apostasy of the Jews. Whilst it appears, at first sight, that God had wiped out and abolished his church in the world, yet there was still a small number that he had gathered to himself, known as his elect remnant (*Isa.* 1:9). Thus, the prophet Isaiah tells us that those who had been redeemed, and who had truly returned to God, ordering their lives in obedience to his Word – these were the children of the church. It is important to notice that the church is not triumphant in this world; she does not shine with the kind of splendour and magnificence that would capture our hearts with just one glimpse and make us her devotees. Often, she is desolate and disfigured. This is all the more noteworthy when applied to the Papists. How must they set out to prove that they are the true church? They surely need some evidence. Yet, all they can point to is their wealth, their popularity, and all their pomp and splendour.

But this is not the way that God desires his church to be known. Rather, the Lord Jesus Christ desires to reign here below, surrounded by his enemies. He has chosen that his disciples must experience those things of which he warned them. In other words, they will be rejected by the world and be despised; people will wag their tongues at them, and trouble them, giving them no peace nor rest in this life (*Matt.* 10:16ff). Therefore, when we speak of the church, let us remember what Paul tells us here: that she is like a barren woman who is alone in her household, and without support or help. She is rejected and ignored, and has one foot in the grave, as it were. But God promises that she will be restored, and will have more children than she that is married and enjoys honour and a good name.

I tell you, we need to bear this teaching in mind today. We see the church trampled upon, and the enemies of the truth acting so proudly and venomously towards her. They have shown fight and charged, standing in triumph over us, as if we were nothing more than dust or smoke. When we witness such things, let us patiently wait for God to gather together his elect, content meanwhile in the knowledge that we are his children, though the world despise and reject us. Thus, if we wish to know what the church is, let us not look for it with an eye full of vanity, like those who seek only pomp and beautiful appearances. On the contrary, let us remember that God will afflict his poor church to the point that it has no beauty or attraction in the eyes of men, but rather appears desolate. Even, as we shall see shortly, if everyone rises up against the church, let us be content to be one of God's children. For if we have been called to God through the pure doctrine of the gospel, we become companions of all our forefathers who were chosen under the law. We are one with all the righteous kings and patriarchs, prophets and martyrs; in short, all believers since the time of Abel as well as those who are to come, to the end of time itself. Yes, the Papists boast that they are a vast multitude, but the prophet Isaiah mocks at all this. Why? Because the important thing is to discern who are the rightful children. What are all the temples of the Papists but brothels of Satan? Everything about them is tainted with filth, and their service for God is corrupt. There is nothing upright about any of it! So then, the Papists, though they call themselves 'the church of God', are born illegitimate, and belong to the brothel, along with their mother and all the synagogue of Satan. This is how it is according to Isaiah and Paul, a faithful expositor led by the Spirit of God, confirms his message. Let us only join those who are the true children of God, who have the infallible seal of the Holy Spirit and refuse simply to follow the crowd. As for those who are wretched, let them go their way to perdition, for they have willingly thrown themselves into the nets of Satan, wandering like poor brute beasts void of knowledge.

However, let us bear in mind that those who are children of the church can still be our fathers in the faith. We have been born again through their message, as we heard the Word of God. It is written that all who believe are sons of Abraham and the true Israel of God, as if we had descended from Jacob (*Gal.* 6:16). Our fathers in the faith, therefore, belong to this same fraternity, though we are known collectively as the sons of God and of his church. Similarly, our Lord Jesus Christ is called our Head. Though he is ultimately the only Son of God, yet by associating ourselves with him and becoming members of his body, we can call ourselves the sons of God, not by nature but because we have been freely adopted. Therefore, Paul tells us that we, like Isaac, are the children of promise. He does not wish us to have any vain confidence in our own merits, nor in our own persons, but rather that we should be devoid of pride when we realise that our dignity has been conferred upon us by the grace and kindness of God alone. In this way, we differ from those illegitimate children who falsely glory in the name of God. They are full of presumption and hypocrisy. All they talk about is free will, meritorious works, penances, the four cardinal virtues, as well as theological virtues, as they call them! In short, they are puffed up with pride. As for ourselves, we are of promise, which means that God has looked upon us in mercy and plucked us out of the abyss of hell where once we were. Through the gospel, he has become our Father, and he has declared that an inheritance awaits us, bought not by ourselves or any other mortal creature, but by Jesus Christ. He, though very God, became man, that we might find in him that which we could never have found in the world.

Thus, Paul concludes here that if we wish to be grounded upon the gospel and enjoy assurance of salvation, we must never entertain thoughts of our own merit, nor believe that we can contribute anything of ourselves, for it is simply a matter of accepting that which has been offered to us. Jesus Christ is not half a saviour, he is *the* Saviour! These are some implications of this promise, as we have already seen at some length. Of course, the law has its promises, but as I have explained, they all have conditions. The promise which Paul refers to here abolishes all human pride, casts man down and reveals that he is lost. The only answer, therefore, is in the Lord Jesus Christ. The only way we can enjoy the blessings of God is by means of the gospel. It teaches us that salvation is to be found in God alone, and that we must return thanks to the One who granted it. It is not a reward that he is obliged to give, for in no sense is God indebted to us.

* * *

At this point, Paul says, 'But as then he that was born after the flesh persecuted him that was born after the Spirit, even so it is now.' Thus, it is inevitable that we will be so treated. Hypocrites and liars, illegitimate children who have defiled the truth and cut themselves off from it, will gloat over us. They will exalt themselves against us, as if we were unworthy even to kiss their feet. They will rise up proudly and persecute us. But Paul is teaching us to be faithful, and not to allow our faith to be shaken by their arrogance; nor are we to be deceived by the cunning of such hypocrites and traitors, who have twisted the Word of God. For in the end, it will be for them as it was for those of the house of Abraham:

'Cast out the bondwoman and her son: for the son of the bondwoman shall not be heir with the son of the freewoman.' All such, though they claim to be believers, and wish to be considered part of God's family, will be cut off as rotten branches, and will have no part nor lot in the inheritance.

There is an excellent message here which ought to be most useful to us, and which confirms that to which I have alluded: and that is, that we are not to be dazzled by the splendour of this world, nor transported with amazement when we see displays of great magnificence. If we were to believe all that we saw with our eyes, the Pope upon his throne, with all his sparkling garments and their trimmings, would seem an idol to be worshipped. It does not surprise us that people stand there aghast, as if they have been hit over the head with a club and are semi-conscious! Why? Because men are inclined to judge carnally, and are less than little children when it comes to the things that concern the kingdom of heaven. Yet, Paul tells us that those in positions of authority, who are filled with self-importance and who are held in awe – indeed, those who might be regarded as the first-born – are often Ishmaelites. They are bastard children, despite what they may claim about their seniority. Now, if Paul lived today, the proclamation of his message would be so unwelcome that he would be burnt a hundred times over! Today, we may write or say whatever we wish, but we could not describe the Pope and his clergy more aptly than in the words of Paul. The implications of this text are that they are a band of Ishmaelites and evil, illegitimate children who fight against God and all his true offspring. Now, the Papists claim that they have not just established themselves today, nor even a hundred years ago. They claim that they have observed their ceremonies and traditions for eight or nine hundred years. Well, it is clear that, even in this, they shamelessly lie to us; but even if the world had not deteriorated in those eight hundred years, the fact that they are the 'first-born' makes them no more important or worthy than Ishmael! With time, they have grown in number and say that we are no more than a handful of people in comparison to them. They say that they have kings and princes among their number, that the whole world agrees with them, from the greatest to the least, and that their rule extends across most of Europe and part of Africa. But even with all this to boast of, it amounts to no more than the seniority of Ishmael. They ought to be looking for other evidence, namely, that they seek to live according to the teaching of the law and the gospel, and add nothing of their own devising; for doing this results in corrupt and illegitimate doctrine. Of course, they will not discuss whether or not they have adulterated the purity of the Word of God. But it is plain enough for all to see! Under cover of being a 'church', as I have been saying, they have audaciously assumed that they have the authority to add and detract from the Word of God.

Thus, we do not need to conduct a detailed examination, nor to possess a special gift of discernment to tell whether or not the Papists are, indeed, children of God. Like Ishmael they are proud to be first-born; they are proud that they have an infinite number of adherents. They say that we are like little runts, in a manner of speaking: we are despised, and we have no dignity or reputation in the world. When they speak like this, it is Ishmael that we can hear. We have great need of patience, therefore; for when the enemies of God occupy the best places in his house, it is a sore trial. They are like straw in the barn, whilst we are hidden away, like seed beneath the soil. It is a miserable condition that is hard for us to bear and, indeed, we have seen many forsake the gospel through weakness. Such poor, simple souls hear the noble titles, such as the Catholic Church, the Apostolic Throne, the Vicar of Jesus Christ, Successor to Saint Peter and Saint Paul, prelates, bishops, etc. With all this placed before them, these poor folk are confused and conclude that they ought to follow. They are captivated by this mask, the same as would horrify little children; but this does not happen to those who are strong and follow God faithfully. Thus, when the Papists claim that they are the 'representative church', they speak the truth, for indeed, they are no more than a representation! In other words, they are like a beautiful medal, but all that glitters is not gold, as they say! We need to know whether they teach the truth.

Take note of what Paul is telling us here. For the ill-treatment of Isaac by Ishmael was not just a one-off occurrence. We see the same kind of thing happening today. The children of God will be oppressed and trodden underfoot by those who, in theory, are the first-born, and many simple souls will be seduced by this very claim of theirs. They cover all their filth and pollution with such pretty colours, do they not? However, let us prepare ourselves for battle, says Paul, and not allow our faith to be overcome by the pride of those who are the enemies of the truth of God. These are domestic enemies, not like the Turks or pagans, but those who are garrisoned within the church, such as the prelates and great leaders. Yet, we must not be surprised, for we have been prepared for it through the example of our father Isaac. We need to persevere to the end, if we have been born again through the pure seed with which God is pleased, for this alone makes us rightful children and heirs of the kingdom of heaven.

Yet it may still be considered strange when Paul says that Isaac was persecuted by his brother Ishmael. For Moses simply writes that on the day that Isaac was weaned, at the feast, Ishmael laughed mockingly (*Gen.* 21:8–9). According to Moses' account, there is no mention of Ishmael persecuting Isaac. He only mocked, being the older child, and considering himself superior to Isaac through greater knowledge. If it was simply a matter of laughter and mockery, why, then, should Paul call this persecution? Well, the persecution that the child of God has to endure is not always by the sword, or by fire, torture, imprisonment, or other bodily suffering. Sometimes he is drowned in a torrent of abuse that unbelievers and enemies of the truth spew out of their mouths. If we are familiar with what it says in the Psalms, we will not find it strange that Paul should speak as he does. We are told that the reproaches that are made against our majestic God will also fall upon us (*Psa.* 69:9). We are to be very particular when the name of God is slandered, or his honour undermined in any way whatsoever. If a person were to attack the reputation of any one of us here, we would be angry and start a quarrel. We would see that it only takes one word of criticism for us to draw our swords in anger, under the pretext that we are defending our honour. If a man were to criticise our parents, such passions would be aroused in us that we would soon be out of control. Therefore, when God is attacked, and when men voice their criticism of him, ought we to suffer it, and not be moved with anger and indignation? This is why it says that the zeal of God's house has eaten us up (*Psa.* 69:9). We are not only to feel anger when a person undermines the majesty of God, or twists the doctrine of salvation, or when the church is full of ungodliness: these things should eat us up within.

To return to what I was saying, it is written that Ishmael persecuted Isaac. We may ask, how? With Gehenna, or with fire? Or did he have a sword with which to cut off his head? Not at all! He simply mocked at the promise that was made to Isaac. It was foretold that Ishmael would live, but not as a child of promise. It was in Isaac that the world would receive blessing (*Gen.* 21:12). Indeed, Jesus Christ was promised through Isaac, and thus, this was a promise of salvation. By mocking, Ishmael was giving a mortal wound to the children of adoption and to all believers, by disdaining and attacking their source of highest good and eternal felicity. Now we understand what Paul intended by this. He wants us to apply his teaching, and to be ready for these internal conflicts. The Turks and the pagans are not the only adversaries of the gospel. There are also many hypocrites, seeking to destroy, as far as they possibly can the doctrine of grace which is offered to them by the Lord Jesus Christ. They would rob him of his dignity and worth, rather than magnifying the wonderful generosity of God, the source of our souls' well-being. Let us be ready, I say, to fight these battles with our internal foes, who claim to be children of God. They say they are our superiors and boast of their seniority, hoping it will make us feel crushed and beaten.

There is another point, and that is that, when we see the doctrines of God twisted in this way, we should be cut to the quick with anguish. By nature, we flee anything that will harm us, or afflict the body. Yet, we should not be so wrapped up in this world that we prefer what seems desirable here below to our heavenly inheritance. Whenever the name of God is blasphemed, or whenever a person seeks to wipe out the doctrines that bring life, we should feel such anguish that we cannot overlook the matter, even more than if we were afflicted in our bodies. If we were to be threatened with having our throats slit, or with enduring all the torments imaginable (the enemies of the gospel today can only satisfy their rage against our poor brothers by torturing, burning, cutting off tongues and the like, as we know) – if this were to happen to us, I say, we are not to take it so hard as when the name of God is ripped to shreds, and attacked by wicked men. But why should they do such things? Well, if they slit our throats, it is not only to deprive us of this fleeting and transitory life, but also to cut us off from the kingdom of heaven. By corrupting the true doctrine, they are turning meat into poison, life into death, light into darkness. This passage is Paul's exhortation and warning to us not to give ourselves over to the things of this world. Our thoughts and affections should be raised heavenward, and centred on the priceless gift which has been offered to us through the gospel. We must fight for this cause more than for our own lives. For truly, a million lives upon this earth cannot be compared to that eternity in heaven which the Lord Jesus Christ has promised. This is what we need to remember: our passion can never be said to be unreasonable if we are reacting to the blasphemies of wicked men against God. For it is by their schemes and devices that they seek to alter and falsify the only doctrine which can bring spiritual life.

Finally, notice what Paul says in conclusion, that all those who boast in this way that they belong to the church today and claim the rights of the first-born will be cast out as bastard children. Do not be deceived by the splendour that surrounds those who strive against the truth of God: their tyranny is maintained by force, by persecution, by gloating and the like. Look to their end: they will be cut off, for they are not heirs. They may well live in the same house, just as we are told that the Antichrist sits in the temple of God (*2 Thess.* 2:4); but they will be scraped off like mud or dung. Now, this does not happen in the sight of men and, therefore, it is hidden from our eyes today. However, we must wait for God to manifest his truth more openly, and for the Lord Jesus Christ to confound his foes by the sword of his mouth, the power of his Word. We need to stand firm with unshakeable faithfulness, that however despised or criticised we are, we might persevere in the holy calling of our God, knowing that we will not be disappointed if we lean upon the doctrines of the gospel. Let us remain grounded therein, until the day that God reveals that which is presently hidden. On that day, we will be truly gathered to his side, knowing that we have not been taught his precious Word in vain. Nor will it be in vain for us to have renounced the foolish inventions of man, and to have sought life only through that pure seed that brings regeneration. This pasture alone can feed and nourish us to the end.

Now let us fall down before the majesty of our great God, acknowledging our faults, and praying that he would make us more conscious of them, so that we are led to true repentance. May we continue to tremble before his throne, and be confounded within ourselves, yet still assured that he accepts us in the name of the Lord Jesus Christ. The remission of our sins is guaranteed if we seek it in true faith, without stepping aside to the right hand or to the left. We must follow the way that he has shown us, and we cannot go astray if the Sun of Righteousness lights our path. May he show this grace, not only to us, but to all peoples and nations on earth, etc.

31

Absolved Only Through the Sacrifice of Jesus Christ

Stand fast therefore in the liberty wherewith Christ hath made us free, and be not entangled again with the yoke of bondage. Behold, I Paul say unto you, that if ye be circumcised, Christ shall profit you nothing. For I testify again to every man that is circumcised, that he is a debtor to do the whole law (Gal. 5:1–3).

Last time, we saw that in order to have an abiding place in the church, we need the Lord Jesus Christ as our foundation. There are many who claim to be children of God who have never been born again through that good seed which enlightens, and brings acceptance with God, who then acknowledges us as his children. We must hold fast to the pure doctrine of the gospel if we desire to be truly united to the Lord Jesus Christ. He, as our Head and our Mediator, unites us to God the Father. We have already spoken about the reason why Paul mentions both the servile and the free offspring. He tells us that those who seek justification through their own good deeds are severing themselves from the grace of the Lord Jesus Christ. For they are binding themselves to perform that which is impossible, that is, to satisfy God by keeping his commandments. Whereas, we are so full of weaknesses that we cannot possibly fulfil the least article of the law, let alone reach the perfection which the law requires. This is why Paul concludes that we must maintain the liberty that was purchased for us by our Lord Jesus Christ.

Now, he is most certainly referring to the ceremonies here, although we should always return to the original purpose and main goal of the law. For if the law were only concerned with keeping a certain feast day or abstaining from a certain kind of meat, this would not be an issue of such weight as to stir up so many contentions within the church. Yet, Paul never wasted his time dealing with trivial or inconsequential matters. He was concerned with doctrine; for to make other matters obligatory was to exclude multitudes from the hope of salvation. If it is a mortal sin to neglect a certain ritual, I become a transgressor if I fail, and there is no remedy for such a sin. God is my judge and will call me to account; there is no means of redemption. Whilst it is true that we all must observe the law, yet there is a remedy if, on account of our shortcomings, we run to the Lord Jesus Christ. Indeed, he submitted to the law in order to buy our liberty. He took our curse upon him in order to set us free. So then, if we impose various additional obligations, and say that to do this or that is a sin, our Lord Jesus Christ will not serve as a remedy for such things in the way that I have said. Instead, we will remain under the curse without hope of deliverance. Thus, Paul has good reason to exhort the Galatians to stand fast and not allow themselves to return to servitude. For this, he says, will rob them of a priceless gift, and they will fall from the grace of God and be separated from the Lord Jesus Christ, the only source of salvation and eternal happiness.

Now, in order to appreciate more clearly the sense of this passage, and also to gather the fruit that is offered here, let us be aware that this word 'liberty' implies that we may walk before God with full confidence that he will always be merciful to us. Even if we are guilty of many wrongdoings, we know that they will be forgiven in the name of the Lord Jesus Christ. Furthermore, it is not in man's power to bind us or hold us captive. We must be willing to obey our God, not because we are constrained or forced to, but like children who submit to their father, knowing that he will not treat them harshly. This is implied by the word 'liberty' that Paul uses here.

However, in case my brief definition has been unclear, I will expound it further. As long as we remain unsure of whether God loves or hates us, we will always experience mental anguish and a worried conscience, and we will remain imprisoned by these thoughts. There will be no freedom in our souls until we are persuaded of God's mercy, that, despite our unworthiness, he will receive us lovingly and graciously. Yet, it is impossible to have such assurance unless we have before our eyes the pardon that was bought for us by the death and passion of the Lord Jesus Christ. Why? Because, as I have already said, we are debtors to God on account of numerous, even infinite, sins. We are bound to keep the law, but a hundred times a day we fail, even without our knowledge. Added to this, there is gross misconduct. However much we try, we can never be assured of the love of God until we are forgiven the debt of eternal death that we owe. Such a gift is bestowed when we are persuaded through the gospel that the blood of the Lord Jesus Christ was shed to cleanse us from all our sinful stains. His death was a sacrifice to appease the wrath of God and blot out the memory of all our offences and iniquities. This is how we are set free, knowing that God mercifully accepts us in the name of the Lord Jesus Christ, and that our sins and shortcomings will not prevent us from obtaining grace at his hand, or from enjoying personal access to him, like a child with his father.

There is a second point. We should never fall over backwards to fulfil scrupulously what men have invented in their heads. No, we are to content ourselves to walk according to the Word of God, knowing that our conscience has been liberated. Whatever man commands or forbids is of no importance. I speak with regard to the spiritual life of our souls and not, of course, in relation to the enforcement of law and order or the things which affect our everyday lives. We are dealing with salvation here; therefore, if a thing has not been forbidden by the mouth of God, then we are free to do it. Although we need to know that we have the Word of God to guide our conduct, and are not to add anything to it, we also need to be sure, as I have suggested, that God accepts our devotion. When he sees our obedience, though there is much that he could criticise, and many weaknesses, though we come limping to him and only achieve inconsequential things (if he were to examine them in any detail), nevertheless, he accepts all of this. Why? Because he bears with us like a father with a son. This is the liberty in which we are to stand fast. Otherwise, we face separation from the Lord Jesus Christ. What do I mean? Well, if we are not assured of God's love, as I have already said (though we are unworthy of it), through having our sins buried by the death and passion of the Lord Jesus Christ, what will happen to us? How will Jesus Christ then profit us? Clearly, if we live with doubt and uncertainty about whether or not our service for God is acceptable to him, or about whether we ought to keep this or that commandment of man – if, I say, we live surrounded by so many questions, we will never have any peace.

Therefore, having exhorted believers to stand fast in the liberty which was obtained for them at such cost, Paul rightly adds that, if they are unaware of this liberty, then 'Christ shall profit you nothing'. He warns them not to allow men to rob them of this freedom. Now, let us be clear that the liberty that Paul speaks of does not mean a licence to do whatever we please. He is not removing the bridle from our neck entirely, as he makes plain a little later on. His intention is only that we may serve God peaceably without complaint or constraint. He desires that we cease to live like unbelievers, who torture themselves continually over various rules and regulations. Such people have not placed their trust fully in the Lord Jesus Christ. Now, in addition to what we have already learnt, we also need to know the goal of such liberty, which is that we can live at ease and at peace before God. Without this, we would be too fearful to obey him, being perpetually troubled within. We would be unable to call upon him, which is the most important duty that he demands of us, and which pleases him above all else.

Thus, we have seen that this issue goes right to the heart of our salvation when we understand its implications. Today, when we talk about our Christian liberty, the Papists say that our aim is to destroy the ordinances and traditions of the church. They say that this would not bother us at all, but each person would be permitted to live according to their own lusts, eating meat every day without any scruples, and caring nothing for such things. Yet, this tells us that they have never realised that you can only serve God if you do so willingly. If we were to study the Papists (though there are so many of them), let us say, the most devoted ones, they champ at the bit by tormenting themselves, and they strive so earnestly to serve God, yet all they do is performed in a spirit of vexation. If it were possible to exempt themselves, they would readily do so. Furthermore, when they have fretted over their foolish acts of devotion, they believe that God ought to be pleased with them. If we were to tell them that nothing they do is acceptable to God, that although their works are good, they have no merit in his sight, then they would spit out their venom (as they do), and blaspheme against God. How different it would be if we were to tell them that their merits make them wonderful people! Whatever we say, we can never make them see or understand what obedience to God entails. Why? Because they have never understood what it is to be at peace. This involves being able to present to God boldly and freely the works we have done; knowing this, that he will accept them only because he treats us with compassion and bears with us as sons. Of this the Papists know nothing; therefore, we must not be surprised that they find it strange when we hold fast our liberty, for they do not know what it is. Thus, Paul has good reason to say these things, and by his words we can see that such freedom is precious and not to be despised. For when Jesus Christ suffered and died and offered himself to God the Father, he was not playing: he was accomplishing a work which surpassed in excellence and importance the very creation of heaven and earth. If Paul shows us that our liberty is a wonderful fruit of the sufferings and death of the

Lord Jesus Christ, then this gift is surely something unique and of great value.

Now, in order to experience the nature and qualities of this gift, we must learn to hide ourselves in God. Let me give an example here. If certain laws and obligations are placed upon us by men, they do not detract from our liberty before God. Whatever belongs to law and order, and is either forbidden or commanded, must be obeyed for the sake of the common good. If a certain duty is required, we ought to do it, thereby serving one another in the community. Notice, therefore, that the things which pertain to law and order require that we interact in a united and harmonious way, having such a strong bond that we will serve our neighbours, and not selfishly look after our own interests. However, when it comes to spiritual liberty, we need to withdraw from the crowd in order to experience its nature and effects. I say that each one of us must come before God personally, for one day we shall give account before our heavenly judge. We are to examine ourselves within and ask, how am I to present myself before the judgment seat of God? If my life is examined according to the law, woe is me! I am guilty of an infinite number of offences, that even if there were a million deaths, it would be insufficient to pay for the sins I have committed. Yet, God desires to show me his favour, and receive me in mercy in the name of the Lord Jesus Christ. When I approach him, therefore, I can come with my head held high, having been acquitted and absolved through the sacrifice of Jesus Christ, who paid for my sin and gave me full deliverance. This is the first thing, the way in which I must serve God. Of course, I must dedicate my life to him, but how do I begin? For I cannot bring him the perfection that he requires, nor even the hundredth part of it! Well, God bears with me, and still accepts and approves that which is imperfect and weak, and even that which is mixed with sin. Why? Because he accepts me in the name of the Lord Jesus Christ as one of his own children. This, I say, is how we are to come before God if we wish to know and experience the fruit of this liberty of which Paul speaks.

When Paul says, 'be not entangled again with the yoke of bondage', he shows that before we had faith in the gospel and understood the significance of the sufferings and death of the Son of God, we were held tightly bound as prisoners and did not enjoy any freedom. Indeed, if Jesus Christ had not intervened and become the Mediator between God the Father and man, our souls would still be tormented and afflicted. For there is not one of us who does not recognise that he is more than guilty, and we would have remained in this condition, drowned in despair, had we not been rescued by the Lord Jesus Christ. Such sorrow would have been ours if we never knew how merciful God would be on us; how he would bestow peace to us, and the boldness to call upon him because Jesus Christ has gone before us. On the other hand, if we do not know that God has truly received us, and is satisfied with the obedience that we seek to render to him (though with much weakness), then we are bound by a second rope, which will strangle us. This is the case with all unbelievers. Now the gospel has shown that God loves us, and that he freely accepts us as his children in his goodness. Therefore, Paul warns us not to be trampled upon by men in their tyranny, but to be delivered from the rigorous obligations of the law which force us into slavery. We are to uphold our privileged position, now that Jesus Christ has set us free.

* * *

Let us now consider the reason that he gives: 'Behold, I Paul say unto you, that if ye be circumcised, Christ shall profit you nothing.' This statement, which tells us that circumcision can cut men off from any share in the salvation purchased by our Lord Jesus Christ, is very harsh. However, we must remember, first of all, that when Paul speaks of circumcision here, he is not referring to the act itself, but to its purpose. The seducers that had infiltrated the Galatians and corrupted the purity of the gospel wanted them to believe that a person had to be circumcised in order to keep the law. Paul stops here, and says that if we are being forced and obliged to perform this task for God and to enter into this covenant with him, Jesus Christ will not profit us. This is well worthy of our attention. Today, we say that it is hellish tyranny to command people to obey certain rules on the grounds that their failure is a mortal sin! Likewise, it is tyranny to forbid something simply because it does not please men. Someone ordained that we should keep Lent, and another, that we should confess all of our sins once a year. Now if we dispute this, the Papists, as I have said, will be thrown into a mad rage, without considering the reasons why we have been stirred up to insist upon this view. Why? Because they look no further than the external act. Yet, we must look more deeply. The Papists command that we obey, on pain of committing a mortal sin, making us think that we are obliged to do it to be acceptable to God; we have entered into a covenant with him based upon doing our duty. Whoever has fulfilled his duty has made God his debtor, according to the devilish doctrines which abound in Popery. We can only obtain grace by our merits, and the memory of our sins and iniquities can be wiped out by making our own satisfaction for sin and thereby appeasing God's wrath. We see, therefore, that if we can obtain our own pardon, Jesus Christ is made of no value and cannot profit us at all. Why? Because Jesus Christ is not our righteousness if we do not seek remission of our sins through the sacrifice of his death. We need to be sure that God is our Father, and that we can call upon him with a peaceful conscience, having been adopted through the Lord Jesus Christ.

Now, it is true that the seducers who deceived the Galatians still desired Jesus Christ to be known as the Saviour of the world. They believed both the law and the gospel, so they upheld all the titles that belonged to Jesus Christ. However, they believed that part of our salvation has to be merited, as a means of appeasing God. Thus, Jesus Christ simply supplied that which was lacking. But this leaves poor souls with troubled consciences still. The same applies today in Popery. The Pope, with all the scum of his clergy, differs nothing from the seducers that Paul is arguing against here, except, perhaps, that they used the authority of the law of Moses to push forward their own notions and make them acceptable. The people that Paul criticises here were arguing that they must observe the rite of circumcision. They said it was necessary for everyone to be circumcised. Why? In order to be guiltless before God; that, having done their duty, they may be acceptable to him. What, then, is the role of Jesus Christ? He acts as a kind of supplement; they are not saying that he has no purpose, but that he supplies the difference, after men have acquitted and absolved themselves, and only if they need extra help! Such is the speech of the seducers who opposed Paul. And what of the Pope? Instead of the ceremonial law of Moses, he says that we must obey what he ordains, and what his councils determine, or decisions of this person or that. He makes such directives compulsory, on pain of committing a mortal sin. If we have offended God, he says we can redeem ourselves through penances, rather than by doing what God has commanded. His idea of penance is not to fulfil that which has been commanded in the law, but to do even more than is required; this is how we are acquitted in God's sight and made acceptable to him. We can see, therefore, that the Pope has retained the same devilish principle that these people sought to introduce. Indeed, his sin is even worse, because instead of using the law of Moses for his authority, he bases it upon his own inventions, forged in his own mind!

Paul opposes all this, and says that Christ shall profit them nothing if they seek such a covenant with God. Why? Because it is as if they are dividing Christ, and only attributing to him half of that which is wholly his own. He is our righteousness and he is our peace (*1 Cor.* 1:30; *Eph.* 2:14). What does this word 'righteousness' imply? It means that God can freely accept us through the Lord Jesus Christ. If we say that we can please God by our merits, and that Jesus Christ simply completes that which we lack, are we not tearing him in two, and dismembering him as far as is in our power? We are not to do such a thing, nor allow others to do so. Furthermore, our Lord Jesus Christ has paid for our sins, and there is no other means of being reconciled to God than the knowledge that he has delivered and rescued us from the penalty of eternal death. If we think that we can purchase our own redemption through our own merits, and believe that the rest will come from him, as a small addition, we are openly mocking him, which is abominable. We see why Paul says that Jesus Christ will not profit in such circumstances; he wants men to stop deceiving themselves by creating a Jesus Christ who only partially fulfils his office. No; we must receive him as he is revealed to us by God the Father. He has been given to us so that we might not trust in anything else, but have recourse to him alone. We are to be content to have him as our Head, and we must serve God the Father with all that we have, knowing that although it amounts to nothing, yet he is pleased with it through our adoption in the Lord Jesus Christ. It is this which makes us ourselves and all our works acceptable to God. Ourselves, I say, though we are worthless, and our works, though they are vain. God is pleased with them because he does not take account of what we are, or of what we have done, nor of the quality or quantity of our works. He is interested in the fact that we have come to him, as members of the body of his only Son, leaning entirely upon the sacrifice by which he bought us.

This is why Paul adds, for the greater confirmation of the same, 'I testify again to every man that is circumcised, that he is a debtor to do the whole law.' If we wish to justify ourselves in this way, he says, Christ will not profit us. We have here a very straightforward and articulate statement of what Paul said earlier, and we must pay attention to it, for it is difficult to persuade people that Christ is of no value at all if they seek to make use of him only in part. For although the Turks and pagans have not even known Jesus Christ, they have a similar view to the Papists, and we will find much conformity between them. For there have never been any pagan people in this world who have believed that we cannot please God. They have always boasted about their good deeds and thought that their salvation depended upon them. Pagans have, therefore, always believed that they can obtain grace and merit favour in God's sight. Hence, they have offered sacrifices to him, unaware that these are a figure of the Lord Jesus Christ, hoping to bring God a propitiation. This, also, was done by the Jews, having defiled and corrupted the true significance of the law. The Papists follow suit today. They are certain that God accepts what they do, and is somehow indebted to them. They enter into a covenant with him whereby he is compelled to accept what they do, though they have failed him. (For on the one hand, they readily accept that they cannot achieve everything perfectly – although, on the other hand, they claim that they can accomplish more than God has required of them, and that this serves as payment!) Now, because it is difficult to persuade men that Jesus Christ cannot serve as part-payment, we must give all the more attention to this passage, where Paul tells us that whoever is circumcised is a debtor to perform the whole law.

Firstly, when Paul speaks of circumcision, he is not referring to that which was instituted by God. Why, indeed, did he ask this of Abraham? It was a seal of the righteousness that comes through faith, as Paul himself says in the fourth chapter to the Romans (*Rom.* 4:11). When Abraham was circumcised, it did not make him a debtor to keep the whole law: on the contrary, it was to obtain remission of his sins, and to assure him that God accepted him as one of his children in the name of the Lord Jesus Christ. Therefore, circumcision set our father Abraham free! Why did he do it? Because it was a sacrament that reminded him of the free mercy of God. Those with whom Paul argues here took circumcision as a meritorious work, hoping to obtain God's favour by it. They saw it as a covenant which said, 'I have declared my allegiance to you by doing this, and now I seek a reward'. If we enter such a covenant with God, then we are debtors to keep the whole law. In other words, Paul is saying that we cannot bargain with God. Men must not imagine that they can please God in part, and that he is, therefore, obligated to them. He is not bound to allow them into his paradise because they have done this or that. No, no, says

Paul, we must reach heaven by very different means; we are not to have this notion of a mutual covenant with God, which makes him obligated to grant us eternal life in return for compulsory observation of the law. If this is what we have believed, then we are debtors to keep the whole law.

In brief, Paul contends here with the Satanic doctrine which holds sway in Popery today. They speak of partial righteousness, which means that part of it proceeds from the grace of God, whilst the other portion is supplied by meritorious works. How could this be? After all, it is quite obvious that there has never been a man alive in this world who has fulfilled the whole law of God. Experience proves this so clearly! Since the Papists realise the truth of this, it being most evident, as I say, that no man can keep all of the law, they have the effrontery to say, 'Oh, we do not believe that a person can be completely righteous in every way, and therefore Jesus Christ is our righteousness and our Redeemer in part. The rest we merit through our good deeds!' Shame, shame, says Paul. If you imagine that you have an agreement with God whereby you have merited something from him, and deserve a reward because you have placed him in your debt; if, I say, you are so mercenary as to say, 'I have done this, now you must do that', you have made yourself a debtor to do the whole law. These are foolish notions; men are deceiving themselves by thinking that God accepts all that they do, yet will ignore all that they have omitted to do. For example, a man owes a hundred pounds, and has to pay it back. Yet, he thinks his creditor ought to be content if he gives him four pounds, and says, 'Here. Take this as payment'. Then he brings him another six, then ten. Finally, after much ado, he has paid him a third or a quarter of the sum owed. Now, if he believed that he had acquitted himself of the debt by doing this, would it not amount to wicked ingratitude? His friend had opened his purse to help him at a time of need, and did not spare anything in order to support him. Yet, he wants to be acquitted of the debt because he has given back I know not what, saying 'Take this as payment', when he has not even paid a quarter of the total amount. We can see that this would be ridiculous. What, then, of those who want to enter into account with God by their merits? For God has said, and Paul has already quoted this for us, that whoever does not keep all the things that are written in the law is accursed.

What, then, are our obligations under the law? To observe it perfectly. And who is able to accomplish this? There is not one who can fulfil even a single requirement to perfection. Yet, what do these hypocrites do, who believe they can be worthy through their own works? They do this and that, hoping to be righteous in part at least. God will accept none of it. He will never retract the following statement, which he made with his own mouth, 'Cursed be he that confirmeth not all the words of this law to do them' (*Deut.* 27:26). This is why Paul insists here that whoever is circumcised is a debtor to keep the whole law. It is as if he were saying, 'Do not deceive yourselves any longer. God does not have two paths. He has declared in the law that whoever does not perfectly fulfil it is accursed.' There is not one who has succeeded, so that leaves us all under this curse. There is but one remedy, and that is to come to the Lord Jesus Christ. It is wrong to believe in the partial value of Jesus Christ, whilst holding on to I know not what of our own. We ought, rather, to confess that we are under the curse until our Lord Jesus Christ has freed us and we have sought all that we need in him. We need to confess that all our works are of no value, and that they stink in the eyes of God, until he owns us as his children, and enables us to walk in liberty of conscience, knowing that our sins are forgiven by virtue of the pardon that he obtained for us. Now, God no longer imputes our sins and iniquities to us, because he sees us as we are in the person of his only Son.

This is how Paul sets out to prove what he said earlier, that Jesus Christ is of no profit to those who have been circumcised. Why? Because, if they seek salvation through works, they must achieve all that God requires, and not bits and pieces (as they say). They must accomplish the whole law, without omitting anything. Who is able to do this? If we were to select the most holy and perfect person that we could find, he could not even perform a hundredth part of that which has been commanded. Thus, men are bereft of any hope of salvation unless they come emptied of all their 'merits' and fully lean on the Lord Jesus Christ, knowing that they cannot be justified by him or by his grace unless they have renounced all those things in which they once trusted.

Furthermore, when Paul speaks of circumcision here, he means the erroneous view of it spread by these seducers, imagining that they were winning God's favour and fulfilling the law. Similarly today, all who keep the papal ordinances are overturning the authority of the Lord Jesus Christ. I am not saying that a man will be condemned for refusing to eat meat on Fridays or on fast days; yet, if he abstains from meat out of superstition, and believes he is meriting God's favour by so doing, then he is rejecting the Lord Jesus Christ. He was given to us as our Advocate, in order to reconcile us to God the Father. He has set us free so that we have no need of human traditions. Many keep the papal ordinances because they believe it is a mortal sin to eat meat on a certain day, and that, by abstaining, they deserve God's mercy because they have satisfied him. They even think that they are honouring Jesus Christ when they make confession, or do this or that! They believe that the door of heaven will remain closed to them unless they open it by confession, thinking that, by this means, they can appease God. Thus, by believing these things, they make themselves debtors (as I have said), and reject the grace obtained for them by the Lord Jesus Christ.

Let us now apply this doctrine to our profit. In the first place, we know that God has declared in the gospel that whenever we come to him (unless we are vexed and perturbed, like reeds shaking in the wind), we are to call upon him freely and openly as our Father, who has adopted us as his children. Secondly, the only way we can be pleasing to him is through having our sins forgiven. How? Jesus Christ has fully paid the price, and given us complete pardon. However, we know that this does not mean that we are to remove our bridles and please ourselves, like wild animals that cannot be tamed by God. No, rather, we must come to him freely, willing to obey him. We need the assurance that he accepts us as his children and supports us so compassionately that he approves of what we do, though it is worthless, because of the fatherly love he bears us. If we do not have this assurance, the thought of serving God will make us grind our teeth. If, however, we are persuaded that God looks upon us favourably; if, though we are weak and can do nothing worthy of his approval, he accepts us in the name of the Lord Jesus Christ, then we will surely be filled with courage. We will be like a ship's sail that has been stretched and filled by the breeze! Thus, our hearts will run to obey him, like a ship driven along by its sail, when we know that God delights in us and accepts our works, not wanting us to be compelled into servitude. He is happy for us to be his children, and that we desire to obey him. Knowing this, we can serve our God with all the more zeal. With his grace as our foundation, we are so filled with his joy that we can offer the sacrifice of praise. Likewise, having sought him in prayer, we can know that he will answer us and, in return, we can thank him for the priceless gifts that he communicates to us every day.

Now let us fall down before the majesty of our great God, acknowledging our sins, and praying that it would please him to make us more conscious of them, so that we are truly humbled, and give ourselves wholly to the Lord Jesus Christ. Having come to him, may we persevere in the faith of the gospel, without drawing back in any way whatever. May he support us in our infirmity, when we are touched with our need for true repentance. May we tremble and groan before him, until the day that he delivers us from this mortal body, which, like a prison, confines us in bondage to sin. Thus, we all say, Almighty God, and our heavenly Father, etc.

32

Not Ceremonies, but Faith Which Works by Love

Christ is become of no effect unto you, whosoever of you are justified by the law; ye are fallen from grace. For we through the Spirit wait for the hope of righteousness by faith. For in Jesus Christ neither circumcision availeth any thing, nor uncircumcision: but faith which worketh by love (Gal. 5:4–6).

We saw last time that those who sought to give equal weight to both their own merits and the grace of God were greatly deceived; for when they are to face judgment, God will deal with them most severely. If we claim to be pleasing to him, and to deserve salvation through our own works, then we must fulfil the whole law, and be irreprovable. But consider whether there has ever been a man who has attained such perfection. It is evident that we all fall far short of it. Therefore, we must come empty to God, that he might receive us mercifully, and declare that he will impute the obedience of the Lord Jesus Christ to our account. We must cast aside all 'merit', and base nothing upon the law other than a simple and clear confession of the fact that we are lost and condemned. This is the case until God takes pity on us and, having buried our transgressions and sins, clothes and equips us with the righteousness of the Lord Jesus Christ, his Son.

Hence, Paul concludes here that those who wish to be justified by the law have fallen from grace, and Jesus Christ will no longer profit them. He does not speak in this way without good reason, for the seducers who had infiltrated the Galatian church tampered with the doctrines of the gospel. They sought to blend two things: that is, the notion that Jesus Christ was given in order to supply our deficiency, with the notion that by endeavouring to do good, we can obtain a partial righteousness of our own. They did not fully reject the Lord Jesus Christ, nor were they saying that God's promises, where he declares that he will forgive the sins of his faithful people through his mercy, are a deception or a lie. However, they wanted people to strive to justify themselves, that is, to win God's favour by their own works. Yet, because man is far from perfect, they needed Jesus Christ to assist them as a kind of second part of the remedy. Such was their conception. Similarly, in Popery today, you will not hear them loudly proclaiming the blasphemy that Jesus Christ is of no value, apart from teaching us the will of God the Father. They will say that he has redeemed us, and achieved the most important work of merit, for he opened the door of paradise for us, that we might enter. They will also say that his sufferings and death profit us daily by reconciling us when we have offended God. Yet, nevertheless, they still want to merit the kingdom of paradise to some extent, and therefore claim that we can pay for our sins in a number of ways. Then come the various penances, and finally, if a man does not succeed in fulfilling his duty during his lifetime, he can accomplish the rest in purgatory! Thus, Jesus Christ has a kind of half-role in helping us to be accepted by God. Yet, they, discount him by making such things as free will, merit, works of supererogation, as they call them, amongst other things, responsible for obtaining at least half of our salvation.

Now Paul tells us that God will not own such a mixture, for we must bring him a full obedience to the law, in which he can delight, or else we will be sentenced to condemnation. If he finds a fault, however small it may be, none of the rest is of any merit, for, as we have declared, God does not promise salvation to those who have half served him, or obeyed to some extent, but to those who have kept the whole law: 'Which if a man do, he shall live in them' (*Lev.* 18:5), and in the negative, 'Cursed be he that confirmeth not all the words of this law to do them' (*Deut.* 27:26). Now it is the case that none of us do what is required and commanded in the law. Whatever righteous zeal and desire we may have to serve God, there will always be much weakness. We will come to him limping, taking many wrong steps, and often we will even wander and stray away. Thus, when it comes to our works, we are all excluded from the promise of salvation. Our judgment is prepared for us and we cannot escape it, for who is so bold as to presume that he has fulfilled the law? If, therefore, we are all found guilty of having offended God, we are all lost forever in the pit of hell, until the Lord Jesus Christ stretches out his hand towards us. It follows, then, that we must forget the righteousness of the law, and tread it underfoot. May it be cancelled out altogether, that we might come to our Lord Jesus Christ naked, to beg, confessing our poverty. We must be unafraid to stand before God in all our shame and ignominy if we are to be clothed in his glory.

These are the main points we are to retain from this passage, for Paul says that Jesus Christ has become unprofitable if men seek to be justified by the law. Such a misconception has been common since time began. In the first place, men simply wished to pay God all that was due to him, and then, seeing that they did not have the faculties or resources within themselves, they resorted to this subterfuge: 'Well, since we cannot do it all, we will do part of it.' But it is not a question of following our own imaginations, for God will judge us by his Word. The proverb says, 'Do nothing without our host', and so we must never presume that God will accept whatever seems right in our eyes. We must recognise that Jesus Christ cannot profit us unless we seek full salvation in him. For it does not say in Scripture that the Father gave him to us in order to help us obtain salvation, but rather that he was given to us to be our righteousness and our life. It follows, therefore, that in our persons, God will only find iniquity and eternal death until in Jesus Christ we recover that which we lost in Adam, and of which we are altogether bereft.

Notice that these two things are placed in conjunction here: that Jesus Christ has become unprofitable, and that we have fallen from grace. Truly, all the grace we are to seek from God is communicated by means of the Lord Jesus Christ. This is a noteworthy point, for everyone will admit that we need to have recourse to God as the fountain of all good. Yet, most go astray on their journey and, instead of coming to God, they turn aside. Just as in Popery, where those wretched bigots and ignorant souls blindly run after their saints and their grotesque images, as they torment themselves over their foolish acts of devotion. They will tell you openly that they do it to obtain the grace of God. Meanwhile, Jesus Christ is left to one side, and no-one notices the fact. They would rather address a statue, which they call 'Our Lady', than the Son of God. How has all this come about? It is because they do not know that God has poured out his grace upon us; neither do they understand how we are to seek him, or the conduct and behaviour expected of us. Once we have discovered that God is our Father, and once we are persuaded that we are to search for all that we need in the Lord Jesus Christ, then we realise that God's grace can never be stifled. It is like an underground spring, which, when uncovered, flows freely so that all may satisfy their thirst. However, it will not flow to us except through the Lord Jesus Christ. In short, all that appertains to our salvation has been placed in the person of the only Son of God; therefore, he must be all-sufficient for us and we must come directly to him, contenting ourselves with him alone. As I have said, keep yourselves from the notion that we can obtain anything through our own merit, for this will only serve to separate us from our Lord Jesus Christ.

* * *

At this point, Paul adds that 'we through the Spirit wait for the hope of righteousness by faith'. He says this to confirm what he had said previously concerning the difference between ourselves and our forefathers who lived under the law. Now, how did Abraham receive God's favour, if not by faith? Yet he differed from us in one respect: he had been given ceremonies to observe because Jesus Christ had not yet been revealed. There were many more ceremonies later when the law was established, because that is the way the people needed to be led and guided. Thus, although believers in all ages have always sought perfect righteousness through God's grace, they were aided by the ceremonies and shadows. This was so because the gospel had not been revealed to them as it has to us, and Jesus Christ, our true righteousness, had not yet been manifested. Let us now look at what Paul says here: he implies that the Spirit dwells with Christians today in order to put an end to all the types and shadows. Paul is saying, in effect, that we are to be contented now that the Son of God has appeared as our righteousness, and at the same time abandon the ceremonies, for, he says, today the shadows are superfluous. It is not in this passage alone that Paul speaks of the Spirit in opposition to the shadows of the law. Now, when God ordained circumcision, sacrifices and the like in former days, he was not seeking simply to entertain the people on earth, for all that is contained in the law is truly spiritual. Think of the pattern that Moses was shown on the mountain (*Exod.* 25:40). It is certain that our forefathers had a spiritual faith like ours, and realised that they could not be washed and cleansed by three drops of water, nor reconciled to God by the sacrifice of a calf or of any other brute beast. They knew that the only cleansing and purging possible was through the Lord Jesus Christ, and that through his sacrificial death they had been pardoned – or would be, in that the task was not yet accomplished. Our forefathers anticipated that which had not been shown to them.

Yet, this is not mentioned without good reason, for Paul is showing that our forefathers could only embrace the grace of our Lord Jesus Christ by observing the means that God had appointed for those days. Thus, when a person had failed God, he would come before him and confess, by offering a sacrifice, that he deserved to die; not that he was seeking reconciliation through a calf or lamb or any such thing, but in Jesus Christ. Thus, the ceremony was intended to prefigure Christ. The same applies to the ceremonial washings and the rest. Today, we have the body, says Paul, and therefore the shadows are no longer required (*Col.* 2:17). If a man is standing right in front of me, why would I want to recognise him by his shadow? It would not be as clear as looking at his face! How foolish it would be to turn away from him and seek out some other means of meeting him! Yet, the same is true of those who return to the former types and shadows. They turn their backs upon Jesus Christ, not realising that when he died, the veil of the temple was torn, thus signifying the abolition of the former shadows and our access into the heavenly sanctuary, which at one time was far from us. To summarise, Paul is seeking to declare here that when he condemns the ceremonies of the law, he is not speaking against our forefathers who observed them, nor God, as their author. Rather, it is because we now have Jesus Christ, their substance and their true fulfilment. Now, the things that were shadowy before are clear, for he is all perfection, and we are to content ourselves with him. Thus much for the ceremonies of the law.

Now, when Paul says that 'we through the Spirit wait for the hope of righteousness', we may find his mode of expression strange. What does he mean by 'waiting for the hope of righteousness'? Well, Paul is intending to draw us away from all that we see around us in this world. We are too much inclined to dwell upon things here below; when we have some object upon our minds, we cannot lift our thoughts above. This is because men are carnal, and want to see everything with their eyes. But God points us to his pure and simple Word in order to test our obedience. The best homage that we could pay him would be to close our eyes to all these things, content with the knowledge that God has made known his will to us, and able to proceed as those who lack nothing. For the word 'wait' implies that we cannot see with our eyes that for which we long, as it says in the eighth chapter to the Romans, even adding the same word 'hope' with it. It is as if Paul were saying, 'My friends, if we wish to know what the righteousness of a Christian signifies, it is that he is a child of God and an heir of eternal life, God accepting him as if he were an angel, without spot or stain.' If we want to see this from the perspective of the world, we will be disappointed, for we see that believers are despised. Other folk scarcely condescend to look at them, except to give a fleeting glance. They also have humble status by the world's standards. Indeed, there is no pomp, no special show in the righteousness that comes from the Lord Jesus Christ. When we say that we cannot stand before God without his mercy, that we depend entirely upon him for all our good deeds, and that we must forget ourselves and seek perfection only through Jesus Christ, we do not say such things in order to be admired! When we speak thus, we are not seeking to be esteemed; we are confessing that we are full of shameful things, and that all our supposed dignity is dung and filth. All our works are corrupt and we are abominable in God's sight; as full of rottenness as poor lepers, that is, until we have been washed and cleansed by the blood of the Lord Jesus Christ and made acceptable to God through him.

The righteousness that believers possess, therefore, is not a thing of great splendour, nor something that causes them to be held in admiration and highly praised; not at all! It implies complete poverty. Hence, Paul says here that the world will mock at our simplicity, when it sees that our hope is in Jesus Christ, and that we humbly condemn ourselves to the pit of hell, that we might be raised up to the kingdom of heaven by the grace of God. However much the world mocks at this, let us persevere in constancy, knowing that we will not be disappointed. For we know who it is that guards our inheritance; and it is he who has promised to bring us to full salvation. Let us walk in this confidence, and embrace Jesus Christ. Once he is ours, we may despise the rest. May we never dishonour and disgrace him by withdrawing into a corner, as it were, and only serving him half-heartedly. Let us acknowledge that our justification is entirely due to him.

We could ask a question at this point, which is, Have the ceremonies of the law been ordained for no purpose? It is true that Paul has already answered this question amply, but because men are slow to respond when it is a matter of keeping to the purity of the truth of God, he feels the need to refer again to the difference between ourselves and those who lived before the coming of the Lord Jesus Christ. His intention is also to close the mouths of the many opponents, for as soon as we preach the mercy of God in Jesus Christ, there are big watchdogs around who bark and advance their slanderous opinions. This is still the case today. If we condemn this hellish trust that men have when they deceive themselves into thinking they can obtain salvation by their own merits, they exclaim, 'Oh! So you are condemning all good works, are you?'. These hypocrites denounce the gospel teachings that we proclaim, as if we were seeking to give licence to evil, as if we were teaching that there is no difference between vice and virtue. When we remonstrate about their ceremonies being nothing but insignificant baggage, and that their boasting about them is abomination to God, they exclaim, 'Oh! So you are banning all acts of devotion, are you? Should not God be served and honoured still?' This is the language and style of the scoundrels around today who cannot accept that the Lord Jesus Christ is the only foundation, and that we must place all our trust in him alone for our salvation. Nor do they accept that we must be governed by the pure and simple Word of God.

* * *

For this reason, Paul says here that 'in Jesus Christ neither circumcision availeth anything, nor uncircumcision; but faith which worketh by love'. By saying that there is neither circumcision nor uncircumcision in Jesus Christ, he means that when God ordained the ceremonies, they were to be temporary. We are always to remember their purpose, which was to give the people hope before the appearing of Jesus Christ. For without those washings, sacrifices and the like, they would have been lost and, judging by man's weakness, would have failed God a hundred thousand times more. Yet, although they did not see clearly the means of their salvation, they had these symbols and vivid pictures in which they could appreciate the grace of God. Thus, these types and shadows served a purpose in their time. Paul does not wish to undermine the authority of God, who established the law for the Jews by saying that all of it was worthless or fruitless. Rather, he is saying that we have reached the fulness of time, now that our Lord Jesus Christ has been made manifest. There is no longer a veil which prevents us from seeing him face to face as we find him revealed in the gospel. For every time the gospel is preached, it is as if we were seeing the Son of God crucified for us, as if we were seeing his blood flowing and were washed in it through the power of the Holy Spirit, as Peter says in his first epistle (*1 Pet.* 1:19). Therefore, now that our Lord Jesus Christ, through his death and passion, has shown us the way to God the Father, we need no longer observe that which was ordained for the period of his absence. It is true that he no longer lives on this earth, but we have his gospel, which contains everything necessary for our salvation. Thus, it is as if he were crucified in our midst, as Paul has already said (*Gal.* 3:1).

Now that we understand what Paul means when he says 'in Jesus Christ', that is, since the gospel message has been preached, let us come to the rest of the statement, which tells us that there is neither circumcision nor uncircumcision. In other words, these things have ceased today, but love remains. Why does Paul mention the word 'love'? To show that Christians could not be lazy and would have plenty with which to occupy themselves, even though they no longer observed the types of the law. Now, God's intention was to bring his people to Jesus Christ when he appointed the sacrifices, circumcision and all the rest. Yet man, because he is depraved, corrupted this. In fact, the Jews thought that by coming to offer sacrifices, they were placing God under an obligation to them. It was quite the opposite, for coming to present a sacrifice meant that you were making a solemn confession that you deserved God's curse, as if you were saying, ' I deserve to die. Here is a poor animal that has been killed, its neck has been slit, and did it deserve it? Not at all!' Here is a man who can see his own guilt there, and he also realises that he must look for salvation outside of himself. Thus, I tell you, the types ought to have led people to such a state of humility that all of them, from the greatest to the least, condemned themselves. Then, having embraced the grace of the Lord Jesus Christ, they were to lean upon him entirely.

In Popery today there is a similar deception by which men misuse all that God has ordained. What do I mean? Look at baptism and the Lord's supper, which were instituted for us to come before God and acknowledge that all that we have is from him. What is the purpose of baptism? It shows us that we must die to ourselves. Why? Because we are corrupt and accursed, children of wrath and completely cut off from God. Thus, baptism excludes all trust in ourselves. At the Lord's supper, we come to seek life in Jesus Christ; we are, therefore, dead. Yet, the Papists still believe that these are meritorious works! Thus, through their hellish abomination of the Mass, they have falsified, indeed, obliterated, all that the Lord Jesus Christ has established. For a work that has been carried out by a man, which has proceeded entirely from him, must, they say, be meritorious. Now, we can see a very glaring error here; yet Paul wanted to take the matter even further by challenging the hypocrisy of those who are given over to external things, just as those in Popery today. Yes, these wretches work hard to serve God: there are no limits to their striving, but what do they achieve? They torment themselves over vanities, things that God has never required and of which he even disapproves. There is much falsehood in what they do. For what does the most devoted of them do, except to dabble in this and that? They will hear evensong and two or three Masses; they will rush to go on pilgrimage, fast during Lent and on other fast days. They observe all this nonsense which has been conceived in the mind of men; for what are all these things? If you put your confidence in these things, you will discover that they are the inventions of the devil; the real sin is that every person is following his own imagination. To God, these antics are little more than tomfoolery. Why? Because he prefers obedience to sacrifice. Therefore, if we wish to obey God, we must serve him spiritually, and not with these children's game.

* * *

Let us come now to the words of Paul, which tell us that circumcision is nothing in comparison with faith, which works by love. By this, he means that when the ceremonies were removed, we were still left with a sufficient task: to fulfil what God has commanded. Now, we are told that all the holiness and perfection of believers lies in love. Love is the fulfilment of the law; it is the end and the goal that God wants us to reach. If, therefore, we have love, we must not think that we are of no value.

Today, we criticise the superstitions that abound in Popery, and we mock them, saying, 'What a lot of rubbish you practise! When you go to church, you sprinkle yourselves with holy water, you bow before an image, you go from altar to altar, you do this and that. Indeed, there is a labyrinth of all this nonsense. Poor souls, do you think all this will count? God will have none of it.' Their answer is, 'What! Must we not serve God? What are we to do for him?' It seems to them that unless they go to Mass, make confession, pay for their sins, and do this and that, there is nothing left for them to do. Yet, we can see that they neglect the most important thing. For even the most committed of them have not stopped being coarse, or blaspheming against God, or stealing and plundering; indeed, when the one who does most of these 'acts of service' sees an occasion to rob his neighbours, he will eat them down to the bone! So cruel are they, that they seem more like wild animals than men! Yet, they appear very refined, and are full of cunning; they will think nothing of perjuring themselves if they can succeed in deceiving someone. For they feed upon such wickedness, and think that God will act as a cloak for it when they compose their faces to look devout. It is this same hypocrisy which the Lord Jesus Christ compares to a den of thieves (*Matt.* 21:13). In other words, it is common for men to forget the most important things when they devote themselves to observing ceremonies. Our Lord Jesus Christ reproaches people for sinning against the commandments of God the Father through their traditions (*Matt.* 15:3). This is what it says in the fiftieth Psalm (*Psa.* 50:13), that God does not desire the blood of brute beasts. If I am hungry, says the Lord, do you not think that the whole world is mine? You ought to offer me the sacrifice of praise, he says.

We have seen Paul's intention here. He is mocking hypocrites who think that all is lost without pomp and finery, that when we come to church, we must do so looking like a banner that is on display. We see them carry out their rituals with their candles, perfumes, candelabra, dressed up in their robes with their images and the like. With all this, they imagine that they are hidden, that God no longer sees them, and that their vices are obscured by the shadows; yet, their rebellion is evident for all to see. Paul mocks such futile opinions and says that, in the absence of all these rituals, there is still plenty that God has for us to occupy ourselves with: namely, love. In short, Paul is expressing here that God's service is spiritual, for in loving our neighbours, we are testifying to the love of God. This is, of course, if we love them aright; for it is not praiseworthy if we love someone in order to profit in some way. But we must love even our enemies, and patiently bear the hurt that they cause us, and seek to do good to those who need help, without receiving anything ourselves, or gaining personal advantage. As members of the same body, we are to support one another as far as possible. If this is the case, then our life will surely answer and testify to the fact that we love God. We cannot love him if we do not know him; love, therefore, is a sure sign and mark of the fact that we desire to serve God, not by presenting him with a bundle of straw, but by loving our neighbours in truth and sincerity. Although the Papists boast as much as they can about their pompous displays and fine appearances, by which they would hope to deceive God, as if they were mocking him, the case will always be as Paul declares here: these things are nothing in the eyes of God. Why? Because if circumcision has come to an end now that the fulness of time has arrived, what need have we of all these things, foolishly devised in a man's brain, with great arrogance usurping that which was neither theirs in the first place, nor lawful for them to do. This is what we are to remember.

Before we go any further, we ought to answer the case that the Papists make here; for they say that because Paul speaks of faith working by love as the aim of all believers, they have won their argument. From this, they conclude that it is not faith alone that is needed to obtain grace, but also love. Imagine for a moment that this was true – how would this benefit them? For all their merits consist in playing children's games, as if they thought they could appease God with a toy. But Paul's intention here is quite different, for as he has described the true way to be acceptable to God up to this point, he would not here wish to base our righteousness or hope of salvation upon our love. What, then, is he saying? He shows us that God has given enough to exercise believers without the ceremonies which hypocrites so mistakenly observe, and regard as so necessary. In brief, we can see that Paul is taking direct issue with the Papists, and does not support them in any way. Seeking to hide behind this text, they regard faith as simply a matter of acknowledging that there is a God, and that Jesus Christ his only Son has appeared for the redemption and salvation of the human race. But this knowledge is without feeling, just as when we have been told a story which we believe, and regard as true. This is how Papists view faith. They say that faith alone is not yet complete in the eyes of God; it needs to be established by heart-felt affection and love for God, they say. But when the Scriptures speak of faith, they mean the knowledge which has been granted to us by the Holy Spirit, not an idea that simply flutters around in our head. It is sealed upon our hearts, which demonstrates that a miraculous work of God had taken place within us before we could be illuminated and established in the faith. For our souls dwell in darkness before this happens. The light must shine from above. We are also inclined to rebellion in every way, and need the Holy Spirit to inscribe upon our hearts that we are truly saved by the Lord Jesus Christ. Furthermore, it is not enough to have a vague knowledge of the fact that Jesus Christ is the Redeemer. Faith means that each of us knows him to be our redeemer. Is this possible unless the Lord Jesus lives and reigns within us, causing his love to burn within us, that we might give ourselves solely to him? The Papists have never understood the meaning of faith, though they warble on about it. A magpie in a cage has some understanding, yet they display such awful stupidity that they reveal, as in a mirror, the terrible vengeance of God; for they have forgotten the work of the Holy Spirit, and know nothing of the Holy Scriptures. They know no more than a pagan or Turk who has lived his entire life in barbarism, and who has never heard of God, the Father of the Lord Jesus Christ. This is where the Papists remain.

Let us note, therefore, that Paul is not thinking of this distorted view of faith that they possess; he is not teaching that love brings us justification. He is simply saying that we have plenty of work to do in order to serve God, without becoming entangled in such trifling matters. To gain from this message (which we must soon end, time not permitting us to go any further), we must learn, for our part, to despise the view that the Papists have today when they boast about their more external service of God, which glitters with more apparent brilliance than ours. Why? Because God does not wish to be served according to the desires of man. This is the first point. What the Papists call divine service consists of ridiculous trifles which they have devised and imagined in their heads; but although men applaud it and rejoice in it, God rejects it all. Let us, therefore, be careful to serve God in the way that he requires. What does he want us to do? We are not to perform useless tasks, but to live a life that, when tested, will not disappoint him. We must behave in an upright and just manner towards our neighbours; each of us according to our ability must help those in need of pity. We must not be selfish, but faithful, loyal and genuine. We must be peace-lovers; if we see someone who is deprived in some way, and needs our help, we are to offer ourselves like a sacrifice for God, knowing that he has called us to show the love we have for him. For if we cannot love our neighbours as human beings, how can we love God (as John says in his letter, *1 John* 4:20), whom we cannot see, who is separate from us, and who is in need of nothing?

Let us learn that in order to serve God well, we must render him the kind of obedience that he will accept, which is that we behave uprightly and with compassion, without cheating, plundering, or deceiving our neighbours. Not only are we to abstain from all harm and evil-doing, but we are to give ourselves to well-doing as far as possible. Those of us who call ourselves Christians, let us learn from the words of the Lord Jesus Christ (*Matt.* 23:23). He says, Woe to you who separate yourselves for the worship of God, amusing yourselves with petty trifles, being scrupulous in every detail, yet forgetting the principal matters of the law, such as faith, judgment, justice and mercy. It is as if he were saying, 'Is it not strange that men mock God in this way, pretending to honour him, as if they took him to be but a little child? They seek to please him with all manner of worthless things, whereas God desires a life that is upright and faithful. He wants us to have compassion, to help the destitute, and not to wrong our brothers. Men are filled with cruelty, deception, and malice, yet they think they can please God by things of no value.' Let us learn, therefore, to serve God in love, that is, to devote ourselves to doing what he has called us to do, and to keep ourselves committed forever to the teachings that are revealed in his Word. Finally, whereas we are to deal justly with men, we are not to forget God. For as I have already said, this is the way he tests our love for him. It is, therefore, a means of revealing the love and respect that we bear him. When we love our neighbours, it does not mean that we neglect to call upon God, for we do not wish to displease him whilst trying to help our neighbours! He must be our desired haven, on whom our eyes are fixed.

Now, to conclude, we must seek to live as God has commanded in his Word, and not occupy ourselves with the pomp, splendour and ceremonies that hypocrites love. We are to walk honestly in purity of life, with all equity and straightforwardness, as I have said. But we are to recognise that when we have done all this, it cannot justify us or obtain God's grace for us. Whilst it is true that he is pleased to accept the desire that we have to honour him, he still only accepts us through the Lord Jesus Christ, as we have explained before. It is here that we are to place our trust for salvation. Thus, even when we have walked in love, and sought to carry out our duty, we must realise that because of our weakness, we cannot approach the standard that God has shown us. We aim to do so, but we need God to look upon us mercifully. Thus, we need not doubt that he is pleased with our works, if they are dedicated to him through the blood of the Lord Jesus Christ, who is the true priest who presents our offerings and makes them acceptable to God. We need our Lord Jesus to intercede, to make our works pleasing to God the Father. Even when we pray or sing praise to him, it would all be dung to him if not purified by the Lord Jesus Christ. Indeed, the apostle says that it is by him that we offer to God the sacrifice of our lips, that is the sacrifice of praise by which he is glorified (*Heb.* 13:15).

Now let us fall down before the majesty of our great God, acknowledging our sins, and praying that he would help us to be more conscious of them. May we truly be convicted by them so that we are brought to a true repentance and seek in the Lord Jesus Christ all that we need. May we be so humbled that we are totally cast down and get rid of all false presumption which we may wrongly have. May our only desire be to be received by the mercy of our God and reach the eternal inheritance. May we so strive to walk according to his commandments, that he will be pleased to support us in our weakness until the day that we are altogether free of it. Thus, we all say, Almighty God and our heavenly Father, etc.

33

Fighting to the End for God's Pure and Infallible Truth

> *Ye did run well; who did hinder you that ye should not obey the truth? This persuasion cometh not of him that calleth you. A little leaven leaveneth the whole lump. I have confidence in you through the Lord, that ye will be none otherwise minded: but he that troubleth you shall bear his judgment, whosoever he be* (Gal. 5:7–10).

If we listen to the Word of God, we can know that God will so order our lives that we need never find ourselves wandering aimlessly. We can know for certain the right path. This is the difference between believers and unbelievers; a person who submits to the Word of God cannot be in any doubt or uncertainty about whether or not God approves of what they do. Who else has the authority to direct our lives but God? He has already proclaimed his will. Thus, as life is compared here to a race, let us learn to follow the route that God has called us to run, and not be like vagabonds, or poor ignorant folk who fret and torment themselves in vain. In this passage, Paul speaks of two forms of race: one which is good and which consists of a straight run, and the other which leads us astray. It is not enough for men to strive – they need a fixed destination. Here we see the true definition of a race which could be termed 'good', and also that of a race where men torture themselves in vain.

Paul's exposition here is reliable and accurate, when he

says that all who obey the truth run well. This statement is a weighty one. From it we gather that when men are given over to their own fantasies, living according to their own notions – or when they receive what they are told without wisdom or discernment, they may, indeed, run fast, but they will not draw any closer to God. Even if they spend their whole lives fretting, they will find themselves further from him than ever before. Therefore, we must begin by listening to God, who has shown us his grace and favour by teaching us; we must recognise that there is no truth but that which proceeds from him. When men follow that which has been devised in their own minds, it can only consist of lies and fables. This is how we are to apply this text of Paul's to our own use. We must realise, firstly, that all the devotions that were ever conceived in the mind of man are the illusions of Satan. All who observe that which is right in their own eyes may trot along, but they will not be progressing along the right path. In fact, they will be moving in the opposite direction! Only obedience to God's truth constitutes running a good race.

Now, if this were widely recognised in the world today, there would not be as much trouble and debate as we see now. Why are we failing to live in harmony with each other, joining hands with our neighbours? Because the greater part of them will not be persuaded to obey God. The true course of a Christian is well described by the prophet Isaiah, when he says that each of us will take the hand of our friend and say, 'Come ye, and let us go up to the mountain of the Lord . . . and he will teach us of his ways' (*Isa.* 2:3). If we were resolved to do this, and had the desire within us to submit ourselves to God fully, then we would all run together, and the first would help those who followed behind. The weakest would not hinder those who were acting as their guides, but would rather encourage them to march on. Although we know that the world is full of rebellion, and that each person is committed to his own opinions, we are to learn from this teaching. We are to hold our minds captive, so that they will not claim an unlimited licence to do whatever they wish. Instead, we are to obey the truth, and acknowledge that the foundation upon which we are to build is the faithful obedience we render to the Word of God.

Now, when Paul uses the word 'truth', he is countering all the foolish presumption and arrogance of men whereby they regard themselves as sufficiently wise to order their own lives. Out of this same pride is likewise born a mass of superstitions. If men saw themselves as they really are, that is, poor, ignorant, blind folk, they would listen to God with all humility, and thus, there would not be so many groupings and sects. But, as I have said, men want to believe that they are wise. Paul seeks to condemn all haughtiness and rid each one of us of our pride and presumption; therefore, he says that truth can only be found in doctrine that has proceeded from God. Whatever confidence we may have can only be folly, unless we are governed by God and live under the complete dominion of his Word. Furthermore, to be submissive is, beyond comparison, a much greater virtue than to be questioning, always wanting to enquire into things that do not concern us and are not lawful for us to know. To have faith is not to be naive, or to believe and accept without reservation all that we are told; but when God speaks, we are to show him reverence by closing our mouths and opening our ears to listen to his revelation, submitting to it all with simplicity. This is the good race which will not lead us aimlessly here and there, for God will show us the way by his Word. Without it, as I have said, we would simply be fretting. Paul gives us such an image here, when he mocks ignorant souls and unbelievers alike for the way they serve God. However much they strive, they are still wasting their efforts.

However, let us also note that Paul is reproaching the Galatians for turning back when they had reached midway along the path. Their fault was harder to excuse because they had begun well, but had not persevered. It is true that the most ignorant people in the world will still be condemned for not following the Word of God; however, we fail more grievously if God has graciously called us to himself and declared his will to us. Having been taught in his school, and having started the race, if we turn back and abandon our holy and heavenly vocation, our sin is doubled and greatly merits a more severe punishment. This is what Paul means when he says, 'Ye did run well'. It is, indeed, a great virtue to be swift to answer in faith, and especially to respond as soon as we have heard the word, but it amounts to nothing without perseverance. If we are so fickle and inconstant that we venture three steps and then run in the opposite direction, wandering from place to place, our actions are more evil than if we had never listened to God at all. For we can no longer use ignorance as an excuse. Those who are brought up in error will say, 'Alas! If we only knew what the truth is, we would not close our ears to it. But we are unsure, and do not know which way to turn.' If people who have begun to follow God, and have received faithful and accurate instruction in his Word, later turn aside or walk in the opposite direction, they prove that they act not through ignorance, but with malice and rebellion, as if they willingly sought to despise God. We must pay good heed to this, especially since God has graciously declared the way of salvation to us; for he has not done this for everyone. Indeed, there are many poor blind souls who run about here and there, not knowing what they are about; nevertheless, they display some desire to honour God. If we were to ask them if they are acting correctly, they would say yes, but it would only be their supposition, and not something of which they could be certain.

As for ourselves, we have the witness of the Holy Spirit sealed upon our hearts, that the doctrine which is preached to us has not been conceived in the mind of man. Holy Scripture sufficiently proves God to be its true author. If we do not add anything to it, we can know that God is our guide. Indeed, there is not a soul who is so stupid or brutish that he cannot be convinced of the truth, and accept the doctrine which is preached and proclaimed. If he does not acknowledge that God is his judge, he is openly declaring war against God. If, therefore, our Lord has given us the privilege of calling us to himself, he is encouraging us daily, and exhorting us to venture further, until we reach our goal.

This being the case, if listening to him vexes us, and we prefer to copy the fashion of following our own tastes, what excuse or escape can we have? We will be condemned along with the Galatians if, having run well and progressed along the right path, we pursue our own course.

We must also notice the words that Paul weaves in here, when he asks, 'Who did hinder you?' He could simply have said (as also at the beginning of this epistle) that they had departed from God, and rebelled like apostates. But, instead, he uses the word 'hinder', to show that it was not enough for them to stress that they had not completely abandoned God. It is already a most pernicious condition, to have been hindered, and not to have gone in a straight line; for they had not consistently pressed towards God. Thus, we need to be on our guard against the wiles of Satan, not only afraid of complete refusal to obey our God, but wise and prudent when the devil is seeking to cool our faith, and hinder us in our race. If we are only limping along, then he has already gained too great a victory over us. This is what we are to retain from this passage.

In order to further accuse the Galatians of ingratitude, Paul adds, 'This persuasion cometh not of him that calleth you.' In the first chapter, he had said, 'I marvel that ye are so soon removed from him that called you into the grace of Christ unto another gospel.' For it is only right that we should listen to God when he has deigned to open his sacred mouth and instruct us. Who are we? Poor earthworms and lice; yet God has made his voice resound from heaven to reassure us, to illuminate us, to guide us that we might not stumble, to cause us to depend upon him entirely and lean upon his truth. If, when God speaks, we prefer to give ear to other voices, so that we 'fly into the air' and give ear to one voice warbling and another that is singing, is it not sheer ingratitude? If a schoolmaster sees that his pupils are chatting together while he is speaking, or 'building castles in the air', and they do not hear what he says, the cane will come out, and quite rightly. Surely none of us would allow our peers and our companions to converse with us and entertain us with other matters; it would be seen as shameful contempt. Here is the God who has called us! If some seducer or other came fawning upon our ears, and we were to listen to him and do as he says, it would be a sure sign that we have no understanding of the majesty of our God or of the reverence that he deserves from us.

We know that the greatest homage that God requires of us is to be attentive in our minds and hearts in order to understand what he ordains and commands. For this reason, Paul says that this persuasion has not come from God, who called the Galatians. Whilst it is the case that he had called them a long time previously, he was not content to have declared on just one occasion the way in which they ought to live. He continuously taught his doctrine and, indeed, we so badly need to have our memories refreshed each day. Now, since God is always prompting us day and night, as the prophet Isaiah says (*Isa.* 65:2), showing that he has continual concern that we be close to him, and helping us to draw closer, it is clear that our crime is more serious if we then 'have one ear in the field, and one in the town', as they say. Instead, we are to be completely devoted and dedicated to him and to his Word. In brief, the true goal of the child of God should be to offer himself entirely to him, and allow himself to be governed, peacefully and with all submission. None of us should ever say, 'This is my opinion or notion', or 'This is what I have been taught'. May we have the obedience of faith. For there is no other lamp that will guide us so well as the Word of God. This is one point.

* * *

After Paul has said this, he adds, 'A little leaven leaveneth the whole lump.' This confirms the point that I have just made, when I said that this situation is not acceptable, even though there has not been an open revolt and God has not been totally abandoned or his Word renounced. It shows that we must remain pure and whole-hearted, for we have been set free in order to persevere. Although Satan may plot and seek to erect barriers in our path to hinder us, we must, nevertheless, endure to the end. It is very important that we give heed to this, because the devil does not reveal his horns at first, as they say, and draw us away from God. He transforms himself into an angel of light. He comes along unexpected pathways; he digs under the earth. This is how we are seduced, for this or that matter may not seem very important to us, and we can pass over things lightly, and strike sail, as they say. We are very surprised to learn that the devil has caught us in his nets. In short, Paul is telling us here that it is not enough for those who have been taught the gospel to profess that they have accepted the doctrine which it contains. They must have integrity in the faith, so that they do not turn to the right hand or to the left. They must not be corrupted by any error or false addition. They must maintain the pure truth that God has revealed to them. This is the argument that we are to gather from this passage.

If ever this warning was useful, it is certainly so today! For Satan is making every effort to cloud, even to debase the Word of God, so that we may no longer distinguish between black and white. He desires that we regard every religion as correct. Those who follow such false thinking are serving the devil, fearing neither God nor religion any more than a dog does. Today, those who are the greatest supporters of the Pope, knowing that his abuses are so gross and so enormous that it is impossible to justify them, say, 'Well, we still do not need the kind of reformation where one seeks to attempt the impossible; we must content ourselves with a happy medium.' But all this is simply a way of covering their filth. Instead of pulling up a poisonous plant, they pull a few leaves off it, and say, 'There, now it has been cut down.' Yes, but the root remains, and the rest of the plant can still do harm! It is just as if it had not been touched. The world today is full of such contaminated vermin. For these middle-of-the-road types who like to avoid extremes, desire to so disguise our Lord Jesus Christ that he no longer fulfils his office. He is no longer recognisable, and the doctrine of his gospel is mixed like soup!

We need to pay all the more attention to what the Holy Spirit is telling us here, that a little leaven makes the whole lump sour. Sometimes, this metaphor applies to men, for it only takes one scabbed sheep to mar a whole flock, as they say. But Paul is referring here to doctrine; he is saying that we must keep ourselves pure, by not allowing anyone to add to the Word of God. As we saw in the second letter to the Corinthians, Paul said that whoever listens to the deceptions of Satan is like a woman listening to a seductive pimp who has come to abuse her (*2 Cor.* 11:3). Once our faith has been corrupted in this way, we find ourselves alienated from the Lord Jesus Christ. We have, as it were, broken faith with our marriage contract as soon as we move away from the simplicity of the gospel. Indeed, note that he uses the word 'simplicity' in that same passage.

Now, he says here that if we add a little leaven to the lump, the whole thing becomes sour. What then? God, in the law, showed the Jews the true way to live, so that they would not have to fret over this and that. In the gospel, he has taught us more perfectly, in that he has fulfilled all those prophecies. This being the case, let us submit to it, though Satan whispers to us from every corner. Let us not be like reeds that sway in any wind. We need to be so rooted in the Lord Jesus Christ that, through faith, he helps us bear all winds and storms, and all the things that beat against us. In other words, if we want to be known as disciples of our Lord Jesus Christ, we must not listen to any other master or teacher than him. For we cannot do him a worse injury than to add to what he has taught us. It is written that he is the one whom the Father has established to be pre-eminent over us; he is the good Shepherd, and those who are his sheep will listen to his voice and ignore the voice of strangers (*John* 10:4). Whatever happens, we must follow God wherever he calls us, without any resistance whatsoever; we must allow ourselves to be guided and steered by him, so that we do nothing other than submit to his Word, as we have already declared.

Thus, although people sometimes find pretty covers to disguise the corrupt views they are advancing, let us remember what it says here, that it only takes a little leaven to spoil the whole lump. Many who would want to make us fall away tell us, 'You are not renouncing Jesus Christ if you keep to the principles of the gospel – that one is justified by the free grace of God, and can call upon him through the name of the One who was promised as our Mediator. When you fail, you have recourse to the "once for all" sacrifice of our Lord Jesus Christ. If there are little spots and stains, you must put up with them and close your eyes.' Those who want to win us over will say in their pride, 'We are only seeking harmony. We are quite happy for you to walk according to the teachings of the gospel, but this is not so important that you have to insist upon it absolutely!' Whenever the devil comes to deceive us through such enticing words, we need to have this text as a shield in order to oppose him: that it only takes a little leaven to make the whole lump sour. In fact, experience (which we call 'the governess of fools') demonstrates how true these words of Paul are in our day. For today we see, in places where the gospel has been faithfully preached, that there are so many different views that it is shameful. From day to day it looks as if it is leading men to ruination, because the gospel is rent in pieces, as it were. Where does all this originate, if not from man's cowardly desire to remain at peace, and to have all that he needs and live at ease. Such people now wander from one thing to another, and accept those who have come amongst them to undermine the purity of the gospel. God has given them the wages that they have deserved. When we see such examples, let us be all the more on our guard, and walk in the purity of the gospel, rejecting all additions, regarding them as an abomination.

Hereupon, Paul adds, 'I have confidence in you through the Lord, that ye will be none otherwise minded'. We have seen the reproaches which have gone before, which were harsh and severe. But when one exceeds the measure, there is always a danger that men will become vexed and discouraged. For this reason, Paul modifies his approach, and seeks to be reunited with the Galatians. Indeed, this is the order that we need to follow if we desire to edify the church of God. It is true that we must not spare our condemnation of sin, especially when we see that doctrine is being tampered with and faith corrupted. Then, we must have an ardent zeal and fight courageously to maintain the cause of our God. Yet at the same time, we must seek to warn those who have gone astray as much as we possibly can, and to help those who are still on the right path, though weak, and not displaying the strength that is required and for which we hope. This is the role of those who are responsible for preaching the Word of God. In rebuking those who have wandered, they must use severity and harshness, yet nevertheless, they must demonstrate some confidence in them, so that the hearers do not, as a result, become angry and decide to reject all sound doctrine. Each of us must apply this to our own specific situation. What causes us often to grind our teeth when God rebukes us, and to be so eaten up with anger that we rebel against him? It is as if we are playing 'double or quits', as they say, and have lost all hope. But our Lord does not rejoice to have to rebuke us, knowing that we are lost souls on our way to perdition. He only wants to win us to himself. However, we do not realise his kind purposes and intentions with regard to us. Thus, we close the door upon him so that he cannot bother us in any way at all. We must remember all the more carefully what Paul tells us here, in order that, next time someone scratches us at a sore point, though we feel aggrieved and are riled to be thus rebuked, we nevertheless yield patiently, knowing that God does not wish to force us over the edge of the pit. Instead, he is calling us to himself.

Following on from this, remember that there is no other remedy for sin than for us to devote our attention to what God is telling us. For Paul presupposes something which is very true; he had proclaimed the doctrines of the gospel faithfully, and had not come like an impostor in order to spread lies and falsehood. He had fulfilled his duty and the commission which he had received whole-heartedly. He assumes that the Galatians will know this to be the case. Therefore, his general advice to those of us who have been poorly taught, or to those whose minds have been darkened by the devil, or who have been led astray by seducers, is that all we can do is close our mouths and simply say 'Amen' to our God. We must be guided by his Word, even though he will not descend from heaven in visible form, nor send his angels, who reflect something of his majesty. He speaks to us through weak men who have no great worth, but we are not, therefore, to neglect to truly obey him. This is what we are to remember.

Now Paul turns his harshest words upon those deceivers who came to sow discord amongst the church of the Galatians. He says, 'he that troubleth you shall bear his judgment, whosoever he be'. By this he shows that if there are some whom Satan has poisoned so completely that they will willingly provoke the wrath of God to fall upon their heads, we are not to be disturbed or moved as a result. This is still a very useful warning. For although we are slow to believe what God teaches us, we are the complete opposite when faced with error; we readily run after it, which shows the perversity of our nature, which is common to all. It is a sin that is most natural to us. Furthermore, we seem more than ready to allow Satan to deceive us, as long as we have some excuse to cover ourselves, though Satan seeks only our perdition. We must, therefore, give heed to what Paul says here, that those who stir up trouble in the church shall bear their own judgment. By this, Paul is warning us that there are many such folk, who have contempt for God, and have no scruples about destroying everything, if they can but make a reputation for themselves in the world. If they can achieve status, it is all the same to them! They care about nothing other than elevating themselves. These people trouble the church in countless ways. Some, through ambition, and in order to be considered very wise and sharp, create new doctrines. This is one kind of seducer. There are others who are so full of malice that they do not know how to have peace or concord; just as we are told that the hand of Ishmael would be against everyone, and that the world, in turn, would make war upon him (*Gen.* 16:12). Such people only seek to bring dissension and quarrelling. Seeing, therefore, that the devil has so many agents who would divert us from the right path, ought not each one of us to look well to ourselves and not be moved? Whatever this or that person babbles on about, we must remain firm in what we already know to be true of our God. This is Paul's aim here; he does not wish us to look, like sheep, to one another. When one sheep goes on ahead, the rest will all jump into the river or into a well. Geese and cranes also follow one another in a line. We are not to be like these. We are never to be moved away from the Word of God. This is one point.

Above all, Paul shows that we are not to be dazzled by the fine appearances of men, when, hiding behind their knowledge, they pervert the pure truth of God, and care nothing about it. They have no religion, no fear to keep them bridled, and sometimes they are more than brazen and reach a position where they have gained command without it costing them anything. It is almost as if they would spit in the face of God. Knowing that such monsters exist, we must wait for God to exercise judgment upon them and thus declare how precious are the souls for which he paid so dearly. Hence, Paul adds, 'whosoever he be'. For he wants to wipe out all the fancy titles which men boastfully claim when they exalt themselves in opposition to God. Today, the Pope overturns the truth of God, and has the diabolical audacity to turn everything upside down, but he still calls himself Servant of the servants of God, Vicar of Jesus Christ, Successor of St Peter. The bishops, calling themselves prelates, think they have a legitimate right to suppress all knowledge of the truth. But Paul shows here that when men mask themselves in this way, they are making themselves nothing more than idols. God does not alter, and neither does he change his nature or his purpose. Though men elevate themselves up to the third heaven, we must still regard them as devils if they seek to mix anything of their own devising with the purity and simplicity of the Word of God. Thus, here we see all human dignity cast down, when it is a question of the obedience of faith. Yes, in the enforcement of law and order, there needs to be superiority, but at the same time, God governs us by his Word. His service is set down there and our faith must conform itself entirely. If all the world rose up, and they made a huge pile of noble titles, higher than the mountains and the clouds, let all this be considered but smoke, or even as dung and filth. This is a summary of what Paul means here.

However, Paul is not excusing the Galatians for their thoughtlessness; he wants to encourage them to return to God. There are many today who think they have escaped the hand of God and are absolved, simply because their prelates and pastors have taught them what they believe. Paul does not accept such an excuse, but he says that they can escape the condemnation which has been prepared for these seducers, if they return to the pure truth of God. Although, for a time, they have fallen away from it, they ought not to refuse to submit. In conclusion, Paul is also expressing how dear our salvation is to God, and on whose recommendation he has it. God refers here to the accountability of those who trouble the church, and speaks of casting them into hell – but what is behind this? It proceeds from an acknowledgement that we are his inheritance, and that he finds all his pleasure in us, as those that he has chosen and adopted. We are like his fulness as Paul has said before. Since this is the case, let us learn to trust ourselves to God, seeing the fatherly care he has for our salvation. At the same time, let us learn to reject consistently all false doctrines with all the fervour we can muster. For we know that God is moved and roused with anger, declaring that he will never forgive those who have thus troubled his own people. Seeing that God displays his indignation towards those who have vexed his church, let us have a corresponding zeal in detesting all false doctrine. If we see people who are only seeking to sow discord, let us regard them as mortal enemies, and courageously make war upon them. May we fight to the end for God's truth, knowing that here is where our life and happiness lies. This is what we are to remember from this passage.

Now, God did at one time call us to himself, and has not

ceased ever since to prompt us daily by exhortations; let us, therefore, remain obedient to him. Though we see many problems, dissensions and conflicts in the world, let us, nevertheless, remain adherents of the infallible truth. Because we are liable to be seduced and deceived, let us pray to God for wisdom and discernment. Let us also be attentive to his Word, which can strengthen us against Satan's deceptions. Let us not be drawn away by siren voices any longer, as it says at the end of this epistle. Seeing, then, that God has established the means by which we may be preserved as members of his church and household, let us persevere in these things. If, at any time, we are ever turned aside through the folly of the flesh, or through carelessness, let us forthwith listen to the warning that is given here. May we tremble because of our sins, and, having trembled, may we serve our God, knowing that he is always ready to receive us. May we guard ourselves well, since there are so many contemptuous and profane men who never cease to corrupt and pervert the doctrines of the gospel, and who have become hardened in their sins. Though, I say, we see such scandalous things, let us not be moved, and let us not follow these people and become ensnared in their condemnation. May we proceed, instead, towards the salvation that has been offered to us, to which God daily calls us.

Now let us fall down before the majesty of our great God, acknowledging our sins, and praying that he would make us ever more conscious of them. Nevertheless, may he support us in our weakness until we have been completely delivered from it, and clothed in the purity of his righteousness, which must increase in us until it is utterly perfected. Thus, we all say, Almighty God, and our heavenly Father, etc.

34

The Zeal That Cuts off God's Mortal Enemies

> *And I, brethren, if I yet preach circumcision, why do I yet suffer persecution? then is the offence of the cross ceased. I would they were even cut off which trouble you. For, brethren, ye have been called unto liberty; only use not liberty for an occasion to the flesh, but by love serve one another* (Gal. 5:11–13).

In every situation, we find that men are so given over to self-advancement, that they will bend over backwards for it and forget about being just or upright. Their eyes have been blinded by avarice and the desire to gain profit and advantage for themselves, to the extent that they lose their good judgment. Especially when it comes to preaching the Word of God, a man will never follow the right course if he cannot forget self, and close his eyes to anything that might distract him in this world from acting according to God's pure ways. Indeed, he will surely stray away from the path, first to one side, then to the other. Hence, God's doctrines are often corrupted because those who ought to preach them are inclined to be malevolent, or to seek the favour of their hearers. They may fear to incur bad feeling or to provoke anger against themselves. Therefore, it is impossible for us to serve God in our natural state; we must be absolutely determined, with unshakeable constancy, to suffer for the doctrines that we preach, and not to let this cause us grief. We must fight under the ensign of our captain, Jesus

Christ, knowing that we cannot share in the glory of his resurrection if we have not first suffered with him, following his example. All believers must certainly strengthen themselves to do these things.

However, this has particular relevance for those who are responsible for teaching and proclaiming the Word. For the devil is always scheming to discourage us, and he finds many who assist him in this world. Indeed, there are numerous people that cannot bear the Word of God to be proclaimed in all integrity. They will not openly say that they would wish to bury the name of God, but they would love to create doctrines to suit their own tastes. In answer to this, we must simply look to what God has commanded and be stalwart in our defence of it. When God instructed Jeremiah to fight, he promised to give him a forehead of bronze, as it were, to come against those who were attacking him (*Jer.* 1:18–19). This is why Paul speaks about preaching circumcision here, and devising doctrines that would please these seducers; for this would have exempted him from all strife and guaranteed the applause of all. At the very least, he would not have been persecuted or troubled by anyone. For the Jews were quite in agreement with him preaching Jesus Christ, as long as they could retain the privileges of the first-born which they enjoyed. These included observing the ceremonies, and regarding the Gentiles as little runts, forced to the back of the queue. This is what the Jews were hoping for. Of course, Paul could have satisfied them, if he had not sought to serve God faithfully and honestly. Conversely, Paul demonstrates that those who sought to destroy the doctrine that he preached, preferred the friendship and favour of men to the discharge of their duty.

Now we see the meaning of this phrase, where Paul says, 'if I yet preach circumcision . . .'. In other words, 'If I agree to such a mixture, where Jesus Christ is obscured, and each person obtains what he desires, I will no longer be criticised by everyone. I will be welcomed by all, and I will have a good reputation. Is it likely that I would want to declare war upon you all and suffer affliction? By this, therefore, you can see that I am not seeking my own advantage. What is it that moves these great teachers to make such a mixture as we see today, except the desire to gratify others and to escape any kind of trouble? Since they are only seeking their own peace and comfort, it is only right that you should be suspicious of them.' Thus, we can see the point that I have only just made, that those who are called by God to preach his Word must be resolved that they will not compromise, even if the whole world were to rise up against them. They must bear all conflicts, knowing that God will help them in their need and always grant them victory, provided they follow their vocation in purity and simplicity. The greatest insult and injury that we can give to God is in yielding to the desires of man, and twisting his Word both left and right. It is not only a question of abandoning our own ideas, but also of constantly upholding God's truth, which is immutable; it must never be altered, however changeable and inconstant men may be.

We must pay attention to this, particularly since most people that have a healthy desire to make God known and to preach his Word aright, will often give way when they hear the reproaches and complaints of men, and the criticism of themselves. Sometimes there will even be a serious revolt, which appears to threaten to destroy everything. But if we uphold God's cause as we should, the slanderers will be ready to brand us as stubborn. Today the Papists accuse us firstly of being too rash. They say that we want to right all the world's wrongs, thinking that we are wiser than anyone else – we who are no more than a handful amongst a great multitude; indeed, amongst people of greater experience, who have seen so much and who are held in high esteem and reputation. They also say that we are too severe, indeed, and too bold, when we teach that everyone else must pass under the yoke. They say that we only desire superiority for ourselves, and humility for others. This is how we are wrongly accused, but we are to accept such disgrace rather than back down. Why? Because it is not a question of making a deal with men. For if two parties were debating over a sum of money, or an inheritance, some of it could be docked off here, and some there, so that peace is restored. But if we give in to the demands of the enemies of God and the preferences of a person who desires his rights to be fully maintained (as indeed they all do), what will become of us? We are, therefore, to be all the more careful to remember the teaching of Paul here when he shows us that if we are to serve God, we must not fear manhandling, nor cutting remarks, nor complaints, nor rebukes, nor anything else. Even if it involves having our lives scrutinised, let us be willing to undergo this. If we are too weak, let us remember that God is calling us to himself and he has the answer to all our infirmities, and can give us sufficient strength to keep ourselves on the right path even in extreme situations. Whatever we do, we must not dishonour him by submitting to the will of man, since, although we are worthless, he has employed us in his service. This is the first thing we are to remember.

Furthermore, we are warned to beware of those who are seeking their own advantage and profit; of all who disguise the fact that they are running with the hare and hunting with the hounds, and who constantly falsify the truth of God in order to please men. For (as I have already declared), we must be prepared for many battles if we wish to serve God alone. We must recall the text where Paul says that if he sought to please man, he would not be a servant of the Lord Jesus Christ, his Master (*Gal.* 1:10). For, as we have said, the devil will never stop making war upon us from every side. Men are naturally disposed to receive flattery and support from others, whilst their vices remain hidden. In short, there is not a person among us who does not seek to be supported and maintained in his mediocrity. Yet, if we wish to befriend man to the extent that we conform to his will and desire, Jesus Christ will no longer be our Master. Not only will we be useless to him, but we will be destroying everything. Therefore, when we see the great zealots of Christianity today seeking their own advantage, we may boldly conclude that they do not deserve to have any authority. There are those who bark loudly in defence of the abuses of the Pope, and constantly slander gospel doctrine, seeking to bring disgrace upon it in the eyes of poor, blind, ignorant folk. What do the majority of such people seek to do? Some seek to preserve their status, in their red cocked hats and crosiers; the others follow on, as in a hunt. Those who follow after, in their poverty and starvation, wish to be valued and merit a reward. Behind them are worthless hypocrites, the filthy vermin, the clergy. Their actions, whatever they may be, flow from one great concern: that their platter may be full, as they say. Thus, they only fight for the sake of their stomach. There are also many mediocre people, content if the gospel is preached half-heartedly. But when it is proclaimed with such rigour and such great severity, the world finds this unreasonable and intolerable.

Why, therefore, do they accept so many ceremonies that originate in superstition and corruption? To this they reply, we must not be so harsh; we are being far too persistent! Today, all who cannot bear us to destroy all the filth and corruption of the Papacy seek nothing more than to avoid and shun persecution. May it please God that such attitudes will become less common. But we also find today an infinite number of people who would be ashamed to resist the gospel utterly, and they will agree with us enough to say, 'Oh yes, all this is true, but we must also be able to tolerate many other things, and proceed with moderation and humanity.' Now, what has encouraged them to be like this? What basis do they have for this? Well, they will say, 'We have seen fires lit in every place, so what good would it do to stir up more trouble when there is trouble enough already? It would seem as if we were vexing the enemies of the gospel even further by ambushing them. They already have the sword in their hand and could destroy us all. Would it not be better to tolerate everything until God grants his church a more peaceful time?' Such people, who seek a truce with those who openly fight against our Lord Jesus Christ, are surely full of treachery. This is the second warning that we are to remember from this passage.

* * *

Moving on, when Paul speaks of 'the offence of the cross' ceasing, he means that the world will no longer be stirred up to reject the teachings of the gospel. For we preach Jesus Christ crucified, but the world chooses to call the preaching of the cross simple-minded. The world always wants to retain its pomp. Firstly, there are many who have itching ears, and desire no more than to hear some pleasing rhetoric or other, or flowery language and the like. Secondly, there are many who are ashamed of the simplicity of the gospel, especially since people of high status are there joined and associated with the lowly. To them, it seems as if its only purpose is to abase the nobility. Must men be spoiled and robbed of their glory in this way? Many are afraid of this. For this reason, Paul says, 'Well, this is the preaching of a gibbet.' It is true; for the Son of God had to bear our curse in order to open the kingdom of heaven to us. He had to endure a shameful death before men. He was even cursed by the mouth of God, for as it was written in the law, 'He that is hanged is accursed of God' (*Deut.* 21:23). Our Lord Jesus Christ had to go these lengths as our substitute. He plummeted the depths, as it were. We know that the prophet Isaiah said that he was disfigured like a poor leper, so much so that we did not dare look upon him or regard him as human (*Isa.* 53:2). In Psalm 22 it says, 'I am a worm, and no man; a reproach of men, and despised of the people' (*Psa.* 22:6). Indeed, even the thief mocked him and put him to shame (*Luke* 23:39).

At first sight, therefore, it would seem that this doctrine does not merit acceptance, but we must remember what Paul said in that other passage, that the world did not know God by true wisdom, and that, therefore, he had to choose another means of teaching us, that is, by foolishness (*1 Cor.* 1:21). For if we were truly wise (as we would like to be considered), we would realise that by looking at the heavens and the earth, we have the best instruction possible. We have there a mirror by which God reflects his goodness, power, righteousness, mercy and infinite wisdom. There we see the greatest treasures of the wisdom of God, which should transport us with wonder. But who profits from these? On the contrary, we see men berating the good things that God has made, and trampling upon them without giving him a thought. Not only this, but also rebelling against the one who has filled their stomachs. When they think they have devoted themselves to serving God, they have really robbed him of his rightful honour by making idols according to their own imaginations. Since the world has not known God through true wisdom, and through the natural order around them, it was necessary for God to use other means, which he has done. For if we were to be guided by our minds, it would, indeed, appear foolish that the Son of God, the Head of angels, the Lord of Glory, the fountain of life, he to whom all majesty belongs, not only became a mortal man and clothed himself with our condition, but also that he emptied himself completely (as Paul says in the second chapter to the Philippians, verse seven), and even submitted to our curse and bore the name of sin, which is even worse. When we express it like this, it might seem strange to us, and, indeed, it does. But let us submit in all humility and know that we have to come to this school, since we did not learn from what God revealed to us at the beginning through the heavens and the earth. Thus much for the text where Paul speaks of 'the offence of the cross'.

Now, in brief, we must learn from this passage that if there is any absurdity about the gospel (according to our way of thinking), we are not to be put off in any way. God is seeking to test our obedience by bringing us to the death of our Lord Jesus Christ, for when we see the Son of God bearing our condemnation, acting as our substitute, and paying our debts, we are brought to see the mouth of hell. Furthermore, his death leads us beautifully to the glory which was manifested at his resurrection. You see, the Son of God suffered infirmity, as God the Father ordained, and yet he voluntarily submitted to such servitude. Having thus suffered, he conquered death by the power of the Holy

Spirit, and attained such victory that now every knee must bow before him, because his name is sovereign. We now recognise that all the majesty of God appears in him and shines through him. This is why we need not be ashamed of the gospel. Above all, let us remember what Paul says in the first chapter to the Romans (*Rom.* 1:16), that he is the power of God to salvation to all who believe. Let worldly people and those puffed up with pride and arrogance, like toads, look down on the gospel as much as they like, and let them perish in their accursed state. Nevertheless, may we embrace the Lord Jesus Christ with humility of faith, for he offers us his presence that we might be raised to glory in the kingdom of heaven.

Moreover, Paul connects the preaching of the gospel with 'offence' here, as if they were inseparable. It is true that we must avoid giving offence as much as possible, for woe to that person by whom the offence comes (*Matt.* 18:7). Nevertheless, Jesus Christ must reign with absolute dominion, though the world sets itself against him. The word 'offence' implies that there will be impediments and obstacles, like walking along a rough, stony road where there are prickles and brambles and other obstructions. This is what is meant by giving offence. It is to be desired that Jesus Christ will advance and be welcomed everywhere, and that the gospel will be preached without hindrance from one end of the earth to the other. I tell you, we must long for this with all our hearts. However, let us appreciate that God is testing the obedience of our faith by handing the reins to Satan, who stirs up a great deal of turmoil and strife. Indeed, our Lord Jesus Christ is not called a 'rock of offence' without cause; he is a stone which people stumble over, thereby breaking their necks (*Isa.* 8:14). In the end (as it is written in Luke's Gospel, chapter two verse thirty-four), this stone will crush them, for it is stronger than their obstinacy.

This is very useful to us, for there are many people around today who are so weak that as soon as someone opposes the gospel, they consider they are exempted and freed in the eyes of God from the responsibility of sustaining the conversation. If kings and princes had declared to the sound of trumpets that people are no longer permitted to fight against the gospel, everyone would pretend to be in agreement. However, today we witness such great cruelty, tyranny, contempt, threatening, and the like. On top of this, most of our enemies are like ravening wolves, seeking to devour us all; disguised as good people, they are in reality seeking to spill innocent blood. Others are inflamed with zeal to wipe out the name of God and fully extinguish all gospel doctrine. What is our reaction to all this? We say, 'Oh, I would not want this to happen to me. What, me? Make myself at enmity with everyone else? Is it not evident that there is only a handful of folk that have accepted this doctrine, and that all the others are their enemies and reject it all, and mock at it, being completely poisoned against them?' Very few are strong enough to bear the attacks upon the gospel once they realise that there are so many hindrances, and that Jesus Christ is opposed by Satan through the devices of his followers. Most quickly decide to draw back. Even today, we hear many say that this doctrine brings them too much trouble. They also give heed to diverse opinions and listen to what is said by others. Thus, when the wicked come to sell their tongues today (much like prostitutes selling their bodies in a brothel), and stand up to blaspheme against God and his Word, they will find some way of covering the fact that they despise and reject the gospel. As a result, they sharpen the tongue of the poor to say, 'We have seen the troubles that this gospel has stirred up.' Yes, but Jesus Christ could no longer live up to his claims in Holy Scripture, unless the gospel stirred up strife. Nevertheless, we must not allow ourselves to be shaken, but must rise above all this.

This is what we are to glean from this passage, where Paul says that we cannot persevere in the faith of the gospel unless we are armed with the determination to let Satan do as he will, and yet not to be turned back from our path. It is true that we must avoid offence as much as we can by anticipating it and warding it off, as I have already said. Indeed, we have already seen how we are to conduct ourselves. Even the prophet Isaiah says, when speaking of the preaching of the gospel, that the way must be straightened out, and that which was rough and uneven must be made level (*Isa.* 40:3–4). Thus, we must put every effort into this. On the other hand, because God would have us to be humble, there will always be difficulties and problems, and Jesus Christ may not always reign amongst his enemies. However, let us press on and frustrate the plans of the devil. Let us not turn from the gospel once we see the trouble that it brings in this world.

*   *   *

Having said this, Paul adds, 'I would they were even cut off which trouble you.' At first, it would seem that Paul is too greatly moved with anger here, when he asks that all who sow discord and error in order to pervert the purity of God's doctrine, be lost and given over to the devil, without ever receiving mercy from God. For this is what the term 'cut off' implies. We are to note, therefore, that the zeal we should have for the glory of God should cancel out all regard we have for man when we balance one against the other. But before we move on, let us firstly notice that Paul is using a metaphor here when he refers to being 'cut off'. For these rogues who had corrupted and falsified the teachings of the gospel were fighting for circumcision! Therefore, he says to them, 'Well then, go ahead and cut! Cut off as much as you wish – your only design is that others should observe such trifling matters. As far as I am concerned, I wish that these seducers were cut off altogether, and that God would destroy them and cast them off; that they would be rejected and condemned by him and have no hope of salvation.'

To return to what I have just been saying, I am telling you that if men are fighting against God and making themselves his mortal enemies, we are to forget about all kinship or friendship with them, or anything else. If we do not, then we are not doing our duty to God at all. For he has called himself our Father, and he has honoured us by accepting us as his children. At the very least, his glory should be our first priority above everything else. But we must take this even further. How majestic our God is, and how precious his truth should be to us! He has linked his glory with our salvation, so that we cannot procure one without the other. However, we can neither advantage or disadvantage God; even if we were as zealous as it were possible to be in maintaining his cause, he has no real need of us. He does not have to rely upon our help, and yet he makes us his helpers. Why? So that we might all seek to profit, not according to this world or in relation to corruptible things, but in relation to the eternal salvation of our souls. This is the reason why God employs us; and yet we are still cowardly and cold. Can such treachery be excused? Let us look at what is written in the Psalms (*Psa.* 69:9): 'For the zeal of thine house hath eaten me up: and the reproaches of them that reproached thee are fallen upon me.' It is true that this was perfectly fulfilled in the person of our Lord Jesus Christ as the Head of the church, but Paul is showing us that we must conform ourselves to him, as our pattern. If we see men obscuring the glory of God, we must oppose them with boldness.

This is the rule that we are to follow; that is, that we put God's honour over all else, even above a million lives if we had them! When men strive with all their powers to trample the name of God underfoot, they may have spared themselves from trouble – but the doctrine of salvation becomes confused, and we no longer know which religion to follow. Furthermore, the peace of the church is destroyed. When we see people applying themselves to this end, is it any wonder that we organise and oppose them? Of course, if it is possible, we should seek to pursue friendship and harmony with others, as indeed Paul tells the Romans (*Rom.* 12:18). But when we see these wicked people rising up against God, and exalting themselves in readiness for a direct clash with him, it is only right that we intervene and show that we are not our own, because our Lord Jesus Christ has redeemed and bought us at such great cost. Therefore, he must, of necessity, reign over us in life and in death. This is why Paul expressed such a harsh desire here, that the people who were troubling the Galatians should be altogether separated from God, and cast into the pit of hell.

Now if we claim that this goes against the golden rule of love, the answer is very simple. Yes, we are duty bound to love our enemies, however much they persecute and harm us, or seek to ruin us. We must, despite this, as far as we are able, pursue their highest good and their salvation, having pity and compassion on them when we see them thus given over to Satan. This is what love involves. Yet God ought to come before anyone else, as we have already said. Love, therefore, is something which we express to fellow human beings; if someone has hurt me, I must forget about it. Even if he still bears malice towards me, I must continue to seek his well-being. However, when it comes to maintaining the cause of God, it is then that men must be regarded as less than nothing, as we have said.

Yet we do the complete opposite! For what is our common reaction? To compromise and strike sail when God is attacked. And yet we defend our own rights to the bitter end. Let me give you an example. We see a man who has committed a very serious crime; he deserves to be punished and if he goes unpunished, it is a terrible breach and corruption of duty. Similarly, we see people in high office and, without taking it too far, even those who preach the Word of God, living dreadful lives: merrymakers, those who only sow confusion and stir up debate. Yet we say, 'We must not cut them off, nor deal harshly with them.' A drunkard would be tolerated, or a bawdy or nasty individual. Disdain for God would prevail, and the gospel would be reviled everywhere; all this, because we claim that we need to show humanity. Yes, but at the same time we have forgotten about honouring God. Anyway, men who are thus humane, or pretend to be, will immediately launch into mortal combat the moment they encounter the slightest criticism of themselves. They will say, 'This person has done me wrong.' They will pursue such a conflict to the end, and yet they will tolerate the followers of the devil as much as they possibly can, even to the point of enduring the shame of a slap in the face, as Paul says to the Corinthians (*2 Cor.* 11:20). Yet they cannot bring themselves to avenge God for the dishonour that he has to suffer.

Now we can see that Paul's zeal was, indeed, under control. If anyone had hurt him personally, we know that he would have borne it patiently. However, seeing that the gospel of God was being mishandled, he could not tolerate this, and therefore opposed it and expressed a wish that such people would be lost. He had no care for himself, but God's honour was more important to him than anything else, as we have seen. Thus we will not waver if we simply look to God, and avoid giving rein to our passions. Instead we must be ruled by a spirit of wisdom and uprightness, that God might help us to decide when we need to fight and when we ought to hold back. If we have such discernment and are governed by the Spirit of God, we can ignore people who want to turn us from the pure doctrines which we have learned – along with Paul, David and all the holy prophets. We can even curse the angels if need be, as Paul told us earlier, when he said that we must ignore even the angels of paradise if they were to rise up against the doctrine which he preached (*Gal.* 1:8). Not that the angels would ever rebel against him, but only if it were possible. It is as if he were saying, 'Imagine that an angel came and sought to destroy your faith; it were better that you send him to hell, and count him as a devil and curse him, rather than be led astray from the right path.' Hence, we are to be rooted in God in everything and every way.

Furthermore, the sentence pronounced against all who were troubling the church ought to put us in fear, as much as if we had heard it thunder from heaven. For, although Paul was speaking, yet his tongue was led and controlled by the Holy Spirit. Though he is only God's instrument, chosen to proclaim this statement, it is still an irrevocable decree which has been given against all who destroy unity in the faith, and the concord and brotherly love which ought to exist between the children of God, and against all who plant errors and heresies which falsify the truth. Indeed, God is declaring here how dear we are to him, (as we said this morning), and he is testifying to the fatherly concern he has for our salvation, when he wreaks such vengeance upon those who would seek our ruin.

* * *

Now, finally he says, 'For, brethren, ye have been called unto liberty; only use not liberty for an occasion to the flesh, but by love serve one another.' For love, he says, is the true fulfilment of the law, and this should govern all our actions. In the first place, Paul shows here that he does not intend us to live at ease, and amuse ourselves with whatever we deem to be good, but he does say that we are free before God. This is very important, for as soon as we hear the word 'liberty', we think (because we live according to our carnal appetites), 'Well then, I can do whatever I wish; there are no longer any restrictions or obligations, nor must I have so many scruples about everything!' Thus, under pretext of this 'liberty', we give ourselves over to carnal passions. Indeed, the devil is very subtle and seduces and deceives us through things which appear to be good, turning them to evil advantage. For (as we have said previously), all who live to fulfil their appetites become poor slaves, held captive in more confining servitude than those restrained in the stocks. How is this? Let us consider for a moment the tyranny of our appetites and passions. If a man were to follow his appetites, he would surely lose all shame, forget himself and become completely brutal. This, then, is the wonderful liberty that all men search for almost by natural instinct! As we have said, the liberty to which Paul refers is quite a different matter. It does not imply amusing ourselves with no bridle to hold us back. Rather, in order to understand what God requires of us, we must be led by his Word, and none must ever usurp his authority and say, 'We ought to do this or that'. For ever since men decided to govern us by their own laws and statutes, they have, in a manner of speaking, created as many cords by which they are strangling poor souls.

Paul shows, therefore, that this liberty which he preached, and which he maintained by constantly opposing these deceivers, does not allow men to exceed all measure, or grant themselves licence to do whatever they feel is right. Instead, it enables them to worship God freely, no longer tortured and tormented with anxiety, like the poor, ignorant people shackled by superstitions, doubts, and scruples. For them, everything becomes a matter for questioning, and they can never be fully resolved in their minds about anything. Such are the Papists, who have a whole host of questions; though this ought not to surprise us because they do not know to which master they must give account. Each person will speak according to the workings of his brain and say, 'It seems to me that this is the right thing to do', or, 'This is the way I am led through my own devotions', or, 'It would be good to do this or that extra thing'. Once they have entered such a labyrinth, they ultimately foster doubts about whether or not to comb their hair, or whether to eat with a certain finger, and the like. In short, there is no end to these things. When Paul wanted to demonstrate what it means to be surrounded by human traditions, he says that, having forbidden the eating of meat, they then forbid the tasting of it! Having forbidden the tasting of it, they then forbid people to touch it (*Col.* 2:21)!

How we need, therefore, to maintain the liberty which was purchased for us through the death and passion of our Lord Jesus Christ. Firstly, we need to know how God desires to be served and honoured, so that we are not tossed about by this dogma and that, not knowing the difference between good and bad. If we know for certain that we are following the Word of God, we will also be assured that we cannot fail.

Secondly, may we serve one another, and not be so devoted to ourselves that we ignore our friends. Rather, may we be so full of compassion that we each consider how we may benefit and help our neighbours. May we avoid all offence, and may none of us ever say, 'I care for nobody'. Instead, may we consider the fact that we are joined together by the Lord Jesus Christ, as members of his church. May we remain firm in this doctrine. First, let us honour and serve God as he commands. Secondly, may there be harmony amongst us, whilst we humbly seek to join together and submit ourselves one to another, enjoying freedom of conscience in the eyes of God.

Now let us fall down before the majesty of our great God, acknowledging our sins and asking him that we might be made more conscious of them. May this cause us to humble ourselves in his sight and draw us to true repentance, profiting by this means more and more, and constantly trembling under the burden of our sins, until we are purged and cleansed from them altogether. May this great God bear with us, and not deal with us according to the severity that we deserve. May he lead us by his Holy Spirit, so that in pardoning our sins, he may also bury them, until the day when they are completely washed away. May he not only show this grace to us, but to all peoples and nations on earth, etc.

35

Spirit and Flesh in Conflict

For all the law is fulfilled in one word, even in this; Thou shalt love thy neighbour as thyself. But if ye bite and devour one another, take heed that ye be not consumed one of another. This I say then, Walk in the Spirit, and ye shall not fulfil the lust of the flesh. For the flesh lusteth against the Spirit, and the Spirit against the flesh: and these are contrary the one to the other: so that ye cannot do the things that ye would. But if ye be led of the Spirit, ye are not under the law (Gal. 5:14–18).

When Moses sought to summarise the law, that we might remember what it teaches and reveals, he said that God would have us love him. Indeed, it stands to reason that we should desire to cleave and be joined to him. There ought also to be a bond of friendship between ourselves that unites us all as members of one body. Our Lord Jesus Christ tells us that by this people will be able to judge whether or not we are his disciples – which demonstrates that the doctrines that he taught were no different from those given by God to his people of old (*John* 13:35). Hence, Paul says here that 'all the law is fulfilled in one word . . . Thou shalt love thy neighbour as thyself'. This does not mean that we can forget about God (as we have already shown), for he must be at the forefront and loved more than anything in creation. Indeed, for his sake we must forget father and mother, wife, children and everything else in this world. Yet, to love God and to love our neighbours are not mutually exclusive things. For when we show love to others, we are revealing the love we have for our God, as we have already said. There is no need for me to reiterate these points further.

To sum up, then, if we are given over to selfish interests, it is a sure sign that we do not know what it is to bear the yoke of God; for we are simply following our natural instincts. Indeed, as we shall shortly consider, men are wholly inclined to evil, and therefore give rein to their appetites, waging war upon God. Their whole life is spent in rebellion against him. This proves that the devil controls our affections: indeed, so much so that God cannot make use of us until he has overcome all that pertains to our nature. However, the person who loves his neighbour demonstrates that he is not looking after his own interests; he is not selfish. This, therefore, is a sure and certain mark of the fact that we are seeking to obey God, and to regulate our lives according to his Word. Moreover, the Lord Jesus begins with this when summarising his own teaching, saying that we must learn to deny ourselves. For if we followed our own natural course, we would undoubtedly walk in the opposite direction to the path set out by God. Thus, Paul has good reason to say in this passage that the law is fulfilled by this one thing: that we love our neighbours.

Now we need to realise that when God uses the word 'neighbour', he does not only include our relatives and friends, from whom we hope to gain some profit or advantage for ourselves, or who deserve some kind of reward from us. He wants us to be aware of the kinship that he has placed between us all. We are all made in the image of God and bear his stamp; we share a common nature. These things ought to maintain a sense of unity and brotherhood amongst us. Of course, many render themselves unworthy of this honour. Some, like foxes, are full of evil and deceit; some are proud, like lions; some are ravening wolves whose only design is to devour everything in sight; others are harmful and injurious. Such people, therefore, cut themselves off as much as they can from the rank and company of 'neighbours', but we must still observe God's command here. However little men may deserve to be regarded as neighbours, yet by showing them love, we demonstrate that God has helped us to overcome all malice towards them. In this way, we can see that even our enemies, who do nothing but rebuke us, are still our neighbours according to the principle that God has established. Our Lord Jesus Christ shows us that if we return a favour to someone who has helped and served us, or if we love people who are pleasing to us or from whom we expect to gain, we cannot call that love. Even the pagans do the same, but not because they are obeying either God or the law (*Matt.* 5:46). When we seek self-advancement, it is not love for others but love for self which is displayed. True love has as its goal God and the sense of community that ought to exist amongst us, as we have said. Therefore, by seeking to do good even to those who are unworthy of it, we are truly proving that we desire to show love for God.

Now, although Paul adds 'as thyself', he is not saying that we must love ourselves first of all, then secondly love our neighbours. No; our Lord is here exposing the disease that prevents us from loving one another. It is just as we were saying before; if people were less devoted to themselves, there would be great love and harmony amongst us all. But we are disposed to love ourselves too much, and this excessive love blinds us and robs us of all reason, good judgment and fairness. This is why God tells us that we must love our neighbours as ourselves. If this had not been said, we could have simply talked a great deal about loving our neighbours, saying, 'Of course we must love them!', but it may have been false. In the same way, hypocrites protest that they wish no evil on their enemies, and even claim to desire their good. Hence, we must employ the test which God has given us here, and examine ourselves to see whether we have excessive love for ourselves, and whether the love that we have for our neighbours is not, in reality, shallow and cold. In short, God is seeking here to remedy the hypocrisy which has blinded us so much. He wishes people to wake up to the fact that they must not flatter themselves, so he says, 'It is not enough to love one another; you must love your neighbours as yourselves.'

This makes us aware of how far short we fall from the perfect standards of the law, and demonstrates that we must struggle against our own natures in order to obey God. How, therefore, should Christians really be exercising themselves? By acknowledging that they have behaved so badly towards God and by trembling because of their many infirmities and sins. Next, they must strive and labour daily to overcome their shortcomings, aiming to be no longer controlled by their fleshly appetites. God ought to have the dominion; then, instead of loving ourselves, we will set out to fulfil that to which he has called us.

* * *

Having shown us the perfection of the law, and having demonstrated that our aim should be to regulate our lives according to the Word of God, Paul now adds that if we 'bite and devour one another' like cats and dogs, we will, at last, consume one another. Paul says this to bring even greater shame upon those who are thus determined to maintain hatred and bitterness, and who refuse to see reason. They do not care about anything but the satisfying of their desire for vengeance. What will you gain from this?, asks Paul. By nature, you seek to preserve yourselves, and this is what you have in common with animals. An animal has no reason or intelligence, yet still seeks to preserve itself and to avoid all danger. People have much stronger powers of reasoning to discern between good and evil; yet they continue to seek self-preservation and to remain in one piece! Now then, hatred brings fighting, quarrelling, dissension, slander and the like in its wake. The end result is that we are all consumed. Therefore, those who abandon themselves to excessive hatred in this way must surely have been robbed of their reason by the devil, since they cannot control themselves to any degree.

In other words, Paul shows, on the one hand, that if there is no law of God, we will have no fear of offending him; but on the other hand, even if we have been well taught and possess a small amount of wisdom, it will in no way be enough to prevent us from squabbling and declaring war upon one another. Indeed, we rush towards our own perdition as if by deliberate intention; therefore, this commandment runs counter to our nature. People become wild when they flare up like this, and thereby invite their own ruin. But why do we hate our enemies? It must be because we let loose our passions; but we excuse it in this way: 'Oh, they wish me ill; not only so, but they deliberately bring evil my way; indeed, have already done so!' Really? So what next? What will you have gained by making two devils out of one, as they say, for you are only kindling a fire in someone who was already sufficiently inflamed. This will embitter him further and make him doubly enraged. You ought to realise that this will end in perdition for you both. However, if we considered this reason alone, it would be insufficient to stop us, for we are far too fleshly in these matters. Even if I were to abstain from all hatred because I saw that it would harm me in the end, I would, nevertheless, continue to seek my own advancement. God wants us to keep our eyes closed to any regard we might have for our own persons, as well as to cast off all ill will and all desire for wrangling. May we trample all this underfoot. Why? In order that he might have the mastery over us. However much men may give us occasion to hate them because of their wickedness, we must maintain unity with them, for God has placed us all together. The homage that God requires of us is that we deny ourselves and love those that hate us.

Now, this warning of Paul's is not superfluous, as I have said. For he wishes to shame those who become so enraged that they refuse, even from the very first instant, to be subdued or restrained by reason. When a man is thus fiery-natured and throws caution to the winds, we need to be able to give him an appropriate reproof, which will make him ashamed and draw him back to obedience to God. Paul, therefore, seeks to extend help to us here, that we might overcome our passions little by little, for they are far too powerful. Then, next time we feel prompted to hate someone, or to avenge ourselves upon him, we will first think, 'What will happen in the end? If we fight like cats and dogs, we will only consume one another!' Have we really taken note of this? Indeed, we could go further and say that even when hatred would be the most useful thing in the world to us, and would mean that we could have greater victory over our enemies when we have come to the end of all our projects and schemes; yes, even when we can only gain by giving vent to our anger, yet we would be provoking the wrath of God if we cannot submit to him so far as to love the unlovable. This being the case, let us fear, and submit to him in all humility. If this is difficult for us, let us strive more earnestly until God has the mastery of us and until we have denied ourselves, as we have been saying. We must leave behind all that pertains to our nature, and preserve the sacred union that God has placed amongst us by designing us to be one body.

* * *

At this point, Paul says that if we do not wish to be under the dominion of the lust of the flesh, we must 'Walk in the Spirit'. He also speaks of a powerful battle going on, which means that we do not do what we intend. Although God has transformed us and given us life, so that we desire to please him in everything we do, nevertheless, we are not perfect, for our nature encourages us to do evil. However, before we proceed, let us understand that by the word 'flesh' Paul means all that a man is, all that he has by birth. Our Lord Jesus says in the third chapter of John's Gospel, 'That which is born of the flesh is flesh' (*John* 3:6). By 'Spirit', he is not referring to the soul of man, but to the grace that God bestows upon us when he brings us to himself in obedience and deals with our sins, together with all that is contrary to his Word. When men are referred to as 'flesh' in the

Scriptures, the term is derogatory. Even in this passage, it is a mark of sin and corruption. Sometimes, when the Scriptures speak of 'flesh', they are saying, 'What is man but flesh?' In other words, he will decay (*Psa.* 78:39). Again, 'All flesh is grass' (*Isa.* 40:6). Again, the Egyptian is 'flesh' and not spirit (see *Isa.* 31:3). By this word 'flesh', therefore, men are taught that they are fragile, made of dust and ashes; indeed, they are no more than vermin. Primarily, this is meant to humble them. But when the word 'flesh' is used in opposition to the Spirit, it does not refer to man as he was created by God in his first state. It is showing him to be corrupted, full of disease and iniquity, without any capacity for good judgment, full of perverse cravings. Our Lord Jesus Christ understands that we are flesh because we are born flesh, that is to say, we are poor and blind and have no understanding to help us to come to God. Although he has given us an instinct within to distinguish between good and evil, yet our minds are still darkened, as it were, so that we cannot come to him. All the reasoning power that we possess renders us without excuse. Since we only crave what is evil, all the desires we have are like so many enemies which fight against all righteousness.

Now the Holy Spirit reveals us as we are: instead of allowing us to glory in our free-will and virtue, as many do, he shows us that we are full of corruption, and that this produces enmity with God, severing us from his righteousness. It is true that our soul is often referred to as 'spirit', for the word 'spirit' implies an invisible essence which cannot be handled in the same way as a body. The angels are spirits, and also the devils; although the latter are corrupted spirits, full of iniquity and, therefore, alienated from God. Similarly, our souls are, indeed, spirits, but they are spirits which have been infected by sin. Through Adam's fall, we changed and became debased, as the image of God in us was effaced. Therefore, there is now a need for restoration. When God transforms us by his Holy Spirit and makes us new creatures, then we can use the word 'spirit', for our minds have been enlightened to understand that which was hidden from us in our natural state. Faith is a special gift of God, since it is impossible for the natural man to understand what salvation is unless God works within him. Therefore, faith is a gift of the Spirit, (as we will see hereafter in due course), so that, had not God taken control of us, we would not even have made a single step towards him, nor towards conformity to his will. But now that he has adopted us, he has given us his Holy Spirit, who is the true mark which distinguishes those who are his children. The word 'Spirit' here includes all that God has given his elect believers to correct their wicked and evil nature.

Now Paul tells us here that we are to 'Walk in the Spirit', and that if we do, 'we will not fulfil the lust of the flesh'. By this, he is issuing a warning to all who revel in their sins and allow themselves licence to do evil, under the pretext that they cannot resist. He stirs them up here and shows them that they have no excuse; that though completely disposed towards evil, they nevertheless ought to search for the remedy. What is it? It is true that we will not find the answer in ourselves, but God is sufficient for these things and will give us grace to fight against our carnal appetites and evil desires. He will make his Holy Spirit reign in us and have the victory. God has no intention of disappointing us when he makes such a promise; flee to him, therefore, like a sick person running to a doctor. In short, Paul anticipates the excuses yet to be made, as well as those to which men are already accustomed. They will say, 'Look at us – we are carnal. Love is an angelic quality; therefore, how can we be expected to exhibit this if wholly disposed to evil and overtaken by sin? If we were not under the dominion of sin, we could be expected to be united under God, but we are too weak for that!' This is what many people say, and they expect to be absolved as a consequence! However, Paul says, 'It is true that we are full of evil, and yet men choose to remain in this state; they are serving the devil and their minds are increasingly darkened. Nevertheless, we are to seek out a remedy. God calls you to himself through the gospel and offers you his Holy Spirit. Therefore, condemn evil and hate it, and then God will work in you and overcome all your fleshly desires.'

This is what Paul meant in this passage, but he also intended an oblique criticism of those with whom he had a quarrel. For we have already said that the seducers who had troubled the church in this region were given over to many petty and unnecessary observances; indeed, they thought holiness was to observe the ceremonial law. Now, God had not commanded them in vain; they were intended for a specific time to prefigure the coming of our Lord Jesus Christ. Yet, since his appearing, they have become worthless things which even hinder us from living as we should. The ceremonies and shadows assisted our forefathers in coming to the Lord Jesus Christ. If we still kept them today, they would cause us to turn our backs upon Jesus Christ. Therefore, Paul had good reason to show earlier that these things are nothing, and do not merit observance; indeed, he speaks of this here again. Now, since he was disputing with those who emphasised the ceremonies, he says to them here, 'Walk in the Spirit'. It is as if he were saying, 'Consider what true service for God involves. It is not about candles, incense or circumcision; not the keeping of certain days, or abstaining from eating certain meats. God does not wish us to be established in such matters, for his service is spiritual.' He says, 'Walk in the Spirit, and ye shall not fulfil the lust of the flesh.' But this is not the whole picture, for as we have said, Paul is also mocking the seducers with whom he has a quarrel (albeit indirectly), because they were impeded by petty, trivial matters which were no more than worldly elements and rudiments suitable for little children. Being so engrossed with these things, Paul tells them they must 'walk in the Spirit'.

Furthermore, Paul sets out here the true way in which we can be united in love, as we have already declared. It is impossible, even if we were to strive mightily, to come to God and forget all enmity. The answer, as I have said, is in God. Therefore, we must pray to him and ask him to increase the graces of the Holy Spirit in us. Then we will find that, although the flesh is wild and spits out rage and impetuosity, though it is like a wild beast that none can tame, yet it is not more powerful than the Spirit of God and the grace that comes from on high, which controls us and brings us under the yoke in submission to our God. In other words, Paul is saying that if we cannot resist our evil desires, this is due to our own indifference and coldness. It is because each of us feeds our evil by empty self-flattery, and we refuse to come to God with the zeal and heart-felt desire which he requires of us. We can only conclude, therefore, that men have no excuse for their vices. They take pleasure in their sins and only ask God to permit them to wallow in them. As far as possible, they avoid the remedy and source of correction, and their minds are so hardened that they do not care if they provoke God's wrath, for they cannot bear instruction in any form whatsoever. From time to time, they profess with their mouths that they wish their nature and disposition to change, yet in reality, they still desire to reach an agreement with God for him to leave them as they are without altering anything! Like a sick person who, when in pain, cries out, 'Oh! I really want to be healed!', but who does not accept the advice of the doctor, or submit to the prescribed diet. The doctor will give plenty of advice and he will also have remedies in his hand to cure the patient, yet the latter will make excuses and say, 'Oh, I'm afraid I have no appetite for such things.' A sick person may be thirsty, but instead of hot drinks, he takes cold, or he may be so intemperate in his appetites that he cannot be held in check, or he may reject all that he is offered to improve his health, even going mad with rage. He may then claim that he desires to be cured, but the evidence points to the contrary! The same applies to those who turn to God, asking him to change them by his Holy Spirit, that they might abandon their evil desires and trample them underfoot, whilst still hoping to remain unchanged and wallow in sin. This is what we are to remember.

However, though we may pray fervently and strive to tame our evil desires, we will always have weaknesses, whatever we do. I am not speaking about hypocrites, but the true children of God. Even those who have increased in holiness can only approach God limpingly, and do not do as they would want to, as Paul adds shortly and as he expounds at greater length in the seventh chapter to the Romans. Yet, believers, once they have become aware of their wickedness, seek the remedy in God, sincerely, and without pretence. They feel the need for his aid to help them overcome their evil desires. Hence, Paul says, 'ye shall not fulfil the lust of the flesh'. This does not mean that, for the rest of our lives, we will never again be tempted by Satan to do evil, or that we will never experience his many promptings. For indeed, our flesh still has many goads urging us to do wrong. Thus, we will be tempted by all kinds of sin, but we can still resist through the grace of God.

Therefore, this statement was added for a purpose, for without this testimony to the fact that God accepts our service, despite our shortcomings and weaknesses, we would not run with the courage that is required. Each of us would feel defeated and eventually collapse in despair, as, indeed, happens to some when they examine their lives. They find themselves to be so imperfect and still so far from God, that it seems as though they have not grown at all, and they become dispirited and reach desperation point. Whilst it is true that we must aim for this perfection and aspire to it at all times, yet we must not forget to seek God. We cannot reach him on our own, and there are many obstacles on the way; sometimes we take the wrong path and sometimes we are held back by our foolish lusts, which hinder us by enticing us away. Nevertheless, let us not allow ourselves to fall, though we be often unsteady. By nature, we cannot walk unhindered as we approach our God, but it is already something if we do not fulfil the lusts of our flesh. Though we feel them, and though they are very vigorous in us, God accepts us and pardons our shortcomings if we seek to overcome them. Paul, exhorting believers not to allow themselves to lose control, speaks of 'the flesh having no dominion over them'. He does not say that evil desires and sinful lusts will no longer dwell within them. For when will we be rid of them? Only when it pleases God to take us to himself. Until the day that we leave this world, there will always be spots and stains within us, and we will always be bent down with the burden of our sins and weaknesses. This is in order to humble us and to show that our life is to be a constant battle. Thus, though sin dwells within us, it must not have dominion, but the Spirit of God must conquer it. This can only happen if we flee to God with fervent zeal, and pray that he will remedy the evil that we cannot change. Also, that he would grant us more of the gifts of his Spirit so that we might overcome all that has weighed us down.

* * *

This is what Paul meant by this particular phrase in this passage, but he goes on to add, 'For the flesh lusteth against the Spirit, and the Spirit against the flesh: and these are contrary the one to the other: so that ye cannot do the things that ye would.' This statement is encouraging us to keep watch, and even to retain our armour in readiness for the enemy. If we were free of all sin, and if each of us obeyed the commands of God without hesitation, we would not need to go to such trouble. Indeed, the angels in paradise do not have this battle, for they are swift to obey all that they are commanded. Since the angels have no rebellion within, there is, therefore, no battle when devoting themselves to the service of God. This is their natural disposition and inclination. However, Paul says that as for us, we ought not to be cowardly when we are called upon to obey God. Why does he say this? Because by nature we are the opposite; we cannot love to do good without violent and forceful effort. Thus, people have to strive, and force themselves to do good, as if engaged in mortal combat with an enemy. Who are these adversaries? It is true that the devil is our chief enemy, and the one who orchestrates the terrible attacks made against us. Yet also our thoughts, our affections, and our desires are as many mortal enemies seeking to lead us into perdition. If they fight against God, then they are also opposed to our salvation. We can see Paul's intention here; he raises the alarm, and shows that if Christians are asleep or indifferent, and seek to serve God at their leisure, they are mistaken. No, they have repeated and endless battles to face, for day and night Satan tempts them through his wiles and treacherous ways. Indeed, he will attack them violently to lead them astray. They must, therefore, fortify themselves carefully, and enter into combat, persevering to the end. They must not expect to have peace or comfort until the day when God takes them from this world. This is what Paul's doctrine here implies.

This exhortation is more than needful for us today, since the majority think that they have done enough for God when they have served him by some small act of devotion; the fact that they are continuing to wallow in filth does not bother them! Others become frustrated when they encounter such difficulty in regulating their lives to do good. They say, 'How is it possible? It seems as though God would press us beyond our capacity, for he is not asking of us something which comes naturally. Indeed, he condemns such things! How will we ever manage to fulfil these requirements? Our instincts move in the opposite direction to his will. He must be mocking at us to expect these things, seeing he has only given us such a disposition and no other.' This is how people, in regard to their sinful nature, blaspheme against God.

Now, in order that none of us should sleep, or think that we have fulfilled God's demands because we have not fallen away completely (though we have only half followed our course), Paul tells us that the Spirit lusts against the flesh, and the flesh against the Spirit. By saying that the flesh 'lusts', he is implying that we can never serve God in peace, for there will always be a multitude of hindrances and we will be tempted to do evil. Even when we are resolved upon full submission to the Word of God and to his righteousness, the devil still has many ropes to drag us in one direction or another. He will surprise us by showing us that our carnal desires are always there to hinder us; not only so, but he will also pull us in a completely opposite direction. When God calls us to go one way, we will be violently compelled to take another path. Since the flesh lusts against the Spirit in this way, let us seek to battle courageously, and not to find this burdensome. Though we desire to be like the angels, who never rebel and whose every faculty is employed in the service of God, yet if we find ourselves often prevented from doing good, let us learn to force ourselves and take control, though we are reluctant to do so. Let us continue to persevere, so that God gets the victory over us. May we learn to hate ourselves and to be angry with ourselves, and to avenge our own wickedness, as Paul says (*2 Cor.* 7:11). For repentance means that men must condemn themselves, hate themselves, and even take revenge upon themselves when they see that their whole life is full of corruption. They must feel holy indignation within, rather than seek vengeance upon their enemies when they have done them harm. May we rather be angry and indignant against ourselves, and avenge ourselves for our own sins if we find that we cannot conform our lives to the will of God.

Now, we might be so distraught that we say, 'Alas! How are we to fight? Where is our strength? We find ourselves so very feeble. We see that the devil is such a powerful and strong enemy that we can never reach our goal. Our lusts are like wild beasts without reason, control or restraint in any measure. This being so, we are defeated, even before we have felt the first blow.' Paul says that the Spirit also lusts against the flesh; in other words, our nature is inclined towards evil, and the devil also pushes us in the same direction, so that we must all the more fiercely resist the temptations which entice and allure us. An answer will be found to all of this. For who is going to win? Who will have the victory and the mastery? Will it be the corruption that lies within us, or will it be the power of God? When God is willing to pour out the grace of his Holy Spirit, he will always be the strongest party and will win the battle, however difficult. Therefore, we must honour God by trusting him to sustain us and help us to prevail in the conflict, marching steadfastly under his ensign and calling upon him with reverent fear and watchfulness. Paul (as we have already shown) did not wish to paint a picture of ease here, because he knew that men are too ready to slow down. Thus, he does not wish to send us to sleep here, but he tells us that if we would serve God well, we must first of all become enemies of ourselves, and fight against our thoughts and affections.

Since this may alarm us and cause us to draw back, saying that we can never achieve this, he asks, 'Do you not believe that the Spirit of God will conquer?' Indeed, yet we do not have the Spirit. Why is this, if not because we have failed to turn to the One who is ready to give him to us according to the measure that he knows we need. Our Lord says through the prophet Isaiah, 'Ho, every one that thirsteth, come ye to the waters, and he that hath no money; come ye, buy, and eat; yea, come, buy wine and milk without money and without price' (*Isa.* 55:1). 'Receive my Spirit', he is saying, 'for I am ready to pour him upon you liberally according to your need.' It is God who has spoken in this way. Our Lord Jesus Christ also shows that he is the true fountain from which we must draw, for with his fulness we may satisfy our thirst. In the seventh chapter of John's Gospel, verse thirty-seven, he says, 'If any man thirst, let him come unto me, and drink.' Whoever does so will have a fountain which flows into streams; he will not only have sufficient for his own needs, but the waters will flow from within him, when he permits Jesus Christ to pour out his Spirit upon him, for he is ready and able so to do. Therefore, though the Spirit of God is far distant from us, yet we will receive from him sufficiently, and God is willing to increase the supply. He will do this because this is what he has promised, and he invites us so lovingly to ask of him; we will certainly receive all that we need. Thus, on the one hand, we are told here that we must engage in a battle and employ our strongest efforts. Yet on the other, we are told that we will enjoy a sure and certain victory if we seek help from God, being convinced of our own weakness and having confessed in all humility that we can do nothing of ourselves. If we come to our God and ask him to be our physician, his Holy Spirit is not too feeble to overcome our fleshly passions, but he will give us grace to persevere to the end, through all the attacks that come against us.

Once again, Paul says that believers cannot do the things they desire to do. He says this in order to encourage us to learn to press on, though we cannot fulfil everything that God has commanded us perfectly. This is vital, as I have said, because otherwise we would be hypocrites, thinking that we were without fault. Such pride is intolerable, but we see many such hounds, who fear neither God nor religion, yet who preach that believers ought to be perfect. This is a diabolical blasphemy which we should hold in abhorrence. Some fall into despair when they find that they cannot fulfil what God requires. Therefore, in order to prevent hypocrisy, as well as to encourage us, Paul tells us that we cannot do that which we desire to do. However, we need to refer back to what I have just been saying, which is that we will not fulfil the lust of the flesh if we are led by the Spirit of God.

Thus, firstly, we need to realise that we are so devoted to evil that we could not even wring a drop of good out of our thoughts and affections; indeed they lead us further than ever from all that is good. This is the first thing. Secondly, we need to entrust ourselves to God, regardless of our sin and rebelliousness, and ask him to give us grace to walk in obedience to him. If we are led by his Holy Spirit, we will experience a power which will enable us to overcome hindrances and obstacles, and help us to pursue the right path, not the one that we follow by nature. Thirdly, if we notice an inner resistance which means that we must force ourselves more and more to do right, and if we find that there are many obstacles which hinder us – even if we fall many times and go astray – let us not lose courage for all this. Let us pursue the holy calling of God, so that, through striving, we learn to die to all our sins. To this end, let us tremble before God and confess our sins freely to him; whatever our case, let us never think that he has rejected us, though our life may be far from perfect. This is what we need to remember – all the imperfections and weaknesses that we feel within ought not to prevent us from yielding to our God, and strengthening ourselves more and more in his fear. However, let us not wear blindfolds, flattering ourselves; let us tremble, rather, and confess how much we owe him, whilst at the same time we aim for that perfection which should be our goal throughout our lives. This involves acknowledging that we are all condemned and lost, unless he comes to our aid in his infinite goodness in the name of our Lord Jesus Christ.

Now let us fall before our great God, acknowledging our sins, and praying that he would make us increasingly conscious of them. May this not only lead to confession with our mouths, but may we be touched with a desire to repent, so that we seek to give ourselves to him with a pure and true zeal, and to mortify the abundance of sin that dwells within us. May we conform to his holy will and serve him in peace and harmony, so that we devote ourselves to magnifying him with one heart and one voice. By this may we show that we are truly united by adoption, as is revealed in the gospel, where he shows himself to be our Father, since we desire to be his true children. Thus, we all say, Almighty God and our heavenly Father, etc.

36

The Spirituality of the Law

> *Now the works of the flesh are manifest, which are these; Adultery, fornication, uncleanness, lasciviousness, Idolatry, witchcraft, hatred, variance, emulations, wrath, strife, seditions, heresies, Envyings, murders, drunkenness, revellings and such like: of the which I tell you before, as I have also told you in time past, that they which do such things shall not inherit the kingdom of God. But the fruit of the Spirit is love, joy, peace, longsuffering, gentleness, goodness, faith, Meekness, temperance: against such there is no law* (Gal. 5:19–23).

We saw this morning that men stand condemned in the sight of God because all that proceeds from man is contaminated and filthy. Now if God is the Author of all perfection, it follows that all that is contrary to his nature or to his Word is totally corrupt. Hence, there is a constant battle of the flesh against the spirit; for if men were left to pursue their own paths, they would be mortal enemies of God throughout their whole lives. For this reason, we can only conclude that men are full of evil and iniquity. When we hear this sentence pronounced, we ought to be utterly ashamed; for here is the decree of our heavenly judge, and it is not lawful to contest it, for God speaks with authority. When he declares that we are evil and perverse by nature, he fulfils his office; for we must give account to him. However, men are so blinded in their hypocrisy or pride that they do not care if they have provoked God's anger against themselves. This is because we all flatter ourselves and feed our sins. Therefore, the only way we can be made truly to acknowledge our sins is by force. Even then, we make use of evasive techniques and subterfuge. What is more, we brazenly seek out frivolous excuses, as if they would be pleasing to God! Therefore, it is not enough for us to hear God's general sentence of condemnation pronounced against us; we need God to reveal our own vileness, to make us ashamed of ourselves. We need him to be specific and point his finger at the sins that are apparent and obvious to the people around us.

Hence, Paul, having said this morning that all the thoughts and feelings of men strive against God, now adds the declaration that we have just heard. He tells us that the appearance of fruit enables us to assess the condition of the tree, though the most important part, the root, is hidden. Just as the tree is known by its fruit, the sin that reigns in us and in our nature is seen by the works that we produce. Thus, we can see why Paul says here that 'the works of the flesh are manifest'. It is as if he is saying that people deliberately close their eyes to obscure their own evil, and deceive themselves into thinking that they are full of nothing but virtue, although they are bursting at the seams with ever so many terrible vices. However much we may protest, seek out different excuses, wipe our mouths and disguise the way things really are, yet we have to return to the fact that our lives declare, loud and clear, the kind of people we are. Thus, the works of the flesh are indeed manifest. Now this is enough to rebuke those who seek to hide behind a layer of make-up, as it were, as if they were innocent in the eyes of God. It is true that Paul does not give a complete list here of the sins that God condemns in the law, but he recites examples by which we may easily judge the rest. Besides, it would have been a lengthy procedure if Paul had wanted to enumerate them in this way. As we shall see, however, this list is sufficient to convict all those who think they stand to gain by their hypocrisy.

In order to have a better understanding of all this, we need to be aware of what it is to walk in obedience to God. In the second chapter of Titus, verse eleven, it says that the grace of God has appeared that we might walk in the world here below in holiness, temperance, and righteousness while we hope for the life that God has promised us, and the coming of our great Saviour, who will gather us to himself in his heavenly kingdom. To this, Christians must apply themselves above all else. They must be exercised in these things; namely, the knowledge that this is not the place of our eternal rest, nor our inheritance. This world is like a foreign land that we must travel through, whilst our eyes are lifted up to heaven. This is the most important thing. Yet this cannot be achieved unless believers call upon God and have recourse to him alone. As for our lives, Paul speaks of three specific things: there is holiness, which means that we serve God with a pure heart, with integrity and honesty, renouncing all the pollution of this world. This is the first point. Secondly, we must not become worldly or profane, but must lead an honest life. The third is that we harm no-one, that we never practise deceit or cruelty, but that we seek, rather, to serve our neighbours. The life of a Christian should be like this.

Now, Paul says here that for those who do not acknowledge that they are wholly at enmity with God, and full of malice and rebellion, a simple test is needed. If we were to examine their lives, we would find that some are given over to fornication, some are drunkards, others are given up to all kinds of wickedness, some are murderers, others are witches, some stir up revolts, others are full of ambition, some still seek only to sow discord and trouble and to create sects that pervert the truth of God by their corruption. This is what we will find if we look into men's lives. Now, what will they gain by complaining against God and seeking to hide their baseness by quibbling? If they do not confess this with their mouths, then their lives will speak. Their lives, with all the works that we see them perform, will be a testimony to what we have said; thus, there can be no further debate.

Moreover, when Paul says that the works of the flesh are manifest, he does not mean that all whom God leaves to follow their natural course, and who are not led by the Holy Spirit, are guilty of each sin named here. It is more likely that a person will be corrupt to the extent that he will be given over first to one sin, then to two or three, as occasion arises. Thus, there are many pagans and unbelievers who have no fear of God, and have never been taught his Word, who yet have some appearance of virtue and uprightness. However, this does not mean that they are therefore free from corruption, for if the infection is hidden and lurking inside them, then they have a tumour which will eventually rot every part of them. For man's nature knows no perimeters, no limits; all is unbounded confusion. This is what we are to retain from this passage; and, in order that none of us should be deceived by hypocrisy, we need to look well to ourselves and examine our lives diligently. Then we will have occasion to cast our eyes downwards, and close our mouths, knowing that we are utterly wretched, and worthy of condemnation. It is true that nothing that Paul lists here is apparent, and maybe we cannot be accused before men; but even if we outwardly appear to be like little angels, we are still evil and perverse, until God has transformed us. It is just that God does not wish us to be without testimony in our lives to cast us down and cause us to condemn ourselves voluntarily.

* * *

Now we will see how to apply this doctrine. If we think we are worthy in some way, and do not perceive our own poverty, let us examine our lives, and make a comparison between our own actions and all that God has proscribed and prohibited. It is then we will have a good picture of our wickedness and filth; instead of us thinking that we are full of purity and perfection as we did before, God will reveal to our eyes that we are full of iniquity. Yet, after we have recognised one sin, then two, then three, we must then conclude that this is not even a hundredth part of it. For we are always bedazzled when it comes to awareness of our own poverty. Even when we see our works clearly, we ought to be able to proceed to their source. Some people are so dense that they think they will be acceptable as long as they have not been guilty of fornication, or as long as their drunkenness remains undiscovered, or as long as their deception has been so secretly and carefully carried out that no-one has noticed it. Paul's intention, however, in saying that the works of the flesh are manifest, is not to flatter men by telling them that a sin can remain uncondemned until it is detected. For, as I have said, one sin leads to another. Thus, if fornication, drunkenness, theft, murders, treachery, blasphemy against God, strife and rebellion, are detestable things in themselves, we can only conclude that the same is true of impiety, ambition, pride, or an inordinate sense of self-esteem and self-worth which remain hidden in the heart. Covetousness, where we desire the things that belong to others and suchlike, is another sin that we must condemn. In short, external actions give testimony to the fact that we are full of infection in the sight of God. Where is this seen? In our desires, in our advice, in our thoughts, and in all our undertakings; we can see that all these things spring from an evil source.

Thus, we are drawn to a knowledge of our sins which makes us utterly ashamed of ourselves before God. God uses the same method of instruction in the law. There God does not forbid fornication alone, but he prohibits adultery. At first sight, it looks as if God does not forbid cheating or plundering. Instead, what does he condemn? Stealing. He does not forbid lying, only bearing false witness. Thus, to those who know nothing of the power of the law, it seems as though they have fulfilled their duty if they have abstained from these specific crimes. For this reason, Paul says that for a time he thought he was most righteous, as if God could have discovered nothing for which to reproach him (*Rom.* 7:7). Thus, hypocrites become drunk with pride and become completely wild if God rebukes them, for they think he greatly wrongs them. Why? Because they do not understand the nature of the law. It is spiritual, says Paul, which means that we must be totally transformed before we can submit to it (*Rom.* 7:14). So long as we follow our carnal natures, all that we think, all that we do and say, can only be sin in the eyes of God.

Thus, we are not to look simply at the word that is used in the law. For when God gives the example of adultery, he was also seeking to make any fornication seem detestable to us, for if marriage vows are broken and violated, it is a perversion of all law and order amongst men. By this word 'adultery', therefore, God is showing that he detests all sexual impurity and immodesty. We are also told, 'Thou shalt not kill'. Is it not, therefore, lawful to fight? Not at all; not even to hate, according to John, who tells us that if anyone secretly hates his neighbour, even if he never torments him, nor lifts a finger against him, he is a murderer in the eyes of God (*1 John* 3:15). Thus, by the word 'murder', God is condemning any harm that we might do to our neighbours. Therefore, even though we may not lift a finger to hurt them, if we hate them or bear them ill-will, we are guilty of murder in the eyes of God. The same applies to stealing; thieves are not just the people we flog and hang, and whose ears we cut off. These, I tell you, are not the only thieves in the sight of God. Even those who seek reputation as good people, and are highly respected – if they deceive and cheat on their neighbours, though they cannot be accused of theft because of their high standing in the eyes of men, they are nevertheless thieves before God. The same applies to all other sins.

In this passage, where Paul says that the works of the flesh are manifest, his line of instruction moves from the grosser sins to the lesser ones. Once we have been convinced of our poverty and sin, and once we have discovered our own shameful condition, so that we are left speechless, we must then be convinced of another point: we need to realise that all of the appetites which lead us to do evil, be it theft and cruelty, deception and perjury, or hatred and enmity – all of these things are equally to be condemned. For the tree is still a bad one, even if we do not see its fruit at first sight; the tree has its own nature, but the only way we can judge the nature of the tree is by its fruit. Now, this is worthy of note because, as I have said, though God compels men to condemn themselves, they will only half do so. They want all that is not apparent to others to be forgotten, so that no mention is ever made of it. The person who is condemned for having done evil will doubtless never excuse his sin if he is forced to confess it. Yet, there is no question of him voluntarily examining himself to feel the judgment of God against him. He does not think about what he deserves, or consider the many temptations he went through before he committed this act, and the hundred or so times that he had offended God before his sin was apparent to all.

We must, therefore, pay all the more attention to this warning upon which I have commented; especially since the Popish doctors display their excessive stupidity by saying that it is not a sin to think evil, or to be tempted, as long as one does not consent to do it. A man could be tempted to wrong his neighbour in some way; he may have a grievance or frustration which makes him want to avenge himself upon the person who has offended him. If the occasion were to arise, he would be delighted. This is not sin, they tell us, unless he has consented to the temptation with resolve. They are only wiping their mouths like whores, or showing their snouts like sows, after they have wallowed in the mire and dirt. A man may murmur against God and be angry with him, and doubt whether God will look after him; he may be troubled by many mistrustful thoughts, so that he cannot find refuge in God; but none of these things are sin according to the Papists. I am not saying that the common herd are the only ones to be deceived in these matters, for all of their schools hold to the doctrine and belief that this is not sin. They do say that all is sin before baptism; but after baptism, all becomes virtuous, however much we may doubt God, or however many grievances we have against him. We may be very impatient with him, or agitated about this matter or that – but we cannot be accused if we have not been moved to practise evil outwardly! In short, if we are inclined to all that God condemns and reproves in his law – all that is unlawful – it is nothing. They are well suited to believe such stupid things! After all, they have made idols and grotesque statues to worship, and now their minds have become darkened as they make merry around their gods, scoffing at us, as at a little child holding forth about righteousness and integrity. We must not, therefore, be surprised if such people behave like this. Because they have falsified the glory of God and destroyed it, they must be completely brutish.

As for us, let us note the words which I have already quoted from the apostle Paul, namely, that the law is spiritual. If we are convicted as rebels against God because of external, visible acts, let us remember that God will find an infinite number, indeed, an abyss of evil desires writhing inside of us, though they are not regarded by men as rendering us guilty. We must, therefore, conclude that in everything and in every way we are drowned in perdition, until God looks in pity upon us, and draws us out. The way to apply this text of Paul's to our instruction is as follows: inasmuch as we are unaware of the sins that lurk within us, it is necessary for God to come and examine our lives. After this, we will learn to humble ourselves. So then, once we see the sins that are known and evident to all, and which cannot be excused, even in the eyes of little children, may we be led even further to sound out the depths, and acknowledge that all our appetites and thoughts are like many rebellions against God. Yet if each of us were more careful to examine ourselves in this way, we would all surely have occasion to tremble and sigh; all haughtiness and pride would be cast down and we would be ashamed of every aspect of our lives. But we know that each of us turns away as much as we can from any knowledge of our sins; we throw them all behind our backs. God does not forget them; though we may want them to be forgotten, he has to keep them in remembrance. This is what Paul attracts our attention to in this passage.

Furthermore, we can see the foolishness and ignorance (or, rather, stupidity) of the doctors of the Papacy, in that they believe that the word 'flesh' refers only to man's sensual nature (as they call it); for this is how they divide it up. They admit that the appetites which they label 'inferior' are very corrupt, but believe that as long as we have free will, there remains some degree of reason and intelligence within us. According to the Papists, the sensuality of man exhibits itself when he is not guided by his own reason, but devotes himself excessively to sexual impurity, or drunkenness or gluttony or some such thing. Yet here, Paul puts ambition on the same plane. Why else is it that men envy one another, and compete for superiority over one another, desiring to be the wisest or most intelligent? Is it not because each one longs to be esteemed in the eyes of the world? Is this less worthy of condemnation than fornication or drunkenness? If a poor lout who loves eating and drinking becomes very drunk, well, he will continue along on his merry way; he does not ask to be a king or a great lord – he simply whiles away his time. Another who is addicted to gambling will go and play with rascals like himself, without being tempted by ambition and the desire for great honour. Therefore, those who are considered to be most honourable, and who think highly of themselves, are the most carnal, says Paul. We saw in the First Epistle to the Corinthians that he accused them of being carnal, because they debated with one another over doctrinal matters, and had a foolish longing to be prized and noticed by men (*1 Cor.* 3:3). Indeed, he mentions 'strife and divisions' there too. If a man troubles the church of God by false doctrines, either out of disdain for others, or out of a desire for acclaim and reputation, the Papists would not say that he was carnal. They would say that he was too clever; but Paul says that heresies, ambition and emulations are works of the flesh. This proves what we said this morning, that the word 'flesh' includes all that pertains to man. We will be completely given over to evil unless we are changed and transformed.

As I have already said, it is true that pagans and unbelievers will always be considered virtuous, though God has let go of their reins and has not regenerated them by his

Holy Spirit. Indeed, we will find some degree of decency present in their lives; at the very least, they will not all be fornicators, or drunkards or thieves. How can Paul say that they are carnal, therefore? Because the heart of man is a deep pit of iniquity, as Jeremiah says, without base or bank; the prophet exclaims, 'What an abyss the heart is! Who can fathom its depths? Only God' (*Jer.* 17:9).

For men flatter themselves, as we know, and commit wicked acts with impunity; they are so hardened in sin that they heap up evil upon evil and sin upon sin, considering their vices to be virtues. Nevertheless, their lives may have a glossy, attractive appearance. Thus, we cannot say that those who have not been taught the truth will be justified. Paul said in the first chapter to the Romans that the whole world is guilty of ungodliness and ungratefulness, since God has revealed himself to all without exception, enough to leave them without excuse (*Rom.* 1:20). He adds, 'when they knew God, they glorified him not as God'; therefore, he gave them up as reprobates, and abandoned them to their own gross, wicked lusts. Paul continues by reciting all the detestable things they do. Amongst other things, he speaks of murder, fornication, and other evil and corrupt things which we ought not to mention. After that, he speaks of envy, as in this passage, and of those who invent evil things; of deceit, backbiting, malignity, contentions and debates. Of course, not all of these are in evidence in every unbeliever! However, Paul tells us that all unbelievers, from the greatest to the least, are ungrateful to God, and have robbed him of the honour that is his due. Hence, they are guilty of sacrilege, because they have removed all that belongs to him. Thus, he gives them the wages that they have deserved, owing to the fact that the seeds of all sin lie in man's nature.

Nevertheless, although men are stuffed full of as many vices as we can imagine, God still holds the reins and does not allow men complete abandonment to wickedness. Because of this, many unbelievers are not controlled by their natural senses, indeed, are chaste and modest; they do not steal another's goods, but are sober and upright. In short, they have many virtues according to the opinion of the world. Why, then, are they condemned along with fornicators, thieves and drunkards? It is because they do not have these virtues out of a desire to obey God, for there is no integrity in their hearts. They are held back out of shame, or for some other reason unknown to us. In this way, God spares the human race, so that things are not in a state of confusion, and men are not totally brutish. God is in control of these unbelievers to the end that all their virtues, whatever they may be, remain vices. Therefore, at the first opportunity, when God releases their reins, they devote themselves to all kinds of evil. We might say that believers could just as easily become debauched. Indeed, but God has promised to strengthen them to persevere. Also, there is a great difference between the children of God, who are led by his Holy Spirit, and unbelievers, who are still carnal. The children of God aim and intend to dedicate themselves to him and to be truly purified by his grace. The others walk aimlessly, and if they are good, they scarcely know why! They will call it 'virtue', but they do not have God in mind because they are far from him. This is what we need to remember from this passage.

* * *

On the other hand, Paul says that 'the fruit of the Spirit is joy, peace, gentleness, kindness, patience', and suchlike things. It is as if he is saying that in view of our great perversity and the fact that we are full of evil and corruption, there is enough here to exercise us to ensure that we will not be idle for the rest of our lives! The battle against our sin is sufficient to occupy us day and night. Yet, we are also commanded to be kind and good-natured, to live sober and chaste lives, and to keep ourselves from being polluted. We are to dedicate ourselves as a sacrifice to God, and to abstain from all that would cause harm. Instead of seeking self-advancement, we are to do all that we possibly can to help and comfort those who need us. When we see that all this is expected of us, we ask, is it possible to achieve this? Not at all; in fact, we need to be transported up to heaven in order to approach God. The holiness that God requires in the law, and all the good works that he demands of us are because he is seeking a union between ourselves and him. But where are the wings to fly so high? For we can neither be chaste, nor benign, nor kind, nor temperate, nor sober, unless we renounce the world and ourselves, and discard all that we are by nature. However, this is beyond our faculties. Therefore, there is much here that could frighten us away.

Hence, Paul concludes by saying that 'against such there is no law'. In other words, if we are truly led by the Spirit of God, we are no longer under the law. Here, Paul encourages all believers, who will feel their own weakness until they leave their mortal bodies behind. God still supports them, and their service is acceptable to him, even though they are not completely renewed to the point of perfection. Therefore, they are to persevere; otherwise, they will be troubled and fall into despair. Paul, therefore, exhorts us to be constant here, telling us that if we are led by the Spirit of God, we will no longer be subject to the law.

However, at the same time, he is indirectly mocking those with whom he has a quarrel, as we saw this morning, for they advertised their virtues with great fanfares! It is so in the Papacy today, where to speak of holiness and the service of God is to speak of nothing more than good deeds and keeping many ceremonies. In other words, they are concerned with trivial nonsense. A Papist will dabble in this and that – he will bow to one statue, and then move on to the next. Bigots will light their candles, apply the holy water several times, make the sign of the cross repeatedly here, there and everywhere, and be sure to keep fast days. They weigh themselves down with all these things in order to redeem themselves, through Masses, or other abominations. This is how God is served and honoured! For the Papists, perfection consists in that which is nothing short of a lie; the candles must be attractive, the organs must sound good, there must be many parades, the statues must be well gilded, they must prepare fragrances and be appeased by all kinds of other follies. This is tomfoolery, indeed, abomination, though they may consider it to be highly virtuous.

As for us, we say that the service of God is spiritual, and that he does not regard that which is seen by men (*John* 4:23–24). God seeks an upright integrity and sincerity of heart, as it says in the fifth chapter of Jeremiah (verse three). However, on the contrary, men persuade themselves that they can satisfy God in their own way and as they please, and thus they transfigure him and imagine that he is absolutely the same as themselves, and will, therefore, agree with their ideas. This should not surprise us, for although they say that they have been taught the law, they never study it and do not really know what it contains. Let us learn, therefore, that if we want to devote ourselves to serving God, we are not to do whatever seems right to us, for our own ideas, as we call them, are simply the deceptions of Satan. We are to give heed to that which God has commanded, and occupy ourselves with the things that he has ordained. Let us make these our study, that we might render him obedience.

We must take good note of the passage that is set before us here, because however hard we strive to observe our own inventions, it does not mean that God will accept any of them. We are following our nature, which is corrupt. What, then, does God want us to do? What does he ask of us? In the first place, that we renounce all perversity, hatred, rancour; all dissensions, deceit, all that causes harm, blasphemies, idolatry, cruelty, violence, treachery, envy and enmity. Thus, we must be good soldiers if we wish to devote ourselves to serving God, fighting against the works of the flesh, rather than against the works that are visible, and which the world either condemns or approves. Our fight is against the hidden lusts. May we be cleansed of this filth, which is stagnating within our hearts. May we apply all our efforts to this end; not that we can achieve this ourselves, but we must be ready to pray to God, and to examine ourselves morning and night. Once we have recognised our sins, may we be moved to tremble and ask for help from the right source. We must ask that God would remedy the evil with which we are stricken. If, therefore, we increasingly strive to live a happy life, to be good-natured, to be patient in adversity, to suffer insults and injuries without seeking vengeance – if, I say, we are like this, we will have a lot to occupy us, and can never be idle.

Let us leave the Papists to get on with their fooling around with God. Why do they fret themselves so much? Because they have never known how God wishes to be served and honoured. According to them, his ordinances are nothing compared to their foolish inventions. Let me give you an example. A man works honestly in order to make a living; though he only has brown bread to his heart's content, he still calls upon God in the morning and praises him in the evening. If he has children, he denies himself as much as possible in order to feed and clothe them. If God sends afflictions to his household, he bears them patiently. If he practises some kind of handicraft, or some other trade, he will refrain from cheating on his neighbours. He would prefer to die rather than to wrong anyone. This man, who lives first and foremost an honest life, will not be arrogant enough to seek self-advancement without restraint. He will not be given over to intemperate habits. He will be modest in his eating and drinking, patient in all adversities. What kind of man is this according to the Papists? 'Oh, he's a secular man; in other words, he is a man of the world.' This is how much they value the pure service of God. We know that the principal service that God requires of us is that we devote ourselves entirely to him; this means that we will glorify him in affliction as well as in prosperity, and that we will follow the vocation we have when we are called, without pride, ambition or envy. God takes delight in this, but according to the definition of the Papists, those who live in this way are worldly!

Where are the Papistical 'angels' then? Within cloisters! When these wicked hypocrites have stuffed themselves full, and gorged themselves with good fare, they do not know what to do with themselves except to gamble or pursue other evils. (For we know that all the convents of the Papacy are full-blown brothels, and would to God that they were only brothels – for they commit such gross and shocking acts there that our hair would stand on end to hear about them!) In other words, their lifestyle would horrify us, and yet these are angels compared to the poor folk who live as we described earlier. Why is this? Because they sing matins devoutly, they sing Mass and separate themselves from the rest of the world. They do not engage in digging earth, nor do they get involved with sewing or tailoring, or anything else. Theirs is a contemplative life, and they are in a state of perfection. Can you not see how the world has been deceived? Such people, who make God into little statues, well deserve the pit for devising such absurd errors.

As for ourselves, let us be aware that our God is Spirit, and that he wants to be served spiritually, as he tells us in his Word. At the same time, let us be wary of becoming trapped in the foolish notions which bewitch these wretches; let us, instead, realise that God speaks with us so that we might have recourse to him in all holiness, righteousness and uprightness. Let us measure our lives against the law and not against our own opinions or those of the world. Let us be concerned with what God commands and forbids, since we have to give account to him, and knowing that we have no other judge than God himself. May we exercise ourselves in all these things, believing that if we do so, we will not be labouring in vain. Leave the Papists to break their legs and their necks, all the while unsure of what they are doing, yet vexing God and provoking him more and more. In order that we do not strive in vain, or wander about here and there following this or that opinion without a fixed destination, let us exercise ourselves in the things that Paul teaches us in this passage. Subsequently, we will not be condemned for occupying ourselves with meaningless things which God disapproves of, detests, and declares to be frivolous.

Now let us fall down before the majesty of our great God, acknowledging our sins, and praying that he would make us increasingly conscious of them, so that we cast ourselves down low. Having condemned ourselves, let us have recourse to him, knowing that he is always willing to help those who are starved of his grace, and who desire it in sincerity. Since he has given us to the Lord Jesus Christ, and views his conduct as if it were ours, may he pour out the treasures and the gifts of his Holy Spirit that we may partake of them. May he increase his grace in us, and may we be so well armed that we achieve the victory in all our combat with Satan, the world, and our own flesh. May he show this grace not only to us, but to all peoples and nations on earth, etc.

37

Our Lifestyle Reveals Our True Spiritual Condition

But the fruit of the Spirit is love, joy, peace, longsuffering, gentleness, goodness, faith, Meekness, temperance: against such there is no law. And they that are Christ's have crucified the flesh with the affections and lusts. If we live in the Spirit, let us also walk in the Spirit. Let us not be desirous of vain glory, provoking one another, envying one another (Gal. 5:22–26).

We saw last time that if we desire to serve God, there will be plenty of opportunity for striving to mortify our sins, when we realise that we are subject to so many corruptions and shortcomings. Paul has set before us the sins that reign in us by nature, in order that we might know how to control our natural affections, thereby enabling us to yield to God and obey him. For we can see that whereas people protest that they are striving to serve God, they are really occupying their time doing frivolous things, fretting constantly and excessively about this or that. Such is wasted and fruitless effort. Indeed, in Popery, what is called serving God is a lot of nonsense forged by man according to his own will. Though they exalt these things and boast of them, they are nevertheless vain. These people never seem to get to the heart of the matter, because the world prefers such byways. God sets before us the right path in his law, and if we sincerely desire true perfection, we must begin by renouncing ourselves. Thus, we must recognise that there is no wisdom in us but that which is cursed; there is no thought but that which is evil; there is no desire but that which is perverse and corrupt. This is why Paul has shown us previously that if men have a true longing to order their lives well, the first thing they discover is that they have much work to do; for they will find that there are many difficulties and wicked lusts to overcome, and this cannot be achieved all at once. In particular, Paul is addressing his remarks to those who observed the ceremonies of the law. For although in general terms they were saying we ought to fulfil the commands of God, they were especially in favour of circumcision and the ceremonial law. This is why Paul has to say that God's aim is for us to be occupied with higher matters; in other words, battling courageously against the many obstacles that drive us from the right path.

In opposition to the works of the flesh, he now adds that 'the fruit of the Spirit is love, gentleness, goodness, meekness, temperance', and the like. When these things are in control, the law no longer has dominion over us, for we are set free and the Lord Jesus, who has liberated us from it, now reigns over us. Paul's overriding aim is that Christians should be set free from slavery to the law. Not those who talk about Christianity with their mouths, and boast of it, but those who show in their lives that they are members of the Lord Jesus Christ, because they are regenerated by his Spirit. For their lives must answer accordingly, or else all that they claim is nothing; they will be condemned as liars unless their works prove that they have spoken in truth and uprightness. Furthermore, Paul is saying that all virtues and all good and praiseworthy things are fruits of the Spirit. By this he confirms what we have shown previously, that if there is an ounce of goodness in us, it is not of our own doing; we cannot take the credit for it without wronging and insulting God. For these are the fruits of his grace, and he puts them all within us by his Holy Spirit. Thus, we are humbled here, and prevented from deceiving ourselves by believing that we have virtue of our own, or temperance, or love or anything else. For until God transforms us, we are like a barren wilderness; indeed, we are full of evil. It is not simply that we can do no good, but we actually produce so much evil, until our Lord cleanses us. We are just like infertile soil, which is not only useless to its owner because it will not produce corn, or wine or any other useful thing, but also because it will, instead, yield only thistles, thorns and weeds.

Now we must note that, as Paul said earlier, love summarises the law, and thus he places it first here. However, he does not wish us to neglect calling upon God, nor to abandon the trust that we ought to have in his promises, nor to forget any of the service that is described in the first table of the law. Paul despises none of it, and therefore does not wish us to reject it; but he is concerned that we testify before men as to whether or not we truly desire to obey God. We have already said that such a testimony is clearly seen if we love our neighbours, and are not devoted to self-advantage. Collectively, we should be trying to foster a healthy and peaceful unity, and to use the faculties and the means that God has given us to serve those to whom his Word declares that we have a responsibility. This is why Paul puts the word 'love' first. He does not mean us to love our neighbours so much that we leave God out of the picture, but rather that we declare our true dedication and devotion to God by the mutual friendship that we have with one another. Of course, this cannot happen unless we have placed all our trust in him, and taken refuge in prayers and petitions. Indeed, since all that is known as virtue, or could be rightly praised as such by men, is called the 'fruit of the Spirit', we will not be equipped to approach God by faith, nor will we have the will to pray to be armed against all temptations, unless the Holy Spirit is at work within us. By nature, we have no ability to understand the gospel, nor are we agile enough to mount up to God and communicate personally with him in prayers and supplications. We need the Holy Spirit to enable us by enlightening us by his grace and encouraging our hearts to call upon God. This is what we need to remember.

Now Paul here adds 'joy' to love; but he does not only

mean that we will be at peace with God, and have cheerful hearts because he has mercifully received us and declared his kindness to us. He speaks of another kind of joy here, meaning that we ought not to grieve or upset one another, nor to alienate ourselves from our neighbours by our disdain for them. We are to be easy-going and friendly, even finding pleasure in being able to help and assist those who require our aid. In the fourteenth chapter to the Romans, verse seventeen, Paul says that the kingdom of God is 'joy in the Holy Ghost'. However, he is using this word in a different sense. For we can rejoice in God when he testifies that we have been accepted in the name of the Lord Jesus Christ; without this, we would be transfixed and numbed with fear, and for this reason we would always be troubled in spirit. Those who have contempt for God may seem happy enough in their pride, but they will never have peace or joy. Inwardly, they are burning, for God pricks their consciences with remorse, so that they are always sorrowful and agitated. Even when they want to rejoice, their minds become increasingly darkened and they have no more feeling; their ability to discern between good and evil is deadened. Thus, when men stray from God in this way, their joy is cursed, and they forget who they are. But, as I have already said, Paul is speaking here of the joy that we have when we relate to our neighbours.

Likewise, the word 'faith' here means faithfulness and integrity. There is a 'faith' that relates to God, which is the certainty that we have about the fulfilment of his promises. It is written that we are justified by faith (*Rom.* 5:1); God begins the process of mortifying all that pertains to our nature. We, therefore, need to be grounded upon the mercy of God alone, revealed to us in the Lord Jesus Christ. How do we enter into the possession of such a gift? By believing the promises of God, and accepting them obediently; also by leaning entirely upon him once we have confessed that we are lost and condemned. Thus, the faith that relates to God is an assurance of his goodness and love, making it possible for us to approach him with confidence because we know that he will hear us. Thus, Paul tells us that those who have such faith trust steadfastly in God, and therefore possess liberty and boldness to address themselves to him. But in this passage, Paul is speaking of our faithfulness to one another when we walk in integrity. We should not seek to cheat anyone out of malice or craft; we should not be two-faced. There should not be any deception in us whereby we seek to influence the simple-minded, but we should treat others as we ourselves would like to be treated. This is what Paul means when he refers to 'faith' as a fruit of the Spirit.

He adds, 'gentleness, goodness'. Without these things, it is impossible for us to unite together; there would be no harmony whatever. For if each of us were determined to be horrible and unkind to one another, we would do better as wild beasts! We must show that we have a desire to communicate with those whom God has placed around us. In short, love must be maintained by the gentleness, goodness and meekness that Paul refers to here. He also mentions 'temperance', which not only means that we must abstain from plundering one another's goods, but also that we must live sober lives, and keep ourselves from intemperance and excess. To summarise, these virtues that Paul sets out here are for Christians; it is as if Paul were saying, 'if we are led by the Spirit of our Lord Jesus Christ, it will be evident and visible in our lives. We will be kept back from wandering like others who lead dissolute lives; we will be loving and kind to all, and will not harbour iniquity, deception or extortion within us. We will be content with that which we possess and will seek to serve one another.' We have seen, therefore, that all good proceeds from the Spirit of God. But we also see here that our Lord Jesus is the fountain from which we must draw water; if we are in him, and belong to him as members of his body, he will demonstrate in our lives that it has not been in vain for him to have received and acknowledged us as his own.

* * *

At this point, Paul concludes that against such virtues (or indeed against the people that are gifted with them) the law has no authority or power. For, as he says in the first chapter of the first epistle to Timothy (*1 Tim.* 1:9), the law was not made for the righteous, but for the wicked and those who are full of evil deeds and offences. If the seducers who were troubling the church in those days only knew the function of the law and the gospel, they would not have sought to enslave believers. Yet, Paul mocks them for their hypocrisy, which they coupled with great impudence, by saying that they claimed to be great zealots for the law, for their lives only revealed disdain for God and ungodliness. The Papist hypocrites today protest loudly that we are destroying good works, and are seeking to introduce a licence to do evil, thus removing all desire to serve God. Why do they say such things? Because we strip men of their vain presumption and arrogance, and show them that there is no other way that a man can have hope in God than by trusting in his goodness in the name of the Lord Jesus Christ. We declare that all that they call merit is an abomination in the eyes of God, because they believe that they are their own saviours. Thus, our doctrine casts down man's pride. It does not mean that we are given liberty to do evil, or that we forget to serve and fear God. On the contrary; but we are saying that Jesus Christ did not only come so that we might obtain remission of our sins before God through his mediation, but also to regenerate us through his Holy Spirit to walk in newness of life. What of those, then, who carefully maintain good works and meritorious deeds? We can see that their lives give off an atrocious stench! If we were looking for profane pleasure-seekers, who have no conception that they will have to give account of themselves – men whom Satan has poisoned – these are the very people!

Now, though they magnify good works, what are these works to which they would have us devoted? We would need to do a lot of babbling, to attend matins and vespers, to trot from altar to altar, to worship grotesque images (which must, of course, be beautifully adorned), to buy a goodly number of pardons, and to run around on pilgrimages. In other words, they would have us openly mocking God, as if his service were child's play. Of course, they would never dare to say that temperance, chastity, sobriety and the like, were not good and praiseworthy virtues. Yet, they can quite easily disregard all this in favour of keeping their superstitions. Indeed, all of God's commands are placed under their feet and trampled upon, as it were, because, to them, there can be no holiness nor true devotion without performing all these 'good deeds', and meaningless works. Hence, the struggle in which Paul was involved has lasted up to this day. For this reason, he says that if the adversaries, with whom he is disputing, wish to maintain the law of God, let them learn how it ought to be applied, and start with themselves. If they seek to make good disciples, let them teach sobriety, meekness, chastity, patience and the like, and let them instruct people to deny all their evil appetites. These are the true duties that we must take pains to fulfil, says Paul. Also, do not close the door upon the children of God, he says, and take away the privilege that God has given them, for now that he leads them by his Holy Spirit, he would no longer have them to be subject to the yoke of the law.

* * *

At this point, Paul adds, 'And they that are Christ's have crucified the flesh with the affections and lusts.' Here, Paul shows that he is not advocating a carnal liberty, as those denigrators of God had falsely claimed. What he demands above all else is that those who speak of Christian liberty must show that they have truly crucified all their sinful appetites and lusts, thereby proving that they are, indeed, members of the Lord Jesus Christ. To enjoy true liberty it is essential that we do this, and follow the legitimate commandments and goals ordained by God. Today, there are many who are Christians only so far as their mouths are concerned, eating meat on Fridays and during Lent. These people despise all such Popish nonsense and declare forcefully that it is a deception and a lie to create strict obligations for people on pain of committing a mortal sin. They speak the truth – if only they were building on a sure and firm foundation themselves! However, although they say these things, they know nothing of the work of our Lord Jesus Christ, nor of his power. They do not know why he came to this earth, nor what grace he communicates through the gospel. They know nothing of the meaning of faith, nor what it is to pray to God. They simply want permission to do whatever they feel is right, and to have the bridle removed from their neck. Even today, we will find many of these 'wild' Christians. The doctrines of God are attacked for their sakes; for the enemies of the truth point out all who live dissolute lives today and say that they do so because of what we preach. This is why Paul responds here to his adversaries and arms and equips us to respond also, in order to silence those who speak evil of us and mistakenly reproach gospel teaching.

Firstly, although the wicked say that we are giving an open licence to those who seek only pleasure for themselves, here Paul is saying that this liberty is only for those who impose laws upon themselves – laws which are in accordance with the death and passion of our Lord Jesus Christ. Now, this ought to serve as a warning to all who imagine that they have liberty to do as they please. They ought to realise that the first thing we need is to become members of the Lord Jesus Christ. Would we like to eat with a peaceful conscience, without scruples? Would we like to be exempted from the kind of ostentatious displays that burden simple, ignorant souls in Popedom today? Then we must know Jesus Christ, and be truly in him. May he reign over us, and may the power and efficacy of his sufferings and death be displayed in every aspect of our lives. This is what we need to remember from this passage.

Once again, Paul shows here that, for the children of God, true perfection consists in denying themselves, so that they are not guided by their own heads or according to their own tastes. For we are utterly corrupt, and are rebels to God throughout our lives until we have mortified all that pertains to our nature, in that it is evil. Thus, firstly, our lives can never conform to the will of God, until we undergo a complete transformation in our thoughts and affections. Secondly, Paul tells us that this cannot happen unless we have a relationship with the Lord Jesus Christ, which is the reason he uses the word 'crucified'. This implies that while we are separated from the Lord Jesus Christ, he rejects us; if we are not united to him by faith, our nature will be producing its own fruit – all of it evil and sinful. Firstly, therefore, the notion of free will is cast down here. Secondly, this reveals that we cannot receive any gift from God or from his Holy Spirit except through the Lord Jesus Christ. Indeed, we have already said that we must all drink from his fulness, for he is the only fountain that can quench our thirst. Any other pathway will only leave us parched and famished. If we feel as if our thirst has already been quenched, we will only be deceiving ourselves with vain presumption. We will remain empty without any good nourishment at all.

At this point, Paul concludes, 'If we live in the Spirit, let us also walk in the Spirit.' This is a simplified statement of all that he has already been saying. Of course, it was enough for him to have declared that we cannot be set free unless we have crucified all of our wicked lusts. However, the hypocrisy of man is so great that he will always find excuses; everyone wants to be thought of as an angel although their life refutes the fact! Hence, Paul adds, 'If we live in the Spirit, let us also walk in the Spirit', to confirm his earlier message. In other words, it is not enough for people to claim that the Spirit of God dwells in their hearts, for he is not idle; if he is there, his presence will reveal itself. If others want to judge whether the Spirit of God lives within us or not, they must look at our works and at our lives; from the way that we are living, people can see who we are, and what we are like inside, judging by external, visible fruit. For example, what if someone wanted me to believe that a statue before me was a living person? There is no movement of the head or the feet. I push it, I hit it, but I can see that it has no soul within. Who will convince me that this piece of stone can move, or that it possesses some virtue, or that it is a living creature with a soul? The same applies to those who claim to be spiritual; for although unbelievers and enemies of God are alive in body, when it comes to spiritual life, they are dead, their souls being totally corrupted. But we are alive to God through the grace of the Holy Spirit. Now, if this grace is within us, it cannot remain idle, as I have said. This is why Paul says that our lives will declare whether or not we are living in the Spirit.

The word 'walk' is used quite frequently in Holy Scripture when referring to our conduct in life. However, in this place it does not only mean 'walk' in this sense. The word that Paul uses here implies more than this; it means marching to order, and yielding in conformity to the will of God and the Holy Spirit. There ought to be an authority controlling our lives, so that people can see that God rules there and that the Lord Jesus has reserved us as members of his own body, and that he truly dwells within us by his Holy Spirit. It is important that this should be clear. Paul also seeks to uncover the insincerity of all those who profess Christ with their mouths, and delude us wonderfully by their zeal, yet whose lives reveal no desire to approach God and no respect for his Word. All such people should be convicted of their deceit and treachery when they read this. Therefore, in order to assess just who are the children of God, we need to examine our lives. Sometimes it is true, as we saw earlier, that poor ignorant folk, who have never been instructed in the law, appear to have some virtue. However, if we were to sound them out at closer quarters we would find that this was but a shadow, and that they neither had any desire to love their neighbours, nor to walk according to God's ways. In short, an examination of our lifestyle cannot lie.

Paul also seeks to confirm what he had said earlier, that if our lives are led by the Spirit of God, we will be careful to observe God's requirements, and not concern ourselves with frivolous things which he will not accept or value. As we have said, those who seek to be the most devout of all never cease to pursue their superstitions, and every night they think that

God is indebted to them because they have worked so hard. Yet it is wasted effort. Thus, Paul tells us that if we know that our life is to be spent spiritually (for this is true), and that God is Spirit, we will also realise that he wants to be served properly and will not tolerate us amusing ourselves with meaningless trivialities and puerile nonsense. Rather, he would have us show loyalty, love, peace, harmony with one another and avoid deceit, malice and theft. If, therefore, we know that the life of which God approves and which unites us to him is spiritual, let us walk in the Spirit, as he says. We have been warned that God only accepts that which is in conformity with his law, which Paul calls 'spiritual' in the seventh chapter to the Romans. Now, the practical application of this doctrine will become apparent as we walk! Thus, instead of being like others, and running around on pilgrimages, let us use our feet in the service of God and of our neighbours. Instead of acting like these poor bigots, consuming all their substance on idolatry, let us be aware of the true sacrifice that God demands of us, and his holy oblations – the dedication of ourselves to him with body and soul. Also, may we use the goods that he has given us, and placed in our hands, in such a way that we demonstrate that we have received all from him. This is what Paul means here.

* * *

Notice that he selects the most deadly of sins here, and those which happened to be all too prevalent amongst the Galatians. He says, 'Let us not be desirous of vain glory, provoking one another, envying one another.' There is no doubt that when people seek to be self-important, all of God's teaching is instantly corrupted. For we can easily see that in the case of these great zealots for the law, who hindered Paul and all the faithful servants of the Lord Jesus Christ, they were driven by foolish ambition and wanted credit and high esteem in the eyes of others. For this reason, Paul addresses them again here, but he also has in mind all the people to whom he was writing, desiring to purge them of all that prevented them from receiving gospel doctrine with simplicity. Let us take good note of the fact that we will never be good disciples of the Lord Jesus Christ unless any remaining vainglory in us is first beaten down. Above all, ambition, the foolish wish to be exalted above other men, is the deadliest plague that a person entrusted with the responsibility to teach others could ever have. When people push themselves forward in society like this, and seek to be famous and to be applauded by men, it is impossible for them not to abandon themselves to all kinds of evil.

However, before we move on, let us comment upon the fact that, in Scripture, all glorying is seen as vain and perverse, if men are seeking esteem for themselves by it. Pagans use the term 'vainglory' to refer to a poor fool who is trying to pass for a clever man, or a poor rascal who is pretending to be a rich man – when a man who is neither dextrous, hard-working, nor honest to any degree, wants to be arrogant and to play at being a wise man. He will be there with his scowling face, belching out great sighs from his big stomach, such that one dare not look! When people deform and disguise themselves to this extent to deceive others, the pagans call this kind of glory vain and foolish. But the Holy Spirit goes even further than this. He says that even if we have intelligent minds, or abundant wealth, or great virtue, or all that it is possible to have to gain renown, and we take the credit for it ourselves, then our boasting is vain. Why? Because it is sacrilegious to rob God of the honour that is rightfully his. If he reserves all the honour for himself, then it is perverse for man to take any of it to adorn his own self. Thus, in order to be cleansed from this sin, let us attribute to God all the praise, knowing that all good things come from him. As we have seen previously, the wise man must not boast about himself, any more than he that is rich, for all the dignity of man must be cast down and all eyes must look to God. All of us, from the greatest to the least, must recognise that all we have has been received from him, and that in ourselves we lack all that is good. If we have begun, it is essential for us to endure to the end, even though every one of us will have spots and stains. All our boasting is in the fact that God receives us in mercy. Furthermore, may we be so led by the Holy Spirit that people will see that we are endowed with his grace.

We have already declared that we cannot be disciples of the Lord Jesus Christ unless we have been thoroughly cleansed from our wicked corruption. This is why Paul addresses his remarks to the whole church, telling us that we must rid ourselves of all foolish lusts, and that unless we beat down all pride in ourselves we cannot approach the Lord Jesus Christ. But, as I have said, those whose role it is to teach in the church must set an example of humility and modesty. For what is it of which even the most noble of us boast? All has been given through the free goodness of God. If they exalt themselves because of it, are they not excessively wicked? Their ingratitude has risen up within them and made them collide with God head on, although they ought to be more indebted to God than others. Therefore, let us make every effort to chase away such an attitude from our own hearts, so that our only goal is that the Lord Jesus Christ should have the pre-eminence. Let all the noble ones allow themselves to be abased, if this serves to magnify the majesty of God and the authority of the Lord Jesus Christ. May we all look to him and cleave to him, and recognise that every good thing comes from him. This is the point to which Paul is leading us.

* * *

In order to help us to detest all vainglory and pride toward God, as well as the desire for personal credit amongst men, he speaks of, 'provoking one another, envying one another'. He is saying, in effect, that if ambition reigns, there will be inevitable conflicts, and each person will provoke his neighbour. For if we are given to vainglory, each of us will strive to be the greatest; thus, it will seem as if we have not achieved what is ours by right until we can look on our neighbours with contempt. This is how pride works. It is not only a matter of exalting oneself against God, but of rejecting those whom we should honour, even if they are beneath our station. For when we have considered everyone, it is certain that even the least should be held in honour by us. Yet, if we are driven by ambition, as I have said, each of us desires to be on top in order to gain the best position. Thus, strife, debate, conflict, revolt, contention and enmity are unavoidable. In short, so long as ambition is in fashion, and permitted to run free, we will always be at war, as experience too often proves. Would to God we had to look far and wide to find examples of this! But as soon as we have the desire to be noticed, we are carried along by ambition, until we declare ourselves at enmity with our neighbours. This is where envy comes from. It is written that love rejoices in the good of others (*1 Cor.* 13:6). Therefore, if God pours out his grace on our neighbours, have we not cause to rejoice? If we earnestly pray for all who are in need, and God grants them a life of ease and prosperity, any subsequent irritation on our part would reveal that our prayers had been filled with hypocrisy and falsehood.

Now, if God distributes some of the graces of his Holy Spirit to a number of us, they are intended for the edification and common good of the whole church. If we are truly living according to the will of God, we will be able to find joy in and through everything; especially if we love to see the well-being and advancement of our neighbours. On the other hand, if we are devoted to ourselves and driven by this accursed ambition and pride, we will only look askance at their success and progress. If God shows himself liberal towards those whom we desire to keep underfoot, we will experience jealousy and malice. This is what we are to retain from this passage: we must understand what it is to be in the Lord Jesus Christ, so that we do not vainly assert that we belong to him. This being so, we will not be accused of falsehood and lies before God and his angels, having foolishly boasted before men. In order to be in our Lord Jesus Christ, we must mortify our appetites and passions, knowing that we overflow with evil and that our nature is wholly inclined to it. We must, therefore, change. Now it is true that this cannot be done through our own strength, but the Son of God is ready and equipped to come to our aid. What prevents us from partaking of the gifts of the Spirit of God, whereby our lives would demonstrate that we have true faith in him? It is the fact that we flatter ourselves in our poverty. Let us, therefore, learn to tremble when we see that we are full of corruption, and yield to the Lord Jesus Christ, that through his sufferings and death, he might mortify in us all evil lusts and inordinate appetites.

To this end, may we know the grace that God gives, that we may thereby serve him freely; no longer under the yoke of the law which would have oppressed us to the end of our lives as an intolerable burden. Rather, led by his Holy Spirit, we know that he approves of our lives and accepts our service if it conforms to the Word of God, though we do not have the great, whole-hearted zeal that is required. Let us be aware of this, and also let us behave in such a way that our lives speak. May our feet, our hands and all our thinking show outwardly that, just as we have been taught in the school of the Lord Jesus Christ, we have also kept his doctrine, which has taken root in us. This does not mean that it is hidden, but rather that it will bear fruit and will bring honour to the name of God, demonstrating that we are not idle or useless, but have been given life by the Spirit of our Lord Jesus Christ. It is he who governs us, and the fruit by and by reaches our neighbours. When the name of God is glorified by us in this way, and when we have thus given testimony to our Christianity, it will be seen that we have been taught in order to impart good to other people. God cares about the whole body of his church, just as he causes his sun to shine on the just and the unjust; he wants believers to endeavour to serve those who are unworthy of help (*Matt.* 5:45). Let us realise this, and at the same time confess that we ourselves are nothing and that all the good things we have are not our own. We have them through the goodness of God alone. Since we have not yet attained the standard of perfection that is required, let us not think that we can be acceptable to God on our own; we can only achieve this if he upholds us until the day we enter his kingdom, the place of complete holiness.

Now let us fall down before the majesty of our great God, acknowledging our sins, and praying that he would make us conscious of them until we tremble before him in true repentance. May we be increasingly set free from sin, and put into practice the doctrines of which we have heard. Thus, if today poor, ignorant, blind souls torment themselves and labour excessively in their foolish devotions, let us learn to keep to the purity and simplicity of God's Word instead. There is no other rule to live by than this, and this is what we must practise, and what we must apply ourselves to study. Let us show others that it by this means that our Lord Jesus desires us to conform to his example. May we aspire and aim to be like him until we are fully united with him, ultimately arriving at that happy meeting when he appears for our redemption. He will then take us away from this earthly pilgrimage, and not only so but he will remove all the corruption and all else that hinders us from truly enjoying our heavenly inheritance. May he show this grace not only to us, but to all peoples, etc.

38

On Rebuking Sin With Gentleness

> *Brethren, if a man be overtaken in a fault, ye which are spiritual, restore such an one in the spirit of meekness; considering thyself, lest thou also be tempted. Bear ye one another's burdens, and so fulfil the law of Christ* (Gal. 6:1–2).

We said previously that there is no deadlier plague than ambition; each person committed only to himself and seeking to elevate himself by despising his neighbours. Ambition knows neither equity nor limit. There is another sin which is related to this, whereby we seek to attack those who have fallen, so that we ourselves, by comparison, are shown to best advantage. This sin is extremely common in the world today, as we know. For we regard the virtues of others as hindrances; they prevent us enjoying the degree of esteem that we covet. Hence, a person spies on his friends in order to debase them, so that he alone has dignity; by such means, he becomes noticed and valued. Because this does not happen very often, we are inclined to be overly rigorous under the guise of zeal. Therefore, Paul exhorts believers to restore one that has fallen with gentleness.

Now, Paul is here exposing human nature. For when we consider weakness, which is common to us all, we ought to be moved with compassion; this he addresses later at greater length. Paul is warning us that we are, indeed, weak by nature, and that, therefore, we cannot claim to be any better than others. Furthermore, he speaks of being 'overtaken', meaning that we must deal with the fault with some degree of kindness when we see a man whom Satan, through his wiles, has taken by surprise. Paul is not speaking about those who have deep-rooted malice in their hearts, who are openly contemptuous of God, profane, and full of acrimony. Such people could not claim that they had fallen inadvertently. Why? Because they are wild beasts who deliberately charge against God, like the many we see who openly defy all commands, and desire to introduce confusion wherever they go. These people are not included amongst the number of those to whom Paul refers here. But even a man who fears God, and longs to devote himself to his service, can be caught out by Satan if he has prepared a net for him. This is how we may be surprised or 'overtaken'. Thus, Paul tells us that we are to show pity in the case of such faults, and support such a man 'in the spirit of meekness'.

We must pay attention to all of the words that are used here, and then we will gather the apostle's intentions. Indeed, there is nothing superfluous here, for each word carries weight. By saying that we must take pains to restore the person who has stumbled, he is showing that the softness with which many flatter the fallen has nothing to do with Christianity. Sins must be rebuked, and we must seek to bring back to God all who have strayed from the right path; for if we support them in their wrong-doing and encourage them, we are in reality betraying them; allowing them to sleep on, and thereby plunging themselves into perdition all the more. Thus, Paul ordains here that we correct a man who fails God, but with a spirit of meekness and gentleness. He could easily have used the word 'meekness' alone here without adding 'spirit', but he uses the two in conjunction to show that we need to have a warm affection for the well-being of those who need warning and exhortation because of their sin. He also seeks to indicate that this comes from God. As he is the fountain of all goodness, he pours out this meekness upon his children, so that they follow him and conform to his example. We know that it is in the style of the

Holy Scriptures to speak, for example, of 'the spirit of truth', 'the spirit of the fear of the Lord', and the 'spirit of wisdom'; these gifts proceed from the Spirit of God, who is the embodiment of all that is good (*Isa.* 11:2).

Here is a summary of what Paul is teaching us here: firstly, we must not love virtue to the extent that we only delight in those whose life is perfect and blameless. We must progress beyond this and show our meekness by supporting those who have sinned because they are not yet as strong in their fear of God as they ought to be. We must aim to bring back to the right path those who have become debauched and turned aside. For if we have no kindness or humanity within, the minute we see someone committing a sin, we will plunge them deep into despair; we see this far too often. This is why Paul says that the children of God must show kindness and gentleness. Then those who have fallen through weakness can be helped up, knowing that we desire their salvation.

Now, I say that there are two extremes here, or two sins that we must guard ourselves against. The first is that we often close our eyes if one of our friends offends God, and creates a scandal; we let it slip by and do not want to stir up ill-will by reproaching them. This is how friendships work today: there is a diabolical plot whereby each person permits and licenses all kinds of evil. No-one wants to have their sore skin scratched, and therefore they will not listen to warning, that is, unless God has touched them and given them an obedient spirit that makes them teachable. Such people would say with David that they would prefer to be scolded harshly, indeed even with austerity, than to have crowds of flatterers around them who would lull them to sleep in their sins (*Psa.* 141:5). However, generally speaking, people want to be spared the shame, and they would not have us utter a word against them, let alone assail their ears with a list of all their vices and transgressions. People are happy with this, yet God is forgotten, and as the Prophet Isaiah says, no man was found in any of the streets who upheld the truth (*Isa.* 59:14–16). There was confusion and worse injustice than ever before, yet they let it all continue unchecked.

Now it is true that if one man were to wrong another, the first would admit that he needs to rectify the situation in which he has allowed himself to act badly. However, it would not be due to his zeal to maintain God's honour, but for his own self-interest and self-esteem. Hence, God cannot find any intercessor or advocate who will fight his cause, because all are given over to self. Let us learn, therefore, that if we see a person fall, it is not showing love if we cover their evil, or pretend that nothing has happened. If we care about the salvation of the person who has thus fallen, we must warn him. If a man is in the mire, we will stretch out our hands and pull him out. If we were to pass by without assisting, would he not think us most cruel and inhumane? This is what happens when we allow sins to be passed by, for a man who carries on unchecked will plunge himself into the depths of hell. This amounts to great treachery on our part, if we willingly allow a man to be lost forever. At the same time, we are showing that we have no zeal for God within us. For if he is our Father, at the very least we ought to be hurt and saddened when others insult or wrong him. Therefore, if the souls that our Lord Jesus purchased at such cost are precious to us, and the honour of God is as important as it should be, we would surely not tolerate or suffer the faults we see, but seek to correct them. This is the first point.

However, there is also an opposite sin: that is, excessive harshness. Hypocrites are like this, for when they see a speck in their neighbour's eye, they cry out in alarm and stir up great turmoil over it, whereas they have a large beam in their own eye which they do nothing about, as our Lord Jesus says (*Matt.* 7:4). Since there are many who enlarge their consciences to swallow an entire camel, yet who strain at a gnat when it comes to the faults of others, we must guard against being too harsh or too severe when we reprove our brothers. There are those who have an ill-considered zeal, which is all vinegar and bitterness; it seems to them that they are only doing their duty correctly if they sound the trumpet loudly when another falls. How many cautionary words today spring from righteous concern? If a person sees his neighbour doing evil, he should, if he has an opening and an opportunity, show him his fault, but we see nothing of this! For, as I have said, each one spies on his friends, and listens out as he keeps watch, to see if he can find anything to reprove, and then he will be severe in the extreme.

However, those who are dealt with severely in this way certainly cannot complain. After all, why is it that such an evil has become prevalent in today's society? No-one is admonished in private any more in order to bring them back to God, but the sins that were hidden are slanderously published abroad. Why? It is only because each one of us closes the door, having itching ears that cannot bear to hear the truth about ourselves. We want to cleave to our sins, as if God has been dethroned and has no more authority or jurisdiction over us. Therefore, because we would all exempt ourselves from correction, this makes us worthy of more severe treatment, suited to enemies, not brothers. Brotherhood cannot exist amongst us without such mutual correction, where we all willingly submit to one another. Hence, because we do not wish to hear any criticism, we merit this rigorous and extreme treatment. This is why Paul tells us the right approach here; that we should care about one another, so that if one falters, he will be restored. How? By healthy warning, this being the remedy that God has prescribed in his Word. Yet, we are not to be so sharp in rebuking others for their sin, that we forget to mix oil with the vinegar by introducing a 'spirit of meekness'. It would be very poor indeed if we were to speak with sugared tongues as so many do, whilst having venom in our hearts. Yet, Paul is not speaking of our tongues alone here and he is not telling us to use attractive language; but he is saying that when we are rebuking our neighbours, we must be fuelled and fired by a desire for their spiritual well-being. If we seek the good of the person who has sinned, we will surely conduct ourselves with sobriety, and this will result in the moderation that Paul speaks of here. In other words, we will not be too sharp, or boil up within and scold the person rashly without care for the outcome. We will come back to these words of

Paul, and be careful to restore the one who is on the wrong path, hoping to bring him back with us to God. Indeed, we will want him to be our brother, that we might worship God together in the way that he deserves. If we have this desire, it is certain that the rest will follow shortly thereafter.

Now by this word 'spirit' we are being warned that we need to conform to God's ways, as I have said, since he has deigned to choose us as his children, as indeed our Lord Jesus reveals. Be like your heavenly Father, he tells us, who pities even those who are unworthy of it (*Matt.* 5:44–45). Thus, if we want to be esteemed and owned as the children of God, we must consider the nature of the One who has called us to be conformed to his example; that is, we must be kind. God, in his gentleness, never praises those who have fallen, for he hates iniquity and will always declare himself at enmity with it. Furthermore, it is written that God corrects his children, and the chastisements that he metes out begin in his own household and amongst his own servants (*Heb.* 12:6; *1 Pet.* 4:17). However, he does not thunder against poor sinners, but he waits patiently for them, exhorts them, draws them, assists them, offers them his grace, and declares that he is ready and has arms outstretched to receive them, if they will come to him. This is the first thing that we have to consider: the need to conform to the example of our God, by not instantly overwhelming those in whom we detect a weakness. Instead, we ought rather to seek to win them, knowing them to be but poor, lost souls.

From this, we gather that those who wish to keep their vice hidden today, or feel that they are acceptable, since God is being so patient and kind, are mistakenly corrupting Holy Scripture. For today, in the case of the most detestable crimes on the face of the earth, people immediately plead for mercy and say that we must show pity. These people are blaspheming against God by asking us to be merciful to them. We know that he is the fountain of all goodness, and it ought to be enough for us to follow him from a distance; if we can draw any closer to him, it is to be greatly desired. But even if we were to strive as hard as we possibly could, it would count for much if we had but a little ray of the mercy of God, which is in infinite supply in him. However, God only promises his grace to those who return to him (*Zech.* 1:3). Whilst it is true that he first touches them by his Holy Spirit and changes their hearts, it is still the case that repentance is linked to the remission of sins. How, then, can men ask to be pitied? They are openly mocking God; they are covering up their evil, and even commending it, thereby rejecting God. They even support those who are ready to commit worse sins. This is an abominable blasphemy, as I have said, when people change good into evil in this way. Let us, therefore, learn to follow Paul's exhortation here and encourage the meekness that comes from the Spirit of God; not to approve of sin and obscure what is right, but so that our correction is moderate.

Let us also learn to pray to God to guide us when we have to rebuke our neighbours, knowing that by nature we are not sufficient for these things. We know that in order to serve God and to employ ourselves faithfully in his service, we need firstly to receive from him all that we lack. If a man were to search within as diligently as he could, he would still not find an ounce of goodness that was his own. But when it comes to correcting others, we are then representing the person of God. If I wish to reprove someone for a fault which they have committed, I do not come in my own name, as if I were superior to that person, but I come in the name of God. Since it is the case, therefore, that we are acting in God's stead when we rebuke those who have sinned, how can we fulfil this role unless God leads and guides us? Let us learn, therefore, to pray for the guidance of his Holy Spirit, that he would take control of us when called upon to warn those who have strayed and to restore them to the right path.

* * *

Now we must also take note of that which I have already said, that Paul is not referring here to those who are steeped in evil, and who despise and rebel against God. He is speaking of people who are 'overtaken'; they have a measure of determination to do good and yet, through weakness, fall. Therefore, we need to proceed with great wisdom and discernment. For if we try to maintain the same approach to all, we will often be harming those who most need our help, whilst at the same time we will be stirring the anger of those who hold God in contempt, making them even more defiant. We must, therefore, as I have said, be able to discern between them. When the prophet Ezekiel refers to a good shepherd, he says that he ought to support any weak lambs, and if there is any disease, he ought to heal them with good medicine (*Ezek.* 34:4). If he were to treat them all the same way without distinguishing between them, how would he be behaving as a shepherd should? The same applies to those who take it upon themselves to warn their neighbours when they have sinned. We must consider the person with whom we are dealing. For example, it may be a shameless pleasure-seeker who rushes into sin daily and pays no heed to the Word of God, who seeks to corrupt the flock like a diseased goat in their midst. Such an evil person, completely devoted to wicked ways, has certainly not been overtaken unexpectedly. Why do I say this? Because he has already left the service of God and altogether thrown off his yoke. As I have already said, he is a wild beast, lifting his horns defiantly towards heaven. Such people do not deserve to be tolerated kindly; thus Paul debars and excludes them in this passage. On the other hand, if we see a poor man overcome by weakness and overtaken by the devil, and we notice that the good seed of the fear of God has not altogether perished, we must be inclined towards showing him pity and compassion.

Now, since we can fail in this at every step, we need to call upon God all the more and ask him to lead us. Indeed, notice that Paul adds, 'considering thyself, lest thou also be tempted'. Here he changes his tune. He had said, 'Brothers, if anyone is overtaken, restore him.' Now he addresses us all, and says, 'Look to yourselves'. This gives his warning greater impact and touches us at closer quarters. For we know that when a person speaks in general terms, everyone thinks that he is referring to others, and all desire to exempt themselves as far as possible. If a person says, 'We are all inclined to do this or that', and is addressing a company, no-one is affected by it as they ought to be. Therefore, Paul deliberately changes his tune here, and is not content to warn the believers and the body of the church in general. He takes each one of us aside instead and says, 'Look to yourselves and examine yourselves within, for you also could be tempted.' There is no better motive that would induce us to be kind to those who have sinned, than a realisation that we also need the help of others. Even pagans have advanced such a notion, for they say that we must be very cruel indeed if we cannot bear with the infirmities of our friends, seeing that we ourselves are just as weak. It would be impossible for two men to live together on this earth without showing patience towards one another, for it would only take two men to disturb the peace of the whole world, if they were not mutually forbearing. Even those who think they are the most perfect people of all still find themselves in need of the support of others. If we were not so stupid, we would surely hate the evil within us. Then we would not need anyone to come and distress us or handle us roughly. We would all be grieved within ourselves and despise ourselves because of our shortcomings. Such being the case, what more is there to say, but that this should induce us to treat those who, through weakness, have stumbled, with meekness and gentleness? This is what we ought to take good note of here.

Indeed, if we were to seek for a reason why people flare up with an excessive ardour, and fly into a terrible rage over the smallest faults, it is precisely because they do not look well to themselves. Hence, this is the order that we ought to follow: firstly, we must condemn evil wherever we find it; this is the first point. For if we only condemn evil in this or that person, and pass by others, it is a sure sign that we are not being guided by upright motives, that is, to serve and honour God. We must have some hidden malice, or grudge; as Solomon says, 'Hatred stirreth up strife' (*Prov.* 10:12). For we all seek to lay blame upon those with whom we already have a grievance. Therefore, the first rule that we ought to observe is that we should condemn evil wherever we find it, simply because it is contrary to the way of God. This is the first point. Secondly, we must each examine ourselves. For the closer we are to evil, the more we ought to hate it. If I see a person clearly showing contempt for God, I will be much more distressed than if I had seen him at a distance of thirty miles and had no knowledge of his sins. Now we must look at ourselves. If we are neighbours, even though we today tend to be independent of one another, we must put into practice what I have been speaking about. We must expose the sin to the person who has fallen; for God has placed us together in such relationships so that, if I have a friend, I will be able to restore him better than if he were a stranger. Yet who can be closer to me when it comes to condemning sin than myself? The only way we can know if we are seeking to honour God and to be cleansed from sin, is if we are harsh and strict with ourselves, to ensure that we keep ourselves bridled. If we wish to reprove others, we must first condemn our own vices, and show that we are displeased with them and are seeking the remedy as far as it is in our power to do so. Thus, we can only be a judge of others if we have condemned ourselves first.

Now, this is not simply a warning about the past, but for the future. Paul, therefore, does not say here, 'Look at how you have fallen on previous occasions.' He says, 'Considering thyself, lest thou also be tempted.' Indeed, we ought always to walk in fear and trembling. This is not to say that we should stop leaning upon the grace of our God, but that we must not be indifferent. Faith does not mean that we do not care about anything, but rather, as Paul says in the second chapter to the Philippians, we can do nothing on our own and we need God to guide us by his Holy Spirit, so that, having given us the desire he would also give us the power to execute his will. Because everything we have comes from God, this is why we must walk in fear and trembling. Looking back on our past sins, and considering our present condition, we will always have occasion to be downcast. It is true that God has granted us grace to be judges, although we deserve to remain silent, for he desires us to have the courage to uphold what is right and condemn what is wrong. Yet, we must also learn to correct humbly the faults within ourselves that we have already identified and condemned, seeing that from day to day, hour to hour, minute to minute, we easily fall. This being the case, let us take pity on those who stumble, for they are mirrors of our own fragility; we see in them the kind of people we are, unless kept by the grace of the Spirit of God. Furthermore, if we inappropriately warn those who have fallen, and speak harshly, forgetting any humanity, we are likely to offend God, as we have already said. Therefore, though the warning of others is a virtue to be encouraged, it could turn into a vice if we do not control it. We need our Lord to restrain us, so that we are balanced, and do not run to either of the extremes I have described earlier. This is what we ought to remember from Paul's statement here.

* * *

Now he especially addresses 'ye which are spiritual'. This implies that if God has strengthened us with his power, we are all the more duty-bound to support the weak, as also it says in the fourteenth chapter to the Romans. Indeed, if God distributes his grace to one man more than to another, it is not to oppress him, but to enable him to help those who cannot make progress. For example, if two men are walking through the countryside, and one finds himself weary and can no longer drag his legs along, surely the one who is robust and strong will not run ahead out of spite? He will keep to the same speed as his friend, and will help him along, saying, 'Come, do your utmost, and I, for my part, will help you along.' In other words, he will do all that he possibly can to comfort the one who is weak. This is how we ought to support each other, for God has called each one of us, and has chosen us on condition that we walk together with one accord, and that we each hold one another's hands.

The prophet Isaiah speaks of the same thing, and says, 'Come ye, and let us go up to the mountain of the Lord' (*Isa.* 2:3). It is not right for those who have received more abundant supplies of the grace of God to oppress others. They ought, rather, to support the weak and be filled with the gentleness of which we have been speaking. This is why Paul says that since our Lord has blessed us more, we have the responsibility to draw others after us.

By way of confirmation of this statement, he says, 'Bear ye one another's burdens, and so fulfil the law of Christ.' By referring to bearing burdens, he is expressing even more clearly that which I declared earlier, which is that he is not speaking about those who despise God and allow themselves licence to do evil, being steeped in wickedness and rebelliousness. He is speaking, instead, of those who aim and aspire to do good, and who have good motives, groaning under their sins, as under the weight of a heavy burden. In order to have a better understanding of this, let us look at the opposite to what Paul implies here. Now, those who have been overtaken in a fault will say that they are bent double under their burden. Why? Because they are angry with themselves, rather than because they are fighting against God in their pride and contempt. It is because they cannot resist Satan as consistently and as forcefully as they would like. On the other hand, those brutes who have fully devoted themselves to evil, whereas they ought to be bent low under their burden, prance around proudly in their iniquities, which they make their triumphs, and elevate themselves in order to defy God utterly. This is the difference between those who are worthy of restoration and those who deserve our rigorous criticism; for the former are bent double because they carry a most heavy burden, which crushes them, as it were. It is these people that our Lord Jesus calls to himself, for he says, 'Come unto me, all ye that labour and are heavy laden, and I will give you rest' (*Matt.* 11:28). Our Lord Jesus does not call everyone to himself without exception, but he sets out the mark of those who can have access to his grace: they must be heavy laden. That is to say, they are not to be those who revel and delight in sin, and proudly boast of it, but those who seek relief and cannot find it in and of themselves. He says that he is ready to be merciful to such.

In the same way, Paul writes in the seventh chapter to the Romans that he does not do the good that he would like to do, but, instead, he does the evil things which he detests. Paul is speaking of himself, even though he lived in this world like an angel of God, and a mirror-image of holiness! Despite this, he still trembles and says that he is wretched. Why? Because he feels like a captive held in prison, in that he does not have liberty to be able to devote himself fully to God. He is prevented from doing so by his sins. Now if this is true of Paul, what of ourselves? At least we now understand the meaning of this word 'burden', when Paul says that we should bear one another's burdens. Paul is exhorting us to give each other mutual support; if anyone is not fulfilling his duty, we must continually err on the side of pity for them, and show the meekness that is spoken of here. In short, he declares that we are to be so united, that if one person is heavy laden and is too weak to bear his load, we must help him in his need and infirmity, as I have already said. We should naturally tend to do this, without having to be exhorted to do so by the Word of God. When we are out walking with others and we see a person who is overly weighed down, we will seek to help out; we will unburden him and each of us will take a part of the load to carry ourselves. Since it is the case that the sins that we commit through weakness are burdens, we need to lend our shoulders in the support of those who are thus encumbered. It is not that we ought to flatter them, as I have told you already, for we must add correction. Indeed, if I act as if nothing has happened when a person offends God and continues in sin, the burden will grow heavier and will eventually break that person's neck. Thus, whereas he had but one burden, he will then have several placed on top which will utterly crush him, simply because we did not warn him. If, however, he had been warned in the first place, he would have been relieved of his burden. Thus, if we overlook sin, we are the cause of the fact that poor souls are never relieved of their load. We are to use moderation, as it tells us here, but in restoring the weak, we must not neglect to cut them to the quick so that they acknowledge their errors, and forsake them.

By way of conclusion, Paul says 'and so fulfil the law of Christ'. There can be no doubt that Paul is indirectly criticising those with whom he has a quarrel here, for we have seen that, at that time, there were many who sought to keep the ceremonial law as a means of attaining holiness and perfection. Therefore, because they always had the word 'law' on their tongues, and thought that they could satisfy God with ceremonies, Paul tells them, 'We have the law of Jesus Christ, who is a faithful expositor of the will of God the Father.' Therefore, if we want to know the true interpretation of the law, we will only find it in Jesus Christ, for he is the eternal wisdom of God, and he was sent to us to lead us to perfect wisdom. Thus, we should especially consider what he has commanded. For the yoke that he has placed on our backs and around our necks is that we must love one another, as it says in the thirteenth chapter of John's Gospel, verse thirty-four: 'A new commandment I give unto you, that ye love one another.' This is the study to which we must apply ourselves: to support those who need our help, and who are overladen; to stretch out our hands to encourage them. This is how to fulfil the 'law of Christ', and when we have fulfilled it, we will confound all who condemn us. Those who fulfil the law of Christ are no longer subject to the ceremonial law, as it is called. Whilst it is true that we can never perfectly fulfil the law of our Lord Jesus Christ, in this aspect or any other, Paul is showing us the goal that we must strive to reach. Although we are still very much '*en route*' while we are in this world, we must not simply run here and there without knowing where we are heading. For Paul is telling us our destination, and we must address ourselves to this. Thus, in order to serve God according to his will, let us learn to devote ourselves fully to him, knowing that he desires us to enjoy great unity with one another because he has joined us with an inseparable bond. May we seek nothing less than to draw our neighbours to him. When we need to correct them, may we be patient and peaceable, yet never encourage sin by flattery or dissimulation.

Now let us fall before the majesty of our great God, acknowledging our sins, and praying that he would make us increasingly conscious of them, that we may tremble before him in true repentance, asking for his pardon. May we always seek to cleave to him, stripped of all the corruptions of the flesh, and clothed in his righteousness. May he support us in our weakness, until he has completely delivered us from it. Thus, we all say, Almighty God, and our heavenly Father, etc.

39

On the Bearing of Burdens

Bear ye one another's burdens, and so fulfil the law of Christ. For if a man think himself to be something, when he is nothing, he deceiveth himself. But let every man prove his own work, and then shall he have rejoicing in himself alone, and not in another. For every man shall bear his own burden (Gal. 6:2–5).

We saw this morning that we must restore the weak, as long as we perceive that they fear God and are born of the good seed, and not if they are determined to do evil. Indeed, we must be kind and compassionate towards people, but if we see that they are proud and provoke God's wrath with their stubborn and angry refusal to obey, then we are not obliged to be gentle and meek with them. If we see them parading themselves around in triumph and exalting themselves against God, we ought, rather, to humble them in their pride. Now we said earlier that in order to keep a reasonable balance when we are rebuking a person who has sinned, we need to consider our own state; we must first judge ourselves, before doing anything else. Seeing ourselves as we are, and that there are many vices that merit rebuke in us, we will humble ourselves and be less rigorous and extreme towards those who need our comfort and encouragement.

Paul now continues this argument by saying that 'if a man think himself to be something, when he is nothing, he deceiveth himself'. We all close our eyes when it comes to a consideration of our faults. It is true to say that if there were but one drop of virtue in us, we would magnify it, whereas if another person were to perceive our failings (and even little children could mock us on account of them), we ourselves say that we see nothing wrong. In order to correct this sin, Paul says although men do not like to be deceived by others, they delude themselves willingly and deliberately, through impertinent, foolish notions. In this way, he brings us back to basics, which, as we said this morning, indicate that if there existed no ambition in men, nor the desire for self-importance, there would surely be a modesty and sobriety, which we do not see at present. Rather, since everyone is swollen with pride, it results in a desire for superiority over everyone else, so that people seek opportunities to trample others underfoot, to make them appear inferior in some way. It is impossible to curtail such excesses, where people desire to rebuke and devour others, unless firstly men are purged of the foolish lust to be important and to hold superior rank.

Whilst folk talk a lot about humility, there are very few indeed who understand this word and what it implies. Therefore, Paul shows us what true humility is here, that is to say, that men ought to be completely self-effacing, and realise that they are worth nothing at all, for then they will truly be humbled. When people commonly refer to humility, they usually mean a kind of feigned lowliness, for though people may say that, in all honesty, they are nothing, they are still bloated like toads with the venom of pride. Paul, however, teaches us a rather different kind of lesson, which is that we must abandon all the regard that we may have for our own wisdom, and all the virtues that we imagine we possess, for here it says in one simple statement that we are nothing. Indeed, the statement which is inserted here should have the following effect on us: if men are, indeed, nothing at all, then those who believe they are virtuous and who glorify themselves are practising wilful self-deception.

Now let us specifically take this part of the text, that is to say, that we are nothing. It is true that God has marked us out, and made us noticeably more dignified and more noble than brute beasts; for he desired to create us in his own image. If, therefore, we consider what God has placed within us, it must, of course, be treasured. Yet it remains true that in our own persons we are nothing, for we are completely indebted to him. Have we merited the good things that we have received? Should we praise and honour ourselves? Our sense of shame ought, rather, to increase when we think that all the intelligence and powers of judgment and discernment within us are corrupted and marred through our own wickedness. In short, people are like damaged and decaying vessels, and the grace of God is like good wine that is poured into them. All is spoilt. The same applies to us: we are vessels, but of what sort? We are diseased because of the corruption of sin. God puts his grace within us in order that he might be glorified. Now do we deserve to receive praise for this in the eyes of men? No; it rather convicts us because it demonstrates that the good gifts that God places within us become corrupted.

Furthermore, when it says that we are nothing, it shows that all the intelligence and reason we have, whereby we wish to be accounted as wise, can only be used for evil purposes. Indeed, God pronounces that we are only evil, and that all our thoughts are like so many vanities, lies, illusions and deceptions (*Gen.* 6:5). Also, we think we have a free will to choose between good and evil, but this will is a slave to sin, and therefore we can only struggle against God. The same is true of our desires. If we happen to have anything which is praiseworthy, it is of God, who distributes gifts as he pleases and, once he has begun, he will continue his good work, as we see in our own experience. How, then, can a clever, sharp-witted man glorify himself, since he has not made himself greater than others, and was not his own creator? We must acknowledge that this has come from God and pay homage to him. On the other hand, those who consider themselves to be the most gifted, and who enjoy the respect of all, so that if they utter one word, no-one dares say anything to the contrary – even such people can be humbled the moment it pleases God to do so.

Therefore, let us conclude that Paul has good reason to blot out any thought that a man may entertain of his own virtue, in order that we might have proper humility, and not think that we are worth anything. This is one point. But he also mocks at the folly of ambition, which takes over our minds. There is no-one who likes to be deceived; indeed, if anyone approaches us in a cunning or feigned manner in order to outwit us, we are annoyed, and cannot tolerate it. However, we will not find any deceivers in the whole world more crude than our own selves. Everyone deceives himself, and everyone brings about his own downfall, and quite willingly, it seems. How foolish! We now see Paul's intention, and the instruction that we ought to draw from this text. Because we all seek our own aggrandisement through belittling our friends, Paul tells us that if we were to make a good and thorough examination of what is within us, we would not find a single drop of virtue meriting praise, that is, in our own persons. For we are nothing, and it would only take one breath to plunge us into the pit. It is, therefore, only foolish presumption that prevents us from walking in simplicity.

Firstly, we need to recognise that we cannot usurp anything without committing sacrilege, because we are robbing God of that which rightfully belongs to him, and that which ought to be reserved for him alone. If we do, it will lead to our own perdition. Indeed, what have we gained by deceiving others, and attaining a reputation far removed from the people we really are? In short, even if we have been idolised, what other result can there be but our own shame and ruin? This being the case, let us learn to fall down and cast ourselves completely prostrate on the ground in order to be strong in the Lord alone. To achieve this, we must learn to magnify none but him. However, should it please him to exalt us, let us, nevertheless, remain bridled by modesty and sobriety, knowing that we have nothing of our own, and that all that God has given us he must preserve in us moment by moment. If we realise that all is from him, let us make sacrifices and offerings to him, seeking to employ ourselves in the service of our neighbours according to the measure of grace that we have received. At the same time, may praise be rendered to the One to whom it rightfully belongs. This is a summary of what we are to retain from this passage.

It is true that it is difficult to bring ourselves to this point. Indeed, today there are so many debates centring upon free will and human virtue, concerned with whether or not we can choose for ourselves, and whether or not we can accept the grace of God and obtain merit thereby. All this is born of the fact that men are so possessed by devilish pride, that they always want to 'be someone' in and of themselves. Therefore, it is all the more vital that we put this doctrine into practice. Indeed, we can never profit in God's school or in the Holy Scriptures, until we acknowledge that we are nothing at all, and draw from the fulness of the Lord Jesus Christ. This cannot happen until we are utterly parched, and confess with David that we are like a 'thirsty land', scorched by the heat, without a drop of rain or moisture except for that which we can receive from heaven (*Psa.* 143:6).

* * *

At this point, Paul adds, 'But let every man prove his own work, and then shall he have rejoicing in himself alone, and not in another': in other words, he is speaking about comparing ourselves with others. Here, Paul provides the answer to another very common sin, which we must confess to be deadly in itself, and which affects us all: that is, the tendency to imagine that we are little angels when we see that others are worse than ourselves, or at least when we see that they are no better. This same sin benumbs many poor people and makes them forget to take God into account, or, indeed, their own salvation. It happens when we notice the rest of the world going along in a higgledy-piggledy fashion. If we were to visit a village and ask the people there how they live, each one would certainly have his own excuses and use them in his own defence, saying, 'I have to follow the pack, you know!' We would find the same in the towns and in the countryside. In short, we are all like coal-sacks, as the proverb says, meaning that we blacken one another. Yet, it seems to us that we are innocent and guiltless in the eyes of God if we can say, 'Oh, this person is not doing as well as I am', or, 'The world is no better than I am, as you can see', or 'Everyone else does this or that'. The fact remains that if we are hardened in sin, despising the judgment of God with a rebellious spirit, as if we will never need to give account of ourselves, it is because we have never been cleansed of our sin.

Thus, we have a very good and very useful exhortation here in this passage where Paul says that we must all 'prove' our work. It is true that we could take the word that he uses here to mean 'approve', but it is not correct, for he is speaking of an examination that we must make without drawing comparisons. In the second letter to the Corinthians, Paul criticises those who measured themselves against others (*2 Cor.* 10:12). Paul tells them, in effect, 'Each of you must consider what he has done, and when you have set all these things before you, you must think about what it teaches you. Each one must come, and sit down at his desk, as it were, and consider what kind of person he is, and what he has done, and then he is in a position to judge well.' Similarly in this passage, we are told that each of us must prove his work. It is as if Paul were saying, 'We want to be better than others; but if one person reproaches another for having fallen, the latter will immediately defend himself by saying that he has many companions in crime.' But this will never be acceptable in the sight of God, says Paul, for we must all separate ourselves and place ourselves each on a rung apart, knowing that before God we must either stand condemned or free, not according to whether we are better or worse than others, but according to the rule of our Judge, that is, his Word. For on the one side, God places his Word, and on the other, our life. This is the true comparison that we must make. We cannot bring a multitude of excuses and say, 'Those people misled me', or 'I followed what I saw', or, 'This is what everyone else did and so I had to do the same', or, 'I was carried along because I could not resist the influence of others'. No; there can be none of this before God and it will be to no avail to say that we have many companions. As I have already said, a true measurement can only be made when God's Word is used as the counterbalance. Even if the whole world entices us to do evil, we will have no excuse if we did not prefer God and his Word to all that is done by men.

Firstly, following Paul's argument here, in view of the fact that we must give account of ourselves, we must be determined to examine our lives thoroughly. A man will never be led to true repentance, and will never acknowledge his sins without hypocrisy, unless he is able to close his eyes to all that others are doing, and ask, 'Now, what does my God require of me? How will I fare before his judgment throne? How will he judge me?' According to his Word. This will fill us with true reverence for God, and also make us uncomfortable in our sin and subsequently humble us: it can only come about if we stop looking at others and thoroughly examine ourselves to see the people we really are. Also, let us be assured of the fact that the Word of God alone reigns, and that we are not to judge according to the ways of the world. This is one point.

However, from this we can extract a more general principle, which is that it is a most serious sin to believe that we can cover and disguise our faults because there are many other people who are guilty of the same crimes. Although this is the common excuse of all today, as I have already said, it does not make it any the less foolish. If we were to ask why the Papists are drunk with such notions, and why they do not listen to reason (it meaning nothing to them), it is because they judge themselves in comparison with others and say, 'Well, everyone else does it'. In short, it seems to them that God has been denied all authority since everyone else lives contrary to that which he has commanded in his Word. They can put forward as many examples as they like, but they cannot influence God to refuse to judge those who have fallen. For even if there were a hundred worlds, they would all be condemned in his sight if they arrogantly came before him saying, 'We want to live in this way'. And who are you? This is the way in which we are to use and benefit from this passage, where Paul asks each of us to examine our work.

Notice that he speaks of 'his own work', that we might be led to a consideration of our whole lives. He does not intend us to take part of it and leave the rest, but, because God has recorded everything in his book, we must thoroughly, and in detail, scrutinise the areas in which we have failed, to see what vices and infirmities lie within us. This is what Paul is referring to by this word 'work'. For it may well be that although we find that in one area we have faithfully served God, yet, nevertheless, there is still much weakness. We are surprised to find that we are riddled with so many imperfections, and we become horrified with ourselves. Let us learn, therefore, to examine our own lives thoroughly before we judge others, for we will only increase our own guilt in the eyes of God if we are harsh and severe with those who have fallen and overlook our own sins. God has honoured us with the privilege of being our own judges.

Now, when Paul says that each one will then have 'rejoicing in himself alone', he does not mean that all who examine themselves will find things in themselves about which they can rejoice, but he is declaring that true rejoicing has solid foundations. It comes about when we know ourselves as we really are, and judge ourselves without resorting to comparison with others. For example, a person with one eye sees better than those who are blind, and amongst the Moors, who are black, a person who is swarthy will seem white! If we tried to judge the colour of a white man in the company of a dozen Moors, he would appear very white indeed; but if we brought him back amongst his own people, we might find that we judge him quite differently! If we say, 'Here is a man who sees very clearly', and yet he is blind in one eye, we mean that compared to those who are totally blind, he sees clearly. However, the fact still remains that he does not have perfect vision. Thus, we can see that to judge by comparison is foolhardy. This is what Paul is saying here.

Paul does not mean that, having examined our lives, we will find good reason to esteem and value ourselves. He is saying that all the rejoicing that men have in regard to themselves is nothing but wind, smoke and lies, for they gaze at themselves in the mirror, as it were, as if others must delight in their image. Take a little child; if you show him a mirror, he does not know whether he sees himself or someone else there, and yet he is completely transfixed. The same is true of those who think they are wonderful. Why? On what do they base these notions, and with what reason, except that they think more highly of themselves than of those who could show them the way? This is what they say: 'Such a person is highly thought of, and yet he has this or that flaw.' The way they scrutinise a man's vices, and condemn him, is nothing but a childish game. Thus, Paul has good reason to say that the only true test is to prove our own selves, in order to have well-founded rejoicing which is justified in the eyes of God.

Now, what if we ask, can a man rejoice in himself? Surely, we have to empty ourselves of all pride in order to obey that which we saw in that other passage, where we are told that our glorying must be in God. Thus, there is no question about whether men are worthy of praise or not. But Paul says, by way of condition, that if we want to be valued by God, we must withdraw to a secret place and acknowledge ourselves as we really are. Then we will no longer foolishly esteem ourselves and say, 'I am worth as much as that person over there; I am no worse than my friend.' Once this attitude has been overcome, then we will see whether there is cause for rejoicing or not. It is certain that we will not find a single cause, at least, not one of our own making. However, we can still rejoice in our God, which is more meaningful than if we were to be lifted above the clouds. For when men deceive themselves with vain opinions of their own grandeur, because all the world applauds them, they feel as if floating on air, but they will inevitably topple and break their necks. This is what happens to us when we are blinded by such presumption. Yet, if we know what it is to seek our joy in

God, then we can be truly united to him and lean upon a sure and certain foundation, through which we know we are valued and prized.

We know that Paul himself glories in all good conscience and in his integrity, when he says that those whom he has won for Jesus Christ through the gospel are his crown. All servants of God can say the same, yet not by way of sharing glory with God, like those who claim to have virtue and merit. Such people make idols of themselves. But believers, having confessed that they are nothing at all except through the free bounty of God, glory in what he has given them, always reserving for him the praise that is his due. If, therefore, we do not claim to have anything except what has been given by God, and instead depend upon him and his grace alone, then we can have this rejoicing, indeed, in ourselves and not in another, as Paul says. When he says 'in himself alone', he does not mean that the cause for rejoicing exists within us, or that we are not sinners. He is concerned with that which I have already declared to you; which is, that whilst we are drawing comparisons between ourselves and others, we deceive ourselves. We think that we are little angels, whereas we are scarcely better than devils! How is this? Because we resemble those who are totally evil and corrupt.

Now, if this warning has ever been necessary, it certainly is today. For although in Paul's day there already existed much corruption, today we see things at their very worst. Indeed, it seems as if all the nations have conspired against God. Thus, we see the world overflowing with rage and fury and making war upon all equity and righteousness. Yet, despite such great confusion, we still remain asleep! Why? Because we say, 'Everyone lives like this!' Thus, God is pushed into the background. Do we think that by our iniquities we can dethrone him or rob him of the authority which is rightfully his to judge the whole world? For we must all, without exception, be assessed as we stand before him, and on that day we cannot plot together and say, 'Stand fast! For we are a great multitude!' With one breath God could send a hundred worlds to their damnation. This being so, let us practise what Paul tells us here and let each one of us keep a careful watch upon himself. When we see that blasphemy and bawdiness are rife, along with many other dissolute habits – drunkenness, gluttony, pillaging, perjury, treason, envy and the like, let us, indeed, groan and sigh, but at the same time, let us never imagine that we are guiltless if the thorns we have to walk amongst have left their marks upon us. We may say that others have caused us to follow the wrong course, and even that we have been carried along as by a whirlwind; but let us not imagine that this will benefit us in any way! We are to follow the Word of God when it is preached to us, and make it our wisdom, and our counsellor; as it says in the one hundred and nineteenth Psalm, the commandments of God are the counsellors of a faithful man (*Psa.* 119:24). If a young man is about to go astray, and he has a guardian to keep him in check, he can be prevented from doing so. Whilst it is true that Satan has many temptations by which to corrupt us, and plentiful means and occasions to do so, yet God has, in his grace, given us counsel. He sets his Word before us; therefore, it is only right that we should do him the honour of listening and submitting to him. What difference will it make if we tell him a hundred thousand times that we have only followed the pack? It is just as if we were saying, 'Well, God was not as important to us as men; we have preferred to follow the world, although it has led us astray and alienated us from all that is good'. Is this a reasonable excuse? Is it not tantamount to spitting in his face, so that he withdraws and moves into the background? We are saying, in effect, that we prefer the company of other people, and feel obliged to copy them and conform to what they do.

* * *

This is the application that we must make today of Paul's teaching, and he adds that 'every man shall bear his own burden'. It is as if he is saying that each person will have enough encumbrances of his own, without helping his friend. This text, admittedly, can be applied in many ways; indeed, even without changing the natural and straightforward sense of Paul's words. If we apply this in the context of his general argument, we have 'every man shall bear his own burden before God'. He uses the word 'burden' to eliminate all excuses, so that we realise that all our subterfuges and evasions are to no avail. This is noteworthy, because we know how audacious we are. We would be ashamed to speak against our fellow creatures in the way that we do against God. Even if he crushes us until we are more than convinced of his power, there are still murmurings and complaints on our part. This is why Paul chooses the word 'burden', in order to say that we cannot accuse God, for we will gain nothing by answering him back. Why? Well, where does the condemnation hanging over us originate? Is it that God has stretched out his arm to show us his power by sending us to the pit? Not at all: 'every man shall bear his own burden'. It is true that God's wrath is compared to raging, all-consuming fire (*Psa.* 50:3). But where has the wood come from for the fire that consumes us? What sets it alight and keeps it burning? It is ourselves, and our sins which are like that wood; our evil lusts have lit the fire. Hence the word 'burden'. It is true that the hand of God crushes the wicked, yet if they were to consider the true cause of this, they would find it to be their sins. Thus much for the word 'burden'.

Having silenced every tongue, and shown that we must quietly accept God's judgment upon us, Paul tells us here that every man must bear his own burden. From this we may draw that which I have already touched upon, that is, we all have enough to hinder us on our own. Paul chiefly declares this because, if I keep harping back to what is customary, and if I say, 'This is the done thing – everyone else does it', I am seeking to exempt myself from judgment. Instead, I must be made to consider whether those whom I propose as guarantors are really that strong, and have broad enough shoulders to bear my burden. God calls me, and it is time to give an account of my life, so I search for substitutes who can make good on my behalf. But who are they? Each person has enough encumbrances of their own; they are all more than guilty already. How, then, can they bear my burden when I throw it upon their shoulders, if they are already so bowed down themselves that they are a hundred times too encumbered? Is it not, therefore, great folly to produce such people as my guarantors when I stand before God? I will be guilty of a hundred thousand faults. I will be standing there amongst the flock with the others, and if I examine myself aright I will find myself more than guilty, as I have said. Yet I seek to satisfy God by saying that I followed the common path. By seeking to exempt myself on account of others, I will find that a thousand, or rather, two thousand people will all attack me, and thus my burden, which was already too heavy for me, will increase and become all the heavier. Thus, we will all stand ashamed.

Now we have seen how foolish it is to exalt men, as if they can help us stand firm against God, so that we are liberated from our deserved condemnation because we have made them shields to protect us from God. As if it were in doubt as to who will win, either the Word of God which abides forever and never changes (*Isa.* 40:8), or our own carnal appetites! Customs, habits, lawful practices (as they call them), ancient rites, and so on – where do all these things come from? They exist because men want to be wiser than God, though they are carried along by wicked lusts, and though they seek only to give themselves free rein and a licence to do evil. Hence, we cannot claim to have sureties who will step forward and set themselves in opposition to God without openly engaging in war against him. In short, as each of us realises more and more that we are laden with our own sins, we will find occasion to humble ourselves; for there is not one of us who will not be utterly put to shame when God calls us to give an account to him and when he demonstrates his severity. Even those who are most righteous will find much in themselves that must be reprimanded, and, therefore, they too will feel ashamed. When we have acknowledged this, let us attribute all the praise to God, and allow him to govern our lives.

Let us also return to what Paul set before us earlier: let us not deliberately deceive ourselves simply because we have enjoyed great boldness in correcting, reprimanding and chastising others. May we not be so foolish as to justify ourselves in comparison to them, considering that God ought to be happy that we have scolded others, and that we, therefore, have some appearance of virtue in us. May we not depend upon any of these things, as we are exhorted here; but let us note that when we are told to bear our own burdens, it shows that we have great need of our Lord Jesus Christ, who carries our load himself. Indeed, he bore all our sins upon the cross, as Peter says in his first letter (*1 Pet.* 2:24). It is true that Paul's argument here is none other than that which I have declared, that is, that we must not think that other people will protect us, since even the most righteous man has enough encumbrances of his own. But to go further, if our Lord had not bothered to help us, we would be altogether crushed under our burden. The fact remains that each of us will have to answer for ourselves, the Word of God being our judge, as I have already said. This is what Paul wants us to know.

However, let us reflect upon ourselves a little more. If each of us must bear our own burden, which of us can fulfil this successfully? We will all be totally put to shame, for even if there is but one sin, a man will be condemned to hell. It is certain that one sin is more weighty than a stone that can break limbs and bones. But we are not talking about either one or a hundred – but an infinite multitude. How, then, can we survive before the judgment of God when he calls us to give account? Who can say that they come to him clean and clear of debt? In short, if there were no remedy in what Paul is teaching here, we would all be damned. We must, therefore, come to the Lord Jesus Christ, for it is he who has carried all our burdens, as we have already explained. It cost him dearly to purchase us, and if we were to search for another means of redemption, either in heaven or on earth, we would find no other that could appease God's wrath. There would have been no other satisfaction for sin had not the Son of God appeared for us. Indeed, the prophet Isaiah declares how he carried our load (*Isa.* 53:4–5). He experienced the sorrows of death, and it was necessary for the Father to treat him as if he held him to be an evildoer, guilty of all the sins of the world. But now we must come to him, as, indeed, he himself has invited us.

However, if we believe that there is a contradiction here, in that Paul says we must bear our own burdens, the answer to this is simple. When the Scriptures speak of the judgment of God, they say, of course, that a man will receive according to what he has done. Paul speaks in this same vein in the fourteenth chapter to the Romans. He says that a man will receive his own reward, according to how he has lived in this world and according to what he has done in his body. This is the approach of Scripture regarding the judgment of God, but it does not exclude the remedy which is given to us in the Lord Jesus Christ, who brings man relief. This is how God provides for his elect, and those whom he reserves for salvation; he stretches out his hand to them after he has chastised them, and restores them after he has put them to shame. In fact, we can never know the worth of the grace of our Lord Jesus Christ, and can never taste it for ourselves, or partake of it, unless we are utterly confounded in ourselves first. Let us learn to so feel our burden that we bow down under it, as we said this morning, and may this lead us to proper humility. Have we felt this intolerable burden? Then let us come to the Lord Jesus Christ, who promises to relieve us if we seek all our rest in him (*Matt.* 11:28).

Thus, we see that when the Scriptures speak of the judgment of God, they do not exclude his grace. We must, therefore, always remember his mercy. It is written that those who have been cruel and who have shown no pity towards others will receive 'judgment without mercy' (*Jas.* 2:13), and by this, James is declaring that our Lord's judgment on the wicked and reprobate is to render to them according to their crimes. Yet he has another approach towards his own; having condemned them in themselves and made them aware of their wickedness in order to bring them to proper repentance, he then restores them. Thus we must first be struck down by the hand of God, and afterwards we can be lifted up by his free promises, for he tells us that we will find all that we need in the Lord Jesus Christ. This, briefly, is how we ought to put this passage into practice. When warning our neighbours in a spirit of gentleness and meekness, indeed humbly and modestly, without any presumption of our own worth, let us make a thorough examination of our own life, so that we tremble daily because of our sins and grow to hate them. May we no longer be deceived by any hypocrisy, and may we seek to withdraw ourselves from the world, so that we no longer imagine that we can escape the judgment of God by our subterfuges. May all these things be true of us, that we might submit to the pure Word of God. Whatever men may do to turn us aside, let us not allow ourselves to be corrupted. To this end, we must take refuge in the Lord Jesus Christ, knowing that, whatever desire we may have to devote ourselves fully to serving God, we are, nevertheless, laden with vices and imperfections that could sink us in the depths of the abyss, if it were not for the One who can pluck us out, that is, our Lord Jesus Christ. He has borne all our sins, and has set us free from them altogether, so that we can approach our God today with heads that have been lifted up.

May we acknowledge our sins with such humility that each of us confesses unfeignedly that we are lost and in despair, except for our great God, who has had pity on us. Let us continue to pray that he would make us recognise our need of the fruit and power of the sufferings and death of our Lord Jesus Christ, not only to cover the sins that we have already committed, and to erase their memory, but also to cleanse us daily by his Holy Spirit. May he continue to uphold us in his infinite goodness until the day when we reach the perfect standard to which we are called, being delivered from the prison of sin, which still surrounds us. May he show this grace, not only to us, but also to all peoples and nations on earth, etc.

40

Men Reap What They Sow

> *Let him that is taught in the word communicate unto him that teacheth in all good things. Be not deceived; God is not mocked: for whatsoever a man soweth, that shall he also reap. For he that soweth to his flesh shall of the flesh reap corruption; but he that soweth to the Spirit shall of the Spirit reap life everlasting* (Gal. 6:6–8).

We have enough evidence to say that, wherever he was known, Paul could not have been suspected of being excessively devoted to his own profit; for although it was quite lawful for him to be fed because he was spreading the Word of God, he abstained from exercising this liberty (as we see), in order to avoid giving offence. He protested that he was constrained to labour day and night with his own hands in order to make a living (*Acts* 20:34). Therefore, he was all the more able to exhort those who were neglecting to do their duty, as we see in this passage, without arousing any suspicion of his motives. He demands that the one who teaches be fed, and that we refuse to allow such a person to be in want of anything. Now, as we have said, if Paul had been an avaricious man, seeking to acquire the wealth of others, or a covetous man who sought esteem by surrounding himself with pomp and feasting, he would have had to remain silent, for everyone would have said that he was speaking on his own behalf, and that this was not devotion to serving God. But since he had shown by example that he was forgetful of self and had no regard for his own person in his efforts to advance the kingdom of the Lord Jesus Christ and edify his church, he could then freely criticise the ingratitude of those who treated their pastors badly, withholding food for the body when they received from them meat and nourishment for their souls.

Now, it is most unkind when a man does not acknowledge that the one who brings the doctrine of salvation to him is like an adoptive father, sent to him by God. At the very least, he ought to endeavour to provide for his bodily needs. When men are indifferent in this area, they display contempt for the Word of God. For even nature teaches us that when we are indebted to someone we must strive to return the favour as far as we possibly can. If we cannot, let us at least show that it is not through want of desire. In this case, we cannot return the same favour, for the Word of God cannot be compared or weighed in the balance with anything else in this world. Nevertheless, those who have been taught ought at least not to withhold their temporal goods, but should feed those who provide them with the priceless treasure of the gospel. We can see that this is one of Satan's schemes to rob the church of God of its good pastors and ministers, by starving them, as it were. The agents of Satan will always be feasting! Indeed, the large stomachs that we see in the Papacy today bespeak idleness. All they have to do is shout out their masses and matins, and then they can become thoroughly inebriated! While everyone else is hungry and thirsty, these men will never see any shortages! They will always enjoy plentiful provision, even while the rest of the world cries out because of famine. The complete reverse is true of those who serve God and demonstrate the zeal and care that they have for the salvation of souls. They are left to their own resources, even though it may appear that they are well looked after by their hearers. 'Well,' they say, 'we have heard him. Now he can go away; he has fulfilled his duty!' Indeed, how many people today sit simmering when they come to listen to a sermon? They would much prefer it if no-one ever spoke to them about God, because it makes them melancholy!

By this, therefore, we can see how the devil uses this to try to abolish all sound teaching, and ensure that only idols remain, and people who do not care in the least about how they ought to behave. Therefore, Paul has good reason to seek to remedy such a sin, telling us that the one who teaches must, at the very least, be fed and given sufficient upon which to live. He who receives the doctrine of salvation is basically obliged to give of his wealth and of his substance to the one who administers spiritual food to him. Paul is specifically referring to the Word of God here, and not to human sciences, which, incidentally, have always been so highly prized that those who have made a profession out of teaching them have been well fed thereby; this makes the Word of God seem less valuable, though it surpasses all else. Thus, Paul accuses men of wickedness, saying, 'Consider the value of preaching the Word of God. Think of the fruit it produces in you. For we are all wretched and accursed until God calls us to himself by means of his Word, which is the power that he pours upon us in order to gather us into his kingdom. This being so, how can you be so mean with the passing possessions of this world, so that those who work for your good and edification are refused the sustenance they need to devote themselves to this work without being distracted by cares, which hinder and prevent them from carrying out their duty?'

The word which Paul uses here means to teach, and is the word from which we derive the term 'catechism'. He literally says, 'him that catechises'; in other words, he that is a faithful teacher, who edifies the people by the Word of God. Such a man must be sustained by those whom he catechises, or instructs, and those whom he leads to God as disciples. Now we have understood Paul's intention here, and from this we can gather, firstly, that today we must only consider those who preach the Word to be ministers and pastors in the church of God. This is the first thing. This is a very useful lesson, because the Papists boast that they are the true church. But, being sheep without a shepherd is not something that would suit the true children of God. What, therefore, are the marks of the church? They are to be a gathered flock, with a pastor that leads the sheep to the Lord Jesus Christ. The Papists also claim to have a hierarchy, that is, a holy and sacred leadership, yet you will not find this to be one of the marks that Paul sets down. These horned prelates and the whole rabble of Papal clergy, possess nothing but their titles. Where is the Word of God? They think it will undermine their dignity! Anyway, it seems to them that it is enough if they observe their ceremonies and other frivolities, for then they have duly fulfilled their responsibilities, when they have really only acted out a farce! These hypocrites do nothing more than fill the world with their deception and falsehood. Let us learn, therefore, to discern the true church from all the synagogues that Satan has established in this world, through which he blinds our eyes. In other words, wherever the Word of God is faithfully preached, we may conclude that God knows and acknowledges the flock that is assembled in that place. Thus, we must distribute the wealth of the church as Paul has shown us here.

However, when Paul says, 'Let him that is taught in the Word communicate . . . in all good things', he does not mean that we should give in such abundance to those who bear and preach the doctrine of salvation that we leave ourselves to starve. Overabundant wealth is a deadly plague; for if several people are moved and motivated by a foolish piety to give their substance to those whom they judge to be worthy of possessing most of the world, it brings terrible confusion. Therefore, we must not think that Paul wants us to make ministers of the Word more wealthy, so that they have the wherewithal to feast themselves intemperately, or lead a dissolute life, with much pomp and great revelling. Paul did not want to make an opening for any of this; he only meant that we must provide for all their needs, so that they will not be destitute. We must remember what he said in that other passage: ' . . . having food and raiment let us be therewith content' (*1 Tim.* 6:8). We know that God takes care of all creatures; how much stronger reason does he have to care for believers? Thus, let us live soberly, taking one day at a time, and not heap up the passing things of this world. Ministers of the Word must take this lesson to heart, that is to say, they should follow modest and temperate lifestyles, and not be tormented or eaten up with the kind of anxiety which is full of unbelief, and leads them to amass more and more wealth. Then they will be content with little. Nevertheless, they will find others to be generous and liberal towards them without them having to ask, and they will have enough to feed and clothe themselves.

Indeed, in addition to his words, Paul put this doctrine into practice himself, and not only so, but he also exhorts his brothers and companions to do the same. In the twentieth chapter of Acts, he specifically points out that he worked hard, and that with his own hands he earned his living, but he also says there that it is more blessed to give than to receive. For, he says, this is what we ought to learn in the school of our Lord Jesus Christ; we will have more pleasure when we find opportunities to do good and to provide for the needs of others, than when we receive and become rich. It is not appropriate for the servants of God to desire to amass wealth. We have seen Paul's intention here; he does not wish to give a free rein to preachers of the Word of God, so that they have a table full of sweetmeats and delicacies, or so that they can be refined according to the world's standards, but that they would have enough by which they may feed themselves with the modesty that becomes people in their position. At the same time, he accuses people of ingratitude, in that those who are indebted to their pastors show themselves to be so mean. It is as if we are asking them almost to disembowel themselves when we speak of providing for those to whom they owe so much, and keeping them from destitution. Let us be aware that Paul has good reason to give us this rule, that those who preach the Word of God should be fed and provided for, seeing that this sin has existed since time began, and the devil (as we have said) is seeking by such cunning means to discourage pastors so that there will no longer be any instruction or doctrinal teaching.

Now in the world today, we see an even greater sin than the one which Paul criticises and condemns here. People who pay nothing out, still insist on muttering and murmuring about ministers of the Word, saying, 'Must we keep them in their idleness?' As if it were idleness to serve God and the whole church! Or they say, 'The apostles did not do this or that'. Indeed, but we can see that the apostles were so led that when they had a need, others would apply themselves to meet it, not only with their faculties, but with their own selves. Rich and opulent people crossed the sea (as we know) to accompany an apostle (*Acts* 27:2). But nowadays, people are murmuring because the servants of God are given meagre support. This demonstrates the ungodliness of those who thus speak; it reveals that they are profane people who prefer to exist in a barbaric and brutish fashion without the doctrine of salvation, trampling this doctrine underfoot and living according to their own desires. Therefore, let us remember what Paul has shown us here, in order that those who are called to fulfil the office and position of preacher of the Word of God would realise that if they are fed and provided for, it is because they have worked, and because their service has profited all the people. By this they ought to be all the more inspired to do their duty with reverence and watchfulness; may this prompt them to be more diligent. Also, we are not to be envious of them in any way, or to murmur against them when they are properly supported and provided for, because God has ordained it, and we have seen the reasons why this is the case.

* * *

At this point, Paul adds, 'Be not deceived; God is not mocked: for whatsoever a man soweth, that shall he also reap.' By telling us that we ought not to be deceived, Paul is clearly showing that since the beginning of time men have used many subterfuges; if they desire to do wickedly or to speak evil, they have always sought to cover themselves in some way. But here he is calling them to the judgment of God, as if he is telling them that though they may be able to satisfy other people and silence them, they must, nevertheless, give account before the heavenly Judge. Then, he says, all their evasiveness will be to no avail, though these excuses are readily accepted by men. And, as I have already mentioned, many people keep their ministers in office, but only so that they can criticise them. They have such itching ears that it is scarcely possible to find one person in a hundred who is happy to listen to such discourses, and either to add some lard, or make a sharper sauce for them! This error is far too common.

Though Paul's teaching here generally extends to include all excuses that we are accustomed to make when we want to justify evil and pretend that black is white, let us firstly consider the specific argument that Paul treats here. It concerns the upkeep of ministers of the Word. He is telling us that we must not deceive ourselves. Why? Because it is a very thoughtless thing to ask, 'Why do ministers not work, since they ought to set an example to others? When they have finished in the pulpit, can they not employ the rest of their time doing some kind of labour, in order not to burden the church?' This argument is easily swallowed by people who babble on in this way, because they think they are following a good cause and acting as zealots for the common good and the maintenance of order in the church. But these people are deceiving themselves, for they are full of malice and it is Satan who has led them to be like this in order to rid the world of the doctrine of salvation, or at least to revile it and put it to shame. We must return to the source of the problem and deal with it. Paul has good reason here to warn the Galatians not to deceive themselves by painting these things in pretty colours.

Secondly, we must apply this warning of Paul's to all the whitewash we use to disguise the way things really are. For if we can be believed, there are always some extenuating circumstances that absolve us. There is none so evil that he does not have a clever way of concealing his shamefulness from men. Indeed, even if we are a hundred times convicted, the devil will still subtly find a way of influencing our imagination, so that a bad motive is painted with make-up when we want to believe it to be a good one. We tend this way by nature, and habit has hardened us therein; thus, we must be all the more careful to observe what Paul warns us about here, so that we do not deceive ourselves and deliberately go astray. For it is certain that hypocrisy can never deceive men unless they willingly delude themselves. Occasionally, hypocrites may be convicted about their own self-deception, feeling such remorse that they are the first to condemn themselves, even though they have been forgiven all. But there are those who have fallen asleep, and think that there is nothing wrong with them. However, they have rough edges within, and though they are blind, God still regards them as guilty; for he has called them and they have sought to wrap themselves up with excuses, such that they themselves do not perceive their own evil, and are not led to repentance. This is the worse kind of hypocrisy in the world, when men deceive themselves by vain flattery, introducing this or that foolish trifle, not only before the world, but also before God.

Thus, Paul says that God will not be mocked. In other words, those who delude themselves with frivolous excuses are self-deceivers and, indeed, fully-fledged mockers of God. For if we have the reverence for God which he deserves, it is certain that in the time remaining before we stand before his majesty, we will sound out the depths of our thoughts and affections, leaving nothing which has not been thoroughly examined. All those who think they will fare so well when they have to come before God, as if he were a little child with whom they can play, reveal by this that they are full of ungodliness. We see, therefore, how useful this passage is.

Here Paul, having exhorted men not to deceive themselves, adds, 'God is not mocked'. It seems as if this does not follow. If we deceive ourselves, does that mean that we are mocking God? Yes, says Paul. To do this, you seek out vain excuses and give yourselves over to them. If you considered the facts aright, and were not so full of malice, you would have better judgment than you now have. What has caused you thus to sleep in your shallow excuses? It is because you do not realise that we must all stand before the judgment seat of God; it is he who fathoms our thoughts, and nothing is hidden from him. But you treat him as if he were an idol, and deceive yourselves into thinking that he will be pleased with your stupid pranks. Because you have deceived others and mocked them, you think that God is on the same level, and indeed, your approach to him is even more audacious. However, be assured that all who flatter themselves and seek to avoid blame are faithless, and show that they are altogether mocking God.

Though this phrase is short, it ought, nevertheless, to make us tremble as much as when we hear loud thunder, or see a thunderbolt fall from on high. Is it a pardonable offence for men, who are rotten through and through, to rise up against God in this way and, indeed, laugh at him? The greatest disrespect that we can show a man is to hold him up to ridicule. If this is not tolerated amongst men, who are nothing, will God allow himself to be mocked? Paul has given us occasion here to examine ourselves more closely, and to walk in simplicity, not following our own pleasures and hoping to improve our account thereby, for we are provoking God. We are defying him, as if we would rob him of his right and have him believe that we can tweak his nose and rail upon him without him noticing.

If people regarded this text, they would show much more reverence than they do now. But look how men defile themselves, even deliberately, and become so hardened that, in matters of good and evil, they have no shame and no decency. With loud mouths, they corrupt and pervert all that is upright, and blaspheme against God. Today, we can see that all tables, all houses and all streets are peopled with mockers of God. From where does this proceed? It is true that many of them are hypocrites who flatter themselves, but the devil has so possessed them that they openly spit in the face of heaven; that is to say, they defy God without any scruples whatever. This proves that they are altogether reprobate and out of their minds. Where does this boldness to rise up against God originate? As we have already said, it comes from that hypocrisy which makes us think that we can hide the way things really are by our subtle excuses and fine answers, so that there is no longer a distinction between white and black. So much the more, therefore, do we need to remember Paul's warning here.

* * *

Here, he continues the argument that he has already introduced, and expands upon it further, saying, 'for whatsoever a man soweth, that shall he also reap. For he that soweth to his flesh shall of the flesh reap corruption; but he that soweth to the Spirit shall of the Spirit reap life everlasting.' Here, Paul is comparing all our labour and our duties, and the efforts that we make, to the sowing that farmers do. For why else do men engage in this or that employment, and work and strive, except because they have some particular end in view? They hope to produce some fruit to meet their needs; this is why they never grow weary of working. For example, a man who hopes to earn much will tolerate hunger and thirst, cold and heat; he will stop at nothing. Why? Because he is transported by avarice, to the extent that he forgets everything else and tortures himself more than he would be tortured in the hands of his enemy. Thus, when a man takes great pains to amass goods, he is like a farmer sowing. He means to reap something in the end, and to produce a crop. If a man wants to be esteemed in the eyes of the world, he will not dare to sleep halfway through a social occasion, but what is he hoping for by keeping himself so alert? He hopes to attain to a degree of honour and dignity, and to have credit in the eyes of others. Well, ambition is like the harvest of those who crave the honours of this world. They want to reap a crop. Of what? Of whatever their nature desires and dictates. The same applies to all the rest. A glutton will work to feed his appetite, even becoming involved in wicked practices such as pimping, and the like. Why? In order to eat and feast himself, or to get drunk. For others, it is that they may indulge in theft and plundering even to the point of becoming bandits. This is where lusts lead men; for they determine to reap a harvest, that is, to get whatever they want, even though this will lead to their ruin and shame. Whatever else is true, if we consider why men give themselves to this or that labour, we will find that it is always because they hope for a harvest. Thus, whatever they do is like sowing, because they work with the intention of receiving something from it.

Paul says here that we will reap according to what we have sown. Then he explains this by saying that some sow to the Spirit and others sow to the flesh. To sow to the Spirit is to withdraw from the things of this world and of this transitory existence and acknowledge that we have been created, not to be attached to things here below, but to rise above them and attain our inheritance. We only live in this world for a short time and then we are carried away, as it says in the psalm that was sung, and will yet be sung again (*Psa.* 90:5–6). We cannot live here for ever, as if this were our permanent abode, for God will carry us away, and will make us do an about turn! As Moses also says in his canticle, 'Return [to dust], ye children of men' (*Psa.* 90:3). This being the case, it is only when we are determined to deny all our carnal appetites, that we can be said to sow to the Spirit. For then we will have realised that we must devote all our efforts to obtaining eternal life, which is what we have been called to do. Hence, some (though it is rare and though they are so few in number) sow to the Spirit, in that they do not bury themselves in worldly cares to the point of being unable to detach themselves from them, but they realise that God is calling them to higher things and they are prepared to make every effort to attain those goals.

Others sow to the flesh, which means that they are so taken up with brutish desires that they think that there is nothing beyond this present life. Indeed, if we consider the goals that men are aiming for, we will find that almost all are captivated by the things of this world. Out of a thousand, there is scarcely one who looks any further, recognising that this world is but a shadow which will vanish, and devoting himself with determination and sincerity to obtaining eternal life. Almost all, therefore, sow to the flesh. It is true that their natures are very different, for one may be lewd, another a drunkard, another niggardly or a teaser, whilst another may be a squanderer. If, therefore, we look at the characters of men, we will find them to be diverse and also incompatible, such that one hates another. Why? Because what is unnatural to me personally seems to me to be improper; but though this is the case, when we examine the matter more carefully, we find that all sow to the flesh. There are, therefore, many ways of sowing, but all are rooted in this world, so that people cannot see that God is calling them, or to what end they ought to apply themselves. Some want to become rich, others to be honoured and held in esteem, others to be comfortable and enjoy great delights, others to possess this or that, but all are concerned with this fleeting life and cannot raise themselves any higher.

Paul tells us that it is only right that we reap according to what we have sown. Those, therefore, who devote themselves to this world and who sow to the flesh will reap corruption, he says. That is, in the end they will recognise that all they have valued so highly amounts to no more than smoke. It is true that we could take the word 'corruption' to mean eternal death, but this is not Paul's intention here. He means that men are devoid of sense and wisdom to let themselves become so entangled in their own stupid anxieties. Why do they do so? If we were to ask them, 'What is this world?', they would say, 'A passing shadow'. 'And what is our life?', 'It is nothing.' 'And what are the things of this world?', 'A dream'. They would all say this, yet they are in reality so taken up with these things that one cannot think of any means to draw them away. The devil has bewitched them, so that even though God cries in their ears, 'You poor people, what has become of you?', they still all plunge into the mire. Although they know that all their lusts are nothing, and that this life slips away very quickly, they still wish to remain here below. God calls out to lead those who have gone astray back to the right path, yet their minds are too dull, and cannot obey the advice or exhortations that they hear. This is why Paul says that those who have thus sown to the flesh will reap corruption.

However, those who have sown to the Spirit, that is, those who know that there is a much more precious life than the one we now live, and who set all their affection there and all their thoughts, will reap eternal life, he says. Because they have been led by the Spirit of God, and have sought to be joined to him and draw close to him, this is the reward which is prepared for them, he says. Firstly, we are being warned here to think more deeply about all our projects and about all that we do, our enterprises and our aspirations and our efforts. We must ask, what is their end? For this image will always hold good, that whenever we apply our labour and industry to a task, we are sowing. Let us, therefore, look well to ourselves, realising that although God desires us to reap corn and wine in this world to feed our bodies, he is calling us to higher things and does not want us to be tied to the things of this world. Let us, then, learn to seek above all else that God should reign and govern, and that we should yield fully to him and to his righteousness. May the cares of this transitory life not dull our minds in the way that we have shown. May this world be nothing more, I say, than means of access to a more important life which is yet to be, that is, in the kingdom of heaven.

In short, God has placed us in this world to sow, not to be idle and fruitless. How? It is true that ministers of the Word ought to sow in order to reap a harvest which they can present to God, as a holy offering. Their sowing involves faithful teaching so that the Word of God produces fruit, and that God's name might be glorified and blessed. As our Lord Jesus Christ said to his apostles, 'I have chosen you, and ordained you, that ye should go and bring forth fruit, and that your fruit should remain' (*John* 15:16). This is something that is peculiar to ministers, and yet all of us ought to sow to eternal life. This involves passing through this world like strangers, having our minds on things above, meditating upon our inheritance, which is our resting place, and the goal which demands all our efforts to attain. Even when we labour to feed our bodies, may it still be because we are pressing towards this goal; as it is written, we must not live just to eat and drink, but we must eat and drink in order to be led through this world into the next life. May we not live our lives in this world in order to remain here, but to reach a higher goal, eternal life.

Therefore, even if a man applies himself to earning a living, be he a labourer, or a mechanic, a merchant, or whatever else; and even if he is taking care of himself and his family, he ought still to aim higher. Indeed, it is a bad thing if a man is occupied simply with earning a living and has no thought of serving God. For he who works to earn a living ought to ask himself, 'How can I make sure that God approves of what I do? How can I make my service acceptable to him? Only if I do not live according to my lusts, and am determined not to harm anyone, and seek to work faithfully in the area in which I am employed.' This is how we ought to sow: we are not to be given over to this world, nor attached to all that is here below, for then we will not be able to aspire to eternal life.

Consider also the way we must sow; it is sowing to the Spirit, says Paul. Let us remember that we are not at all like oxen or asses, who eat and drink after they have laboured, and we feed them (although it is only right and fair that we should do so). Let us remember that we have been adopted by God to attain to eternal life. Let us, therefore, sow to the Spirit, and cast aside all that hinders us from reaching on high. May we throw it away as if it were harmful, realising that all who strive to be valued in this world will be disappointed in the end. Why? Because they will see that it is only corruption. The person who has accumulated a great quantity of possessions will have all the more regret when he comes to die, because he has made this world his paradise.

Thus, he will bare his teeth at God, and fume and be tormented much more than if he had never taken pains to accumulate a thing. This is how those who have sown to the flesh can recognise that they have sown to corruption: corruption is all that they reap. However, it is then too late; therefore let us look well to ourselves.

Now, although we can see that most people are deceiving themselves, and tell their tales as if the happiest life is the one where you receive all that you hope for, the only rule they have to live by is that dictated by their appetites. Therefore, when we see men fuming in this way, let us learn to guard against it in ourselves, knowing that we have been called by God to eternal life, which he has set before us daily in the gospel. Let us make this our only goal, and may all our affections and desires centre upon it. May we strive to gain ever-increasing profit from the doctrine of salvation, that he may raise us up on high, and draw us away from all that is here below. Paul tells us, when he describes the Christian's armour, that we need our 'feet shod with the preparation of the gospel of peace' (*Eph.* 6:15). We must be protected from top to bottom, and armed right down to the feet, since we will very soon be troubled by the attacks meted out by this world. After having said this, I tell you, he then implies that the gospel ought to lift us up on high and pluck us out of the corruption in which we dwell, that we might aspire to the kingdom of God, as we have been exhorted to do. This is what we need to remember.

Now, as for what Paul says concerning those who sow to the Spirit, he teaches that they reap eternal life. Yet, he does not mean by this that we can merit such a precious and excellent thing as our heavenly inheritance. He shows instead that believers, once assured of their calling, will never find themselves to have been mistaken, however poor they appear to be in this world. We know that God, of his free bounty, adopts us; this is that upon which our salvation is founded. He forgives us our sins, and herein consists all our justification. For if he looked upon us in our natural state, he could only reject us as cursed and detestable creatures. We cannot find favour in his sight unless he accepts us through his pure goodness. We also know that our works are always imperfect and soiled with sin, such that they cannot be acceptable to God. When we seek to serve him and to do good, we often do the complete opposite, and are thus always in his debt. However, once God has adopted us as his children and covered all our sins, he declares that he is pleased with our service, though imperfect. Subsequently, he also declares and adds, to crown it all, that if we dedicate ourselves to him and seek eternal life in heaven, we will never be disappointed. Whilst others may ridicule us, and say, 'These people are jokers, tormenting themselves so much! What for? For a life in heaven. And who has brought them news of the place? These people are deceived by some kind of strange religious beliefs. Yet, they are really poor louts, with no intelligence or anything else to speak about.' People today who think they know everything insult us in this way, saying, 'What do these poor simpletons think they are doing?' This is how we are taunted, because we have no desire for self-advancement, or making ourselves of note in the eyes of the world.

However much we are mocked in this way, let us wait on the promise which is given to us here, which is that if we pursue our vocation in sincerity, we can know that God, who began this work, will prove himself to be faithful. He desires our highest good when he is pleased to draw us to himself, but not only does he seek our well-being in and through it all, but also to reveal himself in his infinite goodness as our Father and Saviour. Therefore, let us make every effort to come to him, and to dedicate ourselves to him fully, forsaking anything in this world which would hinder us from coming to him. Let us cast off all this, seeking only that which will lead us on high, and let us continue to do so until the end. If this is our case, our Lord will certainly show us that our harvest is ready to reap. A harvest not of the riches of this world, which are subject to decay, for even the most precious and most costly outfits in this world will be eaten by worms, and there is no gold or silver or anything else which will not eventually perish. When men desire to possess these things in an excessive measure, they may burst at the seams with the goods which they have accumulated, and yet they will be of no value to them, but will cause them to be altogether ruined. Instead of this, we will find that we have good treasure which is kept for us by the hand of God, whose delights we will enjoy when we have finished our course in this world, if we have persevered with our sowing. I mean that we must not be slow to serve our God, fixing our eyes upon heaven, and keeping ourselves from the things of this world as much as lies in our power.

Now let us fall before the majesty of our great God, acknowledging our sins, and praying that he would make us so aware of them that we might be led to true repentance. However, may we not neglect to find comfort and cause of rejoicing in his goodness. Let us not doubt that he will receive us in mercy, provided we have had recourse to him in order to be transformed by his Holy Spirit. He will strip us of all the imperfections and sins of our flesh until, renewed in his image, we reach the perfect standard of righteousness to which we aspire. Thus, we all say, 'Almighty God and our heavenly Father', etc.

41

On Doing Good to All in Need

> *And let us not be weary in well doing: for in due season we shall reap, if we faint not. As we have therefore opportunity, let us do good unto all men, especially unto them who are of the household of faith. Ye see how large a letter I have written unto you with mine own hand* (Gal. 6:9–11).

We have seen the image Paul uses here to exhort us to do good in this world, while God gives us opportunity. For here below we must use all that God has bestowed to serve him and all his own, and even all men in general. As God distributes different abilities and gifts to each of us, we are obliged to use them for those who need us and whom we can help. We must, therefore, make up our minds not to be idle or fruitless in this, and consider the means that God has given us, so that each one of us can use them by way of an offering to him. In order further to encourage us, Paul tells us that by doing this we are sowing. God will not allow us to be disappointed after we have sought to employ ourselves in that which he has commanded. It may seem to us that all is wasted effort, except when we are seeking our own profit and giving ourselves over to self-advantage; yet the opposite is true. For although a person who helps his neighbour loses whatever he has given, he is in fact laying up treasure, like the one who sows seed upon the soil in order to reap a crop in due season.

On the other hand, all is lost when we are too anxious to become wealthy in this life, and only care about our own advancement – then we will reap corruption. In other words, all will perish. Indeed, this entire world is passing away and its shadow is fading, and yet this is the only treasure that those who study to enrich themselves in this world can possess. Just as their lives are transitory and fleeting, so are the goods that they have collected, and all will rot away to nothing. But if we can rid ourselves of earthly cares and consider God's kingdom, though it may seem to us that in well doing we become impoverished and depleted, nevertheless, this treasure will never perish. It will be well guarded by the hand of God until the last day.

However, since the devil presents us with many opportunities to grow cold, or to turn and run in the other direction, Paul adds a most vital warning here. He tells us that we must 'not be weary in well doing'. Then he adds that we must be patient and wait for the right season in which to reap. He says that we must not grow weary, for those who have good intentions and desire to do good will be retarded by the wiles of Satan, and the many difficulties and obstacles that he sets in their path. If a person is preoccupied with pleasing himself, we must not encourage him to persevere. Why? Because he has chosen a well-beaten and attractive path, and he travels at a measured pace. He is completely at ease, because he is not obliged to cover so many miles per day, and he turns back just as soon as the path no longer suits him. This exhortation is, therefore, aimed at those who have many wearisome travelling days to accomplish, not just one or two, for it is important that they persevere. They will have difficult stretches; stony, rough, or miry pathways to tread, as well as mountains and valleys to cross. These people need to be encouraged in order that they might be strengthened and enabled to take the bit between their teeth, as we say, and not to grow weary and faint halfway on their journey.

This applies to us, if God has touched us by his Holy Spirit, and made us inclined to serve him and to do good to those who need our help. Yet, on the one hand, we are held back by our unfaithfulness, for we think that the ground will fall from beneath us if we help someone who needs our assistance; we think that we will fall prey to the same problems and shortages. Thus, we hold back because we are entangled in such anxieties, and have insatiable lusts that make us believe that nothing is ever quite enough, and we are led to seek for excuses. Hence we say that we are not sure if the person who is murmuring really has the problem he claims to have, and if he really deserves such pity. Or we may say that the world is so evil and perverse that we do not know whom to do good to, and that we often waste our goods; we say that there is so much ingratitude that it were better to leave others hungry and thirsty than to give these people an opportunity to offend God by deceiving and mocking us in this way. We will always find plenty of excuses and escape routes when it comes to well doing, as experience too often reveals, chiefly because we are lazy and weak by nature. Therefore, it is all the more important for us to take note of the lesson that Paul is teaching us here, which is to persevere in well doing, without growing weary.

This means that we need to broaden our outlook, and when we have wealth, to use it to provide for our neighbour's deficiency. We know that Paul began by speaking about ministers of the Word, but now he is exhorting all of us in general, seeing that God has placed us all together and has put us in this world on condition that each of us considers how he may help those who need his aid. May we devote our lives to this, so as not to abuse nature's own pattern. However, since we are so lazy and so cold-hearted, and find so many reasons to hinder us and abandon the zeal that we have to fulfil our duty, may we overcome all obstacles, take courage and not faint. Now that the world is more full of iniquity, ingratitude and malice than ever before, we must strive harder to overcome such temptations, looking rather at God than at those who seem unworthy to be supported in their need. For however much evil there is in the world, God's demands never change. Therefore, each of us must consider what he is able to do, according to the means that he has been given. We were not born to live for ourselves; God did not create us with this intention. Therefore, each of us is expected to strive and even constrain ourselves to help those who ask for our support. Even if they do not request it, if we see them in need we must help according to the means that God has given. The pagans are well acquainted with speaking this language, which means that there is double shame upon us when we fail to recognise why God has created us, and why he has been so generous to us. Indeed, he could easily have so disposed matters that there would have been no lack and no destitution in the world, and then we could all have lived independently of one another. Yet he presents us with circumstances that demand our pity and compassion, so that we might demonstrate whether or not there is any kindness within.

* * *

Now we must take good note of the promise that Paul adds: that we will reap 'in due season'. It is true that, even if there were no reward, our responsibilities would be unchanged. The simple fact that God has declared his will should be enough; indeed, it is enough that he has placed us in this world and has generously provided for us. At the very least, we ought to be wholly devoted to him. However, seeing our feebleness and sluggishness to respond, he adds this, that we might be all the more encouraged by the knowledge that in all that we do, nothing will be lost. He accepts it and keeps it in his care, rendering it to us again but with even more than we could hope or wish for in this world. A person with money in his purse will spend here, there and everywhere if he sees an opportunity to profit, because he supposes that he will lose nothing. He assumes that he will receive the original sum again, and more; it will increase because of the profit that he hopes to make. It is true that if a person is to lend money or invest in a business, he will stop and consider time and again until he is reassured. Yet in the final analysis, if the other person is well-off, solvent and honest, his friend is bound to conclude that he can definitely rely on him. However, we do not honour God in this way, by doing everything he has commanded, even though he has whole-heartedly guaranteed that whatever we have entrusted to him will be returned to us, and our profit will be greater than any we could make in this world. Nevertheless, we remain deaf to all this.

Firstly, therefore, in order that we might not be led astray by the ingratitude of others, our Lord says, 'Whatever you do to those who are least, and to those who are the most despised, I accept and own as though it were done to me. In short, I accept it as if I had done it with my own hand' (*Matt.* 10:42). God speaks in this way with regard to the notion of reward. He adds the promise that there has never been any usury or gain as great as the profit that we can hope to receive from him, if we have closed our eyes to the things of this world and refused to be held back by them. Instead, we must use those things that he has placed in our hands, and committed to our care, as he ordains in his Word. God says this, not once or twice, but many times. If there were even an ounce of trustfulness within us, we would surely be convinced of this. Yet, we are still very much rooted in this world and cannot believe or be persuaded that God is speaking advisedly here. Therefore, Paul has good reason to set before us the promise that we will reap. It is as if he is saying, 'Poor folk, you are so eager if you see an opportunity to make a profit. Even if the outcome is dubious, you are still goaded onwards by your lust, and you all willingly empty your purses. And here is God, the only truthful one who cannot lie, assuring us many times and testifying that all that we place in his hands will yield priceless fruit, yet we cannot add faith to these promises of his. Do we know of any other way to insult him more than this? As for himself, he owes us nothing; that which he has promised is out of his good pleasure, without any obligation whatsoever, and yet there is nothing which will induce us to serve him.' This is what Paul sets before us, that each of us might strive to pluck up that accursed root of avarice which is so deeply embedded in our hearts, so much so that if we are to follow what God has called us to do, we must first do violence to ourselves. This is especially the case when it comes to sharing the goods that he has committed to our care, in order to be his faithful stewards.

* * *

Now let us take note of the words which he adds; he says, 'in due season'. This is to establish and strengthen our patience, for we want God to show us overnight, or even instantly, the reward to which he refers. A farmer has to preserve his own patience when he has sown his seed in the soil. He will see that soil frozen over, covered with snow, there will be wind and rain, and cold and heat. Nevertheless, the farmer still has to wait until the arrival of harvest. Those with stores of merchandise place their money and themselves at great risk; their income ebbs and flows, and causes so much worry; yet because they are used to buying and selling, they know full well that they will not make a profit on the first day. They must wait until the time is right. However, when we are dealing with God, we are not talking about expectations or hopes alone. The whole thing ought to be regarded as completely certain. Even the timing need not seem too long if we lift our minds to that eternity in the kingdom of heaven. Yet not one of us is patient. If we have thrown our wealth away to hazard and chance, we can still be at peace; whereas when God declares that he will guard all that we use in his service, it is a great pity that we become perplexed and anxious, thinking that we will lose all when we do not see our reward immediately. This is what we ought to observe about these words: that is, we ought to keep ourselves bridled until the 'due season' arrives. For it is not for us to appoint the day; we must leave this in the hands of God. Let us be content with the fact that he wishes to increase our patience, knowing that the timing will not be prolonged any further than is necessary for us.

Furthermore, Paul seeks to draw us away from this world,

because of our natural demand for temporal rewards. It is true that we are delighted because God has given them to us, but this still shows that we are earthly. The person who gives alms, though he wants to serve God, also desires very soon afterwards to receive a pound or two for his penny. Under guise of these small acts of almsgiving, he is seeking to expand in every possible direction. Because we seek to trade with God in this way, Paul tells us, in order to correct such a vice, that we must consider the end to which God is calling us; a great day when we will all receive our reward. Thus, although it may seem that we will lose everything when it comes to this world and this present life, let us not neglect always to hope in God, who faithfully keeps what we have deposited with him. He will even exceed all that we could hope for, if, for our part, we have patience.

Hereupon, he concludes, 'As we have therefore opportunity, let us do good unto all men, especially unto them who are of the household of faith.' By saying that we must make every effort (while we have opportunity) to do good, he is setting before us the brevity of our life. In this area, we happen to have a serious problem, for a day seems like a year to us. 'Will there never come an end? Must we always continue? Must we do this all over again?' This is how we speak and make ourselves believe that there is plenty of time for doing good. Thus, we say, 'Oh, I'll do that some other time, for if I give all away today, tomorrow when I am approached, I will have nothing left! It is best if I keep this for myself.' But we never find opportunity to do good with our resources; we all prefer it if a friend steps forward first, not so that we can follow his example in well-doing, but so that we can remain tight-fisted. However, Paul shows us that if we were wisely to consider things as they really are, we would see that we will not always have great opportunities throughout our lives. Even if we never ceased, and each of us made every effort to employ himself as much as possible in the service of his neighbours, it would still not amount to much.

Whilst we are in this world, we must take care of others. As children, we were fed and clothed (although we could not have earned the price of a pin), and others had to work for us. Well, have we reached the age of intelligence? Yet, we still have to be assisted and supported often enough; even, I tell you, the most wealthy of us. For an illness arrives or some other adversity which strikes down even those who consider themselves to be the strongest and most robust. Then we require so many things, and are so hampered ourselves, that we can never repay the hundredth part of what we owe to those to whom we are indebted before God. I tell you that even those who are rich, and have many possessions, even with the best will in the world, if all they do is with the greatest of efforts, and they toil ceaselessly, they can never repay the hundredth part of what they owe to those to whom they are obligated.

When all this has been carefully considered, we will not find that we have great opportunities to do good to our neighbours. For when we have reached old age, we will have returned to a second infancy, and will be as helpless as little infants, and we may, indeed, be more demanding than they, in that we may be ill-humoured and difficult to please. Everyone else will have to look after us, because we will be utterly helpless. Hence, we can see that we do not have much opportunity to do good. Therefore, we must strive all the harder, while God gives us opportunity. When a farmer sees the good weather, he says to himself, 'I don't know if rain is on its way; I'd better dig the vineyards, and pull the plough, and sow. I must do this and that while the weather is suitable, for I do not know how long it will last.' A merchant will do the same thing when he has to travel, and so on.

Here, it is a question of the work that God is calling us to do. It is about sowing to the Spirit and to life incorruptible, and yet we say that there is no hurry, and that we can always wait for a year, or two, or even three. Indeed, we will wait for ever, such is our indifference and coldness. Let us, therefore, learn to put into practice the warning that the Spirit of God gives here, to do good while we have the opportunity, for this will not always be the case. If God places in our hands the means by which we may provide for our neighbours, it is a special favour indeed. By this, he is giving us a sign that he acknowledges us as his children; if we can communicate that which he has given us to those who are in need, it is a sign that he has placed his image within us. If we are disposed to serve those who ask for our help when we have the means and the wherewithal to do so, it is God who is giving us this honour. We do not know if this opportunity will always be there, for we have seen him strip people of their possessions when they go about to devour everything. We see him utterly ruin those who are like bottomless pits, until they need to ask for help themselves, but they are not heard because they have shown so much cruelty to those who would have come to their aid, not showing them any compassion. Since this is so, remember that our life is brief, and soon passes, and occasions to do good are slipping by. Thus, we are to employ ourselves in doing good as our Lord gives us the ability, indeed 'unto all men', as Paul says, but 'especially unto them who are of the household of faith'.

Now, when he says 'unto all men', it is to teach us that although we may be so disgusted by others that we do not want to do them good, we must, nevertheless, show kindness because God commands it. As I have already said, we are not to consider what each person is like, or what he deserves; we must rise above this and realise that God has placed us in this world to the end that we might be united and joined together. Since he has stamped his image upon us, and since we share a common nature, this ought to inspire us to provide for one another. The one who seeks to be exempt from the care of his neighbour is disfiguring himself and declaring that he no longer wishes to be a man. For whilst we are human beings, we must see our own faces reflected, as by a mirror, in the faces of the poor and despised, who can go no further and who are trembling under their burdens, even if they are people who are most alien to us. If a Moor or a barbarian comes to us, because he is a man, he is a mirror in which we see reflected the fact that he is our brother and our neighbour; for we cannot change the rules of nature that

God has established as immutable. Thus, we are obligated without exception to all men, because we are made of the same flesh; as the prophet Isaiah says: 'that thou hide not thyself from thine own flesh' (*Isa.* 58:7). It is as if he were saying that those who are mean and niggardly, and who hold back when it comes to doing good, not only display contempt for God and reject his Word, but reveal that they are monsters because they have no regard for the brotherhood that should exist between all men.

This is why Paul particularly says that we must seek to do good to all, even to those who are not worthy, though they are our mortal enemies! It is true that this is hard and against our natural instincts, but this is how God proves us even more. For if we were to do good to those who deserved it, or to those who could repay us, we would not be showing that we desire to serve God at all, for it is possible that we would have an eye to our own profit. As our Lord Jesus reveals, the pagans do as much, and so do the worse people in the world (*Matt.* 5:46). Why? This is how they reason: 'I need to be looked after; therefore, I must acquire some friends.' If, therefore, we seek to distinguish those who are worthy of our good deeds, and have the means to return our favours, this is not proper proof nor a sure test of the fact that we desire to do what has been commanded by God. But if we close our eyes to man's ingratitude, and feel led to pity people solely because of their poverty and misery, then we are serving God. If we are like this, then it is certain that we will seek to do good to all (as I have already said), for we cannot destroy the unbreakable bond by which God has joined and united us. Therefore, even the most distant strangers in the world are our neighbours, although they are neither our relatives, cousins or members of our household. Why? For we are all of one flesh, and we bear a mark which ought to induce us to do all that we possibly can for one another.

Having said this, Paul draws our especial attention to 'the household of faith'. He uses the word 'household' because he wishes to use a comparison which may affect us more powerfully. For although nature itself ought to teach us to assist anyone in need, it is true to say that people who are of the same household are even more inclined and willing to do good to one another. There are degrees of closeness between men. We all know full well that we have a mutual obligation to one another, such that if we fail the furthest strangers in the world, we have forgotten ourselves. Yet, to stretch ourselves in so many directions, far and wide, is a difficult thing, and therefore we are not very motivated to do good to people that we do not know, unless it is a case of extreme necessity. But whatever the extent of our hard-heartedness, we are still moved when we see a man in imminent danger and would all act in order to save him. This kind of pity is so engrained within us that it also extends to animals. There is even stronger motivation to help those who are created in the image of God, as we are. If, therefore, there is extreme necessity, as I have said, we will be all the more eager to help the poverty-stricken of any land. But when we come from the same country and speak the same language, we find that we have more contact with one another, and this increases our affection, which would otherwise be generally cold. This is even more apparent when there is friendship and familiarity within a neighbourhood. Those who originate in the same region will say, 'Since God has put us close together, let us at least seek to serve one another.' Again, those who live in the same street and enjoy friendly communication together have an affinity with one another, like relatives. In an even stronger sense is this the case amongst those who are of the same household, and who gather there like a small body. God is holding them together tightly; he huddles them together in one household, like a father with all his children gathered around him. Therefore, this ought to inspire us to act with even more enthusiasm, knowing that God has united us and knit us together so closely.

Paul tells us in particular that believers, and those who profess to follow the same gospel as ourselves, form a household; in other words, they are of the same house. A member of a household is someone who lives in the same house. Indeed, the church is called the house of God, and he dwells amongst us (*1 Tim.* 3:15). When the Scriptures speak thus, they do not mean that we need to be in this material building in order to be joined together; for even when we are in our own homes, we are still members of the same household (as well as citizens of the heavenly kingdom) because God has truly gathered us to himself. There can be nothing closer than this; nothing that could unite us so well. Thus, when it says that those who are the children of God are all of the same household, it is to show that there is common brotherhood amongst us.

Although earthly brothers separate, and go their different ways, we must always remain in this union established by God amongst us. When we hear these things, are we not worse than stupid, surpassing in cruelty the wild, brute beasts, if we are not moved to use what God has given us to help our neighbours, or rather, should I say, believers? We have now seen Paul's intention here; since God has given us the responsibility of doing good to all men because they are made of the same flesh, may we not be hindered by malice of any kind from striving to carry out our general duty towards those whom God sets before us in order to test our humanity. But since he has gathered us into his flock, and united us in his name, and since we call upon him with one voice as our Father, we must show brotherly love to one another. If we desire that he acknowledge us as his children, we must value our adoption, by which he has chosen us. To do this, let us declare sincerely by our lives that we long to demonstrate that those whom God has called into his household and church are regarded as our brothers. This is what we must remember from this passage.

Let us not use vain excuses any longer and say, 'Oh, I do not know who this person is; I have no idea at all!' This 'person' – is he not known by God? Yet you cannot condescend to open your eyes and see someone of the same image as yourself, whom God counts as one of his children, because you say you do not know him! Yet God condescends to cast his eye over us, though we are so wretched. Indeed, God, who is so exalted and so terrible in majesty that the very angels of paradise tremble before him in all humility – this sovereign God stoops down to see us, though we are nothing but poor earthworms, full of rottenness. Furthermore, he is not content to say, 'I know you'; he declares, 'I adopt you as my children so that you might be my workmanship and my heirs, members of my body.' God speaks thus, but we are so full of pride and arrogance that we despise those who are like ourselves, or, more often than not, who are more worthy than ourselves. Who dares to be this proud? Indeed, those who act like strangers and withdraw from their neighbours, desiring no communication with them, well deserve to be blotted out of the book of life. They deserve to be tracked down by God, and spewed out; to be delivered to the devil, who is their father, who has been a murderer from the beginning, and who is full of cruelty. This is what we need to remember, and how we ought to put into practice this teaching, where our attention has been drawn to the household of faith. Therefore, let us show, if God has deigned to call us to faith, that we value this honour and privilege more than all the wealth in the world. May we also demonstrate that we have a brotherly affection which motivates us to do good to those who need our help, according to the means which God has given us, and the extent of our abilities.

* * *

At this point, Paul says that the Galatians ought to observe that he has written them a long letter 'with mine own hand'. He wants to make them more attentive by showing them the care he has taken over their salvation. He is not extolling the length of his letters because he wants to be paid by the pound (as they say), but in order that the Galatians might realise that he wanted to pour out his heart to them, for they had gone astray and had pursued the wrong path. He so longed that they should not perish, that he could not have warned them by merely one word; he had to reiterate his doctrine to the end that they might recognise that they had been seduced. This is what Paul intended to do. But this passage ought to be a warning to all of us, because our Lord gives us the means and the aids by which we might approach him, in order to strengthen us all the more. If God had simply declared his will to us in one word, there would still not be any excuses for failing to believe and yield obedience, as is fitting. But he has given us the law, and has added an exposition of it. Then he sent us the prophets, to authenticate his doctrine, and to elucidate that which may have been obscure. After the prophets, he sent his only Son, who brought us perfect wisdom. The apostles followed shortly afterwards. Not content with this, God desired that the gospel should be preached, and that this would continue until the end of the world, and he raises up suitable men to instruct us. When we realise that God has done so much for us, and has such concern for our salvation, appealing to us repeatedly and constantly, are we not all the more guilty if we adopt an indifferent attitude and act as if none of this affects us?

Let us not consider Paul as someone to whom the Galatians need not have looked, but let us recognise that God had raised him up, and by reinforcing his doctrine in this way, God is declaring to us how dear we are to him and how precious are our souls in his sight. It is true that there are only five or six pages in this epistle, and at first, we may not consider this to be a particularly long letter. However, if we take note of the content and substance of it, it is certain that we will find matter here to confound the devil and all the schemes that he can invent, so that God, who is our salvation, is victorious. Even if we only had this epistle, we would be equipped and armed to fight against all falsehood, and every deception and lie that the devil could put in our path in order to confuse us. Yet we do not only have this epistle; we have so many other witnesses for God that will put out our eyes, in a manner of speaking, if we refuse to take heed of them. There are also so many reinforcements to help us, that even if we were the most sour-tempered and savage people in the world, we could still be drawn into some knowledge, since God tries to win us to himself by all means. Indeed, he constrains us to come to him, even though we do not desire to come willingly. But if we draw back instead of advancing, is not our rebellion more than intolerable?

Therefore, whenever we read this passage, though it seem that it does not apply to us, and that this was only said for the Galatians, let us remember that God is reproaching us, and saying that his labour will perish and become fruitless in us, unless we grow through his doctrine, since we so frequently hear it preached. However, he is much happier if we come to him in a cheerful spirit, for he will not accuse us or rail upon us if we wisely say, 'Here is my God, who is so worthy that I must run to him the minute I see him beckon to me from afar. He draws me after him so tenderly that I am full of wonder, and he was not content to have opened his mouth on one occasion alone, but sent Moses and all the prophets, and an infinite number of teachers. He sent the apostles and he even sent his only Son, who is his wisdom and his eternal Word. God has been so kind to me, and has raised me up to have such a wonderful dignity, revealing his wisdom to me by every possible means, and seeking through this to win me to himself. If he has done so repeatedly and constantly, morning and evening, can I remain here benumbed, with no more feeling or understanding than a tree trunk?' So much the more, therefore, must we take greater delight in the Word of God, and apply all our efforts to study it. Nothing in it is superfluous, and we need to be encouraged to give ourselves to it, that each of us might be led really to apply ourselves to it. Let us never say that it is meaningless to repeat the same things, but let us recognise that although we may not be hearing anything new, we must nevertheless call to mind this same lesson: that God sent Moses, and then the prophets, and subsequently the apostles, and he then desired that his doctrine be committed to writing. All this was done for our instruction.

When our Lord Jesus Christ was sent in the fulness of

time, he declared all that was needful for our salvation. Since that time, he still raises up people as instruments of his Spirit to proclaim his will and bring us the message of salvation (as is still the case today), to bear witness to that which otherwise would be hidden from us. In the light of these things, may we all be of one mind, and whether we read in private, or are taught in public, let us become stronger in the Word that God has been pleased to communicate to us. This is what we need to remember so that we might have much greater love for his holy Word and give ourselves wholly to it. May we receive it with more reverence, as, indeed, it is most worthy to be received.

Now let us fall before the majesty of our great God and Father, acknowledging him as our judge, unless he buries our sins in his infinite mercy. Let us pray to him that it might please him to accept us in mercy in the name of our Lord Jesus Christ. May he also give us grace to walk in such a fashion that we truly confirm that we are his children, and that he has not called us in vain. May this grace so benefit our hearts that we grow in it and become increasingly enabled to serve and adore him throughout our lives in true obedience to his holy Word. Thus we all say, Almighty God, and our heavenly Father, etc.

42

Ravening Wolves Who Wreak Havoc

> *As many as desire to make a fair shew in the flesh, they constrain you to be circumcised; only lest they should suffer persecution for the cross of Christ. For neither they themselves who are circumcised keep the law; but desire to have you circumcised, that they may glory in your flesh* (Gal. 6:12–13).

It is not without good cause that God strongly exhorts those whose duty it is to preach the Word not to seek grace and favour in the eyes of men. He expects them to close their eyes to human opinions, so that they are not turned to one side or the other, or prevented from properly fulfilling their office. Indeed, we know it to be impossible for us to fulfil our office properly unless we fix our eyes upon God and turn our eyes away from men; for we can easily become corrupted if we do otherwise, and it takes very little to turn us one way or another. Yet the most important loyalty required of those who have the responsibility of preaching the Word of God is that they be not tempted, either through ambition or avarice, to speak to please and satisfy men. They must not be afraid of perils or dangers. For experience shows that, as soon as a man fears for his own skin, or else has an eye to his own profit, he will change in a moment of time.

It is true that those who seek to please men in this way are not demonstrating at that moment that they are evil or enemies of the truth; as indeed, our Lord Jesus shows in the tenth chapter of John's Gospel, where he makes a distinction between the hirelings and the wolves (*John* 10:12). Having spoken of good and faithful shepherds, who seek the common well-being of the flock, he says that there are ravening wolves, or thieves, who seek only to plunder everything, thereby wreaking havoc and confusion. These are people who fight openly with God, and strive and struggle to overturn pure gospel doctrine. However, there are others who run with the hare and hunt with the hounds, and who pretend to be serving God. Yet neither type edify us, not even through their zeal, for they are devoid of integrity. While it costs them nothing, they simply make a fair show. Indeed, so much so that we can often be deceived because we consider them to be ministers of Jesus Christ. However, they only seek the wages and are devoted to filling their own stomachs. This is why, when threatened, they immediately become fearful and they change and alter their approach. Yesterday they seemed to uphold the Word of God, but today they are bending over backwards here, there and everywhere. Why? Because they realise that this will gratify everyone, and thereby be more profitable to themselves.

This is why Paul now warns the Galatians that those who troubled them and led them astray from the right path were given over to their own ambitions; this is why they cast doubt on certain doctrines. Up to this point, Paul has used reason in his debating to show that if we put our complete trust in Jesus Christ, the ceremonies of the law are now superfluous. Their application was temporary; they were designed to show us that, if we are truly leaning upon the grace that was purchased for us by our Lord Jesus Christ, we must not seek justification in the sight of God through our merit or any other foolish notion. Paul has dealt with and settled this argument as far as it was necessary for him to do so. Now, in order that the simple-hearted will be moved even more deeply he comes and addresses individuals, saying, 'Consider why it is that these people with whom I here quarrel mix the ceremonial law with the Lord Jesus Christ. Are they motivated by zeal, or a desire to serve God? Not at all! They have more of an eye to their danger of being persecuted. Therefore, since fear makes them distort the Word of God, it is not necessary for you to make further enquiries or longer investigations into what kind of people they are, and if you can trust them. For you will see how quickly they change and alter simply because they would avoid conflict. Thus, being traitors to God by their fearfulness, do they deserve to be believed, or to have people respect what they say?' This is Paul's aim here.

This teaches all ministers of the Word to have such constancy and faithfulness that they are unconcerned about whether the doctrines they preach are hated or whether they are pleasing to their hearers. They must follow their course, and not strike sail at the slightest sign of wind, nor must they sway like reeds bending here and there. Whatever changes and revolutions occur, whatever trouble and confusion arises, let them continue to serve God. In brief, we must practically apply that which we learnt earlier, which is that if we seek to please men, we are abandoning the service of the Son of God. This is the first point.

However, all believers can draw good, practical instruction from this passage. We are to be wary of those who seek their own profit and advantage, who desire the acclaim of others and want to be esteemed. For such people never have any stability. As I have already said, this may not be immediately apparent, because some are dupes; they even think that it is thanks to them that the Word of God does not appear odious, and is rather applauded. Therefore, they may appear to be on fire, and yet change their minds overnight. If there is some danger and they see that they are being prompted to testify to the Lord Jesus Christ, then they reveal their cowardice, and finally turn in the opposite direction, and turn their coat as the proverb says. Whatever happens, let us always be on our guard, that we might only trust those whose lives are upright, and who do not wander away when they see the world conspiring against them. Even when others are so possessed with rage that they seem to be about to devour them, and even when dangers are most apparent, they ought to continue steadfast and constant. In this way we can distinguish them as servants of God. But those who alter and are counterfeit, who first say one thing, then another (to escape the hatred of men and avoid suffering persecution), we must guard against so that we are not deceived or misled, for they are like deadly plagues. We cannot have any security or support unless we display the good judgment and carefulness that Paul urges us to have in this passage.

Now this message is necessary today. For why is it that so many hypocrites murmur as boldly as whores against the Word of God, and uphold such gross abuses as we see in the Papacy: the superstitions, the idolatries, the errors? It is because they know that if they do not keep the pot boiling, and hold on to certain things, they will simply starve! They also consider the danger of persecution if they uphold such doctrine. They see it condemned by princes and powerful people in this world; they therefore decide to keep themselves hidden away in the shade. This, I tell you, is why an infinite number of people disguise the truth of God, and falsify it; instead, they uphold many corrupt practices. The reason is that they do not wish to endure for the sake of Jesus Christ. It is true that they may not be Papists in the least degree, nor blaspheme openly against the Word of God; yet they desire to create another path, yes, made according to their liking. For they accuse us of being too extreme and too rigorous because we condemn those who attend Mass, and those who convince themselves that they do not worship idols! 'Come now!', they say, 'Provided that they do not have these things in their hearts, do we need to oppress them to the point of creating offence, and cause people to risk death over it? What reason can there be for this? Our life is precious to God, and even if we do commit evil, he will still pity us in our frailty!' Those who speak in this way show for certain that they are motivated by some other reason; that is, that they have noticed that the world is inflamed against us and that it seems we daily run the risk of sinking and perishing. This is why they draw back, and seek to operate as a separate group, when they see the impending danger.

However, because we see weak preachers running away from persecution, not wishing to suffer any conflict for the Lord Jesus Christ, bending and compromising only in order to enjoy peace in this world, we must pay all the more attention to Paul's warning here, and discern who are the true servants of Jesus Christ. They are people who have no thought for their own profit, who do not seek the applause of men, nor the best fare, nor the honours of this world. They are content just simply to do their duty, without concerning themselves about the kind of wind that is blowing, be it a tempest or whirlwind, or be it calm, as long as they profit their hearers and maintain the doctrine that has been committed to them in all purity. If we follow that which is taught us here, it is certain that our faith will not waver. There are many today who do not know what they ought to do, and yet they say, 'I fear conflict and differences of opinion, and the strife that has to be faced in this world.' Some conclude that they must devote themselves fully to the Lord Jesus Christ, but there are others who follow a more gentle route, and who only desire a half-hearted transformation. Whom should I believe?

Simply open your eyes, for those who use such excuses are not seeking to follow the truth. They are quite happy to veil their turpitude, and to seek the flattery of others. But what do they gain? Satan is leading them to perdition, and they desire to follow him! Because they fear what will happen to them in life, they love the shadows, and devote themselves to pleasure and comfort. They must therefore receive the payment that they deserve. Those who deliberately become brutish in this way have been taken over by Satan, Paul declares, and now remain perplexed, not knowing what to do. They do not stop to think that those who simply preach the truth of the gospel are not to be pliable people, but to pursue their course without worrying about whether or not their doctrine is pleasing to everyone else. Since God has commanded them to speak, they do so. On the other hand, simpering people who say that we have to tread carefully and not 'swing beyond our hinges', who claim that it were better to be counterfeits, and double-minded; such people cannot be driven by zeal or affection for serving God. They do not consider either the edification or well-being of the church. In short, their only concern is that they might escape persecution, and retain their comforts; they do not want anyone to attack them. Now this is indeed worthy of note, for those today who remain in their nests and offend God have no excuse. Why? Because Paul gives us a sure mark which distinguishes the true servants of God from the hirelings from whom we are to flee; that is to say, those who seek only to feed their stomachs and enjoy the comforts of this world.

* * *

At this point, he adds 'lest they should suffer persecution for the cross of Christ'. By this word 'cross', there is no doubt but that Paul includes all doctrine, and he is saying that it is very difficult to preach in all simplicity that which is contained in the Word of God, without encountering much conflict. For although God protects us (I am speaking about those of us who preach his Word), and has no desire to put us through trials so rigorous that our enemies come against us with drawn swords, yet it is still true to say that the world has never obediently accepted the gospel, and there have always been murmurers and opponents. Indeed, we still see them today, and shall continue to do so, for our Lord wants to test the faithfulness of his own, and ultimately demonstrate the invincible power of his Word, which overcomes all the obstacles reared up by Satan. As it says in Jeremiah, 'And they shall fight against thee; but they shall not prevail against thee' (*Jer.* 1:19). Thus, God is glorified when the world, together with Satan, makes its strongest efforts, and yet cannot prevent the truth from running its course.

For this reason, Paul says that these motley people, who disguise and falsify the Word of God, are running away from the cross. In other words, they are fleeing from the true message of the gospel, in order to avoid persecution. Once again, this is a badly needed warning for us. For if we desire to serve God and his church, we must always be prepared to undergo danger. Even though the fires are not lit, and the enemies are not armed to execute the cruel persecution that they would like to mete out (or rather, even though our Lord is restraining those who are furious with his Word, and who wish to throw off his yoke), yet we must, nevertheless, suffer the revilings of many people. We will be defamed; there will be murmurings and slanders against us; but let us breathe it all in and then harden ourselves against it, as it were. We see that wherever the gospel is preached, a thousand accusations come against those who seek to carry out their duty faithfully. They are put on trial, and accused of this and that, but it is all pure calumny. In short, all those who wish to pursue their course must prepare themselves to bear many trials; these would lead them to compromise, were they not determined to obey God despite everyone else. Here is one thing.

However, we ought to remember that this extends to the whole body of the church in general. When we hear the message of peace that is brought to us in the name of God, let us not expect to be at rest as regards this world, but always to have to deal with many quarrels and difficulties. If anyone is not prepared for this, he must leave the Lord Jesus Christ, for such a person can never be one of his disciples. As he declares with his own mouth, the one who does not bend his shoulders to carry his burden and his cross is not worthy to be in his school, and indeed all such are excluded (*Matt.* 10:38). Therefore, let us learn that, being called to the Lord Jesus Christ, we must share in his cross as much as pleases him; as it is written, that if we suffer with him, we will also be glorified and partake of the power which was revealed at his resurrection (*Rom.* 6:5). We must still have fulfilled in us, as members of his body, the sufferings that he first endured. It is true that he alone suffered what was necessary for our salvation, but we need to be conformed to his image, as it says in the eighth chapter to the Romans. However, even if God spares us from being amongst tyrants who could torture us, or evil men who could attack us, and he ensures that they only bark at us; yes, even if he leaves us in peace, it is because he pities our frailty and spares us because of our weakness. Let us not flatter ourselves in this meanwhile, but let us pray to God that through his Holy Spirit he would strengthen us. Then, when he calls us to line up ready for combat, we will not act like raw recruits, but will have premeditated long since the fact that we must share in the sufferings of Jesus Christ in order to reach the glory of his resurrection.

* * *

Paul, having thus spoken, now adds, in order to strengthen his argument, that those who are circumcised and who preach circumcision, do not keep the law, but they wish to glory in the flesh of those to whom they taught the ways of Judaism. In this passage, Paul is again accusing his adversaries of being double-minded people, in whom there is nothing but falsehood. Why? Before the coming of Jesus Christ, circumcision was a sign, much like baptism today. For the Jews knew that they were set apart by God as his inheritance. But those who mixed circumcision with the gospel fully believed that they too had to keep the law of Moses because it had been given by God and, therefore, must never be abolished. Thus the excuse they used was that circumcision was a sign that they observed the whole law. But here Paul reproaches them for not keeping the law at all. They were, therefore, deceiving God and man, because this was an exterior sign of something they were not doing; the very opposite was true! We can now see Paul's intention here.

With regard to this expression, 'keep the law', it is sometimes taken to mean accomplishing and observing all that it contains. No-one can 'keep the law' in the sense that no-one can perfectly accomplish all that is commanded therein. There is good reason for it to be referred to as an intolerable burden (*Acts* 15:10). Also, we know how weak we are, and the law reveals God's angelic standard of righteousness. How, then, is it possible to reach it? Therefore, no-one keeps the law if we take this to mean perfect obedience which cannot be criticised. Believers, being governed and led by the Spirit of God, keep the law, that is to say, they walk according to the rule that is given in the law. Not that they run as fast as they ought, nor that they reach their goals immediately, yet they still aim at these things, God supporting them and not imputing their sins to them. Thus, believers keep the law.

However, here he is referring to the ceremonial law (although on previous occasions, Paul has shown us that all the commandments of God can only bring about our condemnation if we do not have resort to the grace of the Lord Jesus Christ). Yet here he is speaking about the ceremonies and shadows. Let us now consider his meaning here. He says that those who are circumcised do not keep the law. He means that whilst they have this sign as a standard, to make others think that they are Jews, in order to avoid hatred and persecution, they do not observe the whole law, for they still allow themselves freedom to despise all that ought to accompany circumcision. The person who is circumcised ought also to sacrifice, and abstain from eating meat that is forbidden in the law, keep the festivals that are appointed therein, observe the various washings and cleansings, and so on. But these people pay no attention to this. When they are alone in secret and not being watched, none of this matters to them, and they have no scruples about showing contempt for the whole ceremonial law. Therefore, we can see that they were not circumcised out of zeal, but because they cared about what others think of them.

Now we must be clear that Paul is speaking here about those who insisted on the circumcision of others as a compulsory act. For on certain occasions, Paul had to be careful to conform to the ways of the Jews, and to forfeit the liberty that he otherwise rightfully enjoyed, so as not to give offence (*Acts* 16:3; *1 Cor.* 8:9). But he always maintained that he was not under any obligation to do so. Thus, since Paul submitted of his own free will, he did not wish to place others in servitude, as indeed he protests, when he says that he would not wish to bind anyone. It is true that this is said in another context, in relation to marriage, but he is still setting out in general terms that he does not wish to cast a snare for the souls that were bought by the Lord Jesus Christ. Thus Paul conducted himself. Now he says here, 'Those who constrain you to be circumcised, in other words, who impose the law upon you, and who tell you that you must keep this ceremony or else commit a mortal sin, needlessly subjugate you.' To sum up, those who wanted to force Christians to submit to observing the ceremonies and shadows of the law of Moses are here accused of double-mindedness. They did not really do these things because God required them but because they wanted to please and gratify others, and thereby escape persecution.

Today, we need the same warning that the Galatians had to have in those days. If we consider the state and condition of our own age, we will easily recognise that this teaching is most necessary, and that the Spirit of God wants to reveal that which he knew would be important for us. For how many people do we find today who strongly and firmly uphold the ceremonies of the law, and see nothing wrong with this? Worse than this, they uphold follies and traditions which have been invented by men; and even abuses, errors and deceits which are more terrible and more foolish than anything else. All of these are insisted upon with extreme rigidity by those who want us to obey them.

When we set before these hypocrites the grace of our Lord Jesus Christ, and tell them that the light of the gospel is obscured by all such observances, or that we are becoming like the Jews (for truly, the Papists have borrowed so many things from the law that it is hard to distinguish between the Jews and those who call themselves Christians) – when we tell them these things, they still maintain that they must keep them to the very end because they have been observed since the beginning of time. If we go further and tell them that these are such follies that even pagans have never stooped to observe such awful or such ridiculous superstitions as they do today, they will reply: 'Oh, but we must keep the traditions of our Holy Mother Church.' They will rant and rave over this matter. But what are these hypocrites doing now, who have incited the rage of both princes and judges against those who faithfully preach the Word of God? Well, as soon as they are amongst their own, they simply mock at these traditions, but when they are engaged in a debate about them, they will say the very opposite to all that they preach and declare in the flesh. By this we can see that they have no zeal for God and no integrity; but they seek to eat their fill, and to feast luxuriously, and then to be at peace and to have all their comforts and pleasures.

We see, therefore, that there are so many people without a single ounce of the fear of God or reverence for his Word, who nevertheless pretend to be great zealots. They allure poor souls, only to strangle them in a manner of speaking; therefore we must pay all the more attention to what Paul declares here. In other words, when we understand that these people who shout and rage do not practise what they preach, let us be on our guard and find out what motivates those we permit to teach us. It is true that if a man does the reverse of what he says, we must not as a consequence allow the Word of God to lose its authority over us. It is not fair to dethrone God from his sovereign position of authority for the sake of one wicked man. If a person leads a dissolute life, or commits a cowardly act, and yet has preached faithfully, we must not allow this to detract from the heavenly doctrine itself. We must not permit the truth of God to diminish in our eyes because a man, fickle by nature, alters and wavers, or if he is a hypocrite and his life does not match that which his mouth proclaims. I tell you right now that whenever we see those who seem champions of the truth, giving themselves permission to do anything and licence to do the opposite of all that they preach, we must consider the situation, and, using our good judgment, refuse to be deceived by false appearances, or led by the nose. Let us search out their doctrine and make a good and thorough examination of it.

If we proceed in this way, we will see that the Papist's doctrine is nothing but a covering that they hide behind so that they can remain at peace in this world. They do not care how things appear to God, and they cannot face changing because they do not wish to expose themselves to the hatred of others. For they always live in fear of bringing trouble upon themselves or having further problems. When we see this, we know it to be an sure indication of the fact that we must guard against Satan's attacks, so that we will not be deceived, at least not inadvertently, as we have been saying.

* * *

Finally, Paul adds that these people want to glory in the flesh of simple-minded folk. This definitely relates to the sign of circumcision. It is as if he is saying, 'They want to leave their mark upon you, in order to prove that they have won you over.' How detestable this makes them, that they would abuse the sign that God gave to ratify the adoption of Abraham and his descendants, and corrupt its true and legitimate use. For God had commanded the Jews to be circumcised. Why? So that they would understand that the whole human race was cursed, there being nothing but pollution within us, and that therefore we must renounce all that pertains to our nature or else forever remain polluted and be condemned before God. This is what the Jews had to learn through circumcision. Yet they received testimony to the fact that their salvation would come through human seed, as indeed we know that we are blessed by God through the Lord Jesus Christ. This circumcision was designed to humble the Jews and cause them to be dissatisfied with themselves and ashamed when they saw that their nature was cursed. And yet it was also a testimony to the grace of God, enabling them to call upon him as their Father, knowing that through the seed promised to Abraham, they would receive salvation.

This, I say, is the true and legitimate use of circumcision. But what did these people that Paul speaks against do? They knew that circumcision no longer applied, and that since the coming of the Lord Jesus Christ, baptism was sufficient. But because the Jews called all who were not circumcised apostates, these scoundrels retained the sign without the reality. We can see, therefore, that they were true forgers, turning this doctrine into something other than God intended when he instituted this spiritual sacrament, simply because they sought to satisfy the world.

The same is true today. Those who seek to overturn God's truth are much worse than Paul's adversaries, for there was some semblance of honesty in their pretext for maintaining circumcision and the figures of the law, in that these had been instituted and established by God. But what about these hypocrites who loudly proclaim that we must keep the ancient rites without the least alteration? Upon what do they base their views? They cannot claim that God is the author of all these things. Men have invented them according to their own fantasies, or, rather, Satan has whispered these things in their ears. In short, there is a confused labyrinth of teachings in the Papacy which they refer to as 'the service of God'. These are dreams put forward by men, and the devil is still their chief source of inspiration. Yet such scoundrels insist that we can take nothing away. What is their motive? They say that these are the means whereby we can obtain God's grace, and that they also inspire men to a greater level of devotion. Then again, they refer to all the foolish inventions that their own heads have devised as 'sacraments', saying, 'You must observe this because it is a sacrament'. When all is said and done, it is obvious that, above all else, they want to please men and preserve themselves. They are forced, in spite of themselves, to confess that all of this is neither here nor there as far as God is concerned, and their service does not please him in the least; he would disown it all, for he seeks to be served by obedience. However, we cause terrible confusion when we suggest removing these things, and when we speak clearly about such matters.

This, I say, is the way they disguise, corrupt and falsify religion and make it a confused mixture of just about everything. They may just say that we can remove the worst and most grievous errors, whilst leaving the ceremonies, which are still admissible. All those, I say, who speak in this way only seek a fair wind and a good profit in this world. This being the case, let us be warned by the Spirit of God to flee such plagues. Although we cannot enjoy victory in this world, and although we are criticised and shamefully accused, may we keep ourselves upright for the sake of the truth of God. May it be enough for us to enjoy the approval of our heavenly judge, even if the whole world regards us as an abomination. However much of this treatment we see, let us be patient, waiting for the day when the Lord Jesus reveals himself as our surety, and gives such victory to his truth that all his enemies stand in shame and silence before him.

Now let us fall down before the majesty of our great God, acknowledging our sins and praying that he would so touch us by his Holy Spirit with a true spirit of repentance, that we might tremble, despairing of ourselves, being emptied and stripped of all presumption. Furthermore, may it please him to increase in us the graces of his Holy Spirit so that we are no longer given over to our flesh and to this world, and hindered and held back by them. May we instead aim to serve him and make every effort to ensure that his name is glorified in us more and more, and that we bear visible evidence of our adoption, that we may be strengthened within ourselves. Thus others will have occasion to glorify the name of our great God, when he has worked in us. May he show this grace, not only to us, but also to all peoples and nations on earth, etc.

43

On Glorying Only in the Cross of Our Lord Jesus Christ

But God forbid that I should glory, save in the cross of our Lord Jesus Christ, by whom the world is crucified unto me, and I unto the world. For in Christ Jesus neither circumcision availeth any thing, nor uncircumcision, but a new creature. And as many as walk according to this rule, peace be on them, and mercy, and upon the Israel of God. From henceforth let no man trouble me: for I bear in my body the marks of the Lord Jesus. Brethren, the grace of our Lord Jesus Christ be with your spirit. Amen (Gal. 6:14–18).

We saw earlier that Paul condemned those whose only desire was to sit on the fence in order to please the world, and escape persecution. For this had caused them to twist the gospel, and we see numerous examples of this today. Having seen that pure doctrine and the truth of God are unacceptable to the world, but that wicked men are incensed against it, these people, I say, seek to find some way to avoid creating bad feeling and incurring hatred. This being so, if we today were to interview people with at least some good sense, we would scarcely find one in a hundred of them who would admit that there were errors in the Papacy. Most would say that we ought not to force them to abandon everything and that it would be enough if they were to get rid of some of their more unreasonable and absurd superstitions, even if they continued to nurture many other corruptions.

Why? Because, as we have said, they desire to be esteemed and highly credited, and because it is all the same to them if they betray the purity of the gospel, provided they can remain exempt from persecution. What is it that motivates them, but the fact that they wish to be valued and to acquire a good reputation? Now the devil, who has stirred up this kind of conflict ever since the days of Paul, continues to this present day, and therefore we need to arm ourselves with this doctrine. The best remedy is the one that Paul proposes here: that we reject all glorying, save that which is in the cross of our Lord Jesus Christ.

In order to understand this clearly, we must firstly remember what is written in Jeremiah, and confirmed here by Paul. In other words, that all the glory of man must be abased in order that God be exalted as he deserves (*Jer.* 9:23, 24). Indeed, in the same way it is written that all the wisdom that men believe they possess is nothing, and will not be taken into account; it must be blotted out, that we might have recourse to God, as the one who has all abundance of good things in himself (*Isa.* 29:14; *1 Cor.* 1:19). Let us acknowledge, I say, that all wisdom proceeds from his free grace, so that we are enlightened by his Holy Spirit, and, being weak, strengthened by his might. Being full of pollution and iniquity, may righteousness be restored in us according to his gift.

Now let us come to the means. It is not enough to know that God is our light, that he is our righteousness, that he is our wisdom, and that he is our strength; in other words, that in his person is perfect life, joy and felicity. This is insufficient, for there is still too great a distance between himself and us. Yet we need to know how and by what means we can obtain all the graces that we seek in God. We know that they are all communicated to us in Jesus Christ, for he descended here below, made himself nothing, and was crucified willingly for our sakes. Therefore, since we must draw all that we lack from the Lord Jesus Christ, we can understand why Paul says that he sought only to glory in the cross of our Lord Jesus Christ. Why? Because he suffered a cruel and bitter death, and even exposed himself to God's judgment on our behalf, receiving all our curse, and in this way was given to us as our wisdom, righteousness, holiness, strength and all that we lack.

Therefore, in the first place, we need to know who we are, before we can prevent all glorying and stay ourselves upon the Lord Jesus Christ. For we see many people bursting with pride who have no grounds for this whatsoever. All that they imagine to be true about themselves is no more than wind and smoke. Yet because they have not examined themselves properly to see what they are really like, they have not sought Jesus Christ; such are these hypocrites, and counterfeits, who are puffed up with presumption because of their 'merits'. Therefore, as I have said, we must consider our condition and see the extent of its wretchedness, that is until the Lord Jesus takes pity upon us. This is how we can prepare ourselves to come to him. This is the first point.

However, this is not all. For there are some who will confess that they are sinners, and that they are full of nothing but vanity, and yet continue to wallow in their filth. Why? Because they do not anticipate the judgment of God, and their minds have been lulled to sleep by the world. All such pleasure-seekers, who abandon themselves to drunkenness, or bawdiness, and the like, cannot excuse their wickedness, and indeed, they ought to be ashamed of it, and yet they seem to take pleasure in sins and continue in them as if hardened. Why? They have been intoxicated by the world, and blindfolded by the devil, such that they cannot see that one day they must give an account of themselves. They have stupidly made themselves believe that they will always remain as they are, pursuing evil things, and that they will never have to sigh and tremble, but only laugh, as if they seek wilfully to show contempt for God. Thus, we can see how it is that some are prevented (indeed, they are fully incapacitated) from coming to Jesus Christ, either because they presume to have their own wisdom, or because they are pursuing a false notion that Satan has placed in their minds, or because they think they are wise enough without Jesus

Christ. These are the reasons why they despise him. Others, of whom there are an infinite number, know that they are poor sinners, and yet do not seek a remedy. Why? Because this world has them in its grip, and they are so caught up in it that they cannot lift their eyes or their minds above to seek for the remedy that has been provided in Jesus Christ.

We must, therefore, be all the more ready to meditate on what I have said, that is, to rid ourselves of all pride and presumption, and to feel so much shame that we have no rest until we have found relief in the Lord Jesus Christ. May we open our eyes to see our depravity and be ashamed of it, and not only so, but also to recognise that this life is nothing, and that God has placed us here as on a journey, so that he can test whether or not we are following him. May each of us therefore come aside, both morning and evening, to consider our sins, and may they be like goads to prick us and encourage us to come to God. May we not be like brute beasts, tied to this world, but may our need lead us to come to the Lord Jesus Christ. This is what it is to glory in the cross of the Lord Jesus Christ.

Paul specifically speaks of the cross here because he seeks to knock down and trample underfoot all haughtiness in man. For we always want to be 'someone' in and of ourselves, and maintain a certain dignity. Therefore, in order to rid us of such a wicked desire, Paul shows us that Jesus Christ, the Son of God, should be our only cause of glorying because he was crucified for us. Following on from this, he adds that we will be crucified to the world, and the world to us, when we have learned to glory only in the grace that our Lord Jesus Christ has brought us. How? Those who are not crucified to the world, that is, those who desire to have a position of some authority, and to be important, and who ask to be held in honour and promoted, in other words those who are diverted here, there and everywhere by their lusts, certainly do not yet know what it is to glory in the cross of Jesus Christ, for they begin at the wrong point. They are confused within themselves.

Therefore, Paul can say with confidence that when his

glorying was founded upon the cross of the Lord Jesus Christ, he abandoned and forsook the world. By 'world' he means all that appeals to our flesh, to men who neither think of God nor of eternal life, but are given over to avarice or ambition. Each one is controlled by his own natural instincts, and not one looks beyond this world. When men follow their inclinations and when God has not touched them by his Holy Spirit or drawn them to himself, it is true to say that though they have all strayed and roamed, yet there is a great variation in their desires, such that, when we examine the matter, we find that one is heading in a certain direction, whilst another is pulling in completely the opposite direction. Thus, it seems as if men are very different from one another. However, they are all alike in one area, that is to say that they want to be important in the eyes of the world, and are given over to their personal profit or pleasure. In other words, they are so enmeshed in things here below that they do not mind being separated from God. But Paul says that if all our glorying is in Jesus Christ, knowing that by means of his cross he has committed us to God the Father, and has secured the kingdom of heaven for us, then it will be easy for us to withdraw from the world and cut ourselves off from it, as it were. Why? Whoever has been cut to the quick and overwhelmed with a sense of their own sin will surely seek the grace offered to him in Jesus Christ, and the world will be worth nothing to him.

Indeed, we treat all the spiritual riches that God has offered us and invites us to share as if they were nothing, because, in comparison to the deceptions and temptations of Satan, we do not value them at all. What is this world, when we contemplate it as it is? Not one of us sees just how fragile our lives are, that they are but smoke which floats past and then vanishes. Men still burn with lust and are transported and carried away thereby. As for God, he calls out, 'Poor people! You have less sense than little children, in that you busy yourselves about wisps of straw, meaningless rubbish, and all kinds of nonsense, and attach yourselves whole-heartedly to these things. Yet when I offer you that which is perfect felicity, you ignore it; to you it is unimportant.' Hence, the reason that we are so cold and so slow to accept the riches that God offers us is that we are preoccupied with the things of this world. Indeed, we value this world too highly. What makes us do this? It is because we do not know what priceless riches God is offering us.

Therefore, let us join together these two things: namely, let us be crucified to the world, and the world to us, glorying alone in Jesus Christ crucified. Now this is easier to say than to do, and yet each of us, wherever we are, must strive to do so; once we have heard this doctrine, we must put it into practice. For if we would be esteemed and accounted Christians before God and his angels, we must conform to what Paul tells us here; indeed, if we were not otherwise-minded, we would find plenty of opportunity to do so, as I have already said. For all those who simply look within themselves and consider what they are really like, and what condition they are in whilst still separated from Jesus Christ, will be terrified of feeling the wrath of God which they deserve. They will feel that they are ruined by their accursed state, and that it would be better if the earth were to swallow them a hundred times, rather than live under this curse for a single day as the enemies of God who cannot escape his hand. Let us therefore learn to examine ourselves. Those who wish to adorn themselves according to this world, especially women, will gaze into a mirror with great curiosity and concern. Yet our poverty and filth will not be reflected there, in order truly to humble us before God, or make us consider what we glory in. The one who recognises his shame and ignominy will certainly seek to remedy it, if indeed the Spirit of God is working deep within him, and he is not (as I have already said) intoxicated by Satan. Let us, therefore, learn to examine ourselves sincerely, without flattery, and when we have acknowledged our poverty and misery, let us come to the Lord Jesus Christ. Since, by means of the cross, all haughtiness, self-worth and boasting is cast down, let us be truly crucified to the world and may it mean nothing to us.

Now, by saying that the world was crucified to him and he to the world, it is certain that Paul means the same thing, yet he wants to reinforce that we can indeed renounce this world and be separate from it, by being crucified to ourselves with regard to the world. This means that all our loathsome desires (which are far too strong in us and consume us like a burning flame, pushing us in one direction, then another), must be mortified, for we know that the Son of God had to suffer such a shameful death on our behalf. Who is he who seeks to have his triumphs and do his courageous deeds in this world, when he knows that the One who is the head of angels, to whom belongs all glory, majesty and authority, hung on a tree and was cursed and hated for our sakes? In this way, all our lusts must be mortified; therefore, may the passion and death of our Lord Jesus Christ be so effectual in our hearts, that our desires do not quiver impatiently within us as once they did. This is the first point.

Also, the world must be crucified to us. How is this? In comparison to the spiritual riches that Jesus Christ brings us, and which we enjoy through him, may we esteem the things of this world as straw and corruption, since all is corruptible. Furthermore, all that men covet so earnestly and with such determination that they become completely hindered by it, are nothing more than nets that Satan has spread in order to catch them. Are they not illusions and deceptions? Yes, this is most certain. Since this is so, let us learn that the world ought to be nothing to us, and let us be completely persuaded and assured of the fact that God is merciful to us, and acknowledges us as his sons and heirs; he has blessed us and without his blessing we would be most miserable. Hence, we are to pass lightly by this world and not be attached to it or held back for anything; this must always be our aim. We know that we must make haste to the place to which God has called us, and if we become enmeshed by the love of this world, we will become alienated from our God. This is what we are to remember from this passage.

* * *

At this point Paul adds that 'in Christ Jesus neither circumcision availeth any thing, nor uncircumcision, but a new creature'. It is as if he is telling us that those who troubled the church in his day were motivated only by ambition. For if the church did not grow, and no-one received any profit in any way as a result of the great trouble they stirred up, it surely proves that they were only seeking to replace the Lord Jesus Christ. For what should our aim be, but to see the Son of God reigning in our midst, and to be ruled by the Word of his gospel, and to know his power, so that all of us, great and small, place our entire trust in him? Following on from this, we aim to have our whole life transformed, that we might live in obedience to God and submit to his Word. For the spiritual temple of God is built upon faith and a new life; faith leads us to pay homage to God for all his riches, and to have recourse to him, and declare his praises – to call upon his holy name when we meet together. This is how we are built up to become the temple of God.

However, we must also be renewed in our lifestyle, and patiently learn to deny ourselves and dedicate our lives to God. This ought to be the message of those who have the responsibility to teach. Those who do not aim at these things reveal that they have no intention of serving the Lord Jesus Christ. Thus Paul declares that the only important thing is to be a new creature in Jesus Christ. In other words, we must come to the point where, as we saw in Second Corinthians, we are new creatures, if we want to be considered to be 'in Jesus Christ' (*2 Cor.* 5:17). For if anyone boasts that he is most eloquent, and another that he is very clever, and another that he is a great scholar, and another that he has good manners, it is all vanity. Let us, therefore, learn to forsake ourselves and this world, and to dedicate ourselves to the one who bought us so that we might be set free. For it is only right that Jesus Christ who obtained us at such cost should possess us and rejoice greatly over us. This cannot be achieved unless we each deny ourselves and reject all that could hold us back amongst men. This is what we need to observe.

Paul speaks here of circumcision and uncircumcision because the dispute and the argument he had (as we have seen previously) concerned the ceremonial law, which he deals with here through the example of circumcision. For the Jews sought to retain all the types and shadows which were only intended to last for a time. Thus, Paul, ridiculing all this, says that our Lord Jesus Christ came, not to encourage us to keep these ancient figures, but, because the veil of the temple was torn in two, and because he is in himself the body and substance of all the shadows that existed under the law, we must now content ourselves with him, circumcision no longer being of any value.

We will derive greater profit from this passage if we apply it to what we see today. For, in the Papacy, there are many pointless rituals in which they place all their trust in order to be holy. When we ask the Papists how they can merit God's grace and obtain remission of their sins, they boast that they have their holy water, their candles, their incense, their organs and choirs, their pilgrimages and this and that. Also, they have their foolish devotions, which involve trotting from altar to altar and from chapel to chapel. Then they must, of course, buy a good number of masses. In short, all that the Papists refer to as the service of God is nothing more than a labyrinth, or an abyss, of superstitions which they have forged in their own heads. Let us come now to consider what these things are worth. God has made no mention of them; but they have been invented by men, in whose ears Satan has whispered in order to corrupt the true service of God. However, the Papists consider that there can be no religion, nor faith, nor service of God, nor zeal unless we too are transported by all their nonsense. Yet Paul, speaking of the ceremonies that God had ordained in the law, says that they are no longer anything. Why? Because God is content if we serve him with a pure conscience, and call upon him, having put our trust in him, knowing that all good things come from him. Let us, rather, live uprightly and honestly with one another, knowing that charity is the bond of perfection, and the end of the law; and let us also so dedicate ourselves to our God that we live chastely and in all holiness, waiting for the coming of our Lord Jesus Christ, as it says in Titus (*Tit.* 2:12–13). This is the starting point of holiness and perfection, as declared by God in his Word.

Yet the Papists will say on the other hand, 'What! And what will become of our lovely devotions? Will they all be abolished? It were better to pull God out of heaven!' This reveals the Papist's folly. We have seen what Paul has exposed here; that even if men are so mistaken about their own inventions that they think they offer God wonderful things, and are held back by these meaningless trifles, it is all worthless. Who has declared this? God, by the mouth of Paul. What, then, ought we to be? New creatures. What is a new creature? We must start by examining our lives and seeing ourselves as nothing in and of ourselves. Then we must offer to God the spiritual sacrifices that we owe him, presenting ourselves to him that he might have pity and mercy upon our misery, and aid and help us. May we be ready to follow him as he calls us, having no other source of wisdom but his Word alone, knowing that he does not wish to be served with pomp or with the fine, glittering external appearances that appeal to the world. He is content if we devote our thoughts and affections to him in sincerity. Moreover, it is our responsibility to understand what Paul is saying here, and to apply his teaching; for it is certain that those who refuse to flatter themselves in their sins, and who look to God, knowing that they must appear before his judgment seat, will forsake all glorying in themselves.

Furthermore, they will know what God demands in his Word, and how he would be served, and what he delights in, so that they will no longer be in danger of being deceived by the meaningless trifles which hypocrites pursue. For it is most certain that when the Papists torment themselves in order to serve God (as we see), it is only so that he will count them innocent, and so that they may escape his hand, and not be constrained to serve him as he has commanded; for they despise the whole law. Yet there are many things which they do regard as vital, and which they desire God to accept.

But (as I have said) their main aim is to believe that their duty to God has been fulfilled, so that he will not oppress them too much. Meanwhile, they follow their own course, allow themselves great licence and grant themselves absolution of all their sins. They think that since they have brought God something (that is, a mere shadow), he dare not speak a word against them and has to remain silent. Now we have seen Paul's intention here.

* * *

Finally, he adds, 'And as many as walk according to this rule, peace be on them, and mercy and upon the Israel of God.' By speaking of this 'rule', he implies that men may believe what they choose, and yet God will not give way to them, for he is immutable and will not yield to folly or be made to retreat. Paul tells us that such alteration is impossible. Whatever happens, the rule that God has established remains as it is, unchanging. This is something which we all accept on the surface of things. For who would not readily accept the fact that God is superior to us? We even feel that to say the contrary is to blaspheme. Thus we are all quite sure that God ought to reign, and that his law ought to be our rule for living. Yet, at the same time, see how men allow themselves to live without restraint! Each person invents this and that, and soon afterwards expects everyone else to hold to their inventions. Everyone wants to have their own separate rules. Whilst it may be true that not everyone in Popery follows the rule of St Francis, or of St Dominic, yet there is not a single foolish old woman or bigot in Popery who has not got his own rule. Just as there is not a single young calf who has not also his own rule for living. For all will say, 'This is the way I do my devotions.' And when they use the word 'devotion', they virtually push God into the background because they are really saying, 'I must have the liberty to do what I think is good, and God must content himself with that.'

What diabolical audacity men have! They compromise here and there, they talk wildly, they deviate first to one side then to the other. It is as if they make for themselves winding and crooked pathways, hoping that God will twist his rules and be pliable enough to bend to suit their own views. Therefore we have all the more reason to observe carefully what is said here, which is that men may torment themselves all they like, but God's rule remains and will follow its own course and direction.

What is this rule? It is that we aim for the perfection that our Lord Jesus reveals in the gospel; not that we can attain this during our lifetime, but rather that we are not to step aside one way or another, to the right or to the left, but to aim always for the goal that God has revealed to us. This is how we can be new creatures, by denying ourselves and dedicating ourselves fully to God. Since this is the case, let us make a decision to submit to this rule, and conform our lives to it. For each one of us immediately picks up our feet and legs to run off here or there; but in order not to go astray, we need to learn to hold fast to all that God reveals and teaches us in his Word. Now when Paul asks that peace and mercy be upon such people, it is to declare that, even if all in the world were foolishly to condemn us, we could ignore it and refuse to let it bother us, pursuing our own course. If God is for us, that ought to be sufficient. For if we are shaken by the foolish judgments of the world, and the opinions that they spread about us, we are not rendering to God the honour that is his due. If folk say of us, 'Those people are not living good lives', and we get upset and seek to conform to their tastes, we will surely be moving away from God.

Therefore, let us take good note of what Paul says here, which is that if men condemn us and find things to criticise in that which we do (and it is obvious that the world will never be in harmony with God), it should mean nothing to us. It ought to suffice us that God has blessed us, and offers us complete happiness in this word 'peace', showing that he will have pity on us, however wretched we may be, and however much others may spit in our faces. Although we do not have all the virtues required of us, yet if we aim to follow God, we will always find him to be merciful. He supports us in our weakness, and aids us in our wretchedness. If we have all this, it ought to be enough. On the other hand, although the Holy Spirit blesses those who submit to God's rule, we also know that he curses and detests and loathes all those who go astray, and who make their own imaginations their law. They seek to have liberty to follow whatever seems right to them, and harden themselves against the Word of God. However valued they are by the world, and however much they are intoxicated with pride and presumption, thinking they are ever so important, we can see that God still regards them as detestable. This is what we need to remember: there is only one rule by which we must live and that is contained in the gospel.

Where does this rule lead us? It will ensure that we do not offer to God that which seems right to us, or that which we have forged in our own heads. Instead, we will submit ourselves fully to him and to his Word. We will recognise that in Jesus Christ we have all perfection. Thus we will be content with him alone, especially since we know he is merciful enough to show us pity, and our lives will be blessed and made happy by him, if we follow him to the place where he calls us. Conversely, we will be cursed unless we follow the rule that Paul speaks of here, no matter what opinion the world has of us, or however much the world may praise us.

Now he adds 'the Israel of God', to prove that those who serve God spiritually, he will always be pleased to acknowledge as his people. For the enemies of Paul, against whom he has a quarrel in this whole epistle, wanted to maintain all the ceremonies, as it seemed to them that these were the marks of the true church, just as the Papists today want to keep the holy oil, and this and that. But the enemies of Paul had much stronger grounds than the Papists, and in comparison their case was stronger. Yet Paul still rejects it all, and says that God does not concern himself with any of this. Whilst it is true that he had ordained the shadows of the law for a time, and they had their function, which was to lead the people to the Lord Jesus Christ, now that we have the substance and the truth in him, we must forsake it all. We have an even stronger reason, therefore, to say that the Israel of God are not those who appear in great splendour before the eyes of men, but those who bear the true mark of God. For when the Papists speak to us of the church, they must include the Pope with his three crowns, and the bishops, who disguise themselves in order to act out their farce. They are like horned beasts, and everything about them glistens; the priests and the monks are among them and they too dazzle the eyes of the simple. This is what the church of God consists of according to the Papists: in pomp and frivolous, useless nonsense. What of the sacraments? No, they need this or that extra thing – in short, they have their own marks which seem quite acceptable to them.

Yet we must look at the gospel. What do we find there? All simplicity. God does not want those who preach his Word and administer his sacraments to wear costumes or to make so many fanfares. Nor does he want the sacraments to be polluted by human inventions, because all these are worthless to God. Let us, therefore, retain the definition that Paul gives here of the true church, so that we are unmoved when people say to us, 'Look, we have many beautiful things here.' It is true, if we judge according to our natural senses, for we are carnal and earthly and are, therefore, more inclined to follow that which appears beautiful to our senses. But it is not for us to decide how we must serve God; we must hold fast to that which he has proclaimed, because his decree is irrevocable, and it is that we should find all our wisdom in Jesus Christ. This can only happen if we obey him, and not before. Thus, we are to recognise that we must no longer be attached to the external things which he ordained at the time of the law; but we are to be content with Jesus Christ alone and the perfection that is in him.

* * *

Let us be sure to notice something else he says at this point: 'The grace of our Lord Jesus Christ be with your spirit.' He exposes here that the world, due to its ingratitude, gives no thought to the riches which are offered in Jesus Christ. The gospel is preached often enough, and yet we all withdraw from it and turn away, as if we have decided to leave the good path that leads to salvation and throw ourselves headlong into ruin and perdition. What is the reason for this? It is because our spirits are empty, and the devil always gains entry; he entices us, he troubles us and makes us flutter about in the air. Indeed, until the grace of our Lord Jesus is with our spirit, we are like swaying reeds, without stability or foundation. This is what we need to aim for, so that God not only pours out his grace upon us, but that we also receive it into our spirit and heart; our spirit must become its throne and the place where it takes root, so that we might not be tied to this earth, but raise our affections and minds to God.

* * *

Now, because there will never be a time when this doctrine escapes contradiction, Paul here challenges those who would rise up against it, and says, 'From henceforth let no man trouble me: for I bear in my body the marks of the Lord Jesus'. When he speaks of the marks of Jesus Christ, he sets them in contrast to all the armouries of princes, to all their diadems and sceptres, and to all that they possess to give them importance, and to obtain the worship and reverence of all. When a prince wants to be seen to be in control of his estate, he must be dressed in such a way that none dare look at him for fear of being bedazzled. They do this more often than not because there is nothing about them worthy of note, and so they need to rely on these borrowed means; the same is true of worldly people who give themselves to pomp and gallantry, and use this and that to acquire a good reputation. In short, the worldly will use any means to get themselves noticed, although these things are vanity in and of themselves. But Paul shows that the marks of our Lord Jesus Christ are, as we know, worth so much more, and far more precious, having more beauty in themselves than all that is cherished by the world.

However, we need to consider what is meant by 'marks'. He has explained this to us before, when he said that he was beaten several times. He had been stoned at one place, put in prison in another, and had suffered hunger and thirst (*2 Cor.* 11:23–27). In other words, he had been regarded as loathsome and was therefore rejected. According to the world, we must flee such ignominy. Yet Paul says that these marks are worth more than all the honour and splendour that we could ever enjoy. He says that because he bears these marks, others must not 'trouble him' by preventing him from following his course and fulfilling his duty.

Now Paul's intention in this passage has been, firstly, to show that if we are Christians and part of the true church of God, we must obey the command to be united to one another. How? Not with each person following their own imaginations; for there are indeed many who have a perverse spirit which makes it impossible for them to co-operate with others. Such people seek to keep themselves separate from everyone else, like wild horses, and it is to be hoped that there are monasteries and cloisters for such people who refuse to unite with others according to the command given to the church. Thus, having separated themselves in their pride from the company of believers, they can only really become monks of the devil! Whatever the case, we know why they hide themselves away: it is because the devil has them in his grip and possesses them. He simply seeks to persuade them to live separately from others so that he might eventually turn them away from God altogether.

Secondly, Paul shows us here that we must aim to keep this 'rule'; the Lord Jesus is to be our example, and we are to seek to conform to his image. When he speaks, may we submit to his teaching, so that each of us keeps his commands. Also, let us help one another. For we can boast about persecution, or this or that, all we like, but unless we seek to help others to enable the building of the spiritual temple to progress, it is certain that we are still serving Satan and are like slaves serving under his tyrannical rule. Let us learn to be of the same mind one with another as we submit to our

Lord Jesus Christ. Furthermore, may those who are selfless and faithful in their walk with God despise all these pompous people who want to elevate themselves in their pride, introducing this or that; for Jesus Christ always recognises his marks. In other words, however contemptible we may be in the eyes of the world, we will always be acknowledged by the Son of God. Therefore, let us continue to walk, and let those who seek to hinder us know that God will beat them down, as we have seen previously (*Gal.* 5:12). It is only right that people should be put to shame and forced to scatter if they disrupt the unity of the church and refuse to serve according to their ability to the advancement of the reign of our Lord Jesus Christ. God must send them to their ruin because of their pride and presumption. This is what we need to remember from this passage if we desire to persevere in the enjoyment of the riches that we possess, which were bought for us at so great a cost, through the death and passion of our Lord Jesus Christ, and which are offered to us daily through the gospel.

Now let us fall down before the majesty of our great God, acknowledging our sins, and praying that they would so grieve us that we would be made to tremble and seek his pardon. Then we will be transformed through true repentance and enabled to battle against all our vices and all the corruptions of our flesh, until he has freed us from them altogether; then he will clothe us in his righteousness. Thus, we all say, Almighty God and our heavenly Father, etc.

Index